AMERICA

CHANGING TIMES

Volume One
to 1877

175 YEARS OF
1807 1982
PUBLISHING

John Wiley & Sons

New York   Chichester   Brisbane   Toronto   Singapore

AMERICA

CHANGING TIMES

TIMES

2nd Edition

CHARLES M. DOLLAR

General Editor

JOAN REZNER GUNDERSEN
RONALD N. SATZ
H. VISCOUNT NELSON, JR.
GARY W. REICHARD

Contributors

REID A. HOLLAND

Assistant Editor

JOHN HAMMOND MOORE

Writer

Production supervised by Jan M. Lavin
Design by Edward Alexander Burke
Photo Research by Rosemary Eakins, Research Reports
Photo Editor: Stella Kupferberg
Manuscript Editor: Martin S. Stanford
Maps by John V. Morris
Cover photo by T. Lennon

NOTE: *America: Changing Times, Second Edition,* is available in a one-volume clothbound edition and in a two-volume paperbound edition. The contents of both editions are the same with the exception of separate indexes. Volume One of the two-volume edition ends with Chapter 15, "Restoring the Union," providing coverage up to 1877. This same chapter is repeated as the first chapter in Volume Two, providing coverage beginning at 1865. The *Instructor's Manual* that accompanies the one-volume edition applies equally to the two-volume edition. A *Study Guide,* available in two volumes, matches the division of chapters in the two-volume edition.

Library of Congress Cataloging in Publication Data:
Main entry under title:

America, changing times.

   Includes bibliographies and index.
   Contents: v. 1. To 1877 — v. 2. Since 1865.
   1. United States—History. I. Dollar,
Charles M.   II. Gundersen, Joan R.
E178.1.A489   1982   973   81-13053
ISBN 0-471-09418-8 (v. 1)   AACR2
ISBN 0-471-09417-X (v. 2)

Printed in the United States of America

10 9 8 7 6 5 4 3 2 1

Preface

America: Changing Times is an effective blend of political and economic history, foreign and domestic affairs, and new insights into America's development. It was prepared by a team of historians with special expertise in various aspects of American history. These specialists, aided by John Hammond Moore, a professional historian and writer, produced a text that focuses on long-established institutions and processes such as the family, business, technology, urbanization, globalization, and the actions of *all* the people involved in the development of America. As the title indicates, the emphasis is on change and continuity—on how generations, past and present, have contended with those forces that give America its zest and vitality.

America: Changing Times, is about people—great and small, haves and have-nots, heroes and villians, movers and moved, shakers and shaken. It's about issues, ideas, confrontations, and disputes that changed the way our forefathers lived and worked and that created our own late twentieth century milieu.

Many improvements have been made in this Second Edition. Twenty-four new biographical sketches have been added while others have been expanded. All have been tied more directly to the textual presentation. Several new essays have been written and all of them relate closely to events covered in the text. These essays develop a particular topic in some detail and link it to other eras and other chapters. The essays at the end of Chapters 7, 15, 22, and 30 emphasize the theme of "turning points" and feature, at the same time, salient aspects of the time periods covered in Chapters 1 through 7, 8 through 15, 16 through 22, and 23 through 30, respectively. In addition to updating all the material to reflect the latest research, other revisions include covering Progressivism in one chapter instead of two, adding a new Chapter 21 on "Culture in a New Society," reorganizing Chapters 23 through 30, and including developments in the new Reagan administration in the final chapter.

The collaborative effort that characterized the first edition of *America: Changing Times* also shaped this Second Edition. Joan Rezner Gundersen contributed the material for Chapters 1 through 7, Ronald N. Satz for Chapters 8 through 15; H. Viscount Nelson, Jr., for Chapters 16 through 22; and Gary W. Reichard for Chapters 23 through 30. And, each contributor exchanged ideas and concepts for every chapter.

We are grateful to a number of readers, including many students, who have reviewed these pages to help us improve the presentation. Special thanks go to all the users of the First Edition who responded to a questionnaire from the publisher regarding strengths and weaknesses of *America: Changing Times*. Their comments and suggestions have shaped this Second Edition.

CHARLES M. DOLLAR
General Editor

About the Contributors, Editors, and Writer . . .

JOAN REZNER GUNDERSEN grew up in the suburbs of Chicago. After graduating from Monmouth College, Illinois, she received an M.A. in history at the College of William and Mary in 1969. In 1972 she received a Ph.D. from the University of Notre Dame and has since completed postgraduate work at the Newberry Library. She has previously published in the fields of colonial and southern history and has taught at Indian University-South Bend and at Vanderbilt University. She is currently Assistant Professor of History at St. Olaf College in Minnesota.

RONALD N. SATZ, a native of Chicago, graduated from Illinois Institute of Technology in 1965. He received an M.A. in history from Illinois State University in 1967 and a Ph.D. in history from the University of Maryland in 1972. He is the author of books and articles in the fields of Native American history and Indian-white relations and a member of the Editorial Advisory Board of the *American Indian Quarterly.* He has taught since 1971 at the University of Tennessee at Martin, where he is currently Professor of History and Dean of Graduate Studies and Research.

H. VISCOUNT (BERKY) NELSON, JR. was born and reared in Oxford, Pennsylvania. After receiving his Ph.D. in history from the University of Pennsylvania in 1969, he taught at UCLA. He taught at Dartmouth College specializing in Afro-American, urban, and social history and recently returned to UCLA. His previous publications have been in the fields of Afro-American and urban history.

GARY W. REICHARD grew up in Newark, Delaware, was educated at the College of Wooster and Vanderbilt University, and received his Ph.D. in history from Cornell University in 1971. He has taught at the College of Wooster and, since 1971, at the Ohio State University, where he has served as Chairman of the History Department. He has published in the fields of recent American history and American political history.

CHARLES M. DOLLAR grew up in Memphis, Tennessee. He completed graduate work at the University of Kentucky, receiving a Ph.D. in history in 1966. He has previously published in the fields of quantitative history and the history of the South. After teaching several years at Oklahoma State University, he joined the staff of the National Archives, Washington, D.C.

REID A. HOLLAND was born in Fort Bragg, North Carolina. He completed his graduate work at Oklahoma State University, receiving a Ph.D. in history in 1972. His previous publications are in the fields of Native American history and instructional techniques in the teaching of history. He has taught at Oklahoma State University, Oklahoma City Junior College, and Grand Valley State College and is currently Director of the Grand Rapids Center of Grand Valley State.

JOHN HAMMOND MOORE received his Ph.D. in history from the University of Virginia in 1961. As reporter, editor, writer, and researcher, he has over ten years of varied experience in publishing and journalism, and as a history teacher, ten years of classroom experience. In addition to feature writing and news experience, he has edited and prepared for publication nine books and over sixty articles in various magazines and journals. His latest books are: *Albemarle: Jefferson's County, 1727–1976* (1976), which received the 1977 "Award of Merit" from the Association of State and Local History, *Australians in America, 1876–1976* (1977), and *The Faustball Tunnel: German POWs in America and Their Great Escape* (1978) and a forthcoming study of American GIs in Australia during World War II. He resides in Washington, D.C.

Contents

CHAPTER 14

THE WAR
TO SAVE
THE UNION

416

CHAPTER 15

RESTORING
THE UNION

448

APPENDIXES

A-1

List of Maps

AMERICA

CHANGING
TIMES

Change is the active ingredient in America's story. Throughout the past four centuries, the land in its harshness and promise; the native Americans — and those who joined them from Europe, Africa, and Asia — in their conflicts, losses, and gains; and the ways in which all Americans have thought and played, sung and ate, fashioned laws and administered justice have undergone — and are still undergoing — transformation. Although the New World has exerted some influence on the Old from the days of Christopher Columbus to the present, the reverse is more startlingly true. For, in their baggage, however limited, all who came to settle in America brought with them bits of their own cultures. Thus a mosaic of untold fragments, fashioned by untold hands, created — and continues to create — a rich, new heritage for all Americans, one in which all can take great pride.

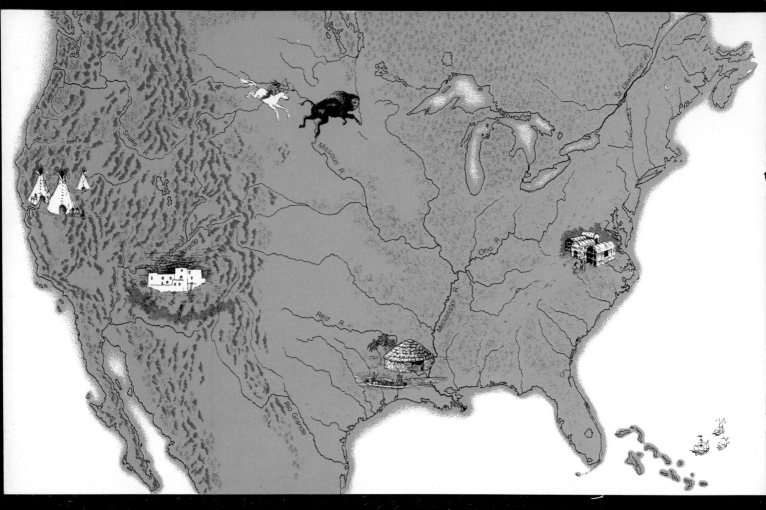

AMERICA ON THE EVE OF CHANGE, 1500-1600
The vast band of continent that would become colonies and then states was, except for the encroachments of the Spanish and other occasional explorers, a land of forests, plains, mountains, valleys, and lakes, homes to a few million Indians with very diverse cultures.

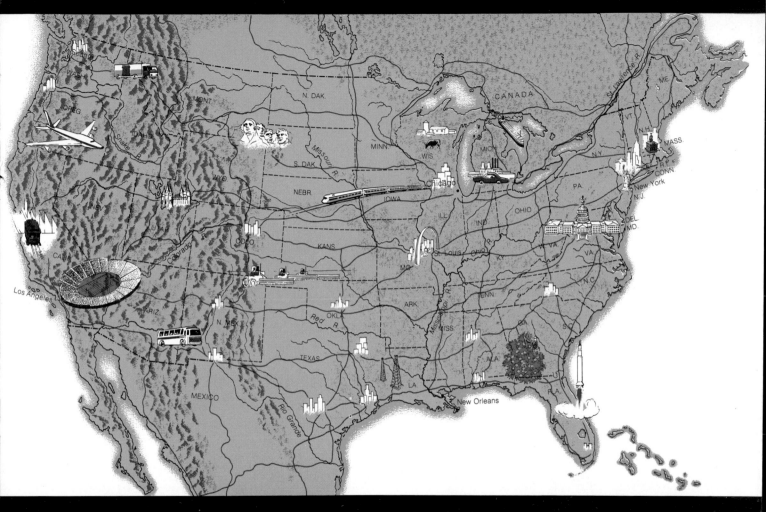

AMERICA TODAY
The same land, subdivided into forty-eight states, the District of
Columbia, Canada, and Mexico, with its cities, industries, and
memorable landmarks, gives tangible proof of development and
change that has occurred in the past four or five centuries.

New York harbor and Manhattan Island through the years—Dutch, British, and American. America's changing face was first glimpsed here by millions of immigrants seeking a new home in a new world.

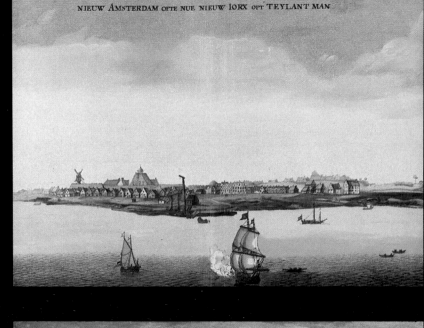

NIEUW AMSTERDAM OFTE NUE NIEUW IORX OPT TEYLANT MAN

The land. Many Europeans came to America to get land, to farm; and there they grew cotton and wheat and raised beef cattle. Until this century, most Americans, in some measure, derived their livelihood from the soil.

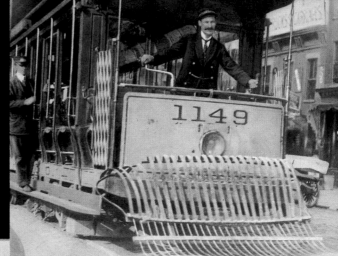

On the move. Traversing the land by saddle horse, ship, stagecoach, railroad, trolley car, automobile, and airplane, Americans have explored and settled their continent. A restless people ever eager to see new places and new things, a handful have already booked passage on the first commercial flights into outer space, whenever that may be.

The urban scene. Philadelphia, Saint Louis, New York, Chicago, Houston
—all are magical names created by first settlers and real-estate promoters.
Through the years, they have come to mean commerce, power, bustle,
confusion, and, above all else, opportunity.

Getting ahead. For many Americans the
route to a better life has been education,
the way West, a trade, a shop of some
sort, or a service demanded by an increasingly urban population. The nineteenth
century peddler, the milkman, the Wall
Street broker, and the owner of a
McDonald's franchise have fulfilled, each
in their separate ways, such needs.

Having fun. Americans have always enjoyed traditional ways of relaxing, alone or in groups. Although organized sports for spectators have attracted millions in the past century or so, voluntary sports for participators such as jogging and sailing have increasingly won dedicated converts from all age groups.

Americans all. Individuality of purpose, unique opportunities, and a rich ethnic mix have created a vibrant civilization, a way of life much of the world seeks to emulate.

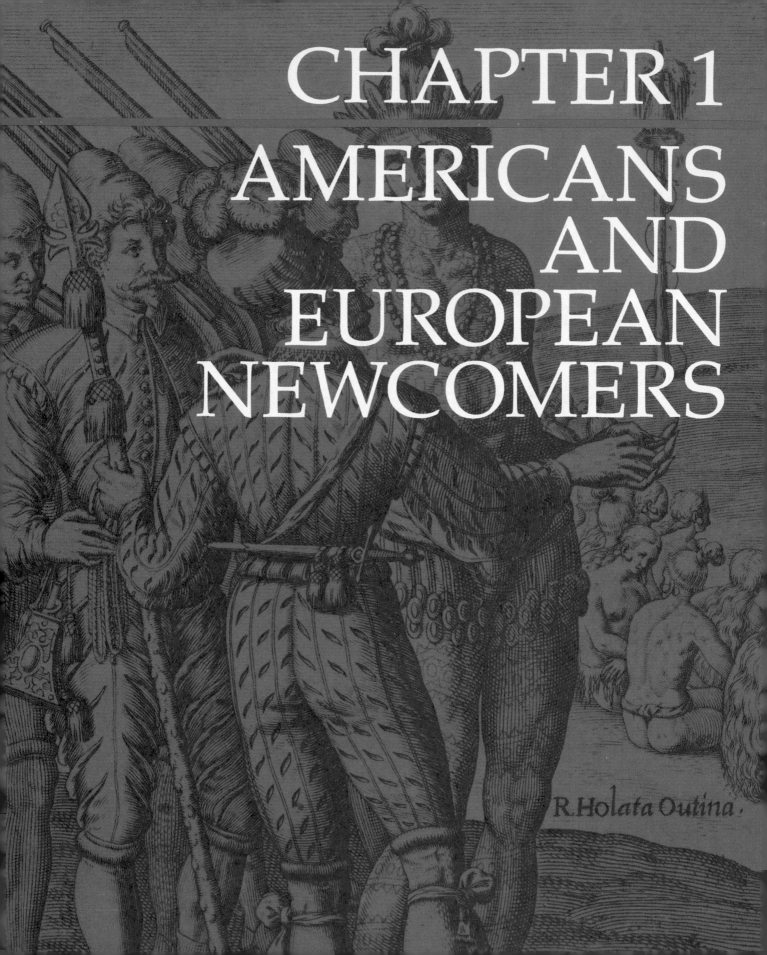

CHAPTER 1
AMERICANS AND EUROPEAN NEWCOMERS

R. Holata Outina

TIMELINE

?–25,000 B.C.
"Original Americans" migrate to North America?

1000
Leif Ericson attempts colonization at Vinland

1000
Hopi Indians build Pueblo Bonito in Chaco Canyon

1200
Plains Indians begin to populate area west of the Mississippi River

1484
Christopher Columbus first proposes an Indies voyage to the King of Portugal

1492
Christopher Columbus lands at Watlings Island after thirty-three days at sea

1494
Treaty of Tordesillas divides New World between Spain and Portugal

1497
John Cabot explores Newfoundland for the English king

1499
Amerigo Vespucci sails with Alonso de Ojeda to Venezuela and provides a name for the hemisphere

1502
Christopher Columbus begins his fourth and last voyage to the New World

1513
Ponce de León lands on present-day Florida

1513
Vasco Núñez de Balboa crosses the Panamanian Isthmus to the Pacific Ocean

1530s
Jacques Cartier undertakes explorations of North America for France

1533
Francisco Pizarro conquers the Peruvian capital at Cuzco

1585
Sir Walter Raleigh establishes the ill-fated colony of Roanoke

1606
James I grants Virginia Company of London and Virginia Company of Plymouth a charter for colonization

1607
English settlers plant the first permanent settlement in North America at Jamestown

1608
French Quebec established

1609
Henry Hudson claims the Hudson River Valley for the Dutch

1609–1610
Colonists at Jamestown survive "the starving time"

1611–1620
Tobacco provides Jamestown colony with a cash crop

CHAPTER OUTLINE

When a sailor, Rodrigo de Triana, spied land at 2:00 A.M. on October 12, 1492, the curtain went up on an astounding human drama. Triana, the lookout on one of Columbus's three ships, thought (as did his captain) that he was about to see the fabled riches of Asia. He had no way of knowing that the world he was entering was far stranger and less comprehensible than anything Marco Polo had seen on his extensive travels.

Columbus, who thought he had found an island just south of Japan, was in fact in the Bahamas, on a small island that he christened San Salvador, that the local inhabitants called Guanahani, and that the British later renamed Watlings Island. As soon as Columbus encountered the inhabitants, he was struck by their physical beauty, generosity, and peaceful ways. As he wrote, "They invite you to share anything that they possess, and show as much love as if their hearts went into it." Their nudity, kindliness, and lack of money led Columbus to think they were in the state of innocence that Adam and Eve enjoyed before the expulsion from Paradise.

These naive impressions of the first Americans encountered by Columbus and his men have been perpetuated in one form or another over the centuries, and a figure labeled "the Indian" has emerged in white American folklore. Depending upon whether one feels sympathetic or antagonistic toward "the Indian," he is either good—a being in tune with nature, democratic, proud, and ecologically minded—or he is bad—a creature warlike when not lazy, set against change and "betterment," and instinctively cruel. *The* Indian never existed, of course. What did exist was a range of cultures as varied as those in Europe, if not more so, and a diversity of language groups as different from one another as Finnish is from Spanish. The Indians of Mexico and Peru lived in empires as hierarchical as that of ancient Egypt. The Natchez and Pueblo Indians of North America, examples of agricultural societies, may well be related to the highly developed corn-growing empires of Mexico. Other North American Indians were seminomadic hunters, living on a simple level of technology but extraordinarily knowledgeable about the forests they inhabited and the game they pursued. Some moved in small bands with virtually no leadership; others formed large confederacies with well-defined borders. Some figured descent through mothers; others through fathers. Some were shockingly sadistic toward prisoners taken in battle; others never waged wars. In short, the differences among them were far greater than the similarities.

This amazing variety of cultures was not perceived by Europeans in their first contact with the New World. It became evident only after prolonged exploration and increasing familiarity. Nevertheless, the differences among the Indians created widely divergent responses to the first white settlers—who themselves, of course, belonged to different nationalities and held different values.

Origins of the Indians

It is safe to say that the Indians preceded the Europeans to the Americas by thousands of years—but their exact origins and the time of their various migrations remain shrouded in mystery. Today, militant Indians insist their ancestors never immigrated to the New World at all but always lived here. However appealing this theory may be in strengthening the claims long advanced by Indians that they are the only true "natives" of the New World, there is little evidence to support it.

When the first Indians arrived in the Americas is not known. Land travel from Asia to Alaska seems to have been possible about 70,000 years ago. Rough estimates obtained from carbon-14 dating of wood artifacts buried with human remains suggest a period perhaps only about one-third as long, some 25,000 years at the most.

In any case, the Indians probably came to the New World in small family groups and hunting parties across a natural land bridge that connected the Chukchi Peninsula of Siberia with the Seward Peninsula of Alaska during the last Ice Age (ending about 10,000 years ago). Doubtless, other Indians came by water. Today only twenty-three miles of water separate the tip of Siberia from Big Diomede Island, and from there it is only another twenty-five miles to the tip of Alaska.

Equally controversial is the question of how many Indians were in the Americas in 1492. One of the traditional European rationalizations for

wresting these two continents from the Indians is that the hemisphere was sparsely populated. This rather specious line of reasoning holds that if the Indians were not fully exploiting the land and resources of the New World, then Europeans had an open invitation, even an obligation to do so. Exact population figures can never be established for certain since neither the Indians before Columbus nor the Europeans afterwards took an accurate census.

For many years historians thought the pre-Columbian population of the Western Hemisphere was perhaps eight to fourteen million, only one million of these individuals living in North America. This estimate was obtained by starting with the population of Indians in this century, calculating backwards to 1492, and taking into account the effects of exploitation and disease. More recent interpretations boost this total from 50 to 100 million and set the figure for North America at perhaps ten to thirteen million. These higher figures are inferred from estimates of thirty million Indians in Mexico at the time of the Spanish conquest. There is obviously no way to reconcile these different sets of statistics nor to arrive at more reliable ones. What is not questioned is that European diseases, especially smallpox and measles, drastically reduced the number of Indians in the Americas.

The Americans before Columbus

From the beginning, Europeans were curious about the origins of the Americans. Were they one of the lost tribes of Israel? Or were they people who had escaped from the mythical island of Atlantis? Were they savages in need of the moral guidance of Christianity? Or were they innocents closer to an original state of purity than any European could hope to be?

Almost all of these speculations were irrelevant, culture-bound, and shrouded in arrogance and ignorance. The civilization of the American Indians was even more diversified than that found in Europe. Some 2,000 languages were spoken in

North and South America. From the Eskimo in Alaska to the Alacaluf and the Yahgan at Cape Horn, virtually every kind of social organization and level of technological expertise was represented.

South and Central American Indians

Indian cultures ranged from highly sophisticated agricultural societies to smaller, more vulnerable tribes of seminomadic hunters and gatherers. In Mexico, the highly evolved civilization that Hernando Cortés (1485–1547) encountered was the Aztec. The Aztecs had established their empire on the ruins of an older civilization, the Toltecs, who in turn had subdued the Mayan empire. Perhaps the Mayans were the most remarkable of these societies. More than 800 sites of Mayan cities and towns have been discovered in the Yucatan Peninsula and in Guatemala. They worked out a solar calendar more accurate than that in use in Europe until the eighteenth century. Between A.D. 300 and 900, Mayan culture reached its peak with a fully developed agriculture and numerous "cities" or ceremonial centers, which were occupied only during certain seasons. Society was divided into classes of artisans and ruled by administrators and priests who lived in sumptuous palaces. Although the Aztecs never rose to such heights of sophistication, they did impress the Spanish with their well-defined class structure, hieroglyphics, and carefully organized economy.

The Incas of Peru lacked a written language, but in every other way their empire rivaled the world's most advanced civilizations. They ruled a territory some 3,000 miles long and as vast as the states that now line our Atlantic seacoast, an area tied together by a well-maintained road system and populated by sixteen million inhabitants who used a system of arithmetic based on units of tens. Like the society of the ancient Egyptians, that of the Incas was divided into a rigid caste system; only members of the nobility could act as priests in the official cult of the sun. Peasants were confined to working the fields, which were laid out and administered with dictatorial precision.

North American Indians

North of Mexico in 1500, some 300 different tribes lived on the deserts and plains and in the forests and mountains. Although each tribe developed in

Courtesy of the American Museum of Natural History.

This Indian painting shows Cortez marching to Mexico City. The Aztecs first thought the Spaniards were gods.

its own way and at its own pace, often making unique adjustments to environmental factors, similarities also existed since all possessed a common ancestry.

Northeastern Woodland Indians The only North American Indians politically organized to a degree even remotely resembling that of the Aztec and Inca empires belonged to the Iroquois Confederacy in the northeastern section of what is today the United States. This league, probably established in the early sixteenth century, included five tribes (Mohawk, Cayuga, Onondaga, Oneida, and Seneca); in 1722 a sixth tribe, the Tuscarora, joined.

Unlike the Indians pictured so often in novels and films, the Iroquois tribes were sedentary and agricultural. Farming was performed exclusively by women, the three most important crops being corn, beans, and squash. The men helped to clear the land but spent most of their time waging war, hunting, and traveling. In winter they hunted deer, beaver, and small game with bows and arrows; in the summer they made long trips in their canoes in order to trade excess corn to other tribes for tobacco and other commodities. The Iroquois lived in villages protected by stockades of upright logs driven

Two examples of pre-Columbian art. An Inca artisan hammered in silver the figure of the standing man. The Aztec statue shows a woman in childbirth. Note the highly stylized features on both.

into the ground. Each village included as many as fifty huts, some of which were 100 feet long and sheltered eight to ten families.

Of all the North American Indians that the Europeans encountered, the Iroquois had the most orderly government, complete with rules determining property inheritance (the women owned the fields), marriage, burial, and even the playing of games (dice and lacrosse were favored pastimes). The basis of Iroquois society was the family, headed and administered by an older woman. Family units were grouped according to clans cutting across tribal lines within which marriage was prohibited. Each clan had an elected civil chief who participated in tribal councils, but only clans possessing hereditary titles had a voice in league affairs. Since descent was traced through women and they inherited all titles, ultimate political power lay in their hands, even though that power was exercised by male officials.

Because the Iroquois were members of a league, strong by virtue of their numbers, and because they had a developed economy based on farming, hunting, fishing, and trade, they were the most potent force the first white settlers had to deal with. Indeed, the Iroquois cleverly played off the French against the English for more than 100 years, and until the time of the American Revolution, they remained an important and sometimes even a decisive element in the balance of power in colonial America.

Surrounding the Iroquois nation were the Algonquian tribes from whose languages we have derived the names of such New England states as Massachusetts and Connecticut. These northern hunters, who had little organized leadership, moved in small bands during the winter, pursuing moose, caribou, small game, and birds as well as deer and beaver. In the summers most of the Algonquian Indians raised corn and fished. They lived in wigwams, which were constructed out of a circle of saplings whose tops were bent and tied together in order to form arches. Over this basic frame work (usually no more than six slender poles) woven mats or sheets of birch bark were placed. One of the northernmost tribes, the Penobscot, built tipis, or conical bark shelters, stretched over an inner framework of poles and reinforced by an outer, matching set of poles.

Indians who spoke one or another of the Algonquian languages lived not only in the Northeast but also further south along the Atlantic seaboard.

One of the Algonquian tribes, the Powhatan of Virginia, was the first to contend with permanent English settlements.

Plains and Mississippi Woodland Indians Although Algonquian Indians could also be found in the Midwest around the Great Lakes and along the Mississippi Valley, the Midwest was a great melting pot of many tribes—the Ottawa, the Ojibwa, the Menomini, the Winnebago, and countless others. Beyond the Mississippi were the Plains Indians. Until 1600 this vast area was sparsely populated by Indians who raised corn. Only after 1600 did enough Indians have horses—animals captured from wild herds or confiscated from Spanish settlements—so that a new nonagricultural way of life could develop. A heterogeneous mixture of Indian tribes from all parts of North America poured into the plains beyond the Mississippi and, mounted on mustangs, hunted herds of buffalo. Among the many tribes who became horseborne hunters of the buffalo were the Blackfoot, Arapaho, Cheyenne, Crow, Comanche, and Sioux. These fierce tribes played a major role in the story of white settlement of the West. At the time of Columbus, however, their distinctive lifestyle, since it depended on the horse, had not evolved.

Southeastern Indians The southeastern Indians, unlike many of those to the north, did not ordinarily don feather headdresses. Rather, the men of the Southeast wore nothing but loin cloths in the summer and cloaks and deerskin leggings in the winter; they pulled out with tweezers the hair on one side of their heads and covered their bodies with elaborate tattoos, signifying success in warfare. The women wore simple deerskin skirts and occasionally shell necklaces.

Until white settlers began to disinherit the Indians of this region, numerous tribes, all pursuing a sedentary and comfortable way of life, inhabited the Southeast. The Creek Indians, whose name derived from the fact that they were found along creekbeds by Indian traders, lived in inland Georgia and Alabama. One group, the Seminole, runaways from other southeastern tribes, inhabited the swamps of Florida where they hunted and practiced agriculture. The Chickasaw, located along the Mississippi River, were related linguistically to the Creek, as were the Choctaw and the Natchez.

One of the tribes flourishing at the time of Columbus, the Natchez, who lived in what is now the

Americans and European Newcomers

state of Mississippi, resembled in some respects the hierarchical societies of Central and South America. For instance, the Natchez had a well-defined social structure composed of four different classes. Their pottery and engravings suggest techniques and motifs derived from Mexico. Their ruler, known as the Sun, was an absolute monarch treated as though he were a god—at his death his entire retinue and wife were killed and buried with him.

At the time of first contact with whites, the Cherokee Indians claimed as their homeland the beautiful mountain areas of the Appalachians from present-day West Virginia to Georgia. A tribe apparently driven southward sometime before Columbus arrived in the New World, they represented a blend of Iroquois and southern Indian cultures. The Cherokee had well-established villages and

The year before this sketch of an Indian was made in Virginia in 1645, the colony there won the last major war against native tribes. Europeans, such as this artist, saw the Indian as a noble savage, however, not a foe.

built substantial log or stick dwellings; the largest, a seven-sided structure used for meetings, stood near the center of each community. Farmers as well as hunters, their basic crops included corn, peas, squash, pumpkin, beans, and strawberries.

Their social and political customs resembled those of the Iroquois, although they had no strong alliances with other tribes and few formal relationships between one Cherokee settlement and another. Cherokee towns recognized no single chief; instead, they had two leaders: one for peace and another for war. Women took an important part in town and tribal matters, and war councils might include a group of women who advised on strategy. Although towns chose men as chiefs, family ties were reckoned through maternal lines. Membership in one of the seven clans of the tribe was determined by the mother's bloodline, and an individual's membership in a clan provided a link of sorts to residents of other towns. Each clan usually had a "mother" town, although members actually lived in every Cherokee town.

Except for possibly brief contact in the early 1540s with the expedition led by Hernando de Soto and for occasional raids on Spanish territory, the Cherokees and whites saw very little of each other until 1700. In the eighteenth century this tribe, which became crucial to the British trade in deerskins, blocked settlement westward into the area now known as Tennessee. Then, new associations with whites brought continous warfare (usually as an ally of Britain) and modification of customs and dress.

Southwestern Indians In vivid contrast to the peoples of the Southeast were the peaceful agriculturalists of the Southwest: the Mogollon, Honokam, Pueblo, and Pima. These various tribes scarcely can be discussed as a unit, since their cultures differed in many important ways. Nevertheless, one characteristic of the region was its peacefulness. When forced to wage war, the southwestern Indians did so reluctantly and never rejoiced in victory. Similarly, there was little competition for positions of leadership.

The Hopi (a word that means "peaceful ones") are the most famous branch of a larger group known as the Pueblo Indians ("pueblo" being the Spanish word for "village"). They lived in terraced apartmentlike houses that sometimes were many stories high; an entire village dwelled within a single building. Construction consisted of piling large stones on top of one another and then plastering them with a mixture of clay, straw, and water, which dried in the sun to resemble brick. Large underground rooms were reserved for religious ceremonies, and the whole complex was serviced by an intricate system of stone drains. Sometimes these buildings were fitted into large openings on high cliffs. One of the largest of these, Pueblo Bonito in Chaco Canyon, New Mexico was built about A.D. 1000. Containing about 800 rooms, it was five stories high and 700 feet long. Many of these impressive Pueblo villages were constructed long before Europeans began to settle in the Americas.

Unlike most of the other North American Indians, the Pueblos were primarily agriculturalists. While other tribes, such as the Algonquian group, supplemented their food supply with farming done by women, the Pueblos of New Mexico and Arizona were farmers first, hunters second. Moreover, the men played an active part in the actual tilling of the fields. The Pueblo men also spun and wove cotton—a domestic activity that most other Indian males would have regarded as contemptible. Pueblo women were expert potters and their polished wares were finer than those produced elsewhere in North America. Since the Indians did not have pottery wheels, bowls were formed out of coils of clay, one laid upon the other; while the clay was still fresh, it was smoothed, painted with a black and white design, fired, and sometimes decorated with an additional layer of paint.

With few exceptions the Pueblos were peace-loving, settled agrarians, and they created a distinctive culture influenced by Mexican tribes. They were ingenious engineers, capable of executing large-scale irrigation systems and erecting impressive apartmentlike complexes. As artisans, they were unusually gifted in producing pottery, turquoise jewelry, and the beautiful painted wooden masks and dolls used in religious ceremonies.

Relative newcomers to this region were the Apaches who moved south from western Canada between A.D. 900 and 1200. They borrowed much from the Pueblo Indians, adapting pottery, weaving, and farming techniques to their own needs. In the nineteenth century, beset by white settlers and rival groups, the Apaches developed into fearsome fighters for whom lightning guerrilla raids became a way of life, a means of acquiring both glory and material goods. A related tribe, the Navajos, which followed a similar migration to the southwest, also had their wars with whites, but generally were more a peaceful people given to raising sheep and weaving rugs. In contrast to most native Americans, they prospered in the late nineteenth century and today are the nation's largest tribe.

Indians of the Pacific Coast During warmer months of each year the Indians of California usually roamed freely in search of food, their route dictated by the supply of seeds, acorns, wild plants, game, and even insects such as caterpillars and grasshoppers. In winter they gathered in small settlements, those in the south living in dome-shaped huts; those in the north in pit houses. Their dress also varied with the seasons. In summer they often went naked or perhaps wore small aprons of buckskin or plant fibers; in winter they wrapped themselves in capes made of fibers, furs, or feathers. Extended families of three or more generations sometimes banded together to form a "triblet" of perhaps 250 individuals. A few California Indians also had clans, but most did not recognize this type of social integration. There were no small towns and no tribal organization comparable to that of Indians east of the Rockies.

Indians of the Pacific Northwest lived in large plank houses and were supplied with food by fishing and whaling. Like the California Indians, they sometimes went naked, but usually they wore skirts, leggings, or cloaks to shield themselves from the wet, cool weather of that region. A conical hat with a wide brim also helped to keep them dry. They had no complex tribal organization similar to that found in other areas; however, each little village had a social-political structure founded upon wealth, the richest man serving as ruler over the common folk and over any slaves taken in raids or acquired by purchase.

During winter months these Northwest Indians held big feasts called "potlaches" at which each host tried to outdo his friends in food and gifts. Lavish hospitality added to one's prestige and also assured a rich harvest at the next "potlach." In contrast to the California Indians, their neighbors in the north lived in a sea of affluence. And, just as Mexican culture influenced the art and life of the Pueblos, so the Siberian and Eskimo cultures had considerable impact on the Indians living along the northern Pacific coast and inspired their extraordinary carvings in wood and stone.

Americans and European Newcomers

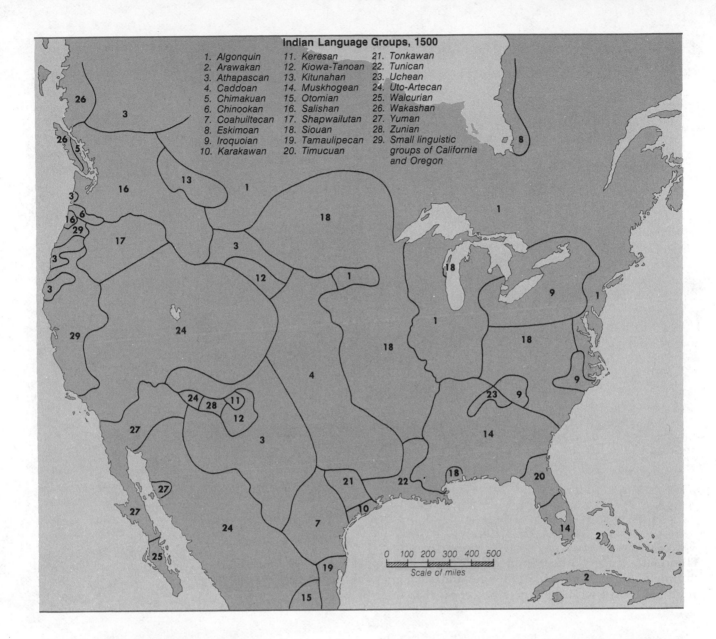

Indian Language Groups, 1500

1. Algonquin
2. Arawakan
3. Athapascan
4. Caddoan
5. Chimakuan
6. Chinookan
7. Coahuiltecan
8. Eskimoan
9. Iroquoian
10. Karakawan
11. Keresan
12. Kiowa-Tanoan
13. Kitunahan
14. Muskhogean
15. Otomian
16. Salishan
17. Shapwailutan
18. Siouan
19. Tamaulipecan
20. Timucuan
21. Tonkawan
22. Tunican
23. Uchean
24. Uto-Artecan
25. Walcurian
26. Wakashan
27. Yuman
28. Zunian
29. Small linguistic groups of California and Oregon

0 100 200 300 400 500
Scale of miles

Predecessors of Columbus

A Scottish prince, an Irish monk, a Phoenician king—all of these figures and more have been championed as the first Europeans to come to North America. The only pre-Columbian voyages that most scholars regard as having taken place are Norse expeditions, one of them led by Leif Ericson to Newfoundland about A.D. 1000. Between A.D. 800 and 1000, the Norse were leaving their homes in great numbers to settle in France, England, the Mediterranean, and Greenland. The gradual destruction of the Carolingian Empire in the West and the Roman Empire controlled by Byzantium in the East disrupted long-established trade routes. And these hardy northern seafarers set out in search of merchants, markets, land, and plunder.

Surveys begun in 1960 by the Norwegian archaeologist, Helge Ingstad, unearthed several large dwellings in Newfoundland that resemble those

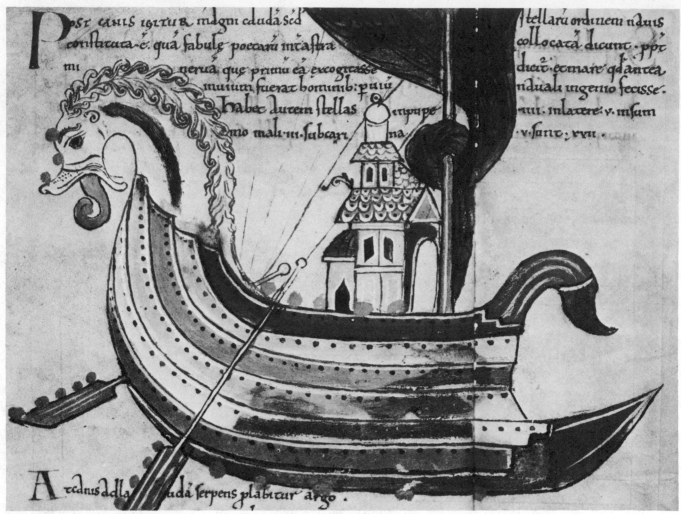

Post canis igitur magni cauda sed constituta e quam fabule poetarum mcastra... neruia que primu ea excogitasse muium fuerat hominib: puu habet autem stellas... mo mali m subcari...

stellaru ordinem induis collocata dicunt... ppt dicit ecmare qd antea nduali ingenio fecisse... m mlatere v insum v sunt xvii...

Arednis adla...uda serpens plabitur argo.

Courtesy of the Arnamagnaen Institution. Copenhagen, Denmark.

This tenth-century illustration of a Viking ship appeared in an English chronicle. Ships were actually longer and more graceful, but the artist was more impressed with the Norse fierceness than their beauty.

built by the Norse in Greenland. In the ruins of the largest house, Ingstad found a late Viking-type spindle whorl used to spin thread from wool. He also discovered four boat sheds along the shorelines. The site, named after a nearby village called L'Anse aux Meadows, is on the northernmost tip of Newfoundland.

Ingstad has several good reasons for thinking L'Anse aux Meadows may be Leif's settlement. For years historians have had difficulty envisioning Newfoundland as Vinland since grapes do not grow that far north. Ingstad suggests that Vinland may be derived from an obsolete term that means "pasturage" and that the wine of the sagas may

have been juice from local red berries. Carbon dating of the timbers of the excavated huts supports the date of A.D. 1000. All other claims for pre-Columbian voyages still seem questionable, and even Ingstad's evidence is at best circumstantial.

Despite the romance of pre-Columbian explorations, their lasting effect, other than in sagas and folklore, is minimal. No one found riches in sufficient quantity to attract others across the broad Atlantic in their wake. No individual representing a European state or nation capable of fostering and supporting such far-flung colonies appeared because, for nearly a thousand years (A.D. 500–1500), the influence of that Continent was shrinking, not

Dr. Helge Ingstad, Norway.

The spindle whorls shown here provided early clues to the Norse occupation of Newfoundland. They also indicated the presence of women, who did the spinning.

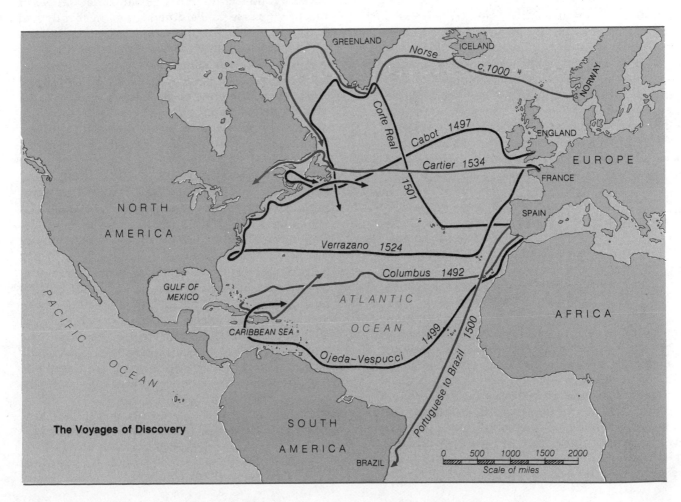

The Voyages of Discovery

increasing. Europe was divided into a patchwork of fiefdoms and principalities warring among themselves and vainly trying to thwart waves of invaders from the north, east, and south.

Gradually, however, a few nobles gained regional power, often by leading successful campaigns against such diverse groups as the Vikings or Moors, and isolated city-states such as Venice waxed rich on trade with the eastern half of the old Roman Empire which, although only a pale imitation of its once-great splendor, remained impressive compared to the chaos of a fragmented Europe. In time, nobles who were able to assert their rule over substantial areas became kings and, through alliances with other powerful elements of the society such as the Catholic Church and well-to-do merchants, curtailed the activities of lesser nobles in their midst. In short, they created modern nation-states ready to expand through colonization, trade, and the export of goods, but they were prepared also to do battle with anyone who opposed them.

Portugal, a compact little country somewhat removed from the hurly-burly of Europe yet superbly positioned for exploration, and Spain, a larger, more complex realm whose rulers soon developed strong dynastic ties throughout the Continent, were the first of these so-called nation-states. And, being the first to consolidate, the Portuguese and Spanish were the first in the Americas as well. This made them rivals for land and gold, not only in the New World, but in Africa, India, and Asia.

The Spanish Voyages

Even though Columbus had a very peculiar notion of the world's true size, he deserves full credit for his first voyage. Born in the Italian city of Genoa in 1451, Columbus was brought up as the son of an unsuccessful clothier. In his twenties he became a sailor and traveled on one voyage as far north as Iceland, where he may have heard tales of Vinland. Later, while sailing for the Portuguese on a trading expedition down the coast of west Africa, Columbus learned a great deal about seamanship from the

skilled Portuguese pilots. By 1484 he was ready to propose to the king of Portugal his great "Enterprise of the Indies."

This project, first submitted to the king of Portugal and later to the rulers of Spain, outlined a scheme for sailing west to the Orient. The Portuguese and Spanish monarchies were skeptical—and with good reason. They and their court scholars did not, as fairy tales would have it, believe that the world was flat. They knew it was a sphere and actually, as it turned out, a much larger sphere than Columbus estimated.

Despite the fact that a royal Spanish commission decided (after years of deliberation) that Columbus's scheme seemed "impossible to any educated person," the Queen, Isabella of Castile (1451–1504), finally endorsed his project. A woman of more than ordinary political vision, Isabella saw the potential of this proposal for providing Spain with an alternate route to Asia since Portugal controlled the route around Africa. She was also influenced by the fact that Luis de Santangel, keeper of the privy purse to Ferdinand, her husband, had become a firm backer of Columbus, willing to raise funds in his behalf. Soon Columbus was fitted out with a fleet of three ships, the flagship *Santa Maria*, and two smaller caravels named the *Pinta* and the *Niña*. The entire crew of the three ships numbered about ninety men and boys. (For more information about Columbus and the expedition see the essay, "Sailing with Columbus," in this chapter.)

The Four Voyages of Columbus

On his first voyage to the New World, Columbus explored the Bahamas and the island of Hispaniola, which today has Haiti on its western half and the Dominican Republic on the eastern. In the following year, 1493, he returned to Hispaniola with a much larger fleet and established the first settlement there. On the third voyage, in 1498, Columbus investigated Trinidad and a section of the South American coast—his first contact with the mainland. Since Columbus refused to accept the fact that he had not reached Asia, he did not know how to account for South America. No traveler to the Orient had ever mentioned this large continent to the south. Columbus's ingenious way of dealing with the continent was to declare that it was Paradise, which he named Gracia, the Spanish word for God's "Grace."

Although Columbus intended to return to South America, in 1502 on his fourth and last voy-

Amerigo Vespucci

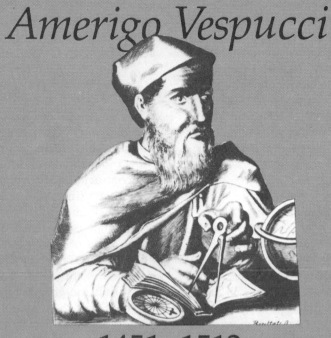

ca. 1451–1512

Born in Florence, this Italian merchant and navigator whose name was given to the New World entered the employ of the powerful Medici family as a young man and in 1491 was sent to Seville where the family had business interests. Giannoto Berardi, who managed the Medici outlet in that city, outfitted Columbus for his first voyage; upon his return, Vespucci probably was among those greeting the famed explorer. When Berardi died in the mid-1490s, Vespucci succeeded to his position.

Between 1497 and 1504, Amerigo Vespucci made several voyages across the Atlantic, just how many is not known, but at least two, during which he became convinced that the land in the Western Hemisphere was not Asia. This assertion dashed the dreams of many Europeans who, stirred by the exploits of Columbus, envisioned quick riches by sailing westward to India. Nevertheless, Columbus, who became acquainted with Vespucci when his firm helped the explorer prepare for his second and third voyages, thought highly of him, and the year before his death wrote that the Florentine native had always shown a desire to serve him and was indeed "an honorable man."

In 1505 Vespucci was summoned to the Spanish court and given a post with the Commercial House of the West Indies; three years later he became that organization's chief navigator, a position of great importance since he had to prepare maps and charts for the Spanish government.

Meanwhile, Vespucci published several letters describing his travels, which were soon circulated and reprinted. In 1507, M. Waldseemüller of Lorraine, produced a pamphlet that included Vespucci's words, as well as some of his own. More importantly, Waldseemüller suggested that the new southern lands be called "America" in honor of Amerigo Vespucci. This proposal won acceptance and the name quickly spread to the northern region, too.

Through his understanding of celestial navigation, Vespucci was able to compute the approximate location of land and water masses on the earth's surface and also establish longitude. His estimate of the earth's circumference, surprisingly accurate and in startling contrast to that of Columbus who thought it was only 3,000 miles from Spain to Japan, missed the mark by only fifty miles. Although the full details of Vespucci's life remain somewhat obscure, he was obviously a man of considerable ability, scrupulously honest, and thoroughly trustworthy; otherwise, as a foreigner, he would not have been given such a sensitive position in the emerging Spanish imperial structure.

age he only cruised past Honduras, Nicaragua, Costa Rica, and Panama. Then he was marooned for many months on Jamaica when his ships sank—the hulls had been honeycombed by shipworms. In 1503 he and his party were rescued. Ill with malaria, disgruntled by Spain's failure to honor its original contract with him (Columbus claimed for himself and his heirs a third of the value of all trade between Spain and the Indies), the great navigator returned disconsolate to Spain. He died on May 19, 1506.

Later Voyages

Other Spanish fleets made frequent crossings of the Atlantic even while Columbus was still alive. One of the most colorful and unpleasant personalities was Alonso de Ojeda (ca. 1468–1514), who led an expedition in 1499. It was he who first saw an Indian village built on pilings above water which he named "little Venice"—Venezuela. The greedy Ojeda attacked other Spanish ships in order to seize weapons and provisions for his own fleet; worse, he treated the Indians he met with intense cruelty and returned to Spain with buckets of valuable pearls he obtained from native Americans at gun or sword point. With him sailed Amerigo Vespucci, a Florentine banker and supplier of ship's stores, whose name was given to the "Americas" in the early 1500s. As Samuel Eliot Morison, the best biographer of Columbus, once wrote: "America was discovered accidentally by a great seaman who was looking for something else; when discovered it was not wanted; and most of the exploration for the next fifty years was done in the hope of getting through it or around it. America was named after a man who discovered no part of the New World. History is like that, very chancy." (For more information on Vespucci, see the biographical sketch in this chapter.)

The Conquests

During their first thirty years in the New World, the Spanish were primarily intent upon establishing a colony on the island of Hispaniola. Although ships returned home with gold, cotton, and Indian slaves, this booty fell far short of the Oriental riches they had hoped to obtain. This disappointment ushered in a new era of exploration, during which the Spanish conquistadores ranged throughout much of the Americas. One Spaniard, Juan Ponce de León (ca. 1460–1521), subjugated Puerto Rico and on April 2, 1513, landed just north of what is now Indian River inlet in the state of Florida, which he thought was an island. In the same year, Vasco Núñez de Balboa (ca. 1475–1519) led an expedition across present-day Panama to the Pacific Ocean.

The great treasures so long sought finally were found in Peru and Mexico. In 1533 Francisco Pizarro (ca. 1471–1541) and his troops overwhelmed the Peruvian capital of Cuzco, where they immediately began to melt down the city's vast stores of gold into portable blocks. Soon the lure of so much gold drew thousands of conquistadores to Peru. The earlier conquest of Mexico and the subsequent taking of Chibcha (in modern Colombia) placed the three wealthiest empires in the New World in the hands of Spanish explorers. Columbus and the first explorers met only the simpler (and poorer) civilizations of the Caribbean, but the Spanish now had not one but three Eldorados at their disposal. One-fifth of all the gold taken in the New World went to the Spanish monarch; the rest was divided among the conquistadores.

The Spanish Empire

Spanish claims in the New World were based upon Columbus's voyages and a treaty signed with Portugal in 1494. The Treaty of Tordesillas, which had the approval of the Pope, divided the new territory between the two nations. Land west of a line drawn north and south between the present forty-sixth and forty-seventh meridians (a straight line from Newfoundland in the north to present-day Brazil in the south) belonged to Spain. Everything east of it, including Africa and the rich trade routes to India and the Orient, belonged to Portugal. The Pope's approval was contingent upon these "heathen lands" being converted to Christianity. Although Portugal maintained its claim to Brazil, it was not an active competitor with Spain in the New World; the Portuguese were too busy developing an exclusive sea trade route with Asia and defending their possessions against the newly independent Dutch.

The Spanish empire, a possession of the throne, was directly administered by the monarch. A Council of the Indies in Spain managed bureaucratic details, but had no independent will of its own. The only restraint on the Spanish king's power was the rebelliousness of the proud colonists themselves; for instance, when the king attempted to put into effect radical reforms in Peru, the conquistadores threatened revolt—and the king was forced to back down.

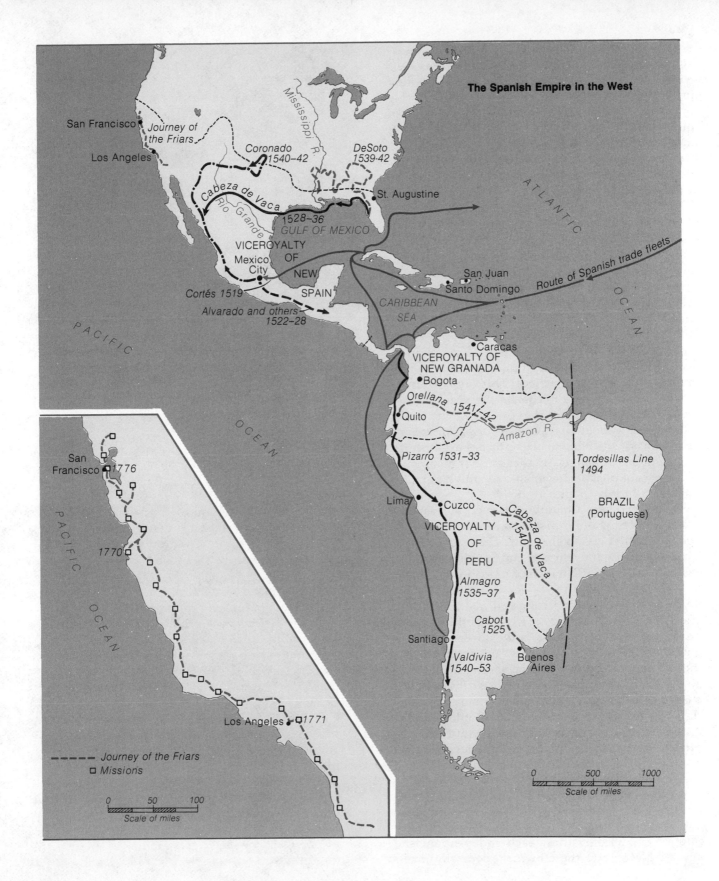

The Spanish Empire in the West

San Francisco
Journey of the Friars
Los Angeles
Coronado 1540–42
DeSoto 1539–42
Cabeza de Vaca
St. Augustine
1528–36
Mississippi R.
ATLANTIC
Rio Grande
GULF OF MEXICO
VICEROYALTY OF
Mexico City
NEW
Cortés 1519
SPAIN
San Juan
Santo Domingo
Route of Spanish trade fleets
OCEAN
Alvarado and others 1522–28
CARIBBEAN SEA
PACIFIC
Caracas
VICEROYALTY OF NEW GRANADA
Bogota
Orellana 1541–42
OCEAN
Quito
Amazon R.
Pizarro 1531–33
Tordesillas Line 1494
Lima
Cuzco
Cabeza de Vaca 1540
BRAZIL (Portuguese)
VICEROYALTY OF PERU
Almagro 1535–37
Cabot 1525
Santiago
Valdivia 1540–53
Buenos Aires

San Francisco 1776
1770
Los Angeles 1771
PACIFIC OCEAN

- - - - *Journey of the Friars*
□ Missions

0   50   100
Scale of miles

0   500   1000
Scale of miles

15
The Spanish Voyages

Dreams of limitless gold enticed the conquistadores to America, while dreams of countless souls to be saved lured the friars. Both succeeded in their quests to a spectacular degree. The friars were able to present Catholicism in terms the Indians often understood and accepted, and native religions, mingled with Catholicism, underwent many accommodations. Thus the Spanish friars came to believe that the Aztec deity, Quetzalcohuatl, was the apostle Thomas, who somehow strayed to the New World to win souls for Christ. Similarly, the Mexicans equated some Catholic saints with the local gods; one of the most celebrated substitutions occurred when the Mexican "Our Lady Spirit" became the patron saint of Mexico—the Virgin of Guadalupe. Much of the success of the Spanish friars was due to their undogmatic outlook in stressing the importance of sincere conviction and faith rather than the formalities of church ritual. This intellectual orientation made the Spanish friars flexible in their assimilation of native American religious attitudes and practices. This outlook also is evident in their efforts to change the Spanish labor policy that forced Indians into peonage. Eventually, through the work of missionaries such as Bartolomé de las Casas, the church began to oppose Spanish mistreatment of native Americans. (For an account of his exceptional achievement, see the biographical sketch in this chapter.)

The very year Columbus arrived at Watlings Island marked another historic event in the fate of Spain, one that was to shape the character of Spanish America. That event was the Spanish conquest of the Moors. In 1492 the last Moorish populations on the Iberian peninsula were subdued by the Spanish monarchs. This conquest had a profound effect on Spanish politics. Knights and aristocrats no longer had peninsular lands to conquer and plunder. Without a source of wealth from warfare, the old feudal Spanish aristocracy (and the king) might have faded into relative obscurity as power passed into the hands of a small, rising merchant class. Suddenly the vast American nations of the Aztecs, the Chibchas, and the Incas were new empires to exploit and plunder, and the feudal values of knightly valor against the heathen were reinvigorated by translation to the New World.

Throughout the sixteenth century, the Americas appeared to be nothing but a godsend for Spain and its king. Initially the New World was divided into several viceroyalties, each independent and answerable only to the crown. Periodically inves-

Bartolomé de las Casas

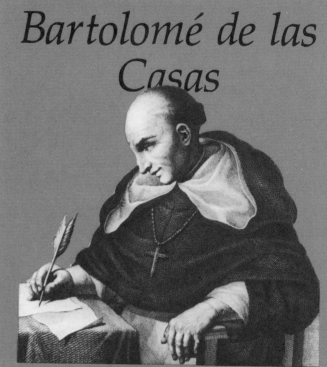

1474–1566

Known as "the Apostle of the Indies," Bartolomé de las Casas was a Spanish missionary who became the first outstanding European defender of the Indians against the conquistadores. The son of a merchant who had sailed with Columbus on his second voyage (1493), las Casas settled in Hispaniola in 1502. At first, having studied law, he was adviser to the colonial governor, but about 1510 became a secular priest. As such, he is believed to have been the first priest ordained in the New World. Meanwhile, in accordance with the practice of the conquistadores, he worked Indian slaves on his estate until 1514. In that year, having come under the influence of a Dominican friar (he joined the order nine years later), las Casas relinquished his lands and began a lifelong struggle to improve the lot of the Indians. What he particularly condemned was a labor system that forced the Indians to work to the point of death on farms and in mines. For the *encomienda* system, which at first was a form of tenancy, quickly became peonage and, in effect, turned into slavery.

To make the plight of the Indians better known, las Casas wrote a massive *History of the Indies* that

John Carter Brown Library, Brown University.

In their eagerness to learn enough about the natives to aid in converting them, Spanish missionaries became recorders of Indian culture. This is the title page of the earliest Spanish-Indian dictionary.

told the tale of Spanish conquest in three volumes up to the year 1520. Fortunately, for later historians, he also copied out Columbus's log of his first voyage; it is the only copy that has survived. In another original work, las Casas refuted the charge that the Indians were "savages" in need of the civilizing presence of Spain. He described Aztec and Inca cities, agricultural methods, industries, religion, government, and laws. He concluded that the Indians "equaled many nations of this world that are renowned and considered civilized, and they surpassed many others, and to none were they inferior."

Unfortunately, the concern las Casas felt for the Indians led him to advocate the use of black slaves to replace Indian slaves. In 1518 he proposed that the Spanish crown prohibit Indian slavery and suppress, in gradual degrees, the forced-service *encomiendas*. Indian slaves and laborers were to be replaced with blacks purchased in North Africa. Las Casas himself apparently owned slaves in Hispaniola as late as 1544. It is ironic that in his zeal to improve the life of the Indians, the "Protector of the Indians," as las Casas was known, contributed to the introduction and establishment of black slavery in the Western Hemisphere.

tigators were sent from Spain to review the accounts and actions of administrators, all of whom had to be Spanish-born and of "pure" Spanish stock.

The original conquistadores were given vast *encomiendas*, but upon their deaths those lands reverted to the throne—and the king issued no new land grants. By the middle of the sixteenth century the throne had established a highly centralized administration over South and Central America. By the time England and France could begin to plant their first miserable and starving colonies in North America, the Spanish empire in the New World boasted impressive cities, a far-flung network of missions, several major universities—and even a high literary and artistic culture of its own. Of

William L. Clements Library, University of Michigan. This watercolor, done for a French edition of *A Very Brief Account of the Destruction of the Indes* by de las Casas, shows Spaniards sacking an Indian village.

course this empire was, from a humane point of view, cruelly oppressive. It was first maintained by Indian labor and then, after the Indians were decimated by disease and exhaustion, by black slaves imported from Africa.

Exploiting And Settling North America

England, France, and Holland did not expand into the New World in the early sixteenth century because all three countries were too fragmented politically and too preoccupied with internal affairs to organize and finance a major expedition. In 1500 England was a minor power still attempting to recover from 100 years of dynastic war, although, Henry VII of England sent John Cabot (1450–ca. 1498) to the New World in 1497. In June of that year Cabot landed in Newfoundland, saw not one native

but was nevertheless convinced he had discovered a land in the north of Asia. The following year he set out for Japan—and never returned. The English, discouraged at finding only codfish, an eagle, and various strange fauna, did not send out new expeditions. After Henry VIII came to the throne, his desire to divorce his first wife to marry another (who might bear him a male heir) led him into conflict with the Pope, who refused to annul Henry's marriage. This conflict culminated in England's break with the Catholic Church. Thus, throughout most of the sixteenth century, Catholic Spain attempted to force England to rejoin Christendom.

Domestic stability returned to England only with the ascension of Elizabeth I to the throne, but throughout most of her reign, the nation continued to be threatened by a hostile Spain—and, much closer at hand, by the separate kingdom of Scotland and a rebellious Ireland. Planting a colony required more money than either the crown or private English merchants were willing to invest.

Early English Settlements
Only one small group of courtiers in England was interested in colonizing. In 1583 Sir Humphrey Gilbert attempted to establish a colony in Newfoundland but was lost at sea on the return voyage. His younger half brother, Sir Walter Raleigh (ca.

1552–1618), next took up the challenge and in 1584 he sent a party of explorers to reconnoiter the coast of present-day North Carolina. These Englishmen claimed the land for the queen, and on their return named the entire Atlantic seaboard Virginia, an allusion to her unmarried state. (The name may have been suggested by the ever courtly Sir Walter Raleigh.)

Encouraged by the reports of these men, Raleigh decided in 1585 to establish a colony, and more than 100 male settlers eventually landed on Roanoke Island. Although the colonists built a fort and cottages, they soon were on very bad terms with the Indians. During the winter, when food became scarce, they declared war on the Indians, and by the summer of 1586 conditions had so deteriorated that the colonists returned to England.

Raleigh's last attempt to plant a permanent colony on Roanoke occurred a year later. Unlike earlier expeditions, this one included women and children. But this party met with even less good luck. When the crew of a relief ship bringing supplies, which was delayed for several years by the Spanish armada, tried to find the colonists in 1590, they had disappeared, leaving behind only the mysterious inscription "Croatoan," a way of suggesting perhaps they had gone to live among the nearby Croatan Indians. It is ironic that the only lasting contribution of the Roanoke Colony was the work of artist and cartographer John White. (What little is known of this artist is given in a biographical sketch in this chapter.)

Jamestown

Conditions had not been right for English settlement in the New World in the sixteenth century. But at the beginning of the seventeenth century a Scottish ruler became James I of England, thereby uniting the two thrones. Moreover, James achieved a new peace with Spain. These stabilizing circumstances encouraged Englishmen to invest in colonies in North America. (Speculation of this sort today would be called expending "venture capital.")

The English pattern of colonization differed from the Spanish in many important respects. The Spanish king, who directly controlled his New World empire, used its vast resources to bolster his position among a restive nobility and usually sent only citizens of high social position and unquestionable piety to the New World. England, on the other hand, set up private companies to settle along the Atlantic Coast of North America and regarded the colonies as a proper dumping ground for paupers, vagabonds, criminals, and religious dissidents. The practice of including families and women in these colonizing groups helped to stabilize the settlements. England also gained some stability at home since the relocation of dissenting religious sects helped to relax religious tensions.

In 1606 James granted a charter shared by the Virginia Company of London, which was to settle what now are the southeastern states, and the Virginia Company of Plymouth, which lay claim to the northeastern areas. In 1607 both branches of the Virginia Company attempted colonization. The Plymouth branch failed; the colony planted in Maine returned after a year, discouraged by a terrible winter.

But the London branch succeeded—if anything as painful, disorganized, and profitless as the first

Thomas Gilcrease Institute of American History and Art, Tulsa, Oklahoma.

This DeBry engraving depicts numerous features of life in a Secotan village. Note the corn, sunflowers, and pumpkins.

John White

dates unknown

Except for a decade or so when he was associated with Sir Walter Raleigh's Virginia colony, little is known about the career of John White. Between 1585 and 1590 this English artist and cartographer made at least three trips to the New World, but his fame rests on his watercolors of the natives and of the flora and fauna he saw near the ill-fated colony of Roanoke. White also apparently made sketches in Florida, Greenland, and the Caucasus during his lifetime, or he copied the work of others who visited those regions.

In 1585, White was one of 107 men who established the original Roanoke settlement on the outer banks of North Carolinia. He sailed from Plymouth on April 9th of that year and fourteen months later accompanied Sir Francis Drake back to England. In July 1587, White went forth a second time, on this occasion as governor. He was accompanied by several relatives, including his daughter Elinor, wife of Ananias Dare, who on August 18, 1587 gave birth to Virginia Dare, the first English child born in America. When Virginia was about nine days old, her grandfather was persuaded, against his judgment it seems, to return to England for provisions.

The following year he set out for Roanoke, but the sailors on his vessel were more interested in Spanish prizes than colonies and tangled (unsuccessfully) with enemy ships and had to return to port. In 1590 White finally got to Roanoke Island, found it deserted, and, denied the opportunity for an effective search, had to put to sea and sail for home. That same year about one-third of the drawings he had made earlier were published in Thomas Harriot's *Brief and True Report of . . . Virginia*. These illustrations, soon copied and adapted, long formed the basis of what much of the Old World knew of the New. Seventy-five of White's original watercolors can be seen at the British Museum in London. Most of these drawings appear to have been done in America and thus provide unusual insight into the natural history and aboriginal customs of the mid-Atlantic region. Harriot's work also included two maps White made of the Virginia coast. These maps influenced European geographers for more than half a century. Indeed, White's "carte of all of the coast of Virginia" was the basis of John Smith's famed map of the same area published in 1612.

years of the Jamestown settlement can be called "success." The purpose of this foothold in the Chesapeake Bay area was to create a permanent colony that would seek gold and silver, convert the Indians to Christianity, challenge the power of the Spanish in Florida, develop natural resources, and achieve a host of other minor goals.

The 1607 expedition was made up of 104 people. During the voyage, no one knew who among them would be their leaders. In an effort to prevent dissension, the identity of the councilors was kept secret until the ship reached its destination, a strategy that backfired and only increased bickering among this band of settlers. Upon arrival in April, the men selected by the company back in London assumed office—and soon began quarreling with one another. Disputes between Edward Wingfield and John Smith (1580–1631) were particularly bitter. Smith was a soldier, explorer, author, and, of course, one of the founders of permanent English settlement in North America. As a youth he fought in the Netherlands, then Hungary where he deluded the enemy with fireworks. Left for dead on a battlefield, he became a prisoner of the Asiatic Turks, escaped to Russia, and returned to his native England three years before setting out for America. In the New World he explored the rivers of coastal Virginia, and perhaps was saved by young Pocahontas. (This incident and her relationship with Smith and other colonial leaders are covered in the biographical sketch in this chapter.) On his return to Jamestown, he was threatened with yet another execution for losing several men during his travels. Spared by the arrival of Captain Christopher Newport from England, Smith soon became president of the little colony's council—in fact, a dictator of sorts since all of the other council members had died or returned to England.

Drastic measures of some sort were certainly demanded, since malaria and other diseases had reduced the original number of settlers to thirty-eight people. Unwisely, the settlers ignored company instructions to build the colony on a high and healthy site and instead chose Jamestown, a peninsula lying between malarial swamps. The Powhatan Indians who lived nearby were alternately friendly and hostile. Having had some experience with bands of Spanish explorers, they mistrusted whites in general and were further antagonized by incessant demands to supply the little colony with food. In fact, it is quite remarkable that relations

Pocahontas

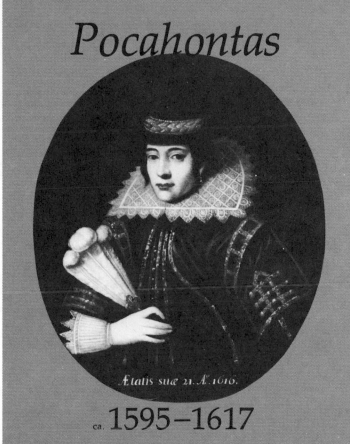

Ætatis suæ 21. Aᵒ 1616.

ca. 1595–1617

Called "wanton" by some Jamestown residents and "naturally precocious" by others, the key to understanding Pocahontas (also spelled Pocohantas) is in recognizing her innate curiosity about the English. In sharp contrast to other members of her tribe, she was determined to learn as much as she could concerning these invaders. As a result, she became a negotiator between two worlds as well as a pawn to be bargained for.

Daughter of Powhatan, ruler of a loose Algonquian alliance, this "American Princess," also known as Matoka, was about eleven years old when the settlers arrived at Jamestown in 1607. She seems to have been fascinated by worldly John Smith, and he, in turn, by her. They taught each other simple phrases in their native tongues, and in December of that year she presumably saved Smith's life when her father's warriors were about to club him to death. That episode led to a shakey truce, although Powhatan, now in his sixties, was wary since he remembered various encounters with the Spanish during his lifetime.

The truce broke down in 1609, and for the next four years there was virtual open warfare. In 1613, Pocahontas was captured by the English and held at Henrico, a frontier parish some 80 miles from Jamestown. The governor used her presence to extract promises from the Indians; meanwhile, she learned more English, was baptized, and fell in love with John Rolfe, the handsome widower who had introduced West Indian tobacco to the little colony. In legend, the bride symbolized the presumed innocence of a new continent and this marriage, the hope of cooperation between natives and newcomers. In reality, although the union ushered in a period of peace lasting until 1622, it signaled recognition by Powhatan of new stability and new strength at Jamestown. The marriage also helped to solidify Powhatan's power and prestige among confederate tribes.

In 1615 Pocahontas gave birth to a son, Thomas, and the following year the family, together with about a dozen of her native relatives, crossed the Atlantic to England. Pocahontas was presented at court and entertained widely. At the same time, the Virginia Company used her presence to promote its colonization schemes. As she was preparing to sail for home after a visit of seven months, Pocahontas died suddenly and was buried at Gravesend. Rolfe returned to Virginia, but their son remained in England until adulthood.

Pocahontas captured the attention of Romantics who idealized her as the model American Indian woman. Unhappily, her experiences were not the opening scene in a tale of Indian-white cooperation. Instead they were merely an intriguing episode in an unfolding drama that would dominate the ebb and flow of European settlement for decades to come.

with the Indians were not much worse than they were. The parent company added to the burdens of the settlement by sending a new supply of colonists at a time when food was scarce. Fire leveled the first fort and feeble attempts to set up a glassmaking industry failed.

Heeding the advice of Smith, who returned to England in 1609 for treatment of gunpowder burns and never returned, the company obtained a new charter from King James. This document, not officially approved until three years later, allowed the company to claim much of North America, to enhance their appeals to investors, and to offer stock and land to each settler over ten years of age. More important, perhaps, Virginia would be ruled henceforth by a single individual, not by a cumbersome council.

Despite the good intentions of Smith and of the company's governors, the winter of 1609–1610—"the starving time,"—almost wiped out Jamestown. The supply of corn was consumed by rats and 440 of the 500 colonists died. When Sir Thomas Gates, the colony's new governor, who was shipwrecked on Bermuda en route from London, arrived the following May, he saw nothing but devastation.

The survivors had decided to leave with Gates and return to England when they learned that fresh supplies and 150 settlers were arriving with Lord De La Warr, the new governor who was to replace Gates, their provisional leader. His auspicious entry on the scene along with a new charter granted in 1609 marked the beginning of success. Slowly the colony began to prosper. Sir Thomas Dale, successor to De La Warr and a ruthless administrator, imposed a militarylike discipline on the settlers. He forced laggards to work the fields, he made peace with the Indians, and under provisions of the new charter, he eventually granted three-acre plots to individuals. Up to this point, the settlers were shareholders working the land jointly. Best of all, in 1611, the colony finally found a cash crop: tobacco. Eight years later Jamestown was shipping 40,000 pounds of tobacco to England and the foundations of economic well-being were emerging.

The French Colonies

Like the English, the French did not begin their first tentative movements into the New World until the second half of the sixteenth century, nor did they plant their first permanent settlement until the early 1600s. And like the English, the French were forced by the Spanish hegemony over Latin America to confine their interests to North America.

There most of the resemblances end. For the French, unlike the English, were eventually more adept in fashioning a workable Indian policy, but less successful in building an agricultural economy. Perhaps their success in establishing relatively amicable relations with the Indians stemmed in part from their failure to appropriate Indian land for substantial farms and for widespread settlement. Also, unlike the English, the French did not encourage Nonconformists to populate the New World; rather, they resembled the Spanish in this regard, eventually permitting only faithful adherents to Catholicism and solid citizens to emigrate.

In the 1530s Jacques Cartier (1491–1557) led several expeditions to the coast of Newfoundland, Nova Scotia, and the Saint Lawrence River. He also spent two winters in Canada, the second time with the intention of establishing a colony. The neighboring Indians dropped hints that were either deliberately misleading (or simply misunderstood) of a great civilization to be found in the interior of Canada. Cartier eagerly set out for this fabled realm where gold, silver, and rare spices must abound. He did find something that looked like gold, but he was forced to return since the colonists were threatened by hostile Indians and winter weather began to claim many victims. When his "gold" was assayed, it proved worthless.

Quebec, the first permanent French settlement, was founded in 1608, only a year after Jamestown. The French colony was essentially little more than a trading post where the French exchanged European goods for Indian furs, especially beaver pelts, which were used in the new French fashion of felt hats. But the fur trade was seen only as a means of supporting the colony until two greater goals were realized: the discovery of a Northwest Passage to the Orient and the development of profitable gold mines. As it turned out, neither ambition was to be realized, but for decades the French pursued these impossible dreams of great wealth.

Like Jamestown, the French colony was backed by a private stock company with a charter from the king. The settlement, indeed the entire French enterprise in North America for the first three decades of the seventeenth century, owed much to Samuel de Champlain (ca. 1567–1635), a sailor, soldier, and administrator, who charted maps of the new territory, established peaceful relations with several Indian tribes, and explored the interior. In 1610 Champlain joined three Indian tribes (the Algonquians, the Montagnais, and the Hurons) in attack-

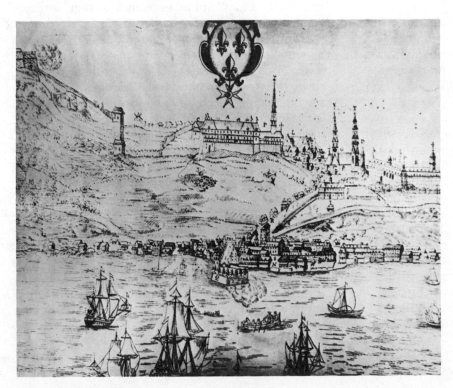

Archives Nationales du Québec.
Quebec's role as the major port for Canada is clearly reflected in this engraving of 1693.

ing and defeating the Mohawks. While this alliance earned the French trading rights with the Huron Confederacy, it incurred the wrath of the Iroquois.

In their early years, Quebec and other French colonies in Canada had a precarious lease on life. They depended on France for much of their food and goods to trade with the Indians. Although the king insisted that the colonists farm, agriculture was slow to start and even slower to expand. While the majority of French settlers became farmers, subsistence farming along with the long winter season, which made export trade precarious, meant that farmers did not have a large cash crop.

Still more serious were threats from the English over disputed territory. Although treaties might be signed in Europe designating lines of demarcation, the actual outcome of colonial rivalries on the frontier in North America depended on the force of arms available on this side of the ocean. England made good its claim to Newfoundland, though France held the areas just to the south; further south, English settlements appeared along the Atlantic seaboard. The English envied French control over the rich fur trade that flowed through the Saint Lawrence River—and in 1621 a Scot, after obtaining a grant from James I, seized Nova Scotia from the French and captured Quebec. But a new treaty signed in Europe returned Quebec to the French. This competition between England and France in the late seventeenth and eighteenth centuries for trade and political power eventually erupted into a series of wars fought in Europe and in America. These wars finally led to the defeat of France and to her expulsion from most of the New World.

Dutch Holdings

The French dominated the Saint Lawrence River, one of the two broad avenues to the fur-rich interior of North America; the Dutch controlled the Hudson River, the other great waterway. In 1609 Henry Hudson, an Englishman working for the Dutch, sailed up the river that now bears his name in search of a passage to the Indies. He stopped his fruitless pursuit at Albany, having laid claim to the entire Hudson River valley, Long Island, and the Delaware Bay for the Dutch. In this vast area the Dutch established their colony of New Netherlands. Within a few years they had developed two strongholds: Albany and the island of Manhattan.

The primary Dutch colony in the New World was in Brazil. This rich prize they attempted to wrest from the Portuguese, but were finally expelled by the middle of the seventeenth century. Enterprising and exulting in their recent independence from Spanish rule, the Dutch were more intent on making money than on establishing settlements. They actually had too small a population to send forth colonists; and their primacy in international trade (especially in the Far East) was too rewarding to encourage them to waste much time or effort on the North American holdings. Fur trade with the Iroquois and Algonquian tribes did, however, prove profitable—as did trade with other European colonists. The Dutch introduced slaves from Africa into French and English islands in the Caribbean, bought the sugar these slaves grew, and throughout much of the seventeenth century traded freely with other English and French outposts.

The Three Empires

Despite the contributions of the Dutch and the Portuguese to the New World, the three most important European powers in the hemisphere were Spain, England, and France.

Each of these three empires took on a distinctive character. Spanish America was administered directly by the king; all important decisions were made in Spain. A static, rigidly stratified social system was grafted onto areas where—at least in Mexico, Peru, and Colombia—such a system already had long existed under native rule. The government was appointed and no local assemblies existed. Few Spanish men migrated to the colonies, and even fewer Spanish women. Consequently, intermarriages existed among whites, Indians, and black slaves. Spanish slave codes even permitted slaves to marry and own property. The resulting gradations of race mixture were officially sanctioned and recognized by the government. But if Spanish America was coherent politically, it was geographically fragmented. Deserts, mountains, and impassable jungles separated one section of the empire from another.

The French settlement in New France (Canada) was originally under the auspices of several private stock companies chartered by the king. By the middle of the seventeenth century, however, the stock companies were bankrupt and the crown assumed control. Conducting the fur trade and converting the Indians to Catholicism became the chief activities of the French. If the French had prevailed, Canada would have been as hierarchical and rigid a society as Spanish America. But there were too few settlers spread over too large a territory to make an autocratic system feasible.

Some French settlers came to Canada to engage in the lucrative fur trade; they were thus constantly on the move in search of Indian tribes from whom they could buy furs. The majority of French settlers became farmers and prospered since the relatively small population consumed most of the agricultural products. Subsistence farming, along with the long winter season that made export trade precarious, meant that farmers did not have a large cash crop. Under these conditions, slavery could serve no economic purpose, hence it played almost no role in New France, though it did on French islands in the Caribbean.

Most of the English settlers, unlike the Spanish and French, were Protestants. Though they had some interest in Christianizing Indians, they did not exercise this talent with the same zeal as their European rivals. Like the early French colonies, the first English settlements were financed by private stock companies chartered by the king; and, in similar fashion, when these companies experienced financial difficulties, the colonies were taken over by the crown. Yet English settlements possessed at least one striking difference: they contained the seeds of parliamentary government. For example, the House of Burgesses, which first gathered in 1619 to discuss company regulations and community affairs, continued to meet after Virginia became a royal colony in 1624. In time, since the king permitted similar assemblies to develop in other colonies, Americans began to view their colonial legislatures as miniature parliaments. This raised basic, fundamental questions concerning the role of Parliament. How much control did it have over the colonies? What was the relationship of these assemblies to Parliament or, for that matter, to the king and his ministers? Here, of course, lie not only the seeds of parliamentary, representative government, but of the American Revolution, too.

In America, the English generally became prosperous farmers because they came in far greater numbers, brought their families with them, and settled in a climate that permitted the development of successful cash-crop farming. By contrast, the French farmer in Canada found no cash crop. Yet he was able to develop a subsistence agriculture that carried little settlements through long hard winters. But in Louisiana and on various Caribbean islands, the French fostered slave societies not unlike those found in the English colonies along the Atlantic Coast.

If the English outshone the French Canadians as farmers, they were, by comparison, dismal failures in working out a practical Indian policy. There were, of course, Englishmen who participated in the fur trade and Indian tribes that got along reasonably well with the English. But for the most part, the English tended to cling to their farms along the Atlantic seaboard for many decades and made little effort to penetrate into the interior.

Settlers in the New World built their homes on Old World models. The Adam Thoroughgood House in Virginia is a perfect example of an Old World style adapted to the New.

Essay

Sailing with Columbus

The ninety men and boys who sailed west across the uncharted Atlantic with Columbus on his first voyage must have been anxious about unknown aspects of the voyage. Although the trip lasted only thirty-three days, less time than required to sail from Italy to England—no member of the crew had any way of knowing that in advance. When Columbus was not stern, he reassured his men with "soft words," as one contemporary put it—but could he be trusted? The trade winds that blew Columbus's three small ships westward were so favorable that soon the crew began to fear they would never find a wind to bear them back home. For days on end the weather was perfect—but even that aroused misgivings. This mad foreigner, the men muttered, this maniac from Genoa, will order us to continue sailing westward until our water runs out. And under a sky that never rains, how will we replenish our supplies?

Other odd phenomena troubled the sailors. On September 16 (the ships having cleared the Canary Islands ten days earlier), the fleet entered the Sargasso Sea, a vast calm pond in the Atlantic covered with green gulfweed. The men were afraid to sail through it lest their ships become enmeshed and becalmed. Columbus, with all the courage of his convictions (or obsessions), ordered them to head on—and his decision turned out to be right, for the gulfweed forms only a slight blanket over the water and could be easily sliced by the prow of a ship. Then a new problem beset the mariners. At night the compass

The New York Public Library, Picture Collection.
This engraving illustrated Columbus's letter of 1493. The ship is not a likeness of one of his three ships, but a stylized version of a carrack from that period.

no longer pointed directly towards the North Star. Until then, sailors had always assumed the North Star marked the True North; in fact, its position relative to the earth shifts daily, and observably so in western latitudes. This peculiar behavior of an old and reliable friend disturbed the sailors.

Sailing conditions during the first voyage were, by and large, so auspicious that the crew had idle time to joke, to troll for fish—and to grumble. To say the sailors were "idle" is, of course, something of an oversimplification, since life aboard a fifteenth-century ship followed a highly regulated schedule. At dawn the men on watch scrubbed down the deck with salt water and twig brooms. The new watch coming on duty were awakened. Arising was a simple affair, since the men slept in their clothes on the planks of the deck or, if it was raining, down below on top of the equally uncomfortable casks of water and wine. (Not until much later did sailors sleep in hammocks, which were invented by Indians in the New World.) Grouchy and aching, the men ate a cold breakfast—cheese, pickled sardines, garlic cloves, dried peas and beans, and hardtack, a tasteless but easily preserved bread. (Dried fruit was a luxury reserved only for officers.)

Since all wooden ships draw water, the caulker and a few hands pumped the vessel dry every morning. The caulker had the responsibility for keeping the ship watertight—by sealing shut (or caulking) seams, by coating the hull with tallow, and by operating and maintaining the pump, a hollow log outfitted with a piston and leather valves at the bottom of the ship.

Up on deck two watches were posted, one in the front (fore), the other at the back (aft). They were on the lookout for brewing storms, for enemy vessels—and, on the first voyage, for land or any hint that land might be near (birds, for instance). The Spanish sovereigns had offered an extra award of money to the first man who spotted land, and a lookout on the *Pinta*, Rodrigo de Triana, collected the prize.

What were the majority of the crew doing? Most of the men were setting sail or taking it in according to the captain's orders. Others were repairing frayed ropes or torn or damaged sails under the direction of the boatswain. The steward might be checking out the provisions, to make certain they were not being ruined by water or rats, or training ships' boys in their duties.

The only hot meal of the day was served at noon, though who cooked it remains a mystery (records of the time never list the position of cook). Food was prepared in an open firebox—that is, an iron tray lined with sand and fed with logs (it was probably in the front of the ship, in the forecastle). Though not sumptuous, the food was no worse than what the average peasant ate on land during the winter: pickled beef or pork, hardtack, sardines, and anchovies. No fresh fruit or vegetables were served, and this lack of vitamins caused a horrible disease—scurvy. Fortunately, Columbus's first voyage was so brief that the disease did not afflict his crew.

Just before the meal was served, a boy chanted: "Table, table, sir captain and master and good company, table ready; meat ready; water as usual for sir captain and master and good company. Long live the King of Castile by land and sea! Who says to him war, off with his head; who won't say amen, gets nothing to drink. Table is set, who don't come won't eat."

In the evening, if the winds dropped, the crew would sit around and tell stories. Then evening prayers would begin. Columbus's men and boys were intensely religious—as were most of the Spanish of that day. The cross was painted on sails, and every change of watch was marked with prayers and pious songs. But the evening ceremony was most impressive. The mariners gathered to recite an "Our Father" and a "Hail, Mary." They then said the Credo and sang an old chant, the "Salve, Regina," addressed to the Virgin Mary, patron saint of sailors.

Columbus sailed with three ships. One was a cargo ship called a *nao* (this was Columbus's flagship, named the *Santa María*). The other two vessels (nicknamed *Niña* and *Pinta*) were caravels. The *nao* and the caravels were the most successful ships for long voyages on the open sea, and their design resulted from the blending of various elements from several different sources. Caravels had square sails, but they also had at least one or more lateen sails, which were triangular sails suspended from a single mast and running from the front to the back of the ship. This design was a departure from traditional European rigging which, since the days of the Roman Empire, had consisted of square sails spread across the width of the ship, from one side to the other. A square sail was fine when the wind was blowing from behind the ship. But the lateen sail, which originated in India, was introduced to Europeans by Arabs. Far more flexible, it could be tilted at many different angles, which greatly increased maneuverability and allowed ships to take advantage of winds blowing from several different directions.

Other new elements of ship construction came from northern Europe. These included square sails with much more flexible rigging and a rudder operated from within the ship. Before the fifteenth century, Mediterranean ships used rudders that protruded from the sides of the ship toward the back (quarter-rudders). The new, so-called "axial" rudder, imported from the North and placed at the back of the boat, was much more efficient.

Combining the slender hull and the lateen sail of the Mediterranean with the unusually efficient square sails and the axial rudder of the North, the Portuguese were able to create a new and effective kind of ship. It had, ordinarily, three masts outfitted with two square sails and one lateen sail. The lateen sail was particularly good for maneuverability along the coastline and for sudden changes of direction; the square sails were ideal for smooth passage across the ocean when the wind was coming from behind the ship. Columbus's flagship, the *Santa Maria*, was rigged in precisely this way: a huge square sail in the center, a much shorter mast in the front with another square sail, and at the back of the ship, a lateen sail.

Skills in navigation also were much improved in the late fifteenth century. This improvement, like the new ship design, resulted from a blend of northern and southern European experience. The navigators who made the first trans-Atlantic crossings were indebted to their Mediterranean ancestors for a tradition of careful navigational records and charts and especially for the compass, an instrument invented by the Chinese centuries before but adopted belatedly by Mediterranean sailors. Southern navigators also had learned how to estimate, even on a cloudy night when stars were not visible, where their ship was. Called dead reckoning, this method involves plotting a course on a chart by correlating direction, time, and speed. Time was measured by a small hourglass. Speed had to be guessed at in the fifteenth century, and

Columbus consistently overestimated the speed of his ships. Further errors in dead reckoning crept in because early navigators did not know how to evaluate the force of ocean currents. Nevertheless, dead reckoning was an intuitive skill raised to the level of an art in the late fifteenth century.

Another valuable navigational instrument was the quadrant. It was a simple apparatus for measuring how far one had moved north or south from an original starting point (latitude). By looking through two pinhole sights at the North Star when the quadrant was held in an absolutely upright position (determined by a dangling plumb line), a navigator could determine the altitude of the North Star—and from that information figure out his own latitude.

From the northern European tradition, navigators inherited far simpler skills, but one proved invaluable—dropping a weighted line overboard in order to measure the ocean's depth. Because Columbus was sailing through uncharted waters and, once he arrived in the New World, piloting his ships from one island to another in the Caribbean, he needed constant measurements of how deep the water was. Without such measurements, he easily could have wrecked his ships on hidden reefs or shallows.

In the final analysis, the success of this remarkable venture rested upon the shoulders of one man, a complex individual whose personality, until quite recently, has seemed vague, imprecise, even contradictory. In the late 1930s, Harvard historian Samuel Eliot Morison began to unravel this mystery. Himself a sailor, a

The Davis quadrant, developed two centuries after Columbus, was a major navigational advance that allowed sailors to use the sun's position to determine latitude.

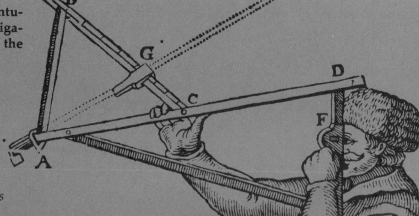

Theodore De Bry's imaginative version of Columbus claiming Hispaniola shows little knowledge of the landscape or native possessions (note the jewels) but a better understanding of ships. Note the rigging of the ship on the left.

skilled writer, and a tireless researcher, Morison followed the routes of Columbus, visiting the same islands and the same ports of call, dug deep into European archives, and produced in 1942 a stunning masterpiece: *Admiral of the Ocean Sea: The Life of Christopher Columbus.*

Morison's Columbus is, above all else, a very imposing figure, a fast learner with an able mind, a devoutly religious man of physical courage, persistence, and strong will. Yet he had defects, too. He was not much of a colonizer; he failed to appreciate the work of subordinates; and he was quick to indulge in self-pity and complain of presumed slights at the hands of kings and princes.

The first third of his life gave no promise of greatness or adventure, and he apparently became a seaman almost by accident. However, once Columbus took up residence in Portugal in 1476 he soon learned how to navigate and how to read charts. Sometime in the early 1480s (following a few voyages to Africa), he became a man with a mission: to reach Asia by sailing west, not east around the southern tip of Africa. Unable to enlist the aid of the Portuguese ruler (despite a propitious marriage to a well-connected young lady), Columbus went to Spain in 1485 to seek the backing of King Ferdinand and Queen Isabella.

For the next seven years he met with various royal committees, which probed his ideas; he also spent long hours in research and study, for which the Spanish court paid some of his expenses. On January 2, 1492, Granada, the last major Muslim stronghold in Spain, was conquered. Overjoyed, Columbus marched in the triumphant procession which entered that city. Then joy turned to despair as court officials for the fourth time said "no"; his schemes were simply too risky, too costly. Furious at this news, he departed for France, but within hours was overtaken by a royal messenger. The keeper of the privy purse to Ferdinand had decided—undoubtedly as the result of his departure—that the royal treasury did indeed have the funds to support his voyage after all. (Morison surmises that the bearing of Columbus, his conviction, and his long battle for approval at Court, not his logic, won him powerful friends who realized that the potential gain from his project far outweighed its probable cost.)

In April, Columbus and royal officials signed an agreement concerning the profits of his explorations, a document that later was the subject of much litigation. During the summer months, the *Nina, Pinta,* and *Santa Maria* were outfitted at Palos, Spain, and on August 3 set sail. The crews included no idlers except a royal butler, a secretary, and an interpreter, taken along in case the three ships encountered a provincial Oriental governor. A month later this trio of ships cleared the Canary Islands and headed due west on a course calculated to take them directly to Japan.

SELECTED
READINGS

General and Exploration Studies

C. R. Boxer, *Dutch Seaborne Empire, 1600–1800* (1965)

Helge Ingstad, *Westward to Vinland: The Discovery of Pre-Columbian Norse House-Sites in North America* (1969)

Samuel Eliot Morison, *Admiral of the Ocean Sea* (2 vols., 1942)

J. H. Parry, *The Age of Reconnaissance* (1963)

David B. Quinn, *Raleigh and the British Empire* (1949)

American Indians

Robert F. Berkhofer, Jr., *The White Man's Indian: Images of the American Indian From Columbus to the Present* (1978)

Alfred Crosby, Jr., *The Columbian Exchange: Biological and Cultural Consequences of 1492* (1972)

Frances Jennings, *The Invasion of America: Indians, Colonialism, and the Cant of Conquest* (1975)

Karen O. Kupperman, *Settling with the Indians: The Meeting of English and Indian Cultures in America, 1580–1640* (1980)

Wilcomb Washburn, *The Indian in America* (1975)

Grace Woodward, *Pocohantas* (1969)

Origins of British Settlement

Wesley F. Craven, *Dissolution of the Virginia Company: The Failure of a Colonial Experiment* (1932)

Wallace Notestein, *The English People on the Eve of Colonization* (1954)

Alden Vaughan, *American Genesis: Captain John Smith and the Founding of Virginia* (1975)

Comparative and General Colonial Studies

Van Cleaf Bachman, *Pelteries or Plantations: Economic Policies of the Dutch West India Company in New Netherland, 1623–1639* (1970)

W. C. Eccles, *France in America* (1972)

Charles Gibson, *Spain in America* (1966)

Carl Sauer, *The Early Spanish Main* (1966)

Clarence Ver Steeg, *The Formative Years, 1607–1763* (1964)

CHAPTER 2
THE GROWTH OF BRITISH COLONIAL AMERICA

TIMELINE

1620
Separatist Pilgrims settle Plymouth Colony

1622
First major Indian uprising against the colonists

1624
Jamestown becomes a royal colony directly responsible to the king

1629
Puritans emigrate to Massachusetts Bay

1637
Pequot War in New England

1638
Anne Hutchinson banished from Massachusetts Bay

1649
Maryland Assembly passes the Act of Toleration to protect Catholics

1659
Richard Cromwell, Oliver Cromwell's son, resigns as Lord Protector

1660
The Stuart monarchy under Charles II is restored

1664
Charles II gives the Duke of York a proprietary grant to a large tract between Maryland and New England

1669
Slavery is incorporated into Carolina constitution

1675
Bacon's Rebellion in Virginia

1676
King Philip's War ends the Indian threat to settlement in New England

1681
William Penn receives a grant from the king to settle Pennsylvania

1685
France revokes the Edict of Nantes

1689
William and Mary promulgate the Act of Toleration

1705
Virginia unifies its various laws on slavery

1732
James Oglethorpe establishes a settlement of debtors in Georgia

CHAPTER OUTLINE

"They say there's bread and work for all," went the line of a popular song English immigrants to North America liked to sing, "and the sun shines always there." To be sure, the promise of improved economic opportunity, if not a brighter climate, was a chief attraction enticing settlers to leave England and come to the original colonies in the seventeenth century. Before 1700, the lure to North America worked most strongly in England itself and Wales. After 1700, it was felt most steadily in Scotland, Ireland, and Germany. And throughout the eighteenth century, the number of black slaves increased to an ever larger portion of the annual arrivals.

Immigrants and Their Origins

Apart from a scattering of Dutch, Swiss, Swedish, Finnish, and French settlers who reached North America in the seventeenth century, the majority of settlers were English, parted from their homeland because of deliberate religious persecution and pervasive economic hardship. Although leaders of English society lacked the techniques of taking an accurate census of the population, many of them sincerely believed that the British Isles were perilously close to being overpopulated. What made this conclusion plausible was the growing number of vagrants caused by the transformation of an agricultural to an industrial society. During much of the seventeenth century, many tenant farmers either suffered disastrous rises in rent or were dispossessed of their lands. Many of the landless drifted to the towns and cities and there formed a large, restless mass of actual or potential troublemakers. It was understandable for the government to treat the colonies as safe and productive places to siphon off these unemployed.

Yet the desperately poor did not find their way to the American colonies. Although fear of vagrants was one reason for the government's cultivation of new colonies, the emigrants who did leave for North America were mostly young men and women of modest but respectable backgrounds. Among the men were former yeomen (small farmers who once cultivated their own land) or husbandmen (workers whom we would now call "farmhands"). Of the 10,000 indentured servants who sailed from the port of Bristol between 1654 and 1685, for example, about thirty-six percent of them were farmers and farm workers; and ten percent were unskilled non-farm workers. Skilled workers and farmers outnumbered common laborers by about five to one. What we can conclude is that the lowest recognized rank of English society, the unskilled laborer, seldom entered the New World, although farmers and skilled workers did come in large numbers—usually in search of land.

The Lust for Land

Tradesmen as well as farmers wanted land in America. To Englishmen of the seventeenth century, land meant security and social position. Tradesmen, moreover, were often the sons of farmers. If they were not working the land, that was generally because there was no land to be had. According to English law and custom, a father's farm went intact to his oldest son, and younger sons were apprenticed to various trades. But they accepted their landless positions only by default. They still wanted real property of their own, a desire that was increasingly thwarted because land was becoming ever scarcer and more expensive.

Few of these land-hungry farmers had the means to pay for their own passage to the New World. More than half of the colonial settlers from England came as indentured servants. Indenture usually required a settler to agree to serve a master in North America for four years in return for free passage across the Atlantic. At the end of his or her term of service, at least during the early seventeenth century, the indentured worker would be rewarded with "freedom dues." More often than not, one of these rewards would be a plot of land, although other freedom dues might include a fixed sum of money, specified tools, clothes, or even food. After 1650, this practice of granting liberal freedom dues fell into disuse.

The terms and conditions of indenture varied considerably, depending upon the age and ability of the servant. Although four years was the usual period of service, indenture could last as long as seven, or even nine, years. Once the worker arrived, he or she generally received no wages, only food, shelter, and clothing, although in some cases skilled artisans also earned small annual wages. The indenture was a legal contract and could be written in many ways. For instance, children frequently were indentured with the understanding they would be given an elementary education or taught a trade.

Today, this system of servitude may strike us as harsh, undemocratic, and unfair, but to a person without property in seventeenth century England, it seemed both fair and normal. The tradition of apprenticeship was an ancient practice, and for hundreds of years apprentices had entered into legal agreements to exchange their services to master craftsmen in return for instruction in one trade or another.

Few farmers in North America could afford to travel to England to select their own workers. As a result, enterprising English merchants filled up ships sailing to the colonies with cargoes of indentured servants. A merchant could turn a profit by selling the servants at a price above the cost of contracting and transporting them. For their part, colonial planters found the procedure profitable, since by buying the labor of many farmhands, they could quickly go beyond merely supplying their own needs to producing large surplus crops. Finally, the English government was pleased with the system since it assured a peopling of the colonies with little or no expense to the state.

In order to attract indentured servants to the New World, colorful and not quite truthful accounts of the "paradise" beyond the Atlantic were circulated in England. Unmarried girls sometimes came in search of husbands. Single young men without property or prospects came in search of both. On occasion the government arranged for convicted criminals to be indentured and deported as a form of punishment and rehabilitation.

Whether they came as indentured servants or paid their own passage, nearly every immigrant wanted land, which could be acquired by many different methods. In their early years, all colonies handed out free land to newcomers. The southern colonies distributed land according to a "headright system," a practice originating in Virginia entitling newcomers to land, the most obvious reason for coming to the New World. A particular number of acres (usually fifty) was given to each person (or "head"). Thus a family of four, two parents and two children, could collect the rights to two hundred acres upon arrival. Sometimes the family was asked to make improvements, but usually they only had to survey and register a claim for land that was available on the frontier; and at this period the

NOVA BRITANNIA.

OFFERING MOST

Excellent fruites by Planting in
VIRGINIA.

Exciting all such as be well affected
to further the same.

LONDON
Printed for SAMVEL MACHAM, and are to be sold at
his Shop in Pauls Church-yard, at the
Signe of the Bul-head.
1 6 0 9.

The New York Public Library, Rare Book Division.

The authors of this pamphlet hoped to attract settlers to Virginia by stressing economic gain. Its stress on "Excellent fruites" is ironic considering the starving conditions of the colony in 1609.

frontier was usually only a few miles inland from the Atlantic coast. As for indentured male servants, they frequently had, as noted earlier, contracts specifying land as a due at the end of their periods of service.

By the eighteenth century, land speculators, who now held most of the unoccupied land in the original colonies, were selling it to new arrivals. The price per acre, however, was still very low since cheap land along the frontier was abundantly available, and was to remain so for many decades even after the prices of property in the built-up coastal areas became relatively high.

Still other settlers passed through two stages in their search for land. First they were tenants, renting small farms from large landowners, who offered them tools, seed, and homes. Later, after a number of years spent in renting, tenants often accumulated enough money to purchase their own land.

After 1700, England was no longer the main source of immigrants. By then, numerous social changes favored stability in Great Britain and made the New World less appealing. The rampant unrest, which had afflicted English life throughout much of the seventeenth century, had subsided, and the great religious questions seemed resolved. Even though the Church of England enjoyed a preferred status after 1689, a general tolerance of Protestant sects decreased the outward flow of immigrants. As forests dwindled, coal mining became a vast growth industry that drew more and more workers into the pits as coal became the major fuel. Other industries that prospered in seventeenth and eighteenth century England were shipbuilding, glass manufacturing, iron mining, and salt processing. As a result, policymakers in government became concerned about the loss of skilled workers and even passed laws to prevent them from going to America.

The new source of immigrants was Scotland and Ireland. Although Scotland and England had the same king after 1603, Scotland did not officially become a part of Britain until 1707. Before then, Scots were regarded as aliens and had to submit to unfavorable arrangements to emigrate to the English colonies. After 1707, however, the New World was easily accessible to the Scots, and they poured into North America. Among them were many Highlanders defeated in various uprisings against the English and many crofters (or cottagers) deprived of their leaseholds. Others were representatives, so-called "factors" or agents of Edinburgh firms eager to do business with the new tobacco wealth of Maryland and Virginia, a trade the Scots nearly monopolized by the 1750s.

Meanwhile, a large number of Scots migrated, not to America, but to Ireland, especially the northern part. These Scots-Irish began to find life in Ireland increasingly uncongenial as they were caught up in the long-standing feud between the colonizing English and the native Irish. The English Parliament passed laws forbidding Irish cloth traders to export fabrics to any area where such products would compete with English cloth—and these laws eventually destroyed the Irish cloth trade. Most Scots-Irish farmers tried to establish themselves as tenants, but rising rents in Ireland soon made emigration again attractive. Finally, although the Scots were Presbyterians, they had to pay a sizable part of their incomes to support the so-called "Church of Ireland," a local branch of the Church of England. This combination of pressures set off the first mass emigration from Ireland.

The Beginnings of Slavery

After 1700, another large group of immigrants came to North America, but these individuals came against their will and in chains. The eighteenth century saw the full development of slavery in Britain's New World colonies as thousands of blacks were forcefully relocated under brutal conditions from their native Africa, a horrifying experience that left dark scars upon that era and has embittered race relations ever since. In 1700 no colony had more than 5,000 slaves; but in 1770 New England had about 13,000 slaves; and Virginia had about 170,000 slaves, who constituted half of the population of the colony. Expressed in other terms, twenty-three percent of the entire population in 1760 were slaves; four-fifths of the slaves, however, lived in the South, generally near the Atlantic Coast. Black population growth was only partially due to importation. For instance, between 1710 and 1769 only 55,000 slaves were brought from Africa to Virginia, although, as noted, by 1770 the Old Dominion had some 170,000 blacks, many of whom were obviously second-, third-, or even fourth-generation Virginians.

The concept of slavery as it developed in North America implied the complete loss of personal freedom. Because it was a lifelong condition and hereditary, it can be contrasted with indentured servitude. The indentured servant traded his services in return for free passage across the Atlantic, and this bargain was carefully regulated by the law of contracts. The servant sold his services, not his body, and only for a fixed period of time. The children of an indentured servant in no sense became the property of that servant's master. In all these ways, slavery and servitude differed.

What was it that made the enslavement of blacks acceptable to English colonists? For English people of the sixteenth and seventeenth centuries, the color black had deep psychological associations with evil which are difficult to analyze with precision. Black was not only the color of physical defilement, of the tortured ways of the human heart, of the Devil, of negation and nothingness, but also the palpable sign of the loss of God's grace, of extreme spiritual deprivation and of utter unworthiness. White, on the other hand, was the color of virginal purity, the emblem of high moral rectitude beyond all reproach, of unblemished integrity fused with consuming intensity.

Also it was easier on the seventeenth century conscience to enslave black Africans because seldom were they Christians. True, the English had an aversion to enslaving their fellow Christians, but

To be SOLD, on the Second Tuesday in October next, at Prince-George Court-House.

TEN choice Slaves, moſt of them *Virginia* born : Credit will be given till the Second Tueſday in *December* next, the Purchaſer giving Bond and Security. And on *Wedneſday* following, will be ſold at the ſame Place, Nineteen Acres of Land, adjoining the Town of *Blandford,* pleaſantly ſituated for carrying on Buſineſs of any Kind. Whoever pays ready Money or Tobacco, ſhall have Five *per Cent.* Diſcount. Any Perſon that choſes to make a Purchaſe of the ſaid Land or any of the Slaves, before the Day of Sale, may know the Terms, by applying to 2 *John Hood.*

Virginia Gazette.
This advertisement, which appeared in the September 19, 1755, issue of *The Virginia Gazette,* makes clear the slave's status as property. Land and slaves are sold on the same terms.

this scruple did not extend to "heathens." African religions, customs, clothing (or lack of it)—all seemed so strange to the English that they could scarcely regard blacks as fellow human beings. In an effort to rationalize their bias against black skin color, the English resorted to the Bible and traced the descent of Africans to Ham, the wicked and disobedient son of Noah. By this reasoning, blacks were by their very nature evil and deserving of punishment.

Other ingredients also must be examined in order to understand how the English evolved the concept of slavery. At least in theory, English writers on jurisprudence recognized that enslavement of an enemy taken in battle could be an alternative to death. Slavery and captivity were equated, and both were seen as one possible destiny for the defeated. On the level of more practical experience, the English were able to observe the enslavement of black Africans as a familiar aspect of Spanish settlements in the New World. For centuries the Portuguese and Spanish had enslaved Moors captured in religious wars; and in the fifteenth century the Portuguese began to carry thousands of blacks back from Africa to Europe. After 1500, Portuguese traders transported black slaves to Spanish and Portuguese colonies in America. That the English tended to regard blacks through the eyes of the Spanish can be deduced from the fact that in the mid-sixteenth century, *negro,* the Spanish word for black, was incorporated into English. Indeed, "Negro" was used far more commonly than the perfectly adequate English word "black."

This brief sketch of the development of slavery in North America should not gloss over the fact that the primary reasons for slavery were economic, not ideological. Throughout the English colonies in the seventeenth and eighteenth centuries, there was a severe labor shortage. To some extent, indentured servitude helped to reduce this problem, but black slavery was the ultimate solution. Tobacco-growing colonies such as Virginia and Maryland needed a form of labor cheaper, more abundant, and more easily managed and identified than freed indentured servants. The first blacks in Virginia clearly were indentured servants and were freed at the end of a term of service. After 1640, however, there is evidence that some of them were regarded as lifetime slaves. For in that year three indentured servants, Victor, a Dutchman, James Gregory, a Scot, and John Punch, a black, escaped and were captured in Maryland. Victor and James Gregory were forced to serve an additional year of indenture, but John Punch was sentenced to serve "for the time of his natural life."

After 1660, slave codes began to be written into law, and by 1705 Virginia had set down a unified compilation of its various laws on slavery. Although slavery developed gradually in Virginia and Maryland, it was written into the very constitution of Carolina in 1669 by settlers who came from Barbados where slave codes already existed. According to this document, each freeman of the colony would have "absolute power and authority over his Negro slaves, of what opinion or religion soever."

In New England and other northern colonies, farming usually had little use for whole regiments of African slaves, yet slaves were found in some sections of New York, Rhode Island, and Connecticut well into the eighteenth century. By the end of the colonial period, Rhode Island had the largest number of slaves per capita in New England. All the same, throughout the colonial period, New England was deeply involved in the economy of the developing slave trade. Merchants from that region often carried blacks from Africa to islands held by the English in the West Indies. And again, at the close of the colonial era, it was Rhode Island that had the greatest stake in the slave trade. Slavery, as it prospered in the seventeenth and eighteenth centuries, was closely tied to and an integral part of an emerging tobacco empire centered in Virginia. (For a general overview of the influence of tobacco on American life, see the essay "Tobacco: The Gift and Curse of the Indians" at the end of this chapter.)

Political and Religious Influences

Many emigrants from England were drawn to America by a hunger for land and the hope of economic opportunity. Another large group came to practice their religion free from English interference, but this freedom proved to be selfish and parochial since each group of colonists denied, with the one notable exception of Rhode Island, the right to others to worship differently in its midst.

Throughout much of Europe, church and local government were closely linked for centuries. Yet the Roman Catholic Church, whose claims were transnational and supratemporal, had to contend with competing dogmas within and conflicting political interests without. The rise of nation-states in the fifteenth and sixteenth centuries precipitated a clash of allegiances that eventually took northern

Europe—and, in time, England as well—into the Protestant fold, while southern Europe, France, south Germany, and Ireland remained predominantly Catholic.

As it evolved under Elizabeth I (1533–1603), the Church of England was sort of a halfway house between Protestantism and Catholicism. This new official state church was supported by tax monies that once were sent to Rome, the English sovereign replaced the Pope as head of the church, and bishops sat in the House of Lords—in short, church and state were closely bound together. Debate over the spiritual value of what had occurred created three distinct groups in opposition to each other but all eager to overturn or to modify the Church of England and, failing that, to emigrate. These included disgruntled Catholics, Puritans (those who wanted to "purify" the new church and to make it more Protestant in form and outlook), and Separatists such as Pilgrims, Presbyterians, Quakers, and Baptists, who, as the term implies, wanted to establish their own congregations free of all state interference—or, perhaps, to set up their *own* state.

As these various groups struggled for supremacy, England experienced constant turmoil throughout the 1600s. For the most part, the confrontation was three-sided: Catholics who wished to reestablish the old ties with Rome; Anglicans who wished to strengthen the state church under the headship of the English monarch; and dissenters, some of whom wished to cleanse the Church of England of popish ritual and others who wanted to allow each isolated congregation to have Christ for its immediate head.

Between 1641 and 1660 England was torn by civil war as Puritans battled monarchists pledged to uphold the new faith. Puritan forces, led by Oliver Cromwell (1599–1658) emerged victorious in 1649 and beheaded Charles I; however, in 1660 his son, Charles II, was restored to the throne. In 1688 his brother, James II, was ousted after a brief reign during which he tried to insure that his male heir (born in 1688) would be Catholic. James was banished and replaced by his Protestant daughter, Mary and her Dutch husband, William.

Ruling jointly, William and Mary promulgated an Act of Toleration (1689); yet for a century or more dissenters were still viewed with hostility. Toleration did not mean complete religious freedom, only that the sovereign would "tolerate" reluctantly the existence of those who dissented from the Church of England, which remained as the established state faith supported by the taxes paid by all, regardless of belief. In addition, those who chose to retain their status as Nonconformists were barred from full civil rights.

Needless to say, such turmoil provided a powerful impetus for migration. Over 20,000 Puritans arrived in Massachusetts Bay, for example, in the early 1630s. Yet one should be aware that in such a fluid situation by no means all of those who left England came to the New World. Many, especially Catholics during the time of Cromwell, went instead to the Continent. Even the small band of Pilgrims who settled in Plymouth in 1620 lived for a time in Holland.

Even though Puritans undoubtedly were the most numerous of the dissenting groups to come to America from England in the seventeenth century, immigrants of those decades also included Quakers, by far the most radical of the Separatists, so much so that several Quaker missionaries who ventured into Puritan Massachusetts were hanged. However, between 1680 and 1710 larger groups of Quakers appeared in New Jersey, Pennsylvania, and Delaware.

Although the fanatical fires of religious faith and their attendant stifling of individual conscience in England may be difficult to comprehend in our age, the English were, in fact, more liberal about religious choice than most other European countries. As a result, English colonies soon became a refuge for religious minorities from France and Germany. During the 1580s and 1590s, like England of a few decades later, France was torn by religious strife. In 1598, when Henry of Navarre had become King of France, he issued the Edict of Nantes assuring Protestants, the followers of John Calvin (1509–1564)—called Huguenots in France—that the state would "tolerate" their faith. However, these Protestants were viewed as an irksome minority in a Catholic realm, and in 1685 the Edict was revoked. The borders of France were sealed and Huguenots were avidly hunted down; nevertheless, thousands managed to escape and flee to Protestant nations in Europe. Some of them settled in the Netherlands, where they fought on the side of the Dutch ruler, William of Orange (1650–1702), against France. When William married Mary, the daughter of England's King James II, and they acceded jointly to the throne of England in 1689, he was in a position to reward the Huguenot refugees who had fought in his behalf. He granted them land in the English colonies and helped pay their transportation costs.

Many of them settled in South Carolina, where they established rice plantations along the coast; others took up residence in Virginia and New York.

German religious groups also began to seek refuge in the colonies. Germany at that time was not a single country but rather a mosaic of many small kingdoms, principalities, duchies, bishoprics, and independent cities—each with its own particular religion that forbade the toleration of all other sects. Some of these states were Catholic, others Lutheran or Calvinist. Each of these major branches of Christianity persecuted the others, and they all hounded small sects such as the Mennonites, the Moravians, and the Amish. Since these sects had much in common with English Quakers, they found a home in the Quaker-dominated colony of Pennsylvania.

Not only religious differences but also the terrors of war drove Germans to the New World. Throughout the seventeenth and eighteenth centuries, the German states were the scene of prolonged dynastic strife fused with contending religious factions. When German princelings were not forcing their subjects to fight their own wars, they were renting them out as mercenary troops to other European powers, or putting them in coalitions for or against the Swedes, the French, the Prussians, and the Austrians.

Two other religious groups also sought refuge in the colonies: Catholics and Jews. The province of Maryland was designed by George Calvert, Lord Baltimore (ca. 1580–1632), an English Catholic, who ruled a large domain in Ireland which was a haven for members of his faith. In 1649 the Maryland Assembly passed an Act of Toleration. This famous document reads in part:

————

"Whereas the enforcing of the conscience in matters of religions hath frequently fallen out to be of dangerous consequence in those commonwealths where it hath been practised, and for the more quiet and peaceable government of this province and the better to preserve mutual love and amity amongst the inhabitants thereof: Be it therefore . . . enacted . . . that no person or persons whatsoever within this province . . . professing to believe in Jesus Christ shall from henceforth be any ways troubled, molested, or discountenanced for, or in respect of, his or her religion, nor in the free exercise thereof within this province . . ."

————

The Act of Toleration did not endure for long since a Puritan majority gained control over Maryland in 1654 and repealed it. Reinstated four years later, the act was gradually modifed to the disadvantage of Catholics by the end of the seventeenth century. With the ouster of James II and the so-called "Glorious Revolution" of 1688, the Anglican

Even Jewish synagogues reflected colonial architectural styles. Touro Synagogue in Newport, Rhode Island, was designed by Peter Harrison for the prosperous community there.

Church in a few years became the official faith in Maryland and received tax support. Roman Catholics were tolerated but could not hold governmental office. In short, events in the Maryland colony mirrored at a distance the fluctuating fortunes of religious factions in England.

The first Jews arrived in the colonies in the 1650s. At its best, toleration in the seventeenth and eighteenth centuries extended only to other Christians. Settling in New Amsterdam, Rhode Island, and Philadelphia, the Jews attempted to remain as inconspicuous as possible in every community without sacrificing their heritage. Yet, as late as 1762, the Superior Court denied fifteen families of Jews in Newport, Rhode Island, the right to be naturalized as citizens.

Patterns
of
Settlement

As communities began to take form along the Atlantic seaboard in the seventeenth century, a few distinct patterns of settlement emerged. Immigrants brought to America against their will—slaves, convicts, and many of the indentured servants—had no choice, of course, where they were to be settled. Families were often split apart and all sense of their original communal life destroyed. By contrast, voluntary immigrants transplanted their past into the present, the Old World into the New. They moved with families and relatives, often to locations where their former neighbors had already established towns or farms. Members of the same generation frequently migrated together.

The joint migration of relatives and neighbors to America helped to preserve Old World customs. The German settlers of eastern Pennsylvania retained their native language, styles of dress, and religious beliefs. In New England the system of landholding in each town was based on the particular practices of the majority of the first settlers. Thus a study of Sudbury, Massachusetts, reveals that, although people came to Sudbury from many parts of England, most of the original settlers were from a section of England where fields were not fenced in and the land was farmed communally, the identical pattern which developed in Sudbury.

The Early Years, 1607–1660

During the decades from the establishment of Jamestown in 1607 to the Restoration in England in 1660, several permanent and eventually successful colonies appeared. The most important of them were Virginia (1607), Massachusetts Bay (1629), and Maryland (1632). Virginia and Massachusetts Bay were joint-stock ventures governed under a charter granted by the king; Maryland, a proprietary grant of land given to the first Baron Baltimore by his sovereign. While settlers at Jamestown and Massachusetts Bay had considerable control over their own affairs, the Baltimore family (or their resident agents) tended to exercise almost feudal power.

The little band of Pilgrim Separatists that settled at Plymouth in 1620, although celebrated in legend, fiction, and Thanksgiving, existed without a charter, grew slowly, and, in time, was swallowed up by the nearby and more prosperous Massachusetts Bay Colony of the Puritans. Stern believers in congregational self-government, this band first settled in Holland for a decade (1609–1619), but about 100 members eventually set out for the New World aboard the *Mayflower*. They secured a land patent from the Virginia Company of London, but then settled outside of the area specified when they made first landfall at Cape Cod in midwinter. After the death of their first leader, Deacon John Carver, William Bradford became governor (Bradford's contributions to this religious settlement are the subject of a biographical sketch in this chapter.)

In 1624, after two devastating Indian raids and considerable financial and political turmoil, the weakened Virginia settlement at Jamestown surrendered its company charter and became a royal colony, a trend that was to be increasingly common throughout colonial history. These three settlements—Massachusetts, Maryland, and Virginia—represent the three types of colonies that evolved in British North America: the charter or jointstock company, the proprietary grant, and the royal colony with resident officials appointed by the crown. Each, in turn, reflected political conditions in England. A sovereign beset by civil strife often had little money to expend on colonial expeditions; hence, stock ventures and proprietary grants then suited his purposes well enough. But, at the same time, he and his advisors fretted over the absence of state control and usually asserted royal authority whenever able to do so; nevertheless, each colony eventually developed a local representative assembly a miniature "parliament" of sorts.

William Bradford

ca. 1590–1657

Brought up by his uncles and grandfather after the death of his father, the future Pilgrim leader William Bradford was a sturdy Yorkshire yeoman who at an early age began to read the Bible and take an unusual interest in Noncomformist beliefs. Braving the scorn of relatives and neighbors, he continued this association and in 1609 joined a congregation that was emigrating to Leyden. Two years later, as Bradford relates, he came into "a comfortable inheritance left him by his honest parents."

During the decade that the Pilgrims were in Holland, Bradford worked as a weaver, and by the time they decided to sail for America, he obviously was one of the group's leaders. That the little Plymouth colony survived at all is a tribute to his stamina, zeal, dedication, and basic good sense. Although he urged rotation in office, he was governor for much of the first quarter of the century (1620–1645) and he also exerted great authority as principal judge and treasurer until 1637. Neither in the colony's records nor in Bradford's famous *History of Plimouth Plantation*, does one see much democracy at work in this government—that is something woven into the Plymouth story later by historians. In 1623 Bradford declared that the colonists would be allowed to share in the government

"only in some weighty matters, when we think good." Two decades later only one-third of the men required to bear arms were freemen.

Bradford's first wife, whom he married in Leyden, drowned in 1620 while the *Mayflower* was anchored off Cape Cod. He subsequently courted by mail and then married in 1623 Alice Carpenter Southworth, widow of a former member of the Leyden congregation. They had a daughter and two sons whose descendants now number in the thousands. About 1630 Bradford began to write his *History*, a work probably intended only for family and friends as a memorial to high enterprise. It was finally printed in full in 1856 and is responsible, both directly and indirectly, for the large role the Plymouth colony plays in American history. Distressed by secular trends he saw on every hand, this undertaking undoubtedly consoled Bradford in his old age as he reflected upon the glory of Plymouth's early years. Lest anyone think him dour and drab, it should be noted that his estate included a red waistcoat, silver buttons, a colored hat, a violet cloak, a great silver "beer bowle," two silver wine cups, four Venice glasses, ninety-seven pounds of pewter dishes, and, not surprisingly, one of the largest libraries in Plymouth.

Expanding the Colonies, 1660–1700

When King Charles II of England assumed power in 1660, he found himself deeply indebted to numerous individuals and consequently canceled these obligations with lavish gifts of real estate in the New World. In 1664 he gave his brother, the Duke of York, a huge proprietary grant covering all of present-day New York, Vermont, Pennsylvania, and New Jersey, half of Connecticut, Massachusetts, and Maine, and various offshore lands such as Long Island, Nantucket, and Martha's Vineyard. The duke had to oust the Dutch from New Amsterdam in order to claim his gift and name it "New York."

The Duke of York, later James II, subsequently gave the provinces of East and West Jersey to two of his friends, Sir George Carteret and Lord John Berkeley, who sold out to other groups that included a number of Quakers. Although proprietors enjoyed absolute power in theory, most permitted some form of representative government in practice in order to attract immigrants. West Jersey, which was settled mainly by Quakers, had, for example, an assembly and enjoyed religious toleration. In 1704 the crown united the two Jerseys into the single royal colony of New Jersey.

In 1681, William Penn (1644–1718), a Quaker, received the proprietary province of Pennsylvania as settlement for a loan his father had made to the Duke of York. Penn also ruled the Swedish and Dutch settlements in Delaware until 1700 when he created the separate colony of Delaware over which

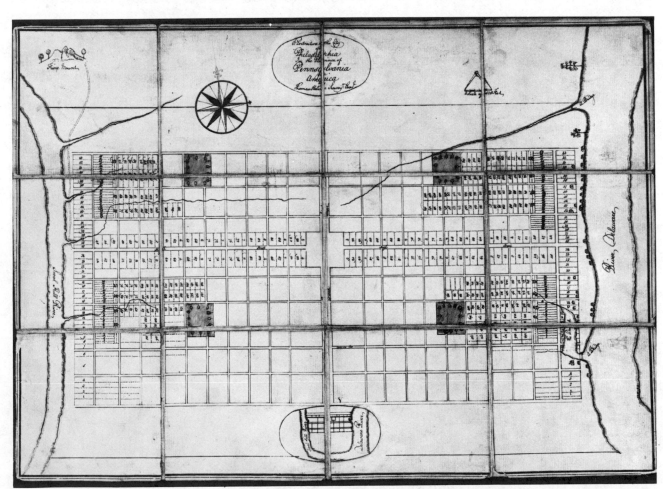

Historical Society of Pennsylvania.

The city plan for Philadelphia represented the growing ideal for order. Its neat squares and numbered streets left their imprint on cities across the United States.

he and his heirs continued to exert some authority. Pennsylvania, well situated and blest with far-sighted leadership, became within a few years one of the most prosperous of the English outposts.

Meanwhile, far to the south, the nucleus of another stable colony was evolving in the Carolinas. Between 1629 and 1670, several attempts, all ill-fated, were made to settle that region. In 1663, a group of distinguished noblemen, led by the Earl of Shaftsbury, received a proprietary grant, but it was not until seven years later that a small band of 140 people from Barbados agreed with the Carolina proprietors to found the city of Charlestown. Aided by social philosopher John Locke, the earl and his friends tried to set up a strange hereditary aristocracy complete with feudal dues, manors and re-

strictive trade policies, which were never fully implemented as settlers succeeded in negotiating changes. Unfortunately, the proprietors proved unwilling or unable to protect their farmers and traders from incursions by the French, Spanish, and Indians. All the same, thanks to rice, indigo, and a flourishing trade with the West Indies, Carolina, like Pennsylvania, became in time an important colonial settlement.

After 1680 the crown, which had until then granted North American lands so liberally to private business and to royal favorites, reversed its policy and tried to assert direct control, a reversal that had its counterpart at home where attempts were made to curb the special privileges of English cities. In 1685 a short-lived Dominion of New Eng-

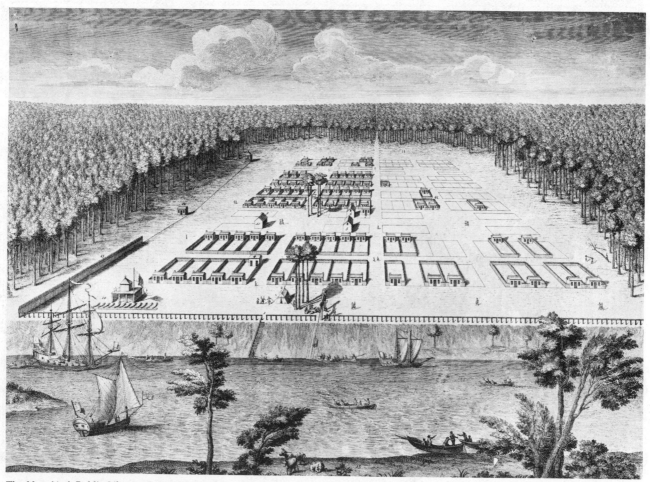

The New York Public Library, Prints Division.
Savannah was a busy port before it had more than a handful of homes. Georgia's status as frontier colony is clear in this 1734 view of Savannah.

The Growth of British Colonial America

land was established encompassing all of present-day New England, New York, and New Jersey. With the "Glorious Revolution" and the overthrow of James II, however, William's ministers, who were busy at home and unfamiliar with colonial matters, permitted the Dominion to dissolve. Connecticut and Rhode Island resumed their old charters. Massachusetts became a royal colony that included Massachusetts Bay, Plymouth, and surrounding territories. And New York and New Hampshire each became royal colonies. Indeed, the latter had been—prior to the Dominion fiasco (1685–89)—a royal colony for about a decade. But the Jerseys were returned to their original proprietors, at least temporarily.

The steady encroachments by royal authority are clear; by the mid-eighteenth century only five of the thirteen colonies that were destined to create a new independent nation were *not* ruled as royal colonies. Pennsylvania, Delaware, and Maryland, which were proprietary colonies, were still the personal domains of the Penn and Baltimore families; Connecticut and Rhode Island, which were relics of the past, continued to exist under charters. Yet even in these colonies the crown managed to exert considerable power, especially after 1696 when a revision of the Navigation Acts required all governors to take an oath to enforce its provisions and a customs service run by the English Treasury appeared in each colony. These agents of the crown could prosecute alleged violators of the law in Admiralty courts set up by the Privy Council (a group of advisers to the king), courts in which the deliberations of juries played no part.

Rounding Out the Colonies, 1700–1750

During the first half of the eighteenth century, the southernmost of the British settlements along the Atlantic Coast assumed more recognizable form. In 1719, when the Carolina proprietors summoned the local militia to stem an Indian attack, the colonists used their arms against their rulers instead. Rather than quell the rebellion, the government in London used the opportunity to buy out the proprietors and to establish not one but two royal colonies, North and South Carolina.

The last of the thirteen colonies, Georgia, was somewhat of an anomaly. In 1732 a group of philanthropists led by James Oglethorpe and Thomas Coram set up a proprietary colony for debtors at Savannah, long after the crown had decided such colonial proprietorships were unworkable. The reason for this exception to royal policy was the desire of the government to create a buffer zone between the Carolinas and Spanish Florida and, at the same time, to rid England of debtors. Like the Earl of Shaftsbury before him, but with far different goals in mind, Oglethorpe tried to create an ideal society. And like Shaftsbury, his efforts also proved a dismal failure. By mid-century, Georgia was a royal colony.

Religious and Ethnic Tensions

Religious dissension, especially in seventeenth century New England, was one reason for the expansion of colonial settlement. The Massachusetts Bay Colony was not founded in order to create religious freedom for every sect but only to preserve the rights of Puritans to practice their own religion. In fact, dissenters who might have found common cause against the Church of England became hostile toward one another once they arrived in the New World. As various religious groups came to disagree with the established order in Massachusetts, they sought freedom in unsettled sections of New England not under the direct control of the Bay Colony. Sometimes these "heretics" withdrew from Massachusetts voluntarily; at other times they were banished. (An illuminating account of a very persistent and unusual "heretic," who was banished, is given in a biographical sketch of Anne Hutchinson in this chapter.)

The Flow of Migration

The simplest pattern of growth and expansion was natural drift; settlers in search of free or cheap land moved away from the older colonies and populated, for example, the hinterlands of North Carolina, New Hampshire, and Connecticut. This expansion almost always flowed along natural "highways" such as rivers and bays. Springfield in Massachusetts on the Connecticut River was settled long before the land between the town and the coast. Because Virginia has such a convoluted coastline—

Anne Hutchinson

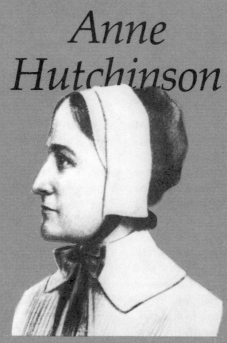

1591–1643

Born into the family of a Lincolnshire minister with Puritan leanings, Anne Hutchinson absorbed much of her father's philosophy and religious outlook. In 1612 she married William Hutchinson, a merchant, and in 1634 moved to Massachusetts Bay where this large family—fourteen children—joined the congregation of John Cotton, whom Anne had known and admired in England.

A wealthy lady, well versed in the subtleties of religious doctrine, she became an important citizen of Boston soon after her arrival there. As a midwife she met many people of that growing community and invited some of them to her home to discuss Cotton's sermons. In time, these meetings constituted a challenge of local authority as Anne, "a woman of ready wit and bold spirit," proclaimed her view that the Holy Spirit could dwell in all "justified" persons. The result was a belief in direct revelation, which Puritans rejected.

She and her followers confidently, perhaps arrogantly, took it upon themselves to proclaim which fellow citizens were of the Elect (slated for salvation) and which were already damned. They denounced all of the ministers in Massachusetts except two, one of them being Anne's brother-in-law; the rest they accused of preaching the false idea that salvation could be won by performing good works.

Soon the colony was split between admirers and enemies, and when John Winthrop was re-elected governor in 1637 he decided to stamp out this heresy. He convened the ministers who examined Anne for her beliefs and then summoned her before the General Court. Winthrop charged that "a meeting and an assembly in your house . . . hath been condemned by the general assembly as a thing not tolerable nor comely in the sight of God nor fitting for your sex." Throughout this ordeal the magistrates and ministers criticized her for not being properly submissive.

Following excommunication and banishment, early in 1638, Anne Hutchinson, her husband and children, and a few friends emigrated to the island of Aquidneck in Rhode Island. Later they moved on to Long Island and then back to the mainland. In the summer of 1643 she and all but her youngest daughter were killed by Indians.

The events of Anne Hutchinson's life are crucial in understanding the early history of the Massachusetts Bay Colony. Her civil trial for "dangerous beliefs" discloses how seriously the Puritans viewed religious doctrine and her fate demonstrates to what extent the Puritans felt called upon to create a society in harmony with their religious beliefs—a harmony that had to be protected forcefully against the slightest threat of disruption.

hundreds of small inlets on the Chesapeake Bay—settlers had little reason for moving inland; for generations they could find farms immediately adjacent to a waterway. As a result, land no farther from the Virginia coast than fifteen miles often remained unsettled. Indeed, as late as 1700, settlement everywhere in North America was limited to a string of occupied areas along the coasts and rivers.

After 1700, immigrants began to move inland slowly. By that time some Indian tribes, decimated by disease and defeated in wars, had retreated so that Europeans could extend their frontiers at least to the eastern foothills of the Appalachians. On arrival, new settlers often found the coastal harbors and river towns heavily populated, with the only free land available to be found inland. Throughout the eighteenth century, immigrants from the European Continent, Ireland, and Scotland outnumbered those coming from England. These "ethnic" groups settled along the western frontier, frequently producing social tensions. In general, the eastern segments of the colonies were settled by the older, English immigrants, whereas the interior was filled by new arrivals, ethnic minorities.

William Penn's Colony

In Pennsylvania, for instance, the Scots-Irish moved to the frontier and there formed a geographically distinct and religiously separate group. These feisty frontiersmen, exposed to the rigors of the wild, were frequently attacked by the Indians. Back in sedate Philadelphia, the Quakers were preaching pacifism—a philosophy that won little sympathy from the embattled Scots-Irish. The Quakers refused to vote funds for military protection against the Indians; indeed, they forbade the formation of a militia. When the enraged Scots-Irish marched on Philadelphia, some Quakers (who were expelled subsequently from their church) took up arms to protect their city against them. A visiting Lutheran minister, unsympathetic to the Quakers, jotted down these notes in his journal for February 5, 1764:

"Toward evening the rumor sprang up that a corps of backwoods settlers . . . were on the march toward Philadelphia. . . . Some reported that they numbered 700, others said 1500, etc. The Friends, or so-called Quakers, and the Moravians ran furiously back and forth to the barracks, and there was a great to-do over constructing several small

fortresses or ramparts near the barracks. Cannons were also set up. Some remarked . . . that it seemed strange that such preparations should be made against one's own fellow citizens and Christians, whereas no one ever took so much trouble to protect from the Indians His Majesty's subjects and citizens on the frontier."

Settlement in the South

After 1730 the interior or back country of the South began to fill up with various ethnic groups. Again, the most numerous were the Scots-Irish; the next largest elements of the population were made up of Germans, Scots, Welsh, and a number of English Quakers. Many of these people originally settled in Pennsylvania or other Middle colonies, but were drawn to the backwoods of Maryland, Virginia, and the Carolinas by cheap land. For many, the Shenandoah and other valleys formed a natural pathway to new and less costly tracts. The average farm in Pennsylvania was expensive and consisted of only about 128 acres. In Maryland a plan was devised to attract newcomers by offering 200 acres to heads of families—and this property was free and exempt from taxation for the first three years.

These tough frontiersmen lived on a bare subsistence level. They built log cabins, grew corn and other vegetables, and fashioned their own wooden furniture, cloth, soap, and candles; the only commodities they bought were salt and iron. Isolated and exposed to dangers, often poorly educated, these backwoods settlers disliked those well-to-do colonists living along the coast, especially those professing a different faith. When an Anglican clergyman, Charles Woodmason, traveled through the Carolina frontier in the 1760s, "ornery" farmers misdirected him, refused to sell him food or lodging, and insulted him wherever he went. In one village they disrupted the Anglican service by releasing fifty-seven dogs in the church. But Woodmason had his revenge.

"What I could not effect by Force—or Reason—I have done by Sarcasm—for at the Time when they sent the fellows with their Dogs, one of the Dogs followed me down here—which I carried to the House of one of the principals—and told Him that I had 57 Presbyterians came that Day to Service, and that I had converted one of them, and brought

Him home—I left the Dog with Him—This Joke has made them so extremely angry that they could cut my throat—But I've gained my Aim, having had no disturbance from them since—for if a Presbyterian now shews his face at Service, our People ask him if he is come to be *Converted*. So shame has driven them away."

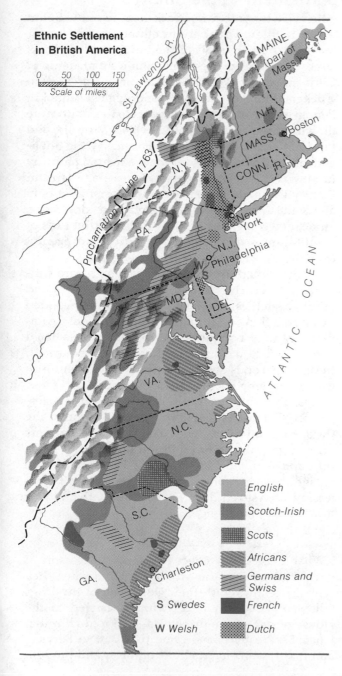

Ethnic Settlement in British America

0   50   100   150
Scale of miles

English
Scotch-Irish
Scots
Africans
Germans and Swiss
French
S Swedes
W Welsh
Dutch

Settlement of the frontier led to political problems in the southern colonies such as North and South Carolina, though for somewhat different reasons. South Carolina, like other expanding settlements, was reluctant to establish local government in the interior or to redistribute seats in the colonial legislature so that the backwoods would be adequately represented. Because settlers were expected to travel several hundred miles in order to vote, to find a sheriff, or to appear in court, they became so embittered against "Low Country" officials that they staged an open rebellion against the government in the 1760s. The South Carolina "Regulators" sought more government, not less, and under pressure Charleston agreed to set up new counties. London, however, disallowed these decisions because those then in power were not eager to see frontier areas expand.

In North Carolina, another group of frontiersmen, who also called themselves "Regulators," was incited to violence by disgust at what was seen as a corrupt coastal elite—judges, sheriffs, attorneys, and other officers almost exclusively of English descent. Taxes, payoffs to county officials, a system of collecting tithes for the established Anglican Church—all of these infringements on the freedom of frontier settlers aroused the wrath of the Regulators. And for a brief time, they drove out the legal authorities and conducted their own court. Finally, however, Governor Tryon put down the rebellion at the Battle of Alamance in 1771 and summarily hanged some of the men who led this outburst.

Indian-White Relations

Throughout the seventeenth century, the expansion of English colonies resulted in friction between Europeans and Indians—and several wars. Initially, the English were impressed by the hospitality of the Indians. Given the advantage of hindsight, we think of the English as having *conquered* North America; yet in many cases the Indians actually received the first colonists with generosity, even pity for their inadequate supply of food. In some cases, an Indian tribe would see the Europeans as potentially useful allies in defeating their rivals. In Virginia, for instance, Powhatan helped the Jamestown settlers survive because he wanted European

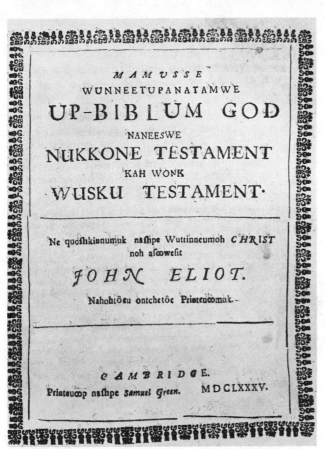

In order to translate the Bible into Algonquian, John Eliot had to devise a system of writing for the language as well as learn it himself. He had his first work printed in New England in 1661.

weapons in his campaign to subdue neighboring tribes. Between 1607 and 1609, Indians and colonists enjoyed an uneasy alliance, as Powhatan increased his supply of armaments and metal and the English relied on the Indians to teach them how to farm in the New World. Similarly, in New England the Pilgrims survived the first two winters because they received food from two friendly Indians, Squanto and Samoset. The Indians taught early colonists how to grow such American plants as corn, squash, and pumpkin.

But there was distrust, misunderstanding, and even contempt on each side from the very beginning. As early as 1607, Captain John Smith, while exploring the James River, observed that the Indians "are naturally given to treachery, howbeit we could not finde it in o'r travell up the river, but rather a most kind and loving people."

The lack of mutual comprehension was heightened by religious differences. Indian "paganism" distressed the English. Since the Indians were polytheistic, some tribes regarded the Christian God as merely another deity. When the chief of one tribe asked an Englishman to pray to his God for rain, since the Indian deities had failed to provide it, the Englishman was confused. Why could this chief not be persuaded to "forsake his false Gods?" Throughout the seventeenth century the Puritans attempted to convert the Indians, but of the 15,000 or so natives scattered throughout New England, only 2,500 were turned into "praying Indians." Granted, the problems of conversion were made especially difficult in New England because the Puritans insisted that every believer be sufficiently lit-

Plans for a college to educate Virginia's Indians were finally effected when the Brafferton Foundation supported an Indian School at William and Mary College. The Brafferton is the building on the left in this early engraving.

erate to read the Bible. As a result, the Puritans built an Indian College at Harvard and established schools in many Indian villages. But acceptance of the white man's God proved hazardous. It meant exposure to European diseases and thus a higher mortality rate among Christian Indians. It also meant that Indians who became Christians aroused the enmity of non-Christian Indians.

Many barriers, of course, continued to separate Europeans and Indians: technology, religion, language, and customs. One of the biggest sources of misunderstanding was the difference in European and Indian concepts of property. Who owned the lands of North America? Even the English were confused over this point. The Indians had some sort of "natural right" to the territories they had long occupied, and yet the English king also had a right to grant patents to colonists in America. Roger Williams—the Separatist who was forced out of Massachusetts and founded Providence, Rhode Island—was one of the few English thinkers to face up to this contradiction. He declared that the king had no right over the American lands at all.

The Puritans attempted to justify their seizure of Indian territory with a tangle of self-serving arguments: God intended Christians to conquer and convert pagans; the king had the political right to grant patents in the lands he claimed; America was

Courtesy The Pennsylvania Academy of the Fine Arts.

Benjamin West, one of America's great eighteenth-century painters drew on his years in Pennsylvania to recreate a scene showing the negotiations of William Penn with a local tribe.

The Growth of British Colonial America

vacant and stood as an open invitation to further settlement. But none of these arguments seemed quite sufficient, and the Puritans prudently took the further precaution of buying land from the Indians. All too often, however, the Indians did not comprehend the full meaning of such sales.

The English also failed to understand the political structure of Indian tribes. Colonists often called an Indian leader the "king," unaware that few chiefs could make important decisions without consulting a council of tribal elders. The muddle in English thought is well illustrated by the varying reactions of the Virginia colonists to the marriage of John Rolfe to Pocahontas, daughter of the Indian chief Powhatan. Some English people dismissed the baptism of Pocahontas as a Christian and objected to the marriage on the grounds that Rolfe was marrying a savage, someone of a different race. Other colonists objected that Rolfe had no right to marry her, since Pocahontas was a "princess" and Rolfe a mere commoner.

Hostility developed openly between Indians and Europeans, especially when colonists found their food supplies dwindling and turned to pillaging Indian granaries. And, as the Indians became more familiar with European firearms and acquired some of their own, they feared white military superiority less and less. Thus, as the colonists penetrated deeper and deeper into Indian territories, the situation grew more and more inflammatory, ready to explode with the first small spark.

Wars in the South

In the South the struggle for land resulted in the first major Indian uprising in 1622. Powhatan's successor, his brother Opechancanough, convinced the Virginia tribes, the so-called "Powhatan Confederacy," that the colonists were devastating their traditional sources of food—berries and game—by planting more and more tobacco fields. Indian warriors of the confederacy descended on the English colonists and nearly succeeded in wiping them out. The attack came as a complete surprise to the English; it resulted in the death of more than 300 settlers and the destruction of almost all outlying farms. In reprisal, the English conducted a war against the Indians that lasted several years. As the English governor succinctly put it, "Either we must clere them or they us out of the Country." The English forces ruined the Indian corn fields, starving their enemies into submission. The Virginia Company used the uprising as a pretext for driving In-

dians off their cleared fields and for enslaving their prisoners. The English even put poison in the cup of wine they offered the Indians after the signing of a peace treaty in 1623. On another occasion in the same year, the English came to an Indian village on a peace expedition, obtained white hostages the Indians were holding, and then opened fire on the village, killing some forty Indians.

In 1644, after two decades of peace, Opechancanough led a second uprising. By now, he was so feeble that his braves carried him onto the battlefield to make a last-ditch attempt to exterminate the colonists. But the uprising failed, Opechancanough was captured, and horrible reprisals were again enacted against the Powhatan Indians. With the peace treaty of 1646, a new era of relations seemed about to begin since a line was drawn between Indian and colonial lands that carefully delimited Indian lands and restricted their movements. Furthermore, the Indians promised to warn the colonists of imminent attacks from other tribes and to pay a yearly tribute to the colony.

Bacon's Rebellion in 1675, however, spelled the end of Virginia's coastal tribes. There were various causes for Bacon's Rebellion. The high-spirited settlers along the frontier had many grievances against the royal governor, William Berkeley (1606–1677), and the English government he represented. In an effort to protect its own merchants against foreign—and especially Dutch—competition, the English Parliament passed a number of Navigation Acts restricting the sale of Virginia tobacco. Only English ships could carry it, and it could be sold only to England. As a result of this restricted market, the price of tobacco dropped severely, and economic depression followed. To force prices back up, the Virginians attempted to forbid the growth of all tobacco in their own colony and in Maryland and North Carolina as well. Lord Baltimore, the proprietor of Maryland, refused to cooperate, and prices continued to sink.

But economic discontent was only a general cause of the rebellion; a more immediate cause was tension between frontier settlers and the Indians. Traditionally, historians have portrayed Nathaniel Bacon (1647–1676), the young leader of the rebellion, as the defender of the poor frontiersmen against the rich grandees of Jamestown. Governor Berkeley has been shown as a tyrant and Bacon as a freedom fighter. Berkeley was charged with refusing to protect the frontier settlers against murderous Indians. As the story went, the fiery rebel

Governor Berkely of Virginia was deeply involved in Indian trade.

Bacon was forced to form a militia that would perform two functions: drive back the Indians and force Berkeley to pass laws that would alleviate the suffering of poor white Virginians.

The facts are simple, even if the interpretation of them is elusive. Some Indians stole hogs from a frontier farm and killed a herdsman. A company of militiamen pursued and murdered many Indians, both friends and foes, which touched off in turn widespread Indian raids along the frontier. Governor Berkeley refused to march against the Indians; instead he offered to build a chain of forts to protect the frontier. Bacon openly rebelled. He temporarily seized control of the government and passed laws that would limit tobacco production. He continued hostilities against the Indians until he died of fever and the rebellion dwindled away.

A close examination of documents shows that, although the rebellion was fought over many issues, the central point of disagreement was over Indian policy. For years Berkeley struggled to con-trol English expansion into Indian territory. When the Virginia assembly stripped him of this power, the governor still tried unsuccessfully to enforce an English law that forbade Indians to sell lands to settlers.

Berkeley's efforts to bridle English greed for Indian lands was what made him so hated. The frontiersmen despised him, not because he refused to defend the colony against Indians but because he would not kill and dispossess *all* Indians, both friendly and hostile tribes.

Although the rebellion was quelled, Bacon's men managed to kill off almost all of Virginia's coastal tribes: the Susquehanna, the Algonkians, the Pamunkey—the Indians of the tidelands. By the end of the seventeenth century, an English clergyman observed: "This is very certain that the Indian inhabitants of Virginia are now very inconsiderable as to their numbers and seem insensibly to decay though they live under the English protection and have no violence offered them."

Conflict in New Netherlands

In New Netherlands a similar tale of European-Indian relations can be told. Between 1614 and 1639 the Dutch, who depended on the Indians for the lucrative fur trade, were on good terms with the local tribes. But a new Dutch governor, Willem Kieft, who arrived in 1638, was determined to humble the Indians, an act that he felt would open up the Hudson River valley to Dutch expansion. When a group of Weichquasekeck Indians sought refuge from another Indian tribe in 1643, Kieft received the refugees—and then slaughtered them. This outrage stirred the Indians to revenge—Kieft's War lasted for several years.

Wars in New England

In New England, relations with the Indians also were peaceful at first. But in 1637 the Puritans of Massachusetts and Connecticut attacked the Pequots, a warlike tribe that had recently moved into the area and posed a threat both to the English and to local tribes. The war was brief and ruthless. The Pequots, who were disbanded as a tribe, were either killed or sold into slavery in the West Indies, or they were handed over as "wards" to tribes friendly to the Puritans.

After the Pequot War, the four Puritan colonies—Massachusetts, Plymouth, Connecticut, and New Haven—formed a military pact called the New

Mary White Rowlandson

THE CAPTIVITY OF MRS. ROWLANDSON.

ca. 1635–1678

"It is a solemn sight to see so many Christians lying in their blood, some here, some there, like a company of Sheep torn by Wolves. All of them stript naked by a company of hell-hounds, roaring, singing, ranting, and insulting, as if they would have torn our very hearts out; yet the Lord by his Almighty power preserved a number of us from death, for there were twenty-four of us taken alive and carried Captive.

I had often before this said, that if the Indians should come, I should chuse rather to be killed by them than taken alive, but when it came to the tryal my mind changed; their glittering weapons so daunted my spirit, that I chose to rather to go along with those . . . ravenous Beasts, than that moment to end my dayes."

So wrote Mary Rowlandson, wife of a Massachusetts minister, as she recalled the horrors of King Philip's War. Early on the morning of February 10, 1676, a band of Wampanoag Indians armed with muskets and tomahawks attacked and pillaged the little town of Lancaster. (Her husband, the Reverend Rowlandson, had been the sole graduate of Harvard College in 1652.) When the Wampanoags struck, the Reverend Rowlandson was in Boston seeking military aid for his community. He returned home to find the frontier settlement devastated, perhaps fifty people dead, and his wife and their three children missing.

During succeeding days, the survivors abandoned Lancaster; Rowlandson returned to Boston to mount an effort to ransom captives. Meanwhile, his wife, a son, and a daughter—Sarah, the youngest, had soon died of wounds and starvation—were being transported from place to place and eventu-

ally became separated. For Mary Rowlandson this trek included twenty different locations and eleven weeks of misery. Her *Narrative*, heavily laced with Scripture, was first published by a Cambridge, Massachusetts, printer in 1682. It tells how she at first detested Indian food, but in time "their filthy trash . . . [became] sweet and savoury to my taste." Although she grieved greatly over the death of her own child, that of a papoose belonging to her new master (Quanopin or Quinnapin) had the "one benefit" of providing more room in the wigwam for others. Mrs. Rowlandson heaped scorn upon the "English Army" as slow and inept, yet she never lost her faith in God since this ordeal, she concluded, was the Lord's way "to scourge and chasten me."

Just how she became a servant of Quanopin and his three "squaws" is unclear, but it is apparent that she existed in a capricious world of "praying" and "heathen" Indians, who would treat her kindly one moment and then suddenly threaten to "break her face" the next. One "praying" Indian even wore a necklace made of his victims' fingers.

In her travels Mrs. Rowlandson met King Philip, who offered her a pipe of tobacco ("a usual Complement now adayes amongst Saints and Sinners"). Being an ex-smoker she declined, noting that tobacco is "a bewitching thing," but with God's help she now had the will power to reject "a stinking Tobacco-pipe."

During these weeks she knitted stockings and made shirts for braves and squaws who, realizing her potential worth, treated their captive reasonably well. Eventually, she persuaded her captors to exchange her for a ransom of £ 20. Her ordeal ended on May 2, 1676, when the ransom was paid. A short time later, her son and daughter also won their freedom. By August the war was over, and Quanopin was captured and executed.

The reunited family lived briefly in Boston, but in 1677 moved to Wethersfield, Connecticut, where the Reverend Rowlandson had accepted a call as pastor. He died in November 1678, and the town voted Mrs. Rowlandson an annual pension of £ 30. Her family reunion had proved shortlived.

What happened to Mrs. Rowlandson after this is unknown, but in 1682 the first edition of her narrative appeared. Supposedly written to instruct her children, it soon enjoyed widespread readership on both sides of the Atlantic. Her vivid language and faith in God's providence, which run throughout the account, provide us with a glimpse of the earthy strength of a Puritan woman and a memorable picture of early Indian-white confrontations in the New World.

England Confederation (1643). Indian policy in New England consisted of pitting one tribe against another and of favoring peaceful allies. And, to assure themselves of immediate protection, most colonies required every English male citizen between the ages of sixteen and sixty to serve in militia units organized town by town.

In 1675 a new Indian conflict broke out, King Philip's War. The new leader of the Wampanoag tribe that had once been so friendly to the Pilgrims, Philip (Metacomet), came to loathe the increasing domination of the English over his people. When three of his braves were hanged by the English for having murdered a Christian Indian who was also an informer for the whites, Philip decided to take up arms. His strategy was to organize several tribes into a league.

The Wampanoags and other northeastern tribes were driven to war by several factors. They resented the erosion of tribal authority and custom by colonial justice; for Puritan authorities, rather than tribal councils', were trying Indian offenders. The introduction of alcoholic drink was further disorganizing tribal life. English farmers and Indian farmers found living side by side fraught with difficulties. For instance, many English farmers refused to fence in their property; as a result, their livestock wandered into Indian fields and ate the crops. All of these contacts with white settlers threatened Indian culture and created considerable uneasiness. The Atlantic seaboard tribes might have migrated further west, but that alternative was closed to them, for there the powerful Iroquois Confederacy ruled supreme.

Hemmed in and frustrated, the Wampanoags attacked settlers before King Philip had thoroughly worked out a master plan for routing the enemy, and the war spread in a disorganized fashion from tribe to tribe. It quickly became the most ferocious Indian onslaught of the seventeenth century. Colonial villages throughout Massachusetts were sacked and burned, one after another. Brookfield was reduced to ashes, Northfield had to be evacuated, Deerfield was taken, and the war spread as far north as Maine, where the town of Saco on the seacoast was assaulted. (For a firsthand account of the survivor of one Indian attack see the biographical sketch of Mary White Rowlandson.)

In August 1676, King Philip was trapped and killed, and soon the war died out, but the losses on both sides were great: 600 English settlers and 3,000 Indians. New England's frontier was pushed back

Courtesy of the American Antiquarian Society.

King Philip appears in this colonial engraving as the warrior-leader. There are no known sketches of him done while he was alive. This reveals the image he had after the Indian war.

some forty miles, almost a thousand colonists lost their lives, and a dozen frontier villages were obliterated. But if the war had frightful consequences for the colonists, it also served to unite them into a tighter confederacy; henceforth the Puritans felt no moral pangs in grabbing Indian lands.

With the breakup of Indian resistance, the tribal life of the Indians began to disintegrate completely. Although the Narragansett tribe of Rhode Island at first maintained an uneasy neutrality, the Puritan leaders waged a "preventive" war against them and trapped their mighty forces in a village that was put to the torch. Of those Indians captured, many were executed, but others were sold as slaves and exported to the West Indies, Spain, and the Mediterranean. Even tribes that supported the English were punished since they were herded into reservations. Just as Bacon's Rebellion spelled the end of Indian autonomy in Tidewater Virginia, so King Philip's War, which occurred at about the same time, reduced the New England tribes to pitiful remnants of their former glory. Severe as the wars of 1637 and 1676 were, the primary cause of the decline of the Indian population was disease.

Colonial Wars

From 1689 to the middle of the eighteenth century, England was involved in a series of Continental struggles, one fracas seemingly spawning yet another. These confrontations included four wars which had reverberations in North America as English, French, and Spanish partisans bribed Indian allies to help them attack outposts of their European foes. During King William's War (1689–1697), one New England expedition occupied Nova Scotia temporarily, but another failed to take Quebec. Meanwhile, the French burned several English towns, among them, Schenectady in the colony of New York. (To appreciate just how these wars might affect the career of a colonial adventurer caught up in this turmoil, see the biographical sketch of Samuel Vetch later in this chapter.)

Queen Anne's War (1702–1713), known as the War of Spanish Succession in Europe, produced more indecisive border skirmishing on this side of the Atlantic. The French ravaged settlements in western Massachusetts, while the Spanish mounted an unsuccessful assualt against Charleston, South Carolina, and the English retaliated with an equally unsuccessful attack on Saint Augustine, Florida. When the dust settled, however, England had made some gains. She acquired title to Nova Scotia, Newfoundland, and the Hudson Bay region and a thirty-year monopoly on the slave trade with Spain's American Empire. The English also pushed the Spanish out of what is now Georgia, thus laying the foundation of the colony launched by Oglethorpe in 1732.

The third confrontation, known as the War of Jenkin's Ear (1739–1742), merged into yet a fourth, the War of Austrian Succession (1740–1748), a general melee of conflicting dynastic ambitions. Jen-

The French fortress of Louisbourg fell to a colonial force led by Britishers Jeffrey Amherst and James Wolfe in 1758. Louisbourg had been a center for French vessels preying on colonial shipping.

kins, an English master mariner, reported in 1731 that Spanish sailors boarded his vessel and cut or tore off his ear. Seven years later he told a committee of the House of Commons of this indignity and even exhibited what he claimed to be his severed ear. A public outcry for revenge, fed by other alleged Spanish outrages, led to war. The conflict over the Austrian succession was justified from the English point of view by the need to protect the balance of power in Europe. The outcome of this dynastic squabble settled nothing and had little immediate impact upon affairs in North America.

In general, these struggles, in which Indian allies played a key role, featured thrusts and counterthrusts by the French and English in New England and neighboring parts of Canada and similar moves by the Spanish and English in the Carolinas and Florida. Yet, for the most part, this ebb and flow had little lasting impact; that is, until after 1750. Then, in 1753 the bad blood of previous decades boiled over once more in the upper Ohio Valley and ignited a conflagration that would alter drastically the course of colonial history. This struggle, known as the French and Indian War on this side of the Atlantic and as the Seven Years' War in Europe, differed markedly from its predecessors. It began in the New World, not the Old, and was no mere series of coastal raids and frontier hit-and-run skirmishes. This war grew into a determined and successful campaign, carefully engineered and well plotted out by those in power in London, to end French rule on the North American continent once and for all.

A Firm Beginning

By 1750 the English foothold along the Atlantic coast of North America was secure. Even the broad outlines of possible control of much of the entire continent could be discerned as the chain of settlements grew stronger and as native tribes withered to insignificance. Unlike the French, whose out-

Samuel Vetch

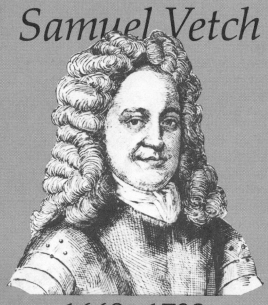

1668–1732

Soldier, trader, and the first man to formulate an adequate plan for the expulsion of the French from North America, Vetch was born in Edinburgh, Scotland. He spent an uneasy boyhood in northern England where his father preached the outlawed Presbyterian faith and conspired against the crown. As a teenager, Vetch received some higher education in the Netherlands and, when William and Mary assumed power, gained a commission in a Scottish regiment.

In 1698 he joined an ill-fated venture in Central America, and a year later when most of the colonists fled to New York, Vetch went with them. There, his handsome and commanding presence won him a bride, Margaret Livingston, daughter of the secretary of Indian affairs; soon Vetch was deeply involved in the Albany Indian trade and its illegal connections with the French at Montreal. A few years later, he moved to Boston, purchased boats, and expanded the growing trade in arms and ammunition with the enemy. However, in 1706 he and his associates were convicted and fined by the General Court of Massachusetts for these activities, but Vetch fled to England, demanded a new trial, and eventually escaped punishment.

While there he concocted a scheme for ousting the French from Canada, which included an attack on Montreal by way of Lake Champlain and seizure of Quebec by land and sea. After those bastions were taken, he believed that other French outposts, and perhaps even some Spanish colonies, would fall easily into English hands. In March 1709, Vetch won the approval of the Whig government in London for his plan and set out for Boston. Within a few months he had three well-trained regiments in the field and the enthusiastic backing of New England and New York, although Quaker Pennsylvania and New Jersey expressed little interest in this undertaking. Then, as a result of the British decision to use its support troops elsewhere and poor execution of Vetch's ideas, the plan faltered. In 1710 colonial forces were able to seize Nova Scotia where Vetch became military governor.

Four years later, at odds with civil authorities, he fled to England once more where he spent the rest of his life in a futile search for a government job. Tempted by the promises of various ministries, he lingered on and died there in 1732, a prisoner for debts he had accumulated.

Vetch's career is reminiscent of those of numerous other colonial adventurers. He obviously was brave, cut an impressive figure, and had considerable ability. But that was not enough to insure success. Changes of ministries, the death of a sovereign, or a shift of military resources because of Continental pressures could dash the best-laid plans of a man like Vetch. Until a distant land represented substantial investment or became a pawn in a serious struggle, it could not long hold the attention of those at the seat of power.

posts were weak, isolated, and scattered, and unlike the Spanish, whose interests focused on South America, Mexico, and the Caribbean isles (some of which London merchants certainly coveted), the English had created in hit-or-miss fashion a necklace of economically sound, prosperous towns, villages, and farms.

Viewed from Mother England, the most important and most valuable possessions in the New World were none of the thirteen colonies destined to rebel but the tiny sugar islands of the sun-soaked Caribbean, often pawns in wars with Spain. The southern colonies (Maryland, Virginia, and the Carolinas), rich with tobacco, rice, indigo, and with turpentine, pitch, and timber ranked next in importance, followed by the Middle colonies (New York, Pennsylvania, New Jersey, and Delaware). New England, a mix of marginal farming, trade, and seafaring, was less valuable in English eyes. Nevertheless, ships from innumerable little northeastern ports were beginning to play a key role in the emerging colonial-imperial economy, messengers of commerce tying diverse parts of the huge Atlantic basin together.

Yet, in growth lay seeds of discord. For, as a colonial economy emerged, the English government often tried to regulate it so as to help merchants at home, not the colonials. Just how much these rules and regulations actually hampered trade and commerce is debatable, since laws promulgated 3,000 miles away often were ignored. Nevertheless, the mere passage of them was sufficient to stir up resentment on this side of the Atlantic, because, once on the books, the possibility of rigorous enforcement loomed ominously.

As the colonists from New Hampshire to Georgia prospered, grew in population, and began to feel their strength, opposition to these trade restrictions became keener and more open. Mingled with this resentment was the age-old suspicion of authority and even abhorrence of *English* authority, an authority that had forced thousands to cross the Atlantic Ocean because of its repressive policies toward dissident believers, marginal farmers, and minor offenders. By 1750, a vibrant, diverse society was emerging along the eastern coast of North America, one that was no longer willing to be tied to the center of empire by mere rules and regulations and made to dance to tugs and twists like a marionette. For thousands of American colonists, England had ceased to be—if it ever had been—a distant but beloved homeland.

Essay

Tobacco: The Gift and The Curse of the Indians

The New York Public Library, Picture Collection.
Early American tobacco advertising, more concerned with presenting an image of refinement than an accurate picture of the tobacco South, bore slogans such as "Best under the Sun."

In recent years, cigarette smoking has been denounced as a major health hazard. Every pack of cigarettes sold in the United States must bear the words: "Warning: The Surgeon General has Determined That Cigarette Smoking Is Dangerous to Your Health." A detailed study by the United States Department of Health, Education and Welfare has documented that cigarette smoking (but not pipe and cigar smoking) is directly related to lung cancer, to circulatory and heart diseases, and to chronic bronchitis and emphysema. The death rate from smoking can be related to such factors as the age at which one begins to smoke and the number of cigarettes one consumes a day. For instance, males who smoke fewer than ten cigarettes a day have a death rate about 40 percent higher than male non-smokers; those who smoke more than 20 cigarettes a day have a death rate that is 90 percent higher; and those who smoke 40 cigarettes or more have a rate that is 120 percent higher. The statistics for females are not yet so complete.

Oddly enough, Europeans originally regarded tobacco as a medicine. One of its first great promoters, Jean Nicot—from whose name the word *nicotine* was derived—thought so highly of the plant's medicinal properties that he sent seeds of the plant from Portugal back to the Queen Mother of France to cure her migraine headaches. Nicotine therapy was soon the rage throughout Europe. For a time, only druggists were allowed to dispense the valuable leaf, which was prescribed as a cure for hundreds of ills.

During the sixteenth and seventeenth centuries, tobacco conquered the whole world, becoming even more popular than another New World product—coffee. It was slow to catch on in Europe, but once it became a medical and social fad, it quickly swept the Old World. In 1558 the plant was first cultivated in Spain. By 1565 the French and English were smoking it. By the end of the first decade of the seventeenth century, its production and consumption had circled the globe, and it was to be found in Russia, the Philippines, Virginia, Java, India, and Ceylon. Almost everywhere it was taken in all three ways—snuffed, smoked, and chewed. At first, smokers used pipes, then switched to cigars, and at the beginning of the nineteenth century turned to cigarettes.

Sir Walter Raleigh enjoyed a great vogue in London when he puffed on his pipe before Queen Elizabeth. So intriguing was this strange practice of inhaling smoke that two Indians were brought from Virginia to London in 1584 to demonstrate it. Dealers soon varied the product by adding other ingredients such as musk, amber, and orange blossom. Dandies were soon entertaining ladies by puffing smoke rings and performing other tricks; learned doctors were recommending a decoction of tobacco leaves, boiled and applied to the face as a lotion, to clear up pimples and blotches.

Not everyone liked the new "medicine." King James I was so irritated by smoking that he published anonymously his *Counterblaste to Tobacco* in which he stated that smoking is a "custome lothsome to the eye, hatefull to the nose, harmefull to the braine, dangerous to the Lungs and in the blacke stinking fume thereof, nearest resembling the horrible Stigian smoke of the pit that is bottomelesse." On this point the Puritans agreed with him and attempted to ban smoking in New England, but with little success.

Who invented this strange custom of inhaling burning smoke? Tobacco is a purely American plant; before Columbus it had not been heard of in Europe, Africa, or Asia. The oldest known evidence of smoking is a Mexican wall sculpture, carved in the seventh or eighth century and portraying a Mayan priest blowing smoke through a long tube. Indeed, tobacco smoking was a religious ritual, or at least a ceremonial act, throughout the New World. Where tobacco was first raised experts have yet to determine; some say in Peru, others in Argentina, and still others claim that the Mayans of Mexico were the first to cultivate it.

Columbus was puzzled when friendly Indians offered him "some dry leaves" as a present soon after landing at San Salvador. The mystery was solved a few weeks later when members of his crew saw natives of Cuba who "drank smoke." Chewing and smoking tobacco at first struck the Spanish as a distasteful practice, as it still must seem to anyone who tries smoking for the first time. By the middle of the sixteenth century, however, Europeans not only were smoking but also had recognized the economic advantages of growing and selling tobacco. For hundreds of years tobacco had been a form of currency among Indian tribes, and in the sixteenth century it became a valuable commercial crop for Europeans as well. Because it was scarce, tobacco at first was worth its weight in silver: in 1600 a pound of tobacco sold in London for a pound of silver.

In the English colony of Virginia, the cultivation of tobacco proved a godsend. Between 1607, when Jamestown was settled, and 1614, the settlers

Tobacco: the Gift and Curse of the Indians

failed to discover an industry or a cash crop that would support the colony. But in 1610 an Englishman named John Rolfe arrived at Jamestown and soon began to experiment with tobacco. The type of tobacco that the Virginia Indians grew was not acceptable to English smokers. Rolfe introduced some seeds of the more attractive variety, *Nicotiana tabacum,* from the Caribbean and raised and cured it successfully. When Rolfe heard that tobacco buyers in London liked his Virginia brand, he felt so jubilant that he immediately informed the other settlers. They abandoned their other efforts and devoted themselves to raising tobacco. By 1627, England was importing half a million pounds of tobacco every year, much of it from Virginia; by 1770, this figure had risen to an astounding 100 million pounds. The future of Jamestown—in fact, of all Virginia and Maryland—was secure. The colonies flourished, some planters became extremely wealthy—and the economy of early Virginians became exclusively bound up with the production of tobacco. This single-crop economy put Virginia at the mercy of fluctuating tobacco prices. When overproduction and English laws restricting tobacco

commerce caused the price to drop drastically in the second half of the seventeenth century, Virginia suffered a major depression.

More tragically, tobacco eventually wedded Virginia to the slave system of labor. The cultivation of tobacco requires an extraordinary amount of care. In colonial times tobacco seed was sown in December in small plant beds. In the spring, after the tobacco plants had begun to sprout, the tender shoots were transplanted to fields thoroughly worked with hoes. Transplanting was a delicate operation. After the transplanted tobacco began to grow, most of its leaves were pinched off so that the remaining leaves would be larger. Insects and particularly worms had to be picked off the plants continually. Harvesting the plants was equally arduous, since they could be cut only at the moment they became ripe and since a whole field never ripened at one time. Drying and curing tobacco was yet another complicated process, the last of several intricate but easily learned steps. All this backbreaking labor required small groups of field hands, and slavery became the most economical means of providing the necessary labor. If cancer has turned

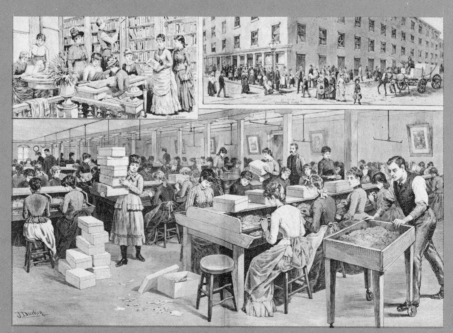

Cigarette girls continued to handroll cigarettes in this Richmond factory in 1887. Production was slow compared to that of a cigarette machine since the best cigarette girl could roll only four or five cigarettes per minute.

The Growth of British Colonial America

out to be one of the curses of tobacco, then slavery must surely be counted as the other.

In the late nineteenth century, cigarette smoking began to be promoted by vigorous advertising and soon emerged as a vast American industry. It came to be monopolized by two brothers, Benjamin and James Duke. In 1883 the Duke brothers replaced the handrolling of cigarettes with a new machine invented by James Bonsack. By the end of the following year, this machine was producing 120,000 cigarettes a day, a rate fifty times faster than that of the handrollers. Mechanization allowed the Duke brothers to cut their prices in half and to sell a box of ten cigarettes for five cents. Joining with several other outflanked corporations to form the American Tobacco Company in 1890, the Dukes became the czars of the industry. In fact, Benjamin Duke was able to invest his enormous profits in many southern industries and thereby became a leader in the South's economic revival after the Civil War.

The success of the Duke brothers must be attributed to two features that long distinguished American industry: advertising and mechanization. Before the Duke brothers adopted the Bonsack machine, it had been turned down by several leading companies on the grounds that it was not reliable and the public would never accept machine-made cigarettes. The Dukes perfected the machine and even boasted of it in their advertisements: "These cigarettes are manufactured on the Bonsack Cigarette Machines." The Dukes spent $800,000 in 1889 on advertising. They tirelessly thought up new gimmicks for their cigarettes, such as sending a polo team on roller skates across the country to advertise one brand and putting the picture of a favorite French actress on another.

Although temperance workers who were fighting alcoholism also condemned smoking, their efforts were futile when confronted by the aggressive business tactics of the Duke brothers and the growing popularity of cigarettes. Religious groups, who abhorred smoking as a vice, and many physicians, who regarded it as a health hazard, attempted unsuccessfully to quell the growing fad of cigarette smoking. For decades "respectable" women thought that smoking was unattractive, but in the 1920s this prejudice was overcome and flappers proudly puffed on cigarettes. Only after the 1950s did the general public become aware of the dreadful damage to health that smoking represents.

SELECTED READINGS

General

Wesley F. Craven, *The Colonies in Transition* (1968)

M. Eugene Sirmans, *Colonial South Carolina: Political History 1663–1763* (1966)

Clarence Ver Steeg, *The Formative Years* (1964)

Immigration and Ethnic Patterns

William Bradford, *Of Plymouth Plantation*, ed. Samuel Eliot Morison (1952)

Carl Bridenbaugh, *Vexed and Troubled Englishmen, 1590–1642* (1967)

R. J. Dickson, *Ulster Emigration to Colonial America* (1966)

James Lemon, *The Best Poor Man's Country* (1972)

George Willison, *Saints and Strangers: Pilgrim Fathers* (1945)

Colonial Frontier

Richard M. Brown, *The South Carolina Regulators* (1963)

Douglas Leach, *Arms for Empire* (1974)

Douglas Leach, *Flintlock and Tomahawk* (1958)

Bernard Sheehan, *Savagism and Civility: Indians, and Englishmen in Colonial Virginia* (1980)

W. Stitt Robinson, *The Southern Colonial Frontier, 1607-1793* (1979)

Wilcomb Washburne, *The Governor and the Rebel: Bacon's Rebellion* (1957)

Labor and Race

Winthrop Jordan, *White Over Black* (1968)

Edmund Morgan, *American Slavery, American Freedom: The Ordeal of Colonial Virginia* (1975)

Gary B. Nash, *Red, White and Black* (1974)

Abbot Smith, *Colonists in Bondage: White Servitude and Convict Labor in America 1607–1776* (1947)

Peter Wood, *Black Majority: Negroes in Colonial South Carolina from 1670 through the Stono Rebellion* (1974)

Puritan Settlements

Emery Battis, *Saints and Sectaries: Anne Hutchinson and the Antinomian Controversy* (1962)

Francis J. Bremer, *The Puritan Experiment* (1976)

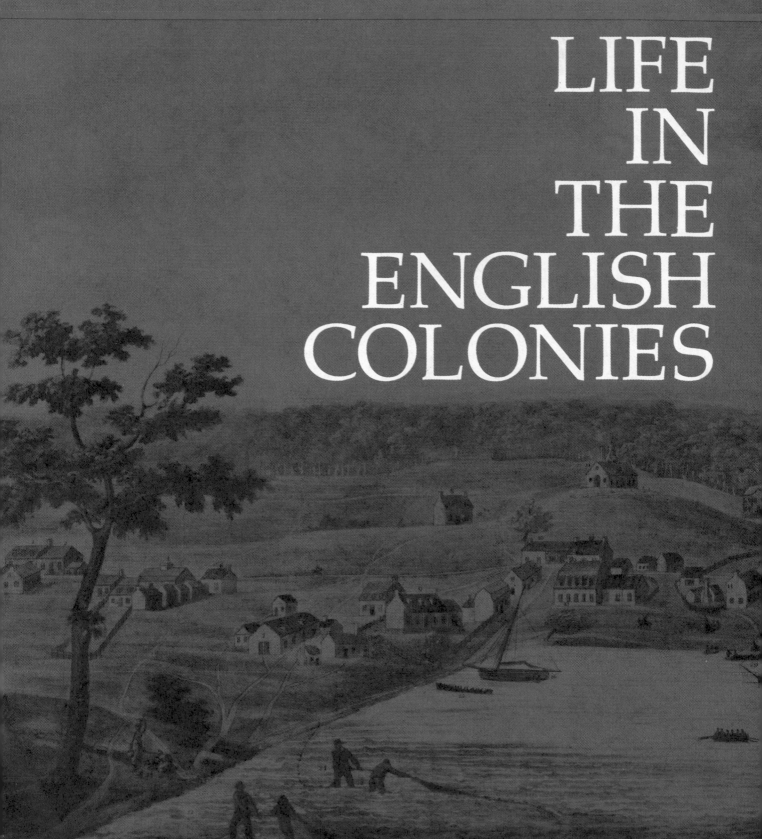

CHAPTER 3
LIFE IN THE ENGLISH COLONIES

TIMELINE

1619
The first blacks arrive in British North America

1637
Harvard College opens

1640
The Whole Books of Psalms published

1650
Beginning of English regulation of colonial trade

1662
The Halfway Covenant established to allow wider Puritan church membership

1692
Salem Village holds witchcraft trials

1699
Wool Act forbids export of colonial textiles

1704
Anglican Church established in New Jersey

1739–40
George Whitefield, an Anglican priest, tours the colonies

1776
Philadelphia population reached 40,000 citizens

CHAPTER OUTLINE

Life in colonial America was marked by startling diversity. In the seventeenth century, Virginia seemed as foreign to most members of the Massachusetts Bay Colony as England itself—possibly more so, since Massachusetts was full of recent arrivals from England. No single style of life prevailed throughout the colonies, no single religion or political structure or economy—not even a unified system of weights, measures, and money. As late as 1724, when young Ben Franklin returned for a visit to his native Boston from his adopted city of Philadelphia, he was quizzed about Philadelphia as though it were a distant land.

Geography isolated the colonies one from another. Roads were few and inadequate, and even travel by water was perilous and slow (Franklin's voyage from Philadelphia to Boston took fourteen days). Various economic systems could be just as isolating. A small subsistence farmer in the backcountry of Virginia had little reason to deal with the outside world at all. If he were Presbyterian and Scottish, he probably was distrustful of the Anglican leadership. The backcountry had less well established traditions of deference than did the Tidewater, the term for those lands served by rivers influenced by ocean tides. And if such enmities could spring up between different regions of the same colony, what would a Virginia small farmer have made of a Puritan merchant in Boston?

Even the leaders of different colonies pursued different lives. For instance, one eighteenth-century Virginia farmer, Robert Carter of Corotoman, owned 300,000 acres, sent his sons to school in England, read Latin and Greek classics from his well-stocked library, but devoted most of his time to managing his estates, selling the tobacco they produced, and speculating in still more land. John Hull of Boston came to Massachusetts from England with his family. As a boy he helped his father on the family farm, but at eighteen he apprenticed himself to a goldsmith. Through perseverance and business acumen, Hull eventually became the owner of a large fleet of merchant ships, built a fine house, but continued working at his trade as a goldsmith. Worldly success and religious piety, far from being at odds with one another, seemed to Hull to be inextricably bound together, and he ordered his captains to be "careful to see to the worship of God every day on the vessel and to the sanctification of the Lord's Day and suppression of all profaneness that the Lord may delight to be with you and his blessing upon you." Both men, Virginian and Bos-

Valentine Museum, Richmond, Virginia.
Shirley Plantation passed into the hands of the Carter family in the eighteenth century. Charles Carter, grandson of "King" Carter, built this home overlooking the James River. Carters still own and occupy this working plantation.

Courtesy Museum of Fine Arts, Boston.
The Isaac Winslow family's status as prosperous colonials was reflected in their dress and in having this family portrait done by Josiah Blackburn.

tonian, were ceaselessly industrious, both spoke English, both were extremely pious, both made money—but there the resemblances stopped. The commercial farmer of Virginia was a representative of the landed gentry. He ruled over a small kingdom of his own and there raised tobacco, operated a gristmill and a sawmill, employed a score of trained craftsmen on his estates, and maintained daily contacts with his black slaves. The merchant of Boston, no matter how wealthy, considered himself to be little more than a successful small tradesman.

The Colonial Economy

For most of its history America has been predominantly an agricultural land, and never was this more true than during the colonial period, when ninety-five percent of the people were farmers.

The Southern Colonies

For Virginia, Maryland, and part of North Carolina, tobacco was the leading cash crop. In the seventeenth century the large planters acted as merchants in England for their own crops, but by the end of the century more and more Virginians were relying on a few large English merchant houses to do the marketing for them. Tobacco was so valuable that in the colonies around the Chesapeake Bay it was a medium of exchange. Salaries were paid in tobacco, taxes were collected in tobacco, rents were figured in tobacco.

In South Carolina the search for a cash crop took longer. At first the Indian trade provided tens of thousands of deerskin hides every year, but no farming surplus was produced until it was learned, after some experimentation, that the hot, wet coastal lands were suitable for growing rice. A young woman, Eliza Lucas (1722–1793), introduced a second cash crop from the West Indies that could be grown in the same coastal areas—indigo, a plant from which a valuable blue dye is extracted. Rice and indigo, then, became the exportable crops of the coast, but the backcountry failed to find a comparable product and remained on a level of subsistence farming.

The varying economy of these regions has led to a theory that there were three distinct colonial Souths, each with its own interests to protect: the tobacco-growing Chesapeake Bay area; the rice-growing coastal lands of South Carolina; and the backcountry throughout the South. This picture of a tripartite South may be oversimplified, but it is a useful scheme for recognizing the various patterns of life. The coastal and Piedmont commercial farmers used slaves, congregated periodically in such cities as Williamsburg and Charleston, and had frequent business dealings with England and

South Carolina Library, University of South Carolina.
Indigo became an important second crop for South Carolina slave owners. Here the dye-producing plant is being harvested.

Philadelphia was well on the way to becoming the second city of the British empire when Peter Cooper sketched its busy port in 1720.

the backcountry. Along the frontier, farmers kept fewer slaves or perhaps none, visited the coast seldom if at all, and had few surplus crops to sell. Pioneers in different colonies along the frontier often had more contact with one another than with residents of the older sections of their own colony. Travel between western and eastern regions was extremely difficult. Few roads existed, the mountains acted as a barrier, and even the rivers could not be used as waterways, since they were broken by rapids at the fall line. North and south travel, by contrast, was somewhat easier, and a north-south trade grew up between Philadelphia and the entire backcountry as far as the Carolinas.

The Middle Colonies

The Middle colonies were the breadbasket of America. Wheat was the principal crop, though other important cash crops such as lumber often were exported. The agricultural wealth of the Middle colonies was increased by trade and industry. Philadelphia was the commercial capital of British North America and of the Middle colonies as well. In 1776 Philadelphia counted 40,000 citizens, which made it the second largest city in the empire, second only to London. New York, Philadelphia's most serious rival, had about 25,000 inhabitants, though it would soon surge ahead. At that date Boston, which grew imperceptibly during the years from 1760 to 1775, had 16,000 citizens.

The chief problem that Philadelphia merchants faced was that the Middle colonies did not produce anything that could be sold in England. Aside from furs, the natural products of the region—and of New York—simply had no market in the homeland. Most of the farms of the region were family-size holdings, not vast estates such as those found in the Virginia Tidewater or Low Country South Carolina. As a result, Philadelphia merchants were obliged to devise more complex and less obvious trade routes. Shipments of provisions (grain, flour, bread, pork, and beef) and lumber (barrel staves, hoops, and shingles) to the West Indies became the backbone of their commerce. Similar products and fish from New England were also shipped from Philadelphia to Portugal. From there Philadelphia ships often carried cargoes of sugar, molasses, rum, or wine to British ports. On the voyage home to Philadelphia the ships brought back British dry goods and hardware and sometimes stopped in the West Indies to pick up slaves as well.

But Philadelphia also was active in intercolonial trade. Iron goods manufactured in Philadelphia were sold to other colonies; furniture from Philadelphia graced the best southern homes. The vast hinterland along the frontier looked to Philadelphia as its supply center, as did Delaware and New Jersey.

The New England Colonies

This region was basically a patchwork of subsistence farms, producing little that could be exported and not unlike those found along the southern frontier. This meant that each year hundreds of able young men turned to the sea or towns such as Boston, Providence, and Newport for their livelihood.

Boston, like Philadelphia, became a commercial center dealing in products from many sources. Molasses (made from sugar) was carried from the West Indies to Boston where it was converted into rum that was then transported back to the Caribbean. Often a rum ship would also carry salted fish, which was fed to slaves in the West Indies, and manufactured items. And in their trade with the Old World, Boston merchants carried fish to the Mediterranean and parts of Africa. In fact, fish was the chief cash crop that Massachusetts could export, though barrels, lumber, and whale oil were other native products that Bostonians sold abroad at a profit. Ships from Massachusetts also engaged in the slave trade. As the vessels worked their way

north from the West Indies, they would stop off at southern ports and sell African slaves bought in the Caribbean. The pattern of trade practiced by ships from Boston, Providence, Newport, and other New England coastal centers cannot be reduced to the simple diagram so well known to school children—the "triangular trade" of rum, slaves, and molasses. Though slaves were sometimes brought directly from Africa to America, more often than not they

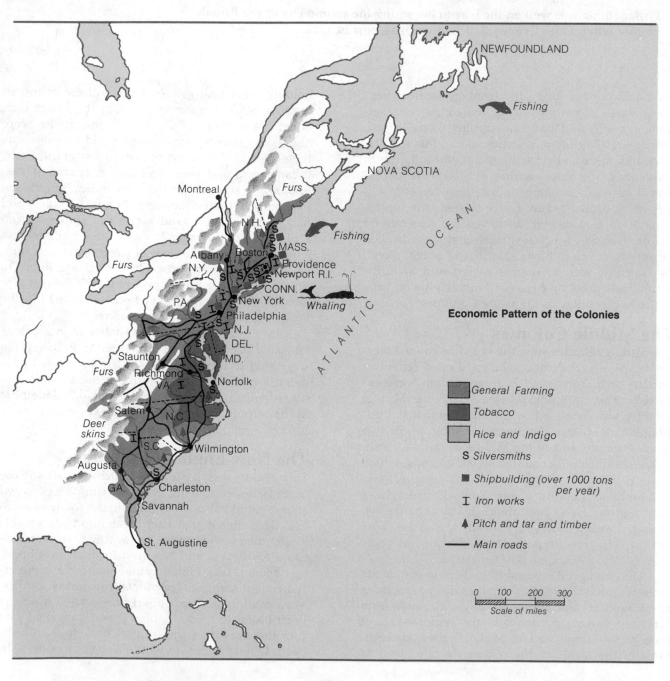

Economic Pattern of the Colonies

- General Farming
- Tobacco
- Rice and Indigo
- **S** Silversmiths
- ■ Shipbuilding (over 1000 tons per year)
- **I** Iron works
- ▲ Pitch and tar and timber
- — Main roads

0   100   200   300
Scale of miles

were purchased in the West Indies. Rum, rather than being sold to Africans in exchange for slaves, was usually shipped to the West Indies.

In the second half of the seventeenth century, a pattern emerged that prevailed throughout the colonial period: agricultural products flowed into Boston from the farms of the colony; and English imports moved in the opposite direction, from Boston into the towns and villages of the hinterland. Rather than sea trade competing with agriculture, the two pursuits complemented one another perfectly. Boston merchants shipped Massachusetts grain, beef, bread, and fish to the West Indies, where, according to John Winthrop, the islanders were "so intent upon planting sugar that they had rather buy foode at very deare rates than produce it by labour." Agricultural produce also was conveyed across the Atlantic. Moreover, cheap Massachusetts foodstuffs were purchased in Boston by foreign vessels; outfitting ships with provisions became a major Boston industry. The entire region profited from this trade—ship chandlers who fitted and loaded ships, butchers who packed and salted beef, coopers who built casks to hold it, millers and bakers who transformed wheat into bread and hardtack, even doctors who sometimes treated injured sailors.

Economic Regulation

European nations recognized the importance of trade to national prosperity and wealth at the time new world colonization began. Most statesmen subscribed to the idea of bullionism, that is, possession of gold and silver was a good measure of the strength of a nation. Acquiring a surplus of gold and silver through trade requires that a country sell more than it imports; in other words, it must achieve a favorable balance of trade. Colonies could help in this search for strength by producing gold and silver (as the Spanish did) or by supplying materials which otherwise would have to be purchased outside of the empire (thus draining off gold and silver). In addition, all colonies, even if they did not produce precious metals, were supposed to be markets for goods made in the mother country. Eventually, these ideas would evolve into a theory called mercantilism, but British trade regulations for the colonies appeared piecemeal long before the final statement of this theory.

The British began to regulate colonial trade in 1650; the regulations were called Navigation Acts. In successive decades more and more such acts were added and gradually became a net of precedents like those of common law. The first Navigation Acts required that all trade with the colonies be carried only by British ships, that is, by ships that were staffed with crews at least half English and that were owned either by colonials or Englishmen. This act was intended to encourage the growth of the British merchant marine and to prohibit Dutch vessels from trade within the empire.

Not only did trade have to be confined to British ships, it also had to be conducted with English merchants exclusively if the transaction involved specified goods. The first such enumeration of specific items was issued in the seventeenth century; but as new colonial crops and manufactured goods became profitable, they, too, were added to the list. As the eighteenth century wore on, the list of restricted items grew quite long.

Careful statistical studies have not yet determined the exact influence the Navigation Acts had on the flow of commerce, though certain generalizations can be safely made. The restrictions inhibited certain colonial industries (finished iron production and hatmaking, for example) and encouraged other activities (growing indigo and making pig iron, for instance). And the Navigation Acts undoubtedly contributed to the widespread depression that occurred throughout the colonies in the second half of the seventeenth century. When a 1673 law placed a duty on tobacco transported from one colony to another, the added cost hurt both the southern colonies and tobacco retail agents in New York. And certainly the Navigation Acts distorted the colonial economy, making it one-sided. The Iron Act of 1750, for example, prohibited the construction of new colonial iron mills. Similarly, the Wool Act of 1699 forbade the exportation of specified textiles manufactured in the colonies, just as the Hat Act of 1732 made it illegal for colonials to export manufactured hats. All of these laws were designed to: (1) prevent colonial industries from competing with favored English industries; (2) build up the British merchant marine; and (3) keep the colonies as a source of raw materials for British manufacturing and as a market for finished British products. To the degree that they were successful in achieving these goals, the laws maintained the colonies as a dependent aspect of the British economy, but understandably they also created a vast army of lawbreakers, colonials who resented such restrictions upon their economic, even their personal freedom.

Farms, Towns, and Cities

Most colonial Americans were, as noted earlier, farmers—so much so that ninety-five percent of all residents of the English colonies earned their living directly from agriculture. But farms, like farmers themselves, came in various sizes and types. Most small farms undoubtedly were hardscrabble, subsistence affairs, their owners eking out a meager livelihood from season to season. Yet a small plot near an urban center such as Philadelphia or Boston might prove highly profitable and be more efficiently organized than some sprawling commercial enterprise teeming with slave or tenant labor.

Farm Life

Today the tenant farmer is generally regarded as an oppressed and exploited agricultural worker, deprived of the fruits of his labor by a greedy landlord. But during the colonial period, tenant farmers were not necessarily poor and in debt, nor were they denied the right to vote. Although suffrage usually was restricted to adult white males who owned a certain amount of property, a twenty-one-year lease of land met the property requirement in most colonies.

When there was so much free land to be had for the asking, why did anyone become a tenant farmer? Because the system had some advantages, especially for the farmer without capital. The landlord provided housing and seed; tenantry enabled recent immigrants to begin supporting themselves immediately while earning money needed for purchasing their own land and basic supplies.

Although there were tenant farmers in every colony, they were more common in New York, Pennsylvania, and other Middle colonies than they were elsewhere. In New York, for instance, vast tracts of land were claimed by landlords. The largest, an old Dutch estate, named Rensselaerswyck, comprised a million acres; another estate, the Philipse Highland Patent, was 205,000 acres; and there were a dozen others several hundred thousand acres large—much of the best land in the colony.

Since most of these immense holdings were sparsely settled or empty (as late as 1720 Rensselaerswyck had only eighty-one families living on it), landlords had difficulty defending their titles. The British government did not look kindly on vacant estates and, when possible, attempted to break them up. There were many opportunities to contest ownership, since Massachusetts and Connecticut claimed territory along their western borders that New York regarded as its own. Moreover, on many occasions New York landlords had been grossly high-handed in land dealings with the Indians. By lavishly entertaining a few chiefs and obtaining their approval of a deed, they claimed control of the land in question although a tribal council had to approve the document for it to be legal. Thus, New York landlords seized Indian territory through fraud, and by keeping descriptions of property deliberately vague, the landlords further infringed on Indians' rights.

These weak or shaky claims to land, however, could be strengthened if landlords could settle their estates. To do so, they made tenantry as attractive as possible. Some landlords collected a mere token rent from their tenants ("three peppercorns" a year, for instance); others charged a rent equal to a tenth of the annual produce of a farm. And in almost every case, landlords assisted lessees by giving them dwellings, livestock, wagons, and tools—surely unexpected blessings for penniless immigrants. Such generous terms were dictated by the real fears of landlords that unless they settled and farmed their estates, they would lose title to them.

This system had drawbacks, however. When a lease expired, the lessee or his heir had to pay a fee to the landlord that was equal to one-quarter or one-third of the price of the farm in order to renew it. Tenants had to agree to grind their wheat at the landlord's mill and to pay him part of the meal for his service. In many cases tenants could not sell crops to the highest bidder but had to offer them first to the landlord.

The small landowner lived in much the same style as the tenant farmer. Every member of the family did chores—the wife, children, and, if the farmer prospered, a servant or slave. If the farm was on the frontier, the farmer's first concern was clearing the land; since digging up tree stumps consumed too much time and effort, crops were usually planted around them. If the land was already cleared and had been functioning for a number of years, then the farmer struggled to maintain its fertility. In the South soil was quickly exhausted by

New York State Historical Association, Cooperstown, New York.

This primitive painting shows a prosperous Pennsylvania farm in the eighteenth century.

tobacco crops; in New England land often was rocky and inhospitable from the start. Knowledge about crop rotation, fertilization, and erosion prevention was meager and uncertain.

Crops were supplemented by poultry, pigs, and vegetables or fruit raised by the farmer's wife, but the diet was monotonous since there was no method of preserving food other than salting and drying. The wife not only kept a garden, prepared the food, cared for the young children, and tended the livestock but she also clothed the family. To do so she had to start from scratch: first by carding, combing, and spinning wool or cotton thread; then by weaving fabric; and finally by cutting it and sewing garments. Although nearly every household

had at least a spinning wheel, looms for weaving were less common, and that process might be done at the home of a more affluent neighbor, for a fee or in exchange for some service or produce.

Few small landowners were able to rise beyond subsistence farming, though in the South they grew tobacco for sale and in the Middle colonies raised surplus wheat. The size of farms also varied with the location. In the South 200 acres was considered a smaller than average holding; in New England the same size farm would be regarded as splendid. Indeed, by the eighteenth century the successive divisions of property through inheritance often had reduced New England farms to thirty or forty acres.

Large-scale commercial farming was a big

Valentine Museum, Richmond, Virginia.

Eighteenth-century Virginia parishes were required by law to furnish ministers with a glebe house of four rooms and an outlying kitchen. This is one of the few surviving glebes and illustrates the middle class standards of the gentry.

business pursued for high profits in several of the colonies. It depended, of course, on hired or enslaved field hands. By the middle of the eighteenth century, Virginia—the stronghold of commercial tobacco farming—had a total population of 293,472, of which 120,156 were black, most of whom were slaves concentrated in the Tidewater area, where large farms often resembled independent villages. William Fitzhugh described one such estate in a letter he wrote in 1686.

"The plantation where I now live contains a thousand acres, at least 700 acres of it being rich thicket, the remainder good hearty plantable land, without any waste either by marshes or great swamps. The commodiousness, conveniency, and pleasantness yourself [*sic*] well knows. Upon it there is [*sic*] three quarters well furnished with all necessary houses, grounds and fencing, together with a choice crew of negroes at each plantation, most of them this country born, the remainder as likely as most in Virginia, there being twenty-nine in all, with stocks of cattle and hogs at each quarter. Upon the same land is my own dwelling house furnished with all accomodations for a comfortable and genteel living, as a very good dwelling house with rooms in it, four of the best of them hung [with tapestry] and nine of them plentifully furnished with all things necessary and convenient, and all houses for use furnished with brick chimneys; four good cellars, a dairy, dovecote, stable, barn, henhouse, kitchen, and all other conveniences and all in a manner new; a large orchard of about 2500 apple trees, most grafted, well fenced . . . ; a garden a hundred foot square, well paled in . . . ; together with a good stock of cattle, hogs, horses, mares, sheep, etc., and necessary servants belonging to it for the supply and support thereof."

The highly colored notion of the southern planter as a gentleman of leisure or his wife as a pampered socialite is misleading. According to this fiction, the planter was an "aristocrat," above demeaning work and trade, who devoted himself to gaming, drinking, hunting, and courting. Actually, the large-scale commercial farmer worked hard, long hours and was often an industrious merchant peddling his own produce. His wife was equally busy since she generally supervised such household activities as the weaving and dyeing of cloth and the smoking of meat.

William Byrd II (1674–1744) was one of the most prominent eighteenth century Virginians but he rose at three in the morning, read till breakfast, then began his round of chores. He supervised the planting of trees, gardens, and crops; he acted as the doctor for his household and servants; he bought the tobacco of neighbors and merchandised it and his own; he operated a gristmill and a sawmill; he arranged for shipments of tobacco to England from Richmond, the Virginia town he built at the first falls of the James River; and in the evenings he usually settled in with a good sermon, though on special occasions he gambled heavily with friends and flirted with their wives. As he confesses in his diary, he kissed a Mrs. Chiswell "on the bed till she was angry and my wife also was uneasy about it and cried as soon as the company was gone."

Colonial Williamsburg Photograph.

William Byrd II was one of Virginia's outstanding political and literary figures. He rose before five to read Greek, after which he pursued his plantation and governmental duties.

The revised picture of the southern commercial farmer that emerges is of a man who was cultivated but not idle. He may have imitated the manners of the English gentry; William Fitzhugh, for instance, though the son of an English woolen draper, researched his family coat of arms and crest, which a servant hired especially for that purpose engraved on all his silver plate. And when his sister announced she would come from England to visit the colony, Fitzhugh anxiously expressed his desire that "she come out handsomely and genteel and well-clothed, with a maid to wait on her." These pretensions, however, did not lead the big Virginia farmers to look down upon trade; Fitzhugh grew wealthy as much by bartering the commodities he picked up from his visiting ship captains as by raising tobacco. And the first William Byrd made money by trading pots, pans, guns, and rum as well as Indian and black slaves.

The New England Town

Farmers in the South often lived isolated lives, but in New England they tended to gather in towns. In many ways these towns resembled—and were an adaptation of—the English parish. In England a parish was defined as the community served by a single church, but it was a unit of government as well as of religion, since the ten or twenty vestrymen (officers in charge of the practical affairs of the church) also acted as local administrators. In modifying this pattern to meet the conditions of New England life, the first settlers of Massachusetts established towns or corporations that were governed by a small number of selectmen, or elected officials.

There were important differences between the New England town and the English parish, however. Puritans believed in separation of church and state, and their New England towns reflected this belief. The church had its elders, but their jurisdiction did not extend into civil matters. Conforming to Puritan ideals, the church was a spiritual assembly of believers and not an imposing building maintained by taxation. In fact, seventeenth-century New England towns had nothing but a plain meeting house where church services and assemblies of any sort could be conducted.

What of the government of the town? The town meeting was the basic political unit. Most adult men in the town could take part in town meetings and vote, providing they were church members. Before 1691 a townsman in Massachusetts had to

The New England meeting house was both town hall and religious center. The architecture reflected this social and theological fact. The absence of towers, bells and crosses at the Rocky Hill Meeting House was a statement of belief.

have at least eighty pounds sterling worth of taxable property and be a church member in order to vote in local meetings; after 1691, however, the General Court (the highest governing body in Massachusetts) lowered the local value of taxable property from eighty to twenty pounds and dropped the church membership requirement.

When a new town was being organized, a number of families gathered together and asked the General Court for permission to occupy previously unsettled territory (usually a tract of thirty-six square miles constituted a township). If the permission was granted, these farmers, who were called the *proprietors* of the town, then built a meeting house and sometimes a school and distributed land to various families. Land distribution was not egalitarian; families received smaller or larger parcels of land according to their wealth, social status, and number of children. When possible, each farmer received a parcel of tillable acreage, including pasturage together with some wooded land. A large portion of the land was kept in reserve for future settlers; this land, owned jointly by the proprietors, was called the *commons*.

In analyzing the evolution of a New England town, a distinct difference can be detected between the community's earlier years in the seventeenth century and its later development in the eighteenth century. During the first fifty years of a town's existence, farming was virtually the only occupation of its inhabitants. The townspeople lived close to one another, a practice designed to facilitate the moral surveillance of the citizens by their elected officials, the selectmen, and the minister.

During this early period, towns were remarkably homogeneous. Most of the adult men were proprietors of the town, and most of them could vote in the town meeting. Since virtually every citizen was a white Anglo-Saxon Protestant, the New England town was unified racially, religiously, and culturally. When a farmer wanted to move to a town, he had to apply for permission from the proprietors. This screening assured the town of continuing harmony and kept out all "such whose dispositions do not suit us, whose society will be hurtful to us."

One Massachusetts community, chiefly Salem Village (now Danvers), gained widespread notoriety in the early 1690s when it was swept by a wave of witchcraft hysteria. Between June and September 1692, nineteen people were convicted and hanged, largely on the testimony of three young girls. After a summer of madness and frenzy, the clergy discouraged the conduct of the court which had tried fifty-five others. A new court using stricter rules of evidence ended the trials. Years later the colony tacitly admitted error by paying indemnities to families of victims.

Why the citizens felt compelled to search out and destroy persons who were "witches" remains something of a mystery. Their reaction may have been triggered in part because Salem Town was becoming a commercial center of importance leaving the village area a commercial backwater. The most enduring and popular explanation sees the Puritans as religious bigots—people so narrow-minded and superstitious that they were easy prey for such mass hysteria. And because the citizens of Puritan towns had little privacy and were encouraged to spy upon one another and to report any signs of irregular behavior, they must have been vulnerable to an invasion of "witches." Recent historians have tried to trace elements of sexual repression and envy in the Salem trials since most of the accusers were young, single women between the ages of thirteen and twenty-six and the accused middle-aged, married women. Other historians have documented long-standing family feuds between the accusers and the accused. And it is quite possible that the "witches" were indeed unpleasant, quarrelsome, antisocial persons. Overall, the soundest explanations are probably to be found in the political turmoil of the times, a sense of failure

as Puritanism declined, all of which led people to search for "witches" rather than try to find a cure for the bewitched.

In the eighteenth century the character of the New England town changed subtly as the old homogeneity disappeared. It remained a preserve of white Anglo-Saxon Protestants, but an increasing number of newcomers created two groups of people: recent arrivals and descendants of the original proprietors who often tried to retain their political dominance by denying certain rights to newcomers. Town meetings appear to have become more contentious; no longer were townspeople willing to let the selectmen make decisions for them. The society, therefore became more democratic and dynamic in the eighteenth century.

The town itself became more dispersed. In the early days, most of the inhabitants lived close to one another, sometimes along a single street, but as the community became more populous, some farmers found it both more convenient and safe to live out of town on their property. Typically, a father might give his son twenty acres a few miles outside of town, or a newcomer might be granted a distant parcel of property. Eventually the settlers in these outlying districts might become sufficiently numerous to start a new town with a church and school of its own. Sometimes the establishment of a new town was a painful strife-ridden bit of surgery and left painful scars.

Although the New England town remained basically rural in the eighteenth century, it did begin to acquire some commercial importance as more and more citizens took up a trade, if only on a part-time basis. Crafts and commerce became necessary means of supplementing wealth since after three generations a New England town that prospered would have less land to bestow on its young citizens. Families did not follow the ordinary English practice of primogeniture (making the eldest son sole heir), but rather divided their property among all the children, including daughters. As a family proliferated, portions of land became smaller and smaller. And, as long as the parents lived, the children had little or no legal control of their land. As a result, families began to provide for their children in other ways—setting them up in trades, acquiring land for them in other locations, or giving them their inheritance early in the form of a cash settlement or perhaps a gift of funds when they married. In a country as vast as America, relocation was the obvious solution to this problem, but people with ties to a village were reluctant to leave. A study of Andover, Massachusetts, has revealed that not until that community's fourth generation did young people move away from it in large numbers.

Cities

Very few Americans lived in cities, but by the 1760s several important urban centers had emerged, chief among them Philadelphia (30,000 people). Boston and New York City were perhaps half as large, and Charlestown, Newport, Albany, and Providence somewhat smaller still. Aside from these major cities, there were a number of secondary centers—such as Wilmington, North Carolina, New Haven, Connecticut, and Williamsburg, Virginia—that played a larger role in the colony's cultural life than population size might suggest. At the time of the Revolution, Williamsburg had about 1,400 people, half of them black slaves. But despite its size, Williamsburg was the cultural center of Virginia, a place where the wealthiest farmers came to socialize, attend balls, and conduct business.

Unlike the homogeneous New England town, the colonial city was a mixture of many social classes. Single women who had to support themselves congregated in cities, where they earned a living sewing, running shops and businesses (even taverns), washing, and cooking. Among the men, a class of day laborers sprang up who represented the beginnings of a free urban proletariat without property. During the eighteenth century there was a growing scarcity of immigrants who came to America as indentured servants. In Boston, for instance, only 250 of the 2,380 people who moved there between 1764 and 1768 were indentured servants. A labor shortage resulted, and as a consequence, poor men without property could earn a living wage by renting out their labor by the day.

This increase of urban life, although infinitesimal by modern standards, nevertheless gave birth to modern urban realities: sanitation, sewerage, fire control, hospitals, libraries, higher education facilities—and crime. For the most part, at least in colonial decades, volunteer organizations and charity institutions tried to meet such needs, not local governments. Cities had their volunteer fire companies, night watches kept an eye on thieves and prostitutes, and the well-to-do gave money to support orphanages, schools, and hospitals.

One of the commonplaces about pre-Revolutionary America holds that it was basically democratic, composed of a huge middle class and devoid of extremes in wealth and poverty. This democratic experience, the theory contends, prepared the way for the Revolution with its assertion of the principles of equality. A statistical analysis of colonial Boston, perhaps the most significant city before the Revolution, tends to challenge this theory. Comparison of the tax lists of 1687 with those of 1771, shows that the distribution of wealth became increasingly unequal. Small property owners—the middle class—became less numerous proportionally, whereas merchant princes at the top and day laborers at the bottom of the social scale became more numerous. In 1687, for instance, the richest five percent of the Boston population had held only 26.8 percent of the city's wealth; by 1771, the richest five percent held 44.1 percent. In some ways, however, Boston may not be a good test case since it was experiencing hard times. Its population grew by only a few hundred souls between 1760 and 1775, and this lengthy economic depression created both widespread poverty and fertile soil for revolutionary ideas.

Social fragmentation in the cities was furthered by two other aspects of the urban experience: the increasing diversity of Protestant sects and the deepening animosity of city politics, which frequently degenerated into demogoguery. The resident in a New England town saw few strangers and pursued the simple and timeless occupation of farming; the city dweller could observe foreign sailors in the port, meet a German Lutheran or French Huguenot or English Quaker at a neighborhood store, and hear a wide spectrum of political opinions.

Each city, of course, had its own character. New York was a free and easy port, careless about promoting the arts, religion, and education but avid in its pursuit of pleasure; thirteen years after Manhattan was settled, one-quarter of the houses were taverns or tobacco shops. Philadelphia, by contrast, was a quiet, Quaker city of compulsive readers and ardent gardeners. As the Quaker merchants became increasingly wealthy, they began to build fine houses and buy handsome coaches, but every display of wordly splendor aroused some disapproval.

In every city, no matter what its peculiar character, there was a social ladder composed of many rungs. At the bottom were slaves and servants. Working alongside the servants were apprentices bound to a master for a period of time in order to learn a trade or business. Above these servants,

The Hand-in-Hand Fire Company was one of the voluntary associations formed to deal with urban problems in colonial cities. This is from a membership certificate of 1762.

slaves, apprentices, and a growing horde of day laborers were the "mechanics"—men who had a trade (printing, say) and practiced it on the free labor market. If the mechanic owned his own shop and was successful, he moved up the social ladder still higher.

A self-employed mechanic or small businessman usually kept his entire family busy working in his shop. The wife often would help out as bookkeeper and the children would perform errands and small tasks. Some women learned trades from their husbands and carried on the business after their husbands died.

At the top of the economic ladder were prosperous tradesmen, merchants, and professionals. In England, "trade" was considered respectable but distinctly and irrevocably appropriate only for the middle classes, low or high. In America, it did not prevent people who engaged in it from rising to the heights of social distinction. For instance, William

Pepperrell, born in 1696 in Maine, joined his father in the family business—selling fish, lumber, and ship's stores. Soon the business was so successful that Pepperrell was able to invest excess profits in real estate and in a fleet of merchant ships that carried products to the West Indies and Europe. In 1730 Pepperrell was appointed chief justice of Massachusetts, though the position preceded his competence; only after he became a justice did he bother to send to London for a set of law books. By leading a military expedition in 1745 against the French, Pepperrell was rewarded by the king: he became the first American-born baronet.

Success, however, did not lead to idleness. Just as the Virginia commercial farmers, despite their wealth, were constantly busy, in the same way the urban merchant princes worked hard for their preeminence. And their women were equally busy. Servants might relieve the upper class wife of the necessity of performing the drudgery of keeping house, but much of her time was devoted to supervisory tasks. What free time she had was spent in the arduous social whirl of cities—paying formal calls on other families, attending parties and musical evenings, and going to balls and formal receptions.

What characterizes modern cities, of course, is that they are industrial centers. But industrialization, or "manufacturing," was thought undesirable by many colonial Americans eager for a piece of land and the independence it presumably bestowed upon them. In addition, the Navigation Acts frequently made industrial activity illegal.

The Human Perspective

Until recently the traditional view of colonial life was that of a rather grim existence. Women were seen as marrying soon after puberty, being constantly pregnant, and dying of exhaustion at an early age. Although men presumably lived somewhat longer, they, too, were seen as having a brief life. If a man reached fifty, he was thought by traditionalists to be old.

This set of assumptions has been seriously challenged in recent years by historians who have analyzed colonial population statistics. Most of these studies have concentrated on settlements in New England. Additional research suggests that although the South had a heavy mortality rate in the first generation, life expectancy rose for the second generation.

First, it appears that the average age of marriage was quite close to the present-day average. In colonial times women were usually twenty-one when they married and men were twenty-three. (In 1970 the average marrying age for women was 20–21 years and for men 23–24 years.) Second, families were neither so large nor pregnancies so frequent as formerly believed. Children were usually born two years apart from one another, and births occurred less frequently the older the mother became. This incidence of childbirth can be explained socially, since couples usually abstained from sex while the mother nursed. The average colonial family had a total of five to seven children. In analyzing seventy households in colonial Bristol, Rhode Island, one historian discovered that almost half were comprised of four, five, and six persons.

Death rates were high by modern standards, though infant mortality accounted for the biggest losses. If someone reached age twenty-one, then the chances were quite good that he or she would live to be sixty. In an era with only the most primitive notions of diet and hygiene and no medicines to prevent or cure infection, ordinary childhood diseases were all too often fatal. Similarly, an epidemic of virulent disease could wipe out a large portion of a town's population.

Epidemics could have long-term influences on the development of a community. For instance, if a smallpox epidemic struck a town and killed half its children, thirty years later there would be few young adults who would inherit larger plots of land, not needing to divide their property with many siblings. A decent inheritance would enable these young adults to marry earlier—and thereby bear more children. Conversely, if a village was spared, an upcoming generation would be more numerous, inheritances smaller, and the age of marriage correspondingly later.

Geographical and Social Mobility

As a land of immigrants, America was, of course, founded on geographical mobility. The movement usually was westward, towards the cheap and previously unfarmed lands along the frontier. But this overall pattern should not disguise exceptions to the rule; in Connecticut, for instance, the eastern part of the state near the Rhode Island border was not settled until the eighteenth century. Settlement remained sparse, both far to the south and far to the north; for neither Georgia nor Maine attracted many newcomers. Though most of the mobility was prompted by the search for cheap land, in some cases urban centers attracted landless young men apprenticed to trades and runaway slaves. Even as small a town as Williamsburg provided protection for an escaped slave, who was often concealed by other slaves. And there have always been Americans who preferred the excitement of city life to the conservative, static existence of the farmer.

The colonies witnessed a few examples of a dramatic rise in social position and many cases of less remarkable advance. From the point of view of social mobility, the colonies offered something of a contradiction, for society was definitely hierarchical but just as surely fluid. That is, social posi-

Museum of the City of New York.

American homes were graced by beautiful pieces of homemade art such as this sampler done about 1800. Young girls learned sewing skills by working on complicated pieces of decorative stitching.

Historical Society of Pennsylvania.

John Singleton Copley's portrait of Mr. and Mrs. Thomas Mifflin shows a prosperous urban family just before the Revolution. He is holding a book. She is using a loom to make fringe.

tion was strictly defined, but a person had opportunities to change the position of his or her birth. Virginia law dictated that only gentlemen could race horses, and throughout the seventeenth century numerous colonies attempted to regulate dress so that no one would be garbed in clothes too fine for his or her station. People could change status, but at any given moment everyone knew quite precisely how far up or how far down he or she stood in the social order.

The colonists made up what has been called by historians a "deferential" society—that is, one in which people deferred to those they regarded as their betters. This view of colonial society is useful, since it explains some startling facts. For instance, although small farmers in Virginia greatly outnumbered the large landowners, nevertheless they consistently voted for these "aristocrats." In traditional England the big landowner had been the local lord, and in America the habit of deferring to the big commercial farmer (no matter how low his original status might have been) persisted despite social differences. But this theory of a deferential society may be only partially true; certainly there are indications that by the 1770s prerogatives of class were breaking down. Just why is not entirely clear, but answers may lie in rising expectations of middle and lower classes, competition among the elite for wider support of their political views, and, of course, the turmoil created by revolution itself. Certainly a tradesman, whatever his class, was not going to defer to a nabob whose views on imperial policy differed greatly from his own.

New World settlers did not start out with an equal degree of wealth. Some came from well-to-do English backgrounds. Others, such as the large number of indentured servants, brought little wealth or prestige with them. Once they were in America, upward mobility could and did occur. Daniel Dulany, to cite an unusually fortunate man, arrived in Maryland in 1703 as an indentured servant from Ireland. Dulany had the good fortune to be sold to a lawyer who needed a clerk. Within ten years Dulany was a lawyer in his own right as well as a landowner. His law practice, his speculation in land, and his marriage to a daughter of a well-to-do family enabled him to accumulate a sizable fortune.

Most social mobility was upwards, but there were cases of people who lost status. None of the families active in Virginia politics before 1660 is important in the later colonial period. In New Eng-

The Maryland Historical Society, Baltimore.

Indentured servants seldom left records behind or rose to prominence. A notable exception was Daniel Dulany who became a noted lawyer in Maryland.

land, the descendants of a prosperous farmer could be reduced by the successive division of lands through inheritance to the level of mere subsistence.

Wealth and prestige are not precisely the same thing, not even in a new land like colonial America. Whereas wealth is comparatively easy to estimate, prestige is harder to define, since it depends on the opinion of contemporaries, which is often irrecoverable. Moreover, there are indications that colonial Americans experienced a degree of confusion about which occupations were the most prestigious, a confusion further complicated by the fact that few well-to-do citizens had a single profession. A man was a farmer, land speculator, politician, doctor, lawyer, everything but an Indian chief. Yet it was his role as farmer that he often prized most highly, and farmers thought of themselves as the most eminent element in colonial society.

But despite this supposedly high status, when American voters (most of whom were farmers) came to elect their leaders, they favored merchants and professional men, who, again, were often farmers of a sort as well. Attitudes towards families that had grown wealthy in commerce were contradictory; the same ambiguity colored opinions about successful lawyers and other professionals.

Slaves and indentured servants were at the bottom of society in terms not only of wealth but also of prestige. Free blacks also suffered from low social status. Artisans, or mechanics, were ranked slightly higher, though not so high that most artisans were not eager to exchange their role for the more prestigious one of landowner or shopkeeper. The professions—doctor, lawyer, and clergyman—ranked higher than the mechanics, but the highest position of all was reserved for wealthy farmers and prosperous merchants.

The Law

Curiously enough, colonial laws varied more from English laws in the seventeenth than in the eighteenth century. While a modern observer would expect the colonies to take an independent course later rather than earlier, the reverse was actually true. In the seventeenth century the colonies were in less frequent contact with England than in the eighteenth century, and this isolation allowed immigrants to drift inadvertently from English standards or steer purposefully away from what were considered corrupt English practices. In Massachusetts, for example, the Puritans deliberately enacted new laws in order to foster their utopian social experiment. Similarly, in Philadelphia the Quakers enacted legislation consistent with their religious views (their strong pacifism, for instance).

In the eighteenth century, closer English supervision and weakening of high, religious resolve caused colonial laws to conform more closely to English standards. Moreover, eighteenth-century colonial lawyers were more knowledgeable about the English legal system than their counterparts of the previous century, a time when lawyers were amateurs. In some cases, Parliament passed laws that applied to the whole empire, which, of course, included the colonies; in other situations, the king instructed the colonial assemblies to pass laws that duplicated English legislation. By the close of the eighteenth century, the laws of the various colonies had come to resemble those of both fellow colonies and the homeland on the most important matters.

There were some appreciable differences between colonial laws and English laws, however. In England the long accumulation of tradition made more than two hundred crimes subject to capital punishment; the colonies reduced the number (depending on the particular colony) to fewer than twenty. English inheritance laws also were usually modified by the colonists. In England primogeniture meant that a father must leave all of his property to his eldest son, and the related law of entail prohibited the heir from selling or parceling out the property he received. Since land was not so precious in the New World, these laws were disregarded. In New England, for instance, children (including daughters) divided the property of their parents equally among themselves. If a widow outlived her husband, she, too, inherited a proportion of the estate by law. In Virginia primogeniture prevailed unless a man wrote a will; as a result, many Virginians made specific provisions for their children. During the first decades of settlement in Georgia, women were not allowed to inherit, since Georgia's original proprietors thought only fighting men should own land. But soon angry landowners with daughters as their only heirs changed that ruling—and many others that did not suit their interests.

Family Life

Some aspects of family relationships were regulated by law in all colonies. There were, however, major differences between colonies. In Puritan areas, marriage was not regarded as a sacrament, but rather as a civil ceremony. Divorce among seventeenth-century Puritans was possible on the grounds of desertion, adultery, or absence from home. A marriage could be annulled if the husband were impotent. Neither husband nor wife could abuse the other.

Outside of New England the situation was different. Anglicans considered marriage a sacrament and divorce was impossible except by legislative act. Legal separations or desertion were the only options. The husband did have a legal right to use physical punishment on his wife, but the records do not suggest this was a common practice.

In general, children were expected to obey parents, and wives their husbands, but all members of a family were expected to subordinate their individual interests to the good of the family. Wives were "helpmeets," not slaves or servants. When one man told his wife that "shee was none of his

Worcester Art Museum, Worcester, Massachusetts.

Elizabeth Freake and her daughter Mary wore their best clothes for this rare portrait done about 1674 in New England. Adult women would not appear in public without some covering on their heads. Aprons were also a standard item of dress, with specially embroidered ones for fine occasions. In this dual portrait the eighteenth-century view of children as miniature adults is strikingly revealed.

wife, shee was but his Servant," eavesdropping neighbors reported the remark to authorities. The husband was fined 40 shillings, despite his wife's protest "that I have nothing Agenst my husband to Charge him with."

Although single women had the rights (except the vote) of men, the rights of married women were merged with their husbands under common law. Thus a husband had custody of his children and controlled his wife's entire personal estate, though in many instances women did retain some control over land. Women and men fared differently in criminal matters. Women more often received physical punishment for adultery; men usually were fined. The most common crime among women was bastardy—giving birth out of wedlock. Paternity was difficult to prove and many women refused to name fathers, hence women often were punished

alone. If the woman was an indentured servant, she had to compensate her master for the loss of service during pregnancy. Eventually the courts became more interested in securing support for the child.

Blacks and Indentured Servants

Blacks had a special—and inferior—place under the law. Not all blacks were slaves, but all were barred from certain privileges, such as the right to bear arms or to testify against whites in court. (An exception, however, was New England where the testimony of blacks was permitted.) Worse, blacks were not allowed to vote. Slaves, of course, had very few legal rights. In fact, the slave had a peculiar position in the eyes of the law. In one sense the slave was regarded as property, much like a piece of real estate; a slave could be owned and sold. But in another sense, the slave's humanity was minimally recognized; laws attempted to protect a slave from flagrant abuse by his or her master. Yet the real estate designation prevailed in the South, as was stated explicitly in 1705 by the Virginia assembly in its statute that "all negro, mulatto, and Indian slaves in all courts of jurdicature, and other places, within this dominion, shall be held, taken, and adjudged to be real estate."

When the first twenty blacks arrived in Virginia in 1619, their status as slaves was unclear. In the first few decades after 1619, some blacks, treated as though they were indentured servants, gained their freedom and bought property. They may have even voted, and at least one possessed one or more slaves of his own. Those blacks who converted to Christianity were often freed, since the original justification for enslaving blacks was that they were heathens. Yet from the first blacks were treated by whites as inferiors, and by the 1640s slavery was the common lot for the blacks in America, though the legal terms of perpetual and inheritable servitude were not clearly defined until 1661.

Servants also had a special and lesser place in colonial laws. The law protected the property rights of owners in the labor of indentured servants. Accordingly, runaways were punished when apprehended by tacking extra time onto their terms of service to make up for periods of absence. But laws also protected servants by spelling out their "freedom dues"—the amount of money, clothes, land, or other property they would receive when the contract expired. Legal remedies were also provided for servants who had been detained in service too long or had been physically abused.

Voting rights were established through legislation, though they differed from colony to colony and from decade to decade. Women were denied the vote, though they may have taken part in elections in the seventeenth century; for example, Virginia did not specifically bar women until 1696, and New Jersey forbade female suffrage only in 1807. Even when women were barred from colonywide elections, they may have voted in town affairs or as members of a religious congregation. Similarly free blacks may have voted until later legislation specifically denied them this right.

White adult males were the voters in the colonies, and the vast majority of men qualified to vote sometime during their lifetime. Qualifications were elaborate and designed to restrict suffrage to the property-owning segment of the population. In the South the voting requirement was the ownership of between 50 and 100 acres of land. Elsewhere the most common requirement was possession of a forty-shilling freehold, that is, land with an annual income of forty shillings. This was not a very high demand, since in the 1760s an income of ten shillings a day was necessary to maintain a Boston family, for instance, in moderate circumstances. Farmland, however, was not the only possession that qualified a man to vote. Men who paid taxes of a stipulated amount, who owned a developed

town lot, or who were master craftsmen qualified under special clauses in many colonies were also eligible to register as voters.

The colonial voter usually stepped up to a registrar and announced his choice orally. Since such a declaration was a public act, the voter's choice was known by everyone; accordingly, the voter could be pressured by the community or by wealthy local candidates into selecting one name rather than another. Moreover, candidates thought nothing of lavishly entertaining voters just before an election. When George Washington ran for office in 1758, his agent in Frederick County, Virginia, supplied 160 gallons of liquor to 391 voters—a quart and a half a voter! And candidates often kept open house for voters on their way to an election, and at least one bold candidate had a cart of liquor drawn up to the very door of the courthouse on election day.

Religion

In the southern colonies (Maryland, Virginia, the Carolinas, and Georgia), the Anglican Church was the established faith, though in North Carolina it received no tax support and scant respect until nearly the end of the colonial period. In Virginia the Anglican parish handled the welfare duties of the state by caring for the old, the infirm, and the

Christ Church in Virginia is a good example of colonial Anglican architecture. The cross-shaped church and the churchyard reflect both the Georgian influence on building and the colonial simplicity of ritual.

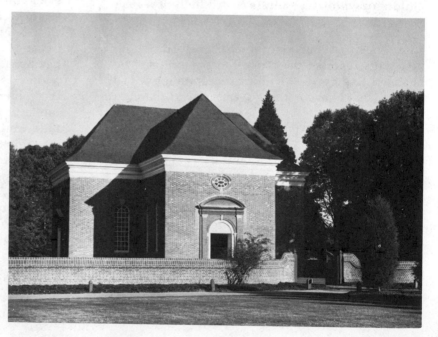

orphaned; the Church even built roads. Governors, who saw the Church as a legitimate arm of government, had the right to send clergy of their choice to parishes.

In New England (except Rhode Island) the established faith was Congregationalism, but in the Middle colonies no single church was legally established. In New York the Anglican Church had a semilegal status, but individual towns were free to make other sects official. When New Jersey passed from the hands of its Quaker proprietors to the crown in 1704, the Anglican Church was partially established there. Pennsylvania, in keeping with Quaker views of toleration, had no legally established church, though in the seventeenth century Quakers were sufficiently influential to legislate such Quaker beliefs as pacifism.

In 1689 England passed the Acts of Toleration, which permitted dissenters from the established church in any colony to choose their own ministers, build meetings places, and worship in peace. The regulations did not, however, relieve dissenters from paying the taxes due the established church, and this inequity led to much political agitation against the collection of church taxes or tithes. And toleration did not extend to non-Protestants. Even Rhode Island, the most liberal of the colonies, denied citizenship and voting rights to Jews and Catholics. Atheists and free thinkers also were banned from holding office, since to qualify one had to profess a belief in the Trinity.

Anglicanism

The Church of England, or Anglicanism or Episcopalianism as it is variously known, was an outgrowth of the Protestant Reformation. When Henry VIII broke with the Roman Catholic Church in 1534, he did little more than reject the Pope's authority. Queen Elizabeth I, however, shifted Anglicanism farther towards Protestantism, though the Church of England remained the most moderate of the Protestant sects. Such Protestant beliefs as the supremacy of the Bible over later church teachings were embraced, but Anglicanism retained many of the old Catholic rituals and traditions (the use of vestments and sacraments, for instance). This emphasis upon ritual and the sacraments, upon the use of the Book of Common Prayer rather than preaching and sermons, clearly distinguished the Anglican faith from others in the Protestant fold. When Jamestown was settled in 1607, Anglicanism was the only faith legally recognized in England.

In the colonies, the Anglican Church enjoyed more independence than it did in England. For instance, there was no Anglican bishop in America during the colonial period, and the distance from episcopal authority allowed parishioners to exercise considerable control over their own churches, even to choose their own ministers with little direction from London.

Methodism, an offshoot of the Anglican faith, has its roots in the work of John Wesley (1703–1791), who stressed piety and the power of sermons, not ritual and sacraments performed strictly to rule. Since Wesley was a chaplain in the new colony of Georgia for only a short time, his views were spread in the colonies by others who worked mostly in Philadelphia and Virginia and other seacoast areas. Methodists, merely a reform group at first, did not become a separate church until after the Revolution.

Congregationalism

Opposition to anything that smacked of Roman Catholicism was carried to much greater extremes in New England than elsewhere. It was settled largely by Puritans and Separatists—that is those who hoped to reform the Church of England from within and those who gave up and withdrew from it completely. English Puritans wanted to eliminate bishops, restore control of ordination to the local congregation, do away with the Book of Common Prayer, and eliminate any symbols of the old religion. When Puritans and Separatists reached the New World, distinctions between them began to blur, since both groups had literally separated themselves from England as well. (The biographical sketch of Samuel Sewall in this chapter offers insight into some beliefs of colonial Puritanism.)

The new faith created in Massachusetts Bay was called Congregationalism because of its stress on the individual congregation as the basic unit of church structure. Each congregation was (at least in theory) independent of all the others. The congregation chose and ordained its ministers.

Membership in a congregation was difficult to obtain. Only those people who were deemed among the elect (that is, those whom God had predestined for salvation) could become members; all the others, though not members, still had to attend services. Members, who believed they were saved and gave signs of salvation in the saintly conduct of their lives, belonged to what the Puritans called the Church Covenant (a covenant, in this case, was the

Samuel Sewall

1652–1730

Sewall was born in England and moved with his family to Boston in 1661 when he was nine years old. After graduating from Harvard College in 1671, he vacillated between entering the ministry and a mercantile career. Eventually, he settled on the latter and about 1675 married Hannah Hull, the first of his three wives, and by whom he had fourteen children.

Although Sewall held many public offices during a long career, he is best remembered as a special commissioner at the Salem witchcraft trials which sent nineteen people to their deaths. Subsequently, Sewall became convinced that he had decided incorrectly in these cases and publicly confessed his wrongdoing. He was the only judge to repent of his decision. His contemporaries apparently did not condemn his error, since he was appointed chief justice of the superior court of judicature in 1718, a position he held for ten years.

Today he is also known for his diaries, which were published late in the nineteenth century by the Massachusetts Historical Society. In three long volumes, the diaries give a vivid picture of a colon-

ial Puritan on the eve of transition to Congregationalism. His Puritan beliefs led him to note with great zeal that people were ignoring Christmas and to regret toward the end of his diary that some misguided souls had revived such "pagan" customs. Sewall combines in one being a zest for money, a morbid preoccupation with death, a deep concern about the passing of old Puritan ways, and a scrupulousness in following the dictates of his own conscience. The same man who could ask for forgiveness for his role in the witchcraft trials also could publish *The Selling of Joseph,* a critique of slavery based on the Bible.

Sewall's wife Hannah died in 1717 and two years later he married a twice-widowed lady who died within several months. He subsequently courted Madam Katherine Winthrop, a member of one of the founding families. But she had fallen away from Puritan ways to such a degree that she wore a wig, and insisted that he keep a coach, neither of which Sewall could accept. In 1722 Sewall married a Miss Gibbs instead. He died eight years later.

agreement with God that He would protect the faithful so long as they obeyed His commandments and remained true to Him). In the early days of the colony, voting was restricted to full members of the Church Covenant, but in the second generation so few people seemed eligible for membership that the ministers in 1662 worked out a new concept—the Halfway Covenant. According to this rule, children of members who wished to belong to the church and who embraced Christian principles could vote on church matters, though they were barred from communion and other privileges of full membership.

Although some conservatives opposed this compromise (the term "Halfway Covenant" was derisive), most congregations had accepted it by 1700. By that time another, still more liberal notion was being propounded by Solomon Stoddard (1643–1729), who taught that communion should be administered to all of "good life and conversation." The ideal of the independence of each congregation also was modified in time. Too much dissension, "heresies" such as those of Anne Hutchinson and Roger Williams, led various congregations to band together; their ministers worked out a more uniform body of church doctrine. (Williams's religious beliefs and his leadership in establishing the colony of Rhode Island, a haven for "dissenters," are discussed in an accompanying biographical sketch.)

Baptist congregations formed both outside of and within the Puritan system but shared the congregational form of organization. Firmly opposed to all established churches, the Baptists emphasized adult conversion and personal religion. More than the members of any other religious denomination in colonial America, the Baptists championed religious liberty. From their traditional center in Rhode Island, they had developed by 1740 more than 150 congregations in America, largely in the Middle colonies. They added converts as their preachers went south after 1740, but the greatest growth came after the Revolution and then at the expense of the former established faiths, Anglicanism and Congregationalism.

Quakerism

The Society of Friends held beliefs that made them suspect in the eyes of all other Christians. Catholics stressed the authority of the Pope and church tradition; Protestants dismissed most of these sources and relied on the authority of the Bible alone; the

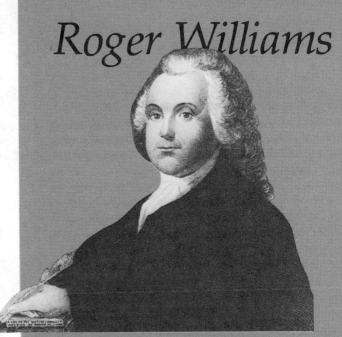

Roger Williams

1603–1683

Son of a well-to-do London merchant tailor with a shop on Cow Lane, Roger Williams was descended from new landed gentry who numbered among their relatives a high sheriff of Hertfordshire and a lord mayor of London. With the aid of jurist Edward Coke, he was able to attend Cambridge, graduating in January 1627. During the next two years he studied for holy orders, became chaplain to a wealthy Puritan family living in Essex, fell madly in love with a young lady whose aunt thought Williams an unsuitable suitor, and married eventually another local girl.

Even before taking a wife, Williams became interested in New England, and in December 1630 he and his wife sailed on the *Lyon* for Boston where he had secured a pulpit. However, he rejected that post and became increasingly critical of the church-state alliance developing in the New World.

He preached for a time in Salem and Plymouth, but because of his avowed Separatist views, he was soon in deep trouble. Williams, a sweet but stubborn man, enraged authorities by contending that the king of England had no authority to grant land to the Massachusetts Bay Company. He also expressed the inflammatory view that the Anglican Church was anti-Christian. Even the government in Boston came under his attack, since he believed civil government had no authority in religious matters and could not even require people to go to church. On every point, Williams was a stickler for an exact interpretation of the Bible, but his reading of the Scriptures threatened the very foundations of New England society.

In October of 1635 the General Court of Massachusetts Bay banished him from the colony, but because of illness and the birth of a second child, he was permitted to remain until spring. Nevertheless, Williams continued to speak his mind and the magistrates decided to exile him to England before he could organize a rival colony.

Williams learned of this plan and in January 1636 set out on foot for Narragansett Bay, an inlet of the Atlantic Ocean southeast of Massachusetts Bay. Here he worked as a missionary among the Narragansett Indians for several months and then purchased land from them and founded the village of Providence. Soon his family and friends who believed as he did left Salem and joined him at Providence. He established what was probably the first Baptist church in North America and established freedom of religion, although his policy of freedom did not include citizenship and voting rights for Jews and Catholics. The Puritan clergy in Boston referred to Providence as "that sewer" in which the "Lord's debris" had collected.

This freedom of religion soon attracted other religious dissenters to what became Rhode Island. Like Providence, these outposts were squatter settlements until a royal charter was obtained in 1644, largely through the personal efforts of Williams himself. However, this document never was fully implemented because of bickering among the settlements. Finally, in 1663 after a second trip to England, Williams secured a new charter from Charles II.

One of the great disappointments in Williams's life was the failure to maintain peace with the Narragansett Indians. Almost from the beginning he enjoyed warm, friendly relations with these Indians and endeavored to protect their property rights at all times. Despite this concern, during King Philip's War the Narragansett Indians joined forces with other Indian tribes against the British. Williams, one of two commanders of local forces, saw Providence burned to the ground and the Narragansett tribe, once his friends, virtually wiped out.

Quakers took a third position. For the Friends, the soul or spirit residing within each believer was the ultimate guide and arbiter in religious matters. Quakers regarded the Scriptures as "a Declaration of the Fountain, and not the Fountain itself."

This belief in the primacy of the Inner Light over the Bible led Quakers to reject the ministry altogether. No longer was there a need for ministers to interpret the Bible to a congregation. Another corollary to the conviction that there is a bit of God in every person was tolerance of all groups—American Indians, Jews, Catholics, Blacks, and so on. This universalist ethic also fostered pacifism—for how could one fight with and kill a person inhabited by divinity?

Early Quakers were persecuted for these unconventional beliefs in England and were hanged in Massachusetts and arrested or banished in other colonies. Finally, William Penn established his proprietary colony of Pennsylvania in 1681 as a refuge for all oppressed people, but especially for his fellow Quakers.

Despite their respect for individual testimony, Quakers were capable of exerting strong moral sanctions against those of whom they disapproved—through social pressure if not direct coercion. At all levels, compliance with group decisions and mores was urged through reason, and people who could not conform eventually were driven out. Although Quakers had no ordained ministers, certain "elders" considered wise or eloquent or particularly spiritual carried more weight than other members during meetings. Thus the original vision of Quakerism became transformed into a church structure that resembled those of other sects.

Because the Quakers did not have an ordained clergy but depended upon inner light, women were accepted as preachers and missionaries. Many of the first converts to Quakerism were women and they served as missionaries. Quaker structure depended upon consensus achieved by discussion at quarterly and yearly meetings, in which women participated.

Presbyterianism
Except for two brief periods during the seventeenth century, Presbyterianism was the established Church of Scotland. Like Puritanism, the Presbyterian Church embraced the Calvinist doctrine of predestination—that God has already decided who shall be saved and who shall be damned and that a person's deeds cannot modify this decision—but,

Quakers at first considered portraits too worldly and vain; but as the group prospered, the wealthy succumbed to the desire for memorials and compromised on silhouettes such as this one of merchant John Reynell.

unlike the Puritans, the Presbyterians favored a strict form of church organization. Congregations were under the control of larger, supervisory presbyteries. Moreover, a doctrinal decision of the church as a whole was binding on all members; private conscience was not the final source of authority among the Presbyterians.

When Presbyterianism was introduced into America at the end of the seventeenth century by the mass influx of Scots-Irish, the newcomers

brought with them a deep hatred of the Anglican Church and the English government, which had repeatedly attempted to make them join the Church of England. Since the Scots-Irish settled along the frontier in the Middle and southern colonies, this pattern meant that the western border sometimes harbored deep-seated animosities against all governmental authorities—a factor that later played a part in the Revolution.

Other Religious Sects

The Dutch of New Netherlands had their own form of Calvinism, the Dutch Reformed Church. While the Dutch retained control of the Hudson River Valley, they made their faith the exclusive religion of the region; after the British takeover, those of Dutch descent often remained adherents to the Reformed Church, though some of the young drifted into the Church of England.

The influx of Germans in the eighteenth century made Lutheranism a significant sect in America. Lutherans had a close affinity to Anglican theology and like the Anglicans were organized under the authority of bishops.

Roman Catholics and Jews were present in the colonies but had little influence on religious affairs. Both groups tried to remain inconspicuous, although in Maryland Catholic missionaries bought up lands for their church. Both groups were viewed with suspicion and suffered political disabilities, the Jews because they were non-Christians and the Catholics because they were considered agents of a foreign power (the Pope) and therefore a threat to the Protestant English throne.

The Religious Climate

Colonial America was characterized by its remarkable diversity of religious groups, but there was one intellectual trend in the eighteenth century that challenged the role of all religions. That movement was Rationalism. Many thinkers in America and Europe, made skeptical of the claims of religion by the advances of science, began by doubting specific doctrines (such as the literal truth of the story of Creation in the Book of Genesis) and ended up by rejecting broader beliefs (such as the idea that God responds to an individual's prayer). In America the very diversity of religions made the claims of each appear somewhat arbitrary. Some educated Americans, such as Benjamin Franklin (1706–1790) and Thomas Jefferson (1743–1826), came to regard the church not so much as a source of absolute truth as a school for the improvement of public morals. Within the traditional sects rationalist ministers appeared; Jonathan Mayhew (1720–1766) and Charles Chauncy (1705–1787) were both Congregationalists who attempted to accommodate rationalism with the beliefs of their religion. Eventually this rationalist branch of Congregationalism split off to form a new church, the Unitarians.

But there was also an equal but opposite force towards what a twentieth-century reader might label "fundamentalism." The first rumblings came from Northampton, Massachusetts, where Jonathan Edwards (1703–1758) began to preach a direct, intuitive apprehension of God in all of His glory. He blamed New England's moral ills upon its assumption of religious and moral self-sufficiency. This force grew into a dramatic rush of evangelical fervor that swept the land and was called the Great Awakening.

The movement was aided by George Whitefield (1714–1770), an Anglican priest with unorthodox views who toured the colonies in 1739–1740, preaching as he went. Although the evangelist was not of a commanding presence, his voice was so huge, melodious, and dramatic that some who heard him said it could melt the most hardened sinner. In complete contrast to the rationalists, Whitefield (pronounced "Witfield") invoked an angry personal God who saw through every person's sham piety into the inner depravity. Even the cool and normally skeptical Franklin was impressed.

———

"In 1739 arrived among us from Ireland the Reverend Mr. Whitefield who had made himself remarkable there as an itinerant preacher. He was at first permitted to preach in some of our churches; but the clergy, taking a dislike to him, soon refused him their pulpits, and he was obliged to preach in the fields. The multitudes of all sects and denominations that attended his sermons were enormous, and it was matter of speculation to me, who was one of the number, to observe the extraordinary influence of his oratory on his hearers and how much they admired and respected him, notwithstanding his common abuse of them by assuring them they were naturally *half beasts and half devils.* It was wonderful to see the change soon made in the manners of our inhabitants. From being thoughtless or indifferent about religion, it seemed as if all the world were growing religious, so that one could not walk through the town on an evening without hearing psalms sung in different families of every street."

———

In Whitefield's footsteps came many other itinerant preachers galvanizing the countryside, winning converts, and criticizing local ministers who did not join in the revival. The result was a period of intense religious strife. Congregational and Presbyterian churches split into "Old Light" (traditional) and "New Light" (revivalist) factions. In New England, the congregations that separated from the traditional religion formed a new sect, the Separate Baptists. In the South, Anglican clergymen were bewildered by fervent missionaries who attacked the established church. Government officials of the Anglican faith fought back by arresting lay preachers (many of the itinerants had not been ordained) and by restricting the number of places where meetings could be held.

Within a few years the Awakening was over. What had the entire movement meant? Some historians ascribe it to an upsurge of democracy among the general run of humanity intent upon enforcing religious toleration on the established church because the Awakening was indeed interdenominational. Other historians suggest that the movement was a conservative backlash marked by its own forms of intolerance (an anti-intellectual disdain for the educated clergy, for instance). Certainly the Awakening struck at the foundations of the two religions in America, Anglicanism and Congregationalism, which had arrived with the first colonists and grown to be the strongest. Also, the mood of this upheaval clearly created some disrespect for all forms of authority, often made a sham of that deferential bow to the local gentry who were pillars of the established faith, and perhaps paved the way for revolution a few decades later. (For a general overview of revivalism on American life, see the essay "Repent, Sinner, Repent" at the end of this chapter.)

Culture and Learning

———

The earliest American colleges were religious and were founded to train clergymen. Harvard College opened in 1637, and by 1650 it had forty undergraduates and ten graduate students. Education always had been crucial to the Puritans, since they saw reading the Bible as the primary act of acquiring the word of God. Although Harvard attempted to be a college for all the colonies, its Puritanism made it unattractive to Southerners; in its first seventy years, not one student came from anywhere in the South, or even from as nearby as the Hudson River Valley.

The College of William and Mary, established in 1693, was an Anglican stronghold in Williamsburg, Virginia. It, too, trained ministers, though for the first decade it was little more than a grammar school and had only a handful of students. Throughout the colonial period one of the deepest fears of the settlers was that their children would not obtain the graces of civilization but would grow up as wild as the land beyond the frontier.

Yale was founded in 1701 by conservative Congregationalists who feared that Harvard had grown too lax in its morality and discipline. By the mid-eighteenth century the Great Awakening and rationalism combined their effects to produce a number of other colleges. The New Light Presbyterians sponsored Princeton (earlier the College of New Jersey); the Dutch Reform Church founded Rutgers (then called Queen's College); the Baptists created Brown (originally Rhode Island College); and the Anglicans and Presbyterians joined forces to found the University of Pennsylvania (then the College of Philadelphia). King's College (now Columbia) became interdenominational by default when it was decided that the president should be Anglican but that the board of governors should represent many different faiths and the school should not exclude any student "on account of his particular tenets in matters of religion." Until a few years before the Revolution, there were no law or medical schools in the colonies, and students had to go to England or Scotland for professional training of any sort.

Most of these colleges, which were in fact simply high schools or academies throughout the colonial era, developed a unique form of administration consisting of an outside board of directors and a strong president. This tended to limit somewhat faculty control of collegiate affairs. By the eighteenth century many clergy, merchants, and some professional men as well were being educated at these colleges, not in England, thus increasing the "Americanization" of colonial life.

Education during colonial times was not, however, primarily gained in schools. The most important training of the day was vocational, and skills were learned through apprenticeships or from parents at home. Even the professions usually were learned on the job by law clerks and medical assistants attending men of established reputation. Tutors also were hired to educate children at home—a system much used by wealthy Virginians who lived too far apart from one another to send their children to a single school.

The New England colonies followed the lead of Massachusetts in legislating public schools. Every town of fifty householders was required to hire a schoolmaster "to teach all such children as shall resort to him to write and read"; every town of 100 householders had to build a Latin grammar school that would prepare students for college. In the other colonies education depended on more haphazard arrangements. Churches or ministers sometimes ran schools. Private individuals sometimes endowed a school or paid for scholarships to be awarded deserving but poor students. Women were educated much less frequently than men: about half of the adult men in the colonies could read; only about a third of the adult women were literate. In Massachusetts these figures were higher, but even there men remained the better educated segment of the population.

Science

Colonial America did not produce any significant scientist or any vital body of scientific knowledge; nevertheless, some individuals began the arduous task of understanding in a *scientific* fashion their new world. Natural science, the collection and description of previously unclassified plants and animals, was one area of scientific endeavor that cried out for the effort of gifted Americans. In the eighteenth century a busy network of correspondence between colonials and scientists in Europe was established. Alexander Garden (1730–1791) of South Carolina was in regular contact with Peter Collinson in England and other naturalists in Pennsylvania, Virginia, and New York. John Bartram (1699–1777), a Quaker botanist of Philadelphia, classified hundreds of plants and also assembled information about Indians and their culture.

The chief medical contribution made by the colonies was the first testing of mass immunization against smallpox. Cotton Mather (1663–1728), a Congregational minister, read about the procedure and inoculated his family and a number of volun-

Anne Dudley Bradstreet

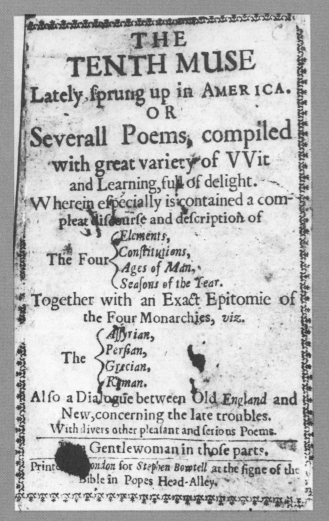

1612–1672

Now say, have women worth? or have they none?
Or had they some, but with our Queen is't gone?
Nay, Masculines, you have thus taxt us long,
But she, though dead, will vindicate our wrong.
Let such as say our Sex is void of Reason,
Know 'tis a Slander now, but once was Treason.

These witty and vigorous lines in praise of Queen Elizabeth were written in 1643 by America's most celebrated poet of the seventeenth century. Born and raised in England, Anne was the daughter of Thomas Dudley, a wealthy steward to the Earl of Lincoln. She led a sheltered childhood, filled with private tutors, the books in the Earl's library, and the intense faith of a Puritan family. In 1628 she married Simon Bradstreet, and two years later the young couple accompanied her parents to the Puritan colony of Massachusetts Bay. Anne went unwillingly; she later said, "My heart rose, but after I was convinced it was the way of God, I submitted to it and joined the church at Boston." Anne followed Simon, first to Cambridge, then to Ipswich, and finally to North Andover in 1644. In this frontier world she occupied a high social position, for her father frequently served as deputy governor or governor, and her husband also played a prominent role in colonial affairs. But despite the demands of public and private life (which eventually included bearing and raising eight children), she found time to write a book of poems, *The Tenth Muse Lately Sprung Up in America*. A brother-in-law, without her knowledge, published this collection in London in 1650. Though well-written, these early poems scarcely reflect her environment. Too often she merely imitated French and English poets whom she admired; or, although writing simply and with genuine feeling, she drew back when close to expressing unconventional Puritan thoughts and took refuge instead in a safe, concluding banality. A posthumous book, *Several Poems Compiled with Greaty Variety of Wit and Learning*, published in 1678, does reveal originality in its blending of the New England countryside, family relations, and Puritan faith. The poem "Contemplations" uses images of fall colors, the dawn, and the growing of day to discuss the dilemma of loving both the world and God. Although such poems established her literary reputation, the irony of Anne Bradstreet's life is that she became famous for describing a countryside she never wanted to see in poems she had not asked to have published. Her whole life was shaped by the decisions of men who surrounded her; yet in her poems, readers find a strong mind and a gracious heart.

teers during an epidemic in 1721. He did so against the advice of most of Boston's doctors, who argued that too little was known about the vaccine and its properties. But the experiment was successful and Mather described the results in a paper that helped to promote the adoption of the technique.

Electricity was another field of American scientific experimentation. A Scottish doctor, Archibald Spencer, toured the colonies lecturing about the topic; when he spoke in Philadelphia, he awakened the curiosity of Benjamin Franklin. Through his famous experiment with a key on a kite string, Franklin established the link between lightning and electricity. He also described electrical current in terms still used today. His published results and his practical invention, the lightning rod, made him an international scientific hero.

The Arts

In the secular twentieth century, Americans find it hard to imagine the interest that their colonial antecedents lavished on religion. The arts, like every other aspect of colonial America, were deeply religious. Sermons were the favorite form of entertainment, instruction, and literary effort. Educated men and women read sermons at home for pleasure, and the public became connoisseurs in the best style of sermon delivery. The *History of Plimouth Planatation*, a historical chronicle written by the early Pilgrim leader William Bradford, is a highly readable and highly religious account of that settlement. The first printed "poetry" in America was *The Whole Book of Psalms* published at Cambridge in 1640. And the best-known colonial poet, Anne Bradstreet (whose life is reviewed here in a biographical sketch), made religious themes the subjects of her meditative works. Two other nonfiction writers of note were William Byrd II, a diarist, and Mary Rowlandson, who began a new genre of literature—the captivity narrative—with a description of her experiences among Indians during King Philip's War.

Bradstreet's first poems were published in England, as were most other colonial works of literature and history. In seventeenth-century America there was only one printing press, which was at Harvard. The first newspaper to endure beyond a few issues appeared only in 1704, again in Massachusetts. But in the eighteenth century, printing developed quickly, and by the time of the Revolution all the colonies (except North Carolina, Delaware, and New Hampshire) had their own newspapers. Philadelphia was the printing capital of the colonies and even had several houses that published works in foreign languages.

In the crafts colonial Americans achieved results that strike the modern observer more and more as the true "art" of the period. For generations, scholars attempted to discover examples of early American triumphs in traditional categories of high art (drama, poetry, painting). Now art historians have come to appreciate the beautiful and vigorous products of artisans working in silver, wood, and glass. Colonial furniture, houses, home utensils, quilts, and rifles—these are the "masterpieces" of a practical people.

The key to understanding and appreciating colonial life is adaptation. Separated from Europe and each other by great distances and by huge expanses of water, forests, and mountains, these first generations in the New World had to adapt their heritage—be it English, Scottish, Irish, Welsh, German, French, Dutch, Scandinavian, Spanish, Portuguese, Italian, or African—to existing conditions. What they realized only after the fact perhaps was that adaptation in the midst of diversity and challenge was creating a new being: the American.

Essay

"Repent, Sinner, Repent"

During the past three centuries four great waves of the revival spirit have stirred the American public. Lasting about a generation or so, each one has been national in scope. According to William G. McLoughlin, Jr.'s *Modern Revivalism*, the first extended from 1725 to 1750; the second, from 1795 to 1835; the third, from 1875 to 1915; and the fourth, from 1945 to perhaps 1970. "In each of these periods," he writes, "a theological and social reorientation coincided with an intellectual and social reorientation in such a way as to awaken a new interest in the Christian ethos which underlies American civilization." Each time, McLoughlin adds, this experience altered both the definition of that ethos and its relationship to our society.

The Great Awakening, which occurred during the second quarter of the eighteenth century resulted from multiple causes, yet it carried in its wake, like all revival movements, the same basic message: organized religion is failing to do its job properly and, as a result, social ills are multiplying on every hand. The Great Awakening clearly knew no distinct bounds and was at home in Europe and America and in both Protestant and Catholic congregations. Theologians saw this phenomenon as a reaction against attempts by the Age of Reason to explain the wonders of Christianity in simplistic, rational terms. Many colonial Americans were disturbed by clergymen who rattled off formal ritual each Sunday, neglected their pastoral duties, and perhaps even led riotous, debauched lives. This scorn increased if a colonial governor forced them against their will to support with hard-earned money or crops an "established" faith alien to their personal convictions.

Prime spokesmen for a "New Birth" of religious life included Theodorus Frelinghuysen of New Jersey; Gilbert Tennent, an Irish-born Presbyterian who preached in the Philadelphia area; Samuel Davies, the most eloquent Presbyterian voice in Virginia; and, of course, New England's Jonathan Edwards and the noted English clergyman, George Whitefield, who toured the colonies, 1739–1740. Although these men and their disciples were accused of displaying too much enthusiasm, stirring up the faithful in parishes where they had not been invited to preach, fostering turmoil and then quickly moving on (all of which was more or less true and, interestingly, constituted the same charges leveled at any revivalist in any age), they set in motion, perhaps unwittingly, a democratizing force that pervaded all realms of colonial life.

In a sense the Great Awakening was a natural outgrowth of the Act of Toleration promulgated in England in the 1680s and tended to loosen denominational bonds still further; but, more importantly, it encouraged political independence as well. Had established colonial churches remained strong, it is quite possible that powerful voices thundering down from scores of pulpits would have snuffed out the seed of separation from Britain long before it took root.

But such was not the case, and the two Protestant groups that profited most by the Revolutionary War, Baptists and Methodists, have never ceased their periodic tilts with Satan. Their cry in mounting tumultuous campaigns is the same heard in the 1730s: much of organized religion is not true to its goals, and sin is rampant in our midst. What distinguished these initial waves of revivalism, however, was true spontaneity. A revival preacher could suddenly ignite an audience and whip to a frenzy those eager to repent their alleged transgressions. Although this aspect of revival meetings persists to the present day in some parts of our nation, as Baptists, Methodists, and Presbyterians gained respectability and numbers their exhortations to the ungodly became quieter and more subdued, and their crusades much more organized.

In August 8, 1801, some 25,000 people thronged into Cane Ridge near Paris, Kentucky, bringing with them children, food, a love of God, and a thirst for social companionship only the loneliness of frontier existence could nuture. Barton W. Stone, a Presbyterian worthy, and his assistants had been working for nearly a month to publicize this gathering and clearly did their job well. Since one man could not possibly address such a mob, according

The camp meeting of the nineteenth century produced emotional conversions such as the one sketched here.

to Daniel Cohen's *The Spirit of the Lord*, eighteen Presbyterian clergymen and a handful of uninvited Baptists and Methodists preached simultaneously.

For three days and three nights the woods and hillsides echoed to the sonorous tones of these men of God, their voices often overwhelmed by the shrieks, uncontrolled laughter, and singing of those possessed by the Holy Spirit. If one listened carefully, he also could learn where to buy a pint of

liquor or meet a damsel eager for a romp in the woods; for, drink and sex were fully as much a part of the nineteenth-century camp meeting scene as prayer.

Although camp meetings that lasted from several days to several weeks remained a vital part of rural America almost to the present day, the true pulse of revivalism was elsewhere in the growing cities. There one could exert more influence, confront more blatant sin, organize bigger campaigns, and attract larger crowds.

During the last century and a half, four men have dominated revivalism: Charles Grandison Finney (1792–1875), Dwight Lyman Moody (1837–1899), William Ashley Sunday (1862–1935), and William Franklin Graham (1918–   ).

Charles Finney, a tall, handsome man with piercing eyes and hypnotic stare, rose to power in central New York state in the 1820s at gatherings not unlike that held at Cane Ridge; but, in 1830 he moved on to Rochester, a growing center of 10,000 crammed with new rich created by the Erie Canal who were not about to shriek, cry, or roll on the ground. Speaking as a liberal Presbyterian, he lec-

tured the anxious and even urged solid church members to look deep into their souls. What Finney did, was "regularize" revivalism. He no longer sought miracles and noisy, on-the-spot conversions to Christ; instead he depended upon efficient organization and more subtle techniques to achieve in a quiet, urbane (and urban) manner the goals desired.

Later Finney spoke in Boston and New York, but with much less success. The fault was not entirely his. Abolition, the consuming issue of the day, was writing an end to the second "Great Awakening" as reform-minded folk pondered how to end slavery, not how to win eternal salvation and sit by the throne of God. In 1835, Finney became

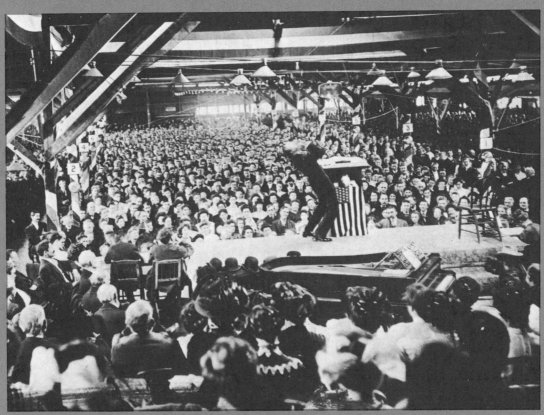

Brown Brothers.

Billy Sunday, like many revivalists, could draw large crowds for his services. Here he is acting out a story standing on a flag-draped platform in a sea of people.

president of Oberlin College in Ohio; and, although he continued to preach, his true revival days were over.

Dwight Moody, cast in the Horatio Alger mold, fled from his rural Massachusetts home at the age of seventeen and went to work in Boston where he became a zealous shoe salesman. Unlike most revivalists, Moody apparently experienced no tortured, mystical rebirth, nor was he tied closely to any faith, although nominally a Congregationalist. Moody brought to the selling of salvation the same enthusiasm and zeal he had once lavished on shoes. For him, conversion was a business just like any other. In 1856 he went to Chicago, became involved in YMCA work, taught Sunday school (despite very bad grammar and sketchy knowledge of the Bible), and in time organized a successful interdenominational church.

When the Chicago fire of 1871 destroyed his church and school, this energy-charged man decided to go to England to conduct revival meetings. With him went Ira D. Sankey, a portly federal tax collector and Christian worker, who played a small cabinet organ and sang beautifully. Moody himself was tone deaf but could appreciate the effect of music and song upon an audience. The English tour started out slowly, but in Edinburgh, home of conservative, moss-covered Presbyterianism, the two Americans were a stunning success. As crowds grew, so did their reputation in both Britain and America, and throughout the rest of the 1870s the Moody-Sankey team thrilled thousands with their simple, no-nonsense approach: come forward and accept Christ as your savior. But by 1880 this brand of evangelism began to pale. Moody never gave up preaching entirely, but turned more to organizational work, devoting much time to the Moody Bible Institute in Chicago. He died suddenly of a heart attack, probably as he wanted to, while leading a revival in Kansas City in 1899.

Billy Sunday, an Iowa farm boy who ran away from home at the age of fifteen and in 1883 became a professional baseball player with the Chicago White Stockings, is a most unusual candidate for the shoes of Jonathan Edwards. His personal habits, until he heard a rescue mission group rendering Gospel hymns his mother once sang, gave no hint

that his future lay in religious work. But Billy followed that little band back to the mission, went forward, got down on his knees, and accepted Christ as his savior. He gave up drinking and gambling, continued to play baseball for a time (no longer on Sundays, however), but eventually quit to work for the YMCA.

In 1895, after several years as advance man for an evangelist, Sunday decided to conduct revival campaigns alone. The result was like nothing seen before or since. This man was a consummate athlete and, not satisfied with merely telling Bible stories, he acted them out. Using sports vernacular, body English, and blazing, near blasphemous invective, he made audiences applaud, laugh, gasp—and repent, too, although his call often was phrased in a jocular manner: "Come on down and take my hand against booze, for Jesus Christ, and for your flag." Sunday brooked no competition as he went through his acrobatics for the glory of God. No one shrieked, rolled, or even uttered an "amen." He had all the lines, it was his show, and it was pure theater, Billy Sunday's theater.

Sunday reached the height of his power during the World War I era. The roaring Twenties, radio, and moving pictures killed him. Of course, they killed vaudeville, too, which is what Billy Sunday really was. He continued to preach and act in small cities and towns, becoming more and more convinced that the world would end in 1935. For him, it did.

Although several individuals tried to take Billy Sunday's place—Sister Aimee Semple McPherson, Bob Jones, Oral Roberts, and Rex Humbard among them, his mantle clearly has fallen upon the shoulders of another Billy—Billy Graham. Born in 1918 in Charlotte, North Carolina, Graham attended several fundamentalist colleges and in 1943 accepted a pastorate in a Chicago suburb. His first break came as a radio preacher; his second, as field organizer for a Youth for Christ movement.

In 1949, while conducting a businessmen's revival in Los Angeles, this young man attracted the attention of the aging newspaper tycoon, William Randolph Hearst, who told his editors to "puff Graham." This publicity, plus Graham's use of radio, movies and television, have produced larger and larger audiences, many thousands that sometimes fill huge football stadiums. No revivalist ever has presented mass meetings so carefully staged, so expertly managed, so appealing to the eye.

Whether one felt Finney's hypnotic gaze, watched the Moody-Sankey team in action, laughed at Billy Sunday's antics, or has marveled at the klieg-light showmanship of Billy Graham, some basic questions remain unanswered. In winning converts, does a successful revivalist, an individual who is often only loosely associated with some established religion, merely reinforce the faith of the faithful for a time? Or does he perhaps exert no significant influence at all? Few evangelists care to speculate about such matters since by claiming huge numbers of converts, a revivalist could exacerbate his or her tenuous relations with local clergy and make future meetings in the same city unlikely. The best evidence indicates that all of these men and women, from Jonathan Edwards to Billy Graham, have been speaking to those solidly within the fold, not to erring sinners. This is not to say that revivalism has failed to achieve some of its goals, yet the recurring waves of exhortations over three centuries lead one to believe that achievement can be neither permanent nor even very significant.

Actually, the greatest and most enduring impact of the sawdust trail has been in the realm of education, not in that of religion per se. Throughout these decades since the early 1700s, the fervent desire to train young ministers in the true faith, or to be certain that one's children drink from the proper spring, has led to the establishment of scores of American preparatory schools, academies, colleges, and universities. Any institution of learning with religious roots at one time or another was the bastion of an old faith or the beacon for a new, upstart rival. Revivalism clearly is a recurring phenomenon given to mounting excess, to gathering momentum, and then to losing it; education, by contrast, is a quiet, ongoing process. Yet, strangely, the classroom owes much to the pulpit-thumping evangelist whose words through the years undoubtedly have built many more schools than churches.

Culver Pictures.
Aimee Semple McPherson was one of the first evangelists to realize the power of radio. Her career in Hollywood was notably theatrical.

SELECTED READINGS

Intellectual and Cultural History

Lawrence Cremin, *American Education: The Colonial Experience 1607–1783* (1970)

Brooke Hindle, *The Pursuit of Science in Revolutionary America, 1735–1789* (1956)

Samuel Eliot Morison, *Intellectual Life of Colonial New England* (1960); earlier title *Puritan Proanos* (1936)

Louis Wright, *First Gentlemen of Virginia: Intellectual Qualities of the Early Colonial Ruling Class* (1940)

Louis B. Wright, *The Cultural Life of the American Colonies* (1957)

Society and the Family

David Ammerman and Thad Tate, *The Chesapeake in the Seventeenth Century* (1979)

Carl Bridenbaugh, *Cities in the Wilderness* (1938)

John Demos, *A Little Commonwealth: Family Life in Plymouth Colony* (1970)

Phillip Greven, *Four Generations: Population, Land, and Family in Colonial Andover, Massachusetts* (1970)

Edmund Morgan, *The Puritan Family: Religion and Domestic Relations in Seventeenth Century New England* (1944)

Michael Zuckerman, *Peaceable Kingdoms: New England Towns in the Eighteenth Century* (1970)

Politics

Daniel Blake Smith, *Inside the Great House: Planter Family Life in Eighteenth-Century Chesapeake Society* (1980)

Patricia Bonomi, *A Factious People: Politics and Society in Colonial New York* (1971)

Jack Greene, *The Quest for Power: The Lower Houses of Assembly in the Southern Royal Colonies 1689–1776* (1963)

Charles Sydnor, *Gentlemen Freeholders* (1952); also published as *American Revolutionaries in the Making* (1965)

Religion

Richard Bushman, *From Puritan to Yankee: Character and the Social Order in Connecticut, 1690–1765* (1967)

William G. McLoughlin, *Isaac Backus and the American Pietistic Tradition* (1967)

William Sweet, *Religion in Colonial America* (1942)

Frederick B. Tolles, *Meeting Houses and Counting House: Quaker Merchants of Colonial Philadelphia* (1948)

Economics and Labor

James Henretta, *The Evolution of American Society, 1700–1815* (1973)

Gerald Mullins, *Flight and Rebellion: Slave Resistance in Eighteenth Century Virginia* (1972)

Richard Pares, *Yankees and Creoles: Trade between North America and the West Indies* (1956)

John Rainbolt, *From Prescription to Persuasion* (1974)

Military

Stephen Saunders Webb, *The Governors-General: The English Army and the Definition of Empire, 1569–1681* (1979)

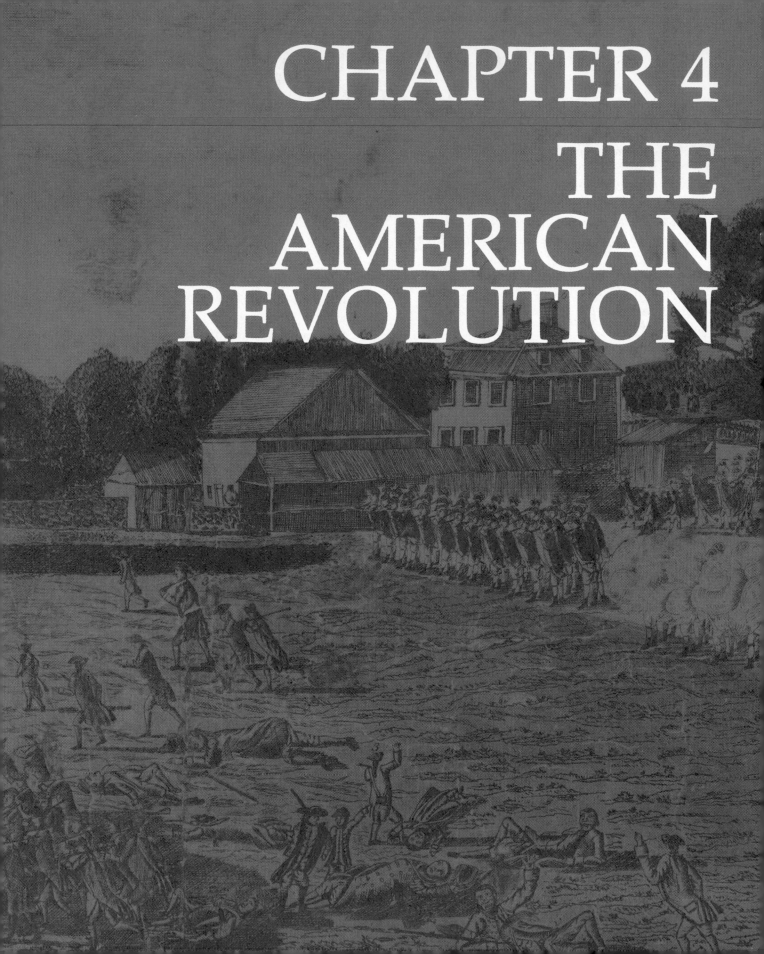

CHAPTER 4
THE AMERICAN REVOLUTION

TIMELINE

1747
Ohio Company established

1754
Albany Congress convenes

1764
Currency Act forbids use of paper money in colonies. Sugar Act tax on molasses and sugar strictly enforced

1765
Stamp Act passed

1767
Townshend Acts place new taxes on colonies

1770
Townshend Acts repealed and Boston Massacre takes place

1773
Boston Tea Party

1774
First Continental Congress convenes

1775
Committees of safety formed

1776
Thomas Paine writes *Common Sense*

July 1776
Declaration of Independence

October 1777
After several defeats, Americans force General Burgoyne to surrender at Saratoga

1781
Cornwallis surrenders at Yorktown

1783
Britain recognizes American independence

1786
First American publication of Phillis Wheatley's poetry

CHAPTER OUTLINE

The War for Independence broke out because the colonies and Britain held different interpretations as to what role America should play in the empire. These differences had deep roots in economic interests and divergent historical experiences; the war was not fought over idle intellectual quibbling. But, on the other hand, blind forces did not impel the combatants to a struggle they could not understand; in the years preceding the Revolution, the inflammatory issues had been widely and articulately debated.

War was not inevitable. There is always the beguiling temptation to read all the events leading up to a major rupture as signposts pointing towards disaster. Throughout the seventeenth and early eighteenth centuries, however, Britain and her colonies coexisted in relative peace, harmony, and mutual benefit. The divisive differences began to appear only towards the middle of the eighteenth century.

The French and Indian War

Between 1689 and 1763 England and France engaged in four wars, each of them fought as a contest over disputed colonial territory. The French and Indian War (called the Seven Years' War in Europe) lasted, despite its European name, from 1754 to 1763 and was the most bitter of the conflicts. In a study of the origins of the Revolution, the French and Indian War is of interest because it pointed up how disunited the colonies were at that time. More importantly, as a result of the war Britain incurred new financial obligations that it attempted to force the colonies to share; this attempt was one of the causes of the Revolution.

The Albany Congress
In June 1754, twenty-three representatives from Pennsylvania, Maryland, New York, and the New England colonies, at the suggestion of the British government, met in Albany, New York, with Iro-

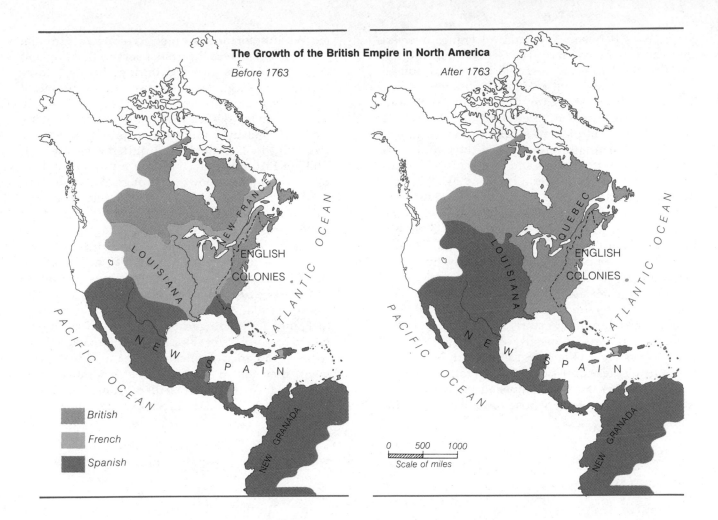

The Growth of the British Empire in North America

Before 1763

After 1763

British

French

Spanish

0   500   1000
Scale of miles

quois chieftains; their goal was to win the allegiance of the Iroquois in the upcoming war against France. The conference with the Indians proved fruitless, but the colonial representatives used the opportunity to discuss an intercolonial defense league against Indian incursions. Benjamin Franklin proposed a plan whereby Parliament would establish a central council composed of elected representatives from each colony and a president-general appointed by the king and responsible for handling all relations with Indians.

When the Congress submitted this Albany Plan to the colonial legislatures for their consideration, it was ignored or vetoed. Two features of the proposal made it unattractive to various legislatures. First, the council would have the right to levy taxes in order to build forts and maintain troops, and colonial legislatures were loathe to surrender their control over taxation to any other agency. Sec-

ondly, the colonies were competing sharply with one another over Indian territories in the interior; a united council might promote the claims of one colony at the expense of a rival.

While the British government viewed the plan as granting too much independence to the colonies, failure of the Albany Congress gave many administrators in England a false impression that the colonies could never act in concert and thus could never present a united front against the mother country.

British Victory

The Seven Years' War was the costliest and bloodiest conflict the modern world had ever witnessed. It was waged in Europe, India, and America, and on each continent France, despite the aid of its allies, Spain and Austria, was roundly defeated by England and Prussia. In North America the major contest was between England and France over an area comprising modern-day Canada and the interior of the United States. The immediate source of friction was ownership of the Ohio River Valley. Based on a 1609 charter Virginians claimed all land west and northwest of their territory. In 1747 a group of Virginia planters, including the brothers of George Washington, established the Ohio Company to trade with Indians and to speculate in western lands. Two years later a grant of 200,000 acres between the Monongahela and Kanawha rivers was made to the land company. Thus in 1754, when the French began to move into that region, Governor Robert Dinwiddie of Virginia, himself an investor in the Ohio Company, instructed twenty-two-year-old George Washington to construct a fort where the Monongahela and Allegheny rivers join to form the Ohio. By the time the expedition arrived French forces controlled the juncture and had begun construction of Fort Duquesne. Washington built a crude stockade, which he called Fort Necessity, about fifty miles south of the French fort. However, on July 3, 1754, he was compelled to surrender to a superior enemy force whose commander permit-

ted Washington and his men to return to Virginia.

This defeat was the first of several that England and the colonies suffered during the next three years. Since England was concentrating its might against France in European battles, the war in America, to the degree it was thought about at all, was regarded by London as an unimportant side issue. But in 1757 England acquired a new leader, William Pitt, obsessed with the future of England as a great imperial power. Through Pitt's intervention, the major thrust of the British war effort was shifted to America. It was Pitt's ambition to drive the French out of North America altogether and to annex the entire continent to the British Empire.

At the close of the war in 1763 a triumphant Britain occupied the French territories of Canada and the West Indies as well as the Spanish territories of Florida. At the peace table England returned to France its holdings in the West Indies but retained control over Florida and Canada. When western Indian tribes learned of the peace settlement, they rallied to the call of an Ottawa chief, Pontiac, to drive white settlers from their lands. Even though Pontiac's forces destroyed a number

National Maritime Museum.
This eighteenth-century engraving shows the final assault by the British on Quebec. Note the troops in the lower left corner using a back trail to the Plains of Abraham where the battle is under way.

of British forts, beseiged Detroit, and killed an estimated 2,000 white settlers, the effort failed. The net result of the treaty with France and Pontiac's abortive campaign was to establish unquestioned British control of the eastern half of North America.

But the very moment of victory foreshadowed Britain's eventual defeat in the Revolution. The French and Indian War, fought in America to secure and expand British frontiers, brought the colonies to the forefront of British consciousness. No longer would the colonies be allowed to enjoy the benign neglect that had characterized earlier British administrations. Now the colonies would be ruled with a tighter hand—and this increased intervention in colonial affairs would bring into sharp focus fundamental differences that were developing between the colonies and Britain.

Evidence of closer supervision of American life is seen in a proclamation designed to simplify relations with Indians and foster orderly colonial growth. The Proclamation of 1763 closed the area south of Quebec, north of Florida, and west of the Appalachian divide to Spanish Louisiana to white settlers. British troops were stationed along this line as a buffer force between Indians and settlers. Colonists looking for new land were encouraged to go to Florida and Canada, newly acquired lands that could be held only if they were populated by English families. Closing the western frontier riled colonists who had been looking avidly toward the rich lands of the Ohio River Valley for years. The belated vigor with which the British government suddenly began to regulate Indian affairs, even appointing special agents responsible to the crown alone, not to colonial legislatures, increased this widespread anger. This anger was not greatly dissipated by the British government's decision that the Proclamation Line of 1763 could be altered through treaties with Indian tribes.

The war served to remind the British of the need for tighter colonial supervision as well. Disloyal colonial merchants had smuggled food and other goods to the French throughout the war, thereby aiding the French military and naval effort.

In another way, equally bad, colonists had undermined the British war effort by quibbling over their financial support for troops. Colonial legislatures begrudged every cent they handed over to the royal army and navy, and only after the British government promised to reimburse the colonies did they produce adequate military funds.

The Constitutional Debate

Unlike the later American Constitution, the British constitution did not exist as a single set of resolutions that had at one time been framed by a group of legislators and signed by them into law. Rather, the "constitution" was nothing more than an accumulation of traditions and documents setting forth the separation of powers between Parliament and the throne.

The Supremacy of Parliament

When William and Mary ascended to the throne at the time of the Glorious Revolution of 1689, they agreed that Parliament could hold regular meetings and elections. (The power to call both formerly resided with the king, and Charles I had once dissolved Parliament for eleven years.) And the new monarchs also agreed that dissenters would be tolerated and that several other important liberties would be vested in the people or their Parliament. This settlement of 1689–1690, the strongest guarantee of parliamentary rights, came to be interpreted differently on the two sides of the Atlantic.

A philosophical, legal, and political question that was much debated in England throughout the seventeenth and eighteenth centuries was the location of sovereignty—that is, who has the ultimate authority to rule? Most theorists on both sides of the Atlantic at least paid lip service to the idea of popular sovereignty—the idea that the people retain the final right to rule themselves. Beyond that point of agreement there was no consensus. The relationship between the people and the king was, according to liberal thinkers such as John Locke (1632–1704), fairly simple: the people agreed to do homage to the king, but if the king overstepped his powers too grievously, then the people's elected representatives in the House of Commons could remove him from his throne. There were conservative politicians in England, however, called Tories, who challenged this interpretation and believed the king should not be subject to the people's will under any conditions. But the opposing party, the Whigs, were much more vocal, both in England and in America, and it was they who stood for the supremacy of Parliament. According to their formula, the location of sovereignty lay with the king-in-Parliament; that is, the king ruled only with the cooperation of Parliament.

Exactly how did Parliament represent the people? The British system of representation was complex. Individual chartered cities (called "boroughs") had the right to elect a stipulated number of delegates, no matter what their current size. Old, chartered cities that had lost most or all of their population retained their right to send representatives to Parliament; new, uncharted cities had no representation at all. Universities sent special representatives and each of the forty shires (or counties) elected a representative. The upper house of Parliament, the House of Lords, represented the privileged classes; any lord of a certain rank and the bishops of the Church of England had a right to sit in that house.

The House of Commons, though it was governed by elected representatives, did not directly represent specific shires or boroughs. Each member of the House of Commons was supposed to vote for the entire empire, including the colonies in America. No member was immediately responsible to his particular constituents, and indeed such a notion of representation would have seemed strange to the English. Representatives were insulted, in fact, if their constituents told them how to vote. Because each representative supposedly had the good of the entire empire in mind whenever he voted, he thought of himself as *virtually* (if not literally) representing every British subject.

The concept of "virtual representation" did not make sense to the colonists. A higher percentage of men voted in the colonies than in England, and in America a representative to a colonial legislature had, by law, close ties to the particular district that had put him in office. (To be eligible for office one usually had to own land in his home district.) Moreover, delegates, at least in New England, were quite used to receiving specific instructions from their constituents on how to vote. Accordingly, the whole theory of virtual representation seemed mere sophistry to Americans. As an editorial in the *Providence Gazette* of May 11, 1765, expressed it: "How trifling then is the supposition, that we in America virtually have such share in the national councils, by those members whom we never chose? If we are not their constituents, they are not our representatives. . . . It is really a piece of mockery to tell us that a country, detached from Britain, by an ocean of immense breadth, and which is so extensive and populous, should be represented by the British members, or that we can have any interest in the house of commons."

But there was another aspect of the constitutional crisis that was seized on as a bone of contention—the supremacy of Parliament. Parliament insisted on its superiority to the colonial legislatures. Soon the argument degenerated into an either-or stalemate: *either* colonial legislatures were superior to Parliament in determining colonial affairs *or* Parliament was superior to them. Because the Whigs felt that parliamentary supremacy was the only guarantee of the commonwealth against the tyranny of the king, the English Whigs viewed the colonists as Tories, reactionaries who favored royal rule over representative government.

That an unbridled sovereign was a threat to representative government was no idle fear. The king was by no means a mere figurehead in the eighteenth century. The crown had a separate income, independent of Parliament's appropriations. Furthermore, the king wielded a great deal of influence within Parliament since he controlled a number of seats in Parliament through his patronage. The king could choose his ministers and they were responsible to him alone; through his ministers the king could attempt to gain a majority in the Parliament. And the king's relationship with the colonies was direct and personal, for the crown's administrative powers included governing the colonies (as well as handling all foreign affairs). Despite this royal prerogative, Parliament never doubted it had the right to interfere in colonial matters; it regarded itself as the supreme protector of all British rights and liberties.

The Authority of Colonial Assemblies

Americans, of course, interpreted their own behavior quite differently. They saw a resemblance between Parliament and their own legislatures. Throughout the colonial period the assemblies had striven for such rights and privileges as choice of their own speaker, the decision on when to adjourn, the initiation of laws, the immunity of members from prosecution during debates, and the right to settle contested elections. Throughout these colonial struggles, both to obtain and to retain specific rights, the opponents of the assemblies were the governors. Just as Parliament gained ascendancy over the king by withholding appropriations, in the same way the assemblies brought the governors to heel through fiscal pressure. Thus the colonists would have contended that their efforts to wrest power from the governors (who represented the will of the monarch) were similar to Parliament's struggles to gain dominance over the king.

The central ideological issue of the Revolution can be seen as the conflict between Parliament and colonial legislatures over sovereignty. Both colonial and British representatives were eager to restrict royal prerogative; the insistence upon the primacy of colonial assemblies in America was as much a Whig characteristic as was the insistence upon the primacy of Parliament in England. The ironic truth of the Revolution is that, in one sense, it was a war in which both sides believed in the same principles. Both the colonists and the members of Parliament claimed to be protecting their Whig heritage.

The Events Leading to the War

The constitutional debate emerged between 1763 and 1765 when the British initiated a number of measures designed to bring the empire more fully under the aegis of Parliament. These measures only raised the hackles of colonists resolved to preserve what they regarded as the status quo, and their hereditary rights.

Writs of Assistance

Writs of assistance were general search warrants authorizing an official of the crown to undertake a search without having to specify the particular goods for which he would search or to identify any particular individual who would be interrogated. Because these warrants could be used against anyone, they were not popular in England, although they had been legal since 1662. When George II died in 1760, all writs had to be reissued; and the

customs officials in Massachusetts applied to the Superior Court of the Colony for the writs. Boston merchants, unhappy with British attempts to strengthen enforcement of the Navigation Acts, hired James Otis to represent them. Otis claimed that the new writs were unconstitutional because they violated a common-law principle that a man should be secure in his home. He lost the case, but used similar arguments three years later against the Sugar Act.

The Currency Act

The colonies, which mined no precious metals, always had been bedeviled by the lack of hard money, or specie. An unfavorable balance of trade with England drained the colonies of whatever specie they might have, much of it derived from trade with the Spanish and French West Indies.

To solve this problem colonial land banks issued paper money in the form of loans to individuals, who put up their property as mortgage. In addition, colonial legislatures printed paper money during time of war to pay for extraordinary expenses. Thus governments met expenses by issuing a paper medium, whether currency or certificates, which could be used to pay taxes and make other payments. This paper could not, however, be exchanged for coin or specie.

Library of Congress.

Both the congress and state legislatures printed paper money during the revolution. This made the money supply impossible to control and assured a rapid inflation.

In 1764 this system was severely curtailed by a currency act that limited certain kinds of paper money as legal tender. Parliament always had been suspicious of the inflationary nature of paper money issued by the colonies; thus, after the French and Indian War, acting through its Board of Trade, Parliament responded favorably to pressure exerted by English merchants, who were complaining of inflated colonial currencies. Franklin later cited British restrictions against colonial paper money as one of the main reasons for the alienation of the American provinces.

The Sugar Act

Another act passed in 1764 was far more obnoxious to the colonies—the Sugar Act. At first glance one might fail to understand why this act should have aroused such a storm, since it *reduced* the duty imposed on molasses and sugar from unrealistically high levels set by the Molasses Act of 1733. But the Molasses Act had been flagrantly abused or ignored by American smugglers. The new Sugar Act was to be strictly enforced. British warships would patrol American waters, and customs officials and naval officers had the right to inspect any cargo on demand. Not only was commerce with other nations so regulated, but intercolonial trade also was affected. A farmer or merchant shipping produce from one colony to another had to report to the nearest custom house, post bond for his cargo, and file a detailed invoice describing his shipment— even when the "nearest" customs house was thirty or forty miles from his home.

Americans in their first objections to the Sugar Act stressed economic hardships it would impose on them. And indeed, the new restrictions on paper money and currency did deepen a depression triggered by the end of the French and Indian War. One businessman writing from Rhode Island observed that "all business seems to wear a gloom not before seen in America," and another, writing from New York City, said, "Business in this town is very much stagnated, Cash excessive scarce. . . . The Prospect is really very discouraging, the Sound of Terror every Day encreasing [sic]."

There were more fundamental reasons, however, for this discontent. Americans were angered because the express purpose of the new acts was to raise revenue to pay part of the expenses of maintaining 10,000 British troops in America. These troops were supposed to defend the frontier against Indian attacks, but as they demonstrated during Pontiac's Rebellion of 1763 near Detroit, they were quite unsuited for Indian fighting. The colonists began to suspect that the real reason for the large standing force in America was to force compliance with new rules and regulations and to put an end to profitable smuggling.

Worse, violators of the Sugar Act were to be tried not in ordinary common-law courts, where they would be judged by a jury of peers and fellow Americans, but by admiralty courts, which handed down judgments without the use of juries. Traditionally, these courts tried cases involving crimes committed on the high seas. In practice, common-law courts assumed the accused was innocent until proved guilty, while admiralty courts proceeded under the assumption that the defendant was guilty until he could demonstrate his innocence. Admiralty courts also were unpopular for less high-minded reasons; they usually convicted smugglers, whereas jury trials almost always let those accused go free. In a long petition sent on October 18, 1764, from the New York Assembly to the House of Commons, colonial legislators, politely but firmly objected to the admiralty courts "who proceed not according to the old wholesome Laws of the Land, nor are always filled with Judges of approved Knowledge and Integrity."

The Stamp Act

The strongest objection of principle to the Sugar Act was that it was a parliamentary law designed to raise revenue. One of the deepest convictions entertained by the colonists was that as Englishmen they could not be taxed except by their own representatives. Although members of Parliament might argue they represented the colonists "virtually," this position, as noted, seemed like arrant nonsense to Americans. Their anger at indirect taxes on merchandise was only a fit of pique when compared to the fury that erupted when they learned of direct taxation to be enforced by the Stamp Act, a law signed by young King George III in March 1765.

This new act stipulated that a tax could be collected on every legal document (or, as the text of the act itself put it, "every skin or piece of vellum or parchment, or sheet or piece of paper"). Every time one American sued another or put up bail or wrote a will or received a college degree or cleared merchandise through customs or surveyed property or sold liquor or performed any other public or legal act, he or she was taxed; a stamp showing that the tax had been paid would be affixed to the document in question. The act also arranged for the taxation of newspapers, almanacs, playing cards, and dice.

To complete the insult, in May 1765 Parliament put through the Quartering Act, which made the government of any colony where British troops were stationed responsible for providing the soldiers with living accommodations, drink, bedding, and basic supplies.

To the English these arrangements, passed through the House of Commons with scarcely any debate, seemed perfectly reasonable. The Seven Years' War, the costliest military venture in British history, left the mother country saddled with an enormous debt. To pay this debt, the government had to invent new sources of tax money both at home and in the colonies. Cider, the drink of the average Englishman, was taxed for the first time, an innovation that set off violent riots in apple-growing districts of Britain. That costly war, in the view of Parliament, the king, and his ministers, had been fought to extend American boundaries, and now that a standing force was required to defend those new lands, it seemed only just that the colonists should pay some of the expenses. (No English leader suggested the colonies should shoulder the whole burden.) England itself had a stamp act that taxed all printed materials and legal documents; the new colonial stamp act was in no way more severe.

The Stamp Act alarmed Americans for many reasons. It was a revenue measure not imposed on the colonies by their own legislature but by Parliament. The money raised by the Stamp Act was slated to support British soldiers in the colonies, and some alarmists in America felt that the law could be used to censor or suppress newspapers by denying them the requisite stamped paper. Finally, the act increased the price of everyday legal transactions, including the transfer of land.

What most Englishmen in positions of power did not realize was that the American colonists were probably the most politically sophisticated people in the world during the eighteenth century. The franchise was not nearly so limited as it was in England; most adult men voted at one time or another during their lives. Complex questions of constitutional rights were discussed openly and intel-

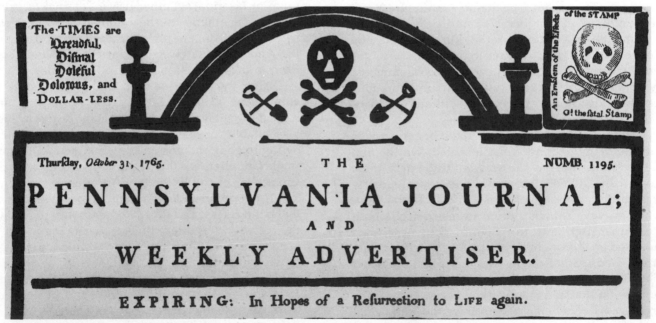

Courtesy of the New-York Historical Society, New York City.
The Pennsylvania Journal expressed its dissatisfaction with the Stamp Act by announcing that it would die rather than use stamped paper. The motto in the upper left reminds readers of another unpopular act restricting colonial currency.

ligently by colonists and, at least in New England, ordinary citizens actively participated in local government.

The Stamp Act aroused a furor of protest in the colonies. The Virginia House of Burgesses approved a petition protesting the act and sent it on to London. Most of the other colonies soon followed this example, and Parliament was deluged with resolutions from the various assemblies.

Riots broke out in many cities, and wealthy merchants and colonists in high positions, men who once dreaded mob rule, now directed the assaults on crown officers. The stamp masters were maligned and mistreated wherever they went. And by appointing Americans to fill such positions, George Grenville made the stamp masters all the more hated. Clubs of patriots named "Sons of Liberty" sprang up, and these radical societies became the first effective means for uniting the disparate colonies behind a common cause. The Sons of Liberty soon set up committees of correspondence that relayed news of the latest British "tyrannies" and created plans for thwarting the machinations of Parliament.

James Otis (1725–1783) conceived a strategy of his own. He proposed an intercolonial congress that would send a joint petition to Parliament opposing the Stamp Act. The Stamp Act Congress met in New York in October 1765 and drew up three documents—a petition to the king, one to the House of Lords, and another to the House of Commons. In the petition to the House of Commons, the Stamp Act Congress stated in unambiguous terms the doctrine of no taxation without representation.

The revolution might well have begun in 1765 had the Stamp Act not been repealed. On the first of November, the day the act went into effect, there were many demonstrations. An effigy of Liberty was burned, many Americans wore black, and thousands of New Yorkers rioted. In resistance to both the Sugar Act and the Stamp Act, Americans mounted a thorough boycott of British manufactured goods. So effective was the colonial boycott that British merchants, already afflicted by the depression that had followed the Seven Years' War, pressured Parliament to withdraw the new legislation. Finally, the crisis was resolved when Parliament decided that repeal was essential for maintaining the health of British commerce. Repeal, rather than being construed as submission to colonial demands, was presented as an act of benev-

olence to British business interests. To drive this point home, Parliament—at the same time it revoked the Stamp Act—passed a Declaratory Act reasserting parliamentary authority over the empire. While the colonies considered the Declaratory Act as a mere face-saving gesture and rejoiced over their triumph, Parliament viewed it as a reassertion of its own authority. This conflict illustrates the growing degree of difference in American and British views on the place and rights of the colonies in the British Empire.

The Townshend Acts

During debate over repeal of the Stamp Act, members of Parliament closely questioned Benjamin Franklin, who made an elegant distinction between internal and external taxes. According to Franklin, the colonists objected only to internal taxes such as those included in the Stamp Act. He asserted that external taxes (duties on imports and exports) did not strike Americans as unjust.

Unfortunately, Franklin misstated colonial opinion. Most Americans had never given a thought to the distinction he drew. If anyone had bothered about the issue at all, it was only to distinguish between raising emergency funds in wartime, say, and regular peacetime taxation. Any sustained program of taxation, whether it was internal or external, was anathema to the colonists. Nevertheless, in 1767 the British ministry decided to impose upon the Americans a new set of duties that would conform to the distinction Franklin had made.

After the repeal of the Stamp Act, George III summoned William Pitt out of retirement and named him first minister once again. Pitt, however, was unable to take an active part in government owing to gout and encroaching madness. The most important man in the realm, therefore, was the Chancellor of the Exchequer, Charles Townshend. Townshend persuaded Parliament to levy duties on tea, paint, glass, and several other luxury items that the colonists imported; this act was inaugurated in 1767. The colonists reacted by erecting a new economic boycott of English goods.

The Townshend duties provided the British Exchequer with very little money and further embittered the American colonists. The preamble of the law specifically stated that the purpose of the duties was to raise money to be used "for defraying the charge of the administration of justice, and the support of civil government" in America. In other words, some of the revenue was handed over to

John Carter Brown Library, Brown University.

This British engraving satirizes the repeal of the Stamp Act. The shops along the way bear the names of English manufacturing towns. The ships in the background bear the names of members of the administration who worked for repeal.

colonial governors and judges formerly dependent on colonial assemblies for their salaries. The Townshend Acts served further to reduce the financial control exerted by colonial legislators over their administrators. The new British ministry vexed the Americans still more by establishing additional admiralty courts and a new board of customs officials. Both the courts and the officials had the responsibility for stopping all smuggling and rigidly enforcing the Townshend duties. Finally, Parliament declared that until the New York colonists complied with the Quartering Act of 1765 all acts of the New York assembly were void.

The dissent that Townshend's measures touched off was heightened by widespread belief among Americans that Parliament was taking only the first steps in a long-range, well-designed course of oppression. If each new infraction of colonial rights was not contested, where would the "tyranny" end? It was this apprehension that in February of 1768 led the Massachusetts assembly to send to the other colonial legislatures a "circular letter" urging united opposition to these acts of Parliament.

Boycotts and a shower of petitions led Parliament to lift all the Townshend duties except the one imposed on tea. This colonial victory, which was accomplished by 1770, reduced American opposition to the British government. However, the political climate remained stormy. Frequent changes in policy, accompanied by the rise and fall of several ministries ousted because of events at home

The BLOODY MASSACRE perpetrated in King—t—Street BOSTON on March 5th 1770 by a party of the 29th REGT.

Unhappy Boston! see thy Sons deplore,
Thy hallow'd Walks besmear'd with guiltless Gore:
While faithless P—n and his savage Bands,
With murd'rous Rancour stretch their bloody Hands;
Like fierce Barbarians grinning o'er their Prey,
Approve the Carnage, and enjoy the Day.

If scalding drops from Rage from Anguish Wrung,
If speechless Sorrows lab'ring for a Tongue,
Or if a weeping World can ought appease
The plaintive Ghosts of Victims such as these;
The Patriot's copious Tears for each are shed,
A glorious Tribute which embalms the Dead.

But know, Fate summons to that awful Goal,
Where Justice strips the Murd'rer of his Soul:
Should venal C—ts the scandal of the Land,
Snatch the relentless Villain from her Hand.
Keen Execrations on this Plate inscrib'd,
Shall reach a Judge who never can be brib'd.

The unhappy Sufferers were Mess.rs Sam.l Gray Sam.l Maverick, Jam.s Caldwell, Crispus Attucks & Pat.k Carr
Killed. Six wounded two of them (Christr Monk & John Clark) Mortally

Engrav'd Printed & Sold by Paul Revere Boston

Yale University Art Gallery, The John Morgan Hill Collection.
The day after the Boston Massacre, Paul Revere had the first copies of this engraving circulating on the streets. Instead of a colonial mob harassing British troops, the engraving shows innocent citizens being murdered by an aggressive military.

and not those in America, tended to undermine British authority on this side of the Atlantic. On the night of March 5, 1770, a mob of Bostonians gathered at the custom house and began to heckle soldiers guarding the customs revenue. "Come on you Rascals," they shouted, "you bloody-backs, you Lobster Scoundrels . . ." When the mob advanced, throwing snowballs filled with rocks, the redcoats panicked and fired. Five Bostonians were killed and a new wave of violence inundated the city. Americans quickly dubbed this event the "Boston Massacre."

An incident involving the *Gaspee*, an armed schooner designed to hunt down American smugglers, demonstrates a continuing enmity towards British authority. When it ran aground off the coast of Rhode Island in 1772, a mob from Providence boarded the helpless vessel, looted it, and put the captain out to sea in a small boat before setting the *Gaspee* afire. When royal commissioners investi-

gated this "attrocious offence" not a single Rhode Islander came up with useful information. The British were unable to find any witnesses.

Soon afterwards two patriots, James Otis and Sam Adams (1722–1803), used the anniversary of the Boston Massacre as an occasion to call for permanent committees of correspondence. Within three months eighty Massachusetts towns set up such committees, and by the middle of 1773 a network of committees, covered all of New England, Virginia, and South Carolina. By 1774, town, country, and regional committees had been formed in nearly all of the colonies, the first step that would soon lead to an American government.

The Tea Act

Charles Townshend died in 1767, still believing that his solutions to the problem of raising colonial revenue were working splendidly. His successor as Chancellor of the Exchequer was Lord North, who recognized that the Townshend Acts constituted an unnecessary irritation to the colonies and a serious threat to the British economy. The chief reason for possessing colonies was so they could supply the mother country with raw materials and buy its finished products. Townshend's duties—and the boycott they incited—negated this whole concept by encouraging Americans to forego English goods and manufacture their own. It was North who suggested that the duties be repealed, with only the tax on tea being retained. Tea could not be grown in the colonies, yet the colonists were inveterate tea drinkers. More importantly, the duty on tea was the only one yielding substantial revenue. London was careful to point out to colonial assemblies that the reason for repealing the Townshend Acts had nothing to do with their boycotts. Parliament was merely working in the interests of English industry.

In 1773 Lord North turned his attention once again to tea. The East India Company, a leading British firm, was on the verge of bankruptcy. It was a huge company and the agency by which England maintained its hold over India. Because duties on the company's imported goods also were a major source of British revenue, North recognized that Britain's role in Asia and the company's solvency were intertwined. One of the main products the company depended upon was tea grown in India and sold throughout the empire. Much of the company's financial distress started at the time of Townshend's original tea duty since Americans ceased buying English tea and began drinking smuggled Dutch tea instead.

North set about to recover the colonial market for the East India Company and, incidentally, to save the company as well. By the Tea Act of 1773, the British government permitted the East India Company to market tea directly in the colonies through agents who were granted a monopoly. Because the company got a rebate on duties paid on tea shipped to America via England, this enabled those agents to undercut competitors. Both by eliminating British and American middlemen and by reducing other costs to the company, Lord North hoped to win back American customers. But North insisted upon retaining the tea duty in order to demonstrate that Parliament still had the right to tax the colonies. Since English tea was now cheaper, even with the duty, than Dutch tea, North hoped the colonists would ignore their principles and pay the tax without complaint.

American leaders, once they learned of the plan, recognized that Lord North's scheme might work—if ordinary citizens in the colonies were given the chance to buy English tea. Accordingly, patriots decided to make sure that the tea was never unloaded from British vessels.

The resistance was remarkably successful. Consignees in American ports were coerced into refusing acceptance of shipments; tea-bearing vessels were turned around before they had a chance to drop anchor. In some cases the tea was unloaded, but merchants who received it were pressured into not paying the necessary duty; as a result, the produce was impounded. Only in Boston did resistance escalate into open violence.

The Boston Tea Party

The royally appointed governor of Massachusetts was Thomas Hutchinson. A man who enjoyed a brilliant political career by staunchly defending British policies, Hutchinson seized upon a legal technicality whereby he hoped to outwit the radicals. He unearthed a seventy-year-old law stating that any vessel remaining in Boston harbor longer than twenty days without unloading could be seized and the cargo impounded until duties were paid. To make sure the three East India Company ships did not sail out of Boston, Hutchinson ordered the Royal Navy to block the entrance of the harbor. The period of grace was coming to an end on December 16, 1773. The ships were still in the harbor and the law required their cargo be unloaded.

But Boston radicals, led by Samuel Adams, concocted a scheme of their own. On the night of the sixteenth, several of them, their faces painted or blackened with soot, their bodies draped in old blankets, boarded the three ships and dumped 342 chests of tea into the harbor.

Parliament's Revenge

The immediate consequences were indeed important—and disastrous. The English were outraged by this destruction of property. Lord North won overwhelming majorities in Parliament as he pushed through several bills—called by the colonists the Coercive Acts—designed to punish Boston and serve as a warning to all of the colonies. First, the port of Boston was closed to all traffic except ships bearing firewood or foodstuffs until the East India Company was reimbursed for its losses.

The second act was the Massachusetts Government bill, which vastly increased the powers of the royal governor. He now could appoint members to the governor's council; previously they were elected every year by the legislature. The governor also could appoint judges to inferior courts. Worst of all was the provision that limited town meetings to once a year and forbade them to conduct any business other than to elect officers and to pass rules for local administration. This last provision threatened the whole New England system of government.

Another stipulation, the Administration of Justice Act, which the colonials dubbed the "Murder Act," decreed that English officials charged with a crime committed in the course of their official activities were given the right to trial in Britain. Not only did this mean few officials would be convicted, but it also implied that colonial courts were prejudiced against English officials. This supposition was manifestly unfair, since Boston courts acquitted several British soldiers involved in the Boston Massacre and pardoned the rest.

As a final bit of tidying up the colonies, Parliament revised the Quartering Act so that it permitted British commanders to use unoccupied town buildings for their troops. Under this act troops were stationed in Boston. The sign (if any was needed) that Boston was regarded as a rebellious city that must be punished was the fact that Massachusetts now received a military governor, General Thomas Gage.

Reactions of the Colonies

The colonists were outraged by Parliament's latest measures. Soon they were able to add yet another "tyrannical" act in what was becoming a long list. Ever since England acquired Canada in 1763, that colony had been under the temporary rule of a military government. Now Parliament, by the Quebec Act, devised a permanent form of government for Canada. The former French colony was to have no legislature, it was to retain the French system of law, and the Catholic Church would keep its privileged position. In fact, the Quebec Act made specific provisions for a Catholic bishop. As though to rile the colonists further, Parliament gave territorial control of the Illinois heartland to Canada, thereby ignoring the claim of other colonies to that land. In every regard the Quebec Act incensed the colonists, who looked upon it as Britain's plot to suppress representative government, favor popery, and limit settlement to the eastern seaboard. The British and Canadians thought it an act of statemanship. Most colonists lumped the Quebec Act with the Coercive Acts and called them the "Intolerable Acts." Amidst colonial calls for a Continental Congress, Virginia's House of Burgesses met illegally after Governor Dunmore dissolved the assembly. They issued a call for a Congress and a new boycott of British goods.

The first Continental Congress met in Philadelphia from September 5 to October 26, 1774. During that time the delegates discussed a plan for union, submitted by Joseph Galloway. The plan proposed establishment of an intercolonial legislature endowed with the right to tax all colonies and to control the appointment of all officials. The Congress rejected this plan on the grounds that it took

Courtesy of the New-York Historical Society, New York City.
This engraving shows the American point of view. A brutal British ministry forces tea down the throat of an American Liberty while Justice weeps. In the background, the British navy bombards Boston.

JOURNAL

OF THE

PROCEEDINGS

OF THE

CONGRESS,

Held at PHILADELPHIA,

September 5, 1774.

PHILADELPHIA:

Printed by WILLIAM and THOMAS BRADFORD,
at the *London Coffee-House.*

The debates recorded in the *Journal* for the first Continental Congress reflect the divided sentiments of colonial leaders just two years before independence.

away too much power from the individual colonies. Had it passed, the colonies would have been saddled with a weak, ineffectual government. Fortunately, the Massachusetts committee of correspondence seized this opportunity to press for much more radical measures. Paul Revere was sent to Philadelphia with a set of resolutions called the Suffolk Resolves. These resolves, adopted by the Suffolk County Convention (created hastily after Massachusetts town meetings were banned), called for total resistance to the Intolerable Acts. According to the resolves, taxes should be collected but not handed over to the royal government until the traditional government of Massachusetts was re-

stored. In a more inflammatory tone, the resolves invited military resistance to British troops stationed in Boston and recommended that citizens be empowered to arrest and imprison British officials if a single patriot leader were taken by the British authorities.

The Continental Congress approved the Suffolk Resolves, although Massachusetts was warned that it must behave peaceably toward General Gage. A declaration of rights set forth the injustices committed by Parliament against the colonies, stated the colonists' view of the constitutional crisis, and denounced the Intolerable Acts. The Congress also petitioned the king to intercede on behalf of the colonies and declared a new Nonimportation Agreement against Britain if the Intolerable Acts were not repealed. When the delegates recessed, they had not been able to agree on a plan to curtail exports but resolved to meet again in May of 1775.

The new Nonimportation Agreements set up local committees of safety to enforce the boycott. These committees functioned as revolutionary cells in each town. They began to gather gunpowder and store it secretly in places unknown to British officials. In Massachusetts local units of revolutionary militia, called minutemen, were organized; they were pledged to defend the colony against British encroachments. By now the colonies formed a powder keg that was ready to explode. Although General Gage recognized that any military move might lead to shooting, nevertheless, upon an order from London, on April 19, 1775, he set out to seize a supply of weapons stored in Concord outside Boston. He also hoped to captured leaders of the resistance.

Every move the British troops made in search of patriot weapons and leaders was reported to the people of Massachusetts by messengers on horseback. The most famous of these, of course, was Paul Revere (whose contributions are highlighted here in a biographical sketch). When 700 British soldiers arrived in the village of Lexington on their way to Concord on the morning of April 19, they found patriot militiamen standing in ranks on the village green. No one knows for certain who shot first, but according to patriot accounts a British officer ordered his men to disarm and disperse the gathering militia. In the following confusion, shots were fired on both sides as the militia fled. The British quickly moved on to Concord where the militia made a stand. Very few supplies were found, and as the British marched back to Boston, they were fired upon by patriots behind walls and trees. Lexington

Paul Revere

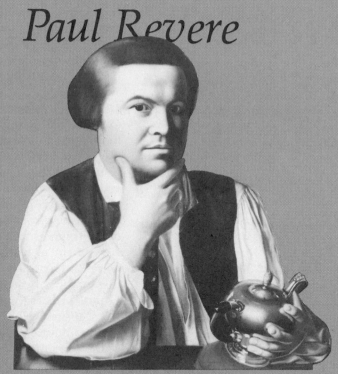

1735–1818

Renowned as the night rider who warned the patriots of the British advance on Concord, Paul Revere was the son of a French Huguenot silversmith (Apollos De Revoire), who anglicized his name so "the Bumpkins should pronounce it easier." The third of twelve children, Paul grew up in Boston, attended local schools, and soon joined his father in the silver trade.

As early as 1765 he was experimenting with copper engravings and executing portraits, seals, bookplates, and coats of arms. He also found time to carve frames for portraits by artist John Singleton Copley and to turn out dental devices, which his ads boasted were "of real Use in Speaking and Eating." However, it was Revere's early interest in politics and an ability to recruit like-minded mechanics and tradesmen which brought him into contact with John Hancock, Samuel Adams, and other local leaders. He helped organize and participated in the famed Boston Tea Party and in 1774 became official courier of the Massachusetts Provincial Assembly to the Congress in Philadelphia. Long before Revere and his horse helped to precipitate the action at Lexington and Concord, the figure of this rider was known to British troops and his name had appeared in the columns of London newspapers.

Actually, on the night of April 18, 1775, Revere reached only Lexington and was detained by the British while trying to reach Concord. Soon released, he made his way on foot back to Lexington, where he gathered up a trunk of important papers that Hancock had abandoned in his haste to elude capture. During the Revolution, Revere designed and printed the first continental dollars and created the first official seal for the colonies and for the new state of Massachusetts, a state seal that is still in use. After the war, he was instrumental in bringing about the ratification of the Constitution, but he also found time to cast bells, make cannon, and furnish Robert Fulton with the copper plates and boilers for his steam ferryboat. Until the end of his long life, Revere continued to wear the clothes of the Revolutionary era through the streets of Boston. His beautifully designed and skillfully executed silver pieces, both flatware and hollow ware, are still highly prized by hundreds of collectors and connoisseurs.

Colonial Williamsburg Photograph.

The news that American women in North Carolina had signed their own agreement not to import from Britain brought this satirical response in England. Note the mannish features on the woman with the gavel.

and Concord may not have been in all respects glorious rebel victories, but these encounters provided the revolutionaries with martyrs.

Organizing a Rebellion

Of course, the colonists did not react in unison to British incursions. One of the first duties of the Revolutionary leaders was to whip up enthusiasm for their cause through propaganda. In the year immediately preceding the bloodshed at Lexington, Americans produced several very able pamphleteers—James Otis, Daniel Dulany, Thomas Jefferson, and John Dickinson. Once the war was under way, the pamphleteering continued. Indeed, in January 1776, Congress actually requested one member to write a pamphlet that would prepare people for independence. This effort, however, was made unnecessary after Thomas Paine wrote a spirited defense of American liberty entitled *Common Sense*. (More information on the life of the author of *Common Sense* and who breathed fire into one, two, perhaps even more revolutions is given in a biographical sketch in this chapter.)

During the course of the Revolution, the rebels relied upon newspaper stories, pamphlets, ballads, and broadsides (printed, posterlike sheets) to win popular support. Mercy Warren was the sister of the Revolutionary leader James Otis. (For more information, see the biographical sketch in this chapter.) She wrote many poems and several plays on behalf of the cause. Rebel preachers thundered

Thomas Paine

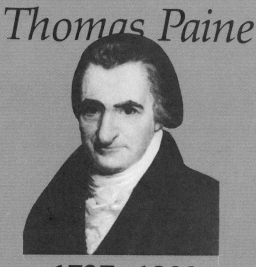

1737–1809

Born into a poverty-stricken Quaker household in Thetford, England, Paine was something of a drifter for nearly two decades (1757–1774). He went through two childless marriages and a variety of jobs, including being a lobbyist for tax collectors. Finally, bankrupt and down-and-out in London, like many contemporaries, he decided to try his luck in America. Although thirty-seven years old when he set out for the New World, Paine brought with him two unique assets: letters of introduction from Benjamin Franklin, whom he had met while working as a lobbyist; and a hard-knocks education firmly rooted in contemporary affairs.

Having dabbled in journalism (as well as being a corsetmaker, schoolteacher, tobacconist, grocer, and excise official), Paine was supporting himself soon after landing in Philadelphia by writing for various local publications. In January 1776, he turned out an anonymous, forty-seven-page pamphlet (price, 2 shillings) entitled *Common Sense*. Arguing that separation was both natural and inevitable, it called for immediate independence from Britain. Within three months 120,000 copies had been sold, and in time an astounding 500,000 were printed. Soon recognized as the author, Paine next launched a series of *Crisis* papers, the first of which opened with the famous words: "These are the times that try men's souls."

During the war years a grateful Congress and various state governments provided Paine with jobs, yet peace found him honored but poor. Until 1787 he lived modestly in New York and New Jersey, working on a scheme to construct an iron bridge. At length, convinced his dreams could not be realized in the New World, he returned to the Old. He spent the late 1780s rather pleasantly in England and France, where he was lionized by liberals as the author of *Common Sense* and a friend of Washington and other worthies. (His bridge eventually was constructed and worked well enough, but Paine lost money on the project.)

After three years of commuting between London and Paris, Tom Paine had become a self-styled missionary of liberal revolt. Then, Edmund Burke's denunciation of events in France precipitated his second masterpiece, *The Rights of Man*, a declaration of equality, liberty, and resistance to oppression. In 1792 he became a member of the French Assembly but was caught up in the crosscurrents of that turbulence and quickly found himself behind bars. There he composed a third work, *The Age of Reason*. Widely known as "the atheist's bible," this actually is an ode to the glory of God as seen by a deist.

Paine returned to America in 1802 and spent his last years among old haunts, largely a social outcast. Denied a Christian burial plot, he was interred on his New York farm.

No patriot stirred such passions in the 1770s as Tom Paine, and few have aroused such controversy since that time. Propagandist rather than a literary figure or philosopher, he has often been reviled and scorned, largely for his repute for licentious living and atheistic beliefs; yet he clearly gave voice to the American Revolution. Without his fiery words, the whole story might well have turned out differently.

forth sermons from the pulpit that stressed natural law, the right to rebellion, and patriotic duty. Tory preachers countered with urgent pleas for loyalty to the king, stating that passive obedience of the monarch was the only moral course to be pursued. When the Tory minister Jonathan Boucher (1738–1804) gave vent to such opinions from a pulpit in Annapolis, he had two loaded pistols at his side so as to ward off interruptions from the congregation.

The committees of safety, which had been set up by the Continental Congress in 1775 to enforce the boycotts against the British, now began to exert pressure on American Tories. Their tactics were embarrassing to a people who claimed they were fighting a war to secure liberty. The committees searched out disloyal books, punished merchants who attempted to break the boycott, and forced out of office Americans who did not subscribe to patriot goals.

Who Were the Tories?

Traditionally, historians have stated that the Tories (persons who remained loyal to England and opposed the Revolution) were wealthy members of the upper class. This conclusion was supported by examinations of the records of those who submitted claims for compensation for property loss at the end of the war; most of the claimants were indeed rich.

But today the general view of historians is changing. First, simple statistics make it impossible that all Tories belonged to the elite. Some 55,000 Americans enlisted in the British army and about 100,000 Tories emigrated from America, some to settle in Nova Scotia, New Brunswick, and the Bahamas, others to live out their lives in Britain. Not all of these people could have been rich.

When Massachusetts banished 300 Tories in 1778, about one-fifth were merchants, members of a profession, or gentlemen who did not work for a living; about a third were farmers; and the remainder were craftsmen, laborers, or small shopkeepers. Other lists of Tories reveal that working-class people always out-numbered the rich.

Divided loyalties turned the Revolution into a civil war in many frontier areas. Tories fought alongside the Iroquois Indians in the North and then raided their former homes. A sizeable number of Tories could be found in the region along the seacoast in the Middle colonies, including Long Island, the Lower Hudson Valley, the counties around Philadelphia, and the peninsula that separates the Delaware Bay from the Chesapeake.

Clearly, not all Tories had English backgrounds. Some were British-born diehards, of course, but many others were Scottish, Dutch, German, and French. Indeed, among the Tory ranks could be counted many members of religious and national minorities who had one thing in common: they felt threatened. This sense of insecurity and uneasiness in the midst of impending change, a characteristic of Tory leaders, was equally evident among the rank and file.

The Tories made up, it seems, about one-fifth of the American population, which was then between two and one-half and three millions. Two-fifths were actively rebel, and the rest either vacillated or remained essentially neutral. Tories were most numerous in the Middle colonies, less so in the South and in New England.

Most of the 100,000 Tories who emigrated from America were forced out. By the end of the war the states, urged on by Congress, passed laws declaring the Tories to be traitors and began confiscating their lands and exiling them. Even before declaring independence, Congress had passed a resolution forbidding its opponents to congregate in large groups or to publish their objections. And, during the war, Tories suspected of aiding the British were jailed, driven inland away from all contact with the enemy, or forced to sign loyalty oaths.

The Tories were, of course, not the only group of Americans who, through the past two centuries, have taken a stand contrary to that of those exerting true power in their community, state, and nation. Opposition of this sort is a fact of life that any people who believe in free speech and peaceful protest (which may become quite *un*peaceful at times) must face. (The essay on "Dissent in Time of War" at the end of this chapter details the nature of this protest in various crises from the Revolution to the present.)

The New Government

Throughout the Revolutionary period, as colonies became states there was a transfer of power from royal to rebel hands. Starting in 1774, few of the colonies experienced untroubled meetings of their legislatures since royal governors invariably dissolved these assemblies as hotbeds of rebellion. While the governors were curtailing legislative meetings for insufficient loyalty to the crown, committees of safety were forcing the resignations of Tory sheriffs, judges, ministers, and other local officials. Sometimes, depending upon local senti-

Mercy Otis Warren

1728–1814

Perhaps the most eloquent female intellectual of the period was Mercy Otis Warren. An early and able patriotic writer, Warren turned her hand to satiric plays beginning in 1772. These plays, meant to be read rather than performed, attacked Tory officials in her native state of Massachusetts. These enemies of liberty she disguised under such caustic names as Judge Meagre, Brigadeer Hate All, and Hum Humbug. Her first play was named *The Adulateur* and it depicted the despised royal governor of Massachusetts, Thomas Hutchinson, as a tyrant.

After the Revolution she brought out a collection of poems that included two dramas in verse, *The Sack of Rome* and *The Ladies of Castile*, both embodying a message on behalf of human liberty. But her greatest effort was a three-volume *History of the Rise, Progress and Termination of the American Revolution*, published in 1805. That she was able to turn out such a massive study while married to James Warren, a merchant and farmer, and looking after her five sons and household chores is a testimony to her vitality and determination. In this work she made such biting remarks about John Adams, whose politics she regarded as too conservative, that Adams was moved to complain, "History is not the province of Ladies."

Until her death at the age of 86, she continued to live in Plymouth, Massachusetts, and to correspond actively with her many friends in public life. At every point in her writing career, Mercy Warren revealed a strong commitment to democracy. In fact, her fight with John Adams broke out when she detected in him a new leaning toward monarchy and a "pride of talents and much ambition," unsuitable qualities in a democratic leader.

ments, the path to statehood was relatively smooth; on other occasions, extremely rocky and rough.

In some colonies the royal governor was removed from office by rebels. William Franklin, Benjamin Franklin's illegitimate son and the governor of New Jersey, was arrested by rebels. Other royal appointees simply fled in the face of mounting violence.

Committees of safety, really interim agencies of local administration, arranged for new elections in their districts, generally retaining pre-Revolutionary voting requirements. The legislators elected served in quasi-legal state assemblies that declared themselves to be the legitimate government of the state and set about writing constitutions.

In the meantime, the Continental Congress had taken on the duties of a central steering committee. The first Continental Congress had provided for the meeting of a second in the spring of 1775 in order to hear the response of Britain to petitions. When the delegates arrived to start the second Congress, the colonies had just received word of Concord and Lexington. The second Congress thus combined reactions to British moves with the running of a war. As state governments came under control of rebels, the delegations in Congress were changed (if necessary) to reflect less moderate positions. The Congress therefore recommended that states form governments, suppress Tories, and create an army. Without any specific authorization, Congress became a central government.

The Declaration of Independence

Between January and July of 1776, state governments, with or without finished constitutions, came firmly under the control of the revolutionary leaders. The creation of state governments that opposed continued union with Britain went hand in glove with establishment of an independent federal government.

As a result, when the Declaration of Independence was finally signed, it did not engineer America's freedom but rather acknowledged officially the independence that already existed. The pressures of waging a war had already turned the Congress into a functioning government, and the various states had already given approval to the idea of independence. In fact, the reason Congress delayed signing the Declaration was the desire to wait until American approval of the document would be unanimous.

A committee to draft a Declaration of Independence was set up in June of 1776 by Congress. Richard Henry Lee had previously introduced a resolution calling for full independence that mandated a declaration, a statement of foreign policy, and a constitution. On July 1 the Lee resolution was submitted to a general vote; it passed, although three states (Pennsylvania, New Jersey, and South Carolina) opposed it and one state abstained (New York). Since this scarcely constituted a united front, the resolution was submitted to a vote again the next day. Private conversations among representatives during the night produced a unanimous vote (New York still abstained since its delegates, though favoring independence, felt they must wait for instructions from the new rebel government just forming in their state). Strictly speaking, it was this resolution penned by Richard Henry Lee and passed on July 2 that officially severed all connections between the thirteen colonies and Britain.

The Declaration itself was prepared by a committee of five delegates appointed by Congress on June 11. Its members were Thomas Jefferson, John Adams, Benjamin Franklin, Roger Sherman, and Robert R. Livingston. Jefferson wrote a rough draft that was corrected by both Adams and Franklin. This corrected version was submitted to the committee on June 28. On July 3, the day after virtually unanimous approval of Lee's resolution, members began discussion of the committee's report. The following day, July 4, the text was approved and put into final form. The actual signing, however, did not occur until some weeks later as delegates, fully empowered to do so by their state legislatures, appended their signatures to the Declaration of Independence, thus assuring that their new nation would henceforth chart its own course and that they would win immortality as its founding fathers.

The Declaration is divided into two parts, the first of which offers a moral and legal justification for rebellion on the basis of natural rights. No longer were Americans invoking their rights as British subjects—a useless argument since they wanted to withdraw from the British Empire. Rather, they were invoking "the laws of nature and of nature's God." Reiterating a belief long held by British political philosophers, Jefferson stated that all governments derive "their just powers from the consent of the governed" and that "whenever any government becomes destructive of these ends, it is the right of the people to alter or to abolish it." In the second part, Jefferson listed the American grievances against the king. Before now, of course,

the colonists had seen Parliament as the enemy. But in the Declaration, Parliament was never named, and it was the king who was singled out as the tyrant. Taking this stand was not only a good strategy for eliciting the sympathy of Europeans, who were more likely to sympathize with a revolt against a cruel king than one against an elected assembly, but the omission of all mention of Parliament also was the final slap in the face against that institution. The colonists were implicitly denying, once and for all, the legal connection between Parliament and America.

The Logistics of War

In 1775, even as the colonies were creating new state governments, a war was in progress. By July 3, 1775, George Washington had taken command of the Massachusetts militia near Boston—and not until eight years later was peace finally secured.

America and its new governing body, the Continental Congress, were peculiarly unsuited for the strenuous tasks of fighting a war. Congress had no power to tax citizens or to draft soldiers. There were no organized armies beyond the groups of local militia. There were few arms and munitions, almost no cash, no military manuals—nothing. And America had no allies.

Financing the war was a challenge that Congress could meet only by issuing paper money in larger and larger amounts until the currency lost virtually all its value. By the end of 1775, Congress already had printed $6 million; by the end of 1776, $25 million; and by the end of 1779, $263 million. Inflation reached such ridiculous levels that at one point 170 continental dollars were worth about only one gold dollar.

The other principal means of raising money was through loans from foreign governments, but until 1780 such aid was limited. France provided the most help—in the form of money, supplies, and material. Total French aid amounted to more than $2 million; Spain contributed about $70,000 and Holland came up with $32,000.

Financial matters were made worse by the corruption and avarice found in all wartime situations. The Quartermaster General, Nathaniel Greene, thought nothing of handing out the best war contracts to his own private firm. Congressmen speculated by investing in privateer ships that preyed on British shipping and turned over the spoils to the investors—no matter that these pirate vessels used up supplies desperately needed by the American navy.

No less disheartening was the struggle to raise troops. Militiamen, as one would expect, remained attached to their own states, and, though they might take up arms to drive the enemy away from their homes, they would not travel elsewhere nor would they sustain any prolonged campaign. Nathaniel Greene, for instance, knowing that his southern militia would not stay in the field through a bloody battle, put them in the front lines, where they might shoot at least once before running.

The only real troops were the "continentals," those who served long-term enlistments and were recruited from each of the state governments. By 1777 the states were unable to fill these quotas through volunteers and were forced to draft men. Unfortunately, the Continental army and the state militias competed for supplies and failed to act together. However, this picture of inflation, corruption, wartime profits, and the scramble for manpower should not overshadow considerable sacrifice, heroism, and devotion to a cause that thousands obviously thought just, worth fighting for, and even worth dying for. The patriot death rate was about twelve percent (the American death rate in World War II was about two percent). The enemy grappled with precisely the same problems and admittedly demonstrated the same valor, the same sense of duty. One of the biggest dilemmas facing rebel leaders was how to sustain interest in a struggle that waxed and waned as it drifted southward from Boston, eventually touching every former colony in one way or another and even involving Canada and various regions not in revolt.

Blacks and the War

When Congress in July 1775 called for volunteers to join state militia units, blacks stepped forward and served, especially in New England. Ten months after Lexington and Concord, however, blacks began to be excluded from the various armed forces; whites were afraid that if free blacks were armed they would stage insurrections and liberate slaves.

Phillis Wheatley

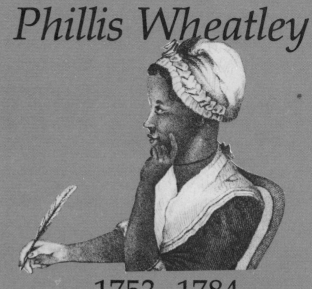

1753–1784

The first black woman poet in America, Phillis Wheatley was born in West Africa, perhaps Senegal, and was brought to Boston as a slave when about eight years old. There she was purchased by John Wheatley, a well-to-do merchant tailor, whose household included his wife, eighteen-year-old twins (Nathaniel and Mary), and a handful of elderly slaves. The family found Phillis alert and eager to learn and within eighteen months Mary taught her English. By the later 1760s she was corresponding with important people and writing poems which Boston, New York, and Philadelphia printers distributed on broadsides or sheets. The novelty of these accomplishments attracted considerable attention and won her special privileges such as light household chores and free time to increase her literary output.

In 1771 Phillis became a member of the Old South Church, and two years later (in an effort to revive her frail health) she accompanied Nathaniel on a business trip to England. While there, the young poet was a guest of the Countess of Huntingdon, whom she had praised in an elegy. Much impressed, the Countess arranged for publication of a volume of her writing, *Poems on Various Subjects, Religious and Moral*. This 128-page booklet includes works on virtue, Harvard College, King George III, and morning and evening. It also includes odes lamenting the demise of persons great and small, all of which brim with classical and Biblical allusions. One of the most interesting poems is this brief personal comment.

'Twas mercy brought me from my Pagan land,
Taught my benighted soul to understand
That there's a God, that there's a Saviour too;
Once I redemption neither sought nor knew,
Some view our sable race with scornful eye,
'Their color is a diabolic die.'
Remember, Christians, Negroes, black as Cain,
May be refin'd, and join th' angelic train.

Phillis's moment of triumph was brief, for she was recalled to America to attend the dying Mrs. Wheatley. After the death of her master four years later, she gained her freedom and married a free black by whom she had three children (two of whom died in infancy). Although talented, her husband proved to be a poor provider; deserting his family, he ended up in a debtors' prison. Phillis took a job in a cheap boarding house, but her health failed; and she and her remaining child died on December 5, 1784.

Nearly everyone is impressed by the achievements of this remarkable woman—a slave girl who learned English and wrote some forty-five poems that won acclaim on both sides of the Atlantic—but the quality of her work has often been questioned. Thomas Jefferson thought her compositions "below the dignity of criticism," words that elicited abuse from abolitionists in following decades. Black historians of today concede her lines are too imitative and too stylized. Nevertheless, considering the handicaps she surmounted, Phillis Wheatley remains a unique figure in American literary history.

The British were not plagued with such fears. Their own difficulties in raising soldiers were formidable. About one-third of the British soldiers were hired mercenaries, mostly Germans; another third were American Tories; and only the remaining third actually British. To keep up manpower, the royal governor of Virginia created what he called his Ethiopian Regiment and issued a proclamation inviting blacks to join. Eventually about 800 Virginia slaves joined the British.

In the end, the patriots were forced to rely on black soldiers and sailors. Whites were permitted to send blacks to the army in their stead if called upon to serve, and by the summer of 1778 the Continental army was regularly enlisting blacks for three-year stints, most of whom came from New England states. All of the states from North Carolina and farther north made provisions for enlisting blacks. Blacks and whites served together in racially mixed units, although blacks generally did not bear arms.

What is important here is that a revolutionary spirit seemed to hold the promise of freedom for all blacks, a better life for all oppressed classes, regardless of color or status. Ominously, the Continental Congress briefly discussed blaming the king for the slave trade while debating the Declaration of Independence, but then dropped the idea. This decision, portent of much serious debate in the future, demonstrates the ambivalent attitude of the founding fathers toward freedom, a "blind spot" the British exploited to the fullest throughout the war.

One black woman, poet Phillis Wheatley, played an unusual role. In October 1775 she wrote to George Washington enclosing a poem, "His Excellency Gen. Washington," which four times referred to the emerging nation as "Columbia" and termed its military leader "first in peace and honours," long before such words were used by others. A few months later, somewhat belatedly, Washington answered, praising her work and inviting her to visit him, which she did at Cambridge in March 1776. (A biographical sketch in this chapter provides more details of this poet's remarkable life.)

Winning the War

Until the end of 1776, most of the fighting was concentrated in New England, where the first conflicts had broken out. After 1776 the war generally drifted southwards, though there were exceptions to this. The most important of these involved the frontier.

American Indians were an immediate concern of both the British and Americans. Throughout the war, the British tried with some success to convince tribes to fight the former colonists while the Americans alternated policies of neutrality with punitive expeditions. The southern states decided in 1776 to mount an offensive to neutralize the Indian tribes. They declared war on the Cherokees and organized devastating campaigns that destroyed much of the Indian food supply. A treaty signed in 1777 committed the Cherokees to peace. Those who could not accept the treaty moved southwest and attacked settlers pushing into Tennessee. Throughout the war settlers moving into Kentucky and Tennessee met stiff Indian resistance, which led Virginia to send George Rogers Clark to the area. Further north, the Iroquois were divided by the war; in the Confederacy the largest number followed Joseph Brandt and Guy Johnson in joining the British. The Iroquois cooperated with Tory troops on a number of expeditions into the New York and Pennsylvania frontiers. The colonists responded with a punitive expedition led by John Sullivan in 1779 that destroyed most of the Indians' food supplies and forced the Iroquois to depend even more upon the British.

Until 1781 the British controlled the seas and could move their troops at will along the American coast. The American and state navies were helpless against this force and played no real role in the outcome, although there were individual high points, especially the exploits of John Paul Jones.

After the defeat at Lexington and Concord, the British troops were penned in Boston by the militia. The Massachusetts militia leaders decided to fortify one of the several hills overlooking the city, Bunker Hill (though, in fact, the men selected Breed's Hill). On the afternoon of June 17, 1775, the British marched up the hill in orderly columns—and when the smoke cleared, it was evident that the Americans had dealt a stunning blow. Of the 2,400 British soldiers, half were hit and 226 were dead, including a sixth of all the English officers who would be killed or wounded in the Revolution. The Americans actually had been greatly outnumbered (there were only 1,600 patriots on Breed's Hill), and of those about 100 were killed and 267 wounded. Despite such losses, the patriots were jubilant. As one officer said, "I wish we could sell them another hill at the same price."

Technically, Bunker Hill was a British victory, for the redcoats drove the patriots off the promon-tory. Shortly after the battle, Washington arrived to take command and to create the Continental army. Of course, the selection of this man was no accident. He had military experience, an imposing presence, was well-to-do, and was living proof of cooperation between Virginia and Massachusetts, two of the most important states in the new nation. What he found were 16,000 badly organized Massachusetts militiamen, milling about and utterly lacking in discipline. Slowly Washington assembled a true army, though throughout the war he was plagued with desertions, mutinies, and rebellions.

In the early months of the war, the Americans scored several successes. Ethan Allen, assisted by Benedict Arnold, took Fort Ticonderoga on Lake Champlain in May 1775. The victory, not especially impressive since the fort was virtually deserted, nevertheless gave the Americans clear access to Canada and provided them with a wealth of cannons, which were hauled overland to Boston. There Washington used the cannons to fortify Dorchester Heights overlooking Boston. The British, realizing their hold on Boston was slipping, withdrew to Nova Scotia, taking with them the first Tory refugees.

Elated, the Americans decided to conquer Canada—if, as the cautious instruction from Congress phrased it, "it will not be disagreeable to the Canadians." The Americans led by Colonel Benedict Arnold and General Richard Montgomery, fully expected the Canadians to join them in battle against the tyrannical British. Nothing of the sort, however, happened, and the patriots, weakened by hunger and disease, were roundly defeated at Quebec.

Although defeated in the North, the Americans made up for their losses by repelling the British invasion of Charleston, South Carolina, in June 1776. The British had been led to believe that the Carolinas were loyal to the king. As the American Major General Charles Lee, a sloppy but jovial man, rushed to defend the South, a British force under General Sir Henry Clinton was heading to the same destination by water. The two armies clashed at Charleston; Clinton's force was augmented by fifty ships and 3,000 men that had come directly from Ireland under Charles Lord Cornwallis. The British, plagued by mosquitos and heat and heavily shelled by the fort commanding the harbor, were forced to give up and sail away, defeated.

Alarmed, Parliament created a new army of

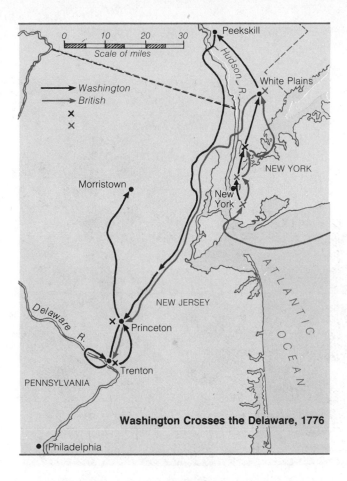

Washington Crosses the Delaware, 1776

Washington
British
×
×

Peekskill
White Plains
NEW YORK
New York
Morristown
NEW JERSEY
ATLANTIC OCEAN
Delaware R.
Princeton
Trenton
PENNSYLVANIA
Philadelphia
Hudson R.

Scale of miles
0   10   20   30

erably. The Battle of Long Island was Washington's first major battle, and he revealed his lack of experience at the encounter when he permitted the enemy to get behind him and nearly cut off any escape route from his island stronghold. And in September Howe easily pushed Washington off the nearby island of Manhattan. New York, the second largest city in the colonies, was surrendered to the enemy.

As winter set in, the prospect was bleak for the new country. Washington was hounded out of the New York area into New Jersey. There he conceived a plan for boosting morale. On Christmas Eve 1776, he made his famous crossing of the Delaware River and staged a surprise attack on Trenton where an encampment of German mercenaries, was taken with little struggle. Washington captured 909 men, whom he led across to Pennsylvania amidst general cheers. While this was a very minor victory, it did wonders for rebel morale.

In the spring of 1777, General Howe, dismayed by Washington's continued resistance, decided to capture the rebel capital of Philadelphia. In July he sailed with 15,000 men from New York to the head of Chesapeake Bay. Congress fled in panic. Washington attempted to stop Howe at Brandywine Creek on September 11, but his defeat at Long Island was repeated, for once again Howe outflanked the Americans. During the winter Howe remained in Philadelphia; there he was so comfortable that he remained "snug as a flea," as a later song put it. Washington moved his headquarters to Valley Forge, where ragged rebel troops suffered unbearably from the unusually cold weather and shortages of food and clothes.

Meanwhile, the British developed a brilliant (on paper) plan to split the colonies and end this troublesome rebellion. Howe was to contain the rebel army at Philadelphia and then move Northward while another British force, made up in part of Iroquois Indians and led by General John Burgoyne, was to advance southward from Canada, and a third army, comprised of Tory troops and Iroquois Indians, commanded by Colonel St. Leger, was to cut eastward across New York state from Lake Ontario and join up with Burgoyne and Howe. Burgoyne, after spending an idle year in Canada, descended upon Fort Ticonderoga, which he easily took. Buoyed up by this victory, Burgoyne pursued the Americans across an overland route. For the British, this trip was slow and arduous, since Burgoyne's personal baggage alone required

55,000 men under General William Howe and his brother, Admiral Richard Howe. As the leaders of such enormous forces, the Howe brothers should have made quick work of the former colonies. But they were saddled with contradictory and confusing orders from the king's ministers. The basic objectives were to subdue New England and destroy the Continental army. The fleet was ordered to support the land troops and also to capture or destroy American ships and ports. The Howes sometimes heeded these instructions, sometimes ignored them (after all, the round trip to England normally required four months, much too long to wait for guidance in fighting a war). The real reason the Howes hesitated in their prosecution of the war, however, was their hope that Americans sooner or later would recognize rebellion was hopeless and would come back into the British fold.

The first encounter between Washington and Howe was a disaster for Washington. When Howe and his men landed on Long Island on August 22, 1776, Washington attempted to stop them with only about 9,000 troops and no navy—and failed mis-

John Trumbull, who made a career of painting the great events of the Revolution, glorified Washington's victory at Trenton with this painting done while Washington was President.

thirty ponderous carts, and the company included a straggling retinue of officers' families and servants. Despite these handicaps, Burgoyne felt certain of success, since he knew that the entire Continental army was with Washington in Pennsylvania. Obviously it would be impossible for the Americans to raise another force.

But the impossible happened. Within six weeks after a new call to arms went out, the American general Horatio Gates was in command of 20,000 men, most of them New York and New England militia. Meanwhile, St. Leger was routed and turned back. Ironically, Howe never received precise instructions from England and remained in Philadelphia. Burgoyne, perplexed and outnumbered three to one, withdrew to Saratoga, his retreat constantly harassed by rebel raids. On October 17, 1777, Burgoyne was forced to surrender. Saratoga was a ma-

jor American victory and it had extremely important consequences; for it convinced European powers that the rebels did indeed have a chance of victory. The French, stinging from the results of the Seven Years' War and fearful that the British might now offer the Americans enough concessions to end the war, soon signed a treaty of commerce and a defensive alliance with the United States. The latter would take effect if Great Britain should go to war with France.

During this same period George Rogers Clark, with the backing of Virginia authorities, embarked upon an expedition against the British, the Shawnee Indians, and the Loyalists who were raiding settlements in the Ohio River Valley, the so-called "Old Northwest." On July 4, 1778, he occupied Kaskaskia; on December 17, took Vincennes; and early in 1779, overwhelmed a British force from

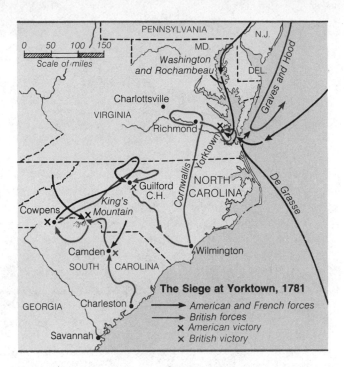

The Siege at Yorktown, 1781

→ American and French forces
→ British forces
✗ American victory
✗ British victory

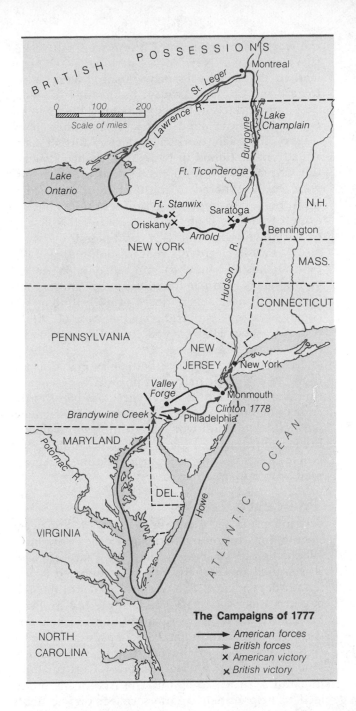

The Campaigns of 1777

→ American forces
→ British forces
✗ American victory
✗ British victory

Detroit. While the campaign had little effect upon events along the eastern seaboard, it gave rebel forces a secure claim to a vast region beyond the Appalachians.

In the spring of 1778 the British, realizing the war now threatened their far-flung empire, deserted Philadelphia and returned to New York, somewhat easier to defend than Philadelphia. By moving there, the British were able to dispatch troops to the West Indies where the French were threatening to seize British possessions. Washington pursued the British army as it made its way to New York, but he was unable to score a victory. The British settled in at New York as Washington kept a wary watch.

Although the British kept New York as their chief base, they conducted raids on the South during the rest of the war. Until now the South had not been the scene of much conflict. In May 1780 Sir Henry Clinton (who had replaced General Howe as supreme commander the preceding spring) conquered Charleston, South Carolina. Horatio Gates was sent south to defend the Carolinas against the British, but he received a thorough drubbing there. Nathaniel Greene replaced Gates and devised a new strategy. Rather than meeting the enemy head on, Greene tried to divide and conquer various army units on sites of his own choice. Week after week the British under Lord Cornwallis lost so

many men that, in despair, Cornwallis at last admitted defeat and turned his attention to the conquest of Virginia. Cornwallis settled at Portsmouth in July 1781 and then, soon afterwards, moved to Yorktown.

The Decisive Victory

At this point a long-awaited French fleet arrived, and with its aid the United States was able to win the war. Washington and Clinton were still locked in a stalemate in New York, but when Washington learned that twenty French warships were sailing toward the Chesapeake Bay, he decided to swoop down on Yorktown, thereby crushing the town between American land forces and French naval might. The plan worked perfectly. British naval squadrons stationed in New York rushed down to the Chesapeake Bay to head off the French, but were badly battered in the encounter and had to limp home for repairs. Washington, leading an army of American and French soldiers, laid seige to Yorktown, which quickly capitulated.

Fireworks went off in Philadelphia, and the bells in Boston churches rang all day. When the young James Madison heard the good news, he observed, "If these severe doses of ill fortune do not cool the phrenzy [sic] and relax the pride of Britain, it would seem Heaven had in reality abandoned her to her folly & her fate."

Diplomatic efforts of Benjamin Franklin and John Jay in Europe helped in no small way to make this astounding battlefield victory possible. Despite clumsy instructions from Congress, they effectively isolated Britain and won, in addition to invaluable French aid, financial loans and considerable good will for a weak, struggling, little republic as it grappled with a giant empire.

The Peace Treaty
Britain's pride had finally been "relaxed" and peace negotiations were opened soon after Yorktown. When the official treaty, called the Peace of Paris, was signed in 1783, the British recognized America's independence. The western border of the new country was to be the Mississippi, the northern border would follow the natural line of rivers and lakes near the fortieth parallel (almost exactly where it is today); but in the South the United States would stop short at the border of Florida which England returned to Spain. The Americans promised to help British creditors collect prewar debts and to cease confiscating Tory property, promises that were not kept for the most part. The British agreed to remove their troops with all deliberate speed.

Something momentous had happened. The world's greatest power had been defeated militarily by the collaborative efforts of a handful of its own colonies, and those colonies were now embarking on a great political experiment—independence and self-government.

Essay

Dissent in Time of War

Dissent is as American as apple pie, perhaps even more so because the thirteen colonies and the nation formed from them were born in dissent. To be truly effective, dissent involves action connoting clear disagreement with the avowed policies of a church, government officials, or a government structure, some agency or organization to which one ostensibly should give support. Balloting is a form of dissent, and all governments (even the sternest of dictatorships) recognize that some citizens inevitably will disagree with those in power. The First Amendment to the Constitution acknowledges the right of protest, the right to dissent and present publicly divergent views: "Congress shall make no law respecting an establishment of religion, or prohibiting the free exercise thereof; or abridging the freedom of speech, or of the press; of the right of the people peaceably to assemble, and to petition the Government for a redress of grievances."

Dissent in time of war, however, creates special problems for the combatants. It matters little whether they are engaged in a revolution, a formally declared state of hostilities resplendent with parchment, ribbons, and signatures, a guerrilla operation, or a "police action." The basic question is the same: to what extent can any government that is locked in what may be a life-or-death struggle permit its citizens to question fixed, ordained policies? Open, defiant criticism may convert others to their point of view, encourage the enemy to press on, and make it impossible for an established state—or a revolutionary force that hopes to supplant it—to defend itself. The rebels of the American Revolution soon uttered the same cry heard during every such upheaval: "All who are not with us are against us!"

But every American war, with the possible exception of World War II, has elicited considerable protest on the home front. American citizens have held scores of mass meetings, burned tons of effigies, thought up countless slogans, and uttered a torrent of angry words. The so-called "little" wars such as the War of 1812, the Mexican War, the

Spanish-American War, and the wars fought in Korea and Vietnam present the clearest examples of organized, highly vocal dissent. In each instance the fighting commenced with high resolves and general (if not totally enthusiastic) approval. Since these undertakings had the backing of a majority of the elected officials sitting in the United States Congress, one is forced to conclude that at the outset they enjoyed the support of the electorate as well.

But initial conditions have a way of changing drastically. In the second war with Britain, for example, New Englanders saw the diabolical hand of Napoleon and soon talked of secession at the Hartford Convention. Only Andrew Jackson's after-the-fact victory at New Orleans and the Ghent Treaty ended a savage threat to disunion. In the 1840s, many Americans questioned the morality of seizing land from Mexico, especially if they were Abolitionists who thought they discerned a scheme to create still more slave states. Henry Thoreau went to jail rather than pay taxes to support that war. His essay

Library of Congress.
Henry David Thoreau was jailed for refusing to pay taxes in protest of the Mexican-American War. While in jail, he wrote *Civil Disobedience.*

Library of Congress.
Jonathan Boucher, an Anglican minister who had taught Washington's stepson, was among the Loyalists who fled to British lines for protection. Boucher went into exile in England.

on "Civil Disobedience" grew out of these experiences. A government of majority rule, he cautioned, cannot be based on justice since the majority, at times, will consider only the expediency of the moment, not conscience. "A minority is powerless while it conforms to the majority; it is not even a minority then; but it is irresistible when it clogs by its whole weight. Under a government which imprisons any unjustly, the true place for a just man is also in prison."

The Spanish-American War, as it was very brief, aroused little outcry until it was over and the United States decided to keep the Philippines. Then a wave of anti-imperialism swept the nation as Mark Twain and other well-known voices railed in protest, one spokesman noting that all wars of conquest evoke the phrase, "My country, right or wrong!" "That spirit," he thundered, "ridicules morality, cows religious teaching and is the forerunner of national decay."

The Korean and Vietnamese experiences began quite differently but soon developed marked similarities. The Korean affair in 1950 burst like a thunderclap for all to hear; the quagmire in Vietnam started quietly in the early 1960s and gradually engulfed more and more of our national resources until it brought down a president and fractured American society. By the time a peace of sorts came in Korea, it was seen as a "no-win" war, a precursor of what happened in Vietnam a decade later.

What is striking about these five confrontations is that those who dissent strike two very familiar chords, one sounded by those on the left, the other by those on the right. The first group says the conflict is immoral and unjust; the second, that it is being carried on in a stupid manner. Those who protest are not allied with the enemy nor are they (for the most part) conscientious objectors opposed to war in principle. They apparently would fight in a moral war, if one could be found without too much trouble, or they might even join in the current sacrifice of money and blood if it were only conducted in a fashion more to their liking. These "little" wars clearly delineated the "ins" from the "outs." The established government was pursuing

policies that the Hartford Convention, the sage of Walden Pond, Samuel Clemens, those opposed to "limited" war in Korea, and millions perplexed by the agony of Vietnam (and America) did not like.

The two world wars present somewhat different aspects of dissent, as do the American Revolution and the Civil War. In each of the twentieth-century conflicts there was widespread conscription of manpower that met with some resistance, just as a rather capricious draft during Korea and Vietnam fed the fires of protest. Deferring college students, for example, permitted those who could afford college to buy their way out of serving their country. However, not hearing the request of the state to bear arms is a very old, rather personal game, even a semirespectable maneuver during an unpopular war; and, unless resistance to the draft becomes a highly organized, active force encouraging general disregard for the law within the nation itself, it cannot be classified as true dissent.

During World War I, Woodrow Wilson's government passed two sedition laws signaling that active opposition to wartime programs would be tantamount to treason. The American minister to the Netherlands even suggested that all dissenters be hanged. Under the terms of this legislation, some 1,500 citizens were arrested and many of them ended up behind bars. Ironically, in 1918 the producer of a movie, *The Spirit of '76,* about the American Revolution received a ten-year sentence for stirring up anti-British feeling!

The best-known of these World War I dissidents was Eugene V. Debs (1855–1926), five times Socialist candidate for president. In June 1918, Debs spoke in Canton, Ohio, where he stressed the deeply engrained opposition of all Socialists to war. Since men of draft age heard his words, under the terms of Wilson's new laws he was charged with sedition, convicted, and sentenced to ten years in prison. While there, he campaigned for the White House and got an astounding 920,000 votes. On Christmas Day, 1921, the man who won, Warren G. Harding, granted him a pardon.

Dissent during the American Revolution and the Civil War was a complex phenomenon, for both conflicts were, in fact, revolutions. The problem is, from a practical standpoint, as long as hostilities are underway, to whom does one actually owe allegiance? A Tory living in rebel-dominated Virginia might refuse to swear allegiance to the new regime. One of his grandsons living in the same state perhaps viewed the Confederacy with equal disdain, while another residing in Maryland gave it his wholehearted support and scorned federal rule. Of course, once peace came this dilemma was solved. The Tory had either to move elsewhere or to stay and accept a new way of things, and both of his descendants found themselves under firm federal authority once more. But during the war years, the Tory, the Confederate sympathizer, and the Unionist could maintain—and with considerable justification—that the governments about them, not they themselves, were in dissent.

If these individuals expressed their strongly held views within the confines of their own homes and made no effort to organize resistance to the rule of such men as Patrick Henry, Thomas Jefferson, Abraham Lincoln, and Jefferson Davis, then their antiregime stance should have concerned very few, except perhaps some overpatriotic neighbors. But this was not always the case. The state governments of Revolutionary War days and the Confederacy were new, unsure of themselves, and eager for the aura of respectability, and Lincoln's wartime administration was extremely sensitive to the threat posed by disloyalty. As a result, nonbelievers often had a rough time of it.

Even before the Declaration of Independence— in January 1776—the Continental Congress encouraged suppression of dissent by passing a resolution urging every state to act vigorously against those favorable to England and critical of the patriot cause. Six months later the Congress suggested that the states consider opposition to the war as treason, and some states declared that those suspected of British sympathies should forfeit their property without a hearing.

The Revolutionary War editor, as Arthur M. Schlesinger has tartly observed, enjoyed little "liberty of speech" unless he spoke "the speech of

liberty." Ministers whose sermons did not please rebel leaders had to seek out new pulpits. Loyalty oaths were commonplace in hundreds of colonial communities, and governors often used the state militia to maintain order (as they interpreted the word), seize dangerous Tories, and rout any groups suspected of aiding the enemy. Yet some prominent Tories—Ralph Wormley of Virginia and Daniel Dulany of Maryland among them—lived unmolested throughout the war. Apparently they posed no direct threat to the rebel cause. Editors and ministers, being more active and able to influence public opinion, clearly did.

During the Civil War, Lincoln's government arrested 13,000 citizens for antienlistment activity or aiding the enemy. Twenty-one newspapers were shut down. Early in July 1863, at the time that the crucial Battle of Gettysburg was running its course, an antidraft riot with racial overtones left hundreds dead in Manhattan. In Ohio, Indiana, and Illinois, Lincoln also harassed the "Copperheads," groups of disgruntled Democrats who wanted to preserve the Union by negotiation, not through open conflict. Although much maligned by their Republican critics, these dissident Democrats forcefully proved they were not rebel sympathizers by joining in battle against Confederate forces that invaded their homelands. Nonetheless, like the citizens who later on were opposed to our involvement in Korea and Vietnam, the Copperheads urged that peace be reached through give-and-take at the bargaining table, not through blood-and-death on the battlefield.

When eleven states seceded from the Union in 1861, they took with them a hard core of pro-Unionists who soon became openly critical of the Confederate cause, especially as the tide of war began to turn. One state, Virginia, was split asunder by secession, and another, Tennessee, almost went down the same road. Within a year or so "peace societies" began to appear in Arkansas, Texas, Alabama, Georgia, and North Carolina, complete with secret grips, passwords, and special oaths. Unlike Lincoln's federal government, which grew stronger, the Confederacy became steadily weaker,

The antiwar leaders of the North are satirized in this cartoon, which suggests that the Confederates found their terms and conditions for peace extremely offensive. (Note the pious figure of Lincoln behind the humble bearer of the peace offer.)

so much so that during the last two years of the war the manpower and resources of entire sections such as northern Alabama and the mountain counties in several other states were denied to the southern cause.

It is obvious that (1) the United States Constitution recognizes the right of dissent, (2) a nation cannot defend itself in time of war if dissent becomes too pervasive, and (3) conflicts that drag on and become unpopular inevitably foment more and more protest. They may even reach a point at which some individuals become firmly convinced that righteousness actually lies in the cause of the enemy, not in that of their own nation. This occurred in the Revolutionary War, in the Civil War, in Vietnam, and perhaps in other conflicts as well. As Abe Fortas, a former U.S. Supreme Court justice, wrote at the height of the Vietnam holocaust, "Wars tend to create danger or the fear of danger to the state, and the state is always apt to respond to fear by taking measures which its officials consider necessary for its defense, and which sometimes are far more drastic than justified."

This, then, is the basic dilemma posed by dissent in time of war, especially in a republic that prides itself on free speech, a free press, and the right of peaceful protest. To stifle criticism a government may resort to controls that transform the state into a replica of the enemy. At that juncture citizens may well ask: "Why fight?" Although Fortas does not say so, what is essential to a republic engaged in war—if it is to remain a republic—is *not* to respond to dissent in so unjustified a manner that it changes itself into a dictatorship. For, if it shelves basic freedoms "for the duration of the emergency," a government may discover it, too, is put aside by its citizens because they value those freedoms highly. When a citizenry can no longer tell the difference between its own government and that of its adversary, then a war is effectively lost, regardless of what the enemy may do.

SELECTED READINGS

Background to the War

David Ammerman, *In the Common Cause: American Response to the Coercive Acts of 1774* (1974)

Oliver M. Dickerson, *Navigation Acts and the American Revolution* (1951)

Benjamin Labaree, *The Boston Tea Party* (1964)

Pauline Maier, *From Resistance to Revolution* (1972)

Edmund Morgan, *The Stamp Act Crisis: Prologue to Revolution*, rev. ed. (1962)

John Shy, *Toward Lexington: the British Army in the Coming of the American Revolution* (1965)

Participants in the War

Robert Gross, *The Minutemen and their World* (1976)

Ira D. Gruber, *The Howe Brothers and the American Revolution* (1972)

William Nelson, *The American Tory* (1961)

James H. O'Donnoll, III, *Southern Indians and the American Revolution* (1973)

Benjamin Quarles, *The Negro in the American Revolution* (1961)

Paul Smith, *Loyalists and Redcoats: A Study in British Revolutionary Policy* (1964)

Jack Sosin, *Revolutionary Frontier* (1967)

Conduct of the War

Howard Peckham, *The War for Independence* (1958)

Eric Robson, *The American Revolution in its Political and Military Aspects* (1966)

Marshall Smelser, *The Winning of Independence* (1972)

Growth of Constitutional Thought

Bernard Bailyn, *The Ideological Origins of the American Revolution* (1967)

Carl Becker, *The Declaration of Independence* (1922)

David Hawke, *Transactions of Free Men: Declaration of Independence* (1964)

Merrill Jensen, *The Articles of Confederation* (1940)

Gary Wills, *Inventing America: Jefferson's Declaration of Independence* (1978)

Gordon Wood, *The Creation of the Republic, 1776-1787* (1969)

Diplomacy

Samuel Flagg Bemis, *The Diplomacy of the American Revolution* (1935)

Richard B. Morris, *The Peacemakers: Great Powers and American Independence* (1965)

Richard Van Alstyne, *Empire and Independence: American Revolution* (1965)

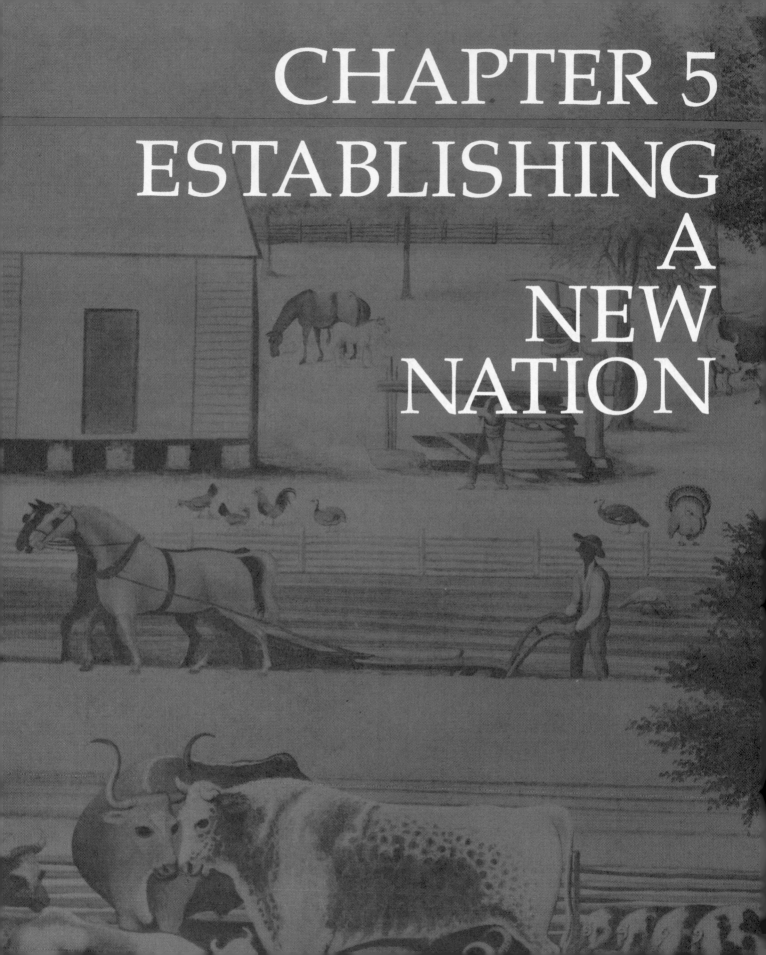

CHAPTER 5
ESTABLISHING A NEW NATION

TIMELINE

1775
Settlement of Kentucky

1776
Declaration of Independence

1777
Articles of Confederation drafted

1781
Ratification of Articles of Confederation

1783
Treaty of Paris

1784
Ordinance of 1784

1785
Land Ordinance of 1785

1786
Shays' Rebellion

1786
Annapolis Convention

1787
Northwest Ordinance

1787
Constitutional Convention

1789
Constitution takes effect with George Washington as President

1791
Philip Freneau established *National Gazette*

1791
Bill of Rights

1791
Establishment of the Bank of the United States

1792
Washington reelected President

1794
Whiskey Rebellion

1794
Jay's Treaty

1795
Treaty of Greenville

1795
Treaty of San Lorenzo or Pinckney's Treaty

1796
John Adams elected President and Thomas Jefferson elected Vice President

1797
XYZ Affair

1798
The Alien and Sedition Acts

1800
Jefferson defeats Adams in presidential election.

CHAPTER OUTLINE

In the years following the Revolution, American leaders were deluged with problems. The solutions they came up with have influenced all subsequent national history. The travail of those exciting years contributed to the settling of the Old Northwest, establishing a strong central government under George Washington, developing a two-party system, creating a foreign policy, and making something we now call our "national character." In 1787 Dr. Benjamin Rush (ca. 1745–1813), a well-known Philadelphia physician, saw clearly the task ahead for the nation.

"The American war is over, but this is far from being the case with the American Revolution. On the contrary, nothing but the first act of the great drama is closed. It remains yet to establish and perfect our new forms of government; and to prepare

Courtesy of the University of Pennsylvania.
Dr. Benjamin Rush of Philadelphia wanted to shape the new nation. He urged the education of women and an end to slavery as two reforms needed to create a virtuous republic.

the principles, morals, and manners of our citizens for these forms of government after they are established and brought to affection."

Western Expansion

During the Revolutionary era the states functioned as nearly autonomous powers and nowhere was this more evident than in territory some of them claimed beyond the Appalachians. From 1781 to 1789, the United States was (or rather *were*) governed under the Articles of Confederation, a document that placed virtually no restraints upon the states. In fact, the Articles were designed specifically to protect states' rights against those of a central government.

The first settlers moved into Kentucky in 1775, and throughout the Revolution westward expansion continued. At every point the conflicting claims of states led to squabbles and even bloodshed. In several cases original settlers who held claims from one state were violently dispossessed by those who held claims granted by another.

The dissolution of ties with England did not resolve any of these disputes, for the states based their claims on long-established royal charters. These charters had created an inequity from the very beginning, since Georgia, the Carolinas, Virginia, Connecticut, and Massachusetts all received the right to lands west of their own boundaries—sometimes all the way to the Pacific Ocean; the other colonies had few territorial claims beyond their borders.

Land disputes figured so prominently in American politics that they delayed ratification of the Articles of Confederation until 1781. Maryland refused to sign until Virginia ceded her western lands to the national government.

These disputes became acute since the population in the West was growing steadily throughout the Revolutionary era. By 1790 there were more than 100,000 settlers in the territory beyond the Appalachians. The frontier needed protection, government, and a legal system. It especially needed to be defended against Indian tribes who resented this usurpation of their traditional lands.

Because the national government was too weak to aid the settlers, they frequently took matters into their own hands. Kentucky pioneers created their own legislature in 1776 but petitioned for statehood to no avail. Virginia offered the area the status of a county and maintained Kentucky as a private possession until 1792. Settlers in eastern Tennessee set up an independent government, but North Carolina refused to recognize the independence of the area and made it a county as well. At one time North Carolina ceded Tennessee to the Continental Congress, then withdrew the offer. The settlers of Vermont, although active as patriots in the early years of the Revolution, eventually entered into secret talks with the British government in hopes of gaining recognition as an independent state or country.

The first step toward achieving ratification of the Articles of Confederation and thereby promoting a national government of sorts depended upon solving the problem of the western lands. By making Congress sole owner of most of those lands, the states not only reduced their own rivalries but also provided the national government with a source of income. The Continental Congress was not allowed to tax Americans; but by selling off western lands, it could raise badly needed funds. And, perhaps most importantly, the cessions constituted a strong move toward nationalization.

Although the Articles of Confederation provided for some sort of central authority, this government had little power. Only with actual implementation of a new constitution in 1789 did the nation in general and the West in particular have a strong hand at the helm. Nevertheless, under the Articles, Congress did begin to work out a national land policy. The Ordinance of 1784 divided lands north of the Ohio River (the Old Northwest region) into sixteen districts, established a pattern of limited self-government, and arranged for a logical process leading to statehood when the population of each district reached 20,000. Although later repealed, this legislation drafted by Thomas Jefferson is important because it introduced the fundamental concept of territorial government. The Ordinance of 1785 set up a plan for surveying western lands so they could be sold more readily. Each entire region was divided into ranges, sections, and townships, all divisions being made in square units. A township, was six miles square and was broken up into thirty-six units, each one square mile. Every sixteenth section of a town was set aside for the maintenance of a school. This plan has imposed a grid pattern on most of the American landscape.

The imprint of the Northwest Ordinances is still obvious throughout the Midwest. Roads and farm fields follow the old section and range lines.

Finally, the Northwest Ordinance (1787) revised the earlier 1784 Ordinance in order to give Congress greater control over the frontier and to delay statehood until each area was more adequately settled. It decreed that no less than three nor more than five states could be carved out of the Northwest. During the initial years of settlement a territory would be ruled by a governor, a secretary, and three judges, all appointed by Congress. When the area had 5,000 free adult male citizens, it could send a representative to Congress, but that representative would not have the right to vote. The territory also could elect a legislature and begin the process of self-government, but that body had to submit all of its proposals to the governor. Only when the territory had a population of 60,000 could it become a full-fledged state. Slavery, although at first permitted, was forbidden throughout the Northwest Territory after 1787 and religious freedom was guaranteed.

These three ordinances embody an orderly process by which new states, once they have sufficient population, can join the republic on a par with the old. This means that, instead of creating a central-ized empire with a galaxy of dependent and politically inferior colonies, the United States of America became a constantly expanding republic. Also, these acts gave Congress complete control over frontier growth and helped to unify a young, struggling nation.

Creating
a
Government

To a large extent the American Revolution was fought over the constitutional question of the power of the British Parliament. The American colonies argued that their own legislatures should be supreme in deciding internal affairs. Each colonial legislature was regarded as a parliament in its own right. When the states attempted to form a national government, they were wary of yielding their hard-won authority to a central congress. As early as 1774 a Continental Congress convened, but it merely passed resolutions, not laws. With the outbreak of war Congress took on more power and created a Continental army and navy, although it had not been authorized by the states to do so. When Congress drew up the Declaration of Independence in 1776, it also decided to write a framework for central government. A year later that document, known as the Articles of Confederation, was completed, and Congress began to act under its provisions even though it was not ratified by all the states until 1781.

The Articles provided for a very weak central government. The state legislatures jealously guarded their right to tax, and Congress received funds only through state appropriations. Moreover, Congress was not given any means to force its decisions on the states. There was no chief executive, although the President of Congress could act as a ceremonial head of state, and there was no judiciary. The sovereignty of the states was underlined by the fact that each state, no matter what its size or population cast only one vote in Congress.

The Articles did concede to Congress a number of specific powers that later would be incorporated into the Constitution. Congress controlled foreign affairs, including the signing of treaties, and the army. And it could issue currency and borrow money. The legislators themselves were granted immunities similar to those enjoyed by the members of Parliament in Britain. They were guaranteed freedom of debate, the right to decide on the length, place, and dates of their own meetings, the right to choose their own officers, and the right to be free from arrest except for major crimes.

The two chief powers that the Articles denied the national government were the power to tax and the power to regulate commerce. Nevertheless, Congress was not totally impotent. It conducted a successful war against the British; it worked out a viable foreign policy whereby the United States formed military and political alliances with other countries and received large foreign loans; and it wrote the various ordinances that regulated western expansion.

The shortcomings of the Articles, however, were manifest. The legislators formed many small committees through which all important business was conducted. The committee system became so tangled that soon Congress decided to reorganize itself; in 1781 the plethora of committees was reduced to a few executive departments. But no amount of reorganization could combat the problem of absenteeism. Toward the end of the rule of the Congress, there were several months during which it could not get a quorum.

Since Congress relied upon appropriations from the states for its funds, it was unable to deal with the huge national and foreign debt. To meet interest payments on foreign loans, Congress was forced to borrow money from Dutch bankers—which, of course, only increased the deficit. In 1786 the United States defaulted on interest payments due French citizens. The money owed to Americans, on the other hand, was paid after each state assumed the responsibility for paying its own citizens.

The Critical Period

Historians have long debated over the period from 1781 to 1789, during which the national government functioned under the Articles of Confederation. These years were first called the "Critical Period" by John Fiske (1842–1901), who wrote a book by that title in the 1880s. Fiske argued that the difficulties of this period led the Founding Fathers to write the Constitution in order to ensure a much stronger form of government. According to Fiske, the Constitution saved America from civil and financial disorder and crowned the Revolution with a strong national government.

One manifestation of civil and financial disorder came in an outbreak of violence among frontier farmers who were protesting foreclosures on their farms in western Massachusetts. Under the leadership of Daniel Shays (about whom more information can be found in a biographical sketch in this chapter), a small army prevented the state supreme court from meeting and attacked the arsenal at Springfield. Eventually, the uprising was put down, but not before many Americans became gravely concerned that this anarchy and violence might spread to their communities. This concern about the crisis in Massachusetts was heightened when it became apparent that legally Congress had no right to assist the state of Massachusetts in putting down what became known as Shays' Rebellion.

Later historians, led by Charles A. Beard, challenged Fiske's interpretation of the 1780s. In particular, Beard's follower, Merrill Jensen, stressed the positive aspects of the Articles of Confederation and suggested that they were more democratic than the Constitution. According to this thesis, the so-

Daniel Shays

ca.1747–1825

A humble Massachusetts farmer, Daniel Shays, led an insurrection in western Massachusetts in the 1780s that is known to history as "Shays' Rebellion." This uprising of the poor was so distressing to propertied Americans that it strengthened their resolve to draw up a Constitution that would ensure orderly, stable government.

The date of birth and early life of Shays remain obscure, but it is known that he served gallantly during the Revolution and was commissioned a captain in 1777. He seems to have been popular both with subordinates and fellow officers. Shortly before fighting ceased, Lafayette presented Shays with a handsome sword, which he subsequently was forced to sell when he fell upon hard times.

In 1780 Shays settled in Pelham, Massachusetts, where he became a member of the Committee of Safety and was elected to various town offices. Several years later a depression aroused widespread unrest among the poor farmers along the frontier. In 1786 the people of western Massachusetts met in several conventions and lodged objections to their high land taxes. A band of insurgents prevented the court of common pleas from acting against debtors. Shays, commanding 800 men, finally agreed to let the court sit if it would agree not to convict farmers unable to pay their mortgages.

During the winter of 1786–1787, Shays and his men realized their grievances would not be settled peaceably. He attacked the arsenal at Springfield and was defeated by the Massachusetts militia, which finally routed his troops at Petersham. Shays was captured and condemned to death by the state's supreme court, but he was soon pardoned.

After this brief moment of notoriety, Shays moved to New York, where he spent the rest of his days as a farmer. Although he had little education, Shays proved he possessed leadership qualities and could arouse loyalty among the discontented. He clearly was convinced that the rebellion of 1786–1787 was merely another stage of the Revolution, and many observers—men in positions of power in a newly independent United States of America—feared that ex-Captain Daniel Shays of the Fifth Massachusetts might be right. During the ratification debate in Massachusetts, Jonathan Smith referred to Shays' Rebellion as "a black cloud that rose in the east last winter and spread over the west. . . . People that used to live peaceably, and were before good neighbors, got distracted and took up arms against the government." Smith emphasized that the Constitution was an obvious cure "for these disorders", and many of his fellow citizens agreed.

called "critical period" was not truly critical. The states were beginning to pay off the national debt, and Congress was about to receive independent income from the sale of western lands granted to it by the states. Lack of a strong central government actually was a blessing, since the powerful state governments were more responsive to the electorate than any national congress could have been.

Recently a more subtly shaded interpretation of the period has emerged. Today historians recognize that the Articles of Confederation functioned reasonably well, especially during the late 1780s. And there were many Americans, independent small farmers, for example, who suffered little during this period. Nevertheless, in the opinion of these present-day historians, the nation faced grave problems that Congress under the Articles could not solve. Britain refused to leave frontier posts, state duties hampered interstate trade, and all efforts to amend the Articles to grant revenue to the national government failed.

The Constitutional Convention

The convention that wrote the Constitution began its meetings in May 1787, but it was far from a formal, full-dress affair. In fact, the gathering happened almost by accident, and deliberation of the Constitution was well under way before most of the delegates completely understood and accepted what they were doing.

In September 1786 five states sent delegates to a convention in Annapolis called by the Virginia legislature to discuss trade regulations among the states. This meeting clearly was illegal since only Congress had the power to convene such a meeting. Nothing was accomplished—except Alexander Hamilton (1755–1804) recommended that the states should send delegates to Philadelphia the following May "to devise such further provisions as shall appear to them necessary to render the Constitution of the Foederal [sic] Government adequate to the exigencies of the Union." The purpose of the Philadelphia convention, therefore, was to revise the Articles of Confederation, not to write a new Constitution. Congress specifically limited the upcoming convention to "the sole purpose of revising the Articles of Confederation."

The first meeting of the Federal Convention was held on May 14. Even when the convention was in full swing, no delegates from New Hampshire appeared since that state had no funds for representatives. Rhode Island never named or sent

delegates. Some states chose as their delegates to the convention men who were members of Congress, which met in New York.

Nevertheless, once the convention began to function, it was quite obviously a collection of the most distinguished men in the country. Nine signers of the Declaration of Independence were among the company. George Washington, who at fifty-five was universally revered as the hero of the Revolution, presided over the session.

Almost as famous as Washington was Benjamin Franklin who, at eighty-one, could look back on almost sixty years of accomplishment. He was a seasoned negotiator, having helped to draft the Declaration of Independence and draw up the peace treaty with Britain. Missing, however, were four well-known Revolutionary figures. Patrick Henry refused to attend and later led the antiratification forces in Virginia. Thomas Jefferson, minister to France, followed the proceedings with avid interest and, unlike Henry, strongly favored the new document. John Hancock, at first opposed to the Constitution, at length gave it his support as presiding officer of the Massachusetts ratifying convention. Samuel Adams, also a member of that body, followed the lead of Hancock, his political rival. Assured that a bill of rights would be added, he eventually backed ratification.

Almost all of the delegates who did attend had served at one time or another as congressmen—and this experience gave most of them a nationalistic outlook. New York had as one of its delegates thirty-year-old Alexander Hamilton, the supreme advocate of a strong federal government.

The other members of the assembly included ministers, doctors, and the governors of several states. They were a highly educated, relatively young group (average age forty-three), and for the most part represented the propertied interests of the new nation. This was the rising class of state and national leaders who, thanks to the departure of royal government and royal appointees, had moved into positions of power. And with this new prominence came money, land, and a somewhat more conservative outlook than that evident a dozen or so years earlier when these men were rebels against King George III. Virginia undoubtedly had the most distinguished representatives, and outstanding among them was James Madison (1751–1836). He spoke frequently and kept careful notes on the debates, which many years later were published. Madison, instrumental in arranging the

Annapolis convention, arrived at Philadelphia with very firm ideas concerning how to reform the Articles of Confederation. Even before the sessions got under way, he wrote to Washington and others describing his scheme for a strong central authority, the so-called "Virginia Plan," which actually went beyond mere reform and created a new governmental structure.

Constitutional Compromises

The convention almost immediately decided to keep its sessions totally secret—ostensibly, according to George Mason of Virginia, because secrecy was "a necessary precaution to prevent misrepresentation or mistakes," but in part because secrecy allowed the delegates to consider far more extensive governmental changes than any state would have permitted them to make. Secrecy also permitted freewheeling discussion and compromise. At the same time, the body could present a unified front to the public. From the outset members agreed that each state would vote as a unit.

Throughout the convention one of the main subjects of debate was Madison's Virginia plan, a sweeping call for constitutional change. This plan divided the government into three branches: executive, legislative, and judicial. A national, two-house legislature would choose a chief executive for a single seven-year term. Each state would be represented in that body by a number of delegates proportional to its population. While adult male citizens with the franchise would elect the lower house, that body would choose the upper from among candidates proposed by the state assemblies. The executive branch would have the right to veto bills passed by the legislature. The most striking feature, other than proportional representation, was that the legislature could veto state laws which it thought prejudicial to the national interest.

All of these changes (still called "amendments" to the Articles of Confederation) would be ratified by state conventions elected by the people specifically for that purpose, not the state legislatures. This provision had both ideological and practical repercussions. It effectively bypassed the state legislatures, seen only as agents to carry out powers delegated by the electorate. The Virginia plan was based firmly on the will of the people themselves.

The plan was discussed, revised, and attacked during the Convention, but the states that favored the plan consistently outvoted those that disap-

Virginia State Library.

George Mason of Virginia considered the Virginia Bill of Rights one of his most important contributions to law. He opposed the federal Constitution for not including a similar grant.

proved of it. The one aspect of the plan that drew the most wrath from the smaller states (led by New Jersey and Connecticut) was the decision to base representation on population. States with smaller populations and little chance of growth feared that their interests never would be adequately represented in such a Congress.

William Patterson of New Jersey introduced an alternative proposal. According to this plan, basically a mere revision of the Articles of Confederation, the national legislature would represent the states and not the people. Each state would have only one vote, no matter how large or small it might be. Northern states generally supported Patterson's "small-state" scheme. The bigger southern states objected on the grounds that, since the new Congress would have the power to tax, it was unfair for a few people to decide what the majority must pay. Benjamin Franklin neatly summarized the conflict.

"The diversity of opinions turns on two points. If a proportional representation takes place, the small States contend that their liberties will be in danger. If an equality of votes is to be put in its place, the large States say their money will be in danger. . . . Both sides must part with some of their demands, in order that they both join in some accomodating proposition."

After careful discussion the problem was turned over to a committee, which worked out a compromise. The lower house would be left proportional, but in the upper house states would have equal representation. This arrangement aroused the anxiety of Madison, among others, who believed that once states were recognized as independent entities, the whole concept of a strong federal government would collapse. But these fears were somewhat misplaced: the delegates agreed that the members of the upper house (the Senate) would vote as individuals; they thus emphasized that the Senators were accountable to the people they represented, not to their respective state governments.

At this point, the end of July, the convention adjourned for ten days to give the Committee of Detail time to write a draft of the new Constitution. But once the draft was prepared, debate broke out anew. The conflicts were now clearly sectional. Southern states feared that the congressional power to regulate commerce might be used against them and in the interest of merchants in the North. The South wanted the passage of bills regulating duties to be decided in Congress by a two-thirds majority. Many northerners were interested in banning the slave trade, not only for humanitarian reasons but also because northern farmers did not want to compete with slave labor, especially in the western territories. But more immediately a dispute arose over two questions: should slaves be counted as population in determining a state's representation in the House? Should the value of slaves be included in computing taxable property?

The solution to this dispute required two trade-offs. Duties, like all other bills, would be passed in Congress by a simple majority, not by a two-thirds majority (a victory for the North). In return, the slave trade could not be abolished until after 1807 (a victory for the South). Slaves would be counted for purposes of taxation (a point for the North), but also for determining representation (a point for the South). However, slaves would not be counted in the same way as free white citizens. Only three-fifths of the slave population in each state would be counted for representation or taxation purposes. This ratio was not pulled out of thin air. Under the Articles of Confederation, Congress had, in a similar fashion, been using that ratio (3:5) to determine the amount of money each state had to contribute to the federal government.

The final issue to be settled was the presidency. Many people were wary of the seven-year term proposed by the Virginia plan (a term that could not be renewed through reelection). Since the President was to be given impressive powers, infrequent elections would allow him to assume the authority of a monarch. Alexander Hamilton was almost alone in not being adverse to a powerful executive. In fact, he wanted the President elected for life, as well as the members of the Senate, and, according to Hamilton, the states themselves should be under the rule of the federal government, which would appoint the various governors.

During August and September, the convention discussed the powers and duties of the President and finally agreed that his term of office would be not seven years but four and that he could be reelected. The first draft of the Constitution, as prepared by the Committee of Detail, stipulated that the President be elected by Congress. But this plan, some of the delegates objected, would make the executive branch dependent on the legislature. If various state legislatures were allowed to elect the President, that method would make the federal government dependent on the states—and neutralize the centralizing trend of the Constitution. Though the best solution would be for the people to elect their leaders directly, the members of the convention by and large distrusted the judgment of the people, who they feared would choose a rabble-rouser. Finally, in a compromise, the convention decided that a special electoral college composed of the same number of electors as each state had representatives in Congress would elect the President. The electors would meet in each state and cast their ballots by mail for a President. The runner-up would be Vice President. The House of Representatives would count the ballots. If no one had a majority, the House would decide the election, but each state would have only one vote in the matter.

This plan had two advantages: it placed the decision in the hands of the people's representatives; but it also gave a voice to each state, especially when no one had a majority.

Ratification

For the Constitution to go into effect, only nine states had to ratify it. The Constitution now appears such a solid, inevitable and "respectable" document that it is difficult to conceive how it was regarded otherwise in the 1780s. In fact, a pitched battle was fought between those who supported ratification and those who opposed it.

Supporters were called Federalists, although logically they should have been termed Nationalists or Centralists since they favored a strong national government. Opponents, known as anti-Federalists, actually favored a true federalism in which the states wielded great power. Of the two camps, the Federalists were far better organized. They knew how to publicize their position (most notably in a series of brilliantly argued papers by Alexander Hamilton, James Madison, and John Jay, *The Federalist*), how to change the minds of delegates, and when to push and when to back off. They were able to create a ground swell by securing four quick ratifications, three of which were unanimous (Delaware, New Jersey, and Georgia). In Pennsylvania the Federalists were not above resorting to bullying. The Pennsylvania legislature was predominantly in favor of ratification and was prepared to call an election for choosing delegates to the special ratifying convention. But the opposition boycotted the meeting of the legislature, thereby preventing a quorum and passage of the call. To achieve a quorum, a Federalist mob hunted up two of the missing anti-Federalists and dragged them to the legislature, forcibly retaining them until the motion passed. When the Pennsylvania convention met, it ratified the Constitution after some debate.

Connecticut easily ratified the Constitution by a vote of 128 to 40. But in Massachusetts passage was more difficult. Skillful lobbying and reasoned argument finally ensured passage by the narrow margin of 187 to 168. Here as in other states promise of amendments, especially a bill of rights spelling out basic civil liberties, carried the day. Maryland was the seventh state to ratify, by a six-to-one majority. South Carolina followed suit, and New Hampshire became the necessary ninth state in June 1778.

New York and Virginia, however, had not acted and they were among the most populous and wealthy states in the country. In Virginia Patrick Henry vehemently opposed the Constitution on many grounds. He felt that a republican form of government was suitable for only a very small, homogeneous territory. No other large country, he insisted, ever had successfully attempted the republican form of government. Henry, like many other Americans, was alarmed by the fact that there was no bill of rights.

Nevertheless it was Madison's quiet, reasoned argument that won the day—that and the support of John Marshall and Governor Edmund Randolph, once the latter agreed to work for a bill of rights.

New York state distrusted the Constitution, but New York City was so in favor of it that the city threatened to secede from the state unless ratification won out. Although Hamilton, Madison, and Jay were publishing *The Federalist* in New York, it was too subtle to influence popular support. The governor, knowing that the Constitution would not permit the use of import duties as a source of state income, opposed the Constitution. But while the New York convention was debating the question, news of Virginia's approval reached the delegates. Ratification in New York passed by the narrow margin of thirty to twenty-seven.

North Carolina did not ratify until November 21, 1789, after the new government already had been formed and a bill of rights was under discussion. Rhode Island, vexed by economic problems of its own, did not approve ratification until the following May, and even then it acceded only because the new Congress was threatening to levy a tariff on trade with the "foreign" domain of Rhode Island.

Anti-Federalist Fears

Arguments against the Constitution reflected fear that the proposed new government would reinstate a tyrannical rule similar to the one Britain had imposed on America. After all, the new government would possess four great powers: the right to wage war; the right to regulate commerce; the right to tax; and the right to decide the fate of the western territories. At the same time, the Constitution enforced economic restrictions on the states.

The problem of centralization seemed particularly acute in a republic. The people would feel out of touch with a distant central government where they were inadequately represented. Their lack of interest might lead to the emergence of tyranny.

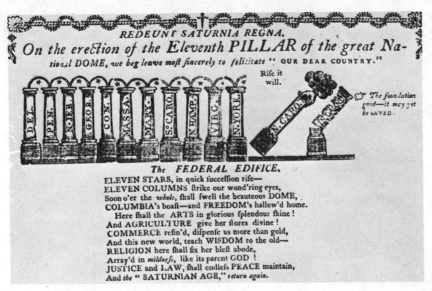

REDEUNT SATURNIA REGNA.
On the erection of the Eleventh PILLAR of the great National DOME, we beg leave most sincerely to felicitate "OUR DEAR COUNTRY."

Rise it will.

The foundation good—it may yet be SAVED.

The FEDERAL EDIFICE.

ELEVEN STARS, in quick succession rise—
ELEVEN COLUMNS strike our wond'ring eyes,
Soon o'er the whole, shall swell the beauteous DOME,
COLUMBIA's boast—and FREEDOM's hallow'd home.
Here shall the ARTS in glorious splendour shine!
And AGRICULTURE give her stores divine!
COMMERCE refin'd, dispense us more than gold,
And this new world, teach WISDOM to the old—
RELIGION here shall fix her blest abode,
Array'd in mildness, like its parent GOD!
JUSTICE and LAW, shall endless PEACE maintain,
And the "SATURNIAN AGE," return again.

Courtesy of the New-York Historical Society, New York City.

This cartoon celebrates the ratification of the Constitution by the eleventh state (New York). The symbolism of the classical columns reminds readers of an earlier republic.

"From the moment we become one great Republic," one anti-Federalist essayist wrote, "either in form or substance, the period is very shortly removed, when we shall sink first into monarchy, and then into despotism."

Finally, the anti-Federalists believed the Constitution would promote an aristocratic (or even a monarchical) form of government. Some of those who held this view pointed to the upper class background of the men who framed the Constitution. Others argued their case from the contents of the document itself. Elections, instead of taking place once a year as under the Articles, would be held every two years for representatives and every six for senators. These long terms of office would separate Congress from the people. Behind many of these objections was a conviction that human nature is basically selfish and consumed with a lust for power. Only rigorous checks and balances could hold this lust within bounds.

Historians have offered two basic theories to explain the split between Federalists and anti-Federalists. One theory focuses on social and economic backgrounds of the two groups. The anti-Federalist bloc was made up basically of small inland farmers; the Federalists were merchants who lived in the cities and were generally better educated. The other theory highlights ideological differences. For instance, some historians believe that Federalists had a national outlook, while anti-Federalists were more narrow and parochial in their views. The Federalists may well have been businessmen and "aristocrats" with a more cosmopolitan outlook based on broader experience. Many anti-Federalists were small farmers with limited incomes who feared a federal government that would have the power to tax. Suspicious of "foreigners" from other sections of the country, these untraveled anti-Federalists had little vision of the possible future greatness of a united country.

Using the Constitution

Elections for the new government were held in 1788 and Congress met for the first time in 1789. The first few months of activity were devoted to organizational matters. The House chose its Speaker and counted the electoral votes, and George Washington, as everyone had expected, was the overwhelming choice for President. John Adams had the second highest number of votes and accordingly became the Vice President. In the new Congress the Federalists had won the day. There were only eight anti-Federalists in the House and only two anti-Federalists in the Senate (both elected by Virginia). These election returns clearly demonstrated the people's confidence in the great experiment.

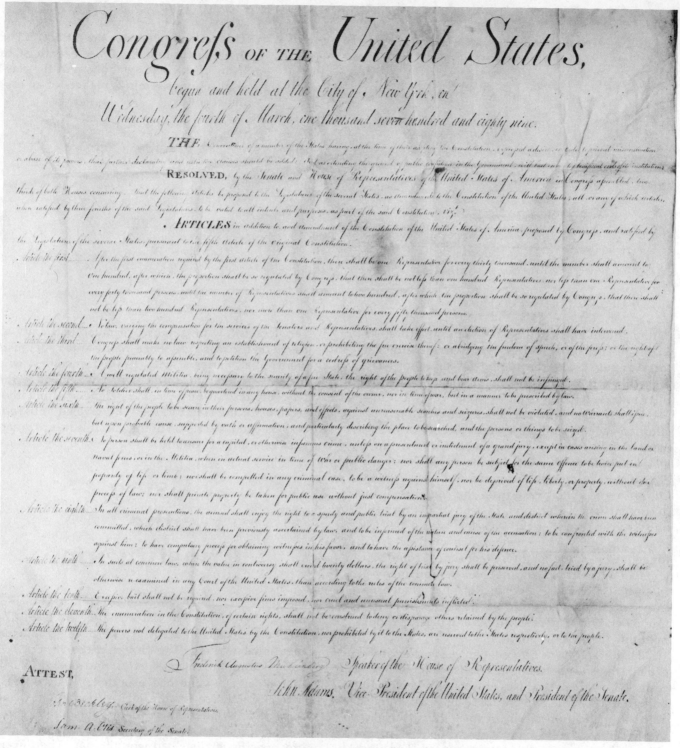

The Bill of Rights as sent to the states for ratification included twelve amendments. Only ten received the approval of the states. This is the formal draft sent to each state and thus lists all twelve. The first two were the ones defeated.

The Bill of Rights

Lack of articles guaranteeing specific freedoms and rights had been one of the chief objections to the Constitution. Following the ratification vote, six states suggested that a bill of rights should be added by the first Congress. The ten amendments, passed by Congress and eventually ratified by the states, protected such freedoms as the right to trial by jury; freedom of religion, speech, and the press; the right to assembly; and the right to petition the government. As safeguards against the sort of actions that precipitated the Revolution, the Bill of Rights forbade quartering of troops in private residences. Cruel and unusual punishments, excessive bail, and general warrants also were forbidden. The Tenth Amendment, drawn up to mollify defenders of states' rights, reserved powers to the states which were not specifically given to the federal government.

While the process of ratifying the Bill of Rights was going on, three new states joined the union (North Carolina, Rhode Island, and Vermont). Had they not become states, the Bill of Rights would not have been ratified, since three states (Massachusetts, Connecticut, and Georgia) failed to approve the amendments.

The Presidency

Article II of the Constitution states that all executive power is vested in the President. It says he will command the army, navy, and any state militia called to national service, may grant reprieves and pardons, carry on foreign relations, appoint numerous officials (including Supreme Court judges), veto laws passed by the Congress, convene either or both houses of that body, and should they disagree with respect to adjournment "he may adjourn them to such time as he shall think proper." He also is required "from time to time" to report to the Congress on the "State of the Union" and "recommend to their Consideration such Measures as he shall judge necessary and expedient," words most Presidents have interpreted as an invitation to submit proposals for new legislation. It is very doubtful if the Founding Fathers would have endowed this office with so much power if it had not been assumed that Washington—wise, impartial, widely respected—would be the first President.

Although the Constitution named only a Treasury Department, other "executive departments" were mentioned. The President was granted the right to appoint "Heads of Departments" and other officials with the Senate's approval. Washington created the positions and filled them with old friends. Alexander Hamilton, the young Federalist, became the Secretary of Treasury. Thomas Jefferson was recalled from France and made Secretary of State. Edmund Randolph became Attorney General

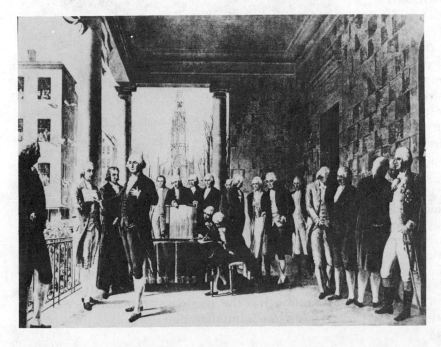

Washington set the first of many precedents by taking the oath as President before the newly assembled Congress.

and Henry Knox, Secretary of War. The most pressing problems facing the executive branch were finances, foreign policy, and westward expansion. In all three areas, of course, the President could act only in conjunction with Congress.

Financial Policy

During the Revolution the federal government as well as the state governments contracted enormous foreign and domestic debts. The new central government was determined to settle these debts, but most members of Congress wanted to pay back only a percentage of the money borrowed. After all, they reasoned, the domestic debt was owed to only a few citizens, many of them speculators. Why should the population as a whole pay taxes to enrich the few?

No one questioned that the foreign lenders (France, Spain, and Holland) should be repaid in full; repayment in this case was considered a sacred responsibility. But of the entire national debt of $50 million, some $40 million was owed to American citizens.

Alexander Hamilton took an entirely different approach that drew upon recommendations of Robert Morris, Superintendent of Finance under the Articles of Confederation, and upon precedents set by the Bank of England. He proposed in his "Report on Public Credit" that the federal government pay back all debts in full, both foreign and domestic (called "funding"). Moreover, the federal government also should assume all state debts incurred in waging the Revolution (called "assumption"). By repaying these debts at full face value, Hamilton was making the national debt as large as it possibly could be. Although it might enrich speculators, payment in full would also set the highest standards of financial reliability for the new government. Equally important, assumption of state debts would exert a strong centralizing influence on the country since many more people would have the new government's interests at heart.

Both of Hamilton's proposals—to pay all debts at face value and to assume state debts—met with stiff opposition. The opponents were led by James Madison, who objected to the first proposal on the grounds that full repayment would enrich the few and to the second on the grounds that some states, including Madison's own Virginia, had already paid off their war debts. Under Hamilton's plan debt-free states would share the cost of repaying

the debts of states less prompt in meeting their responsibilities.

Despite vehement attacks on the scheme, Hamilton prevailed and Congress passed his plan, which raised the national debt from $50 to $100 million. While it did enrich both American and many foreign speculators (some of whom were Hamilton's friends), it also restored American credit. By 1792 the United States was well on the way to repaying its debts, and the price of government securities soared to something close to face value.

Hamilton next turned his attention to chartering a national bank. The bank would draw on federal funds, but most of its capital would come from private investors. The bank would print bills and lend money, thus providing the nation with capital for industrial and commercial development and a much-needed currency for its daily business. Madison and Jefferson both opposed the idea by pointing out that nowhere in the Constitution was such

Independence National Historical Park Collection.

Alexander Hamilton's drive and energy are obvious in this portrait by Charles Willson Peale. Hamilton was the single greatest influence on the Washington administration.

an institution mentioned. Hamilton said the bank could be justified by referring to the clause that gave Congress the right "To make all Laws which shall be necessary and proper for carrying into Execution the foregoing Powers, and all other Powers vested by this Constitution in the Government of the United States, or in any Department or Officer thereof." Since a bank was "necessary" for collecting taxes and regulating commerce, it was clearly constitutional. Furthermore, the Constitution did not specifically prohibit such a bank, a matter of some consequence in the Supreme Court's affirmation of the constitutionality of the Bank in 1819. Hamilton's position was the first instance of the "broad construction" of the Constitution; Jefferson and Madison, by contrast, at least on this occasion, stuck to a "strict interpretation."

Hamilton finally won the day, though the victory cost him the support of his former friends, Jefferson and Madison. Many American leaders began to see in Hamilton, who was born in the West Indies, the very personification of the monarchical Federalist that so many anti-Federalists feared would develop.

Traditionally historians have written that during the dispute over the assumption of state debts, Hamilton struck a secret bargain with his opponents from the South. Hamilton reputedly agreed to the removal of the national capital from New York, where it was originally located, to the South in return for support of his fiscal policies. Recent research has shed doubt on this story. The permanent location of the capital, however, was undoubtedly a matter of concern. The Constitution provided that the permanent seat of government would be a district (not more than ten miles square) where Congress, not the states, would "exercise exclusive Legislation." Eventually that body worked out a compromise that appeased various sections of the country. The capital would remain in New York for a while, then move to Philadelphia. The permanent site would be land deeded to the government by Virginia and Maryland. If this new city (present-day Washington, District of Columbia) were never built, the government would remain in Philadelphia.

Indians and the Frontier

Although the Northwest Ordinance of 1787 set up procedures for the settlement of the western territories and their admission to statehood, it did nothing to solve the difficulties with Indians in that region, and problems continued south of the Ohio River as well. Indian tribes still held on to the land, and sporadic but bitter fighting continued between Indians and settlers in Kentucky and Tennessee especially. Most settlers were convinced these outbreaks were inspired by the British who still illegally held forts in American territory.

Indian resistance also met white expansion in the Southwest. Creek Indians blocked the growth of Georgia and threatened sparse, exposed settlements in Tennessee. When the United States met these Indians in battle, the results were dismal defeats. In the Old Northwest, Indians under the leadership of Miami Chief Little Turtle (1752-1812) defeated General Josiah Harmar in 1790. In the following year, with the aid of guns supplied by the British, the Indians completely routed a much larger force under the command of Arthur St. Clair.

The government's failure to defend the frontier prompted many settlers to consider seceding from the Union. Only some successes through arms and diplomacy stemmed this drift toward anarchy. In 1794 "Mad" Anthony Wayne bested the Northwest Indians at Fallen Timbers, and one year later the Indians ceded most of the present state of Ohio to the United States by the Treaty of Greenville. At last the West was truly opened to intensive settlement, though subduing the Indians had cost the country $5 million between 1790 and 1796—one-sixth of the total federal budget.

The Whiskey Rebellion

One outbreak of violence in the West was launched by frontiersmen not against the Indians, the British, or the Spanish but against the United States government. In order to raise federal revenue, Hamilton instituted, among other taxes, an excise tax on whiskey. This levy aroused a rebellious spirit in four of the western counties of Pennsylvania beyond the Alleghenies. Along the frontier, whiskey circulated in place of currency, and more than one minister received his salary in flasks of distilled spirits. More importantly, whiskey was the most common product derived from corn. It did not spoil and it could be easily transported.

By 1794 open resistance to the tax erupted. Mobs pursued federal tax collectors and a federal marshal who tried to summon offenders to court met with violence. Washington, relying on Hamilton's advice, viewed the incident as an opportunity to demonstrate the new government's authority. He and Hamilton rode out at the head of 15,000 troops—but found not a single rebel. Washington pardoned the leaders of the rebellion and the incident was soon forgotten.

Foreign Affairs

Although President Washington relied upon the counsel of his Secretary of State, Thomas Jefferson, he also solicited the advice of Alexander Hamilton and other national leaders.

Jefferson was pro-French and Hamilton was pro-British, though neither man's allegiance was as straightforward as historians have sometimes asserted. Jefferson, who had lived in Paris, was very sympathetic to the French Revolution, which broke out in 1789, even welcoming its excesses for a time. Hamilton, on the other hand, felt American trade and commerce needed British connections in order to prosper. He did not see these ties as permanent or subservient; but, for the moment, he believed they were necessary. The success of his funding plan depended on duties on British imports, which supplied nine-tenths of all U.S. tariff revenues. To offend Britain, Hamilton thought, would invite economic disaster.

When Britain and France became embroiled in war in 1793, these sympathies clashed head-on. Hamilton, Washington, and Jefferson all agreed that the United States should remain neutral. But beyond that single point of agreement, radical differences arose. Hamilton advocated a much stricter neutrality than Jefferson proposed. According to Hamilton, Washington should not receive the minister Edmond Genêt, whom the French revolutionary government sent to America. Moreover, Hamilton wanted Washington to revoke the treaties of alliance that the United States had signed with France in 1778.

Jefferson offered very different advice. He wanted Washington to recognize Genêt as a legitimate minister and not to declare publicly America's neutrality until the best diplomatic terms were wrested from both France and England.

Hamilton had Washington's ear, and the President followed his advice, though he tempered it with Jefferson's suggestions. Genêt was formally recognized and treaties with France were not revoked, but Washington revealed America's neutral stance (without actually using the word). Genêt, showing deplorable judgment, complicated these diplomatic maneuvers. He did not go directly to

New York to report to Washington but instead made a triumphant tour of the South, telling wildly cheering crowds about the French Revolution. At Charleston he commissioned American ships to sail under the French flag and raid British vessels. Washington was forced to demand Genêt's recall; but, as it turned out, Genêt was terrified he would be guillotined if he returned to France. Washington reluctantly granted him asylum.

Jay's Treaty

Many Americans sympathized with the French Revolution, which they saw as similar to their own, and this sympathy was increased by new conflicts with Britain on the high seas. The British stood behind their so-called "Rule of 1756," which held that if, during peace time, any power (France in this case) refused to let another power (America in this case) trade with its colonies, then, during wartime, the same restrictions must prevail. But, now, the French had opened their islands in the West Indies to American vessels, and it was this trade that the British denounced. Americans, by contrast, held that neutrals could trade nonmilitary goods with any nation on earth. The English, accordingly, began to seize American ships in December 1793. This action infuriated the American public, as did allegations of British encouragement of Indian raids along the American frontier. Jefferson resigned as Secretary of State in December 1793; shortly before doing so, he recommended restrictions on trade with Britain.

Hamilton did not resign his post until a year later, but before he left the government he convinced Washington to avert war with Britain by sending John Jay on a special mission to England. Hamilton's concern for peaceful relations with Britain led him to secretly inform the British minister that the United States would not join an "armed neutrality" coalition to resist British maritime policies. Therefore, Jay found the negotiations very difficult since the British would make no concessions. He came back with a treaty that Washington signed with great trepidation, that the public denounced, and that Congress almost rejected.

Indeed, Jay did make extraordinary concessions in this much maligned treaty. He renounced the American principle of the freedom of the seas and subscribed to the Rule of 1756. America would not sell provisions to Britain's enemy (France) nor trade in naval stores. And American ports would not welcome privateers threatening the British navy. In exchange, very small American vessels (scarcely larger than fishing smacks) could trade with the British West Indies, though not in certain key commodities (sugar, molasses, coffee, or cotton). British possessions in India also were partially open to American trade.

The remaining terms were equally distressing. The British promised to withdraw their troops from American soil if British merchants could continue to trade with the Indians. Americans whose ships had been seized in the West Indies would be compensated for their losses only if the American gov-

ernment reciprocally compensated British creditors for debts owed them from the period before the Revolution. No guarantees were given that the British would cease impressing American sailors into the English navy.

Jay's Treaty was the most unpopular act of Washington's administration, and the House of Representatives insisted that some of the terms (the list of excluded commodities) be modified before it appropriated funds necessary to pay the pre-Revolutionary debts owed British creditors. In addition, members of the House of Representatives asked to inspect the documents concerning the negotiations, but Washington refused, invoking executive privilege, a kind of presidential step the Founding Fathers had probably not anticipated and proof they had created a stronger presidency than they envisioned.

Luckily for the Washington administration, in 1795 a much better treaty, the Pinckney Treaty (or the Treaty of San Lorenzo) was worked out with Spain. This treaty was inspired by Spanish fears that Britain and the United States might join arms and seize the Spanish possession of Louisiana. Thomas Pinckney was thus able to open the Mississippi to American navigation and win for Americans the right to deposit goods in New Orleans until cargo could be reshipped to ports throughout the world. The Spanish agreed that America's western boundary would be the Mississippi and its southern boundary the thirty-first parallel, leaving only Florida and a slim crescent of the Gulf Coast to the Spanish.

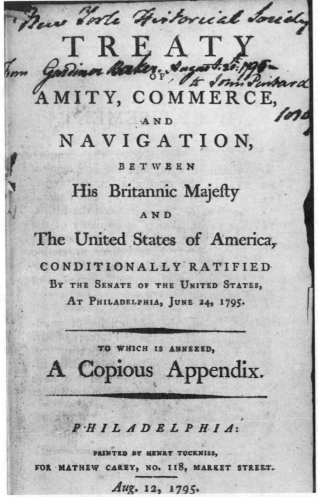

Courtesy of the New-York Historical Society, New York City.
Printer Mathew Carey lent his support to the debate over Jay's Treaty by printing this copy of the terms along with a series of comments in the appendix.

The First Party System Is Born

Most of the framers of the Constitution envisioned a government devoid of factionalism and united in patriotism. But soon after Washington's inauguration two parties began to grow. Significantly, they

149

AMERICAN POLITICAL PARTIES SINCE 1789

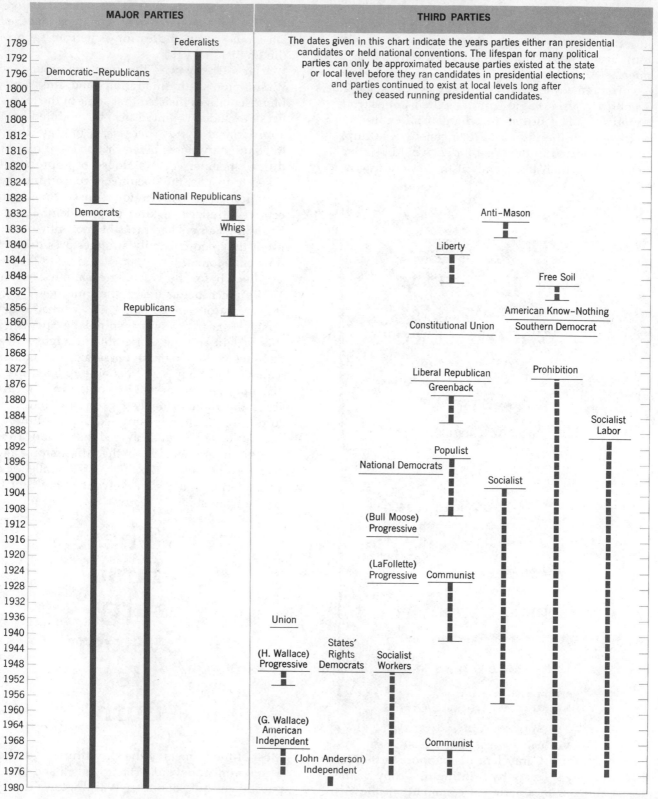

MAJOR PARTIES	THIRD PARTIES

1789
1792
1796
1800
1804
1808
1812
1816
1820
1824
1828
1832
1836
1840
1844
1848
1852
1856
1860
1864
1868
1872
1876
1880
1884
1888
1892
1896
1900
1904
1908
1912
1916
1920
1924
1928
1932
1936
1940
1944
1948
1952
1956
1960
1964
1968
1972
1976
1980

Federalists

Democratic–Republicans

Democrats

National Republicans

Whigs

Republicans

The dates given in this chart indicate the years parties either ran presidential candidates or held national conventions. The lifespan for many political parties can only be approximated because parties existed at the state or local level before they ran candidates in presidential elections; and parties continued to exist at local levels long after they ceased running presidential candidates.

Anti-Mason

Liberty

Free Soil

American Know-Nothing
Southern Democrat

Constitutional Union

Liberal Republican
Greenback

Prohibition

Socialist Labor

Populist

National Democrats

Socialist

(Bull Moose) Progressive

(LaFollette) Progressive

Communist

Union

(H. Wallace) Progressive

States' Rights Democrats

Socialist Workers

(G. Wallace) American Independent

(John Anderson) Independent

Communist

appeared first among the people's representatives in Congress. These factions developed in reaction to programs and events initiated by Washington's administration.

Federalists and Republicans

One group, the Federalists, was led by the Secretary of the Treasury, Alexander Hamilton, and it was his plan for fully funding state and federal debts incurred during the Revolution that first aroused opposition. Most Americans were dismayed and disturbed as these legislative divisions grew into political organizations. Washington tried to remain aloof, but was unable to do so because his administration, made up almost entirely of Federalists, had firm control of federal offices and the flow of information. The opposition, lacking tradition, was in a difficult position. Congress represented the will of the people and attempts to thwart that will were, in the eyes of many Americans, tantamount to treason. Nevertheless, as congressmen took stands on Hamilton's policies, treaties, and other issues, they discovered that these political factions were coalescing into definable groups. Since the Federalists were in power and excluded the opposition from federal offices, these divisions soon became obvious to all. Those aligning themselves with Madison and Jefferson could not use government posts to create a party structure, so they reached out to voters with promises to dispense future rewards once they had gained power.

The second party was not yet established as a clear entity in 1792 and Washington and Adams were returned easily to office. But in 1793 foreign affairs became stormy, and disagreements about America's position vis-à-vis France and England deepened the domestic rift. The second party, headed by Jefferson in the Cabinet and Madison in Congress, came to be known as the Democratic-Republicans or Jeffersonian Republicans.

Differences between the two parties were founded on personalities, ideologies, policies, and tastes for invective. Though both Hamilton and Jefferson were well educated and well-to-do, Hamilton represented the interests of northeastern merchants and financiers, and Jefferson identified himself with the cause of farmers and the "common man." Hamilton was articulate and quick-witted; Jefferson was far more retiring and reflective. Hamilton was a declared foe of local government and an ardent Federalist; Jefferson distrusted centralization and advocated minimal government in-

THE PROVIDENTIAL DETECTION

Anti-Jefferson propaganda is summed up in this cartoon, which shows the American eagle preventing Jefferson from burning the Constitution on an altar to French despotism.

tervention. Hamilton saw the American future as depending upon trade and industrialization; Jefferson saw the American future as bound to agrarian pursuits and their encouragement. Hamilton was pro-British because he felt that England was America's best commercial ally: Jefferson was pro-French because he felt that only Revolutionary France shared America's republican ideals. In fact, he and Madison built upon the grass-roots support of some forty Democratic societies formed in imitation of Jacobin societies in France.

The contrast between the two men has sometimes been overdrawn, and certainly they both responded to the exigencies of practical politics. Nevertheless, beneath their divergent political stands lay different views of human nature. Hamilton distrusted people in general; Jefferson believed they would make wise decisions, at least in the long run, and took a much more benign view of the populace, especially the majority tilling the soil.

Competing newspapers soon fueled this growing controversy. Before 1791, the *Gazette of the United States,* published in Philadelphia by John Fenno, was the only journal that reported political events extensively. It was solidly Federalist, as Hamilton intended it to be. The arch-Federalist Fisher Ames said of the editor, "No printer was ever so *correct* in his politics." Jefferson and Madison quickly founded a rival voice, the *National Gazette,* edited by the poet, Philip Freneau. (His activities as a political journalist in behalf of Jefferson are recounted in an accompanying biographical sketch.)

The Adams Administration

In the election of 1796, John Adams became the second President of the United States and Jefferson, as the runner-up, Vice President. The campaign brought factionalism out into the open, both between and within parties. Adams refused to campaign openly and was the choice of most Federalists, some of whom did not like Hamilton. Meanwhile, Hamilton backed Thomas Pinckney of South Carolina who, he thought, might undercut Adams's support in the Electoral College; however, this maneuver failed.

Party spirit of the times should not obscure more important signs of harmony. In September 1796, Washington framed his famous "Farewell Address," a valedictory statement explaining why he would not seek a third term and counseling all Americans on steps to be taken in the future. He cautioned against the dangers of the party system, stressed all citizens must obey the Constitution, and warned against permanent alliances with foreign powers, especially European states, which had "a set of primary interests" and are "engaged in frequent controversies, the causes of which are essentially foreign to our concerns." With these words, later frequently quoted by isolationists to support their views, Washington charted a foreign policy course adhered to for a century and a half. He also bequeathed to his successor an adequate bureaucratic system.

Nevertheless, Adams inherited a far from peaceful situation. His Vice President was captain of the opposition party and his Cabinet, dominated by friends of Alexander Hamilton, wasted little affection on Adams. And the world situation was even more perilous. The French government was far from satisfied with the American policy of neutrality, having expected the United States to grant

Courtesy Massachusetts Historical Society.

John and Abigail Adams, whose portraits were done early in their married life by Benjamin Blythe, found themselves caught in a torrent of partisanship while presiding over the nation. It alienated them from old friends such as Mercy Warren and Thomas Jefferson.

Philip Freneau

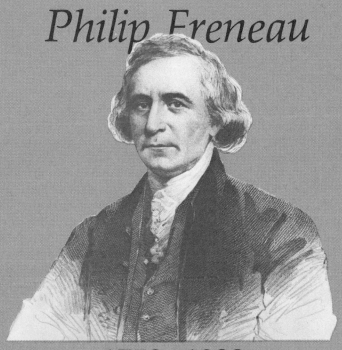

1752–1832

Educated at Princeton, where he perhaps was a roommate of James Madison, Freneau longed to become a poet and composed a remarkable ode, "The Rising Glory of America," which he read at his graduation exercises in 1771. A year later it was published in Philadelphia.

For a time Freneau taught school, but with the outbreak of hostilities his pen became active once more, so much so that his satires (eight anti-British phamplets in only a few months) won him a reputation as "the poet of the Revolution." However, poetry provided neither income nor glory, and this young man took a promising job as secretary to a prominent planter in the West Indies. While there, he turned out some of his most significant work, several romantic poems, long before the literary movement known as "Romanticism" came into flower in Europe.

During the final years of the Revolution, Freneau returned home, was captured by the British, and spent a ghastly period in a prison ship in New York harbor (an experience later described in verse). After regaining his health, he worked in Philadelphia for three years and then went to the Carribean once more.

Marriage in 1789 halted his roving momentar-

ily and ushered in several years of highly partisan journalism, briefly in New York and then in Philadelphia. In 1791, backed by Jefferson (who got him a lucrative State Department clerkship), Freneau launched the *National Gazette* as an antidote to the highly aristocratic *Gazette of the United States*. In its pages he not only cut Hamilton to ribbons but also praised Jefferson as "that illustrious Patriot, Statesman and Philosopher." Hamilton became so angry that he begged President Washington to choose between him and Jefferson. Washington persuaded the two cabinet ministers to remain in office—but the newspaper war continued at full force until 1793, when a yellow fever epidemic drove Freneau out of Philadelphia and forced the *National Gazette* to close its doors. Jefferson later said that Freneau's editorials "saved our Constitution, which was galloping fast into monarchy."

Freneau dabbled in newspapers for a few more years, then returned to poetry, his New Jersey farm, and occasional ocean voyages. Probably best known for his brief sally into the political realm, he was actually a figure of considerable significance in American letters. Not only a precursor of revolution and Romanticism, Freneau also was the first American poet to incorporate the Indian into his work.

it the status of most-favored nation. Instead, the Americans signed the pro-British Jay's Treaty. In retaliation, France began to seize American ships bound for British ports. Moreover, the French began to treat Americans serving on British ships as pirates.

This turn of events of course delighted Hamilton and his allies, the High Federalists, who hoped the United States would declare war on France—a step that would place America firmly in the British camp, where Hamilton believed his country's material interests would be best served. Adams, however, opted for a more moderate policy. The new President sent three men to France, though the trio he chose seemed unlikely to secure a peaceful settlement. John Marshall was a well-known Federalist and an enemy of Jefferson and

Madison. Charles Cotesworth Pinckney was a leading South Carolina Federalist and older brother of Thomas Pinckney. The third member of the delegation, Elbridge Gerry, was a nominal Federalist but acceptable to Jefferson.

The American mission to France ended in disaster. Talleyrand, the French Minister of Foreign Affairs, devised a clever way of lining his pockets—extortion. He routinely required foreigners to bribe him in order to receive an appointment. To the Americans he sent three of his agents (later referred to by Adams in a report to Congress as X, Y, and Z); the agents said they could arrange for a meeting with Talleyrand if the United States would pay him $250,000 under the counter and lend the French government $12 million. "Not a six-pence," Pinckney declared. He and Marshall returned to America,

This cartoon shows the anti-French feeling following the XYZ Affair. The three American ministers reject the French demands for money. The black at the table is to remind people of the rebellion of Haiti.

Establishing a New Nation

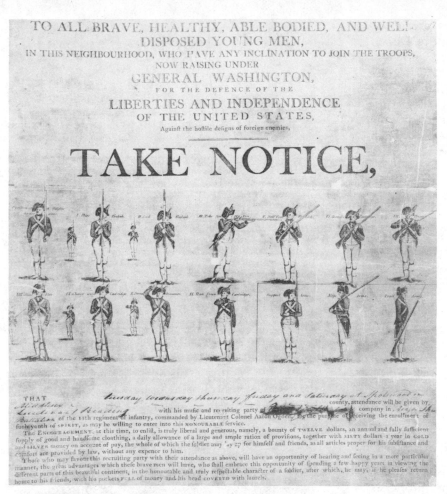

Historical Society of Pennsylvania.

This recruitment poster used the appeal of George Washington's name to try to convince men to join the army that was raised during the 1798 war scare with France.

leaving behind Gerry, whose passport Talleyrand withheld.

The Alien and Sedition Acts

The XYZ Affair seemed to make war with France inevitable and opened the way to suppress the opposition to government policy as treasonous. President Adams suddenly became a national hero, and the most popular songs were "Adams and Liberty" and "The President's March." Indignation against the French—and the pro-French Republicans—was so strong that Federalist leaders were able to persuade Congress to appropriate money to build up the army and the navy and to pass legislation designed to crush all opposition.

These measures, known as the Alien and Sedition Acts, were defended as necessary wartime laws. Two of the alien acts hit hard at part of Jefferson's growing constituency—newly arrived Americans. The time for naturalization (and therefore for voting) was increased from five to fourteen years and the President was empowered to imprison or deport foreigners in time of war. Adams signed the bill, but did not like its provisions and made no concerted attempt to enforce them.

More serious was the Sedition Act of 1798, which curtailed freedom of the press. The law defined sedition as uttering or writing or printing any false, scandalous, or malicious opinions about the government or the President. The government indicted fifteen offenders under the Sedition Act and convicted and punished ten of them. All four of the leading Republican newspapers were attacked and the three most influential Republican editors were convicted of wrongdoing.

Prosecutions under the act were highly selective. The first victim was Mathew Lyon, a Vermont congressman, charged with having questioned the government's French policies. Lyon was convicted, assessed a fine of $1,000, and sentenced to four months in jail. There were fifteen indictments and ten convictions under the Sedition Act.

The courts, with Federalist judges presiding, willingly went along with the trials. The Democratic-Republicans reacted with outrage. Jefferson and Madison persuaded the legislatures of Virginia and Kentucky to pass resolutions stressing that states had the right to oppose clearly unconstitutional federal laws. The Republicans resorted to the state legislatures because the Supreme Court had not yet established its practice of declaring laws unconstitutional—not that the Federalist court of the time would have judged the laws unconstitutional in any event. Although the Virginia and Kentucky resolutions dramatized Jefferson's alarm, the acts endangered the whole federal system by investing the states with extraordinary power. Fortunately for the health of the central government, no other states followed suit.

Washington reluctantly agreed to come out of retirement to command the army, but only if a true emergency arose. Many officers asked for commissions but few privates enlisted, and popular opinion gradually turned against the war. Jefferson and his followers, certain that the troops raised were being trained to attack his Virginia supporters, began to arm and drill an army of their own to repel a Federalist invasion.

When Gerry returned in 1798, he informed Adams that the French did not want to fight and would negotiate a treaty. Adams' son, John Quincy Adams, sent the same news home from Europe, as did the American minister to England, Rufus King. Sensing a shift in public opinion and assured that France did not want to fight, Adams dispatched a new minister to Paris who concluded an agreement with the French government (the Convention of 1801). This infuriated High Federalists and stirred up discord within the party but greatly increased the popularity of Adams throughout the young nation and averted hostilities.

An Exciting Generation

The Revolution improved the lot of the common man in some measure. Independence opened up the West for settlement and created new opportunities in business, the army, and government. In

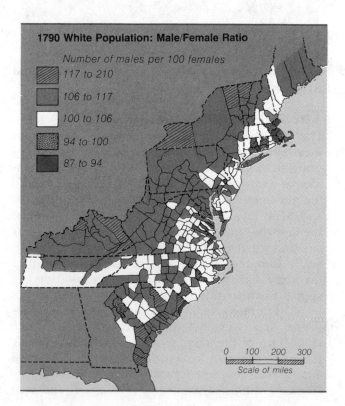

Courtesy of the Charleston Library Society.

Academies for boys and girls sprang up in the late eighteenth century. This advertisement makes clear that girls of middle and upper class families were being trained more as graceful ornaments than as practical helpmates.

a practical sense, the right to vote had little immediate impact, but in time men such as Thomas Jefferson would lead political upheavals that demonstrated the true worth of the ballot. What impact independence had upon the status of specific groups within colonial society such as women and slaves is less clear. During much of the eighteenth century, American women worked hard on farms and in small shops, and in colonial days they were not specifically barred from voting. However, as the colonies matured, the role of women became more ornamental. True, more academies opened to "educate" young women of the well-to-do classes, but there they learned how to sew, to speak and write politely, and to appreciate the decorative arts. State constitutions denied them the suffrage (the last women of this era to vote in New Jersey did so in 1806), and as shops moved out of the home and became factories, women had less opportunity to learn meaningful trades.

Perhaps one of the most significant but least understood social changes set in motion during this period occurred in the American family. Historians date the "demographic transition" or the point when traditional large families began to get smaller at approximately 1800. For example, the birth rate among whites, which is based on the number of live births per 1,000 females of child-bearing age, was 278 in 1800, 274 in 1810, 260 in 1820, and 240 in 1830, a decline that continued throughout the nineteenth century. Explanations for this remarkable phenomenon range from abstinence, primarily on the part of wives, to the easy access for unrestricted abortion during the early months of pregnancy. Historian Carl Degler has suggested that a growing interest in and concern for individualism contributed to a declining birthrate as women may have consciously chosen to have smaller families in order to have more time for themselves or their children. Whatever the explanation, it seems clear that beginning around 1800 more and more Americans approved and practiced some kind of family limitation.

The Founding Fathers had mixed feelings concerning slavery since they believed in class differences and harbored racist views. Nevertheless, all of them thought legal equality a prerequisite for the preservation of freedom and thus found themselves on the horns of a troublesome dilemma. Slavery, in short, made them very uncomfortable. Pennsylvania approved a system of gradual abolition in 1780: adult slaves were not freed, but their children be-

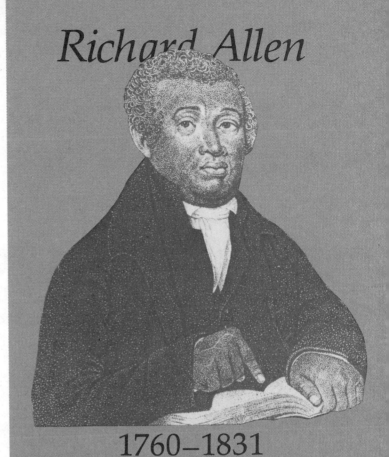

Richard Allen

1760–1831

Born in slavery in 1760, Richard Allen became the founder of the African Methodist Episcopal Church, an organization which by 1836 controlled property worth $125,000 and was a major force in the antislavery movement.

As a youth, Allen, the property of a farmer residing near Dover, Delaware, was converted by the Methodists. Because of this strong interest in religion, his master permitted him to hold prayer meetings in his home. As a result, the master also became a Methodist and a firm believer in emancipation, thus enabling Allen and his family to escape from slavery in an era of increasing toleration and religious freedom.

In an effort to educate himself, Allen labored at a variety of occupations, while continuing to preach the Gospel to blacks and whites alike. He was accepted as a minister in the Methodist Church at a general conference held in Baltimore in 1784. After traveling with Bishop Asbury, he began to hold services for blacks in Philadelphia. His magnetic style attracted many blacks to the Saint George

Methodist Church in which he occasionally preached; but, after a particularly insulting racial incident when a white worshiper pulled blacks up from a kneeling position and banished them to the gallery, black church members organized a "Free African Society." That group soon split up, but Allen influenced one of the groups to establish an independent Methodist church. Eventually this church merged with sixteen similar black churches to become the African Methodist Episcopal Church, with Allen as bishop.

Although the church never had any influence in the South, it spread widely in the northern states east of the Mississippi. By 1836 there were eighty-six churches, serving 7,594 members. Allen's influence made this organization a source of inspiration for many. Originally only a religious force, the church he founded became a major voice in the antislavery movement after his death in 1831. It was an integral part of both the underground railroad and the battle for emancipation.

came free at the age of twenty-eight. Soon Connecticut and Rhode Island followed suit, the latter deciding all children born to slaves after March 1, 1784, would automatically be free. A year earlier, the Massachusetts Supreme Court, noting that the phrase "all men are created equal" appeared in the new state constitution, ruled that slavery did not exist there. All other states, except South Carolina and Georgia, either abolished the institution or considered steps to modify it. Yet a few blacks managed to gain considerable prominence during these years, as in the case of Richard Allen (whose career as a Methodist minister is described in an accompanying biographical sketch).

The trend of the times, however, did not favor widespread abolition. Owners of blacks were convinced they needed their labor, a view that became more entrenched as the Cotton Kingdom expanded after 1800. Moreover, no one came forward to propose a feasible plan of compensation if slaves were set free. Also, ex-slaves themselves showed no wish to migrate to Africa. What was to become the great question of the nineteenth century only festered and grew ever more threatening.

Economic problems resulting from the American Revolution at first seemed insurmountable. No longer could Americans trade legally with the British empire, especially the rich islands of the West Indies. Other European nations either prohibited numerous U.S. exports or taxed them heavily. These regulations hit tobacco extremely hard. In 1783 the young republic had some four million inhabitants (700,000 of them slaves) widely dispersed and served by inadequate roads, few banks, and an unworkable currency. Only a decade or so later conditions had improved markedly. Several factors help to explain this turnabout, among them shrewd leadership, Europe's involvement with its own affairs, and unexpected wartime demand for American goods. As some citizens plunged westward into the wilderness and as others began to develop factories and mills to serve a growing population, the nation expanded and grew strong. It was an exciting age beset with problems, but it was also a time rich with promise.

In addition, it was an age when Americans set about consciously to create an "American" culture, something here in the New World apart from and, they hoped, better than what was found in the Old. In this venture they encountered both success and frustration. (For a general discussion of their quest see the essay on "Creating An American Culture.")

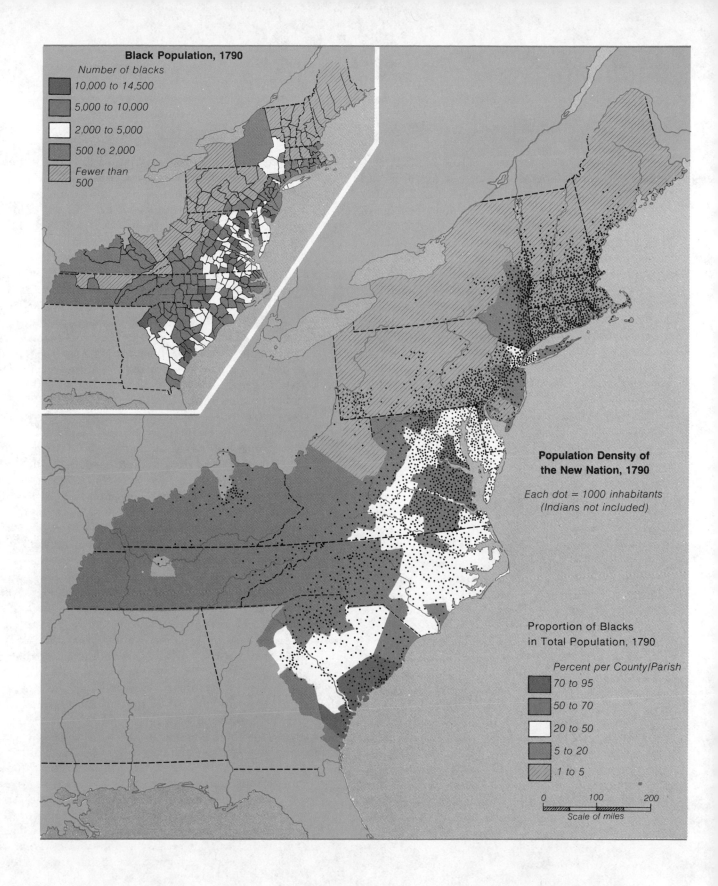

Black Population, 1790

Number of blacks

- 10,000 to 14,500
- 5,000 to 10,000
- 2,000 to 5,000
- 500 to 2,000
- Fewer than 500

Population Density of the New Nation, 1790

Each dot = 1000 inhabitants (Indians not included)

Proportion of Blacks in Total Population, 1790

Percent per County/Parish

- 70 to 95
- 50 to 70
- 20 to 50
- 5 to 20
- 1 to 5

0   100   200

Scale of miles

Essay

Creating an American Culture

In some respects, a root cause of the American Revolution was an independent frame of mind on this side of the Atlantic long before independence became a political reality. As children of the Age of Reason, most eighteenth-century Americans believed strongly in rationalism, science, and the pervasive power of the laws of nature. They also had deep misgivings concerning attitudes based solely upon tradition and established order; for they had seen their little colonial world grow, prosper, and change. Although often using outmoded European ideas in a different setting and for different purposes than originally intended, they gradually evolved an eclectic culture that served them well during their first half-century of nationhood.

This culture, the glue that holds a society together, had diverse goals, for the young republic stressed, above all else, individuality—all men are created equal and have an unalienable right to Life, Liberty, and the Pursuit of Happiness. Yet most Americans of those years could agree on general notions such as the perfectability of man and his prospects for progress in the decades ahead. Within this context they saw the need for several basic steps or innovations. These included the expansion of education, the professionalization of various professions with the aid of societies dedicated to research and learning, and the diffusion of general knowledge to the citizenry at large so as to inculcate the values of a new nation and shake the corrupting influence of unrepublican European ways.

But even a desirable goal such as greater educational opportunity encountered immediate obstacles. Schooling for the masses was impossible. It cost too much and was also impractical. Slaves and children of the poor could not attend classes because they had to work long hours; as a result, most states merely encouraged additional outlays for existing elementary schools and academies, a mode of operation that continued in some regions until the Civil War. Higher education fared somewhat better, perhaps because those allocating funds or making bequests were themselves college educated and believed that a "trickle down" approach might bring the desired results.

No new colleges were started during the heat of battle, but even before the Peace of Paris was signed no less than two colleges named after Washington appeared—one on Maryland's Eastern Shore, the other in the Shenandoah Valley (formerly Liberty Hall, now Washington and Lee University). By the turn of the century, fifteen more institutions of higher learning were chartered, among them, Hampden-Sydney, Dickinson, St. John's, Williams, Bowdoin, Union, Middlebury, and the universities of Georgia (Franklin College), North Carolina, Vermont, and Tennessee (Blount College). Most were poor, struggling little frontier schools that faced hard times indeed before they even granted their first diploma.

By 1825, when the University of Virginia began classes in the unusual setting created by Thomas Jefferson, nine state universities had been chartered, largely in the South and West. Of this group, only Virginia tried from the outset to maintain high standards but, soon—like its contemporaries—it had to rely upon nearby preparatory schools to tutor unqualified students. Others, such as Georgia, established "junior" schools, while Michigan set up regional "branches" where freshmen could begin their collegiate training. Each institution—and this was true of older centers such as Harvard, Yale, William and Mary, and Dartmouth—struggled with the problem of uneven preparation at lower levels, a shortcoming that would continue to plague college administrations for a century or more. (In fact, some professors and students might agree that it still lingers on today.)

The trend in all of these colleges and universities, regardless of when they were founded, was toward a more practical course of study. Latin, Greek, and Hebrew had to share the spotlight with modern languages and more attention was given to scientific pursuits. For the first time some students could choose among three or four programs, even if true election of courses was not yet possible. And institutions unwilling to adapt to change quickly faced competition from academies set up to teach navigation, bookkeeping, geography, mathematics, and similar skills demanded by a changing society.

The University of Virginia was one of the colleges created after the Revolution in order to provide an American version of higher education.

Women benefited to a degree from this educational fervor. Some revolutionaries debated the role of women in the new republic and urged that education was necessary to prepare women for their role as mothers of citizens. Thus, although higher education remained the exclusive domain of men and boys, a few women attended male academies, and numerous female seminaries also opened their doors, especially after 1800. But young ladies, whether they attended coeducational institutions or not, took less demanding courses of study and were expected, for the most part, to perfect the female graces in preparation for marriage. A basic dilemma plaguing post-Revolutionary leaders was the realization that it was necessary to educate the female mind so that it could exert a good moral influence in thousands of households; at the same time, many of them feared that such freedom might "de-sex" their daughters and encourage them to forsake the role of homemaker.

Nevertheless, by 1830 the seeds of several important ideas were beginning to take root in the educational world. First, concern for the "de-sexed" female was abating as a generation or so of experience demonstrated this was an unfounded fear.

As a result, schools such as Emma Willard's in Troy, New York, and Mary Lyon's in Mount Holyoke, Massachusetts, soon were offering courses equal to those found in many male institutions of higher learning. Second, and perhaps of greater importance, education was gradually becoming a *public* responsibility. In 1821, for example, the first truly public high schools (open to the public at large and wholly supported by public money) opened in Portland and Boston. For the good of the nation as a whole—to develop civic responsibility, provide economic security, give moral and ethical training, create a common culture—the state, it seemed, would have to play an ever greater role in education; and with participation at taxpayer expense came, of course, both public responsibility and public control.

Professional men—doctors, lawyers, scientists, and so on—were especially hard hit by war. Many of those most prominent and influential cast their lot with the Tories and, at the time of Yorktown or sooner, chose to depart from the new United States. Their actions were, in fact, a mixed blessing that created both a great void and opportunity for patriots with similar training. The latter, however, often had forsaken their careers to wage war and now found everything in disarray. Colleges and hospitals had been closed, libraries ransacked, journals and research abandoned, contact with European contemporaries disrupted.

The most active and yet the most confused branch of science in the postwar decades was medicine. Neither Americans nor Europeans could agree upon general theories, clinical techniques, or even the classification of diseases. In addition, there was considerable outcry if anyone experimented with or did research upon human bodies. As a result, physicians and surgeons (really two distinct fields of endeavor) learned whatever they could in their day-to-day work as the medical world floundered about aimlessly, awaiting the development of laboratory facilities and a means of testing both theories and purported cures for disease.

Despite this confusion, regional medical societies and medical education prospered. The organization of societies, primarily a postwar phenomenon, increased markedly after 1780. The earliest was probably New Jersey (1766), followed by Massachusetts (1781), New Hampshire (1791), Connecticut (1792), and Delaware (1798). Before 1776 only King's College in New York and the College of Philadelphia offered medical training, but by 1800 similar study was available at William and Mary, Harvard, Pennsylvania, Rutgers, Dartmouth, and Transylvania. In 1797, Samuel Mitchell's *American Medical Repository* appeared and within a decade or so had been joined by six other journals. By 1835 thirty-five such publications were broadcasting new medical knowledge throughout America.

Despite the uncertain state of the medical world, the average American enjoyed reasonably good health, largely because of an abundant supply of food and a widely scattered population. Epidemics were a constant threat, yet perhaps caused fewer deaths here than in Europe and frequently led to improvements in general sanitation such as street cleaning, food inspection, and sewage disposal.

Two other scientific fields of special interest to Americans were agriculture and geography. Farmers Washington and Jefferson tested new crops, crop rotation ideas, and fertilizers. In agriculture, as in medicine, state societies were formed in an effort to both pool and dispense information. And,

in turn, agricultural journals such as Samuel Deane's *New England Farmer* (1790) began to publish the results of experimentation and research. Geography, of course, had utilitarian application for a people exploring and moving westward across a great continent, and development of this field was heavily subsidized by a federal government anxious to find out just what riches the Louisiana Purchase, for example, actually contained. A similar need was evident on the high seas as Americans tried to revive a commercial life stunned by the loss of British ties, a need admirably fulfilled by Nathaniel Bowditch's famous *New American Practical Navigator* (1802).

Several trends are apparent in the realm of American science during these decades. It was fast breaking up into a variety of fields—medicine, geography, chemistry, engineering, astronomy—and was no longer viewed as a unified body of knowledge that any one human mind could encompass. The variety of nature was too great, the flood of data too overwhelming. No longer was science the plaything of a jack-of-all-trades dabbling in electricity, fossils, seeds, and comets. At the same time, each of these individual fields was being taken over by professionals who had the ability and the time to specialize. The term "engineer," for example, meant little to most Americans until after 1800. At the grass-roots level, practical inventions paved the way for the age of steam, canal locks, railroads, cotton mills, and machine tools. As one writer has observed, in less than half a century Americans leaped from despair to "Yankee brag." Artisans who in 1780 thought that half-done was good enough were boasting by 1820 that "any American can do anything better than anyone else."

These changes in education and science, so vital to the creation of a new culture, for the most part affected only the upper levels of society. And, until the advent of true public education and the demise of slavery, it is difficult to see how the third goal of post-Revolutionary America (diffusion of general knowledge to the public at large) could be realized. People unable to read have little use for the printed page, and those tied to a region by poverty or slavery benefit but little from scientific wonders such as canals and steamboats. Yet, in truth, we are dealing here, not with a democracy, but a republic and must view the efforts that were expended in that context.

Textbooks stressing American values and adopting a moral rather than a religious tone quickly replaced British imports. Noah Webster's *American Spelling Book* (1783) was soon joined by his *American Reader* and *American Grammar*. His goal, he said, was to create a uniform, pure language and "to promote the interests of literature and harmony in the United States." Webster, a one-man industry in behalf of Americanism, also turned out schoolbooks in history, geography, and science.

At the adult level, editors and writers made a conscious effort to create an American literature. Numerous literary journals appeared, especially in Boston and Philadelphia, but even such powerful organs as the *North American Review* (1815) could not produce immediate results. For the most part, the histories, biographies, novels, and dramas of these years have for us today merely an antiquarian value. Not until James Fenimore Cooper began to write in the 1820s did an author discover how to mine the American past and make it both interesting and entertaining. Similar frustration is evident in such fields as art, architecture, and music where classical or European models smothered attempts to produce anything "American."

Despite these shortcomings, by the 1820s an American culture of sorts was taking shape. In some areas, such as science and invention, it demonstrated considerable vigor; in others, much less. The goals established in 1780 were, of course, too ambitious and often contradictory in nature. In the intellectual realm, complete independence from the Old World was neither possible, as it turned out, nor desirable. It takes time for a people who rebel successfully to sort out their cultural priorities and their needs. Also, time alone can erase both the alleged and the real scars of colonization and war. Perhaps only a people without such memories can build a true national culture; if this is so, then such work had to await succeeding generations.

SELECTED READINGS

Confederation Period

James Ferguson, *The Power of the Purse* (1961)

Merrill Jensen, *The New Nation: A History of the United States during the Confederation* (1959)

Jackson T. Main, *Political Parties before the Constitution* (1973)

Forest McDonald, *We the People: Economic Origins of the Constitution* (1958)

Curtis Nettles, *Emergence of a National Economy, 1775–1815* (1962)

Constitution Making

Max Farrand, *The Framing of the Constitution of the United States* (1913)

Leonard Levy, ed., *Essays on the Making of the Constitution* (1969)

Jackson T. Main, *The Anti-Federalists* (1961)

Linda De Pauw, *Eleventh Pillar: New York and the Federal Constitution* (1966)

Robert Rutland, *The Birth of the Bill of Rights* (1955)

Gordon Wood, *The Creation of the American Republic* (1969)

Federalists in Power

Reginald Horsman, *Expansion and American Indian Policy* (1967)

Stephen Kurtz, *The Presidency of John Adams: The Collapse of Federalism, 1795–1800* (1957)

John C. Miller, *The Federalist Era, 1789–1801* (1960)

Richard B. Morris, *John Jay, the Nation and the Court* (1967)

James M. Smith, *Freedom's Fetters: Alien and Sedition Laws* (1956)

Leonard White, *The Federalists* (1948)

Diplomacy

Samuel Bemis, *Pinckney's Treaty*, rev. ed. (1960)

Alexander De Conde, *Entangling Alliance: Politics and Diplomacy under Washington* (1958)

Bradford Perkins, *First Rapprochment: England and the United States 1795–1805* (1955)

Women and the Family

Carl Degler, *At Odds: Women and the Family in America from the Revolution to the Present* (1980)

Linda Kerber, *Daughters of Columbia: Women, Intellect and Ideology in Revolutionary America* (1980)

Mary Beth Norton, *Liberty's Daughters: The Revolutionary Experience of American Women 1750–1800* (1980)

CHAPTER 6
ADOLESCENT AMERICA

TIMELINE

1800
Spain transfers Louisiana to France

1800
Washington, D.C., becomes the national capital

1801
Jefferson inaugurated as President

1803
Louisiana Purchase

1803
Lewis and Clark begin expedition

1803
Marbury v. Madison

1804
Burr-Hamilton duel

1804
Jefferson reelected President

1806
Lewis and Clark expedition returns

1807
Burr's conspiracy

1807
The *Chesapeake* incident

1807
Jefferson places embargo on American trade

1807
Robert Fulton invents a steamboat

1808
Madison elected as President

1808
Slave trade ends officially

1811
Battle of Tippecanoe

1816
African Methodist Episcopal Church organized

CHAPTER OUTLINE

The years from 1800–1812 were among the most difficult and exhilarating our nation has experienced. The Revolution was now history, and the problems of the United States were those of adolescence and youth. The republic was, in fact, a gangling youngster, brash, boastful, secretly unsure, but brimming with outward confidence, bright dreams, and high hopes. At home there was an unexpected turnover in political leadership, the first time that "the rascals were thrown out," a development which those who framed the Constitution had not anticipated and one which raised hard, serious questions. Would Jefferson and his followers try to reshape the national government? Could they change policies and programs set into motion by the revered Washington and his successor, Adams? Might they, for example, gain control of the courts by removing judges from the bench?

A New Party Takes Over

"Let us then fellow citizens unite with one heart and mind, let us restore to social intercourse that harmony and affection without which liberty, and even life itself are but dreary things. . . . But every difference of opinion is not a difference of principle. We have called by different names brethren of the same principle. We are all republicans; we are all federalists."

This call to reconciliation in Thomas Jefferson's first inaugural address was in response to the bitter partisan battle of 1800, an election which reminded Americans that they truly had embarked on an amazing experiment in government. That campaign was disturbing to many Americans not only because it whipped up partisan furies and dire predictions of doom should candidates of the opposing side prevail but also because it demonstrated an unpalatable truth. The leaders of competing political organizations are most likely to make decisions based on the needs of their party, not on those of the nation as a whole.

Both Thomas Jefferson and his opponent, John Adams, were nominated by a congressional caucus, the first procedure devised for placing presidential candidates before the public. In 1796, once Washington announced he would not seek a third term, the Federalists in Congress met secretly and agreed to support John Adams and Thomas Pinckney for President and Vice President. The Jeffersonian Republicans then convened and named Thomas Jefferson and Aaron Burr as a rival slate. Four years later members of the two parties who held seats in Congress met openly, not in secret, and pledged their support to Adams and Charles Cotesworth Pinckney and, once more, to Jefferson and Burr. Jefferson, of course, was then Vice President, having defeated Thomas Pinckney for that office in 1796. During the next two decades, the congressional caucus system controlled by two political parties faced mounting criticism; many thought it was virtually unconstitutional—or at best undemocratic—for representatives and senators to nominate presidential candidates without consulting the electorate. In 1824 only about a fourth of the members of Congress attended a caucus that nominated William H. Crawford as the Republican candidate for President. This was the last such meeting ever held. During the succeeding decade, the more familiar national convention system developed.

Adams campaigned for reelection by being President and carrying out established Federalist programs. Jefferson, who lacked oratorical talents, disclosed his political views in letters to friends, who then dispersed them to an eager populace that came to see him as the spokesman for the common people and Adams as the representative of men of property, portraits that are much too simplified. Although both John Adams and Thomas Jefferson believed fervently in an independent United States of America under a constitution that promoted liberty and preserved order, disagreement over the means to such goals interrupted a long friendship, which was renewed only when both were very elderly statesmen.

There are numerous reasons for the defeat of Adams, a proud, doughty patriot. Among them were Federalist moves that alienated large blocks of voters (Hamilton's fiscal measures, the Whiskey Rebellion fracas, the Alien and Sedition Acts, and the alleged schemes to declare war on France), and among some of Hamilton's followers there was strong opposition to Adams for his alleged weakness in dealing with France. In addition, the fractured Federalists failed to build up support among voters who had newly gained the franchise, especially among those lower-class and middle-class elements living outside of the Northeast. In short, they ignored changing conditions and virtually committed political suicide.

This head-in-the-clouds (or sand) attitude not only caused a political turnabout with profound reverberations but it also produced something the men meeting at Philadelphia in 1787 had not anticipated: party voting in the Electoral College, where, according to the Constitution, the top votegetter would be President and whoever came in second, Vice President. An equal number of ballots (seventy-three) for Jefferson and Aaron Burr, ostensibly candidates for the presidency and the vice presidency on the Democratic-Republican ticket, threw the election into a lame-duck House where the Federalist opposition still wielded considerable power. Some of these disgruntled congressmen considered installing Burr as a puppet president, but after thirty-six ballots Jefferson won. Ironically, Jefferson's victory owed much to the efforts of Alexander Hamilton, who, as Burr's keenest rival in New York state, had told his followers to support Jefferson.

Although he disliked both men, who long were his political foes, Hamilton respected his Virginia adversary much more than he did the unscrupulous, handsome Burr. Yet all this uproar and Burr's tragic downfall a few years later should not disguise a crucial fact: the winners had hit upon a political partnership that has demonstrated considerable power ever since—southern agrarians hand-in-hand with urban politicians of the Northeast.

Having experienced two confusing national elections that put a President and Vice President of rival parties in office for four years and nearly turned a vice-presidential candidate into a President, the Congress decided something must be done. Before the next election the Twelfth Amendment to the Constitution was ratified; it was now clear that the electors must vote separately for the two offices and specify which position they were voting for.

Jeffersonian Triumphs

On March 4, 1801, Thomas Jefferson, (whose long and productive career is highlighted in the accompanying biographical sketch) rose at sunrise, soaked his feet in cold water for five minutes, washed, shaved, selected a green outfit with gray stockings and gray waistcoat, and went downstairs to breakfast in a boardinghouse located about a half hour's walk from the Capitol. The other boarders quietly awaited his arrival and tried to seat him in a place of honor at the head of a large common table, but he declined, noting he was about to become the president of a republic, not the sovereign of a kingdom.

To their surprise this fifty-eight-year-old Virginian did not ride to the Capitol in a carriage; he walked and rubbed shoulders with his fellow citizens along the way. In the Senate chamber there was a brief ceremony, not especially impressive. Those present included a few close friends and two men who were not: Chief Justice John Marshall, whose duty it was to administer the oath of office, and Aaron Burr, the new Vice President, a man Jefferson did not trust. Among the missing were John Adams and nearly all of the Federalist congressmen who had hurried out of town rather than witness what they were certain were the initial death throes of the American dream.

The Cabinet

Although the Republican victory in effect witnessed the birth of a long-lasting and successful political partnership between southern agrarians and urban politicians of the Northeast, Jefferson and Burr themselves did not get along well. Aware that Burr was eager to reward his New York political machine with jobs, the President did not consult with him concerning cabinet appointments, and the distance between himself and his Vice President increased daily. Both were extremely able, brave men, but Burr craved excitement, intrigue, action. Jefferson liked repose, books, pleasant conversation, and philosophy. Their personalities were so different that cooperation was virtually impossible.

James Madison, Jefferson's associate for over a quarter of a century, became Secretary of State and the most important member of the Cabinet. Swiss-born Albert Gallatin (1761–1849) eventually was Secretary of the Treasury, but not until a new Senate took over since his confirmation by Federalist stalwarts was in doubt. Besides Madison and Gallatin, Jefferson's official family included General Henry Dearborn as Secretary of War, Levi Lincoln

The new capital was in the rough countryside, with mud roads and a few boardinghouses nearby. This view of the capitol was painted in 1800.

Thomas Jefferson

1743–1826

One of the most important leaders in Revolutionary America and the decades that followed was Thomas Jefferson. A rather shy, loose-limbed, redheaded youth, Jefferson was the son of a well-to-do frontier planter whose wife, Jane Randolph, was related to the most distinguished families in colonial Virginia. Young Jefferson first lived near Richmond, but at the age of nine, shortly before his father's death, the family moved west to Albemarle County. After being tutored in the classics, he entered the College of William and Mary in 1760, graduated two years later, began to practice law, and in 1769 was elected to the House of Burgesses. There Jefferson immediately joined the strong anti-British faction and helped to create the Virginia Committee of Correspondence.

In 1772 he married a twenty-four-year-old widow, Martha Wayles Skelton, who bore him six children before her death ten years later; however, only two daughters, Martha and Mary, lived to maturity. In 1774 he penned a set of resolutions titled *A Summary View of the Rights of British America*, a document that spelled out many of the legal and political doctrines that Americans would use to justify their rebellion. Just as the Saxons conquered England, Jefferson reasoned, in the same way British colonists seized the American mainland—and this immigration in no way indebted the colonists to England. Rather, it was a "natural" right of conquest. Jefferson also denied Parliament's authority over the colonies and insisted that the only link between America and England was the colonists' voluntary submission to the king. However, the most widely read composition Thomas Jefferson ever wrote was the Declaration of Independence, in which he expressed his belief that a government ruled only by popular consent, a notion he had derived from the English philosopher John Locke.

In 1779 Jefferson was elected governor of Virginia, a job he performed reasonably well until the British invaded his state in the spring of 1781. This military action, coming at the very end of his term, inspired political rivals to level charges of unpreparedness, accusations that were renewed when he emerged as a presidential candidate in 1800.

The most versatile of the founding fathers, Thomas Jefferson built a stunning mansion on a hilltop near Charlottesville, his beloved "Monticello," where he experimented with fruit and vegetable culture, tinkered with scientific pursuits, played the violin, and accumulated probably the best private library in America, which later became the nucleus of the famed Library of Congress. After his White House years (1801–1809), Jefferson returned to Monticello where he conceived, designed, and brought into being the University of Virginia, the last of many achievements to flow from a truly brilliant mind.

as Attorney General, Robert Smith of Baltimore as Secretary of the Navy, and Gideon Granger as Postmaster General (not a cabinet-level post until 1829). Dearborn, Lincoln, and Granger were New Englanders, proof that the new President was trying to give his Cabinet a regional balance. A harmonious group of men, the Cabinet was clearly dominated by the President, Madison, and Gallatin.

One of Jefferson's first decisions involved the hated Alien and Sedition Acts. Those jailed under the acts were set free and their fines returned and the two laws were allowed to lapse. The Naturalization Act, which set a fourteen-year residence requirement for citizenship, was repealed and the original five-year residence requirement restored. Jefferson, who was distressed by both the size and the existence of the national debt, told Gallatin to keep finances simple and reduce costs. Like any good farmer of his own day, he believed that the federal government should pay its own way. In two years Gallatin cut the debt by $5 million and out-

lined a scheme for eliminating it entirely within about a decade and a half. Most of this saving resulted from cuts in military spending, but some jobs created by the Federalists were also eliminated.

Patronage and Spoils

Despite his statesman's image, Jefferson was no stranger to patronage. Sudden expansion of various departments, one way to create jobs the party faithful thought they had earned, was obviously in direct opposition to his philosophy of strict economy and small government. After much deliberation Jefferson concluded that only those who had abused their powers, men who had enforced the Sedition Act, for example, would be ousted. Adherence to Federalist principles alone was no cause for dismissal. Vacancies, he said, would be filled by Democratic-Republicans until they held half the places, thus equalizing the number of officeholders. Yet by mid-1803 only 130 Federalists remained

Courtesy of the New-York Historical Society, New York City.
The American navy ended extortion against U.S. vessels after this attack on Tripoli in 1804. This engraving, done the next year, commemorated the new nation's first successful naval operation.

in 316 positions over which the President had appointive power. Since Jefferson was an adroit, consummate politician, "equalization," to no one's surprise, meant a 40–60 percent split, with his followers clearly in the majority.

Taming the Barbary Pirates

As minister to France in the 1780s, Thomas Jefferson had urged war on a number of small Moslem states along the southern coast of the Mediterranean. An assortment of pashas and beys who lived in that part of North Africa demanded, and usually got, payment from both small and large powers in return for letting their merchant ships pass unmolested. He subsequently tried without success to interest President Washington in an international blockade that would smash this crude protection racket.

Shortly after Jefferson became President, the Pasha of Tripoli demanded an increase in his annual subsidy. When the United States turned him down, the Pasha declared war. Angered by this effrontery, Jefferson dispatched Commodore Richard Dale to protect the interests of the nation in that region. Dale and the local consul arranged a blockade of sorts along the coast of Tripoli. The so-called Tripolitan War, which dragged on until 1805, was marked by occasional exploits now celebrated in legend and song. The U.S. Navy got a handful of heroes, notably Stephen Decatur. (An account of Decatur's tumultuous life can be found in a biographical sketch in this chapter.)

On June 4, 1805, fearing internal disorders and further American attacks on his city, the Pasha signed a treaty of peace with the United States. Although the terms were reasonable, they included $60,000 in ransom money for the release of American prisoners he held. (A decade later Decatur returned to North Africa once more, crushed a new outbreak of piracy, and ended for all time payment of tribute by the United States to these Barbary pirates.) The importance of this episode is twofold. Though a costly affair, the war gained new respect for the young republic on the high seas and provided invaluable experience for the naval commanders who were soon destined to grapple with a much mightier foe.

The Frontier

Although Jefferson naturally was interested in the course of the Tripolitan War, he had to face a potentially much more dangerous enemy than the

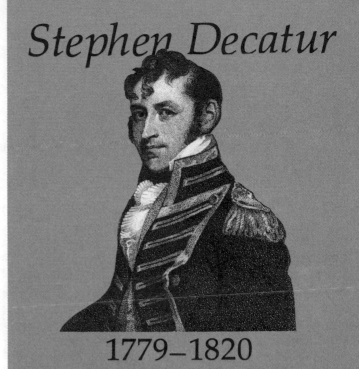

Stephen Decatur

1779–1820

Son of a naval hero bearing the same name, Stephen Decatur grew up in a comfortable Philadelphia household; as a youth, he was never far from the sea, controversy, and excitement. Impatient with the classroom, he became a midshipman in 1798 and sailed forth to do battle in the on-and-off naval war with France. Tall, erect, athletic, handsome, full of daring, he proved to be a good officer, despite a propensity for duelling.

In the so-called Tripolitan War (1804), Decatur achieved full-fledged hero status and rose to the rank of captain. Skill in close combat (during which his younger brother was slain) and a natural flair for leadership made him easily the most striking figure to emerge from those rough-and-tumble encounters with Barbary pirates.

After helping negotiate peace with the Bey of Tunis, he sailed home in triumph to Norfolk, Virginia, where he met his future wife, Susan Wheeler, daughter of a wealthy merchant who was then mayor of that city. During the next four years Decatur commanded a gunboat flotilla in Chesapeake Bay and also was head of the Norfolk Navy Yard. As commander of the *United States* at the onset of the War of 1812, he scored an impressive victory over the British warship *Macedonian* near Madeira; but two years later, now captain of the *President*, he came out second best when he tried to break through the enemy blockade that had sealed up Long Island Sound. Briefly interned in Bermuda, Decatur nevertheless returned a hero once more. A naval court of inquiry decided his capture had resulted not from enemy action but from damage to the *President* as it crossed a sandbar into open water. The court declared that Decatur had, in fact, achieved victory over the *Endymion*, the most persistent of the enemy warships in pursuit of the *President*.

In 1815 Decatur went back to North Africa with a squadron of nine ships to settle a dispute with the Dey of Algiers. In quick order he negotiated a treaty that ended tribute for all time and required payment for recent damage to American ships. The squadron then moved on to Tunis and Tripoli where similar agreements were signed.

During the last five years of his life, as a member of the Board of Naval Commissioners, Stephen Decatur was a prominent figure in Washington society. Financially secure as the result of prize money awarded to him, he invested heavily in local real estate and erected a substantial mansion that still stands on historic Lafayette Square. In 1818 he was second in yet another duel and two years later was mortally wounded when he met Commodore James Barron at the famed Bladensburg duelling ground near Washington.

This disgreement arose when Barron, suspended for five years for his role in the *Chesapeake-Leopard* affair in 1808, tried to reenter active naval service. Decatur, a member of the court-martial board which handed down that decision and now a U.S. Navy commissioner, vigorously opposed Barron's request for sea duty. In deference to the latter's poor eyesight, Decatur stood only eight paces away and apparently intended to merely wound his adversary. Barron had other plans.

Forty-eight hours later official Washington attended a stately funeral for the hero of Tripoli. Commodore Barron, seen as the villain in the piece and devoid of support, lived out the remainder of his unhappy life ashore on "waiting orders." When he died in Norfolk in 1851 at the age of 82, he was the U.S. Navy's senior officer.

Pasha of Tripoli long before it ended. North America hardly figured in Napoleon Bonaparte's schemes for conquest and power, yet his influence upon Jefferson's administration and the development of the United States was profound indeed. For a brief moment it appeared that he might seize the heartland of the continent and end all dreams of expanding frontier growth.

The lands beyond the Appalachians, source of considerable Democratic-Republic support, were of special concern to Jefferson. New territories and states were appearing there almost every year. Kentucky became a state in 1792; Tennessee, four years later; and Ohio, in 1803. Meanwhile, territorial governments were being organized in Indiana, Illinois, and Michigan. By 1800 some 400,000 citizens, many of them from New England or eastern regions of the South, were carving out homesteads in the new territories. In 1796 the Federalists cut the minimum purchase to 640 acres, then in 1800 to 320, also reducing down payments to 25 percent with the balance due in four years, not one. The price of land, however, remained the same, $2 per acre. Four years later the Jeffersonians lowered the minimum purchase to 160 acres, with the down payment set at only $80.

These reduced requirements for land purchase aided small farmers who swarmed in, erected simple log structures in a day, only partially cleared eight or ten acres of their property, raised a few crops, let their stock run wild, and moved on, often within a few years. To be successful in the wilderness, of course, one needed money, land, seed, and basic tools. The frontier, therefore, never was a haven for the extremely poor. Such folk tended to remain in eastern cities where they became day laborers or factory workers or, if they somehow got beyond the mountains, became squatters who were subsequently displaced by those who acquired legal title to the land.

The Louisiana Purchase

Pinckey's Treaty (or the Treaty of San Lorenzo, 1795) gave Americans the right to use the broad Mississippi and to deposit goods on Spanish soil for reshipment to the rest of the world. Soon after taking office, however, Jefferson learned of a secret treaty transferring New Orleans and the vast Louisiana Territory to France. The ambitious French emperor wanted Louisiana because, thanks to a momentary peace with Great Britain, he could turn his attention to the restoration of the New World

City Art Museum of Saint Louis.

George Bingham made the crew of an Ohio flatboat the subject of this painting in 1857. The crew is killing time while tied up to a dock.

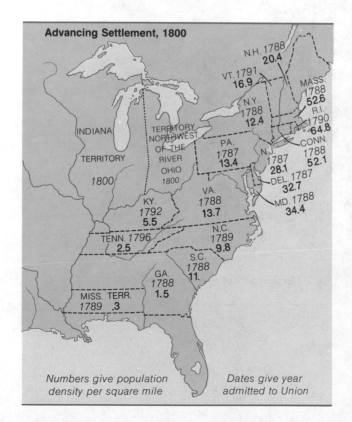

Advancing Settlement, 1800

INDIANA TERRITORY

TERRITORY NORTHWEST OF THE RIVER OHIO *1800*

N.H. *1788* **20.4**

VT. *1791* **16.9**

MASS. *1788* **52.6**

N.Y. *1788* **12.4**

R.I. *1790* **64.8**

PA. *1787* **13.4**

CONN. *1788* **52.1**

N.J. *1787* **28.1**

DEL. *1787* **32.7**

MD. *1788* **34.4**

KY. *1792* **5.5**

VA. *1788* **13.7**

TENN. *1796* **2.5**

N.C. *1789* **9.8**

S.C. *1788* **11.**

GA. *1788* **1.5**

MISS. TERR. *1789* **.3**

Numbers give population density per square mile

Dates give year admitted to Union

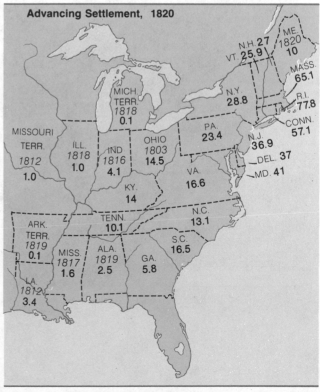

Advancing Settlement, 1820

MICH. TERR. *1818* **0.1**

N.H. **27**

VT. **25.9**

ME. *1820* **10**

MASS. **65.1**

N.Y. **28.8**

R.I. **77.8**

MISSOURI TERR. *1812* **1.0**

ILL. *1818* **1.0**

IND *1816* **4.1**

OHIO *1803* **14.5**

PA. **23.4**

CONN. **57.1**

N.J. **36.9**

DEL. **37**

MD. **41**

KY. **14**

VA. **16.6**

ARK. TERR. *1819* **0.1**

TENN. **10.1**

N.C. **13.1**

MISS. *1817* **1.6**

ALA. *1819* **2.5**

GA. **5.8**

S.C. **16.5**

LA. *1812* **3.4**

empire France lost in 1763. Louisiana, he thought, could provide foodstuffs for Haiti and other tropical islands he planned to add to his realm.

Alarmed by this news, Jefferson asked Robert Livingston, minister to France, to find out what was going on. He told Livingston to discourage the transfer of Louisiana if it were not completed and to obtain West Florida for the United States if it were. The French, however, were unwilling to discuss these matters, and Jefferson clung to the hope that international complications would prevent Napoleon from actually taking possession of Louisiana. As it turned out, these hopes were realized,

but not before Jefferson experienced some extremely anxious moments.

In October 1802 the acting Spanish intendant at New Orleans suddenly terminated the right of Americans to deposit goods there, duty free, for reshipment. Beset by angry frontiersmen from Kentucky and Tennessee crying for war and by political adversaries eager to embarrass the administration, Jefferson dispatched James Monroe as a special emissary to both France and Spain. Monroe had orders to determine the precise borders of Louisiana and was authorized to offer up to $2 million for control of New Orleans and as much of the Floridas as pos-

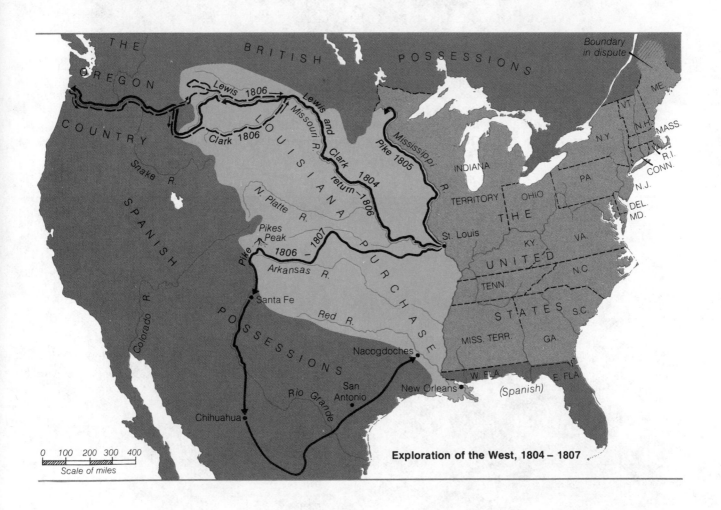

Exploration of the West, 1804 – 1807

New Orleans was already the main port for the growing Ohio River Valley
of the United States when Louisiana was purchased in 1803.

sible. If he had no success whatsoever, then he was free to approach the British concerning an alliance against France.

By the time Monroe arrived in Paris in April 1803, Napoleon had changed his plans completely. After some initial success, his West Indies armies were bogged down by disease and revolt. Spain refused to give up the Floridas, without which defense of Louisiana was difficult, and because of bad weather, the expedition outfitted to set up French administration in Louisiana never departed from a Dutch port. Of greater importance, Napoleon did not want a rupture with the United States since he was planning to resume his war with England. The British navy, he fully realized, could seize Louisiana easily enough once hostilities began.

For all these reasons, Napoleon decided to sell; even before Monroe got to France, he offered Livingston the entire territory of Louisiana, although no one was quite certain how much land actually was involved. Somewhat taken aback, the two Americans exceeded their original instructions and quickly agreed to pay France $11.25 million and to assume claims totaling $3.75 million by U.S. citizens against France.

At a cost of about $15 per square mile Livingston and Monroe more than doubled the size of their nation and struck a death blow to lingering European hopes of somehow containing the young republic along the Atlantic seaboard. Yet signing a bill of sale with Napoleon Bonaparte, a very sly negotiator, was only the first of several possible hurdles. The French legislature and Spain might not sanction this transaction since Napoleon had promised not to hand Louisiana over to a third power. Also, President Jefferson at first believed that acquisition of so much land might require a constitutional amendment. However, he dropped this proposal and acquiesced in the argument that the President's war and treaty powers covered this question. In October of 1803 an enthusiastic Congress controlled by Jeffersonian Republicans gave its approval, notwithstanding the opposition of Federalists from New England. Two months later a special French commissioner dispatched to New Orleans handed Louisiana over to the United States.

Meanwhile, even before Napoleon offered to sell this vast territory, Jefferson had sent a combined scientific and military expedition westward to find out what lay beyond the Mississippi River. Alarm over Spain's decision to end the right of deposit at New Orleans prompted this move, and what the President probably had in mind was an alternate route for western produce, or at least to ascertain if such might exist. Heading this group of explorers was his former personal secretary, Meriwether Lewis (1774–1809), a young man who idolized him, and William Clark (1770–1838), the younger brother of George Rogers Clark who had won fame in the Revolutionary War.

This small, well-equipped expedition, secretly financed by Congress since its goal was to explore lands then owned by foreign powers, set out in 1803. All of the military men were required to keep journals of their daily observations, which added to the natural history notes recorded by trained observers who accompanied them. The party followed the Missouri River nearly to its headwaters and then crossed the Rockies, finally reaching the Pacific Ocean in November 1805. Part of the way, they had as guides a French Canadian trapper, Touissaint Charbonneau, and his Indian wife, Sacajawea (whose contributions to the success of the expedition are discussed in an accompanying biographical sketch). The Lewis and Clark expedition returned to St. Louis, now American soil, in September 1806, loaded with journals, samples of flora and fauna, and much valuable knowledge about the great Northwest. (An essay on "Jefferson, Lewis and Clark, and the West" at the end of this chapter provides more information on the expedition.)

During these same months another army officer, Lt. Zebulon M. Pike, set out on two expeditions in the West. Like Lewis and Clark, Pike departed from the St. Louis area each time. In 1805 he went up the Mississippi into what is now Minnesota in an effort to find the headwaters of that great river. He collected a wealth of information but failed to achieve his goal. The following year Pike and a small party headed for the great Southwest.

Sacajawea
ca. 1787–1812

Born in a Shoshone village in present-day Idaho and daughter of a chief, Sacajawea was captured in 1800 by a war party of a rival tribe, the Hidatas. Along with another Shoshone girl, she was sold to Touissant Charbonneau, a Canadian trapper who lived with her captors. He subsequently married both of them according to local Indian rites. In the winter of 1804–1805, Lewis and Clark appeared in the region and hired Charbonneau as an interpreter and guide, with the understanding that both he and Sacajawea would accompany the famous explorers. In February 1805 she gave birth to a son and, less than two months later, with the papoose strapped to her back, set out for the Pacific.

Sacajawea proved her worth to the expedition in many ways. She was visible evidence to the various Indian tribes encountered on the journey of the peaceful nature of this expedition, and her knowledge of Indian dialects made her an invaluable aid to communication with those natives. She was instrumental in gaining the aid of her kinsmen in leading the expedition across the Continental Divide and without their help it is quite possible that Lewis and Clark never would have reached their objective.

William Clark later took Sacajawea's son into his care, and provided for his education. Clark also helped Charbonneau and Sacajawea to settle in St. Louis. However, both desired a less "civilized" life and returned to a life of fur trading.

The legend of Sacajawea as sole guide of the Lewis and Clark expedition arose from a novel based on the expedition. Few women have been honored by so many memorials, and her character and exploits have evoked great praise. She was an early heroine of the suffragists, and the celebrations marking the centennial of the Lewis and Clark Expedition added to her fame. Lewis only mentions her once in his journal, rather disdainfully in fact, but Clark obviously thought very highly of her. He nicknamed her "Janey" and called Jean-Baptiste "Pomp," a name he also bestowed upon Pompey's Pillar on the Yellowstone River.

Missouri Historical Society.

This building was one of the earliest trading posts.

Pike and his men made it to southeastern Colorado, where they camped during the winter at what is now Pueblo, Colorado, and then in midwinter crossed the mountains and constructed a fort on the Conejos Creek near its entrance to the Rio Grande. Later, they were captured by Spanish troops based at Santa Fe and taken to Chihauhua for questioning by Mexican officials. Eventually, Pike and his men were escorted back to American soil unharmed.

John Marshall's Court

Alexander Hamilton remarked in 1788 that "the judiciary is beyond comparison the weakest of the three departments of power," and indeed the Supreme Court was of minor importance under the Federalists. It heard few cases and only a very small number were of any significance. The justices met in the basement of the Senate, the designers of the Capitol having forgotten to build special quarters for them. Shortly after the election of 1800, Chief Justice Oliver Ellsworth quit. His health was poor, but the Democratic-Republicans believed he stepped down so Adams could install a younger, healthier man to keep bright the flame of Federalism.

John Jay, who had been the first Chief Justice (1789–1794), refused to accept the position again, and Adams eventually appointed John Marshall, his Secretary of State, to head the court. Federalist

Chief Justice John Marshall used his personal charm and strong mind to shape the Supreme Court into a force for nationalism. Rembrandt Peale caught the gentle force in Marshall's eyes in this 1834 portrait.

stalwarts in the Senate were not impressed. Marshall was a Virginian, a simple, modestly dressed person, democratic in bearing and close to Adams, then much out of favor with the party regulars. Reluctantly they confirmed the man who would preside over the Supreme Court for the next thirty-four years.

Marshall wasted no time in organizing the court so as to produce maximum results. It was his aim to use it to strengthen the national government; to do so, the position of the court itself would have to be enhanced considerably. Marshall saw the future of the nation as being determined by the ability of the Constitution to accommodate to the changing forces of daily life and to harness those forces to the national purpose. He contended that the Supreme Court had the final power *and the responsibility* to interpret the Constitution, and he was determined to succeed in securing that authority for his court.

To project a strong, unified voice to the public, Marshall persuaded the justices to forgo traditional individual opinions and through private conferences to forge differing views into an official decision, usually penned and delivered by Marshall himself. In this way the pronouncement became the verdict of an institution rather than the random thoughts of a handful of men.

The opening round in Marshall's drive to increase the powers of his court began as soon as the Democratic-Republicans assumed control of the national government. The Judiciary Act of 1801, passed just six days before Jefferson took the oath of office, set up sixteen new circuit courts, thereby creating jobs for sixteen judges and a host of marshals, attorneys, and clerks. This act cut the number of Supreme Court justices from six to five, the actual reduction to occur upon the next vacancy. This meant two justices would have to retire before Jefferson could name anyone to the court. It also permitted Adams to appoint as many justices of the peace as he wanted to. Before his precipitious departure he managed to make forty-two such appointments, all of them, of course, solid, sturdy Federalists.

The Department of State, headed by James Madison, found a stack of commissions signed, sealed and ready to be handed over to new Federalist office-holders. These so-called "midnight appointments" (John Adams presumably stayed up late on the evening of March 3, 1801, to complete this task) were not delivered before the Democratic-Republicans took office, and Jefferson told Madison not to do so. William Marbury, finding himself unemployed, asked the Supreme Court to issue a writ forcing Madison to give him his commission. Madison ignored a preliminary order to do so, and in 1803 the court turned to the Marbury matter in earnest.

This famous case, *Marbury v. Madison*, presented the justices with a complex dilemma. If they ordered Madison to award the commission, might he not again refuse to comply and thus make the court lose face since it had no way to enforce its decisions. If the justices ruled in favor of Madison, then they would be helping their political foes. Marshall's way out was shrewd indeed. The court, he said, did not have the jurisdiction to issue the writ sought by Marbury since the provisions of the Judiciary Act of 1789 granting such powers were unconstitutional. Marshall then proceeded to lecture the administration on the *justice* of the case, informally urging James Madison to give William

Marbury what he wanted. In short, Marbury should get his post as a justice of the peace; but, because a 1789 law was defective, the Supreme Court lacked the power to issue the desired writ.

For the first time the court had declared a federal law unconstitutional, and this decision suggested an answer to the sticky question of how to protect the people from unconstitutional acts by the executive and legislative branches of the national government. Virginia and Kentucky tried to assert, when the Alien and Sedition Acts were passed, that a state could rule on the constitutionality of federal laws. In his opinion, Marshall said, the Supreme Court was the final arbiter, a view that would keep the states out of national affairs. During the same session, the Marshall court ruled that Jefferson's Circuit Court Act of 1802, which restored membership on the high bench to six and established six circuit courts with one Supreme Court justice assigned to each one, was constitutional. Thus, the Chief Justice gained public respect for what appeared to be impartiality, while actually reasserting the court's awesome power of judicial review.

Unmoved by the court's approval of the 1802 act, the Jeffersonians were firmly convinced that they must somehow restrict judicial power. At issue, in their opinion, was the ability of six Federalists to thwart the will of the majority of American voters. The only method of unseating federal judges was, according to the Constitution, impeaching them for "high crimes and misdemeanors." The first case sent to the Senate for trial involved Judge John Pickering of New Hampshire. Pickering was charged with malfeasance and general unfitness because of excessive drinking and unstable behavior. The administration won its case despite uncertainty over whether unstable behavior was a "misdemeanor" and thus impeachable.

The administration then set out for bigger game, Justice Samuel Chase of the United States Supreme Court. Chase, an arch-Federalist, had not been impartial in the Alien and Sedition cases he had heard, and in 1803 criticized the administration before a Baltimore jury, charging that Congress was jeopardizing the independence of the judiciary. His trial, held in 1805, with Aaron Burr as a disgraced, lame-duck Vice President presiding, was a disaster for the Jeffersonians. The defense, ably conducted, held to a strict interpretation of impeachment; the administration argued for a loose construction of what the Constitution said. Although Jefferson's party enjoyed a substantial majority in the Senate,

the leaders could not gain a conviction, which required a two-thirds vote. With Chase's precedent-setting acquittal, the administration abandoned this route and concentrated instead upon appointing the right men whenever vacancies occurred.

Burr, Hamilton, and the "Essex Junto"

Despite occasional setbacks, Jefferson's first term was a success. His inexperienced party grasped the reins of national government, provided generally constructive legislation, and proved it was not the demon Federalists had feared it would be. More importantly, the Jeffersonians demonstrated that the transfer of power in a republic was indeed possible without bloodshed. They had also "shown the flag" in North Africa and, incidentally, more than doubled the size of the nation with an unexpected and very successful real estate deal. Not surprisingly, Jefferson was reelected by a huge majority in 1804, carrying every state except Connecticut and Delaware. His running mate, was not Aaron Burr, but another New Yorker, George Clinton.

Burr's troubles began four years earlier when he was suspected of permitting the Federalists to use him in an Electoral College scheme to supplant Jefferson as President. This crude ploy, which ruined him in the eyes of most Jeffersonians, seemed also to end his usefulness on the national scene. Aware that he would not be renominated on the ticket with Jefferson, Burr listened to the siren song of some disgruntled New England Federalists known as the "Essex Junto." This small band of malcontents, led by Senator Thomas Pickering of Massachusetts, viewed with alarm the admission of new Democratic-Republican strongholds such as Ohio to the United States and the national rule of southern aristocrats. They were certain their party was doomed. The solution, they thought, was to secede and form yet another republic.

These New Englanders first sounded out Alexander Hamilton as a leader, but were turned down. Burr, however, was interested and agreed to run for the governorship of New York, a position that would lend prestige to this disunion movement. It was a bruising campaign with Hamilton and other Federalists, who feared Burr's intriguing mind, solidly behind his Democratic-Republican opponent, Lewis Morgan. Morgan won, and angry words uttered during the campaign led to a duel between Burr and Hamilton near Weehawken, New Jersey, on the morning of July 11, 1804.

Courtesy of the New-York Historical Society, New York City.

Aaron Burr combined ambition and political maneuvering both to build and to destroy his own political career.

The two took their positions thirty feet apart, Burr (the challenger) aimed and fired. So did Hamilton but his shot skittered off harmlessly into some tree branches as he tottered and fell, fatally wounded. The ensuing uproar stunned Burr. New Jersey and New York authorities issued murder warrants since dueling was illegal, and he agreed to surrender if they in turn would allow him to post bail. When no such arrangement proved possible, he fled to the South where dueling was a more respected pastime but returned to Washington to preside over the Chase trial.

This affair was a tragedy of epic proportions. Hamilton, a truly brilliant individual who neither understood the public mind nor cared to, died—as he had lived—amid controversy. Yet during the formative years of the 1780s and the early 1790s, he was the indispensable man. Burr, a handsome, engaging conniver, potentially Jefferson's only rival

for national leadership, was now thoroughly discredited.

Jeffersonian Troubles

The issues and personalities shaping Jefferson's first four years in the White House continued to dominate his second administration, but somehow the magic touch was gone. Nothing seemed to go well. Burr out of office was more of a problem than when in, escalation of hostilities between England and France created one incident after another on the high seas, and worse yet, the administration's policies breathed new life into the Federalist party. Like many of his successors who have been returned to office by huge landslides at the polls, Thomas Jefferson learned that public acclaim can be transitory and that sustained political success is a difficult feat.

The Wilkinson-Burr Conspiracy

The full dimensions of this scheme are not totally clear even today since Burr told different people different things at different times, but it apparently included a plan to attack Texas with volunteers raised in Kentucky and Tennessee and possibly an attempt to lure the West out of the Union. While still Vice President, Burr became closely associated with General James Wilkinson, governor of the Louisiana Territory, political opportunist, and Spanish intelligence agent. The two pored over maps of the Southwest, dreamed dreams, and began rallying sympathetic politicians to their cause. The Burr net, cast widely and loosely, touched the governor of Tennessee, the territorial governor of Indiana, and some Federalist senators. Even Andrew Jackson was taken in for a time, thinking that the Secretary of War, Henry Dearborn, was behind the plot; however, he soon realized his error and severed all ties with Burr.

As Aaron Burr sought funds from various foreign ambassadors and began organizing a fighting force, word of these maneuverings crept into the press. Harman Blennerhasset, an active conspirator, indiscreetly talked with editors and reporters, and before long Jefferson dispatched investigators westward to find out what was up. Meanwhile, one of Wilkinson's friends alerted the Spanish government to a scheme to liberate Mexico. Although the desired war with Spain seemed unlikely, Burr seized upon a military buildup along the Sabine River as an excuse for action and set out for that region. Wilkinson, who had decided to betray Burr in order to gain a more important post with the American government, notified both Jefferson and the Spanish of the impending attack, and early in 1807 Burr was arrested.

The original charge against Burr was merely the misdemeanor of organizing an assault against foreign territory, but a grand jury increased the offense to treason. Burr was brought to trial in Richmond in a circuit court presided over by John Marshall. From the moment the proceedings began this episode took on new importance, for the real battle now was not over Burr's alleged crimes but was between the President and the Chief Justice. Marshall, still smarting over presidential threats to the judiciary, was eager to embarrass Jefferson. In the process he abandoned impartiality and in effect became the leading lawyer for the defense. Jefferson offered pardons to anyone incriminated by evidence they gave to the prosecution, spoke openly of Burr's guilt before the trial, and allowed publication of data relevant to the proceedings.

Marshall issued a subpoena for Jefferson to testify, but he refused to comply, noting that to do so might make the executive branch of the federal government subservient to the judicial. Marshall's masterstroke of partisanship was his charge to the jury, defining treason in the strictest possible terms. This man, normally an advocate of broad construction, suddenly found it expedient to advocate the opposite approach. Acccording to the Constitution, conviction required two witnesses to an overt act of war or an open confession by the accused. The prosecution could produce neither, and Marshall's charge assured Burr of acquittal.

The administration immediately sought a new trial outside of Marshall's jurisdiction on lesser charges, but Burr jumped bail and fled to Europe. Only one man in Burr's entourage was convicted of any crime and he paid a twenty-dollar fine and spent three hours in an Indiana jail. The final irony of this fiasco is that if Jefferson had not secured repeal of the Judiciary Act of 1801, Marshall would not have heard the case. No one involved—Burr, Wilkinson, Jefferson, or Marshall—emerged from this sordid mess with his reputation enhanced. But the Chief Justice defined treason so tightly that rarely has anyone since been accused of that crime.

Instead the federal government has seen fit to press for conviction on the lesser charge of espionage.

Trouble on the High Seas

England and France resumed their war in 1803, and by 1805 England controlled the high seas while France was winning on land. America, her shipping industry caught between two world powers, found herself in a very uncomfortable position. Each nation resorted to economic pressures in an attempt to weaken the other. Neither could tolerate neutral trade with its adversary. To maintain control of the seas, England needed a massive number of able seamen and increased greatly the practice of impressment or forced enlistment. Under British law, any able-bodied subject of the king could be conscripted for emergency service in the navy. The British navy thus began to search American vessels for deserters and any other Englishmen who might be subject to impressment. American captains resented the delays involved, loss of some crewmen, and searches of their ships by a foreign power.

Modern estimates of the number of illegal impressments are lower than claims made at the time, but they suggest that some 10,000 seamen were seized between 1793 and 1811. Since the British refused to recognize naturalization, English-born American citizens were seized. The British also impressed American-born sailors. Although there were more than enough British deserters, British subjects, and Americans to keep ships properly manned, national pride was wounded.

For their part, the British resented the success of the American carrying trade, which was growing by leaps and bounds while their maritime strength was tied up in naval warfare. With the Americans taking over markets once theirs, the British began enforcing the Rule of 1756. Seizure of cargoes under this rule, an infuriating reminder of former colonial status, was extensive and damaged American commerce severely. In retaliation, Napoleon issued his Berlin Decree (1806), a paper blockade of the British Isles, and French privateers began taking possession of all ships loaded with goods bound for Britain. The British answered in kind by prohibiting neutrals to trade with ports from which their own ships were barred, unless such vessels first stopped in the British Isles and paid British duties. In his Milan Decree, Napoleon warned that any ship that did so would be considered denationalized, henceforth a British vessel and subject to seizure as a prize of war.

Impressment, meanwhile, was becoming a much more troublesome issue. For months the *H.M.S. Leander* had been working the coastline just off New York, often detaining a dozen ships at a time pending search. In 1806 its seamen accidentally killed an American while firing a warning shot across the bow of a merchantman. Riots erupted in Manhattan, and Jefferson barred both the *Leander* and its sister ship, *H.M.S. Cambrian,* from port. Later that year the *H.M.S. Melampus* destroyed a French warship within the Virginia capes, clearly American waters.

The following year the British accused an American navy vessel, the *U.S.S. Chesapeake,* of enlisting two British deserters, charges that were probably true. The U.S. Navy refused to return the men, and when the *Chesapeake* left Norfolk, Virginia, the *H.M.S. Leopard* stopped the ship before it was able to mount its guns. When the American commander did not immediately comply with orders to permit a search, the British opened fire, killing three and injuring eighteen seamen and severely damaging the ship. Following the surrender of the *Chesapeake,* the British seized four of its seamen said to be deserters. Jefferson closed all American ports to the British navy. As a result, the British established a virtual blockade of the Chesapeake Bay and began ravaging the coast of Maine.

President Jefferson clearly did not want to be drawn into a European war, but he could not permit American rights to be ignored. Sadly, the nation was in no position to fight: the economy-minded Jeffersonians had done little to build up defense installations or to increase naval strength. As relations with London worsened, the President tried to negotiate, using American trade as a bargaining tool. On the last day of 1806, the British agreed to a treaty allowing "broken voyages," that

is, the reexportation of goods. In exchange the American negotiators said their nation would not place any restrictions on commerce for ten years, thus blunting their only true weapon in such talks. Americans were to ignore French decrees, and their country was granted "most-favored-nation" status and given a promise that the British no longer would stop unarmed U.S. ships within five miles of the American coast.

These provisions clearly put the United States in a very unneutral position, while actually imposing no restrictions on the British. Jefferson was so disgusted that he did not even present the document to the Senate for ratification. He said he was willing to continue talks, but the British thought they already had been too generous. The President reacted by putting into effect the Nonimportation Act passed by Congress earlier in 1806. This act included a suspending clause allowing Jefferson to invoke nonimportation whenever he deemed it advisable to do so. This ended importation of certain British goods and aroused considerable animosity in the British Isles. At the same time, Jefferson quietly prepared the nation for war. Forts were armed, the navy spruced up, and the militia readied for action. Yet he clung to the hope that the wide-ranging European conflict would end before fighting broke out.

The Embargo of 1807

In one last attempt to avoid hostilities, Jefferson asked Congress to enact an embargo to prohibit American ships from sailing to foreign ports. This measure hurt the British more than the French since the British naval blockade already sealed off the continent of Europe. The British, however, depended upon American food and raw materials. Although the President did not actually rally support for this measure, most citizens obeyed the new law, at least at the outset.

The full effects of what would become known as the "Obnoxious Embargo" are hard to assess. It ended an American shipping boom, and the American merchant marine lost its prominent role in world trade. There was widespread unemployment in many ports, but New England merchants soon became masters of evading the letter of the law, shipping goods to Canada and from there to Britain. Additional measures passed by Congress then barred overland export. The Federalists claimed these acts were unconstitutional, but the Marshall Court disagreed.

> ## British Barbarity and Piracy!!
>
> The Federalists say that Mr. Christopher Gore ought to be supported as Governor—for *his attachment to Britain.*—If British influence is to effect the suffrages of a free people, let them read the following melancholy and outrageous conduct of British Piracy, and judge for themselves.
>
> The "LEOPARD OUTSPOTTED" or Chesapeak Outrage outdone.

Courtesy of the New-York Historical Society, New York City.
This broadside linked the outrage of national pride over the Chesapeake-Leopard incident to other impressments, in this case an incident in Macao.

The British, of course, encouraged smuggling and opened their West Indian ports to American ships willing to go there. Some Yankee captains, once they learned of the embargo, never returned home and spent many months trading from one foreign port to another, piling up profits as they went. The embargo clearly failed as a weapon of foreign policy. Colonies of the great powers, caught in a general war, needed American goods much more than their mother countries; and, just as American ports were closing, the British found substitute commerce in Spanish colonies throughout the New World. English manufacturers stockpiled some cotton, located a plentiful source in Asia, and got still more from American smugglers eager to make money. London was not even interested in an American offer to rescind the embargo in return for relief from British restrictions on U.S. trade.

Although New England merchants complained the loudest, the commercial farmers of the South actually suffered the most. What the embargo really did at home was to encourage the growth of American manufacturing, but the transfer of investment capital to factories took time and, in the interim, thousands were out of work. The embargo became a very hot political issue and revived the Federalist party in both New York and Maryland, giving that political organization a momentary reprieve. It also split the Republican party into warring factions. This controversial measure was repealed shortly before Jefferson left office and replaced by the Non-intercourse Act (1809), which opened trade with all nations except Britian and France and held out the possibility of removing those restrictions on either country agreeing to respect American rights.

The Election of 1808

Despite the furor over the embargo (something many Federalists were certain was designed in Paris) and bickering among the Jeffersonians, the President's handpicked candidate, James Madison, won easily in 1808. Yet it was no landslide. C. C. Pinckney, once more the Federalist standard-bearer, got nearly three times as many electoral votes as in 1804, and New England resumed its solid Federalist stance. George Clinton, Jefferson's Vice President, and James Monroe both were a bit miffed because Madison received the nomination instead. Although Madison, a founder of the Democratic-Republicans and an early foe of the Federalists, had certainly earned the nomination, he lacked the personal appeal of his mentor, Jefferson. The first choice of the congressional caucus, Madison did not enjoy similar support among state branches of his party, some of them badly split by Jefferson's policies and personal factionalism.

Nevertheless, the Democratic-Republicans retained a respectable, if diminished majority in the Congress, and Madison was elected. Despite his credentials as party leader, he was very much a

Courtesy of the New-York Historical Society, New York City.

In this satire of the Embargo of 1807, the embargo is represented by a snapping turtle called the "Ograbme," which is embargo spelled backwards.

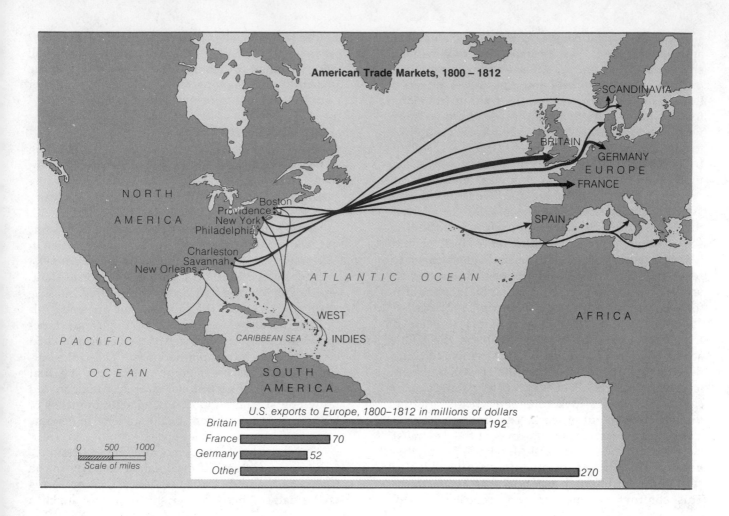

American Trade Markets, 1800 – 1812

SCANDINAVIA

BRITAIN

GERMANY
EUROPE
FRANCE

SPAIN

NORTH AMERICA

Boston
Providence
New York
Philadelphia
Charleston
Savannah
New Orleans

ATLANTIC OCEAN

AFRICA

PACIFIC OCEAN

WEST
CARIBBEAN SEA
INDIES

SOUTH AMERICA

U.S. exports to Europe, 1800–1812 in millions of dollars

Britain	192
France	70
Germany	52
Other	270

0   500   1000
Scale of miles

creature of Congress, unable to exert the influence Jefferson had displayed. This dependence was unfortunate since his administration would face new crises on the world scene.

The last months of Jefferson's second term were among the most distressing in his long life. Even his own party refused to support the embargo and, as noted, it became a nonintercourse scheme. The triumphs against the Barbary pirates, the Louisiana Purchase, the Lewis and Clark expedition, and other earlier successes seemed insignificant in the light of the ill will generated by a policy designed to maintain peace. What Jefferson failed to realize was how interdependent the United States and Europe really were. This fact, more than any conscious desire on the part of the American public for peace or war, doomed any plan that interfered with this close, natural relationship.

Jeffersonian America: An Overview

Political infighting, foreign dilemmas, and domestic intrigue should not disguise the growth and development of the United States during the first decade of the nineteenth century. In 1800 the nation had a population of 5,308,483; a decade later, 7,239,881. Every state and region demonstrated substantial growth, although the Middle Atlantic

POLICE OFFICE, *NOTICE.*

The Landlords, Tenants, and Occupiers of all houses of ill fame, situated in and about the neighbourhood of East George-street, in the Seventh Ward, are hereby notified, that all houses of the above description, found west of Rutgers-street, from and after the first day of May next, will become the particular objects of the vigilance of the Police, until they are suppressed.

January, 1813.

Printed by Hardcastle & Van Pelt, 86, Nassau-street.

Museum of the City of New York.

America's growth brought it the problems of cities and poverty, including prostitution, as noted in this warning from the New York police.

states (especially New York), Kentucky, and Tennessee registered the most dramatic gains.

Despite agricultural practices often thought primitive by Old World standards, farm output had increased sufficiently by 1800 to permit very impressive wheat exports to overseas markets. The South was in the midst of the switch to cotton. This crop, seldom seen prior to the Revolution except on the Sea Islands of Georgia and South Carolina, now was grown from Virginia southward into the growing frontier. Invention of the cotton gin by Eli Whitney in 1793 made it possible for a man to process as much as 50 pounds of the hardy upland variety in a single day. As cotton, almost a mania, became increasingly important in the new western territories of Alabama and Mississippi, even to the point of being accepted as currency, many planters abandoned traditional crops. Eight times as much

cotton was produced in 1804 as in 1794, and by 1810 Georgia and South Carolina were growing enough of the staple to account for nearly one-fourth of all American exports.

Since those expanding fields demanded gang labor, pressure to revive the slave trade grew apace. South Carolina, which because of hard times had placed a ban on foreign slave trading in 1787, decided to discard its anti-importation law in 1803. While Congress prohibited the importation of slaves in 1808, some smuggling of human cargoes continued after that date. Between 1790 and 1810, influenced largely by cotton, the number of blacks in South Carolina alone rose from a fifth of the total population to a third.

Other areas of American agriculture were expanding, too. Spanish sheep of the fine Merino strain appeared in 1802, and within eight years a strong wool-producing industry was evident in New York, Pennsylvania, and some parts of New England. The opening of new lands aided this agricultural upsurge. By 1810 more than a million Americans lived west of the Appalachians, many of them using rivers as their highways to spread settlement and transport supplies. At the same time, the beginnings of a transportation revolution were apparent in the East. By 1810 some 200 turnpike companies had been chartered in New England, and many other areas were quick to follow this example. In an age when transportation was crucial, privately constructed roads, paid for by the collection of tolls, provided one way to fulfill obvious needs. Several inventors were experimenting with steam-powered craft for inland travel. In 1807 Robert Fulton's steamboat made its way upstream in the Hudson River, and soon afterwards he inaugurated commercial steamship service.

Speculation in lands, so common during Jefferson's administration, continued under Madison. Under constant pressure, Indian tribes made further cessions, especially north of the Ohio River where 100 million acres were ceded between 1801 and 1810. As they were pushed closer together and further west the Indians found themselves caught between the frontier and the hostile Sioux and Chippewa. Those living in the Old Northwest found a leader in the Shawnee chief Tecumseh (ca. 1768–1813), who warned Indiana's territorial governor, William Henry Harrison, that he intended to form a confederation of tribes to resist further incursions. In late 1811 Harrison marched on an Indian town on the Wabash River, but Tecumseh had

The Public Library of Cincinnati and Hamilton County.

The City of Cincinnati grew as a result of its strategic position on the Ohio River, where it could tap the agricultural wealth of the Midwest and South. This early photograph (1848) shows the relationship of the river to the city's growth.

Courtesy Burton Historical Collection, Detroit Public Library.

The British gave up the fort of Detroit very reluctantly, despite its location on American soil. The reason is clear in this 1794 watercolor—Detroit was a major center of Indian trade.

departed for the South to find new allies, leaving his half-brother, the Prophet, in command. A battle ensued on Tippecanoe Creek, which Harrison won despite heavy losses. Tecumseh returned, mobilized the survivors, and sought out British help. When the War of 1812 erupted, he would seek his revenge.

Similar pressures existed in the Spanish Floridas where runaway slaves sometimes joined forces with hostile Indians. Nevertheless, Americans were flowing into West Florida (a coastal strip later apportioned among Mississippi, Alabama, and Louisiana), and in 1810 they staged a revolt against Spanish rule. Madison immediately announced annexation of the region. Spain was too weak to do more than protest, but two years later the Spanish threatened war when Madison tried to seize East Florida. This time the Americans backed down.

There is in these experiences in the Floridas a theme frequently repeated during ensuing decades. Restless American settlers moved on to foreign soil—land that was distant from the capital of the ruling power, saddled with weak colonial administration, and lacking military and naval installations. Within a few years, a decade at the most, as their numbers increased so did pressure for annexation by the United States. Eventually the foreign power either bowed to the inevitable and negotiated the best deal possible or went to war.

If there is one word that epitomizes Thomas Jefferson's America, it is expansion. The Louisiana Purchase was merely emblematic of what was transpiring in agriculture, population trends, transportation, and, thanks to the "Obnoxious Embargo," even in manufacturing. This was not the path of development that the Squire of Monticello had in mind, nor was it precisely what Alexander Hamilton had anticipated.

It is often said that the United States of America has been a fortunate land isolated from Europe's woes and profiting from them. To a degree this observation has merit, but America in 1810 was still very much a part of Europe in spite of its independence, the wide Atlantic, and a republican government. Soon those bonds, twist and turn as Americans might, would lead to war, a struggle some of them entered with great relish, but one that all Americans were delighted to see end.

Essay

Jefferson, Lewis and Clark, and the West

At the turn of the nineteenth century the land beyond the Mississippi River comprised an intriguing unknown, a mysterious land in which some men thought even the most fantastic forms of fauna and flora might exist. Its inhabitants, geographical features, and mineral wealth were only rumor and speculation. Although the southern and eastern boundaries of the vast area known as Louisiana were defined, it was uncertain just how far north and west the unexplored wilderness extended. English and Scottish trappers and traders were operating in areas just south of the Great Lakes region, and the Russians, Spanish, and British had begun to explore sections of the Pacific coastline; but, except for the port city of New Orleans and Spanish settlements in what is now New Mexico, Texas, and California, white settlers and explorers had exerted little influence in the area.

The Mississippi River, eastern boundary of this region, was becoming the major artery for commerce in the rapidly expanding American frontier. The fur trade long had depended upon the Mississippi for access to the outside world, and the increasing importance of agriculture in the territories and new states west of the Appalachians increased the need for fast and easy transportation routes to the markets.

As the river trade became more important, control of the port of New Orleans became an issue of increasing significance. Clearly, whoever controlled the port dominated the river and easily could determine the economic destiny of families living in Kentucky, Ohio, and Tennessee, not to mention those in the mushrooming American territories as well. However, as long as Louisiana was held by the weak Spanish government, these Americans felt reasonably certain that the Mississippi would remain open.

Although well-known for his actions as a patriot and statesman, Thomas Jefferson deserves to be equally well-known for his serious interests in nat-

The Lewis and Clark expedition had numerous encounters with bears. This illustration of a bear hunt appeared in Patrick Gass's *Journal*.

ural science and the unexplored western lands. While minister to France, he was approached by the enthusiastic John Leyard, an American who had attempted unsuccessfully to reach the western coast of North America by way of Siberia. Leyard wanted Jefferson to help him obtain aid in his efforts to explore the area between the Mississippi River and the Pacific Ocean. Jefferson agreed to do what he could, but Leyard died before any plans were formulated. Later, while Secretary of State, Jefferson encouraged the French botanist André Michaux to organize an expedition to explore the wilderness. He suggested to Michaux the possibility of mammoths inhabiting the vast Louisiana Territory, since remnants of their bones had been discovered in Kentucky; he also expressed hope that the easily

domesticated South American llama had migrated into the North American continent. Unfortunately, Michaux's political ambitions were greater than his scientific interests; and, before the venture got off the ground, he was discredited by his efforts to organize an independence movement in the trans-mountain territories.

Although President Jefferson had no idea that the United States was about to purchase Louisiana and thereby double its size, he continued his plans to explore the French-held western territory. In a "secret" message to Congress in January 1803, he requested a grant of $2,500 to finance an expedition staffed by members of the U.S. Army.

Jefferson appointed Meriwether Lewis to act as leader of this expeditionary force. The Lewis family, neighbors of the Jeffersons in Virginia, moved to upper Georgia when Meriwether was young. Life as a planter's son afforded Lewis a great deal of time to spend in the wilds, where he became a fine hunter and skilled observer of natural scientific phenomena. Although he returned to Virginia to pursue a classical education, the death of his father cut short his academic career when he was eighteen and Lewis enlisted in the army. During the Indian wars in the Northwest Territory, he fought under William Clark. After several years of military service, Lewis became private secretary to President Jefferson, who listed Lewis's "knowledge of the Western country, of the Army and of all its interests and relations" among the reasons for his appointment.

It seems that the search for the Northwest Passage was a common topic of conversation for Jefferson and Lewis, and the two shared the enthusiasm that eventually set the expedition into motion. Lewis chose William Clark, with whom he served in the Indian wars, to assist him in the leadership of the expedition. Clark was the son of a Virginia planter who moved to Louisville in 1785. While his older brother, George Rogers Clark, was making a name for himself as a military patriot, William was learning about frontier life. Although he received little formal education, Clark became proficient in surveying and the drawing of maps, and developed a keen interest in the activities of animals. After seven years in the army, Clark resigned, returning to private life until summoned by Lewis.

Although the two leaders had similar backgrounds, the success of the venture rested on the combined special talents of each. Lewis had higher military rank and actually was in command; he led his band of explorers with a sense of humane responsibility that echoes throughout the pages of his journals. Clark had more wilderness experience, and his resourcefulness was of incalculable value. He was both the illustrator of flora and fauna found enroute and the chief mapmaker.

In a detailed letter of instructions sent to Meriwether Lewis on June 20, 1803, Jefferson outlined the objectives of the expedition, itemizing provisions to be taken along and giving advice pertaining to the return trip. They were to make careful observations of all manner of geological, botanical, and zoological phenomena and supply detailed reports of natives encountered, complete with as much anthropological detail as could be gathered.

Lewis went to Philadelphia for crash courses in celestial navigation, geology, and emergency techniques of surgery and medicine. Lewis already had set out for the West when news of the purchase of the entire Louisiana Territory reached him, negating any further need for secrecy.

After unexpected delays in the construction of the flatboat which was to be home base to the travelers for much of the venture, Lewis and his party shoved off from Pittsburgh on August 31, 1803. The delay made this first leg of the journey difficult; for the Ohio River was nearing its seasonal low-water mark, and the vessel, although designed by Lewis with this problem in mind, encountered shoals shallower and more numerous than expected. Heavy fogs further impeded progress. After several minor incidents, the party reached Louisville where Clark joined it on October 26.

During a winter spent encamped on the eastern bank of the Mississippi about eighteen miles from St. Louis, Lewis questioned traders passing through the area about minerals and other features to be encountered on their trip. On May 14, 1804, the party, now numbering about forty-five men and one Newfoundland dog, set out up the Missouri.

Although the river provided the men with an abundant supply of fish, it was often treacherous, and even with both sails and poles, the party sometimes made only a few miles a day. There were disciplinary problems and a few accidents, but the Indians and trappers they met at the outset proved to be friendly, and the expedition proceeded much as planned.

The party wintered among the Mandan Indians at the junction of the Knife River and the Missouri in what is now North Dakota. Fort Mandan, their home until April 7, 1805, was of crude log and mud construction but had fieldstone fireplaces for heat and eight-foot walls for protection against possible Indian attacks. The explorers got along well with the Mandans, trading them the usual beads and trinkets, whiskey, and tobacco.

As the ice began to thaw after the severe winter, the flatboat went back down river with ten of the party and various specimens to be delivered to

On several occasions the expedition faced near disaster. This rough sketch from the *Journal* of Patrick Gass depicts one near disaster—a canoe accident.

the President. These included live birds, squirrels, and plants, as well as samples of Indian clothing and the bones and skins of various animals.

The rest of the group pushed on in canoes and the larger keel boats, carrying with them an interpreter, Touissant Charbonneau, his Indian wife, Sacajawea, who was to prove very helpful before the journey ended, and their son, Jean-Baptiste, born at Fort Mandan in February. Although the going was rough because of ice in the river and bad weather, the trek proceeded without a hitch until the Missouri River forked and the leaders could not decide which branch to take. After several days of scouting and decision making, they correctly chose the southern branch and soon were within sight of the majestic Rockies.

As the terrain became progressively more rugged, game grew scarcer. Now Lewis and Clark were especially anxious to contact Indians, for they thought that the Shoshone (Sacajawea's original tribe) had horses, which the expedition badly needed. The explorers also were fearful of spending the winter in an unfamiliar wilderness. In August a lone Indian on a horse was encountered, but after a brief, frustrating meeting, he rode away. Several days later, after crossing the Great Divide and dis-

covering the first westward-running river, the party made successful contact with a group of mounted Shoshone; one of the chiefs turned out to be Sacajawea's brother.

Lewis and Clark managed to get about thirty horses from the Shoshone, but no food. The Indians were close to starvation themselves and spent most of their days foraging for edible roots and whatever game could be found. They told Lewis that the small river he had discovered eventually flowed into the Columbia but that much of the intermediate waterway was impassable. Winter was arriving early (there was a heavy frost on August 19), and the expedition set out hurriedly to cross the mountain barrier. Now near starvation, they had to slaughter horses for food.

On September 19 a Nez Percé settlement was discovered. These hospitable Indians literally saved the explorers' lives. After recovering from near disaster, the leaders decided to continue by water, even if the going became difficult. They built canoes in the Indian fashion, left their remaining horses with the Nez Percé, and set off westward.

It took the shabby band another month to reach the Pacific. Their trail, the Kooskooskee River, consisted of a long series of rapids, and the Sanke, into which it emptied, was no easier to navigate. The Indians met along this leg of the journey were shrewd traders. As the expedition approached the mouth of the Columbia it encountered Indians who were familiar with the white man, according to D. B. Chidsey in his account of the expedition, and one was overheard to call another a "son of a pitch [sic]." Fleas, syphilis, and English vernacular expressions such as this gave evidence that these folk had been "blessed" by contact with the white man.

It rained incessantly during the first week that was spent near the Pacific. When the weather finally improved, the men set about building Fort Clatsop (named after the local Indians). There they spent the winter. The party became relatively friendly with the Clatsop, and much space was devoted to their customs in the journals of the explorers. There were only twelve days without rain

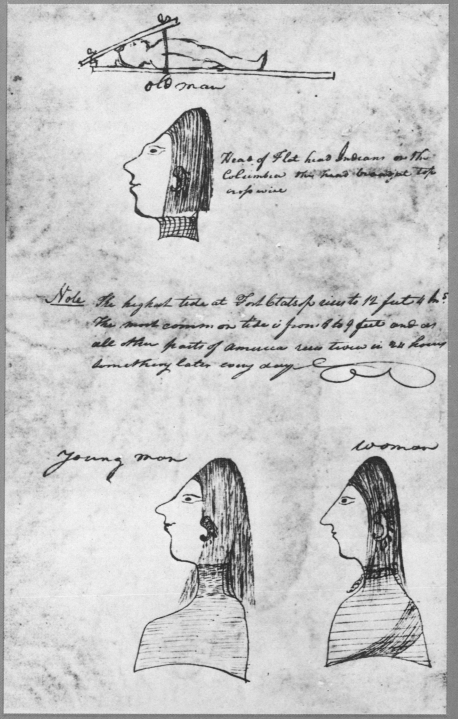

old man

Head of Flat head Indians on the Columbia this head brought top crosswise

Note The highest tide at Fort Clatsop rises to 12 feet 4 Ins. The most common tide is from 8 to 9 feet and as all other parts of America rises twice in 24 hours something later every day

Young man

Woman

William Clark's *Journal* **of the trip included this careful diagram of the Indian custom of headflattening.**

during the four-and-a-half-month stay at the mouth of the Columbia, and the winter was bitter indeed.

Several descriptions of the expedition were distributed to various Indian chieftains with instructions to give them to any traders or trappers they met; Lewis and Clark hoped some record of the expedition would reach civilization even if the party did not survive. The trip back was difficult, but not so arduous as the initial westward journey since the explorers had made friends with several tribes that could be counted upon for guidance, provisions, and assistance.

After crossing the Rockies, the expedition split into three groups in order to collect more data. In this fashion they were able to explore both the Yellowstone and Missouri rivers. The band led by Lewis had a frightening confrontation with hostile natives, and he was painfully injured in a hunting accident before the groups rendezvoused on the Missouri above Fort Mandan. The trip down river was basically uneventful, and the expedition arrived in St. Louis on September 23, 1806. Its return was celebrated in St. Louis, Louisville, and Washington with much pomp, and the explorers were the celebrities of the day, being awarded acclaim much like that given to twentieth-century aviators and space travelers. Lewis and Clark had explored territory that would become ten states. They had discovered twenty-five hitherto unknown varieties of fish (including the anchovy), six species of birds, five reptiles, and four amphibians. They had greatly expanded the body of scientific knowledge of the western lands as the Louisiana Purchase had expanded the physical limits of the United States.

This epic undertaking ended all speculation concerning a water route via the Louisiana Territory to the Pacific but provided Americans with insight into what they had bought for $15 million. Both Lewis and Clark resigned from military service shortly after this famous expedition ended, and both subsequently became territorial governors. There the similarities end. Clark, twice married, was active in the War of 1812 as chief executive of the Missouri Territory and led an assault against allied British-Indian forces in Wisconsin. He spent his last years quietly in St. Louis where he was host to numerous Indian delegations and carried on a substantial correspondence with gov-

ernment officials in Washington on their behalf. His home became a museum of sorts, filled with many Indian and natural curiosities. This collection, bequeathed to the St. Louis Natural History Society when he died in 1838, has now virtually disappeared.

Jefferson's reward to Lewis was the governorship of all of the Louisiana Territory north of the state bearing that name. Lewis proved to be an able administrator, but in the fall of 1809 he decided to go to Washington to straighten out some tangled personal finances. Accompanied by two servants, a black and a half-breed Spaniard, on the evening of October 11 Lewis arrived at a crude inn located in central Tennessee. The next morning he was dead. Just what happened is not clear even today. Jefferson, who knew Lewis well, assumed he committed suicide. Others believed he was murdered.

During the last century or so numerous monuments have been raised to Lewis and Clark, but none are necessary. Their exploits, their deeds, and their journals assure them of prominent places in the annals of American heroes.

And Jefferson, who lived to see several states from the Louisiana Purchase enter the Union, could bask in the reflected glory of his bargain, one of the most important real estate deals in American history. Strangely, at the time of acquisition in 1803, a benefit that he foresaw and a personal plan he cherished, both long forgotten by most historians, did not come to pass. In July of that year the President wrote to his good friend, Philip Mazzei:

"The acquisition of Louisiana, besides doubling our extent, and trebling our quantity of fertile country, is of incalculable value, as relieving us from the danger of war. It has enabled us to do a handsome thing for Fayette [sic]. He had received a grant of between eleven and twelve thousand acres, north of Ohio, worth, perhaps a dollar an acre. We have obtained permission of Congress to locate it in Louisiana. Locations can be found adjacent to the city of New Orleans, in the island of New Orleans, and its vicinity, the value of which can not be calculated. I hope it will induce him to come over and settle there with his family."

SELECTED
READINGS

Federalist Politics

David Fischer, *Revolution of American Conservatism: Federalist Party in Jeffersonian Democracy* (1965)

Linda Kerber, *Federalists in Dissent: Imagery and Idealogy in Jeffersonian America* (1970)

Jeffersonian Politics

Noble Cunningham, *The Jeffersonian Republicans in Power: Party Operations, 1801–1809* (1963)

M. J. Heale, *The Making of American Politics* (1977)

Leonard Levy, *Jefferson and Civil Liberties: The Darker Side* (1963)

Marshall Smelser, *The Democratic Republic, 1801–1815* (1968)

Leonard White, *The Jeffersonians: Administrative History, 1801–1829* (1951)

Development of Law

Richard Ellis, *The Jeffersonian Crisis: Courts and Politics in the New Republic* (1971)

Robert K. Faulkner, *Jurisprudence of John Marshall* (1968)

Kent Newmyer, *The Supreme Court under Marshall and Taney* (1969)

Foreign Relations

Bradford Perkins, *Prologue to War: England and the United States, 1805–1812* (1961)

Louis Sears, *Jefferson and the Embargo* (1967)

Glen Tucker, *Dawn Like Thunder: Barbary Wars and the Birth of the U.S. Navy* (1963)

Special Incidents

Thomas Abernethy, *Burr Conspiracy* (1954)

John Bakeless, *Lewis and Clark, Partners in Discovery* (1947)

Francis Beirne, *Shout Treason: Trial of Aaron Burr* (1959)

Reginald Horseman, *Expansion and American Indian Policy 1783–1812* (1967)

CHAPTER 7

WAR AND PEACE

TIMELINE

1810
Macon's Bill No. 2 removes trade restrictions

1810
Napoleon revokes Berlin and Milan Decrees

1812
Congress declares war against Great Britain

1812
Madison reelected President

1813
Perry's naval victory on Lake Erie

1813
Chief Tecumseh killed

1814
Andrew Jackson defeats the Creek Indians at Horseshoe Bend

1814
British army captures and burns Washington

1814
"The Star-Spangled Banner"

1814
Treaty of Ghent ends war with Great Britain

1814
Hartford Convention

1815
Battle of New Orleans

1816
Second Bank of United States chartered

1816
James Monroe elected President

1819
Panic of 1819

1819
Tallmadge amendment opens slavery controversy

1819
McCulloch v. *Maryland* upholds constitutionality of the National Bank

1820
Missouri Compromise

1821
Florida acquired from Spain

1823
Monroe Doctrine promulgated

1824
House of Representatives elects John Quincy Adams President

The War of 1812 spelled the end of the Revolutionary era. James Madison, who led the country through the war, was the last of the Presidents to have played an active role in founding the nation. The next two Presidents, James Monroe and John Quincy Adams, were the last prominent politicians to have served in government before the Constitution was written. After the War of 1812, the first political parties began to disintegrate and new ones came to the fore. Also following the War of 1812, the economy prospered and then entered a serious recession—thereby setting a pattern of boom-and-bust that would plague the American people into the twentieth century. And by 1820, sectionalism, which would burst forth within two generations into the great conflagration of the Civil War, had already begun to smolder.

The Path to War

During the twenty years preceding the War of 1812, the United States was caught between two superpowers at war, Britain and France. These two nations engaged in an on-and-off contest for empire in which the combatants repeatedly interfered with trade on the high seas. Both the French and the British forbade American captains to enter enemy ports, but America was not willing to withdraw from the arena of conflict because it found trade with the belligerents far too profitable. Nevertheless, after 1800 British action brought the Jefferson administration to the brink of war. But the President decided to impose the Embargo of 1807 on his own country rather than fight. The Democratic party replaced the unpopular Embargo with a Nonintercourse Act shortly before Madison became President. This permitted American ships to trade with any nation except Britain and France.

Violation of American Neutrality
England controlled the seas and most of the incidents that provoked war were maritime. By 1812, the British had seized some 10,000 Americans from

U.S. ships and impressed them into their service. Worse, Britain refused to recognize America's right as a neutral to trade with any nation. Although France under Napoleon seized 600 American ships between 1801 and 1813, by 1811 the British had virtually destroyed the French navy. As a result, provocations by France on the high seas became fewer and fewer, but high-handed British action continued unabated.

When the Nonintercourse Act proved unworkable, the United States government issued Macon's Bill No. 2 declaring that if either England or France would remove restrictions on American trade, then the United States would favor the complying nation and impose an embargo on the other major power. In 1810 Napoleon ordered his foreign minister to announce in an ambiguous letter that he would revoke his Berlin and Milan decrees and respect American neutral rights. Despite warnings by John Quincy Adams that Napoleon was not to be trusted, Madison announced that the French had complied with Macon's Bill No. 2. This apparent triumph of American policy led the President to ban trade with Britain. Yet when Madison sought concrete guarantees that France would honor American rights, Napoleon was evasive.

The British, unconvinced that Napoleon had complied with American demands, asked for proof. The Americans then decided to subject the British to commercial restrictions. Madison revived the Nonintercourse Act against Britain; that nation could neither ship goods to America nor import produce and products from there. The United States was therefore for all practical purposes Napoleon's ally against Britain.

Impressment and interference with American trade were not the only British crimes. The Americans suspected they were deliberately stirring up anti-American hostility among the Indians of the Old Northwest. And indeed the Shawnee leader Tecumseh and his brother, known as "The Prophet," received aid from British officers in Canada after 1807. Because of the Embargo (although they blamed the British navy instead), Americans in the West were suffering from an economic depression after 1808; their produce brought low prices and imported goods were expensive. To some, a war seemed an excellent way to cure these ills—and, in the process, to smash the British-Indian alliance in the Northwest. War might even provide an opportunity for seizing Florida from Britain's ally, Spain.

Dolley Madison

1768–1849

On September 14, 1794, Dolley Payne Todd, a vivacious young Philadelphia widow of Quaker background, married James Madison, a forty-three-year-old Virginia bachelor. Perhaps it was inevitable that this lively lady who lived only one block from where Congress was meeting would marry one of its eligible members, but her choice of slender, stiff, five-and-a-half-foot Madison was something of a surprise.

Dolley (or Dolly, the spelling varies) was born in North Carolina, but her family later moved to a house once owned by Patrick Henry in Hanover County, Virginia. In 1782 her father, unhappy with slavery, freed all of his blacks and went to Philadelphia to open a starch business, an enterprise that collapsed seven years later. To keep the family going, her mother opened a genteel boarding-house, which enabled Dolley to meet numerous eligible young men. She soon married a Quaker lawyer named Todd who died of yellow fever in 1793, leaving her with a son, John Payne Todd.

Dolley's subsequent marriage to Madison (a non-Quaker) resulted in her expulsion from the Society of Friends. However, the Paynes were not in especially good standing since she was the sixth member of that clan to be ousted in five years. Her marriage to James Madison turned out to be a very happy union as respect and affection blossomed into love.

The place in history of this "fine, portly, buxom dame," as Washington Irving described her, was assured by her long reign as White House hostess from 1801 to 1817. She served unofficially in that capacity for the widower Jefferson and then in her own right during her husband's administration. The key to Dolley Madison's popularity was not elegance or brilliance but an innate friendliness that sometimes won her husband the political support he badly needed.

From 1817 until James Madison's death in 1836, they lived at Montpelier in Orange County, Virginia, a lovely estate that her wayward son managed to ruin. Dolley Madison spent her last years in Washington, beset by financial problems, yet a gracious reminder of an earlier age and a living link to America's Revolutionary past.

These tensions created serious problems for Madison, a smallish, dour man who was aided immeasurably by his vivacious wife, Dolley. Her Wednesday afternoon levees quickly assumed political importance for both diplomats and Congressmen. On one such occasion, nearly all of the Federalists stayed away, only to discover that Madison's backers had turned out in full force to demonstrate support for the President. Nevertheless, as war seemed increasingly imminent, a Representative observed: "By her deportment in her own house you cannot discover who is her husband's friends or foes." (For more details about Dolley Madison see the accompanying biographical sketch.)

The War Hawks

Those most eager for a fight were known as the "War Hawks," politicians who wanted to end Brit-

National Portrait Gallery, Smithsonian Institution.
John C. Calhoun was a southern nationalist during the War of 1812. By the 1820s, when this portrait was made, his intense intellectualism had led him to a sectional stance.

ish meddling on American soil and defend the nation's honor as well. Men from New Hampshire, western New York state, Kentucky, Tennessee, South Carolina, and Georgia led this group, notably Henry Clay (1777–1852) of Kentucky, Felix Grundy (1777–1840) of Tennessee, and John C. Calhoun (1782–1850) of South Carolina. Young, patriotic to the point of being chauvinistic, they resented wrongs done by both Britain and France (occasionally talked of fighting both) and scorned efforts to accomodate either power and maintain peace. In addition, almost without exception they possessed a vision of a great United States encompassing all of North America.

Declaration of War

In Madison's war message, issued on June 1, 1812, the President stressed impressment and violations of American neutrality rights as the principal causes for hostility. Despite these charges and a decade or more of provocation, Madison's call for action faced stiff opposition. Eighteen days later Congress declared war, but the vote was close—19 to 13 in the Senate, 79 to 49 in the House. New England, the last bastion of the dying Federalist party, and the Middle Atlantic states generally opposed the war. The South and West were for it. Coastal and mercantile folk were cool, even downright hostile to this campaign to protect trade on the high seas. Citizens in some New England towns and cities flew flags at half-mast, while those living farthest from the Atlantic Ocean cheered loudest.

At the beginning of the twentieth century, historians dismissed some of Madison's motives as mere rhetorical camouflage for America's deeper lust for new land. They pointed out that if freedom of the seas had been the true cause of the war, then surely East coast merchants would have been the most bellicose element of the population. The South and the West, this interpretation said, longed to annex Canada and Florida to the United States, and these expansionist ambitions were the underlying reasons for war. The classic statement of this position is *The Expansionists of 1812* by Julius Pratt.

In the last fifteen years, historians have taken a new look at the War of 1812. One view is that Madison and Congress truly feared Britain might reduce the United States to colonial status once more. From 1807 to 1812 America tried to solve problems with Britain peacefully, but the British, underestimating the anger such acts engendered,

Courtesy of the New-York Historical Society, New York City.
As a War Hawk and peace commissioner, Henry Clay would help both to begin and end the War of 1812.

continued to violate U.S. rights. Some Jeffersonian Republicans eventually concluded that, if America did not use force, Britain might reassert its dominion over the young republic. Another view is that the war was fought to ensure American economic freedom. The West and the South were suffering a real depression because of British interference with Atlantic commerce. American shipowners might be humiliated by British policies, but all the same they were making money by supplying British armies in Europe. American farmers, however, blamed low farm prices on Britain and saw that nation's arrogance as a threat to American independence. This undoubtedly is not the last word on the causes of this brief, confusing, but rather important conflict, for debate continues. Nevertheless, most historians agree that this war can be seen as "the completion of American independence."

The War of 1812

Although not all Democratic-Republicans backed the war, it was essentially their struggle, and as the war went on, more and more stood behind it despite a lingering apathy. Taking a strong states' right approach and a narrow view of the Constitution, Federalist leaders obstructed Madison at every turn, a stance that lost them sympathy and badly damaged the party.

New England was so opposed to the war that it flirted with treason in 1814 when the Hartford Convention convened to discuss the grave issues of the day. Delegates from Massachusetts, Connecticut, and Rhode Island recommended several amendments to the Constitution. One would diminish the power of the prowar Republican South by basing representation and taxation on the number of free people alone (under the Constitution three-fifths of the slaves were counted for this purpose). A second amendment limited embargoes to no more than sixty days—clearly a way to avoid a repetition of Jefferson's Embargo of 1807, which had been so harmful to northeastern commerce. A third amendment barred naturalized citizens from holding federal offices; this resolution struck hard at the Democratic-Republican party, whose greatest strength was in the new states and among naturalized citizens everywhere. A fourth amendment required a two-thirds vote of both houses of Congress to admit new states, an obvious effort to restore the region's national political power.

The convention expected to meet again after Congress responded to these demands, but when the three-man delegation arrived in Washington early in 1815, the war was over. In the general jubilation of peace, Americans soon forgot the proposals forged at Hartford, but this action virtually ruined the Federalist party. Never again was it a factor in American politics.

Yet the Democratic-Republicans under Madison had problems, too. Political maneuvering within Madison's party forced him to accept a cabinet that did not please him. Robert Smith, Secretary of State

Albert Gallatin, Secretary of the Treasury to both Jefferson and Madison, saw his frugal budgets destroyed by war. This sketch was made when he was part of the peace commission at Ghent.

until 1811, was most famous for having substituted bourbon whiskey for rum in the navy ration when he served as Jefferson's Secretary of Navy. The President wanted Albert Gallatin to head the State Department, but the Senate never would confirm the appointment because Gallatin had uncovered and publicized graft in the Senate. Gallatin remained as Secretary of the Treasury until 1813, when he resigned in disgust after learning that Madison, out of political expediency, had named an incompetent person as Secretary of War and other incompetents to lucrative posts as well. During the war years, Madison's only able cabinet member was James Monroe, who replaced Robert Smith in 1811 as Secretary of State.

Despite this confused state of affairs in both cabinet and Congress, the voters did not repudiate the Democratic-Republicans in the election of 1812, although Madison faced stiff opposition. A coalition of eastern antiwar Democratic-Republicans and Federalists supported DeWitt Clinton of New York who carried all of the northeastern states except Vermont and Pennsylvania. The Federalists even increased their strength in Congress momentarily.

Although constant disaster led to a major overhaul of both the army and navy as soon as peace returned, events in the economic and political realms (both before and during the war) probably had more impact on American life than those on the battlefield or high seas. Several factors help to explain an upsurge in manufacturing, especially in New England. Various machines such as the spinning jenny, improved casting techniques, steam engines, and both the assembly line and the use of interchangeable parts paved the way for rapid innovation. Jefferson's Embargo, plus nonintercourse schemes and war, cut European imports and created unprecedented demands for finished goods. Considerable capital flowed into new factories where quick profits were realized. Cotton mill spindles increased at least sixteenfold (1807–1815) and the value of factory-made woolens, nearly five times, from $4 to $19 million (1810–1815). The war clearly was the watershed of Jeffersonian democracy. It ruined the Federalists but also changed the outlook of their opponents. Embarrassed and sobered by bungling defeat and disaster, they realized that many basic Federalist tenets—higher taxes, a strong army and navy, a federal bureaucracy, factories, and industrial urban centers—were necessary for the total well-being of a growing nation. Agriculture alone was not enough. In short, the Democratic-Republicans ended up embracing many planks in the platform of their vanishing foe.

The Canadian Incursion

Once the Americans declared war, the only British soldiers they could easily attack were in Canada. Canada had a much smaller population than the United States and was even less well prepared for war. There were only a few thousand British soldiers there, and England was unlikely to send more since the much larger struggle against Napoleon was entering its final stages.

Despite all these advantages, the American invasion of Canada proved to be a humiliating fiasco. A sorry set of bunglers led the American army, and various militia units refused to obey them. General William Hull, stationed in Detroit, advanced on Canada but turned back without firing a shot when he heard that Tecumseh had joined the Canadians.

The Canadian general, Isaac Brock, pursued Hull, besieged Detroit, and forced the Americans to surrender without a fight. Loss of control of the Northwest meant that military campaigns could only be mounted in the East and that later in the war Americans would have to win back their own land.

The next major front of the war was the area around Niagara Falls. An American army decided to attack the capital of Upper Canada, York (modern Toronto), but once more the Canadians routed the invading force. Finally, a campaign up the Lake Champlain corridor to Montreal ended in similar chaos. When General Henry Dearborn tried to follow this route, his men refused to travel more than twenty miles.

The campaign against Canada would be remembered as pure farce were it not for the splendid victory of Captain Oliver Hazard Perry (whose brilliant naval career is reviewed in a biographical sketch in this chapter). Working feverishly, early in 1813 Perry began to construct a small navy on Lake Erie using supplies hauled across mountains and floated on barges upriver. But all the work paid off handsomely, for in September Perry smashed the British fleet at Put-in-Bay on Lake Erie. Elated, Perry reported: "We have met the enemy and they are ours." Perry's victory forced the British to abandon Detroit and surrender control of the Great Lakes. General William Harrison's defeat of the retreating British helped nail down this American triumph. During this encounter the Indian leader Tecumseh was killed, and with his death the Indian confederacy of the Northwest collapsed.

Pursuing their winning streak, the Americans advanced on York, seized it, and burned the houses of Parliament. Nevertheless, American leaders, convinced that they could not subdue Canada, retreated back to their own borders. By the end of 1813 the United States had a secure hold over its own territory, but it had made scarcely a dent in Canada. If anything, the American invasion served to stir patriotism among Canadians as they defended their homeland against foreign enemies.

The Sea Battles

At the beginning of the war, the entire American navy consisted of sixteen vessels; the British had more than 100 frigates (intermediate war ships) and about the same number of ships of the line (huge three-deckers, all of them mounted with at least seventy-four cannon). Yet, in the first year of the war, to the bewildered astonishment and the ec-

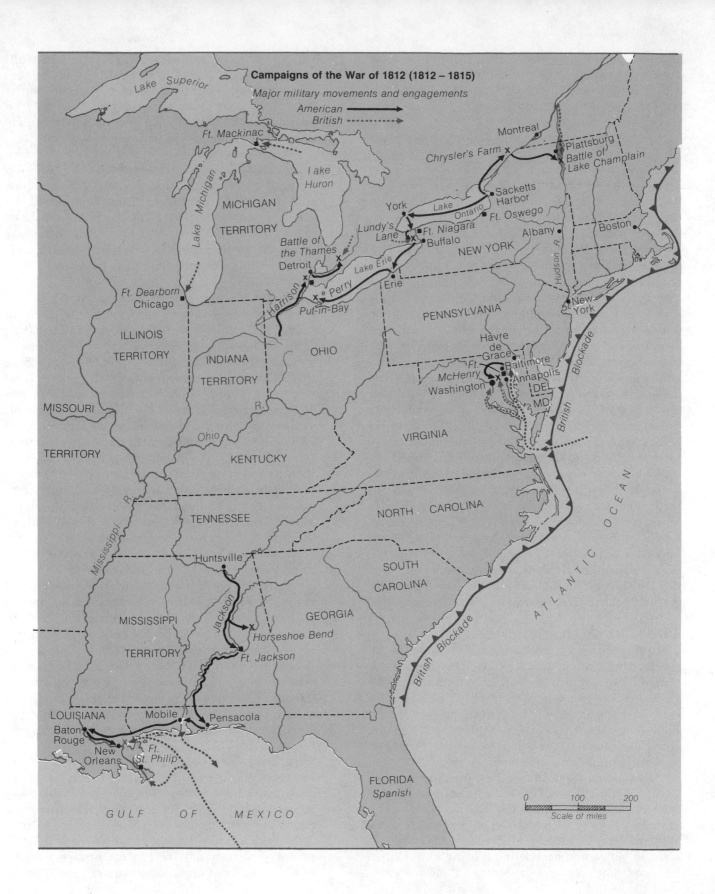

Campaigns of the War of 1812 (1812–1815)

Major military movements and engagements

American →
British ⇢

Lake Superior

Ft. Mackinac

Lake Michigan

Lake Huron

MICHIGAN TERRITORY

Montreal

Chrysler's Farm ✕

Plattsburg
Battle of Lake Champlain

Sacketts Harbor

York

Lake Ontario

Ft. Oswego

Albany

Boston

Lundy's Lane

Ft. Niagara ✕
Buffalo

NEW YORK

Battle of the Thames

Detroit ✕

Harrison

Perry

Lake Erie

Put-in-Bay

Erie

Hudson R.

New York

Ft. Dearborn
Chicago

ILLINOIS TERRITORY

INDIANA TERRITORY

OHIO

PENNSYLVANIA

Havre de Grace

Ft. McHenry
Washington

Baltimore
Annapolis

DEL

MD

British Blockade

MISSOURI TERRITORY

R.

Ohio R.

KENTUCKY

VIRGINIA

TENNESSEE

Huntsville

NORTH CAROLINA

SOUTH CAROLINA

ATLANTIC OCEAN

Jackson

MISSISSIPPI TERRITORY

Horseshoe Bend ✕

Ft. Jackson

GEORGIA

British Blockade

LOUISIANA

Mobile

Pensacola

Baton Rouge

New Orleans ✕

Ft. St. Philip

FLORIDA
Spanish

GULF   OF   MEXICO

0   100   200
Scale of miles

Anne S. K. Brown Military Collection, Brown University Library.

The news of spectacular one-on-one victories at sea such as the *Constitution's* over the *Guerrière* helped to distract Americans from defeats on land.

static delight of the Americans, their tiny navy held its own. Hundreds of merchant vessels became privateers (that is, they were armed and their captains authorized to seize enemy craft) and attacked British commercial ships sailing between London and the colonial ports in the New World. Some of them even raided British ships in the English Channel and off Ireland.

Far more troubling to British morale, however, was the contest between the American frigate, the *Constitution* ("Old Ironsides"), and a British ship, the *Guerrière*. The two ships sighted each other about 450 miles southeast of Halifax, Nova Scotia, on the afternoon of August 19, 1812. They were almost equally matched, though the *Constitution* had six more guns and nearly 200 more men. The *Constitution* totally disabled the *Guerrière*, and the British ship surrendered without further resistance. Fifteen crew members were dead and sixty-three wounded (the *Constitution* had seven dead and seven wounded).

The *Constitution* scored another stunning victory in December when it destroyed the British frigate, the *Java*, off the coast of Brazil. Earlier a third frigate, the *Macedonian*, was lost to the Americans.

Humiliated, the Royal Navy sent more and more ships to America, and early in 1813 British vessels succeeded in bottling up American ships in their home ports. A tight British blockade of the East coast proved effective in stopping the depredations of the American navy. American privateer vessels, however, continued to stage raids; by the end of the war they had captured more than 1,300 British ships valued with their cargoes at more than $40 million.

The Burning of Washington

In April 1814 Napoleon abdicated, and the war in Europe was over. Now the British could turn their attention to the United States. In August, 10,000 European veterans arrived on American shores. Their chief goal was to secure Canada and to win a new boundary that would include the Great Lakes, Lake Champlain, and northern Maine, but the Battle of Plattsburg (September 11) dashed these hopes. An American naval captain, Thomas Macdonough, had ordered his men to fashion ships out of Vermont timber, an arduous task they were able to accomplish in a few short weeks. Suddenly the Americans had a navy on Lake Champlain—four warships and ten gunboats confronting four British warships and twelve gunboats. In the ensuing conflict, Macdonough commanded with such brilliance (except when he was knocked unconscious for a moment by the flying head of a decapitated sailor) that all four British warships were destroyed. Sir George Prevost, commander of the British forces, retreated to Canada and gave up plans of encroaching on American territory.

Events elsewhere, however, cast a pall over this stunning triumph. President Madison had worried about the lack of defenses for the city of Washington, but Secretary of War Armstrong assured him there was no danger. The Secretary was wrong, for in August 1814, 4,500 redcoats moved up the Chesapeake Bay and fought the ill-equipped, poorly trained, and cowardly militia of Maryland and the District of Columbia. The battle ended quickly as the Americans fled in panic, an encounter some wits dubbed "the Bladensburg Races." Madison departed in such haste that his dinner was still

Oliver Hazard Perry

1785–1819

Perry, born into a Rhode Island family with strong ties to the United States Navy, was the son of a naval officer impressed by the British for a time during the American Revolution and brother to four other naval officers (among them Matthew Calbraith Perry, the man who established trading rights with Japan in 1854). When young Perry was fourteen, he became a midshipman aboard his father's ship, *The General Greene*. He saw active service in the naval war with France and, during the dispute with Tripoli (1802–1806), was stationed in the Mediterranean. In 1807 Perry won his lieutenant's commission and for two years built gunboats in Rhode Island and Connecticut, finally receiving command of his own schooner, the *Revenge*, in 1809. With this vessel he cruised the southern coast of the United States where he looked for American ships seized by the British; he also surveyed the harbors of New London and Newport. In 1811, while stationed in the latter city in command of gunboats once more, he married Elizabeth Champlin Mason, by whom he had five children.

Handsome, polite, and extremely ambitious, Perry was eager for glory when the War of 1812 broke out. He traveled to Washington, D.C. to ask for a command and was eventually put in charge of the naval forces on Lake Erie. In the spring of 1813, he and his men built a small fleet of ten ships. Put-in-Bay, near the present city of Sandusky, Ohio, became his headquarters, and it was there that he fought his famous battle with the British commander, Robert H. Barclay.

The encounter took place between noon and 3:00 P.M. on September 10, 1813. The two navies were about equally matched. When Perry's flagship was so battered by enemy fire that he was forced to abandon it, he transferred to another vessel. Fifteen minutes later the entire enemy fleet surrendered. Barclay lost forty-one sailors; Perry twenty-seven.

This was the first time that an American had ever captured a British fleet, and the feat made Perry a national hero. More importantly, it secured American control of Lake Erie for the rest of the war. After elaborate fetes in his honor in several American cities, Perry took command of a small force of seamen along the Potomac.

In May 1819 Perry was sent to South America. There he protested the piratical raids of ships from the republics of Venezuela and Buenos Aires on American vessels, but he died of yellow fever a few days after completing his negotiations. His body was buried first on Trinidad but was later transferred to Newport.

Library of Congress.
This version of the burning of Washington was published in 1814 in England. Although the facades of the public buildings are recognizable, the rest of the town is based on the artist's fancy rather than an observed fact.

warm on the table of the White House when the British commanders sat down to eat it. After finishing Madison's meal, the redcoats set fire to the White House and the Capitol—retribution for the American sacking of York and Dover in Canada.

Leaving a stunned, smoke-scarred Washington, the British marched on Baltimore. There they met a more resolute militia force, which turned back their assault, and a short time later these invaders departed. In the midst of this highly embarrassing episode, really a nuisance raid to teach the upstart Yankees "a lesson," America's national anthem was born. On the evening of September 13, Francis Scott Key (1779–1843), a young lawyer, went aboard a British warship to secure the release of a Maryland physician. Before they could depart, the bombardment of Baltimore began. Through the long night Key watched in agonized suspense; but, to his delight, at daybreak the Stars and Stripes still flew proudly over the ramparts of Fort McHenry, so he wrote the poem that was later set to the music of a British tavern song.

The Hero of New Orleans

Throughout the War of 1812, American forces in the South whittled away at Spanish Florida, a goal of young War Hawks from Georgia and South Caro-

lina. In 1812, an American force gained control of part of West Florida, the section that rimmed the Gulf Coast from New Orleans east to the present state of Florida, thus annexing the important outpost of Mobile.

These moves alarmed the Indians of the Southeast. Traditionally they played off one nation against another and precariously maintained hegemony over their lands, but now the French had pulled out of the area, the Spanish were powerless, and the British were concentrating their interests in Canada and along the eastern coast of the United States. White American settlements were pressing in around the Creek, Cherokee, Choctaw, and Chickasaw Indians—and more and more bloody incidents occurred. When Creeks friendly to Tecumseh staged a raid on Fort Mims (near Mobile) in August 1813 that left over 200 whites dead, white Americans had a pretext for a massive reprisal. In March 1814, Andrew Jackson (1767–1845) defeated hostile Creeks at Horseshoe Bend on the Tallapoosa River, killing over 800 and forcing them to cede two-thirds of their lands.

The American militia was in firm control of the Southeast when rumors began to circulate that the British were planning an attack on Louisiana. On his way to defend New Orleans, Jackson burned

This primitive engraving was sketched during the morning of the bombardment of Fort McHenry. The bombs fired on the fort from British warships attracted not only this artist but also the poet Francis Scott Key, who had witnessed the bombardment from its beginning the night before.

Pensacola in West Florida on November 7 so that the British could not use it as a base.

In the first move of the Battle of New Orleans, the British won a point by marching through the bayous rather than taking the easier river route to the city—the one Jackson planned to defend. But then the British waited too long for reinforcements, and Jackson had time to reorganize his defenses. Commanding a motley army of bedraggled Tennessee militia, free blacks, former French pirates,

and New Orleans citizens, Jackson seemed an easy mark.

But when the British troops, led by Sir Edward Pakenham, advanced in a rigid frontal attack, the slaughter was terrifying. In five crucial minutes Jackson's twenty cannon killed 2,036 redcoats, Pakenham, and another general. Only 8 Americans were killed. The massacre was so total that the British hastily withdrew.

This dazzling victory quickly made Jackson a

The New Orleans Museum of Art.

This painting of the Battle of New Orleans was done by a participant. Note the heavy guns in the front of the American lines. These produced the most casualties among the British.

national hero and launched him on the path to the White House. It also helped Americans to forget many months of inglorious defeats. Although serious negotiations were under way long before Pakenham and Jackson met, news traveled so slowly that neither was aware that a peace treaty had been signed. Perhaps of greater importance than the outcome of this belated triumph itself was the strategic advantage it gave Americans. The British, weary of war, had no heart to renew this faraway contest.

Peace Negotiations

Even during the first months of the war, peace talks were already under way between Britain and the United States. In fact, in the first week of the conflict Russia, England's ally against Napoleon, offered to act as an intermediary. President Madison, willing to consider this route to peace, sent two American representatives to Russia—James A. Bayard and Treasury Secretary Albert Gallatin.

When Russian mediations failed to interest

The Harry T. Peters Collection, Museum of the City of New York.
Andrew Jackson's defense of New Orleans became the crowning triumph remembered by Americans. This engraving, done while Jackson was President, shows his appeal as a military hero.

Britain, Bayard and Gallatin went directly to London for negotiations. Early in 1814 the British decided to begin peace talks and Madison added the fiery, hard-drinking Henry Clay and Jonathan Russell, the American chargé d'affaires in London, to the official delegation. The peace talks, which at length opened at Ghent in Belgium, started off on an inauspicious note when the Americans insisted that the British promise to abandon the practice of impressment. The British balked—and a stalemate seemed inevitable over the old question of American rights on the high seas. But fortunately Madison, recognizing that now the European war was over the British would have no need to continue impressing American sailors into their navy, sent new instructions to his delegates: they need no longer discuss the issue at all.

The British demands were ominous because they revealed that the British, unable to face the reality of American independence, clearly intended to undo the treaty of 1783. England wanted to create a buffer state for the Indians of the Old Northwest, a scheme that would take a large bite out of America's northern boundary since the proposed territory would lie north of the Ohio River. When the Americans flatly refused this demand for an Indian state, the British pressed for a new, more southern Canadian boundary that would include much of Maine and the Great Lakes.

The treaty talks easily could have broken down at this point and war continued. But external events suddenly made the British more reasonable. News of Macdonough's victory and failure of the British invasion of the Northeast arrived. Then the Duke of Wellington, the English military genius who defeated Napoleon, shrewdly observed that no victory was possible in America unless the Royal Navy could gain control of the Great Lakes. Finally, the simultaneous Congress of Vienna that was settling the fate of Europe in the wake of Napoleon's abdication was experiencing some uneasy moments. Renewed war in Europe seemed possible, and Britain had no heart for a continuation of hostilities in two hemispheres.

As a result, the British softened their hard line and on December 24, 1814, signed the Treaty of Ghent. Impressment and neutral rights, though these were the stated reasons for Madison's declaration of war, were not even mentioned. Neither were questions of fishing rights, trade regulations, or indemnities. Americans were neither granted nor denied the right to trade with British India; the British did not gain specific permission to navigate the Mississippi (one of their fondest hopes). All of these unsolved problems were referred to joint commissions for future discussion, and the Treaty of Ghent is as notable for what it did not spell out as for the terms it did.

The treaty simply returned everything to where it had been before the war, the status quo ante bellum. As Adams put it, "Nothing was adjusted, nothing was settled—nothing in substance but an indefinite suspension of hostilities was agreed to." Some Americans (Henry Clay most vociferously) considered the treaty worthless, but the majority rejoiced in the fact that the new nation had held its own against mighty Britannia.

And, as history has demonstrated, the treaty was a remarkably good one. Never again have the United States and England gone to war with each other. The joint commissions that handled the unsolved problems won many advantages for America and established a precedent for settling Anglo-American disputes in the future. The Canadian boundary, as far west as the Rockies, was established along the forty-ninth parallel. Another agreement arranged for both Americans and Canadians to settle in what are now the states of Oregon and Washington. A commercial treaty opened the entire British empire (except the West Indies) to unrestricted American trade—a complete reversal of England's long-held mercantilistic policy of maintaining the mother country and her colonies as a closed economic system. A pact limiting both Britain and the United States to only four armed ships each on the Great Lakes defused any threat of renewed hostilities in that region.

Postwar Developments

During the next decade (1815–1825), momentous but subtle, far-reaching changes occurred in American life. Various statesmen, for the best of reasons, charted a course that, while it did not make civil strife inevitable, certainly heightened sectional tensions. Although Madison and the Democratic-Republicans were committed spiritually to the Jeffersonian ideal of America as an agrarian paradise, they were realistic enough to recognize the importance of the nation's infant industries.

In 1816 Congress passed a mild protectionist tariff to guard American industry against British competition—the first U.S. tariff not designed simply to raise revenue. At the time, this action won widespread support because even men like the aging Jefferson, who ostensibly abhorred factories and cities, realized the young republic must have some industry. However, England, fast becoming the world's leading industrial power, was alarmed. Its mills had to have American customers. To dissuade America from pursuing a protectionist course, England passed a series of trade laws making America's business dealings with England more profitable. Though John Quincy Adams, Secretary of State, acknowledged these favors with a few gracious nods, America actually was unimpressed and went on to pass a still stiffer tariff bill in 1824.

Although these measures tended in time to divide more settled parts of the United States into a factory North and a plantation South, intense national feeling created by the outcome of the war with Britain muted these experiences. And no national voice boomed louder than that of Chief Justice John Marshall as he and his fellow justices handed down decisions strengthening federal power. The disarray of the Federalists as they faded into oblivion accentuated this national mood; political party lines became so blurred and indistinct that some historians call these years "The Era of Good Feelings." However, this supposedly euphoric mood did not extend to voters in the listless national election of 1816, when three-fourths of the congressmen lost their seats. Because few Federalists were extant, the electorate that elected James Monroe as Madison's successor, simply replaced one set of Democratic-Republicans with another. The reason? The lawmakers had just passed a bill raising their own salaries, an unpardonable sin in the eyes of Americans of those days.

Monroe's two campaigns for the White House cannot be termed stirring or dramatic. In 1816, despite a general lack of enthusiasm for Monroe in the congressional caucus, Jefferson's protégé and one-time neighbor received the nomination. Monroe went on to win 183 electoral votes to 34 for Rufus King, the candidate of the discredited Federalists, who carried only Massachusetts, Connecticut, and Delaware. Four years later Monroe got all of the electoral votes except that of a New Hampshire man who cast his ballot for John Quincy Adams.

Acquisition of the Floridas, 1815–1821

After the Battle of Horseshoe Bend, the defeated Creeks fled into Florida where they found a safe haven from which they could dart across the Georgia border and harass American settlers. Skirmishes and reprisals occurred constantly. When the American commander in Georgia burned a Seminole village, the Seminoles retaliated in 1817 and seized an American hospital ship and killed thirty-six soldiers, six women, and four children.

The American reaction was outrage. Early in 1818, acting on vague instructions from Washington, Andrew Jackson decided to track down the Creeks in East Florida. He put two Indian chiefs to death on the grounds that he *suspected* they might have encouraged raids.

Next, Jackson made Fort Saint Marks his base of operations, sending the Spanish garrison fleeing to Pensacola. In his march through Florida he arrested two British subjects, tried them, and convicted one for writing letters to European and American governments on the Indians' behalf and the other for aiding and comforting the Indians in their war on the United States. The first man was hanged; the second, shot. Now Jackson returned to Pensacola, the scene of his earlier triumph, and seized it. By late May he had wiped out all Spanish and Indian opposition and captured the Spanish governor, Don José Masot.

When the news of Jackson's actions reached Washington, the President and his cabinet favored disowning General Jackson. Clearly Jackson had violated international law by putting two British subjects to death in Spanish territory. Worse, negotiations with Spain concerning acquisition of Florida and the boundary between Spanish Mexico and the Louisiana Purchase might break down.

Only John Quincy Adams saw the diplomatic hay to be made out of Jackson's antics. Instead of apologizing profusely, Adams went so far as to suggest coolly that the Spanish government ought to pay the United States for the expense of policing its unruly colony. Adams cleared Jackson of all blame and announced that the two British subjects Jackson killed had been plotting a war both against Spain and the United States. All of this Adams knew to be untrue.

But this strategy worked. The Spanish, weakened by European wars and revolts in many parts of their empire, accepted the inevitable, and in 1819 the Adams-Onís Treaty, was drawn up. Spain agreed to turn Florida over to the United States in return for $5 million, which the American government would pay to settle its citizens' claims against Spain. The Spanish were willing to make this settlement in order to establish the boundary between Spanish Mexico and the Louisiana Purchase. The original terms of the Louisiana Purchase had been vague, and Adams was willing to withdraw claim to that territory (Texas) if Spain would cede to the United States all claim to the Oregon country.

The Monroe Doctrine

Turmoil in Spain's dominions in Central and South America and belated British recognition of the true role of the United States gave birth to a document that meant little when issued but eventually became a cornerstone of American diplomatic policy.

As early as 1811, Simón Bolívar led a revolution that freed Venezuela from Spain. In the following years the vast Spanish empire in Latin America dissolved into a series of republics.

In 1815 at the Congress of Vienna, the victors over Napoleon—Great Britain, Russia, Prussia and Austria—pledged to combat republicanism and preserve monarchical rights. Spain's loss of her South American colonies concerned them greatly and the Quadruple Alliance theoretically was duty bound to restore those lands to their former king. The sovereigns of Russia, Prussia, and Austria, while not willing to go to war to subdue the South American republics, did support the Spanish cause. England, however, was less interested in protecting royal prerogatives than in capturing new markets—and South America, freed from the closed mercantilistic system of the Spanish empire, was a very tempting market indeed.

As a result, Britain wanted to keep South America independent, free of Spanish control, and this concern increased in 1823 when a French army marched into Spain with the ostensible purpose of protecting King Ferdinand VII from his own rebellious people. If the French gained control over Spain, might they not take the next step and attempt to recapture former Spanish colonies?

Britain offered to announce, in conjunction with the United States, a statement saying that neither nation could stand idly by and watch French interference in Latin America. John Quincy Adams, however, thought joint action would make America a mere instrument of Britain's will. There were other disadvantages, too. Any pledge of noninterference might stand in the way of eventual acquisition of Cuba, an island Adams thought should belong to the United States. Finally, in Adams' opinion, America's true rival for control of the New World was not France but Britain.

Adams convinced President Monroe to issue a unilateral policy; after some hesitation (Monroe was always slow to make up his mind), the President did so in a speech to Congress delivered in December 1823. The Monroe Doctrine, written by Adams, stated two basic principles: European powers could not create new colonies in the New World; and European powers could not intervene in the affairs of the Americas, nor should the New World attempt to intervene in those of the Old.

This doctrine was aimed as much at Britain as at the other European powers. At the time, the Monroe Doctrine scarcely interested, and certainly failed to intimidate, any European nation, since the United States was a third-rate power incapable of

Culver Pictures.
By 1901 the Monroe Doctrine had a more vigorous meaning. This cartoon has Uncle Sam as the king of the roost keeping the European hens in their coop and watching over the Latin American chicks, two of whom are about to fight.

backing up its strong words, and it was actually the British fleet, not this doctrine, which stymied European meddling.

The Bank of the United States

On December 5, 1815, Madison submitted his seventh State of the Union message to Congress. It was not a ringing document, but clearly reflected change both present and future. The President called for a "uniform national currency" administered by a national bank if state banks could not do the job, a tariff to protect infant industries from foreign competition, and a program to create roads and canals "which can best be executed under national authority . . . requiring national jurisdiction and national means." Had he not been in his grave for over a decade, Alexander Hamilton could have written these words himself.

Especially representative of the changing views of the Democratic-Republicans was their attitude towards a national bank. Under Jefferson the Democratic-Republicans opposed Hamilton's first Bank of the United States as unconstitutional and as an undemocratic ally of merchants and financiers in the Northeast. Indeed, the party allowed the bank's charter to expire in 1811—even though its financial help obviously would be needed to pay for the upcoming war. In 1816, however, the party reversed its position and, as Madison suggested, chartered a second National Bank. The government would deposit all of its revenues in the bank, and that institution, in turn, would provide a stable currency for the country. Legally, the bank was a semi-

private corporation managed by a board of directors, a few appointed by the government, though the majority would be elected by private stockholders (only American stockholders could vote; foreign investors could not directly influence bank policies). The bank's charter would expire after twenty years. Establishment of such an institution required a great deal of tenuous justification from a party that had denounced the first bank as illegal and dangerous. Unfortunately, the new bank, poorly administered, helped to bring on several financial panics by overextending credit.

The newly chartered bank would pay out a substantial part of its dividends to the federal government, and some congressmen suggested that these funds be invested in improving or building roads and canals. Kentucky's Henry Clay led the drive for this program. Although Madison called for internal improvements, he thought a constitutional amendment was needed. Thus, he vetoed a bill that established a federal improvements program. Congress was left with the option of appropriating funds for transportation projects to be carried out by states and communities.

The Panic of 1819

The postwar boom, inflated by events in Europe and peacetime expansion at home, collapsed into a depression within five years. Crop failures in a Europe already ravaged by war brought a demand for American produce, and English mills once again were free to buy American cotton. Since the price of crops was high, Americans wildly bought up farmland in the West. State banks, which increased in number from 89 to 250 between 1811 and 1816, tried to take up the slack between the demise of the first National Bank and creation of the second. Far from curbing reckless speculation in crops and lands, they encouraged it by issuing their own notes, even if they lacked assets to back up the paper.

In 1819 the mirage of boundless and endless national prospeity evaporated. The most profound cause of the Panic of 1819 was worldwide and beyond the power of the United States to temper—a shortage of hard money. The gold and silver mines of Mexico and Peru, the chief sources of the world's specie, were scarcely functioning during the revolutions in those countries against Spain. More significantly, national treasuries were hoarding the world's stock of precious metals as governments everywhere became fearful of economic collapse and the sudden devaluation of paper money.

But there were two other important reasons for America's depression. One was that the demand for American farm produce, especially for American cotton, was slacking off as Europe returned to normal agricultural production. The other factor, however, was nothing less than incredible fiscal mismanagement within the United States, especially in the booming West. Irresponsible banking practices and feverish land speculation created an iridescent bubble that could only burst.

The second Bank of the United States made the situation all the more precarious by permitting state banks to trade their paper money for hard federal coin. But instead of retaining these metal coins to back up the paper being issued, they continued to issue more and more paper to fuel the boom. When the new National Bank belatedly got around to calling in its loans, ending its liberal credit policies and submitting state bank notes for settlement with those who issued them, boom turned to bust. As one man said: "The Bank was saved and the people were ruined." Although that sentence neatly expressed the sentiment of most angry Americans, it ignored the fact that speculation and depressed cotton prices were the most immediate causes of the panic. That the crisis was severe cannot be doubted. In Baltimore rents dropped to half their previous rate; in Virginia land was almost worthless; in Pennsylvania some 14,000 cases of debt were heard; in Pittsburgh almost a third of the population, finding no livelihood, deserted the city for the country; and in Cincinnati the city government was forced

to repossess everything from stores to stables. Everyone caught in this downward spiral called the bank "the Monster." The majority of Americans were farmers, more used to barter than banking, and they were especially resentful of an institution controlled largely by Philadelphia financiers.

The Marshall Court and Centralized Power

The panic prompted a major Supreme Court decision. Several of the states had concurred with popular hatred of the National Bank by levying taxes on the bank's branches or on notes they issued. The Baltimore branch was one of the most poorly run in the country, and on February 11, 1818, the state government passed a law requiring all federal notes issued in Maryland to be printed on stamped paper bought from the state. The Baltimore branch of the National Bank ignored the law, whereupon Maryland sued a federal cashier, James McCulloch. The case quickly worked its way up the judicial ladder to the Supreme Court.

In *McCulloch* v. *Maryland* John Marshall, the Chief Justice, wrote a decision that greatly strengthened the authority of the federal government. He declared that the National Bank was constitutional since it was necessary for the fulfillment of the government's stated power "to lay and collect taxes; to borrow money; to regulate commerce; to declare and conduct a war; and to raise and support armies and navies." This broad construction of the Constitution clearly validated the most general interpretation of the federal government's implied powers. More startlingly, Marshall and the other justices, went on to announce that, though a state could legally tax an individual or organization, the federal government could exempt itself from state taxation. Marshall relied upon the supremacy clause of the Constitution, arguing that a supreme national government's will could not be thwarted by state taxation.

Marshall and his associates strengthened this nationalistic outlook in other court decisions such as *Dartmouth* v. *Woodward* (1819), in which the court ruled that a charter granted by the King of England in 1769 to the college was a contract between the state government and the institution— the state could not violate the terms of the original agreement. This decision gave great powers to any chartered institution or business and freed it from state control. From the political point of view, any loss of states' rights was a gain in federal authority.

ROBERT FULTON'S CLERMONT · 1809
COPYRIGHT 1909 BY IRVING UNDERHILL, NEW YORK

Library of Congress.
Fulton's successful run of the Clermont meant that Americans would be able to tap their extensive network of rivers. The early boats still depended on sails and gave little shelter to passengers, as illustrated in this artist's drawing of the first steamboat.

Still other cases asserted the right of the Supreme Court to reverse the decisions of state courts.

Among the most important rulings of these years was *Gibbons* v. *Ogden* (1824). Ogden, who held a monopoly license granted by the state of New York to operate steamboats to New Jersey, tried to force Gibbons, a man with a federal but no state license, out of business. If Ogden prevailed, then states, not the national government, would have the power to regulate such operations. Marshall and the court interpreted the constitutional provisions relative to commerce broadly to include not only buying, selling, and bartering but also navigation and other forms of intercourse as well.

They seized on a federal licensing statute regulating sea going vessels as a means of ruling that the state law conflicted with the national law. So, Ogden lost. Any state monopoly on river travel that crossed state lines was invalid. This opened up rivers to intense development by competing steamboat lines.

Emerging Sectionalism

Apart from Louisiana itself, Missouri was the first territory within the Louisiana Purchase to petition for statehood. Missouri first applied for statehood just after the Congress agreed to admit Alabama. Transformation of Alabama from territory to state (a formality not complete until December 1819)

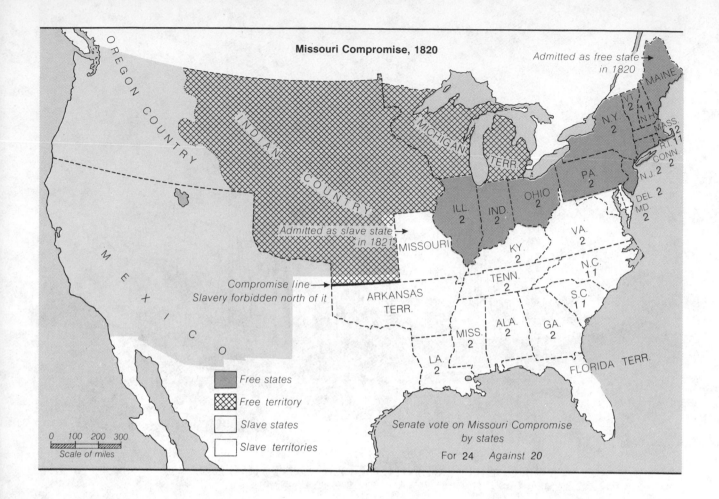

Missouri Compromise, 1820

Admitted as free state in 1820

OREGON COUNTRY

INDIAN COUNTRY

MICHIGAN TERR.

Admitted as slave state in 1821

MISSOURI

Compromise line →
Slavery forbidden north of it

ARKANSAS TERR.

MEXICO

MAINE
VT. 2
N.H. 1
N.Y. 2
MASS. 2
R.I. 1 1
CONN.
PA. 2
N.J. 2
OHIO 2
DEL. 2
MD. 2
ILL. 2
IND. 2
VA. 2
KY. 2
N.C. 1 1
TENN. 2
S.C. 1 1
MISS. 2
ALA. 2
GA. 2
LA. 2
FLORIDA TERR.

☐ Free states
☒ Free territory
☐ Slave states
☐ Slave territories

0 100 200 300
Scale of miles

Senate vote on Missouri Compromise
by states
For 24   Against 20

meant the number of slave and free states would then be equal. Missouri obviously would be yet another slave state (there were 10,000 slaves in Missouri in 1820). This fact troubled Northerners, but the full problem surfaced only when James Tallmadge of Poughkeepsie, New York, offered an amendment to the Missouri statehood bill on February 13, 1819, that prohibited the importation of any new slaves into Missouri and stipulated that all children born of slave parents automatically would be free at the age of twenty-five. Although the House passed the amendment by a narrow vote after violent debate, the Senate struck it down. Voting in both the House and Senate followed strict North-South sectional lines.

Late in 1819 the possibility of a compromise emerged when Maine applied for statehood (it was then part of Massachusetts). Southern congressmen made the admission of Missouri as a slave state a necessary condition for the admission of Maine as a free state. That proposal might have seemed at-

tractive—except it did not settle the greater question of whether slavery would be permitted in the rest of the Louisiana Purchase. Fights raged back and forth in 1820 over this question and the other issues to which it was linked.

During the prolonged debate in Congress, the most violent insults were hurled by Northerners against Southerners and vice versa. "The words civil war and disunion," Henry Clay confessed wearily, "are uttered almost without emotion." Although a few Northerners at this time were genuinely opposed to slavery on moral grounds, the animosity of most was less idealistic. Northern politicians feared that soon slave states would outnumber free and thereby control Congress. The constitutional arrangement whereby one slave equaled three-fifths of a single citizen in determining representation in Congress had always angered Northerners. The issue of states' rights also was germane. The Virginian John Taylor was not alone in fearing that if the Supreme Court could establish the legality of a national bank, it also could order the emancipation of slaves. Taylor declared that slaves were private property not subject to government jurisdiction of any sort.

The agonizing deadlock was finally broken when Henry Clay arranged a compromise. The Kentucky statesman linked the admission of free Maine to slave Missouri but prohibited slavery in the future in the Louisiana Purchase north of 36°30′N, Missouri's southern border. Since the struggle over Missouri was threatening to disrupt the unity of the Democratic-Republicans, the Missouri Compromise came as a welcome expedient to some congressmen who formerly had insisted on banning slavery from the entire Louisiana Purchase. Even so, Clay, Speaker of the House and a wily tactician, had his plan voted on in two sections and thereby drummed up differently composed majorities to pass each section.

Although Monroe had misgivings, he eventually signed the bill, thus establishing the precedent that Congress indeed could exclude slavery from lands acquired after 1789. But the controversy still was not over. When Missouri presented its constitution to Congress for approval, the document prohibited the entry of free blacks and mulattos into that state. Northerners once again were up in arms, this time arguing that the clause violated that part of the federal constitution granting citizens of one state all privileges and immunities bestowed by another.

Charles Pinckney of South Carolina, who claimed authorship of that provision, insisted that it never was intended to cover free blacks. Finally, Clay came forward with yet another compromise. He argued that the state constitution should be accepted as written but with the proviso that the state of Missouri would agree never to pass a law preventing persons coming to and settling in the said state, "who now are or hereafter may become citizens of the States of this Union." In 1825 the Missouri legislature effectively repudiated this agreement by excluding all blacks and mulattos without naturalization papers, documents that none of these individuals could get because the states where they were regarded as citizens had not naturalized them.

All the painful and heated issues that would eventually result in the Civil War were touched on in the controversy over Missouri. North-South sectionalism became more rigid, as did regional East-West differences. The North roundly condemned the southern way of life, and formerly moderate

Edward Coles

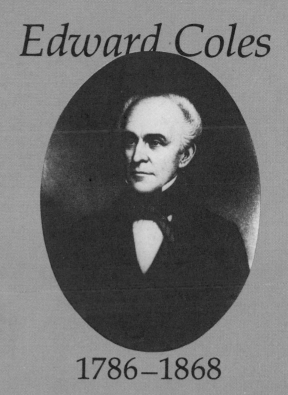

1786–1868

A neighbor of Thomas Jefferson and private secretary to President James Madison, Edward Coles was a well-to-do young man who at the age of twenty-one inherited a farm in Albemarle County, Virginia, and twenty blacks. Fresh from lectures at the College of William and Mary where he began to question the morality of slavery, Edward (the youngest of nine children) shocked his family by announcing plans to free his slaves. To evade the letter of Virginia law which said emancipated blacks had to leave the state within a year or face possible reenslavement, he planned to retain these workers as hired hands and grant them final freedom at the time of his death. He soon realized, however, that his family and friends would not tolerate such a scheme.

As Coles wrestled with this dilemma, an older brother, Isaac, private secretary to Jefferson, suggested he take a similar post with the incoming chief executive. Edward Coles, a second cousin to Dolley Madison, knew the Madisons well and eventually agreed to take the job, thus deferring any emancipation plans for a time. In 1814 he wrote Jefferson urging him to lead a manumission movement and "put into practice those hallowed principles contained in that renowned Declaration, of which you were the immortal author." Jefferson replied he was much too old; this was work for younger men, he added, such as Coles himself. Keenly disappointed by these excuses, Coles told Jefferson he should consider the notable example of Benjamin Franklin who was very active and "usefully employed after he had passed your age." Jefferson, then seventy-one, subsequently asked several younger men in the neighborhood to form a "phalanx" to eradicate slavery. But no "phalanx" appeared, and Edward Coles realized that if he wanted to be a pioneer abolitionist he must act alone.

After two visits to Illinois, in 1819 he secured a post as Register of the Land Office in Edwardsville and soon took his blacks to Pittsburgh and from there down the Ohio River. En route he gathered the slaves around him and told them they were free—free to leave, go where they wished, or remain with him. Some of them were shocked. How would they live? Where would they go? As the hubbub subsided, Coles said he was willing to hire them as free laborers and would give the head of each family or any male over twenty-one 160 acres of land. A few days later, Coles took up his duties at the Land Office, and his ex-slaves began working on their own property about three miles from Edwardsville.

In 1822, Edward Coles became governor of Illinois and used his powers to thwart all attempts to revise the state constitution so as to permit slavery. It was a savage fight, but the antislavery forces won. This was a key victory in a very important state and undoubtedly had profound effect upon the slave-free debate throughout the upper Mississippi Valley. A few years later Coles lost a bid to become a member of Congress and, still a bachelor, moved to Philadelphia. At forty-seven he married, raised a family, and occasionally visited relatives in Virginia; but, as the abolition fury increased, it was obvious he could not live there. However, Robert, his eldest son and the apple of his father's eye, succumbed to the charms of the South, moved to Albemarle County in 1860, and became master of slaves. In February 1862, as a Confederate officer, he died in action at Roanoke Island defending the institution his father fought to abolish.

Southerners, who conceded the evil of slavery, began to defend and justify the institution. An active abolitionist movement emerged in the North, made up largely of ex-Federalists of the middle and upper classes. Of course, one should never forget that sectionalism had profound effects at the personal level. (For details of how it influenced the course of one man's life, see the biographical sketch of Edward Coles in this chapter.)

The 1824 Election

The decade of the 1820s was a crucial, confusing era. Solid issues were emerging which laid raw sectional differences. Older regions, accustomed to running the republic, had to share that privilege with younger, bumptious upstarts west of the Appalachians. And, to make matters worse, political party structure provided no guideposts. "The Era of Good Feelings," an ironic name for a decade that gave birth to the fury of abolition and charted a course to war, had destroyed the original two-party system.

The voters of 1824, all of them ostensibly Democratic-Republicans of one shade or another, clearly were looking for both a leader and a platform. Many candidates tried to capture their attention. William Crawford, though seriously ill, was nominated by the "Old Republicans" at a legislative caucus in Washington, the last time this method would be used. John Quincy Adams had the blessing of James Monroe; Adams had served as Secretary of State, and that position had become a stepping stone to the presidency. Andrew Jackson and Henry Clay both had followings in the West, but only Clay worked out a clear program, his "American System" that called for internal improvements and encouragement of business. John C. Calhoun had presidential ambitions but he recognized they were futile and announced for the position of Vice President.

Andrew Jackson, the hero of New Orleans and of the Florida campaigns, won more votes than any other candidate, but no one received an electoral vote majority. The choice therefore went to the House, which would elect one of the three leading candidates (Adams, Crawford, or Jackson). Clay, the most influential member of the House, feared Jackson as a political rival in the West; and, although he and Adams had many differences, Clay himself and the delegations of Ohio and Kentucky switched their support to his camp. Yet, despite Clay's efforts, the whole game almost went up in

Courtesy of the New-York Historical Society, New York City.

John Quincy Adams began his diplomatic experience as secretary to his father during the Revolution. He used that experience to good advantage as Monroe's Secretary of State.

smoke when the large New York delegation in the House was deadlocked, 17–17. The tie breaker, Stephen Van Rensselaer, an elderly Federalist, bowed his head in prayer as voting began and, he said later, saw an Adams ballot at his feet which he interpreted as a sign from heaven. According to some historians, however, Daniel Webster produced an omen somewhat earlier when he informed Van Rensselaer that if Adams prevailed he promised to end a ban on appointment of old Federalists to federal jobs. Had New York voted differently, then on the second ballot Maryland and several other states planned to desert Adams, and many feared that if

balloting dragged on Calhoun might yet emerge as a compromise President.

Whether Clay, Webster, or a ballot carefully dropped at the feet of a wavering old politico decided this strange election, Adams won. When the new President named Clay as Secretary of State (and thus seemingly heir apparent to the presidency), Jackson accused Adams and Clay of corruption. But the real lesson to emerge from the election was that the Democratic-Republican party could no longer contain the competing ambitions of so many political figures who espoused divergent views. The old order was ending.

Essay

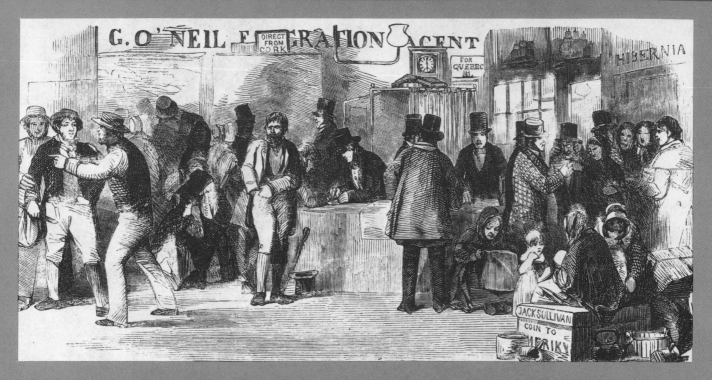

Turning Points:
The Old Order Was Ending

The concluding words of this chapter delineate a turning point in American life, that is, a time when old attitudes and old habits are giving way to new. Yet no "ending" is final and complete; certain themes prominent in the centuries and years before the 1820s continued to exert considerable influence long after that decade came to a close. Several even became more powerful in altered form as the nineteenth century ran its course, among them, immigration, westward expansion, and confrontation with the Indians. In fact, these three phenomena—movement of peoples across the Atlantic from Europe and Africa to North America, exploitation and settlement of this continent (first along the rivers and bays of the East coast and then moving inland, usually in a westerly direction), and, as a result, clashes and intermittent warfare with displaced natives—dominated America's historical development from 1600 to 1830. And to these we must add a fourth, the creation of an independent system of government.

In a sense, the business of cutting loose from Great Britain was so lengthy and painful a series of events that the emotions engendered tended to obscure vision for a time. Even today it is not entirely clear how many Americans actually were furious enough at the Mother Country to shoot and kill and how many wanted merely to chart an independent course and stand on their own two feet. Of course, wherever fighting began, a blow by one side invited retaliation from the other; feelings became convictions and tempers mounted. Nevertheless, for several generations British generals, American patriots, Tories, envoys in two capitals, War Hawks, and men such as those who attended the Hartford Convention danced a strange minuet. Despite bloodshed and recrimination, the ties binding the emerging American nation to the British Isles were strong indeed, among them, a common language and a common heritage. In the midst of the Revolution, for example, Thomas Jefferson could entertain at his dinner table officers of George III cap-

Frank Leslie's Illustrated Newspaper caught this scene of Irish immigrants in 1856 arranging to come to America.

tured at Saratoga, and as soon as peace was secured Congress quickly dispatched John Adams to London to restore diplomatic relations.

During the years from 1775 to 1814, Americans were, in fact, much like a child growing up and becoming an adult—sometimes valiantly, sometimes awkwardly trying to assert independence, not only from Britain, for also from Europe as well. Quasi-wars with France, petty disputes in the Mediterranean, a confusing and generally inconclusive second round with London, and the language of the Monroe Doctrine—all underscore this truth. In the 1770s, size, population, distance from Europe, and economic potential were powerful arguments for a separate, go-it-alone course. Even if fundamental political-philosophical disagreements on how best to run an empire had not surfaced, change was in the wind.

A half-century later change was again evident. The land mass had more than doubled, and population had grown at least three fold: from 3.9 million in 1790 to 12.8 million in 1830. In fact, every census from 1800 to 1860 revealed a ten-year increase of about thirty-three percent. In 1810 New York became the first city of over 100,000. Thirty years later it had been joined by Philadelphia, Baltimore, Boston, and New Orleans, and in 1860 it became the first metropolis with one million inhabitants.

New York was the first city of America by the time this picture was painted in ca. 1840.

Hidden in these statistics is the beginning of urban-industrial America. In 1790 only 5.4 percent of the population lived in communities of 2,500 or more; by 1860, 20 percent of all Americans were considered nonrural. This urban world—safe from Indian war whoops and free from the dictates of European despots—could turn its attention to commerce, making money, educating its children, and reforming virtually every aspect of day-to-day life from religion and dress codes to eating habits and slavery.

One important theme of these decades, only faintly perceived in some aspects of American life, was an independent, individualistic frame of mind. The Revolution certainly gave full expression to such views in the political realm, but one can sense similar attitudes throughout society as a whole—democratic trends in dress, speech, and manners; efforts at least to 1800 to ameliorate or abolish slavery; and some concern for the status of women. This emphasis upon the individual was even felt in the most intimate recesses of the family itself, for at some point in the late eighteenth century, parents decided to have fewer children. It is impossible to say whether this step was prompted by a regard for their own welfare or by a desire to provide more adequately for a smaller family, but in any case it is an expression of concern for the individual. In 1790 the average American family (slaves were not counted as families) had 5.7 persons, ranging from 5.4 in Georgia, a frontier area, to 6.1 in Delaware, a long-established community. Throughout the years that followed—despite vast waves of immigration and economic expansion creating thousands of jobs and great opportunities—the average family became ever smaller. By the end of the nineteenth century, it had decreased to 4.6 persons. Put another way, in 1790, 35.3 percent of all households (not necessarily families) consisted of seven or more persons; a century later only 23 percent were that large.

So, what in fact was ending in the 1820s? What were the earmarks of the "old" order that was passing from view? For one thing, it exhibited an aristocratic attitude closely tied to landed wealth, long-established families, educational attainment, and experience in positions of power. Andrew Jackson, who became President in 1829, may have owned a plantation and lived in a fine house, but his background differed radically from those of his predecessors. Born in obscurity in either North or South Carolina (the two states long fought over this matter, although South Carolina seems to have been the victor), he never was a cabinet member nor did he ever hold any high government post before entering the White House. In addition, Jackson came not from Virginia or Massachusetts, the traditional suppliers of chief executives, but from across the Appalachians in Tennessee.

This doughty old general was, in many ways, merely a symbol of what was occurring, for the United States over which he presided clearly was becoming more democratic, less concerned with blood lines and family background, and more interested in its internal affairs. No longer so sensitive to external pressures, Americans could turn their attention to exploiting their continent and perfecting their world. Because this was largely a "white male" democracy that was coming into being, one offering little to women and blacks, not everyone was pleased with these trends. And even among those who benefited most, there was discord, for different individuals had conflicting views on what constituted a "perfect" social order. The emerging slavery issue and the spirit of sectionalism it fostered were, for example, especially disturbing in decades ahead. Thomas Jefferson, in his famous "firebell in the night" letter to a Massachusetts congressman, sounded an extremely despondent note. In light of the Missouri Compromise of 1820, which sought, in his opinion, to divide the nation on the basis of principle and not geography, he thought all of the great sacrifice in 1776 had been "useless."

The "old" order also represented generations who had known firsthand both colonial status and the struggle for independence that Jefferson feared was being demeaned. On November 5, 1831, Alexis de Tocqueville, famed French-born student of American habits and attitudes, met with ninety-

Utah State Historical Society.

Restless Americans had moved to the Far West by the middle of the century. Here a group approaches South Pass in Wyoming.

five-year-old Charles Carroll of Maryland, the lone survivor among those who had signed the Declaration of Independence. Carroll, who owned 13,000 acres of land tilled by 300 slaves, was accustomed to wealth and power. To Tocqueville he seemed an English aristocrat of sorts who somehow had acquired certain democratic habits during his long and illustrious life.

Looking back over the years, Carroll (who had been educated in France) told his visitor that the men of 1776 did not actually anticipate independence even after the famous document was signed. Attachment to the Motherland remained very strong, and most signers saw the Declaration only as a bargaining point, but events, he added, proved it to be otherwise. Carroll closed the interview with a word of warning: "A mere democracy is but a mob. The English form of government is the only one suitable for you; if we tolerate ours, it is because every year we push our innovators out West." Of course, this was not true, for some innovators (such as Andrew Jackson) were coming back East, and growing urban centers (Baltimore, for example) were fast becoming vehicles for change.

In a confused state of mind, the French aristocrat left the venerable Catholic patriot, bemoaning the fact that such men and their cultivated manners were fast disappearing.

"The people is becoming enlightened, attainments spread, and a middling ability becomes common. The striking talents, the great characters are rare. Society is less brilliant and more prosperous. The various aspects of the progress of civilization and enlightenment, which are only hinted at in Europe, appear in the clear light of day in America. From what first cause do they arrive? I do not yet see clearly."

There was no *first cause* for the changes occurring throughout the United States in the 1820s, and neither Tocqueville nor anyone else should search for it. American society, even in that era, was far too complex, too vibrant, too individualistic to permit easy generalization. We can point to themes that dominated American life before 1830—immigration, westward expansion, Indian warfare, and independence from the Old World, but who is to say what type of civilization and what kind of people they might create in a new and different environment?

The 1820s were, then, as much as anything else an end of adolescence. Revolutionary veterans were fast disappearing, and so was the world they had created. Their sons and daughters, for the most part free of European bonds, could now go about the task of forming a uniquely American way of life. For the first time, Americans were clearly on their own; with strength and true independence also came responsibility for one's actions. No longer could they blame others for failure to reach desired goals. And the task ahead was formidable indeed, for there was little general agreement on just what "new" order was going to replace the "old."

SELECTED READINGS

General Studies

George Dangerfield, *The Awakening of American Nationalism, 1815–1828* (1965)

George Dangerfield, *The Era of Good Feelings* (1963)

C. S. Forester, *The Age of Fighting Sail* (1956)

Robert V. Remini, *Andrew Jackson and the Course of American Empire, 1767–1821* (1977)

Marshall Smelser, *The Democratic Republic, 1801–1815* (1968)

Charles Wiltse, *The New Nation* (1961)

War of 1812

Charles Borkks, *Siege of New Orleans* (1961)

Roger Brown, *Republic in Peril* (1964)

Harry Coles, *The War of 1812* (1965)

H. S. Halbert and T. H. Ball, *Creek War of 1813 and 1814* (1970)

Reginald Horseman, *The Causes of the War of 1812* (1962)

Glen Tucker, *Tecumseh: Vision of Glory* (1956)

Politics

Ronald Banks, *Maine Becomes a State: Movement to Separate Maine from Massachusetts, 1785–1820* (1970)

James Kehl, *Ill Feeling in the Era of Good Feeling* (1956)

Philip Klein, *Pennsylvania Politics, 1817–1832: A Game Without Rules* (1940)

Shaw Livermore, Jr., *Twilight of Federalism: Federalist Party, 1815–1830* (1962)

Glover Moore, *The Missouri Controversy* (1953)

Murray Rothbad, *The Panic of 1819* (1962)

Foreign Policy

Samuel F. Bemis, *John Quincy Adams and the Foundations of American Foreign Policy* (1949)

Bradford Perkins, *Castlereagh and Adams: England and the United States 1812–1823* (1964)

Dexter Perkins, *A History of the Monroe Doctrine*, rev. ed. (1963)

CHAPTER 8
THE GENESIS OF INDUSTRIAL AMERICA

TIMELINE

1807
Robert Fulton develops first practical steamboat

1808
Albert Gallatin calls for federal road system

1811
Construction of Cumberland Road begins

1815
Cotton boom in Lower South

1817
Construction of Erie Canal begins

1819
Dartmouth College v. *Woodward*

1825
Erie Canal opens

1827
Mechanics' Union of Trade Associations organized

1828
Steampower replaces waterpower in factories

1830
First American railroads

1835
Samuel Colt mass-produces revolving pistol

1837
Charles River Bridge v. *Warren Bridge*

1839
Charles Goodyear vulcanizes rubber

1844
Samuel F. B. Morse demonstrates telegraph

1845
Elias Howe perfects sewing machine

1848
Gold discovered in California

CHAPTER OUTLINE

The first four decades of the nineteenth century witnessed the beginnings of industrial growth in the United States, a phenomenon that was part of a general development of machines, factories, and working classes which was common to many parts of the North Atlantic basin. After 1815, both Europe and America enjoyed two generations or more of peaceful relations during which barriers to international trade relaxed somewhat and the movement of goods was encouraged. In this milieu, favorable to the growth of both domestic and international commerce, the young republic had several factors in its favor: a steady flow of inward migration that provided workers and, in turn, lured European investment capital; a series of bumper crops of grain and cotton; and a willingness—even a dynamic Yankee eagerness—to tinker, to experiment, to improve, and somehow to produce more, faster.

The Transportation Revolution

In these years, more so than after mid-century when the United States had become somewhat self-sufficient, the economic health of the country depended upon trade, which in turn was linked to transportation. Although "transportation" may sound like a specialized and rather abstract topic, it was in fact vitally associated with almost every facet of American life—the migrating of whole populations into new regions, the choosing of sites for cities to be built, the developing of manufacturing and agriculture, and the improving of the standard of living of citizens everywhere.

Roads

Before and after the War of 1812, farsighted leaders sought to link the larger centers in the Northeast with each other and with the growing settlements in the West. As early as 1808, Secretary of the Treasury Albert Gallatin called for a comprehensive system of federal roads. After much controversy about the constitutionality of such a federally sponsored project, the government began to build a highway (known as the "Cumberland Road") from Cumberland, Maryland, to Wheeling, Virginia, a town located on the Ohio River, now a major city in West

Improvements in transportation played an important role in the genesis of industrial America. This painting by Leila T. Bauman depicts several of the modes of transportation utilized by Americans during the first half of the nineteenth century.

Virginia. Construction took place between 1811 and 1818; later the road was extended to Vandalia, Illinois. The original road cost $1.7 million at the rate of about $13,000 a mile. The Cumberland Road (also called the National Road) was raised in the center for drainage and had a ditch on each side. Most early dirt roads were rutted in dry weather and a sea of mud in wet weather. The rock roadbed of the National Road permitted year-round travel at relatively high speeds.

Westerners, not satisfied with only one overland link to the East, persistently called for more East-West highways. The lack of such roads meant that few commodities could be transported be-

tween the two areas, and those carried overland were extremely expensive.

Despite the obvious advantages of building more and better roads, several sectors of the nation objected. Many politicians in the eastern states feared that improved East-West transportation would enable factories in the West to compete with those in the East. New, improved roads also threatened to lure more and more eastern workmen and their families to western settlements. Southerners had their own fears about federal roadbuilding. They were apprehensive that an expensive federal transportation project would lead to high tariffs, which would impede the flow of trade between the

227

The Transportation Revolution

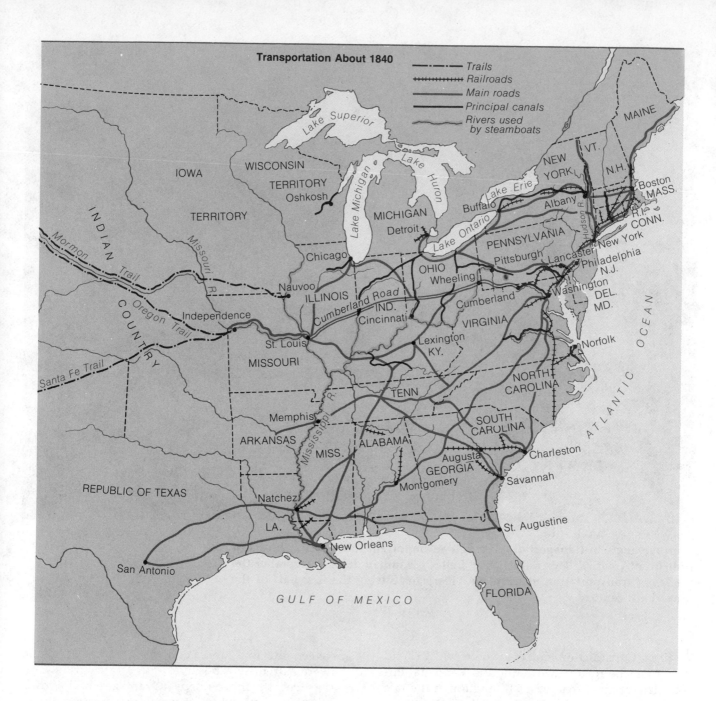

Transportation About 1840

Trails
Railroads
Main roads
Principal canals
Rivers used by steamboats

South and Europe. Finally, some national leaders were troubled by the constitutionality of federal roadbuilding.

This question was almost as old as the republic itself and goes back at least to Alexander Hamilton's plans for internal improvements at federal expense. At issue was whether national funds could be used for the direct benefit of a region or of a class, such as businessmen, when those outlays might, at best, only be for the very indirect aid of the total popu-

lation. This point was one of fundamental disagreement between some Federalists and Democratic-Republicans; and many Jeffersonians still viewed such undertakings with considerable skepticism.

As a consequence, the government did not build roads on a full-fledged scale. The job was left to private turnpike companies, which were especially active between 1789 and 1830. Turnpikes (or toll roads) did not constitute a lengthy system of roads; most of them could be found only in the older, more settled parts of the country. Among the best-known were those linking Philadelphia and Lancaster in Pennsylvania and the Old Post Road between New York and Boston.

Water Transportation

From the earliest times of white occupation of North America, water transport was the most common way to convey goods. The cost of transporting goods 100 miles overland (an average of $10 a ton) was not much less than shipping them from America to Europe. Water transport was considerably less expensive, though it, too, had disadvantages. Most river freighting ran with the current, usually from north to south in the United States; up-country freighting, by contrast, relied on wagons and packtrains or, along the coasts, on sloops and schooners.

The trouble with transport by water was that it restricted trade to the patterns prescribed by the natural system of rivers and bays, and even these networks were often not navigable in winter. In good weather a trip upstream could be very long; on the Ohio-Mississippi river route, for instance, the journey downstream from Pittsburgh to New Orleans took six weeks; the same journey upstream required nearly three times as long. High river banks made sailboats ineffective, and much slower barges, flatboats, and rafts, all poled or paddled, had to be used.

Two innovations—steamboats and canals—completely changed the nature of water transportation shortly after the War of 1812. As early as 1807, Robert Fulton constructed the first practical steamboat, the *Clermont*, a vessel 133 feet long and 7 feet deep equipped with a steam engine, a twenty-foot boiler, and two side paddle wheels, each fifteen feet in diameter. On its first voyage up the Hudson River to Albany, New York, the *Clermont* rushed

Denver Public Library, Western Collection.
Water transportation on the Ohio River in the 1830s. Here steam power and muscle power are both at work. Before the coming of railroads, water transportation was predominant on America's expanding frontier.

along against the current at the astounding speed of about five miles an hour! After the war, Fulton established a regular service of steamboats between New York City and Albany. Although ingenious men had been working out the details of steam navigation since 1790, Fulton deserves credit for bringing the various mechanical features—engine, boiler, paddle wheels, and hull—into the proper functioning balance.

Soon steam vessels were plying the Mississippi, and New Orleans, the port near the mouth of the river, became one of the world's major trading centers. By 1852 steamboats had transformed the commerce along the Mississippi River Valley into a business worth more than $650 million annually. Along the eastern seaboard, steamboats facilitated rapid passenger transportation. Cornelius Vanderbilt operated numerous coastal vessels after 1829 and made a fortune doing so—within seven years he was worth half a million dollars.

The most dramatic effect of the steamboat was on the Mississippi, Ohio, and other rivers of the Old Northwest (Illinois, Ohio, Indiana, Michigan, and Wisconsin). By 1830, these craft were traveling all of the main rivers of that region and many of the principal tributaries as well. The resulting commercial traffic made the West an integral and very vital part of the national economy.

While steamboats were improving the flow of commerce in the West, the construction of canals was providing a direct link between the Northeast and the West. The Erie Canal was the first and by far most important of these projects; in fact, it continues to carry a substantial amount of freight even today. A massive undertaking, the canal covered a distance of 364 miles and connected Albany on the Hudson River with Buffalo on Lake Erie. Begun in 1817, the canal was finished in 1825 at a cost of $7 million to the state of New York. The first voyage was taken by New York's governor, DeWitt Clin-

Museum of the City of New York.
The opening of the Erie Canal as a toll waterway connecting the Hudson River with Lake Erie was a joyous occasion in 1825. It set off a nationwide craze for canal building.

Cooper's *Tom Thumb*, the first efficient steam engine locomotive built in the United States, races a horse-drawn car on the Baltimore & Ohio Railroad on August 28, 1830, and wins.

ton, who traversed the canal from Buffalo to Albany and then went down the Hudson on a steamboat to New York City, where he poured a keg of water from Lake Erie into the Atlantic, symbolizing the marriage of the Great Lakes to the ocean. The marriage turned out to be a highly profitable one; New York became the country's major city, outstripping Philadelphia, Boston, and New Orleans. Western lumber, flour, whiskey, and some manufactured items, such as pig iron, were conveyed to New York; the trade from the East to the West, however, was still larger. Moreover, the canal carried thousands of settlers to the West and greatly increased the value of land there.

Traveling along the canal was slow, since ordinary speed was only about three miles an hour. Brightly painted canal boats were dragged along by one or more mules or horses, which walked beside the canal on tow paths. The cost, however, was low; the rate on a small boat that did not offer sleeping accommodations or food was one cent a mile, which was much less than the cost of travel by stagecoach; the rate for larger packet boats with bunks and food was about five cents a mile. Of greater importance was the movement of crops and freight. Thanks to the Erie Canal, much of the Great Lakes region now had easy access to the Atlantic Ocean. Freight charges between Buffalo and New York dipped 85 percent and shipping time shrank

from eight to less than four days. Two years after the Erie opened, a Georgia governor complained that wheat grown in New York state sold for less in Savannah than that produced only 100 miles away in inland counties of his own state.

Philadelphia, recognizing that the Erie Canal was diverting western business to New York, sought to compete by building its own canals. The terrain of Pennsylvania, however, was much hillier, and the Pennsylvania system of dams, locks, stagecoaches, and horse-drawn railroad cars may have been ingenious but proved to be impractical. Other East coast canals were similarly costly and unsuccessful; few ever reached their avowed goal, and most of them eventually gave way to railroads.

In the Old Northwest, "canal fever" was rampant, and many canals were started. The most ambitious and useful one was the Ohio Canal, a 308-mile undertaking that connected the Ohio River with Lake Erie. Western canals fostered urban growth and expanded the economy, but these waterways also led to the eviction of Indian tribes, such as the Miamis and Potawatomis, who blocked the path of the white man's "progress."

Railroads

Canals and the steamboat were only harbingers of a true transportation revolution ushered in by the steam-powered railroad. In addition to creating a huge demand for workers, materials, and supplies, railroads virtually eliminated the confining restraints of weather and topography. No longer did one have to be so concerned with snow, rain, and mountains. Seasonal layoffs because of icebound rivers and canals were a thing of the past, and both invested capital and labor could be used much of the year around. Railroads, although expensive and time consuming to build, were direct, relatively fast, and in continuous operation, factors that had a profound effect upon growing American industry in general.

The first efficient steam locomotive in the United States was built in 1830 by manufacturer Peter Cooper (whose extraordinary career is summarized in a biographical sketch in this chapter). Cooper's steam engine, "Tom Thumb," demonstrated that steam locomotion was practical. In the following decade, railways assumed local and, after 1840, national importance. Nevertheless, until 1840 inland waterways remained the country's main arteries of transportation. In the early years of steam locomotion, construction was hindered by the opposition of canal owners and other vested interests, who tried to persuade state governments to limit railroad traffic to passengers. Carrying freight, they claimed, should be permitted only in areas where canals did not exist.

Among the pioneer railroad companies in the United States were the Baltimore & Ohio and a line between Charleston, South Carolina, and the town of Hamburg near Augusta, Georgia. In 1833 the South Carolina railroad had 136 miles of track, the longest stretch in the entire world. By 1840 railroads were operating more than 2,800 miles of track in the United States, which was more than that found in all of Europe. For the most part, these were short lines of varying gauges designed to haul inland produce to the port that had promoted the railroad. Little or no thought was given to connecting them with rival centers; that would come later. At the same date, the nation had 3,326 miles of canals; but, unlike railroads, canal construction was ending, not beginning. Virtually no canals were dug after 1840, although for a decade or so their backers expended millions in a last ditch effort to thwart the rise of the "iron horse."

Construction of all kinds ceased for a time following an economic panic in 1837. But after the economy improved in the 1840's, the railroad-building pace picked up again and reached boom proportions in the 1850s.

Peter Cooper

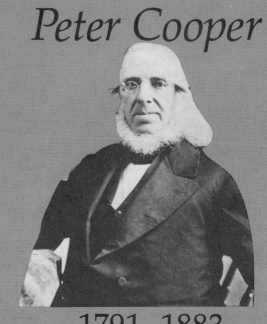

1791–1883

Coachmaker, traveling salesman, grocer, producer of glue (as well as iron, steam locomotives, and wire), inventor of an amazing variety of machines, and—above all else—the philanthropist who created New York's famed Cooper Union (also known as Cooper Institute), Peter Cooper lived his ninety-two years to the fullest. Although he had only a year of formal education, soon after the War of 1812—following varied experience in the business world—this young New York City native decided that the future lay in manufacturing. He bought a local glue factory and soon was monopolizing a field previously crowded with European imports.

In 1828, with funds earned from glue and isinglass, he joined two partners in an iron works located on 3,000 acres of land in Baltimore. This plant, to the surprise of a skeptical English engineer, hammered together America's first steam locomotive (the so-called "Tom Thumb" or "Teakettle"), which saved the troubled Baltimore & Ohio Railroad from disaster. That railroad's growth aided Cooper's iron enterprise, and when he sold some of his lands to the B & O eight years later, he accepted as payment company stock, which soon soared in value.

Within two decades Cooper's holdings included not only glue and iron, but a wire-rolling mill, blast furnaces, foundries, mines, and a New Jersey factory, which in 1854 turned out the first structural iron for fireproof buildings. He served for over twenty years as president of the New York, Newfoundland, and London Telegraph Company and also headed up the North American Telegraph Company, an organization that once controlled or owned over half of the lines in the United States. As head of the former, he was the chief backer of Cyrus Field and never lost faith in that man's persistent attempts to lay a transatlantic cable.

As an inventor, Cooper might have rivaled Edison, had he possessed technical training. His first successful effort (a washing machine) was followed by devices to mortise wheel hubs, to propel ferry boats by compressed air, and to use ocean tides as a source of power. He also somehow found time to be a New York City alderman, reform numerous aspects of Manhattan daily life (such as police and fire departments, schools, and the municipal water supply), and run for President of the United States on the Greenback party ticket in 1876.

Yet Peter Cooper is remembered today chiefly as a philanthropist, the creator of a famous institute offering free courses in art, general science, chemistry, electricity, and various branches of engineering. It was almost as if having been somewhat thwarted in his own efforts to perfect still more inventions, he was determined to make the path easier for others. Although Cooper's story is not really a rags-to-riches tale, his career incorporates many themes found in the development of America's burgeoning Northeast during his lifetime: boundless energy, innate personal drive, monopolistic tendencies, and an inventive mind, as well as a dedication to public service, an interest in politics, and an eagerness to aid others. At a reception given in his honor in 1874, Cooper said: "I have always recognized that the object of business is to make money in any honourable manner. I have endeavored to remember that the object of life is to do good." When Cooper died on April 4, 1883, he was sincerely mourned in New York, a city that he had served so well.

Government and the Economy

After 1815, economic expansion and scientific improvements in America were promoted by both federal and state governments. In the past, many historians believed that during this period the federal government seldom intervened to determine economic policy or to plan and finance internal improvements. Now this view has been revised. Americans did spend a great deal of time discussing whether the Constitution granted Washington officials the right to give government aid to local projects, but much of this debate centered on whether or not state or national authorities should act. Americans were not opposed to government aid; some simply wondered whether the Constitution permitted *federal* money to be given to specific projects.

Government Intervention

One way the federal government affected economic life was by passing tariffs designed to shelter such young industries as the manufacture of cotton and woolen goods from foreign competiton. Such regulations, which produced considerable revenue, began with a moderately protective tariff in 1816, which was revised upward in 1824 and again four years later, so much so that critics called the Tariff of 1828 "the Tariff of Abominations." These maneuverings, though they aided industries in the Northeast, angered Southerners, who were convinced that this protection hurt their trade with foreign markets; imported manufactured goods, they said, cost more, and foreign merchants were more reluctant to buy southern cotton and tobacco.

One of the biggest businesses in the county was the United States Post Office; the federally built National Road also was a giant enterprise. Until the government's Indian trading posts, or "factories," were abolished in 1822, they sold supplies to Indians and bought their furs and animal hides. By arranging for the removal of Indian tribes from states and territories, the government aided the economic activities of white citizens. The federal government influenced the economy in a very real way by regulating the sale of public lands. Congressional legislation protected the merchant marine by excluding foreign vessels from domestic trade along the Atlantic and Gulf coasts and often provided substantial sums for internal improvements, despite the debate such measures aroused. Washington stimulated industries by handing out large government contracts—for instance, to the manufacturers of pistols and rifles.

The United States Patent Office encouraged and protected inventors by ensuring their rights to the profits earned by their discoveries. This vitally important bureau was organized in 1802 when a single individual in the Department of State was designated as the superintendent in charge of patents.

In the short run at least, whatever steps the national government took tended to aid one section or region at the expense of another. The sale of cheap public land encouraged westward movement and caused problems for the economies of some settled areas of the East. This could mean labor shortages and perhaps even diminished political power if population decline led to reduced representation in Congress. Federal aid for turnpikes, canals, and railroads bestowed few immediate benefits upon some coastal inhabitants or upon communities already blessed with functioning transportation systems. And, as noted, nonindustrial areas such as the South and West deeply resented tariffs designed to protect burgeoning factories of the Northeast.

One response to sectional jealousies was a scheme of "trade-offs" or compromises, which would give each area something while none reaped all of the rewards. As a rising young politician, Henry Clay, spokesman for the new West, devised his "American System" to do just that. He proposed the creation of a great domestic market by means of a protective tariff to stimulate industry, federally funded internal improvements to aid the commerce of all sections, and a national bank to regulate credit and the transfer of funds throughout the nation. Of course, the bank appeared (1816), and so did the tariffs (1816, 1824, 1828), but somehow the balance wheels of Clay's "American System" were missing. The result was constant competiton among rival sections, bitterness when one region won what residents of another viewed as unfair advantages, and recurring efforts at compromise.

The Role of the Judiciary

Working hand in hand with Congress was another branch of the federal government, the Supreme Court, which wielded enormous influence in deciding political questions. In the first half of the nineteenth century, it determined policies that were largely economic in nature. Under Chief Justice John Marshall, who presided until he was succeeded by Roger B. Taney in 1836, the Court viewed the business community as an important agent of progress—and decided many cases in favor of private enterprise. The Marshall court's decisions in cases such as that involving the Dartmouth College Charter (1819) and *Gibbons* v. *Ogden* (1824) came down solidly in favor of private enterprise and the businessman. The Taney court continued to side with business, but it stressed the role of business as an agent for social change and growth.

One of Taney's most famous decisions was the *Charles River Bridge* case. In 1785 the Massachusetts legislature had granted a company a charter to build a toll bridge; when a second company received a charter from the legislature to build an adjacent toll-free bridge nearby, the first company took the second to court. The question involved was whether or not the original charter conferred a monopoly that the new bridge encroached upon, thus violating the contract clause of the Constitution. Taney and four justices in 1837 decided in favor of the second company; they did not think that the Supreme Court should protect the exclusive claims of one enterprise when such protection would work against the interests of the public, which was obviously better served in this instance by having the use of more than one bridge. As Taney put it: "While the rights of private property are sacredly guarded, we must not forget that the community also have rights, and that the happiness and well-being of every citizen depends on their faithful preservation." Taney's modification of Marshall's earlier rulings defending the sanctity of contracts—notably in the Dartmouth College case—was based on the belief that any ambiguities in the contract must be interpreted in favor of the public.

The Influence of State Governments

The state governments appear to have played a larger economic role than Washington during the antebellum period. Conferring charters that allowed businesses to incorporate was one of the chief economic functions of state governments. In addition, states granted tax benefits to certain favored enterprises and some exempted workers from militia or jury duty so as not to disrupt industries where they were employed.

Aside from granting corporate charters, providing tax benefits, and conducting regulatory activities, the states intervened in the economy by supporting internal improvements. A careful analysis of the railroads built before 1860 in the South, for instance, reveals that almost three-fourths of the financing came from public sources. Local and state governments had to pay for railroads, since only they could raise the necessary capital. The State of Pennsylvania invested more than $100 million in its public works system, especially in canals and railroads. Power to grant corporation charters gave states obvious influence over both banks and transportation companies; and, in many cases, the corporation itself was a "mixed" institution—that is, partially public and partially private. Pennsylvania's state government not only invested heavily in many corporations but also placed public directors at the head of these enterprises; by 1844 there were some 150 "mixed" corporations in that state.

The Factory System

Englishman Charles Dickens, a bitter foe of the evils of industrialization in his own country, was quite favorably impressed by what appeared to be much better working conditions in America. Factories in Lowell, Massachusetts, that he visited in 1842, did indeed exemplify careful organization and farsighted planning, though they were not typical; and, had Dickens looked elsewhere, he would have found many factories all too reminiscent of what he deplored in his native England.

Factories were by no means the predominant mode of American industry until mid-century. Small household manufacturing operations continued to play a major role, although by the 1840's factories were becoming more and more common, especially in the Northeast. The factory system can be distinguished by a few distinctive features that set it apart from the craftsman's shop. A factory turns out a substantial quantity of standardized items. Secondly, a factory is manned by an assembly of workers ruled by rigid discipline. A craftsman might be relatively free to set his own hours and working conditions; the factory laborer adheres to an unvarying schedule and usually performs only one step in a process of many stages. The factory worker is not self-employed and does not directly enjoy the full profits of his or her own labor. A single entrepreneur or a group of investors owns the physical plant, the machinery, and the tools. The owners reap most of the profits; the worker receives a fixed salary.

The first American factory was established by Samuel Slater (1768–1835) in 1790 in Pawtucket, Rhode Island. Backed by a mercantile partnership in Providence, Slater (an English immigrant and a mechanical wizard) succeeded in setting up a cotton-spinning mill that was fully operative by 1793. Twenty years later there were many such mills throughout southern New England, almost all of them located along streams and rivers since their looms were driven by waterpower. A growing influx of skilled English laborers aided these New England ventures; the newcomers were attracted by the high wages they could earn in the United States.

Before the War of 1812, the factory system grew slowly in the United States, hampered by a shortage of skilled machinists, an inadequate knowledge of factory management, and a lack of capital for buying the necessary equipment. What American capital was available was going into such areas as commerce and trade, real estate, and building. More significantly, new enterprises, particularly in textiles, faced strong foreign competitors, especially the more efficient and well-developed English factories that could undersell those in America. Moreover, marginal domestic manufacturers, scattered in thousands of homes were still much more important than factory producers of the same items.

The years preceding and during the War of 1812 aided industrialization. The Embargo of 1807, the Nonintercourse Act, and the interruption of trade with England during the war itself all served to seal off British competition temporarily and to make Americans dependent on their own resources for manufactured goods. The enormous profits acquired by Yankee merchants of the period also provided New England with the capital necessary for building factories and buying machinery.

But the industrialization of the Northeast was not based on such transitory factors alone. Even when the war was over and British industrialists were free to compete for the American market once more, factories continued to spring up there because that region had decided advantages in this movement towards industrialization. One of these "advantages" was actually a shortcoming—the soil was so poor in New England and the average farm so small that many farmers needed to supplement their meager incomes by sending their wives, sons, and daughters to work in factories. Most of the young women Dickens saw at Lowell, for instance, were recruited from impoverished farms in communities where females outnumbered males by a substantial margin. In addition to having a ready labor force and capital, New England had numerous rivers gushing toward the sea, rich with power easily harnessed to run looms and mills. Soon, large brick and stone structures were dotting the banks of the Merrimack in northeastern Massachusetts; the Naugatuck, Quinnipiac, and Housatonic in Connecticut; the Blackstone in Rhode Island; and the Androscoggin in southern Maine.

Manufacturers in the Northeast were also blessed with easy access to raw materials. Pennsylvania had rich resources of iron and coal, essential to smelting. The chief manufactured goods were made of cotton which, though grown in the South, could be shipped inexpensively up the Atlantic coast to Boston, New York City, and other ports of the Northeast. For all of these reasons, factories spread in the Northeast, and manufacturing gradually replaced commerce after 1815 as the economic mainstay in urban communities throughout the region.

In 1828 steampower replaced waterpower at the Slater cotton mills in Pawtucket. Soon steam was powering many other American industries, freeing them from the necessity of having to be located beside a stream or river.

Yankee Inventions

By 1840 only England was more highly industrialized than the United States. Considering that Americans had a late start, their success can be partially attributed to such factors as an everexpanding population, growing prosperity, and plentiful natural resources—but these factors should not obscure the importance of "Yankee ingenuity." American industry was aided greatly by American inventions.

The major American inventions are too numerous to list, but a few milestones can be mentioned. In 1819 Jethro Wood perfected a cast-iron plow made of three replaceable parts; by 1825 this plow, despite unfounded fears on the part of some farmers that iron would "poison" the soil, came into general use. A plow, along with an axe, seed, a gun, and a few animals, accompanied practically every frontiersman as he moved westward. Wood's plow (later improved somewhat by a blacksmith named John Deere) literally was the cutting edge of settlement and its iron—then later its steel—blade proved more than equal to the task of slicing through tough prairie grass and virgin soil tangled with roots. After 1820 food storage changed radically with the introduction of canning. At first sea-

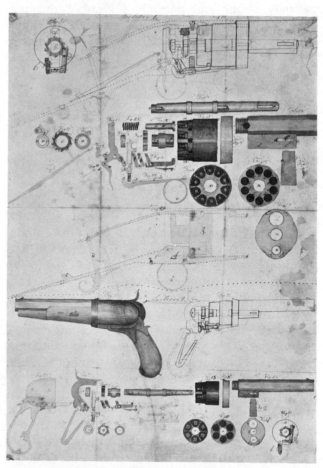

Colt Firearms Collection, Museum of Connecticut History, Hartford, Connecticut.

The 1835 patent drawing for Colt's revolving pistol, using interchangeable parts.

Eli Whitney's cotton gin revolutionized the cotton industry and consequently increased the demand for black slaves.

foods and later, vegetables and fruits were sealed in glass bottles or tin cans and preserved for future use. This process introduced seasonal variety into diets at low cost and made the foods of one region available in another.

Cyrus Hall McCormick and Obed Hussey, working independently of each other in the 1830s, perfected the reaping machine, a device that allowed one worker to cut about ten acres of grain a day. Soon McCormick, who built a plant in Chicago in the heart of the grain-raising part of the country, was manufacturing about 40 reapers a day. The innovative policy of selling to farmers on the installment plan, a strategy adopted earlier in the century by clock manufacturers in New England, increased his business substantially.

In 1835 Samuel Colt began to mass-produce the revolving pistol. In the following years Americans got their first glimpse of other inventions and processes. Rubber, for example, was "vulcanized" by Charles Goodyear (1800-1860) so that it would hold up under extremes of heat and cold. Goodyear's feat actually resulted from an accident in 1839. While experimenting, he spilled rubber heated with sulphur on a hot stove and found, to his delight, that it retained its elasticity. However, fame and fortune eluded him and he died a poor man. The telegraph that Samuel Morse (1791–1872) dem-

onstrated to Congress in 1844 eventually put every section of the nation in touch with every other region. The sewing machine that Elias Howe perfected in 1845 revolutionized the textile and clothing industries. (More information about Howe and his invention is given in an accompanying sketch.)

New inventions especially benefited the textile industry. In 1790 the various stages of producing fabric—the preparing and cleaning, spinning, weaving, and finishing—were all done by hand; by 1815 machines performed these tasks. The cotton gin mechanically separated seeds from fibers. Two other American inventions, "pickers" and "willows," cleaned the raw fibers and pulled out burrs. After 1826 yet another American invention, the Goulding condenser, not only carded wool but also compressed the various fibers into a single strand ready to be spun into yarn. After the War of 1812, power-driven jennies did the spinning. The jenny consisted of a belted spinning wheel to one side of a horizontal loom with bobbins, which reproduced the work of hand spinners as waterpower or steampower turned the belt and wheel. The manufacture of textiles involved many small steps, some quite intricate, and at almost every point Americans either invented new devices to do the work or improved already existing techniques. As a result, factory-made cotton and woolen cloth soon became

237
The Factory System

Elias Howe

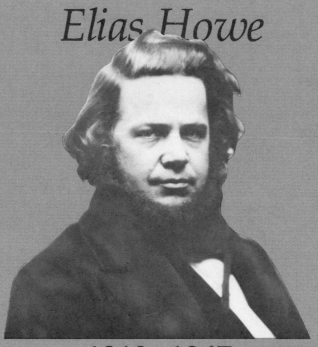

1819–1867

The inventor of the sewing machine led a life that sounds as though it had been written by Horatio Alger—a true rags-to-riches saga. Born in Massachusetts, the son of a poor farmer, Howe was hired out to a neighboring farmer when he was twelve because his family was too poor to feed or clothe him. When he was sixteen, young Elias was apprenticed to the machinery shop at the cotton mills in Lowell, Massachusetts.

After a number of other small jobs, Howe ended up two years later as an apprentice to Ari Davis, a maker of precision instruments in nearby Cambridge. One day Howe overheard Davis say that the next important invention would be a machine that could sew automatically. Armed with the technical skill he had acquired in Davis's shop and inspired by this suggestion, Howe began to work on this invention. The first attempt was a total failure, but in 1844 he made a new stab at a sewing machine, incorporating principles he had observed in the power looms at Lowell. He quit his job with Ari Davis in order to devote full time to the project. Howe's father provided free room and board, and funds for supplies and equipment came from a

friend, George Fisher, who with an investment of $500 became a partner. By April 1845, Howe had perfected a sewing machine that operated swiftly and efficiently and could make 250 stitches a minute, faster than the speed of five people sewing by hand. This invention soon revolutionized the manufacturing of clothing.

Howe registered his invention with the United States Patent Office in 1846, but no one in America seemed interested in producing the machine. Later that year Howe sent his brother to London where William Thomas, a corset manufacturer, bought the sewing machine and all British rights for £250. Howe himself traveled to England where he adapted the machine to sewing leather.

Meanwhile, back in America, manufacturers who had learned of the machine's favorable reception in England started producing sewing machines without giving Howe credit or royalties. Only after a long battle in the courts did Howe win his case in 1854; every machine that had been turned out or that would be manufactured in the future was to earn him royalties. During the Civil War, Howe sometimes was earning as much as $4,000 a week.

so cheap that household production of fabrics declined, undersold by industrial competition.

These improvements in the textile industry had far-reaching results. A secondary industry sprang up to produce textile machines and related equipment, and this industry in turn spawned a third—shops to make machine tools.

The Cotton Boom

The effects of the textile industry were not confined to the Northeast. Many parts of the Southeast greatly increased the cultivation of cotton. Indeed, when territories opened up along the Gulf of Mexico after the defeat of hostile Creek Indians during the War of 1812, most of these lands became cotton plantations. After 1815, cotton was king in much of the Lower South—an arc of states stretching from South Carolina westward to Texas and Arkansas—although states below the Mason-Dixon Line continued to produce other crops as well. Maryland and Virginia grew considerable amounts of wheat and corn. Tobacco also flourished in those states and in North Carolina. Kentucky and Missouri raised hemp; Louisiana, sugar; and small, subsistence farms could be found throughout the entire area.

The regional supremacy of cotton had national, even international repercussions. Since so many southern whites turned their fields over to cotton, they had to purchase some of their food from the West. Northern merchants profited from handling the transportation and insurance involved in shipping southern cotton to domestic and foreign markets. English fabric manufacturers looked to the South as a prime source of raw cotton. The three main regions of the country—the South, the Northeast, and the West—became increasingly specialized and interdependent.

In time, as a one-crop mentality gripped much of the Lower South and manufacturing loomed ever more important in the Northeast, the Mississippi Valley became the great breadbasket of the nation, a role once enjoyed by the Middle Atlantic region. It is no accident, for example, that although McCormick perfected his reaper in Virginia, he produced those machines in Chicago. It is easy to oversimplify this three-sided portrait of the American economy after the War of 1812, but by the 1830's cotton clearly was one of the foundation stones. The Northeast provided its manufactured goods and various services; the West, food; and, the Lower South, cotton, which became a basic ingredient in this interchange.

During the years immediately after the War of 1812 and again in the 1830s cotton was a crucial factor in American economic expansion. By midcentury, however, the boom was over. An analysis of land sales, cotton prices, and cotton production between 1833 and 1843 reveals what was happening in the so-called "Cotton Kingdom." After 1836 the sale of lands dropped sharply and prices began a slow downward trend, while production generally continued to climb. One could make money in cotton, but no longer expect quick, spectacular returns. As a result, investment capital turned elsewhere—to newer and bigger factories in the Northeast and California and its gold fields after 1848. The Far West, more industrialization, and the first big wave of immigrants (few of whom settled in the South) fueled the expansion fires of the 1850s, not cotton.

While it lasted, the cotton boom had a dramatic impact indeed. Production rose by leaps and bounds. In 1820, the South was producing 335,000 bales, each weighing approximately 500 pounds; by 1840, the annual crop rose to 1,348,000 bales and would triple by 1860. Several unique factors frustrate efforts to estimate the profits of a cotton plantation: the soaring cost of new black workers, the birth of offspring to slaves already living on the plantation, and income derived from sources other than cotton. In the 1820s, for example, a prime Georgia field hand averaged about $700; in 1860, about $1,800.

More impressive than columns of annual prices are census statistics that reveal how many people were lured to the Lower South by cotton. Between 1790 and 1860 the population of the South rose from two to more than eleven million. Alabama, for example, had 1,250 residents in 1800, 964,201 in 1860. During the last two decades before the Civil War, expanding American factories used up one-quarter of the cotton crop, yet that commodity still accounted for half of all U.S. exports and helped mightily to pay for imports and attract foreign investment across the Atlantic to America. Widespread cultivation led to increased demand for slave labor; picking cotton had to be performed by hand, and slaves, for the most part, did this work. As a result, slave trading within and between states became a flourishing enterprise.

Although Southerners made a few efforts to

build textile factories, first in the 1790s and again after the War of 1812, these attempts were largely halfhearted. Several factors tended to discourage their growth. The Northeast, with its know-how, capital, labor resources, and waterpower, surged so far ahead in industrial capabilities that it usually was cheaper to buy whatever was produced than to emulate this development and compete. So much money could be made in cotton that many Southerners invested their capital in land and slaves, leaving little for factories. By tradition the South was a rural, agricultural region, not eager to welcome urban masses and the resultant problems found wherever workers congregated. In addition, as the abolition fury grew, the prospect of an influx of "nonbelievers" caused considerable unrest. Perhaps the key factors militating against industrialization lay simply in habit and attitude. The South had labor, capital, raw materials, and waterpower. If it had wanted factories badly enough, it could have had them, as later decades demonstrated.

Improvements in Industry

American industry took an important step toward assembly-line mass production when goods with interchangeable parts appeared. This innovation first occurred in the firearms industry. Whether Eli Whitney (the inventor of the cotton gin) or the less well-known Simeon North (1765–1852) first came up with the concept of interchangeability of parts is not known, but the two men, working independently, both made major contributions to the method. Interchangeability requires another, equally important concept and practice—subdividing the production of a product into many small steps.

In 1813 Simeon North signed a government contract to make 20,000 pistols. In the contract North wrote this provision: "The component parts of pistols are to correspond so exactly that any limb or part of one Pistol may be fitted to any other Pistol of the twenty thousand." Each one cost $7. For a decade or more, North, Whitney, and other gun manufacturers in Connecticut had been turning out interchangeable parts. Working with these components, their laborers could assemble guns in a fraction of the time previously required. The assembly line later was introduced into other industries as well. By the 1850s items ranging from watches to locks were being mass-produced by scores of workers, each doing one simple task over and over. (For an in-depth analysis of how one

Yale University Art Gallery, Gift of George Hoadly.
Eli Whitney, inventor of the cotton gin and proponent of the concept of the production of machines with interchangeable parts.

group of entrepreneurs—the Boston Associates—used these techniques, see the essay on "The Birth of Mass Production" at the end of this chapter.)

America was slower than England to industrialize, primarily because it was a newer, developing land and because American entrepreneurs lacked the capital to purchase expensive machinery. Even after the War of 1812, despite the remarkable successes of the American factory system in the production of cotton textiles, local craftsmen and traveling artisans were still providing most of the nation's manufactured goods, items such as pianos, tin utensils, shoes, cigars, hats, clothes, and hundreds of other necessities and luxuries. Development of centralized production in what we now call factories was far from orderly or systematic. By their very nature, some commodities fitted quickly into such a scheme of things; others did not. Reacting to increased market demand created by an evergrowing population, a producer often went through three steps: enlarging his shop or handicraft output, spreading the growing workload among various households (the so-called domestic or putting-out system), and eventually constructing a much larger shop complete with laborsaving machinery, perhaps powered by a waterwheel or steam; in short, a factory.

In the early days of industrialization, most factories catered strictly to local needs and did not produce goods for distant markets. Even in the most rural parts of the country, local entrepreneurs turned out flour, lumber, brick, ironwork, cheese, and liquor to satisfy community needs. If one of these operations reached a larger market, this increase in business did not necessarily entail a departure from traditional methods of production.

Capital needed for mechanization was in short supply. The number of banks willing to extend credit to American businessmen increased from 300 to 1,000 between 1820 and 1840, but this proliferation did not stimulate industrialization as rapidly as one would expect. The public distrusted banks, and this distrust deepened when nearly half of the recently founded banks in the country failed by 1825; twenty years later a similar proportion of new banks founded between 1830 and 1840 collapsed.

Nevertheless, banks did play a significant role in financing American industrialization. Bank credit, for instance, helped Eli Whitney to set up his mass production of firearms, and banks helped to finance the business interests of Peter Cooper, who in 1828 established the Baltimore ironworks that produced America's first steam locomotive.

The corporation was another mode of financing industrialization after the War of 1812. A corporation is a legal entity that provides investors with the benefit ot "limited liability." If two or more people enter into a partnership, each partner is fully responsible (or "liable") for debts incurred by the enterprise as a whole. But in a corporation, by contrast, each stockholder is legally responsible for the corporation's debts only to the extent of his or her own investment. This form of organization evolved through the centuries in Europe, and in America it had proved to be a convenient means of attracting large numbers of investors to such enterprises as building turnpikes, bridges, and other large and expensive types of internal improvements. Only after 1815, however, did the corporation begin to play a major role in industrial life.

Like banks, corporations were regarded with suspicion by the general public and even by many entrepreneurs. Since individual investors had limited liability and in many cases did not participate directly in running the company's affairs, the corporation was associated with corruption and the undermining of individual enterprise. The very success of corporations was seen as evil, since their size, wealth, and efficiency enabled them to drive out smaller businesses and create monopolies.

Before 1837 businessmen eager to incorporate their enterprises faced legal difficulties. Each group interested in forming a corporation had to petition a state legislature for a special act of incorporation. As a result, businessmen with money and political connections had an advantage over those lacking leverage with lawmakers. This inequitable situation awakened protest and led to a demand for the general enactment of revised laws of incorporation enabling any group, once it met certain minimum requirements, to obtain a charter. Connecticut passed the first such general act in 1837, and in the following years the chief manufacturing states revised their own statutes accordingly.

Extensions of Industrialization

By mid-century virtually every American household had been influenced in some measure by changes in transportation, business, and industry; and many U.S. wares were being sold overseas as well. These included, among other things, cotton and woolen goods, shoes, boots, clothing, rubber products, various machines and agricultural implements, and processed foods. Interestingly, one invention often spawned others. Preservation of meats, fruits, and vegetables by sterilization and enclosure in airtight receptacles (begun in the 1820s) led within two decades to a canning machine, a process for storing milk through evaporation, and the utilization of glass jars with screwtop lids.

The sewing machine of Elias Howe inspired Isaac Merrit Singer (1811–1875), a superb salesman, to build a foot-operated version for use in the home. The two men fought legal battles over in-

Elias Howe's sewing machine revolutionized the textile and clothing industries. Here Howe is shown in Boston watching a contest between sewers working by hand and one operating a machine.

fringement of patent rights, and in 1854 the courts ruled in Howe's favor. This was a hollow victory since by this time Singer's company enjoyed a dominant position in the industry and played a major role in setting up a "combination" that shared patents. Howe actually was deeply indebted to Singer, who understood merchandising techniques much better than he did. Singer's goal, one he almost achieved, was a sewing machine in every home. His sewing machine and McCormick's reaper were two inventions that elicited considerable praise overseas. In 1851 the reaper gave a spectacular demonstration at a farm near London's Crystal Palace Exhibition and quickly attracted more attention than the fabulous Kohinoor diamond.

Technology in the Classroom

The mechanization of American industry made applied science a subject of great interest to the educated public. Traditional education in the United States had devoted little attention to science of any

sort, but in the early nineteenth century this neglect came to an end.

One of the leading crusaders in behalf of science education was Benjamin Silliman (1779–1864), a professor at Yale University for more than half a century. Beginning in 1808 Silliman occasionally opened his lectures to the public in New Haven. In 1818 he founded the *American Journal of Science and Arts,* which became one of the world's great scientific journals, and served as its editor for many years. Later, in the 1830s and 1840s he became a famous public speaker, addressing Boston and New York audiences on geology and chemistry. Each chemistry lecture in Boston typically drew crowds of 1,500, and most of the speeches had to be repeated for those who were turned away. Still later, Silliman toured the country to address throngs in New Orleans, St. Louis, and other major cities. At Yale University he founded the forerunner of the Scientific School which became by the 1850s the center of scientific inquiry in America.

In 1824 another school of technology was established. The Rensselaer Polytechnic Institute in Troy, New York, was dedicated to applying science to "the common purposes of life." This school pioneered the laboratory method of classroom instruction and, in 1835, became the first engineering school in the United States to grant degrees.

Industrial Workers

Government support of business was not accompanied by corresponding concern for the welfare of industrial workers. Although American workers usually were far better off than their European counterparts, nevertheless their situation was often

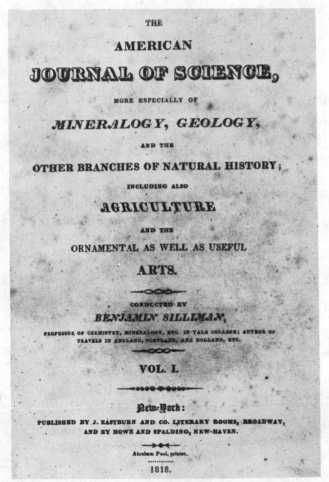

THE

AMERICAN

JOURNAL OF SCIENCE,

MORE ESPECIALLY OF

MINERALOGY, GEOLOGY,

AND THE

OTHER BRANCHES OF NATURAL HISTORY;

INCLUDING ALSO

AGRICULTURE

AND THE

ORNAMENTAL AS WELL AS USEFUL

ARTS.

CONDUCTED BY

BENJAMIN SILLIMAN,

PROFESSOR OF CHEMISTRY, MINERALOGY, ETC. IN YALE COLLEGE; AUTHOR OF
TRAVELS IN ENGLAND, SCOTLAND, AND HOLLAND, ETC.

VOL. I.

New-York:

PUBLISHED BY J. EASTBURN AND CO. LITERARY ROOMS, BROADWAY,
AND BY HOWE AND SPALDING, NEW-HAVEN.

Abraham Paul, printer.

1818.

The Beinecke Rare Book and Manuscript Library, Yale University.
Between 1818 and 1846, *The American Journal of Science and Arts,* popularly known as "Silliman's Journal," helped to promote interest in natural and physical science.

grim—and the government did little to ameliorate it.

In colonial times and in the days of the early republic, the scarcity of labor meant relatively high wages. Laborers of those decades, often apprentices, worked at the side of their boss who usually owned the shop and perhaps had in his employ sons, daughters, nephews, and other assorted relatives. These factors tended to create good working conditions. Even in 1830 the American urban working class was still fairly small, since nearly three million of the country's four million laborers (including men, women, and children) worked on farms. Indeed, prior to 1830 the urban wage-earning class was going through a transitional period from an earlier era when jobs had been performed primarily by self-employed craftsmen to an era increasingly dominated by large factories. In this process the employer became separated from the individual worker, and personal bonds, which once gave them common interests and common concerns, disappeared.

Industrial Paternalism

Many European visitors were quite favorably impressed by the working conditions of American laborers. They were particularly delighted with the industrial paternalism practiced by the Boston Associates in Waltham and Lowell, Massachusetts. Their so-called "system" involved the recruitment of hundreds of young women who lived in boardinghouses or dormitories under the careful supervision of matrons—a precaution against immorality. Most of these women were from rural families. The textile mills offered them an excellent opportunity for earning an income and supplementing the often meager livelihood of their families and at the same time enjoying a more exciting life than at home. (The biographical sketch in this chapter of one "Lowell girl," Lucy Larcom, offers insight and understanding into this aspect of industrial paternalism.)

Although mills following the Waltham or Lowell system employed women only, other New England factories hired whole families; in fact, in 1832 about half of the factory workers in New England were families. Newspapers frequently carried industrial advertisements seeking families of five or six children. Workers in the family-system mills were supposed to be of good moral character. "Those who are in the habit of profanity and Sabbath breaking and intend to continue these practices," one advertisement warned, "are invited not to make application." Each person in the family was put to work at a task deemed suitable for his or her strength and maturity, and all members lived together in company-constructed tenements.

Industrialization required a large pool of labor and a work force with specialized skills. European immigrants provided the country with both these necessities. Some 425,000 immigrants came to America between 1790 and 1830; most of them became farmers, but some stayed in seaboard cities to work as skilled laborers in textile mills, in machine shops and founderies, and in factories manufacturing shoes and boots. In the 1840s and 1850s, some four million immigrants crossed the Atlantic. Most of them were unskilled workers who were welcomed by American industrialists as a cheap source of labor. Before long, immigrants were settling in cities and towns and displacing white and free black workers in mills, factories, and other urban establishments.

Working and Living Conditions

Even in the supposedly idyllic environment of the Lowell factories, young women worked an average of seventy-five hours a week and earned only a dollar or two a week. In most American urban industries, working hours lasted from sunrise to sunset, with only a half hour off for meals, and wages varied from $1 to $6 a week.

Both living and working quarters were often cramped, stuffy, and noisy, and even skilled workers watched fearfully as larger and more complex machines appeared—mechanical monsters that they knew would soon take over their jobs. In one industry after another during the pre-Civil War period, mechanization put thousands of craftsmen out of work.

The hard life of factory workers was reflected in the crowded dwellings in drab factory towns. In Philadelphia, for instance, working families lived in tenements, one room for each family. Not only were laborers plagued by bad living conditions, they also were faced with other concerns. Most factory workers watched their children grow up ignorant, unable to read or write, for education cost money. Only in some New England communities or in towns located in states dominated by Yankee settlers (Ohio, for example) was basic primary education provided free of charge. Even where classrooms did exist, attendance often was poor. Agri-

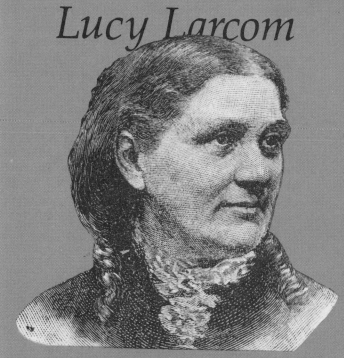

Lucy Larcom

1824–1893

The career of Lucy Larcom has elements common to the lives of many "Lowell girls." Born in Beverly, Massachusetts, the next to the youngest in a family of seven girls and two boys, she lived a normal existence until her father died in 1835. The Larcom family was not destitute and there were numerous relatives in the area, but this loss forced her mother to become a boardinghouse keeper at the Lowell mills. Looking back over half a century, Lucy Larcom, recalled in *A New England Girlhood* (1889) that most of the boarders were from New Hampshire and Vermont and had "a fresh, breezy sociability about them which made many of them seem almost like a different race of beings." At first, Lucy did housework and attended grammar school; but she soon was working at the mill to aid her family, only occasionally returning to the classroom. Within a year or so formal education ended and Lucy Larcom was a full-fledged "Lowell girl."

At the mill, working up to twelve hours a day, six days a week, she moved from bobbin girl to spinner to warper in a dressing room but, finding the latter task too difficult, transferred to the cloth room where she kept books. Confinement indoors became "wearisome," and Larcom disliked the noise of machinery. Whenever she looked at her drab coarse apron, she feared she was becoming a "drudge."

The decade during which this tall, stately young woman was making her way up the mill ladder was, nevertheless, an exciting era. She remembered visits by Dickens, Emerson, Daniel Webster, John Quincy Adams, and especially John Greenleaf Whittier with whom—as the result of a passion for poetry—she developed a lifelong friendship. Larcom recalled the strange scene created by Penobscot Indians who came upriver each summer in canoes to camp in the shadow of the mills. Those were the days, she wrote, when steamboats and railroads were changing American life and mesmerism, phrenology, and Millerism ("Oh, dear! Oh, dear! We shall be no more in 1844!") were in vogue.

About 1840 her older sister, Emiline, emerging as the leader of the family, organized a discussion group called "The Improvement Circle," which met each Saturday evening in the boardinghouse attic. This activity encouraged Lucy to compose verses, and, in time, the Circle's little newspaper developed into the famous *Lowell Offering*, a mill publication that flourished during the 1840s.

Some girls, Lucy noted, came to Lowell with a romantic vision of mill work. "Instead of Arcadia, they found a place of matter-of-fact toil, filled with a company of industrious, wide-awake girls, who were faithfully improving their opportunities, while looking through them into avenues toward profit and usefulness, more desirable yet." Those "avenues" usually led to the altar or classroom, since western and southern schoolmasters looked upon Lowell as a likely place to recruit teachers. And it was the wedding of sister Emiline which ended Lucy Larcom's Lowell days. Emiline married a local grammar schoolteacher who in April 1846, to improve his health, decided to go to Illinois. Lucy went with them, taught school for three years, and attended Monticello Seminary in Godfrey, Illinois for three years. In 1852 she returned to Massachusetts and two years later joined the faculty of Wheaton Seminary (now Wheaton College). Meanwhile, she began to publish books of verse, which in the later 1860s enabled her to become one of the editors of *Our Young Folks*. Her last years were spent in the Boston area.

There are two unusual circumstances in the life of Lucy Larcom. She gained regional acclaim as a minor poet, yet today is known for her memoirs, *A New England Childhood* which completely ignored labor unrest in Lowell. An explanation may lie in the fact that Larcom was associated with the *Lowell Offering* (attacked by some as nothing more than mill-owner propaganda) or because she either was absent from or about to leave the mills when labor agitation began. Nevertheless, Larcom painted a unique picture of Lowell and she suggested why many farm girls were so eager to go there. Not only could they earn money, be independent, get an education, and perhaps find husbands, they could live a more exciting existence than at home. "One great advantage which came to the stranger girls was to go out of themselves and enter into the lives of others."

cultural demands and a family's need for factory pay frequently took precedence over the three Rs— reading, writing, and arithmetic.

The Early Labor Movement

The modern labor movement in America began with the founding of the Mechanics' Union of Trade Associations in Philadelphia in 1827 (a "mechanic" was an artisan). This organization was an outgrowth of an abortive strike by Philadelphia carpenters for a ten-hour day; the failure led various craft unions to band together into a larger body. Though unionization continued among skilled artisans in the urban Northeast, the growing number of unskilled factory workers there remained unorganized.

In the mid-1830s, the number of unions representing skilled workers grew rapidly, largely in response to the pressures of inflation. Though wholesale prices nearly doubled during that period, wages advanced very little. Unions lost their old fraternal character and became fighting instruments intent on raising wages and reducing hours. More and more craftsmen were organized, including milliners, handloom weavers, and plasterers; and craft unions also sprang up in cities in the West and South.

Labor parties also appeared, though they were short-lived. Almost all of them attempted to secure free public education for children of workers and abolish imprisonment for debtors. The most successful of these, the Workingmen's Party, sprang up in Philadelphia in 1828. It published the first labor newspaper, the *Mechanic's Free Press*. Soon more than fifty labor newspapers were being printed from Maine to Missouri. By 1832, however, most of these early labor parties ceased to exist.

The parties enjoyed brief, chaotic lives because most Americans of the times—including laborers themselves—did not perceive the working class as a distinct entity. In a sense, early labor parties failed for the same reason that labor unions experienced difficulties: they lacked an ideology and a program that appealed to a sufficient number of workers to sustain any sort of labor movement, whether it was a political organization or a class-structured association. Native-born or immigrant, the American worker of those decades did not see himself tied to a class, and the political issues that interested him often had little relevance to how he made his living.

Nevertheless, some of the Workingmen's Party planks were built into the platforms of the major political parties. Goals such as the ten-hour day, public education, and abolition of debtors prisons were achieved in some states by 1840, as were many of the other reforms urged by workers: universal male suffrage without property qualifications; laws to protect hired workers against default on the payment of wages by employers; restrictions on child labor; state regulation of all banks; reform of the tax system; and abolition of compulsory state militia service. The militia system, the workers argued, was unfair, since rich citizens, when punished for not serving, had only to pay a fine; poor

THE MECHANIC'S FREE PRESS.

A JOURNAL OF PRACTICAL AND USEFUL KNOWLEDGE

EDITED AND PUBLISHED BY A COMMITTEE OF THE MECHANICS' LIBRARY COMPANY OF PHILADELPHIA.

| VOL. I. | PHILADELPHIA, OCTOBER 25, 1828. | NO. 42. |

The goals of the Workingmen's Party were ably expressed in the pages of labor newspapers such as *The Mechanic's Free Press.*

workers, unable to pay the fine or take off from their jobs to serve in the militia, received jail sentences.

Workingmen's parties and unions of the 1820s and 1830s signaled a false dawn in the American labor movement. The main reason they failed to survive can be traced to the Panic of 1837; this depression forced rebellious workers to accept poor working conditions and low wages, which were preferable to unemployment. But the early movement also lacked cohesion and did not include the female work force.

To some extent, the early labor movement may have been undermined by the lure of the frontier. In 1893 historian Frederick Jackson Turner (1861–1932) propounded a theory, later called the Frontier Thesis, which held that the abundance of cheap land in the West acted for generations as a "safety valve" for discontented factory workers from the East. Recently, historians have attacked Turner's thesis and pointed out that few eastern workers had the money to move West. Nevertheless, cheap land in the West did at least attract some farmers from the East who, had they not moved, might have joined the labor pool in the Northeast. The frontier, in addition, did give some recent immigrants a place to go; had these newcomers not headed west they would have settled in the East, swelling the ranks of laborers and driving down wages still further. Even as an escapist fantasy, the frontier worked a powerful spell; thousands of factory workers, farm boys, tired apprentices, and overworked immigrants *thought* they could eventually go to the West and start life anew. Although they might never actually pack up and go, that dream alone somehow made life more bearable.

Workingmen who remained in the East seldom moved up the economic or social ladder in a dramatic way. There were very few self-made wealthy men, and the gulf between the working class and the rich was widening. Although Andrew Jackson, in appealing to newly enfranchised voters from the working class, employed the rhetoric of equality, in fact his was not an egalitarian age. Wages did not keep pace with inflation in the period between 1827 and 1840, and John Quincy Adams expressed the opinion that although in the North there was "a great equality before the law . . . it ceases absolutely in the habits of life. There are upper classes and working classes."

Abject poverty may not have been the lot of most American workers, who were certainly better off than their European counterparts, but their hours were long, their salaries low, their lives tedious, their homes crowded and unhealthy, and their opportunities few. Industrialization was bringing greater wealth to the nation as a whole after 1815, but it also engendered exploitation of women, children, and immigrants and meant the loss of independence for the artisan.

The Rise of Cities

New modes of transportation, new factories, new inventions, new immigrants—even the new lands of the West to a surprising degree—all contributed directly to the growth of an urban America. Between 1820 and 1860 cities grew more rapidly than in any earlier period in our history, three times as fast as the rate of the nation as a whole, and by the eve of the Civil War 20 percent of Americans were living in communities of 2,500 or more. The shift to an industrial society—for that was what was beginning during these decades—required considerable capital, managerial skills, a good supply of labor, a specialized work force, and an extensive transportation network. Four of these factors are found only in cities, and the fifth (transportation) by its very nature obviously is related to and depends upon them.

The basic ingredient in the rise of cities was the factory, but it could take many forms such as textiles in New England, flour milling in Baltimore and Rochester, New York, iron castings in New Jersey and Pennsylvania, clocks and guns in Connecticut, and steamboats in Cincinnati. Water and rail connections fed these behemoths, collecting whatever they needed from all parts of the nation and later distributing their products to eager customers. These networks, in turn, created cities at points where tracks converged and canal, river, and oceangoing boats docked. The end of a line, "the jumping off place," often developed a momentum of its own for a time, especially in the West. There settlers departed for new farms and homesteads and returned with goods to be shipped to market.

URBAN GROWTH IN SELECTED CITIES, 1800–1840

City	1800	1810	1820	1830	1840
Baltimore, Md.	26,514	46,555	62,738	80,620	102,313
Boston, Mass.	24,937	38,746	54,027	85,568	118,857
Charleston, S.C.	18,824	24,711	24,780	30,289	29,261
Louisville, Ky.	—	—	4,012	10,341	21,210
Memphis, Tenn.	—	—	53	663	1,799
Mobile, Ala.	—	—	—	3,194	12,672
New Haven, Conn.	4,049	5,772	7,147	10,180	12,960
New Orleans, La.	—	17,242	27,176	46,082	102,193
New York, N.Y.	60,515	100,775	130,881	214,995	348,943
Norfolk, Va.	6,926	9,193	8,478	9,814	10,920
Philadelphia, Pa.	61,559	87,303	108,809	161,271	220,423
Portsmouth, N.H.	5,339	6,934	7,327	8,026	7,887
Providence, R.I.	7,614	10,071	11,767	16,833	23,171
Richmond, Va.	5,737	9,735	12,067	16,060	20,153
St. Louis, Mo.	—	—	—	4,977	16,469
Savannah, Ga.	5,146	5,215	7,523	7,303	11,214
Trenton, N.J.	—	3,002	3,942	3,925	4,035
Washington, D.C.	3,210	8,208	13,247	18,826	23,364

Library of Congress.

Chicago's history is the remarkable story of how profit-minded and public-minded boosters helped to transform a frontier outpost into a thriving city. In 1830 (top) its population was 50. By 1853 (bottom) it had grown to more than 60,000.

Although many of these communities were not large by modern standards, they were significant.

This phenomenon of urban growth was not limited to any region. During these decades, the South, often thought of as rural, lagged only behind the North and Great Britain in urbanization. St. Louis, Memphis, Louisville, New Orleans, Mobile, Savannah, Richmond, Washington, and Baltimore all registered impressive population gains, usually because of the influence of cotton or the success of rail lines funneling raw materials, manufactured goods, and people into their midst. The only traditional center that lagged behind was Charleston, stifled somewhat as the "Cotton Kingdom" moved ever westward and new rail lines leading to municipal rivals diverted business from it.

One result of this urbanization surge was a quickening faith in the American future, a sincere belief in what the promoter of each "new Athens" had to say. Sometimes their blarney rang true. In 1835 William Ogden, a resident of upstate New York, moved to Chicago, a town of 3,200 residents. Two years later he became that community's first mayor. Convinced of Chicago's future greatness and aware of benefits railroads could bring, he wisely invested in land and made a fortune. By 1850 Chicago had 30,000 inhabitants, ten years later nearly four times that number, and Ogden was worth several million dollars.

Thomas Jefferson warned in 1800 that cities were "pestilential to the morals, the health, and the liberties of man." A half-century later Horace Greeley observed that "we cannot all live in cities, yet nearly all seem determined to do so." Despite Jefferson's words, he spent considerable time in cities—Paris, New York, Richmond, Philadelphia, and Washington—although the nation's capital was little more than a strung-out village during his White House days. Editor Greeley, the man who told everyone "to go West" (he only went from New England to Manhattan himself), was nearly as far off the mark as Jefferson. America still was overwhelmingly rural at mid-century, but few could ignore the trends set into motion by industrialization. The city, regardless of what it did to morals, health, and liberty, was fast becoming an integral part of the American landscape. And so was the fortresslike factory surrounded by a sea of tenements filled with thousands of workers, many of them willing refugees from villages and towns that had lost out in the struggle for turnpikes, canals, and railroads.

The Birth of Mass Production

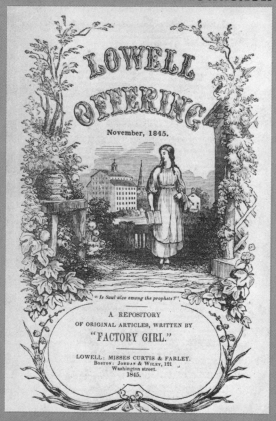

Massachusetts Historical Society.

The female workers at the Lowell mills had their own literary magazine. The editors of the *Lowell Offering* published stories of moral uplift and left such matters as hours and wages in the hands of the directors of the company.

The industrialization of America in the early nineteenth century was intimately connected with the accumulation of large supplies of capital. In the South, the leading citizens were planters who sank all ready cash into land and slaves; in the Northeast, the leading citizens were merchants who had accumulated, after years of speculation in commerce and trade, sufficient money to make the big initial outlays that industrial development required. Moreover, the business experience of successful New Englanders had conditioned them to wait years for full returns on their investments and to plot with care and imagination every step of the industrial process, from the building of plants to the merchandising of final products.

Development of world trade was, in the long run, another key to this success story. Cotton for textiles and hides for boots and shoes could be brought to New England from Georgia, Egypt, and South America. And the same ships that gathered raw materials could distribute finished products to customers in all parts of the world.

In a unique fashion, New England's disadvantages proved blessings in disguise. Lacking rich soil and abundant minerals, she was not tied to any tradition-bound enterprise and could experiment freely with new ways of doing things. Even the turmoil fostered by Jefferson's Embargo and the War of 1812 tended to aid the movement toward large scale production. Labor and capital which, temporarily at least, could not go to sea or move west quickly sought and found new outlets.

The most efficient and successful of the pioneer industries in the Northeast was founded by a rich Boston merchant, Francis C. Lowell. Lowell, a well-to-do young man, was suspended from Harvard in 1789 for lighting a bonfire in the historic College Yard; however, he continued his studies under private tutors and graduated with his class in 1793. Lowell then worked in his family's import-export business until ill health caused him to travel to England in 1810. There he was deeply impressed by textile machinery he saw in Lancashire. When Lowell returned to the United States in 1812, he formed a corporation for the manufacturing of cotton textiles. Among the other members of the New Boston Manufacturing Company were Lowell's brother-in-law, Patrick Tracy Jackson, and Nathan Appleton, whose family's trading firm was dissolved on the

The Waltham Mill operated by the Boston Manufacturing Company was the first factory in the world to manufacture cotton cloth by power machinery enclosed in one building.

eve of the war with England, since the conflict signaled an end to international trade. Appleton invested $5,000 in 1813; by 1840 the company owned mills worth $12 million.

These men, the Boston Associates, quite literally were the fathers of American big business. In their petition to the Massachusetts legislature for an act of incorporation, the investors sounded much like modern businessmen: "Your petitioners believe that a great capital, always at the command of the manufacturer, is essential to his success." This capital, accumulated quite rapidly, amounting to the astounding sum of $300,000. In an astute move, the members of the corporation decided to invest only two-thirds of the money in mills and machinery and to reserve the remaining $100,000 for operating expenses.

Their innovation did not stop there. The Boston Manufacturing Company reorganized virtually all aspects of the factory system. They placed every

step of the manufacturing process, from bleaching thread to printing calicos, under one roof. Based on rough sketches of equipment Lowell saw in England, a mechanical genius named Paul Moody was able to construct an efficient power loom (all other mills in New England still used handlooms). In 1813 they built their mill on the Charles River at Waltham. It was the first completely self-sufficient cotton-manufacturing plant in the world.

Although the success of the Waltham enterprise can be attributed in part to its handsome capitalization and efficient plant organization, in addition, the owners tapped a new source of labor. Rather than hiring poor families and employing children, as so many other mills did, young women formed the bulk of their labor force. These workers, usually the daughters of impoverished farmers, worked at Waltham for a year or two and then, after accumulating some small savings, returned to their homes. Though temporary, these laborers were hardworking and efficient—and their wages were low.

At the time, those who organized this "boardinghouse" system were convinced that America would never have a permanent factory class, and Waltham and similar communities became show places that drew hundreds of visitors each year. The well-groomed young ladies lived in spacious homes where they had ready access to religious life, learning, and lectures. Of course, New England soon had grubby factory towns where workers lived in squalor, but here was an ideal to which both labor and management could aspire.

The Boston Manufacturing Company also devised a new way to merchandise its goods. Instead of placing their fabrics on consignment with a large number of merchants scattered here and there, the company set up a separate sales organization and worked through agents who received a commission of only 1 percent but received in exchange the exclusive right to merchandise Waltham goods in a certain area.

Perhaps the most astonishing thing about this undertaking, which goes far toward explaining many differences between American everyday life in the nineteenth and twentieth centuries, is that no one had done it before. Waltham produced nothing strange or exotic, only cotton cloth. This

Alert and neat-looking young women at work in New England mills impressed foreign visitors and American dignitaries alike with the new world of the factory.

was little more than the successful marriage of the experience of others, efficient machinery, good labor practices, and shrewd distribution techniques. And to the amazement of Old World visitors (and perhaps to Americans as well) the world's most advanced form of industrial organization had appeared unheralded in a "backwater" area of civilization along the rocky streams of New England.

The postwar depression of 1819 destroyed many competitors, but the Boston Manufacturing Company prevailed—and in doing so set the pattern for later American enterprises. By 1820 the Associates were ready to expand. They bought land bordering the Merrimack River at East Chelmsford and dubbed the new community Lowell, in honor of the founder of the company, who had died in 1817. As business revived throughout the United States in 1821, the new factory at Lowell thrived.

In this enterprise and others that soon emulated its success, executive management, sales, and production functioned independently. Each segment—decision making, sales promotion, and work on the looms themselves—was organized so as to reap maximum benefits from mass production. In this manner the Boston Manufacturing Company was able to turn a country hamlet into the industrial city of Lowell. Also, in this new community Moody developed a machine works that was soon turning out new and improved cotton machinery to be used in Lowell, Waltham, and other cities that would try to duplicate their success.

By 1830 the expanding corporation solved yet another problem—transportation. The Middlesex Canal and turnpikes serving Lowell were inadequate, and Patrick Tracy Jackson, one of the original members of the corporation, suggested a railroad be built between Boston and Lowell. The company soon laid out a line of track—a big but ultimately rewarding investment.

In the 1840s an influx of cheap immigrant labor changed the paternalistic relationship between employer and employee; nevertheless, the early years at Waltham and Lowell served as a prototype for the modern corporation.

Two aspects of this pioneer enterprise are especially revealing: versatile management and specialized machines. The three men who started it—Lowell, Jackson, and Appleton—had virtually no experience with textiles or with manufacturing, but they knew how to organize a business venture and were not afraid to experiment with new techniques. Second, the machines developed for their factories and others that appeared throughout America became more and more and more specialized, not the workers.

Both management and labor were, in effect, interchangeable parts and could adapt quite easily to scores of enterprises, no matter how diverse their needs might be. This attitude has, of course, influenced American industrial life to the present day. One experienced in sales, advertising, or management can move quite easily from a job in the automotive industry to an allied or quite different field of endeavor. Much like the assembly line, this versatility of management and labor—a willingness and an ability to work almost anywhere and at anything—became an integral part of the emerging process known as mass production.

SELECTED
READINGS

General Accounts

Richard D. Brown, *Modernization: The Transformation of American Life, 1600–1865* (1976)

Stuart Bruchey, *The Roots of American Economic Growth, 1607–1861: An Essay in Social Causation* (1965)

Douglas T. Miller, *The Birth of Modern America, 1820–1850* (1970)

Douglass C. North, *The Economic Growth of the United States, 1790–1860* (1961)

Robert E. Riegel, *Young America, 1830–1840* (1949)

The Transportation Revolution

Leland D. Baldwin, *Keelboat Age on Western Waters* (1941)

Louis C. Hunter, *Steamboats on the Western Rivers: An Economic and Technological History* (1949)

Ronald E. Shaw, *Erie Water West: A History of the Erie Canal, 1792–1854* (1966)

John F. Stover, *The Life and Decline of the American Railroad* (1970)

George Rogers Taylor, *The Transportation Revolution 1815–1860* (1961)

Government and the Economy

Carter Goodrich, ed., *The Government and the Economy, 1783–1861* (1967)

Oscar and Mary Handlin, *Commonwealth: A Study of the Role of Government in the American Economy: Massachusetts, 1774–1861* (rev. ed., 1969)

Louis Hartz, *Economic Policy and Democratic Thought: Pennslyvania, 1776–1860* (1948)

James Willard Hurst, *Law and the Conditions of Freedom in the Nineteenth–Century United States* (1956)

R. Kent Newmyer, *The Supreme Court under Marshall and Taney* (1968)

Malcolm J. Rohrbough, *The Land Office Business: The Settlement and Administration of American Public Lands, 1789–1837* (1968)

Industry, Technology, and Workers

Thomas C. Cochran and William Miller, *Age of Enterprise: A Social History of Industrial America* (2nd ed., 1961)

Alan Dawley, *Class and Community: The Industrial Revolution in Lynn* (1976)

Thomas Dublin, *Women at Work: The Transformation of Work and Community in Lowell, Massachusetts, 1828–1860* (1979)

Paul W. Gates, *The Farmer's Age: Agriculture, 1815–1860* (1960)

Constance McLaughlin Green, *Eli Whitney and the Birth of American Technology* (1956)

Herbert G. Gutman, *Work, Culture and Society in Industrializing America: Essays in America's Working Class and Social History* (1977)

Hannah Josephson, *The Golden Threads: New England's Mill Girls and Magnates* (1949)

Edward Pessen, *Most Uncommon Jacksonians: The Radical Leaders of the Early Labor Movement* (1967)

Nathan Rosenberg, *Technology and American Economic Growth* (1972)

William A. Sullivan, *The Industrial Worker in Pennsylvannia, 1800–1840* (1955)

The Rise of Cities

Robert G. Albion, *The Rise of New York Port, 1815–1860* (1939)

Stuart M. Blumin, *The Urban Threshold: Growth and Change in a Nineteenth-Century American Community* (1976)

Constance McLaughlin Green, *American Cities in the Growth of the Nation* (1957)

Allan R. Pred, *Urban Growth and the Circulation of Information: The United States System of Cities, 1790–1840* (1973)

Richard C. Wade, *The Urban Frontier: The Rise of Western Cities, 1790–1830* (1959)

Samuel B. Warner, Jr., *The Urban Wilderness: A History of the American City* (1972)

CHAPTER 9

RACE, SEX, AND NATIONALITY

TIMELINE

1777
Vermont emancipates slaves

1793
Congress adopts first fugitive slave law

1800
Gabriel Prosser slave revolt

1811
Battle of Tippecanoe

1816
Congressional committee reveals that two-thirds of factory workers are female

1822
Denmark Vesey slave revolt

1830
Removal Act authorizes transfer of eastern Indians to locations west of the Mississippi River

1831
Nat Turner slave rebellion

1832
Worcester v. *State of Georgia*

1834
New York Female Moral Reform Society combats the "double standard"

1836
Maria Monk publishes alleged account of life in a Catholic convent

1838
Cherokee Indians travel the "Trail of Tears"

1838
Sarah Grimké publishes *Letters on the Equality of the Sexes and the Condition of Women*

1840
World Antislavery Convention in London rejects female delegates

1844
Protestants riot against Irish Catholics in Philadelphia

1845
Potato famine accelerates emigration of Irish

1848
Seneca Falls Convention

1849
Elizabeth Blackwell becomes first female to graduate from medical school

1851
Treaty of Fort Laramie

1853
Elizabeth Blackwell opens clinic for the poor

CHAPTER OUTLINE

One of the most important ideals of the American Revolution was the promise of equality, liberty, and happiness for all, yet in the first half of the nineteenth century the nation clearly denied legal and economic equality to blacks, Indians, women, and many recent immigrants. The factories of the Northeast, in their search for cheap labor, exploited women, children, and immigrants. As the textile industry called for more and more cotton, southern farmers turned increasingly toward cotton cultivation—and the use of slave labor. As the white population grew, valuable lands held by Indians in the South and in the Old Northwest became increasingly attractive to settlers. Finally, the government removed most of the Indians living east of the Mississippi to land in the West so white settlers could get what they wanted.

Black Americans

The first Americans to face up to the problems of race relations were the Quakers of Pennsylvania, who, in time, became the spearhead of an abolition movement. Blacks were also active in efforts to gain freedom for their race. Such blacks as Phillis Wheatley, the poet, Benjamin Banneker and Thomas Fuller, both mathematical geniuses, Richard Allen and Absalom Jones, both very able ministers and writers, Prince Hall, the founder of the Black Masonic Order, and James Derham, the pioneer physician, achieved fame, engendered admiration, and also aroused support for the cause of abolition by their impressive accomplishments.

Although slavery knew no sectional boundaries on the eve of the American Revolution, it was dying a slow death north of the Potomac River. The new state constitution of Vermont abolished slavery in 1777. Perhaps the high-water mark of the antislavery movement that began during the Revolutionary period was reached in 1787 when Congress banned slavery in the Old Northwest. By 1805 every northern state had abolished slavery or had made provisions for eventual emancipation.

Yet no national emancipation movement developed and hopes generated by the Revolutionary War began to fade. Why? The principal reason, the stumbling block frustrating all such efforts for the next few decades, was that no one could answer some hard questions: How would former masters be compensated for the loss of their slave property? Where would the ex-slaves live? How would they be cared for during the initial months and years of freedom? What would happen to the nation's social and economic life if one-eighth of its inhabitants—most of them uneducated and familiar with little except agricultural labor done under the direction of others—suddenly were free to do as they wanted?

From 1783 to 1800 the new, independent republic was struggling to stay afloat. The last thing needed was debate over an issue that obviously would exacerbate regional differences and perhaps lead to disunion. During those same years, several events occurred to strengthen slavery and to slow the momentum toward racial equality. These included the invention of the cotton gin, revulsion against the excesses of the French Revolution, and a constant demand for cheap labor in the South.

As the black population in the South increased, a growing fear of slave rebellions and the concurrent anxiety that freed blacks would seek revenge against former masters snuffed out an incipient abolition movement in that region. In the 1790s Southerners heard with alarm of a black uprising in Haiti against French rulers. In 1800 a young slave, Gabriel Prosser, convinced some 1,100 slaves to take an oath to fight for their freedom. The blacks planned to seize the arsenal in Richmond, Virginia, and to launch a general slaughter of their white oppressors. The plot was discovered at the last moment and put down, but it inspired hysteria in southern whites everywhere. As a result of the attempted revolt, some three dozen blacks were executed, though no whites had been killed. Caught between paranoia and economic pressure, southern whites responded to the abolition movement by generating a copious literature defending slavery. Between 1800 and 1810, southern legislatures tightened legal controls over slaves. In 1806, for instance, Virginia adopted a law making it more difficult for a white master to free slaves. The humanitarian flood that had swept the country, even parts of the South, in the wake of the Revolution subsided.

In the period before the Civil War, as southern farmers moved into the Gulf states and started cotton plantations, the slave population followed this trend in settlement. Older Atlantic seaboard states in the Upper South, such as Virginia and Maryland, which had considered abolition just after the Rev-

Although the slave trade was outlawed in 1808, slave ships continued to smuggle cargoes of Africans in southern ports during the antebellum period.

olution, now supplied slaves to the cotton-growing areas in the Lower South.

Between 1709 and 1810, the number of slaves nearly doubled, increasing from 697,897 to 1,191,354, and during each succeeding decade another 550,000 or so would appear. By 1860 there were nearly four million slaves in the United States. The free black population kept pace, rising from 59,466 in 1790 to 488,070 in 1860. Although the number of whites grew even faster in those years (3,172,464 to 26,957,471), it is apparent that the institution of slavery was becoming ever more deeply enmeshed in American life.

State Laws

Congressional measures such as the fugitive slave law of 1793, the Compromise of 1820, which led to the admission of Missouri as a slave state and Maine as a free state, and the Compromise of 1850, which enacted stringent fugitive slave regulations and admitted New Mexico and Utah as territories

Percentage of Slaves in Total Population, 1800

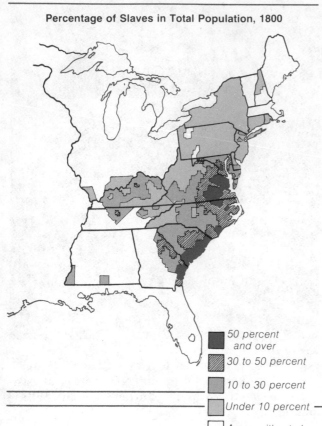

- **50 percent and over**
- **30 to 50 percent**
- **10 to 30 percent**
- **Under 10 percent**
- **Areas without slaves, or unsettled**

without restrictions on slavery—all governed and gave legal sanction to slavery.

But it was the state laws in the South that spelled out the details of black servitude. Southern slave codes were designed to perpetuate a rigid system of social control. They relegated slaves to the status of chattels (that is, movable property). Slaves could not legally own anything themselves. They were compelled by law to submit completely to their masters. Although the codes prohibited brutal treatment, a master or an overseer usually was not held responsible for the death of a slave who was receiving or resisting "just" punishment. All slaves had to show respect to all whites, even to total strangers. Patrols of white men frequently rode through the countryside checking passes to make sure that each slave was on his master's plantation or had permission to be elsewhere. Such patrols also sought to prevent slave uprisings and to capture runaways. Before the Civil War much of the South was like a prison in which all whites, re-

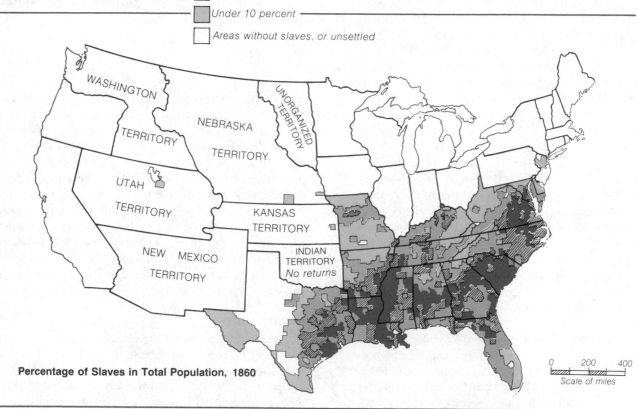

Percentage of Slaves in Total Population, 1860

Scale of miles
0   200   400

gardless of their wealth, status, or social class, were jailers supervising black inmates.

Slave codes restricted the legal movement of blacks unless they could produce a pass authorizing their travel. A slave who traveled alone by train sometimes had to get two passes: one to be deposited at the point of departure; the other retained to show if accosted. Contact with slaves from adjoining farms and plantations—and particularly with free blacks—was limited unless it took place under white supervision. Slaves were prohibited from owning books or printed matter of any sort, and no one was supposed to teach a slave to read, though this law was often ignored. Slaves could not testify against a white person in court. There was no legal recognition of slave marriages or divorces; marriage was regulated by whatever rules a master chose to devise. Some masters assigned mates to their slaves, though most permitted them to choose their own husbands or wives. Slave couples and families usually were broken up when one member was sold; a slave preacher in Kentucky joined couples in wedlock "until death or *distance* do you part." As a result, the family did not provide slaves with the security afforded whites. Nevertheless, there is evidence of many long-lasting slave marriages, and the names of children reflect family connections.

Of course, the system of social control embodied in the slave codes was not always observed. The individual master could treat his property more kindly or more harshly, depending on whim or temperament. Even southern judges and courts occasionally made decisions that contradicted the codes. One of the prime factors mitigating against extreme cruelty was simple economic self-interest; unless consumed by sadism, a master had no motive for destroying the spirit and health of his property. In fact, some slave masters frequently employed hired labor, usually Irish or German immigrants, to perform the most dangerous tasks. Such an expedient avoided the risk of losing the year-in, year-out labor of a costly slave.

Slave Life

By 1850 there were 3,204,313 slaves in the United States (including southwestern territories that had not yet achieved statehood). Only 12 percent of the slave population lived in cities or towns. The remainder (some 2,800,000) worked in agriculture; of these, 1,815,000 lived on cotton plantations, and the rest cultivated tobacco, sugarcane, rice, and hemp.

About one out of every eight people in America was a slave.

Between 1790 and 1860 both cotton production and the number of slaves rose dramatically. In 1790, for instance, 3,000 bales were produced in the South, and there were fewer than 700,000 slaves. By 1830 cotton production had risen to about 732,000 bales and slaves numbered about 2,009,043. By 1860 the South was turning out about 3,841,000 bales and there were nearly 4,000,000 slaves. These statistics are surprising since slave importation was outlawed after 1808. Although some blacks were brought over illegally from Africa after 1808 (the number is estimated at between 54,000 and 270,000), the majority of nineteenth century slaves were American born. This ability to reproduce itself set the South's slave society apart from others in the New World. American masters often encouraged slaves to reproduce by giving rewards for the birth of a child and not punishing promiscuity. The slave community developed its own sexual standards that allowed intercourse before marriage but encouraged fidelity in marriage. Both practices helped to increase the black birth rate.

Slaves who were agricultural workers typically labored under the gang system on cotton, sugar, and tobacco plantations, that is, they worked in groups on a general project. Most field hands rose before dawn, cooked their meals, sometimes looked after the livestock, and then hurried to the fields before sunrise. There they labored till dusk, planting, hoeing weeds, picking worms off plants, and finally harvesting. At night some slaves attended livestock again, cooked meals, and performed other chores before retiring.

Discipline was maintained through physical punishment. But most planters preferred to keep control by merely threatening corporal punishment or by withholding privileges and imposing such penalties as solitary confinement, additional work, public humiliation, and demotion from easier, more prestigious jobs to lower, more menial ones. Good behavior was rewarded with free time, better tasks, and other benefits. A system of rewards and nonphysical punishments, however, was more likely to exist on a plantation with fewer than ten slaves, where the master was personally in charge; once a plantation had more than 30 slaves, overseers were hired, and they all too often treated slaves brutally.

Aside from agriculture, slaves engaged in a

Black house servants dressed in plain clothes serve their master's household. Note the elegant dining area, furniture, and clothing of the white family.

host of tasks. Some were skilled artisans, mechanics, lumberjacks, mining and construction workers, and laborers in factories producing cotton textiles, turpentine, and iron or in factories processing tobacco. Still other slaves served as dockworkers, loading and unloading ships, or as deckhands. But the most important category of rural nonagricultural slaves was that of house servants. The butler, the cook, the maid, and the nurse were all slaves of rank and privilege in the eyes of the white family. Through prolonged contact with whites, the domestic servants often learned to read and keep accounts; more subtly, the household staff absorbed white values to some extent and often became loyal to the family they served.

House servants ate the leftover food of their masters and wore the hand-me-downs of the white family, but the life of a field hand was at a subsistence level. Living quarters were small, cramped, and crude, clothing was of poor quality, and the diet sometimes was so bad and deficient in protein that it failed to provide the workers with enough stamina for the manual labor demanded of them. As a result, slaves built up little resistance to disease and were more than normally susceptible to infection. The diet consisted mainly of salt pork, corn meal, and molasses—filling but not very nourishing food. Medical care usually was administered by the planter's wife.

Hunting and fishing were favorite pastimes, as was producing such handicrafts as woven baskets,

dolls, clothes, and other useful items, which slaves sometimes sold or bartered for profit. On some plantations slaves were allowed to have their own gardens. Saturday nights could be joyous occasions when slaves danced to a fiddle or a banjo or an improvised rhythm band. On holidays and Sundays slaves amused themselves by dressing up in their best clothes and visiting with slave friends. Listening to folktales was another exciting entertainment, and storytellers invented for their audiences episodes in the lives of the deceitful Br'er (Brother) Rabbit, the bumbling Br'er Bear, and the shrewd Br'er Fox, who, despite his craftiness, always was outwitted by Br'er Rabbit.

Fiddling, dancing, and raucous merriment did little to mask the boredom, agony, and frustration of a barbarous system. These activities merely provided temporary release from a degrading, confining world. Even Br'er Rabbit was telling a moral tale. He was the personification of the smart slave shrewd enough to outwit his master, Br'er Fox.

Though free blacks in the North had their own churches, slaves in the South were forced to attend services with whites or were preached to by white ministers at special services. Nevertheless, many of them held secret religious meetings. Whether these services were legal or illegal, religion was generally a matter of intense emotionality and fervor for the slaves, who found personal meanings directly applicable to their lives in Old Testament accounts of Israel's release from bondage and in the New Testament doctrine of release from suffering through belief in Jesus Christ. The haunting spirituals of the slaves ("Nobody knows the trouble I've seen") expressed the pain they felt and their longing for redemption. On some occasions religion was used by slave leaders to foment rebellion, but Christianity had another impact on slavery. Although it may have strengthened the bonds of some slave communities and thereby provided a source of unrest and rebellion, the church, with its promise of reward in the afterlife, also may have reconciled some slaves to their existing status.

Urban Slavery

The slave system was static, closed, and self-perpetuating on the plantation where the two main classes were black slaves and white owners. But in the city the institution of slavery soon began to decay.

Urban slaves sometimes traveled by day performing various errands without close supervision. Owners often hired out their slaves as laborers or skilled workers in construction gangs, factories, shops, and on riverboats. Some owners even permitted slaves to make their own hiring arrangements in return for part of the wages received. In addition, some slaves arranged and paid for their own living quarters. Clearly urban slavery offered freedom of movement not permitted under plantation slavery. (Some dimensions of this latitude are apparent in the accompanying biographical sketch of Simon Gray, a slave riverboat captain.)

Because of this latitude, slaves in cities had many opportunities to mingle with free blacks and with whites, and the line between slavery and freedom became blurred. The urban master's dilemma was how to control his slave when the day was done or as he moved about the city doing various tasks. While busy on the job, he was no problem, but in the evenings city slaves would gather in homes, churches, grogshops, and around dock areas, regardless of ordinances to the contrary.

Another problem for the "peculiar institution" (as slavery was called) was fraternizing between whites and blacks, and between slaves and freemen. More than a third of the free blacks in the South lived in the larger cities; there were more than 10,000 in New Orleans and 25,000 in Baltimore in 1860. At that time the South had some 385,000 slaveholders who were owners of nearly 4,000,000 blacks. In their midst lived nearly 262,000 free blacks.

In an attempt to stamp out the social familiarity between whites and blacks, segregation was introduced in southern cities and efforts made to reduce the black population, both slave and free. On the plantation discipline was the private domain of the owner or an overseer. But in the cities, where blacks were less clearly in subordination to whites, segregation separated whites from blacks by the 1830s in public means of transport, public facilities, churches, jails, parks, hospitals, cemeteries, and elsewhere. Blacks, both free and enslaved, sometimes were moved from the centers of cities and

Playing musical instruments and dancing provided entertainment for black slaves.

Simon Gray

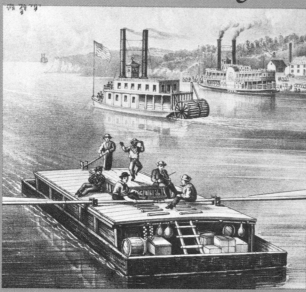

dates unknown

Although Simon Gray was not famous, he is of interest because his life as a slave suggests that regulations governing the lives of slaves involved in trade and commerce may have been much more lenient than those restricting plantation slaves. Simon Gray belonged to Andrew Donnan of Natchez, Mississippi, who rented him out to Andrew Brown at the rate of 75 cents a day.

Gray's job was to convey lumber on flatboats down the Mississippi to New Orleans. He began his career in 1835 working in Brown's sawmill, but by 1838 he was directing a rafting crew, and by 1845 he had been promoted to the rank of flatboat captain. As a captain, Gray had authority over crews of ten to twenty men, some of whom were slaves, others hired whites. Gray himself employed the whites, paid their salaries and expenses, and kept their work records. For this work Brown paid Gray a salary of $8 a month plus a $5 bonus for each trip to New Orleans.

His responsibilities were numerous. On some occasions he would deliver lumber from the Natchez mill to a New Orleans lumberyard. At other times he would go on trips lasting two or three weeks and sell lumber to plantation owners. Gray solicited orders, quoted prices, and collected money. His business records reveal that he was literate and trained in simple mathematics.

In 1850 his employer bought Gray's wife and children for $500 and allowed him to live with them in a rented house in Natchez; Brown did not make use of the family and simply purchased them in order to please Gray. In 1853 Gray himself appears to have been freed by his old master, Andrew Donnan, informally if not legally. After this date, Simon Gray's monthly wages rose from $8 to $20, and he began to do jobs on the side for profit. On the eve of the Civil War, he was wealthy enough to be able to spend $1,000 at Hot Springs, Arkansas, where he took treatment for his rheumatism. Sometime in 1863, after the fall of Vicksburg, his name no longer was listed in business transactions of his employer. It is not known if he died or moved elsewhere.

Simon Gray's life was so different from that of the plantation slave that he must be described as "quasi-free." He earned a salary, he knew how to read, made business trips, was a manager who employed whites, and was allowed to live apart from other slaves. Perhaps other nonagricultural slaves—those employed in construction, in factory work, in the mines, and on riverboats—enjoyed something of the same sort of relative freedom.

forced to find housing on the peripheries. On the job, free and enslaved southern blacks were pushed out of one line of employment after another in the last few decades before the Civil War; increasingly new immigrants, especially Irish and Germans, took over jobs formerly held by blacks. The exclusion of blacks from crafts, trades, and other positions requiring skill usually was enforced by city ordinances; even the less-skilled positions, such as those of household servants, sometimes were handed over to white immigrants.

Yet one should keep in mind that pre-Civil War segregation, like that which would rise in the 1890s, was a mosaic of custom, ordinances, state laws, public pressure, and convenience. It was awash with absurd contradictions, and its rules and regulations interpreted in a capricious manner. The avowed goal was to keep the white and black races separate and to prevent what most people knew was happening. In fact, police blotters, bits of gossip in newspaper columns—even a short stroll down the streets of almost any city or town—revealed the failure of segregation, for miscegenation was a fact of southern life. Of course, racial mixing was occurring in the countryside as well, but there it was frequently greeted with a veil of silence or a sly wink.

Slave Trading

Planters moving into the lower Mississippi Valley and Gulf states took their slaves with them. If they prospered, they quickly needed more manpower, and this need was fulfilled by the domestic slave traders. These businessmen drove slaves in chains overland or shipped them by river or ocean steamers or by train to the markets at New Orleans, Mobile, Natchez, or Galveston, where purchasers bid on them in exactly the same manner as they bid for livestock at auctions. During these auctions slave families often were split apart. Virginia farmers who generally were turning from tobacco to wheat and planters in the Carolinas now had an excess of blacks, many of whom were sold "down river." Some masters, however, refused to sell their slaves to men who planned to take them to Alabama, Mississippi, and the new lands of Arkansas and Texas.

The domestic slave trade was a vile business, but its horrors were exceeded by the foreign slave trade. Slaves were shackled together in dark, stuffy hulls of slaveships for days, allowed little exercise and fed sparse, often rotten food. Before 1807 more than 20 percent of those who left Africa for America died en route. And, when that trade became illegal in 1808, the risk to these unwilling immigrants increased dramatically, for a captain pursued by federal authorities might jettison his cargo to get rid of the evidence. Nevertheless, some Africans continued to be smuggled into a few southern ports throughout the antebellum period. The domestic trade, however, was far more active.

Historians View Slavery

During recent decades historians have hotly debated the effect of slavery on antebellum blacks. Ulrich B. Phillips began modern research with the publication of his major works, *American Negro Slavery* (1918) and *Life and Labor in the Old South* (1929). Born in Georgia, Phillips took the position that the plantation actually had benefited blacks and provided a naturally backward and childlike race an opportunity for acquiring civilization.

Herbert Aptheker, a Marxist historian, took a very different stand in *American Negro Slave Revolts*, published in 1943. Far from being the lazy and contented child that Phillips portrayed, the slave actually was rebellious and discontented—or so Aptheker asserted. In the 1969 edition of the book, Aptheker argued that "American Negro slavery was a monstrously cruel system of exploitation and that its victims despised it and sought in every possible way to oppose it."

In 1956 Kenneth Stampp published *The Peculiar Institution: Slavery in the Ante-Bellum South* in which he stated that slavery was a thoroughly cruel and brutal system of social control. In contrast to Phillips, who assumed black inferiority, Stampp argued that "Negroes *are,* after all, only white men with black skins, nothing more, nothing less." Blacks responded to slavery just as white people would have done if they were placed in the same situation—they resisted it.

Writing in 1959, Stanley Elkins (*Slavery: A Problem in American Institutional and Intellectual Life*) contended that the dominant black personality type under slavery had been docile and passive—the "Sambo" stereotype so pervasive in white southern literature and folklore. But Elkins, unlike Phillips, did not attribute these qualities to innate traits of black slaves. Rather, Elkins argued, blacks became docile because of their environment, just as imprisonment in German concentration camps supposedly reduced inmates to a childlike, confused docility. Elkins emphasized that slaves had few contacts, except in cities, with free society; the mas-

Following an auction, these slaves are being sent "down river" from Richmond. While the whites complete their business arrangements, the blacks say goodbye to relatives they may never see again.

ter established himself as the all-knowing figure who determined every slave's activities—and his self-image as well. Elkins concluded that slaves came to accept their alleged inferiority to whites as a result of deliberate efforts on the part of slaveholders to encourage infantilism in blacks.

John Blassingame has contended in *The Slave Community: Plantation Life in the Antebellum South* (1972) that Stanley Elkins' concept of the slave personality type ignores entirely the accounts that slaves have left of their own lives. While conceding that it is impossible to know objectively how discontented slaves really were, nevertheless, Blassin-

game points out that judicial records of the period show that slaves frequently fought back, assaulting, robbing, and even murdering their own masters.

In 1974 Robert W. Fogel and Stanley L. Engerman published their highly controversial quantitative study, *Time on the Cross: The Economics of American Negro Slavery*. Using economic statistics (and a methodology that has been denounced from several quarters), the authors maintain that neither southern planters nor black slaves fit the concentration camp model depicted by Elkins. Indeed, Fogel and Engerman state that plantation slaves were not typically lazy or inefficient, nor were planters intent on maintaining perfect submission. The plantation was a business, and masters were interested primarily in making it pay. Since slaves provided a very productive working force, they generally achieved their goals. Fogel and Engerman believe that the Sambo myth may not only have been perpetuated by the racism of slaveowners but also by the unconscious prejudice of abolitionists.

To Eugene Genovese, however, the slave society that developed in the United States was "first and foremost . . . a record of one of history's greatest crimes." His *Roll, Jordan, Roll: The World the Slaves Made* (1974) argues that although slave masters had hegemony over slaves, paternalistic control over individual slaves made them more and more dependent upon their oppressors. Paternalism, therefore, reinforced the exploitation of blacks and narrowly defined the "living space" in which blacks could survive spiritually as well as physically. Genovese claims that plantation slavery with its paternalism "made white and black southerners one people" who shared one life.

In 1979 Paul D. Escott offered a partial refutation of Genovese's assessment of antebellum slavery. In his *Slavery Remembered: A Record of Twentieth-Century Slave Narratives*, Escott argues that there was an autonomous and viable antebellum slave community and culture even though the South's "peculiar institution" was a harsh and heavily exploitative social system. Contrary to Genovese, Escott maintains that master and slaves lived in different worlds and that "paternalism related more to talk about the plantation than to what actually went on there."

Another issue that has received the attention of scholars is the question of whether slavery was truly profitable. There is considerable evidence that it was. The steady movement of slavery into the cotton and sugar cane land of the Southwest contributed to the rising cost of prime black field hands. In 1840 such a slave cost about $700 in Georgia; in 1850 the cost had risen to about $1,000 and by 1860 it was nearly $2,000. Funds invested in slave labor brought high return to most owners. Indeed, the purchase of a black woman often yielded a high return on the original investment because her offspring could either be sold or used as additional labor.

Slaves and Slavery

Some slaves may have acted in a Sambo fashion in order to pacify their masters; house servants may have identified with their white masters; and still others may have become deeply frustrated with their status. (Many documents of the antebellum period mention stammering and stuttering in blacks—sometimes regarded by clinical psychologists as signs of frustration.)

Driven by desperation, some slaves mutilated their own bodies or sabotaged their master's property. Resistance could take much more subtle forms. Slaves knew their labor benefited only the master, so they were often clumsy, inefficient, passive, and smiling. Such tactics possessed several innate advantages: the satisfaction of "hitting back" without fear of retribution; a record of minimal work output that they could not be expected to exceed; and the possibility a dissatisfied, cruel owner would sell them.

And some slaves periodically banded together in rebellion. The most famous of these uprisings were those planned by Gabriel Prosser in 1800, Denmark Vesey in 1822, and Nat Turner in 1831. Turner, after allegedly hearing a voice from heaven commanding him to lead an uprising, joined with four other slaves in killing the white family he was serving. He and his comrades then moved from house to house in Southampton County, Virginia, killing whites and liberating other slaves. Turner's group swelled to seventy blacks; they killed sixty whites before they were captured. Over forty blacks, including Turner, died as a result of the revolt.

Such bloody rebellions were rare in the antebellum South, but many whites feared the prospect of slave revolts. The lack of organized resistance, however, may have encouraged some whites to regard blacks as Sambos. Not only did this way of looking at blacks provide a convenient defense of slavery against northern abolitionists ("Our slaves are happy"), it also helped allay persistent white fears of a black revolution.

Whether or not slavery converted blacks into Sambos, it did undermine their basic human dignity. Winthrop Jordan suggests in his definitive study, *White Over Black: American Attitudes Toward the Negro, 1550–1812* (1968), that white males invented the myth that black men wanted to rape white women as a coverup for their own erotic attraction to black women. Slavery also led most Southerners to regard manual labor, especially if performed by a hired hand, as a demeaning task unworthy of a white man; this attitude discouraged poor whites and any white immigrants who went South from working as field hands.

Free Blacks

By 1860 there were nearly half a million free blacks in the United States. Many had bought their freedom; others had been granted it, frequently at the death of their masters; still others had been born into free black families. Forty-six percent of the free blacks lived in the North, while the remainder lived south of the Mason-Dixon line. In general, free blacks preferred to live in cities or towns where their unique status was well-known and recognized.

In the eighteenth century and the first two decades of the nineteenth, free blacks in the South could own property, retain their earnings, marry legally, and participate in their own churches and various mutual aid societies. But a growing fear of conspiracies among free blacks and slaves led southern whites to impose more and more restrictions on free blacks until they became only "quasi-free."

The free black's second-class status was ensured by any number of discriminatory measures. Free blacks could not enter most southern states—or leave and return for a period of more than ninety days. Whatever schools existed were segregated, not only in the South but in the North, as were most churches, transportation facilities, and public accommodations.

Although free blacks were subject to taxation, more and more of them were being barred from polling places in all parts of the nation by the time of the Civil War. The movement to disenfranchise the free blacks gained ground throughout the early nineteenth century. Yet if a political party needed their help, free blacks might continue to cast ballots, regardless of what state legislatures decreed. This was true in Maryland and Ohio, and until 1860 free blacks of Rapides Parish, Louisiana, were mustered to the polls by various local factions.

The condition of free blacks was far from being ideal in the North. Not only were free northern blacks subject to a host of restrictions, but they also encountered mob violence. In 1829, Cincinnati whites drove a thousand blacks out of the city. Five years later whites in Philadelphia instigated a three-day reign of terror, during which they beat up blacks and burned their houses. Similar outbreaks occurred in several northern cities, especially during times when blacks and poor whites were in competition for jobs. As Fanny Kemble, a foreign visitor, wrote about northern blacks: "They are not slaves indeed, but they are pariahs, de-

The New York Public Library, Picture Collection.

Northern free blacks could generally only find employment doing menial labor such as sweeping up at the close of business on Wall Street in New York City.

barred from every fellowship. . . . All tongues . . . have learned to turn the very name of their race into an insult and a reproach."

In response to oppression, free blacks in the North held conventions with increasing frequency between 1830 and 1860. At first, participants at these assemblies sought to encourage blacks to start their own businesses and to educate their children, but after 1840 the movement became more political. Some leaders even proposed black militancy and separatism as the only ways to combat white racism. One of the first to speak out was David Walker, a Boston merchant. Walker, born in North Carolina in September 1785 to a free black woman and a slave father, published his famous *Appeal* in 1829.

In four, closely reasoned articles he examined the history of slave societies, quoted profusely from the Declaration of Independence, and called upon white Americans to reflect upon the words "All men are created equal."

In 1843 black Presbyterian clergyman Henry Highland Garrett of Troy, New York called for southern slaves to rise up in rebellion: "Strike for your lives and liberties. . . . You cannot be more oppressed than you have been—you cannot suffer greater cruelties than you have already. *Rather die freemen than live to be slaves*. Remember that you are FOUR MILLIONS."

Neither the convention movement nor the work of abolitionists could eradicate the deep prejudice evident everywhere in America. This bias assumed that blacks were either savages, ready to rape white women, or that they were children, incapable of managing their own lives.

This child/savage image of blacks came to represent to white Americans everything that their nation was not or should not become. It performed an

WALKER'S

APPEAL,

IN FOUR ARTICLES,

TOGETHER WITH

A PREAMBLE,

TO THE

COLORED CITIZENS OF THE WORLD,

BUT IN PARTICULAR, AND VERY EXPRESSLY TO THOSE OF THE

UNITED STATES OF AMERICA.

Written in Boston, in the State of Massachusetts, Sept. 28, 1829.

SECOND EDITION, WITH CORRECTIONS, &c.

BY DAVID WALKER.

1830.

Library of Congress.

David Walker's *Appeal* was an early expression of black nationalism. It called upon white Americans to remember the lofty words of the Declaration of Independence, "All men are created equal," and urged slaves to rise up against their masters. Note the classical garb and the heaven-sent message in Latin.

identity function for white Americans, northern and southern, who were groping for self-identification. They were civilized; the slave was not. In the age of Andrew Jackson, a time of very rapid change, for example, the slave helped to define the norms of white society. Yet that society—made up in part of rough frontiersmen, Indian fighters, slave traders, religious zealots, rapacious entrepreneurs, die-hard nativists, uncompromising abolitionists, and a great mass of uneducated and unschooled adults—often seemed bent upon breaking every rule in the book and discarding whatever pretensions to culture, refinement, and social mores the young republic had acquired.

Indians And Indian Policy

Congress signed a treaty in 1788 with the Delaware tribe, thereby recognizing Indians as foreign nationals; this policy was continued and greatly expanded under the federal government. President George Washington began the practice of providing friendly Indian tribes with clothes, agricultural tools, and teachers to instruct them in the various "arts of civilized life." Treaty commissioners inserted provisions for such items in the documents they negotiated, and Congress appropriated the money. In 1819 Congress established a separate Civilization Fund that remained in effect until 1873. With the aid of missionaries, Bibles, hoes, and trinkets, and by ignoring the role of agriculture in many Indian societies, Washington officials hoped to convert hunters into farmers. The latter supposedly would need less land and thereby cause less trouble; however, that land could not be in areas where whites wanted to settle.

In the early 1800s substantial numbers of Indians were still living in the Old Northwest and the South. The cotton boom sealed the fate of the Indians in the South. Planters in that region were eager to appropriate the vast Indian holdings within their borders and convert these lands into cotton plantations. Moreover, southern whites disliked the presence of an alien people in their midst, es-

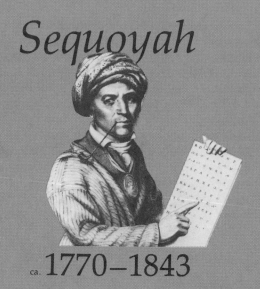

Sequoyah

ca. 1770–1843

Sequoyah has been hailed by white Americans as perhaps "the finest intelligence of the American Indians." The wise, able offspring of a white man, who soon disappeared, and an Indian mother, he grew up among the Cherokees of Tennessee, thoroughly indoctrinated in their ways and customs. As an adult, Sequoyah gave up hunting for fur trading and became a silver craftsman, turning out jewelry and various ornaments for friends and neighbors.

Although he neither spoke nor wrote English, Sequoyah was intrigued by the white man's printed pages ("talking leaves") and about 1809 began to construct a syllabary—a set of characters that stand for syllables, unlike the letters of the alphabet, which stand for individual sounds. Despite considerable ridicule, within a dozen years he completed the work, and this system of writing quickly spread throughout the Cherokee Nation. The Cherokees thus became the first North American Indian tribe to develop their own written language.

This unique contribution gave great impetus to the spread of literacy among the Cherokees, and Sequoyah was much honored by his people. As a result of his invention, Cherokees in the East and those like Sequoyah who had migrated west of the Mississippi River were able to communicate in writing. Sam Houston, who lived for a time with the Cherokees in the West, told Sequoyah that his syllabary was "worth more than a double handfull of gold" to each Cherokee Indian.

Sequoyah went to Washington in 1828 as a member of a delegation of Western Cherokees seeking redress for grievances against the United States.

While in Washington, he posed for Charles Bird King (see the illustration opposite). When the Eastern Cherokees traveled the Trail of Tears to Oklahoma in the late 1830s, Sequoyah helped to moderate differences between various tribal factions and secure adoption of an Act of Union forming "one body politic" designated as the Cherokee Nation. In 1841 the Cherokee Nation bestowed an annual income for life in honor of his many achievements and efforts in behalf of his people.

In the ensuing years, Sequoyah dreamed of reuniting all Cherokees and of finding enough similarities among various Indian languages to enable him to devise a writing system for all Indian peoples. While engaged in an effort to locate a band of Cherokees that supposedly had settled in the Southwest in earlier times, he died in 1843.

The traditional account of this aboriginal genius recently has been challenged by an Indian who claims direct descent from the "true Sequoyah" and relates a quite different story. In *Tell Them They Lie: The Sequoyah Myth* (1971), Traveller Bird maintains that the existence of a Cherokee syllabary was known to whites as early as 1792 and certainly was not invented by Sequoyah. Bird writes that for a quarter of a century this rugged, full-blooded warrior, born in 1776, fought against white encroachment. As the only scribe remaining among the Cherokees, he taught his people their language in a vain effort to thwart alien influence; he also led several groups westward to Spanish soil.

According to Bird, in 1816 Sequoyah was captured by "progressive" Cherokees receptive to white ideas and, because of his activities, convicted of witchcraft and mutilated. Missionaries among the Cherokees, alarmed by this turn of events and unable to suppress the syllabary, fostered a legend that comported well with federal schemes to "civilize" the Cherokees. The man subsequently honored as Sequoyah, says Traveller Bird, was a white-created impostor named Thomas Maw. The real Sequoyah supposedly went west once more; he died in July 1839, cut down by soldiers' bullets while crossing the Brazos River.

Indian and white scholars have denounced Bird's book as a hoax, and the fame of the man known as Sequoyah in the early nineteenth century seems secure: Oklahoma has placed his statue in its capitol, giant redwoods (Sequoias) honor his memory, and generations of Americans have been certain that the man whose picture is here is not one Thomas Maw, but Sequoyah.

pecially because fugitive slaves could hide out in Indian country; as whites came to fear the prospects black uprisings more and more, their hostility toward Indians increased.

President Thomas Jefferson had instructed government agents to encourage Indians to purchase more goods at U.S. trading posts than they could pay for with furs or animal pelts. Jefferson hoped that Indians would run into debt and, in order to pay the government, would be forced to sign land-cession treaties and move into the newly acquired Louisiana Purchase west of the Mississippi River. At the same time, he urged the "civilization" of the Indians. Ignoring the tribal traditions of Indian farmers in the South, Jefferson insisted that Indians would have to learn the white man's agricultural practices and give up the custom of communal ownership of the land in favor of private ownership. If the Indians made these changes, Jefferson believed, then they would be more easily assimilated into American society. Even more important, assimilation presumably would lead Indians to take up trades and give up their surplus lands to white settlers. What actually happened, however, came as a complete surprise. The Cherokees in the South did in fact adopt many of the patterns of white society, but they made these societal changes in order to preserve their tribal integrity and lands from further encroachments. Cherokee acceptance of white patterns of living was facilitated by the spread of literacy, made possible by the development of a written language. The inventor of this written language was a Cherokee named Sequoyah (whose invaluable contribution is discussed in greater detail in a biographical sketch in this chapter).

The Old Northwest

The Indians of the Old Northwest also encountered persistent pressure from white Americans to give up their lands. In this region in the early nineteenth century two Indian leaders appeared who attempted to unite the Indians all the way from Canada to the Gulf of Mexico into a single confederacy that would stop the westward advance of the United States.

These men were Tecumseh, a man of Shawnee and Creek background, and his brother, the Prophet. They used the twin appeal of Indian nationalism and religious vision while preaching that the deteriorating condition of various tribes was caused by the white man's whiskey and ways and by the failure of Indians to maintain their own traditions. Tecumseh was particularly opposed to land-cession treaties.

Tecumseh, the Prophet, and their followers gathered at an old Indian town on Tippecanoe Creek in the Indiana Territory known as Prophetstown, which by 1811 housed about a thousand warriors from various tribes who had joined the cause. But when Tecumseh traveled south in the summer of 1811 to recruit tribesmen there, the Prophet disobeyed his brother's instructions and allowed some warriors to attack a nearby American military camp. General William Henry Harrison retaliated by attacking Prophetstown, burning it to the ground.

Nevertheless, Tecumseh seemed a force that could not be stopped. He eventually gathered un-

An 1832 painting by artist George Catlin of the Sac and Fox warrior Black Hawk.

der his banner braves from numerous tribes, though the allegiance of these particular warriors did not assure the support of their tribes. When the War of 1812 broke out, Tecumseh hoped that the Anglo-American conflict would end the westward migration of the whites. Instead, it spelled his downfall. During the Battle of the Thames in Canada in October 1813, American soldiers killed Tecumseh. Then, on March 27, 1814, General Andrew Jackson subdued Tecumseh's Creek allies in the South by wiping out over 800 of their finest warriors at the horseshoe bend of the Tallapoosa River in Alabama.

Jackson's victory helped to pave his way to the White House in 1828. Old Hickory was interested primarily in southern Indian removal, but events in the spring of 1832 precipitated action in the Old Northwest as well. In April a group of Sac and Fox Indians, under the leadership of a proud, old warrior named Black Hawk, left Iowa Territory and crossed the Mississippi into Illinois. Their destination was an ancestral village and adjacent cornfields, land that the United States had acquired by a treaty that Black Hawk had denounced. Although this band, which included women and children,

Tecumseh, wearing an English uniform and medal. This Shawnee leader had a vision of uniting the Indians against the Americans. When the War of 1812 between the British and Americans broke out, he joined the British and fought with his supporters against the Americans.

did not constitute a war party, a short bloody confrontation provoked by panicky white militia ensued. The Jackson administration used this "invasion" as an excuse to seize Sac and Fox lands beyond the river and push other tribes westward, too. If the Indians failed to provide a motive for action, then soldiers simply used brute force.

The Removal Policy

The War of 1812 and its aftermath proved a disaster for Indians in the Old Northwest and in the South. Neither Tecumseh nor the British had been able to stop the westward migration of whites, and when the war was over, the United States continued to seize Indian lands. Even tribes such as the Cherokees and Choctaws who had fought on the side of the United States were forced to relinquish territory. Presidents James Madison, James Monroe, and John Quincy Adams advocated removing the Indians to locations west of the Mississippi, but the actual dispossession was accomplished largely through treaties secured by President Andrew Jackson under the Removal Act of 1830. This legislation authorized him to provide eastern Indians with unorganized public domain in the West in exchange for their eastern land. This was to be accomplished on a voluntary basis.

The fact that Jackson had long advocated Indian removal was one of the reasons he swept the South in the 1828 election. His Indian policy was in harmony with his belief in American expansion. Jackson was, curiously enough, both a nationalist and a champion of states' rights; his Indian policy suited both sympathies, since it made room for a growing nation and simultaneously asserted the supremacy of the state governments of Georgia, Alabama, Mississippi, North Carolina, and Tennessee and the government of the Florida Territory over the Cherokee, Choctaw, Chickasaw, Creek, and Seminole Indians within their boundaries. Although Jackson was opposed by powerful pro-Indian humanitarians, he won a majority of the Congress to his side by stressing that removal was itself a humanitarian measure "actuated by feelings of justice and a regard for our national honor."

Since the 1790s the War Department had used economic coercion as a means of pressuring Indians to sign land-cession treaties by only paying them the annual interest on money owed under treaty obligations. Thomas Jefferson established the precedent of withholding these annuities as a lever for social control, and during the administration of

Jackson, American officials found that withholding annuities was a very convenient means of inducing tribes to sign removal treaties and to emigrate westward. Jackson was no admirer of what he referred to as the "erratic" ways of native life, yet his actions were governed not so much by any personal animosity towards the Indians, but by his great concern for the growth, unity, and security of the nation. So long as Indian enclaves remained within the states, the President argued, the potential for an explosive confrontation between armed militia and Indian warriors, or between state and federal authorities, clearly existed.

During the years of Jackson's presidency, the United States acquired through removal of Indians about 100 million acres of land east of the Mississippi, in exchange for about $68 million and 32 million acres west of the Mississippi, which were given to the Indians. In order to secure this excellent bargain, the government removed some 46,000 Indians from their tribal lands in the South and the Old Northwest by 1837, while a little more than that number had treaty stipulations calling for their removal. Although some Indians in both regions managed to avoid eviction, only a few scattered tribes, mostly in New York and the Great Lakes region, escaped without treaty stipulations requiring their removal.

The South

Typical of Indian dispossession, and in many ways a precedent for the emigration of other tribes, was the Choctaw removal from Mississippi. Despite government promises to make the move as comfortable and orderly as possible, the first wave of Choctaws to depart in 1831 was handled by the War Department with total confusion and inefficiency. Washington did not send the necessary funds, which caused long delays that pushed the migration into the winter of 1831–1832 and exposed the Indians to severe storms. Subsequent Choctaw removals were planned better, but still were executed poorly and took place during unexpected attacks of cholera. Some Choctaws took advantage of a treaty provision allowing them to stay behind in Mississippi and receive land allotments if they submitted to state laws, but they became victims of flagrant fraud, intimidation, and speculation. Hounded by avaricious land speculators, most of the Choctaws sold their land for fifty cents an acre. (By an act passed in 1820, the federal government was selling land for $1.25 an acre.) Among the beneficiaries of

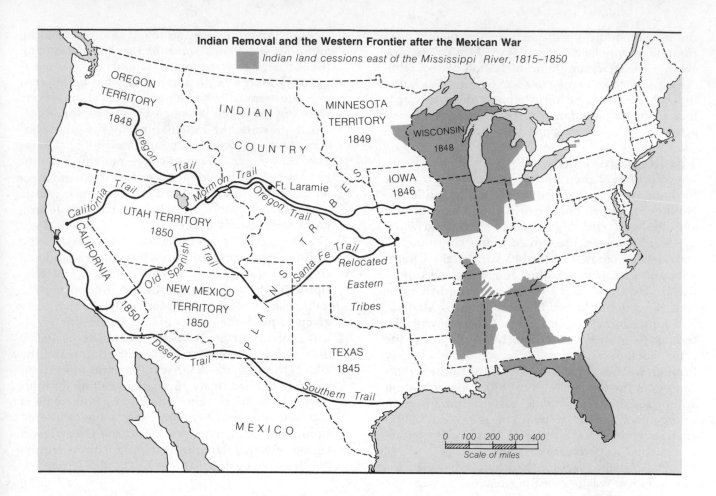

Indian land cessions east of the Mississippi River, 1815–1850

OREGON TERRITORY

1848

Oregon Trail

INDIAN

COUNTRY

MINNESOTA TERRITORY

1849

WISCONSIN 1848

California Trail

Mormon Trail

Ft. Laramie

Oregon Trail

IOWA 1846

UTAH TERRITORY

1850

Santa Fe Trail

Relocated

Eastern

Tribes

CALIFORNIA

Old Spanish Trail

NEW MEXICO TERRITORY

1850

1850

Desert Trail

P L A I N S   T R I B E S

TEXAS

1845

Southern Trail

M E X I C O

0 100 200 300 400
Scale of miles

this swindle were politicians in Jackson's party, federal marshals, and friends and relatives of agents in the General Land Office.

Following the passage of the Removal Act, the Cherokees came under strong pressure from politicians in Georgia and neighboring states to relinquish their landholdings and to leave the Southeast. Anti-Jackson politicians like Henry Clay, David Crockett, and Daniel Webster encouraged the Cherokees to appeal to the U.S. Supreme Court for protection of their treaty rights. In *Cherokee Nation* v. *State of Georgia* (1831), Chief Justice John Marshall declared that the Indian tribes were "domestic dependent nations" that were "in a state of pupilage" and therefore "wards" of the federal government. As "guardian" of the Indians, the United States was responsible for their welfare, but Marshall rejected the petition of the Cherokees because they had incorrectly filed suit as a *foreign* nation.

Georgia officials then stepped up their campaign of intimidation and even arrested Reverend

Samuel A. Worcester and other missionaries residing among the Cherokees. Marshall rallied to their support and in *Worcester* v. *State of Georgia* (1832) ordered the missionaries released and ruled that Georgia's extension of state laws over the Cherokees was unconstitutional. Although the missionaries soon were free, technicalities in federal laws relating to enforcement of Supreme Court decrees left the Cherokees at the mercy of Georgia. President Jackson did not, as many historians have claimed, actually refuse to enforce the Supreme Court ruling in this case, but he was certainly pleased that its decision "fell still born."

Increased pressure from state and federal officials led a minority faction of the Cherokees to sign a removal treaty in 1835. The vast majority of the Cherokee people, however, refused to abide by what they called the "fraudulent treaty." When the deadline for removal arrived in 1838, only 2,000 had emigrated westward. The remaining 15,000 Indians and their black slaves were rounded up by the army and placed in temporary internment camps. The "lawless white rabble" on the frontier and some militiamen treated the Indians in a manner so hair-raising that one Georgia volunteer said years later, "I fought through the Civil War and have seen men shot to pieces and slaughtered by thousands, but the Cherokee removal was the cruelest work I ever knew."

Under orders from President Van Buren, General Winfield Scott began the forcible ejection of the Cherokees in the summer of 1838. After about 3,000 captive Indians had departed under military escort, Scott agreed to suspend the operations until the hot summer season was over. Scott, a Whig favorite, rival of Jackson, and a man sympathetic to the condition of the Cherokees, worked out a compromise with Cherokee chief John Ross. Between October 1838 and March 1839, Ross led the remaining Cherokees to the trans-Mississippi West. Some 17,000 Cherokees and their slaves traveled on a virtual Trail of Tears to present-day Oklahoma under the terms of the treaty of 1835. About 4,000 Indians died as a result of the circumstances surrounding their capture and detention before emigration began or as a result of the hardships on their trek to the West. Those who left the South under the guidance of Ross fared better than those who had embarked earlier under military escort.

Other southern tribes also faced eviction. Between 1835 and 1842, the Seminoles in Florida developed hit-and-run guerrilla warfare to an art as they sought to evade removal. Only after suffering some 1,500 casualties and spending over 40 million dollars was the federal government able to force all

Woolarc Museum, Bartlesville, Oklahoma.

Robert Lindneux's painting of "The Trail of Tears" shows Cherokees emigrating westward under military escort. As a contemporary observer noted, the faces of the Indians carried a "downcast dejected look bordering upon the appearance of despair."

but a handful of the Seminole people to emigrate to the West. When some Creeks in Alabama responded to depredations by whites with violence in 1836, the majority of the tribe was forcibly removed by the army. The Chickasaws in Mississippi, on the other hand, accepted the inevitability of removal and emigrated westward in 1837–1838.

Public Opinion

Many Americans considered the Indian removal policy of the 1830s as morally wrong, but the evidence indicates that there was no official policy of racial extermination or genocide perpetrated against the Indians by the government. Though Indian policy was not deliberately brutal, it was characterized by ethnocentricism, mismanagement, inept planning, and, too often, hypocrisy. Members of both major political parties condemned and supported it, and some of the most outspoken critics—Daniel Webster, Edward Everett, Caleb Cushing, and Ralph Waldo Emerson—were among those who nevertheless speculated in what once had been Indian land.

The American people in the Jacksonian era were a restless people accustomed to moving every generation or so. To many people there seemed no reason why a band of "savages" could not exist just as well on one plot of ground as another. Their wants were supposedly few and the supply of land in the West apparently inexhaustible.

Between 1845 and 1848, the United States acquired nearly 1.5 million square miles of new territory. Instead of solving Indian-white relations, the removal policy greatly complicated those relations. By 1850, the "permanent" homes granted to eastern tribes in areas west of the Mississippi River by treaties negotiated under the Removal Act of 1830 formed a barrier between white settlements and the new lands which included Texas and California as well as the New Mexico and Utah Territories. At the same time, these expansive acres were the home of still more Indian tribes.

During the late 1840s and early 1850s, American officials in the Office of Indian Affairs had determined that the Indian barrier to westward expansion created by Jacksonian Indian policy would have to be removed; Indians everywhere in the West would be placed on "reservations." In the Treaty of Fort Laramie (1851) between the United States and the tribes of the central plains, American

officials designated specific areas as reservations for the various tribes—despite the fact that such boundary lines violated the traditional migration patterns of these peoples. In the future this arrangement would permit whites to force individual tribes onto more restricted areas without upsetting other nearby tribes. Henceforth "removals" might cover shorter distances, but the consequences were no less devastating.

Women
And
Women's
Rights

Feminism as an American political movement had its beginnings in the 1830s and 1840s. It was not an isolated phenomenon, but rather integrated with other events of the era, in particular industrialization, abolitionism, and an upsurge of general interest in reform.

Industrialization affected women both directly and indirectly. Its direct effect was the fact that women formed a significant portion of the working population; as early as 1816 a congressional committee discovered that of 100,000 factory workers in the United States, nearly two-thirds were women and girls. But these individuals received less than men for the same work and were kept from rising in the factory hierarchy. Worse, whole categories of industrial work (usually the better-paying jobs) were closed to women. One of the leading feminists of the era, Sarah Grimké, remarked in 1837 that American society's disdain for women

------

"bears with tremendous effect on the laboring classes, and indeed on almost all who are obliged to earn a sustenance, whether it be by mental or physical exertion—I allude to the disproportionate value set on the time and labor of men and women. . . . As for example, in tailoring, a man has twice or three times as much for making a waistcoat or pantaloons as a woman, although the work done by each may be equally good. In those employments which are peculiar to women, their time is estimated at half the value of that of men. A woman who goes out to wash, works as hard in proportion as a wood sawyer, or a coal heaver, but she is not generally able to make more than half as much by a day's work."

———

Indirectly, industrialization, by increasing the wealth of the middle class, increased the leisure time of women in that social stratum. At the same time, foreign immigration to America made Irish and other European servants more plentiful and thereby gave some middle class women considerably more time for outside interests and activities. From this emergent leisure group came many of the members of the early women's rights movement.

If the Industrial Revolution provided some women with the time to devote to feminism, it also increased the plight of most women. For, as the nineteenth century wore on, women were increasingly relegated to a minor role in society. During the colonial period and in the early years of the republic, most Americans were engaged in a hard struggle to survive; on a small subsistence farm a man's wife and daughters worked hard and, as a consequence, had considerable say in the conduct of family affairs. But in the city and among the middle classes as the decades passed, women no longer played an important economic role—and, correspondingly, their independence and authority diminished. This loss of status was disguised in a deceptive cult of "true womanhood." In the period before 1850, middle class women were taught that obedience to the husband and to male-dominated society was a positive feminine virtue; the qualities most admired in women were piety, purity, submissiveness, and domesticity.

The position of women in antebellum society was one of great inequality relative to men. By 1807 states had stopped relying on custom and specifically limited the vote to males. Harriet Martineau, an English visitor to America, wrote in 1837 that in America women had a "political nonexistence."

Legally and economically, women also were at an extreme disadvantage. Every cent a married women earned belonged to her husband. If a woman divorced her husband, he usually retained custody of the children. Married women were not allowed to write their own wills. In fact, in most states married women could not legally hold property in their own names. As Alexis de Toqueville wrote: "In America a woman loses her independence forever in the bonds of matrimony."

The "Double Standard"

The meager wages offered to lower-class women as workers drove many of them into a better-paying, if more demeaning, occupation—prostitution. A statistical study of New York taken near the end of the antebellum period revealed that half of the city's prostitutes formerly worked as seamstresses or servants. Women forced by economic necessity into prostitution were victims of sexual mores that ignored male promiscuity but insisted on chastity in "respectable" women—the double standard.

The New York Female Moral Reform Society, organized in May 1834 by a group of women who met at a Presbyterian Church in Manhattan, declared open war on the city's houses of ill fame and tried to convert prostitutes to Christianity. Despite a lack of success, the society's members were among the first women of this period to question the well-known double moral standard and to indict the sexual behavior of American men. The organization never embraced feminism overtly, but it did urge women to unite in denouncing male behavior and in proclaiming female moral superiority. By mid-century the society abandoned its attack on prostitution and instead took up the cause of working women in general, even urging them to join unions.

Pioneers in the Professions

Although most recognized professions were closed to women during the antebellum period, more and more women were becoming school teachers. Like women workers in the textile mills, however, female teachers received less money than their male counterparts. And teaching, never a high-status profession in America, had fallen a few notches farther in public esteem by the time women outnumbered men teachers in 1850.

The more prestigious professions, such as law and medicine, were closed to women. Indeed, when doctors formed the American Medical Association in 1846, they specifically excluded females. Some women, however, broke through these barriers. Elizabeth Blackwell (1821–1910) became the first woman to graduate in medicine. She received

Courtesy New York Infirmary, New York City.
Elizabeth Blackwell, the first woman in America to receive a medical degree.

But as young ladies they traveled to Philadelphia, where the views of the Quakers and their strong abolitionist stand changed their lives. Both of the Grimké sisters moved north, became Quakers, and took up the antislavery cause.

When Angelina addressed mixed audiences in New England in 1837, she created a scandal; the Congregational Ministerial Association of Massachusetts objected in a circular letter. Angelina quickly saw that they must secure their rights as women before they could fight slavery effectively. Sarah responded to attacks on their right to speak by publishing *Letters on the Equality of the Sexes and the Condition of Women* (1838) and by lashing out boldly in the columns of *The Advocate of Moral Reform,* a publication of the New York Female Moral Reform Society.

When Sarah Grimké used *The Advocate* to attack the Protestant ministry and its standard inter-

her degree in 1849, after finishing the course of study at a small medical school in New York where she was admitted as a prank. For the next seven years she found it difficult to establish her practice in New York, where she was barred from hospitals and attacked by anonymous letter writers. Nevertheless, in 1853 she opened a one-room clinic for the poor, and there she treated 200 indigent women in the first year alone. Soon she was joined by two other women doctors, one of whom was her sister. In 1868 she established a medical college of her own, although by that time there were also medical schools for women in Boston and Philadelphia.

Among other prominent women of the period were Sarah (1792–1873) and Angelina Grimké (1805–1879) who became active in abolitionist circles in the mid-1830s. The sisters were born into a wealthy Huguenot family in South Carolina (their father was equivalent to chief justice of the state), and they were accustomed to the services of slaves.

Library of Congress.
Angelina Grimké was an active abolitionist who came to realize that women had to secure their own rights.

pretations of the Bible, both of which, in her opinion, denied woman's true role, the result was a wave of angry letters that convinced the editors · never again to overtly assault traditional family structure or orthodox Christianity. Nevertheless, the Grimkés became leaders of both the abolitionist and the feminist movements.

Abolitionism was also the immediate vehicle for other women to recognize that their own rights were being denied. In the summer of 1840, the British held an international meeting of the World Antislavery Convention in London. When several women, delegates from antislavery groups in America, tried to be seated, the majority of the delegates, who were men, ruled that the women could not participate but would have to watch silently from the galleries. One of the delegates shunted upstairs was Lucretia Mott (whose work as an active feminist is summarized in a biographical sketch in this chapter). Elizabeth Cady Stanton (1815–1902), whose husband was a delegate, also had to watch from the galleries. After their humiliation in London, Mott and Stanton both became active feminists.

Library of Congress.
Frances Wright was denounced in the press as a "bold blasphemer and voluptuous preacher of licentiousness" for her so-called radical views.

Lucretia Coffin Mott

1793–1880

Outstanding reformer and Quaker preacher, this energetic, cheerful woman was born on Nantucket Island. Her mother, whose family had been staunch Tories, and her father, a somewhat more democratic sea captain, were members of the Society of Friends. When she was eleven the family moved to Boston (her first trip to "the Continent," she later recalled) where her father became a businessman. She briefly attended local public schools, but at the age of thirteen was sent to boarding school near Poughkeepsie, New York. This was her home for four years as student and teacher.

In 1811 she rejoined her parents, now living in Philadelphia, but soon married James Mott (1788–1868), a fellow teacher at the Poughkeepsie school. Mott, later a distinguished abolitionist and unique in his early advocacy of women's rights, recently had joined Lucretia's father in the cut nail business.

Although a Quaker background developed Lucretia Mott's antislavery sympathies, several experiences sharpened this interest and also piqued her concern for women's rights. The death of an infant son in 1817 caused this highly intelligent woman to reflect seriously concerning religion; and, as she began to speak at meetings, she easily won recognition as an acknowledged minister. Her views supported those of Elias Hicks, and in time she and her husband became associated with the "Hicksite" branch of the Quakers, a group with Unitarian-like leanings.

As her reputation as a speaker spread, she directed her attention to temperance, peace, antislavery, and women's rights. Concern for the latter seems to have stemmed from her brief teaching career when for the same work she received half as much money as her male counterparts. When officials at a worldwide antislavery convention held in London in 1840 refused to recognize Lucretia Mott and several other American women as official delegates, her interest in the rights of women increased markedly. Eight years later, together with Elizabeth Cady Stanton, she helped organize the famous Seneca Falls meeting (held in a Methodist church) which launched the women's rights movement in America. Despite this step and the fame it bestowed upon her, Lucretia Mott's first devotion as a reformer was to abolition. After passage of a new fugitive slave law in 1850, her home became a stop on the underground railroad to freedom.

Mott was a sprightly, impulsive woman who displayed both firmness and courage in behalf of whatever causes she espoused. She is a good example of how Quaker upbringing and practical experience could convert an agile mind into a multipurpose reform spirit. Also, Lucretia Mott is an early example of a woman who gracefully managed a public career without sacrificing a private life.

The feminism these women embraced was not without precedent. One of the earliest and most articulate women to speak about feminism before American audiences of men and women was a Scottish writer, lecturer and reformer, Frances Wright (1795–1852). Originally Fanny Wright, as she was known, was caught up by a desire to bring about the emancipation of slaves, and she proposed a plan whereby slaves could work large tracts of public lands, and with the profits, buy their freedom. When she turned to feminism, Wright became far more radical than perhaps any other woman of her time. She aroused hostility and ridicule when she advocated free love, equal education for women, liberal divorce laws, and birth control. Today her positions strike many people as rational, but in the 1820s they were shocking in the extreme, especially when coupled with her efforts to set up an interracial utopia in West Tennessee and her attacks on racially segregated schools, organized religion, and marriage.

Frances Wright's views alienated most American women, but she did stimulate other feminists to consider the merits of suffrage for women, equal educational opportunities, and liberal divorce laws. Margaret Fuller (1810–1850), a teacher and Transcendentalist writer, never identified herself with the feminists but one of her books, *Women in the Nineteenth Century* (1845), argued for equality of opportunity. In speaking about women's careers, Fuller said: "If you ask me what offices they may fill, I reply—any. I do not care what case you put; let them be sea captains if you will."

Seneca Falls

The high-water mark of early feminist agitation, which was aimed at making people aware of the barriers to women in the legal, educational, economic, and social spheres, was the first feminist convention held at Seneca Falls, New York, in 1848. Led by Elizabeth Cady Stanton, nearly 300 reformers (including forty men) proclaimed that women were the equals of men and should be free to speak in public, write, teach, and participate equally "in the various trades, professions and commerce." Stanton offered a resolution declaring: "It is the sacred duty of the women of this country to secure to themselves that sacred right to the elective franchise." Even among the enlightened people at Seneca Falls, the suffrage resolution seemed too extreme. Many present argued that such a resolution was premature and would arouse antagonism and division. Only with support from Frederick Douglass, an ex-slave and prominent abolitionist, did the measure pass. The Seneca Falls convention adopted a Declaration of Sentiments and Resolutions modeled after the Declaration of Independence, which stated that "all men and women are created equal" and listed the "injuries and usurpations" women had endured at the hands of men.

Although women did not obtain the right to vote or hold elective office in any state until the last decades of the nineteenth century, they did make some gains. In 1838, for instance, Kentucky granted widows and single women with taxable property the right to vote for district school officials. In 1839, Mississippi granted married women the right to control their own property. And by 1848, New York recognized that women had certain rights in controlling property. Other states followed the New York example. Meanwhile, some state legislatures made divorce laws less stringent. Yet the equality of women spelled out by the delegates at the Seneca Falls Convention remained an ideal rather than a statement of reality for women in antebellum America.

The battle for women's rights, especially the ballot, was a long, uphill struggle, not only for women but for all those Americans who believed they should be allowed to vote and to participate in the political process. Most of those turned away from polling places maintained (with considerable justification) that the privilege of casting a ballot was an inherent right in any republic based upon the ideals of liberty, equality, and justice. (For a general overview of this struggle, see the essay on "The Struggle for Full Citizenship" at the end of this chapter.)

Immigrants

Before 1830, many of the new arrivals in America were Protestant artisans and well-to-do farmers from England and the six northern counties of Ireland. After 1830, however, the number of impoverished Catholic peasant immigrants from southern Ireland increased dramatically until, in the 1840s, most of the people moving to the United States were either Irish or German. Smaller groups of foreigners came from Scandinavia, France, England, Canada, Holland, Poland, Italy, Hungary, and China. The ethnic flavor of America also was enriched by the inclusion of large numbers of Mexican Catholics, who were incorporated into the United States after the Mexican War (1846–1848).

Irish and German Immigrants

Irish peasants came to America to escape from extreme poverty and misery. A potato blight began to destroy Ireland's primary subsistence crop in the 1820s, and the island experienced a severe famine in 1845 and 1846 when rot destroyed stored potatoes to be used as food and seed for the next crop. By 1845 almost a million Irish had moved to the United States; by 1860 there were more than 1,611,000 people born in Ireland living in America (almost 40 percent of all foreign-born residents).

Because they were unskilled and quite different from most Americans in their religious, social, and linguistic customs (many of the Irish peasants still spoke Gaelic or heavily accented English), they gathered in ethnic enclaves in ports such as Boston. Cities were not well suited to most of the Irish, who were rural people, but the newcomers preferred staying close together in the shadow of the Catholic parish church rather than dispersing through the countryside and encountering hostility from other ethnic groups; moreover, the Irish seldom had enough money to buy a farm or farm equipment, livestock, and seed.

The Irish came to Boston because it was a major port for British ships. Many stayed there because they could not afford to move elsewhere. Before 1830 the total number of immigrants entering Boston never exceeded 2,000. But between 1840 and 1849 the number increased rapidly from 3,396 (1840) to 28,917 (1849), and most of these arrivals were Irish. By 1850, some 35,000 Irish lived in Boston, far outnumbering the next two most numerous minority ethnic groups—free blacks (2,085) and Germans (about 2,000).

Of course, the Irish clustered in large numbers in other cities besides Boston—among them, Lowell, Hartford, New York, Philadelphia, Albany, Buffalo, Cleveland, Cincinnati, Chicago, and St. Louis. In general, they followed the canals and railroads (often helping to construct them); they also settled in southern ports such as Baltimore, Charleston, Savannah, and New Orleans. The Irish were, in fact, urban pioneers and their ghettolike enclaves gave them considerable political clout, which they quickly used. And the same muscles that helped lay railway ties, dig ditches, and keep the foes of their political boss patron away from the ballot box

Courtesy of the New York Historical Society, New York City.

Hard times in Ireland and the prospect of a new life in America brought a great influx of Irish to America in the antebellum period.

on election day soon were carrying arms in the local militia, fighting fires, and bringing the law (if not true order) to bustling city wards.

Unskilled Irish peasants, willing to work for low wages, provided Boston with the labor that helped to create a new industrial economy for the city. Because the men were paid such low wages, their wives were forced to seek employment as domestic servants. By the mid-1840s many Irish were seeking better jobs, but they often were met with prejudice. Newspaper advertisements offering employment frequently stipulated "None need apply but Americans."

Even the free blacks of Boston fared better than the Irish on the job market. Although it was difficult for blacks to acquire an education, skills, or capital, many did become traders, barbers, or seamen; and some even rose into the professional ranks. The Irish, by contrast, remained at the bottom of the occupational hierarchy.

The Boston Irish were hired by southern planters looking for cheap labor to perform jobs deemed too dangerous for expensive slaves. New railroad companies used them to lay miles and miles of track. In the late 1840s and well into the 1850s, Boston's Irish provided factory owners with labor so inexpensive that industrialists could reap enormous profits. Many industries, held back from expanding by high wages, could now grow as a result of the abundance of cheap Irish labor. For the Irish immigrant, the independence of a peasant's life had been exchanged for fifteen-hour working days and a ceaseless scramble for survival. In America the Irish were no longer haunted by starvation, perhaps, but they had become, to use George Fitzhugh's phrase, "wage slaves." Fitzhugh (1806–1881), a Virginia lawyer and proslavery propagandist, became a confirmed defender of slavery after a visit to the North in the 1830s. He claimed that the conditions of plantation slaves were preferable to those of northern workers. Life was indeed bleak for Irish in the North. Nevertheless, they endured as free people.

Excluded from participation in the normal affairs of the white Boston community, the Irish responded by developing an ethnic consciousness. They sought to preserve their own cultural heritage in churches, parochial schools, Irish newspapers, and social organizations such as the Charitable Irish Society and the Shamrock Society.

On the West Coast, the Irish generally were more assertive, competitive, and aggressive than their counterparts in Boston. The Irish in San Francisco, for example, were part of a subculture, but the interactions between these Roman Catholic immigrants and the contemporary residents of the city dispel the stereotyped notion that all Irish immigrants suffered from such traumatic conditions as alienation or despair in America. Certainly not all Irish immigrants suffered as outcasts and as a ruthlessly exploited source of cheap labor, but the Boston experience indicates that many of them did.

During the 1840s and 1850s, another group of immigrants, who like the Irish had been coming to America for generations, suddenly increased their numbers dramatically. These were the Germans. In 1851, 72,482 Germans often called the "Forty-Eighters" because of the failure of liberal revolts of that year, arrived in American ports. For the most part they were a relatively well-to-do group who turned their back on Europe for political, not economic reasons. During the next two years another

288,000 of their countrymen came to America. Although many remained in cities, more so than the Irish these folk tended to become farmers in states such as Ohio, Wisconsin, Illinois, and Texas. Their arrival created a special religious problem. Since many were Catholic, they keenly resented Irish domination of church affairs. And Protestant Americans were equally critical of their Sabbath custom of a "Continental Sunday," that is, going directly from church to a beer garden or saloon for an afternoon of pleasant sociability. Despite the middle class ideology of most German immigrants, many Americans viewed them as atheists or radicals.

Among these newcomers were a considerable number of Jews who settled in the larger cities, especially New York. In 1840, there were only about 15,000 Jews in the United States out of a total population of more than 17,000,000. At that time about half of them lived in New York, Philadelphia, Milwaukee, and Richmond. By 1860 their numbers had increased to 150,000, largely because of the revolts of the late 1840s which shook not only Germany, but Austria, Italy, and France as well. Unlike Catholic immigrants, the Jews were such a tiny minority that attacks upon them as a group were rare.

Anti-Catholicism

Native Americans were alarmed by the clannishness of all these immigrants, but they were most frightened by the Catholicism of the Irish. Samuel F. B. Morse (who later invented the telegraph) was Professor of Sculpture and Painting at New York University in 1834 when he published a rabid anti-Catholic tract, *The Foreign Conspiracy Against the Liberties of United States*. Morse contended that America was about to witness an epic struggle between the Pope's followers and the Protestant defenders of liberty. According to Morse, the Catholics (that is, the Irish) intended to take over the government and destroy the separation of church and state. For many Americans—Morse's predictions seemed grimly plausible.

The bewildering social changes racking America after the War of 1812 gave focus to a general but totally unfounded fear of a Catholic conspiracy. These tensions found release in a series of mob actions. In 1831 rioting Protestants burned St. Mary's Church in New York. On August 10, 1834, a mob of forty or fifty Bostonians, excited by an anti-Catholic speech, burned a convent in Charlestown. In 1836 a sensationalist book, *The Awful Disclosures*

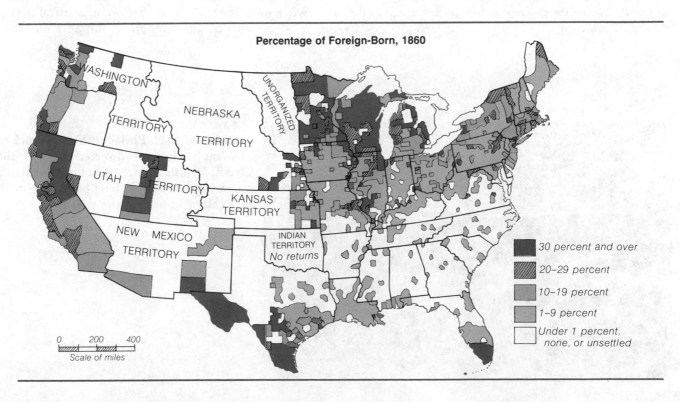

Percentage of Foreign-Born, 1860

30 percent and over
20–29 percent
10–19 percent
1–9 percent
Under 1 percent, none, or unsettled

of the Hotel Dieu Nunnery of Montreal, appeared. Written by Maria Monk (1816–1849), a Canadian adventuress, the book pretended to be the account of ordeals suffered by a nun forced to submit to the sexual advances of priests. Even after the public learned that the author actually was a Protestant imprisoned for picking the pocket of her companion in a house of prostitution, the book continued to sell well. In fact, more than 300,000 copies were sold before the Civil War, and the book was widely circulated by anti-Catholics well into the twentieth century.

Between 1840 and 1844 the anti-Catholic movement took on a new form. At that time the Public School Society, dedicated to teaching students the "sublime truths of religion and morality contained in the Holy Scriptures" and endorsed by Protestant groups, operated the "public" schools of New York City. Catholic parents did not want their children exposed to the King James version of the Scriptures, which was not in accord with Catholic dogma, nor did they approve of religious instruction that openly mocked Catholicism. When Catholics, led by New York's Bishop John Hughes (1797–1864), attempted to obtain state tax funds to institute their own educational system, a great debate erupted. Bishop Hughes then switched tactics and campaigned for nonsectarian public schools, from which religion of any sort would be excluded, but he only aroused more Protestant ire.

When Catholics demanded that their children be allowed to read their own version of the Bible and not be forced to receive Protestant religious instruction, the American Protestant Association responded with fanatical antipathy. This group, organized in November 1842 by about 100 local ministers, was convinced that "Popery" was trying to gain control of the Mississippi Valley and cited letters of the reigning Pope supposedly attacking such freedoms as those of conscience, opinion, and the press and bewailing separation of church and state anywhere in the world. In May 1844 clashes broke out in Philadelphia between Irish Catholic workers and militant Protestants; during three days of mob rule, several Catholic churches were burned, thirteen citizens killed, and many more wounded.

Rioting was only the most overt expression of anti-Catholicism. Beginning in the mid 1830s and continuing through the next decade, nativists organized politically and fought to limit the influence of immigrants, especially Catholics, in every aspect of public life. In many states, ministers and local politicians, seeking instant public sympathy from their Protestant constituents, quickly embraced the banner of nativism. However, the Philadelphia riot cooled the ardor of many Americans, who thought the movement had gone beyond the bounds of reason. Yet nativism did not die out. In the 1840s, when its adherents saw that open political action was ineffectual in combating immigrants, they

Library of Congress.
In May of 1844, Philadelphia was rocked by mob violence directed against the Irish. In this scene, militant Protestants wearing tall beaver hats battle the militia called in to stop the rioting.

formed secret societies such as The Native Sons of America, the United Daughters of America, and The Order of the "Star-Spangled" Banner.

The great influx of immigrants to America during the antebellum period certainly aroused strong tensions that still have not been entirely resolved. But the phenomenon was not without its more positive side. Before the controversy over religious instruction in the schools occurred, Protestant teachers had freely used the Bible as a textbook. The objections of Catholics to this practice led at first to a strong parochial school system and in the twentieth century to a secularization of education and a truer separation of church and state, and undoubtedly created widespread interest in true public education. If nothing else, this controversy awakened all Americans to the many problems immigration brings in its wake, and those who arrived quickly learned a basic lesson in democracy American style: how to use the ballot box to get what they wanted.

Essay

The Struggle for Full Citizenship

For all practical purposes, citizenship is much like good health and the ability to walk or talk. It is something most Americans take for granted and rarely reflect on except when going to the polls or traveling abroad. The ballot, passport, and an occasional burst of pride during a Fourth of July parade or when some celebrity sings the national anthem at a sports event are the most common expressions of a rather intangible concept.

Citizenship is, in essence, the relationship between an individual and a state as prescribed by the laws of that state. It is a condition acquired at birth or by naturalization, that is, choosing to renounce one's native land for another. In the modern sense, citizenship is a byproduct of the American and French revolutions and represents an obvious attempt to discard the word "subject" with its connotations of feudal service and inequality.

The tempestuous 1770s created countless problems concerning just who was and who was not an American citizen. Throughout the middle decades of the eighteenth century, London had pursued a contradictory policy of encouraging immigration to the New World but had balked at naturalization of aliens by the colonies themselves; instead, those running the empire wanted foreign immigrants to take an oath of allegiance to the Crown before they departed for America. Nevertheless, until 1773 the government generally permitted naturalization by colonial officials, providing still more evidence of "benign neglect." The decision of George III to change this practice led to one of the many "He has" phrases in the Declaration of Independence: "He has endeavoured to prevent the Population of these States; for that purpose obstructing the Laws of Naturalization of Foreigners."

That next great document, the Constitution, failed to define citizenship, either because those writing it assumed everyone knew what the word meant, or because this was an expedient means of sidestepping what could have been an explosive issue. In any case, the Founding Fathers implied that anyone who voted in national elections had to be white, male, and at least 21 years of age. They left the determination of citizenship to the individual states but gave federal authorities sole power of naturalization, thus creating a potentially awkward situation. In theory, any state could admit aliens to virtually all privileges of citizenship and, at the same time, refuse those rights to individuals properly naturalized by the central government.

In 1789, David Ramsay, a well-known South Carolina historian, published a carefully phrased, eight-page document entitled "A Dissertation on the Manner of Acquiring the Character and Privileges of a Citizen of the United States." In Ramsay's view, any person living in a state or country was an inhabitant or resident, not necessarily a citizen. Blacks, he observed in passing, clearly were not citizens; concerning women, he was silent.

There were, Ramsay emphasized, few paths to U.S. citizenship. Those who were party to the original compact were clearly citizens, that is, adults who were present in the new nation on July 4, 1776, and who gave active support to the break with Britain. Others who swore "an oath of fidelity" to one of the several states in the next dozen years or so were also citizens. And still others had acquired that status by tacit consent or acquiescence (such as coming of age after 1776), by birth and inheritance, and by "adoption" (naturalization).

Colonial Americans who on July 4, 1776, were orphans less than twenty-one years of age, Ramsay argued, were still British subjects unless they had subsequently taken an oath to a state or had been naturalized. Because no one could say whether their parents would have been Tory or Patriot, they could not claim citizenship merely by the fact of birth on what was now American soil. Pointing to little-noticed provisions in the Constitution, he stressed that U.S. citizenship did not exist before July 4, 1776. That document required members of the House of Representatives to have been citizens for seven years before their election and Senators to have been citizens for nine, but the President (only to be an individual who was a citizen at the time of the adoption of the Constitution or a natural-born citizen, not a naturalized citizen, a barrier which still exists) had to have been "a Resident within the United States" for fourteen years.

David Ramsay, the noted South Carolina historian, was serving as a member of the State House of Representatives when he wrote his famous publication.

It is readily apparent that any revolution gives rise to numerous dilemmas concerning citizenship, the most notable being: Where does one's allegiance lie? Citizenship is, after all, merely one of several obligations. An individual also has ties to family, church, locality, region, and the old regime, all of which may seem more important than the ones to an amorphus and perhaps ineffective, embryonic national entity. Yet the greatest impact on the nature of citizenship in our own Revolutionary era was the failure of the Founding Fathers to define its scope, thus precipitating an ongoing battle by disfranchised white males, blacks, women, and immigrants to achieve what they termed *full* citizenship.

Throughout the first six decades of the nineteenth century, these groups enjoyed varying success, most of their assaults being directed at state laws that restricted the right of suffrage. As older and newer states vied for population, property qualifications and other regulations restricting some white males from voting disappeared. Also, as territories changed into states, all white residents were welcomed as citizens *en masse*, but the status

Greenwood Leflore, mixed-blood leader of the Choctaws.

of women, blacks, Indians, and other ethnic minorities remained unclear. They sometimes were viewed as citizens, depending on treaty provisions, state laws, and local customs, but they were rarely given the vote. There were occasional exceptions to this. For example. Greenwood Leflore (1800–1865), a mixed-blood Choctaw chieftain who elected to remain in Mississippi when the majority of the tribe moved to the West beginning in 1831, became a U.S. citizen under the terms of the Treaty of Dancing Rabbit Creek. Eventually he became a wealthy planter and served as a member of the Mississippi Senate. But the rest of the Choctaws who remained in Mississippi became outcasts who struggled to survive as squatters on marginal lands unoccupied by whites.

In 1857, the Dred Scott decision shattered any hope for participatory citizenship for blacks. Scott, a slave born in Virginia about 1795, was taken by his owner to free territory and then to slave Missouri. Later Scott sought his freedom on the basis of his prolonged residence in Minnesota. A majority of Supreme Court justices ruled that a black was not a citizen and could not bring suit in federal courts. They went on to state that even if Scott could have sued, he would not have won his freedom since the Missouri Compromise of 1820, which outlawed slavery in much of the Louisiana Purchase, was unconstitutional. Congress, they added, had no power to exclude slavery from the territories. Although this decision hardly caused the Civil War, it did little to calm rough waters and clearly made imperative a definition of citizenship by federal statute.

Actually, this decision of 1857 should not have come as a great surprise. The previous year the Department of State informed a New York City resident that his repeated requests for passports for "eleven colored persons" would not be honored since blacks were not citizens of the United States.

"The question whether free negroes are such citizens is not now presented for the first time, but has repeatedly arisen in the administration of both the National and State governments. In 1821 a controversy arose as to whether free persons of color were citizens of the United States within the intent and meaning of the acts of Congress regulating foreign and coasting trade, so as to be qualified to command vessels; and Mr. Wirt, Attorney-General, decided that they were not, and he moreover held that the words 'Citizens of the United States' were used in the Acts of Congress in the same sense as in the Constitution. This view is also fully sustained in a recent opinion of the present Attorney-General."

Nevertheless, the State Department was willing to issue certificates stating that the eleven blacks were free, native-born, inhabitants of the United States, "and that the Government thereof would regard it to be its duty to protect them if wronged by a foreign Government, while within its jurisdiction for a legal and proper purpose."

Three years after Appomattox the Fourteenth Amendment was ratified. It recognized "all persons born or naturalized in the United States, and subject to the jurisdiction thereof" as citizens of the United States and the state where they lived. Although this amendment implied that only males twenty-one years of age and older (except Indians not taxed) qualified for full citizenship, in 1871 suffrage pioneer Susan B. Anthony and several other women invoked its provisions to cast ballots in an election held in Rochester, New York. They subsequently were indicted by a federal grand jury for voting illegally and, with the aid of the judge, convicted. The judge, while addressing the jury, drew a strict distinction between citizenship and suffrage: all women now were citizens, true, but state law conferred the ballot only upon men. The women refused to pay the fines levied, and at that point the federal government abandoned the proceedings.

The Supreme Court ruled three times in the 1870s on matters relating to women's citizenship. A Missouri woman sued an election official for refusing to let her vote. When the case reached the Supreme Court, the judges ruled that women were not covered by the Fourteenth Amendment, at least for voting rights. A later test, brought by a woman claiming rights under the Fifteenth Amendment, also was disallowed. Although the Amendment did not mention gender, it was deemed to apply only to males. In the same decade, the Supreme Court, following common law, also ruled that married women had no legal existence. This decision was prompted by an audacious "she-lawyer" who sued the Illinois Bar for the right to practice law. Finally, the Nineteenth Amendment, ratified in 1919, gave women the right to vote.

Yet the citizenship status of a few women remained somewhat obscure for three more years. Until 1922 any American woman who married an alien assumed the nationality of her husband. In fact, if he was ineligible for naturalization, this situation persisted until 1931. For the most part, these laws, while unfair, attracted little attention, until prospective voters discovered they actually were foreigners and no longer U.S. citizens.

Margaret Fuller, noted social reformer, journalist, and critic, lost her citizenship by marriage to an Italian nobleman. However, since they perished in a storm on the eve of their return to New York City, the issue of citizenship never arose. President Grant's daughter, Nellie, married an Englishman in 1874; and, when he died twenty-two years later, she returned to live in America. To clear up her legal status, she petitioned Congress to restore her citizenship, a request that was granted in 1898. Ruth Bryan Owen, daughter of William Jennings Bryan, ran into some difficulty as the result of her marriage to a British subject. She and her husband came to America at the close of World War I, and the 1922 law mentioned earlier clearly restored her U.S. citizenship; however, when she won a seat in the House of Representatives six years later, her defeated opponent charged she had not been a citizen for seven years before the election. This claim ultimately was rejected by Congress.

In 1924 all Indians became citizens. Theodore Roosevelt had claimed in 1901 that some 60,000 Indians living apart from their tribes already were U.S. citizens, but the Indian Citizenship Act of 1924 completed the process. However, unlike other minorities, most Indians were more anxious to retain tribal identities than to gain the right to vote. Efforts of those Indians desiring to retain their tribal identities were promoted by Indian Commissioner John Collier in the 1930s.

Several late nineteenth century letters demonstrate the attitude of State Department officials toward the citizenship status of women and Indians:

"Referring to your letter of April 30, asking whether the daughter of a naturalized citizen of the United States who has married an alien may obtain a passport through her father's citizenship, you are informed that, inasmuch as a woman's citizenship follows that of her husband, she is not a citizen of the United States and can not, under the law, receive a passport."

"The woman merges her nationality in that of her husband upon marriage to a foreigner. In case of legal separation, the practice places her in a position similar to that of a minor child, born of foreign parents, who has been adopted by a citizen of the United States, upon reaching majority. The wife may elect whether to preserve the foreign nationality acquired by her marriage, or reacquire her former American citizenship."

Published in *The Wasp,* a humorous weekly from San Francisco, this 1879 cartoon stereotypes what some Americans believed to be "Uncle Sam's Troublesome Bedfellows." These bedfellows include a Mormon polygamist (on the floor), a Chinaman (receiving a kick), an Indian (poking his finger in Uncle Sam's ear), a black, and an Irishman (asleep with a whisky bottle in his arms).

This late nineteenth-century cartoon by Thomas Nast depicts Secretary of the Interior Carl Schurz showing the wonders of the ballot box to a group of Indians visiting Washington. Nast pokes fun at the Secretary's opposition to extending political rights to the Indians before their "civilization." The posters hanging on the wall portray stereotypes of other ethnic groups that had been "civilized" by the ballot. Not until 1924, however, did Congress grant citizenship to all Indians, and even then several states continued to deny suffrage to the Indians until the 1960s when new legislation on civil rights was enforced.

"I have to acknowledge the receipt of your No. 506, of the 11th ultimo, reporting the application of Humper Nespar, or Wadded Moccasin, a Sioux Indian, for a passport."

"In reply, I have to say that Indians are not citizens of the United States by reason of birth within its limits. Neither are our *general* naturalization laws applicable to them, but various Indian tribes have been naturalized by *special* acts of Congress."

———

Even Asiatics, despite the Chinese Exclusion Act of 1882, scored a few victories. Wong Kim Ark, a laborer born to Chinese parents who lived in San Francisco and enjoyed dual citizenship, made a trip to China in the early 1890s to visit relatives. On his return, federal officials barred his reentry. This case eventually reached the Supreme Court in 1898, the justices ruling in Wong's favor: he was a native-born U.S. citizen and could not be deported or excluded from his homeland.

Despite the struggle of disfranchised white males, blacks, and women to be recognized as full-fledged citizens, citizenship by naturalization remains a dramatic experience. In the late nineteenth and early twentieth centuries, this process of Americanization reached its peak as millions of immigrants studied manuals designed to prepare them for citizenship. These volumes usually included a brief, simplistic overview of American history and government and a list of questions that were frequently asked before one could swear an oath of allegiance to the United States of America: What is a republic? What is the meaning of citizenship? How are bills passed in Congress? Who is the lieutenant-governor of this state? What did John Cabot do? How do presidential electors vote? Who can become a Senator?

During World War I whole units of servicemen were naturalized, 1500 U.S. Navy men in one New York ceremony, for example. Two decades later, although immigration laws were more strict, thousands of aliens serving in the armed forces once more became American citizens.

Today, as far as the responsibility of the federal government is concerned, little difference exists between citizens and so-called "nationals." The Immigration and Nationality Act of July 27, 1952, designates as "nationals" both citizens and those who owe permanent allegiance to the United States. Inhabitants of American Samoa are the only remaining noncitizen nationals. They enjoy diplomatic protection and can enter the United States freely, but have no political rights.

Some efforts have been made in recent decades to cancel U.S. citizenship under certain conditions, especially the citizenship of naturalized persons who live overseas for extended periods. Anyone who votes in a foreign election, serves a foreign power, goes outside of the United States to avoid the draft, or commits treason or desertion runs considerable risk; however, for the most part, the Supreme Court has declined to approve congressional legislation depriving both native-born and naturalized individuals of their citizenship.

The cautious, restrained wording of the Constitution as written in 1787 is a far cry from the amendments of 1868, 1919, and 1971 extending the right of suffrage to blacks, women, and eighteen-year-olds. For some, it has been a long, hard struggle; for others, the right to vote, if that is what full citizenship means, came easily indeed. If the road had been harder, they perhaps would value this prize more highly.

SELECTED
READINGS

Black Americans*

Ira Berlin, *Slaves without Masters: The Free Negro in the Antebellum South* (1975)

James H. Dormon and Robert Jones, *The Afro-American Experience: A Cultural History Through Emancipation* (1974)

Herbert G. Gutman, *The Black Family in Slavery and Freedom, 1750–1925* (1976)

James O. Horton and Lois R. Horton, *Black Bostonians: Family Life and Community Struggle in the Antebellum North* (1979)

Lawrence W. Levine, *Black Culture and Black Consciousness: Afro-American Folk Thought From Slavery to Freedom* (1977)

Leon F. Litwack, *North of Slavery: The Negro in the Free States, 1790–1860* (1961)

George P. Rawick, *From Sundown to Sunup: The Making of the Black Community* (1972)

Richard C. Wade, *Slavery in the Cities: The South, 1820–1860* (1964)

*(See other studies mentioned in this chapter)

Indians and Indian Removal

Robert F. Berkhofer, Jr., *The White Man's Indian* (1978)

Grant Foreman, *Indian Removal: The Emigration of the Five Civilized Tribes of Indians* (new ed., 1953)

Donald Jackson, ed., *Black Hawk: An Autobiography* (1964)

Jack F. Kilpatrick, *Sequoyah of Earth & Intellect* (1965)

Gary E. Moulton, *John Ross: Cherokee Chief* (1978)

Francis P. Prucha, *American Indian Policy in the Formative Years: The Trade and Intercourse Acts, 1790-1834* (1962)

Ronald N. Satz, *American Indian Policy in the Jacksonian Era* (1975)

Robert A. Trennert, Jr., *Alternative to Extinction: Federal Indian Policy and the Beginnings of the Reservation System, 1846–1851* (1975)

Glen Tucker, Tecumseh: *Vision of Glory* (1956)

Dale Van Every, *Disinherited: The Lost Birthright of the American Indian* (1966)

Women and Women's Rights

Nancy F. Cott, *The Bonds of Womanhood: "Woman's Sphere" in New England, 1780–1835* (1977)

Ann Douglas, *The Feminization of American Culture* (1977)

Ellen C. Dubois, *Feminism and Suffrage: The Emergence of an Independent Women's Movement in America 1848–1869* (1978)

Eleanor Flexner, *Century of Struggle: The Woman's Rights Movement in the United States* (rev. ed., 1975)

Blance Hersch, *The Slavery of Sex* (1980)

Katharine D. Lumpkin, *The Emancipation of Angelina Grimké* (1974)

Anne Firor Scott, *The Southern Lady: From Pedestal to Politics, 1830–1930* (1970)

Barbara Welter, *Dimity Convictions: The American Woman in the Nineteenth Century* (1976)

Immigrants and Nativism

Ray Allen Billington, *The Protestant Crusade, 1800–1860: A Study of the Origins of American Nativism* (1938)

Kathleen N. Conzen, *Immigrant Milwaukee, 1836–1860: Accommodation and Community in a Frontier City* (1976)

Michael Feldberg, *The Philadelphia Riots of 1844: A Study in Ethnic Conflict* (1975)

Oscar Handlin, *Boston's Immigrants: A Study of Acculturation* (revised and enlarged ed., 1959)

Marcus L. Hansen, *The Atlantic Migration, 1607–1860: A History of the Continuing Settlement of the United States* (1940)

Leon A. Jick, *The Americanization of the Synagogue, 1820–1870* (1976)

Ira M. Leonard and Robert D. Parmet, *American Nativism, 1830–1860* (1971)

Carl F. Wittke, *Refugees of Revolution: The German Forty-Eighters in America* (1952)

CHAPTER 10
RELIGION, REFORM, AND UTOPIANISM

TIMELINE

1800
Second Great Awakening in Kentucky and Tennessee

1817
Organization of American Colonization Society

1819
Elihu Embree begins publication of *The Manumission Intelligencer*

1821
Kentucky outlaws imprisonment for debt

1825
New York establishes reform school for juvenile delinquents

1825
Robert Owen founds New Harmony

1826
American Society for Promotion of Temperance formed

1826
Charles G. Finney begins revival campaign in upstate New York

1828
American Peace Society established

1830
Joseph Smith founds the Mormon Church

1833
American Anti-Slavery Society organized

1836
John Humphrey Noyes forms Oneida Community

1836
Georgia Female College, the first woman's college, founded

1837
Elijah P. Lovejoy killed in Alton, Illinois

1837
Horace Mann becomes Secretary of the Massachusetts Board of Education

1841
Brook Farm organized

1843
Dorothea Dix exposes treatment of mentally ill

1843
Racial segregation on trains in Massachusetts ends

1846
Maine adopts Prohibition

1847
Frederick Douglass begins publication of *The North Star*

Tiger '66

CHAPTER OUTLINE

During the decades from 1820 to 1850, the United States was caught up in a frantic wave of reform inspired by the near universal conviction that on this continent, free from the decayed, restraining hand of Europe, Americans could create a perfect civilization, at least something more perfect than what they and their forefathers had known in the Old World. Political independence seemed assured and the inhabitants of the republic could now get on with "the great experiment." The preamble to the Constitution, before it digressed into a mundane catalog of facts detailing how the machinery of government would work, held out the hope of "a more perfect Union," justice, domestic tranquility, and "the Blessings of Liberty." Paramount among those blessings was the exhilarating opportunity to reshape society according to one's own wishes.

Different people had different designs and the result was a hodgepodge of contradictions that did anything but "insure domestic Tranquility." For example, hostility towards blacks, immigrants, Indians, and some women reformers was widespread because either their presence or programs conflicted with what many Americans thought a "perfect" society should be. At the same time, millions were susceptible to evangelical appeals that fed one of the greatest outbursts of humanitarian reform our nation has ever known.

Why America should have experienced a great wave of humanitarian concern at this time is far from clear, but surely one of the causes was the traumatic social change brought about by industrialization. Urbanization and the growth of factories and an industrial economy were generating very visible extremes in wealth and poverty, attracting droves of immigrants not easily assimilated and separating people not only from the soil but also from one another. These departures from traditional American living patterns only served to point up contradictions between practices and ideals. Despite the fact that the agrarian idealism of Thomas Jefferson was still widely accepted and the greater part of the population was still rural and self-employed, in the years preceding the Civil War America was developing an industrial base. Even though America did not emerge as an industrial power until the late nineteenth century, the social strains and stresses resulting from immigration, urbanization, and industrialization were clearly visible from the 1830s on.

Rather than reacting to these social changes by seeking political and institutional solutions, Americans responded with their hearts. While Europe was witnessing the birth of socialist parties calling for radical reform or even revolution, the United States (which had already had its Revolution) was undergoing a great revival of religion. Even utopian experiments that disavowed traditional religion harbored a guiding philosophy that was unmistakably religious in that it depended upon awakening the individual conscience rather than on engineering large social movements.

The most prevalent single idea in antebellum America was that of progress, which had its roots in the Enlightenment philosophy of natural rights. This concept was confirmed by Romanticism, an enthusiastic mood that fused easily with the exuberant optimism of the period. Romanticism, a major development in European thought during the first half of the nineteenth century, stressed that the free individual could move toward the comprehension of the eternal truths and translate them into action. Evangelical Protestantism, with its emphasis on the free will of the individual and salvation for all believers, helped to promote both confident nationalism and an all-pervasive spirit of reform that characterized these decades.

Religion

That religion was able to enter into so many aspects of American life is at least partially attributable to a new direction in theology. Calvinism, the prevailing orientation of the New England Puritans and of many other Protestant sects in the seventeenth and eighteenth centuries, preached a stern, unrelenting determinism—or, more exactly, a fatalism. According to Puritan theology, God had predestined—even before people were born—who would be saved and who would be damned. During the eighteenth century, however, Calvinism was challenged by beliefs more in keeping with the views and hopes of an optimistic people imbued with Enlightenment principles and encouraged by scientific progress. One such challenge was Deism, the belief that God created the universe as a rational, self-perpetuating system. Humanity was gifted with reason, and if it behaved in an enlightened fashion, society would reward virtue.

The Deists rejected the notion of a personal God who answers prayers, watches over individuals, and intervenes in human affairs. Because the deity proposed by this philosophy seemed impersonal, Deism did not attract many people besides intellectuals. More widespread was Arminian theology, which stressed a person's ability to achieve salvation and, together with Deism, argued that performing good works was "the most acceptable service of God."

Revivalism

Just as America had been seized in the 1730s by a revivalist spirit, in the same way the country experienced a Second Great Awakening that began in 1800 in a series of camp meetings (open-air religious convocations) held in Kentucky and Tennessee. The new wave of revivalism lasted until 1837, and before it ran its course exerted a mighty impact on antebellum life.

About the time this movement began, seven religious bodies dominated the American scene, all of them having been battered to some extent by disestablishment, war, and the fast pace of events since 1775. These were (in order of approximate numerical strength) the Congregationalists, Presbyterians, Episcopalians, Methodists, Baptists, Quakers, and Roman Catholics. The Congregationalists and Presbyterians were virtually one faith; the Methodists, a society within the Episcopal fold until 1784. The latter, stunned by disestablishment and loss of the Methodists, failed to set up churches in new areas. In 1820, for example, there was no Episcopal minister in Indiana, Tennessee, Illinois, or Missouri, and probably none in any territory either.

At the outset of the Second Great Awakening, the Congregationalists and Presbyterians were the leading religious bodies in the United States, but because of doctrine, internal disputes, and poor leadership, neither reaped substantial benefits from the fervor that ensued. The Congregationalists tended to sit self-satisfied in New England, and the Presbyterians, although they certainly tried to convert the frontier, were hampered by their rejection of emotionalism, insistence upon an educated clergy, and general unwillingness to adapt to the needs of the backwoodsman and his family.

Quaker scorn of slavery meant the Friends had little following in the South, and, like the Congregationalists, they made only feeble efforts to follow

The Smithsonian Institution.

Outdoor revivals such as this Methodist camp meeting were emotional affairs led by preachers who emphasized personal redemption.

the course of migration westward. The Roman Catholics, in addition to traditional bases of strength in Maryland and various port cities, developed surprising strength in Kentucky (nineteen churches with 10,000 faithful in 1815), picked up hundreds of French and Spanish believers with the purchase of Louisiana, and gained even more adherents with the increasing flow of migration from Ireland and Germany.

Yet the two faiths that profited most from revivalism and grew by leaps and bounds in all parts of the country were the Methodists and Baptists. The key to the success of the Methodists, the leading religious body at mid-century (1.2 million), was the circuit rider. Close behind (with 750,000) were the Baptists who, free of ecclesiastical machinery, could establish a church almost at will and present God and Jesus Christ in down-to-earth terms that the common person could understand.

The most powerful revivalist of the Second Great Awakening was Charles Grandison Finney. Wherever he preached or spoke, whether from his pulpit in New York's Broadway Tabernacle or later from his office as president of Oberlin College in Ohio, he inspired religious enthusiasm. According to another evangelist, Lyman Beecher, some 100,000 Americans joined churches in 1831 alone, and Finney was the man who moved many of them to repent. The most intense area of religious zeal was upstate New York, especially during Finney's revival campaigns there in 1826 and 1831.

Finney, like other evangelists, stressed that redemption was possible for everyone. By repenting of past sins and believing in Jesus Christ, salvation could be secured. Finney rejected Calvinist determinism and advocated the idea that both sin and salvation are freely chosen behavior. By 1831, Finney had welded his evangelism to the general reform movement in America as he dwelt upon the sins of men in society rather than the specific sins

Religion, Reform, and Utopianism

Charles Grandison Finney was an immensely successful revivalist whose emphasis on benevolence was a factor in shaping the reform spirit in antebellum America.

of the men themselves. This concept of social responsibility or moral stewardship would have a direct impact on the reform impulse of the ensuing years.

Benevolent Societies

Since religion is part of the life of almost every element in society, it cannot be said to represent any one set of interests alone. Indeed, the religious impulse that eventually gave rise to reform initially manifested itself as a politically and socially conservative movement. Between the War of 1812 and 1830, conservative moral reformers established a number of benevolent societies.

Among these benevolent associations were the American Education Society, founded in Boston in 1815 to subsidize the education of future ministers, and the American Bible Society, which in 1816 began distributing millions of copies of the Bible throughout the nation. In 1824 the American Sun-

day School Union was established in Philadelphia to send missionaries to set up schools; between 1825 and 1860 the American Tract Society issued some 200 million religious books and pamphlets; and in 1826 the American Home Missionary Society began to subsidize poor congregations, giving them funds with which to pay their pastors. The purpose of all these societies was to perpetuate established interpretations of morality and decency in a period of great social change. The moral tenets of Christianity somehow would "civilize" and subdue the West and pacify the urban poor, seething with unrest.

Lay officers of these societies were men of rising social and economic station such as industrialist Anson G. Phelps (1781–1853), whose firm was involved in manufacturing, railroads, and copper and iron mining, and Theodore Frelinghuysen (1787–1862), a New Jersey lawyer who served as United States Senator from 1829 to 1835 and delivered a six-hour speech condemning the Indian Removal Bill in 1830. His objections to the bill earned him the nickname, "Christian Statesman." From 1846 until his death in 1862, he was president of the American Bible Society, and at other times he served as an officer of the American Tract Society, the American Sunday School Union, and the American Temperance Union.

Unitarianism

During the 1820s and 1830s the bulwark of Calvinism was thoroughly dismantled by a little man who was an invalid all his life. William Ellery Channing (1780–1842) may have been sickly in body, but his mind reshaped American theology. Born in Rhode Island, raised by stern Calvinist parents, and educated at Harvard, Channing became the minister of Boston's Federal Street Congregation in 1803. From his pulpit he preached a new doctrine that human beings had free will and were rational ("God has given us a rational nature and will call us to account for it," he said). At the same time, he retained the idea of a personal God, the authority of Scripture, and the existence of miracles.

Channing, however, was more impressive for the spirit of his beliefs than for his theological innovations. Squarely on the side of the ordinary citizen, Channing created a religion of optimism and common sense for the average American. He was father of Unitarianism (so-called because he and his followers rejected the belief in the Trinity as a concept not justified by Scripture and impossible to understand). Although the Unitarian denomination never became numerous, it exerted a great influence on such New England thinkers as Ralph Waldo Emerson and ultimately on a vast Christian public. The main thrust of Channing's religion was its emphasis on man's divine nature, his resemblance to his maker. Even God was refashioned from a stern Puritan patriarch into a true nineteenth-century Democrat.

Transcendentalism and Perfectionism

Unitarianism was, however, too much the faith of established, well-to-do New Englanders to reach the masses. But its tenets reached a broader audience through a philosophical movement known as Transcendentalism.

The leader of Transcendentalism was Ralph Waldo Emerson (1803–1882), the descendant of a long line of ministers who himself served the Second Church of Boston until 1832, when he resigned because he felt he could no longer administer the bread and the wine in the Lord's Supper—articles of faith in which he no longer believed.

Emerson was thirty when he traveled to England and became a friend of the historian Thomas Carlyle, the poet Samuel Taylor Coleridge (who had introduced the English to German idealism), and the poet William Wordsworth. His contact with English Romanticism (and indirectly with German philosophy) gave him a new approach to nature. When he returned to Boston, Emerson made public addresses in which he advanced the Romantic idea that human beings are at the center of the world, godlike creatures who can fully realize their divinity by immersing themselves in lessons to be drawn from nature. In the place of organized religion, he exalted instinct, insight, and intuition. Transcendentalism stressed that the mind and soul can go beyond all intellectual limitations and grasp intuitively the realities of life. The Transcendentalists assumed that human nature is perfectible—and this stand naturally linked them to the reform movement. In the 1840s Emerson allied himself (though with reservations) with the abolitionists; he thought slaves must elevate themselves and doubted whether this was possible. But, by the late 1850s his antislavery position was no longer equivocal, and Emerson openly championed emancipation.

The Transcendentalists with whom Emerson associated included George Ripley, Bronson Alcott,

National Archives.
Ralph Waldo Emerson, the Leader of Transcendentalism.

James Russell Lowell, Henry David Thoreau, Nathaniel Hawthorne, and Margaret Fuller. These Transcendentalists were experimenters whose search for truth and reality led them to challenge the legitimacy of such institutions as slavery, education, property rights, and the position of women. (One of the most striking Transcendentalists was Margaret Fuller whose brilliant career is discussed in a biographical sketch in this chapter.)

Humanitarian Reform

While benevolent societies used reform and religion as a means of social control, as a way of preserving the status quo, a more dynamic and liberal reform movement sought to change American society radically for the better. These reformers had a high, undauntable sense of optimism. They were certain that America's mission was to set a moral example for the rest of the world, and they were eager to make that example as glowing as possible. Emerson asked, "What is man born for, but to be a Reformer, a Remaker of what man has made?" and many of his fellow Americans could only agree with this sentiment. Science, technology, and democracy were all American pursuits that were prospering and that suggested progress was boundless. The great rebirth of religious fervor contributed to the growing sense that human nature was perfectible; if only the conscience of the sinner could be awakened, he or she could be made to reform. Once saved, the sinner could demonstrate salvation by performing good works.

The Temperance Movement

One of the most energetic reform activities in the antebellum period was the temperance movement (not necessarily total abstinence from all alcoholic intake). The crusade against "ardent spirits" was launched in the pulpit by evangelists who warned that excessive drinking was sinful. Others argued that drinking made voters unsuited for choosing their leaders wisely.

The most popular argument against drink was that it directly contributed to poverty. Not only did alcoholism keep the urban worker in his wretched state, incapable of rising in the world and barely retaining his miserable job, but it also imposed great suffering on his family. Employers complained of frequent absenteeism and accidents owing to liquor. Much of the violence of the cities, temperance workers argued, could be attributed to drunkenness.

Modern commentators on the temperance movement sometimes discuss it with a smirk, as though it were merely an outgrowth of "Victorian" prudishness. But a closer look reveals that the problem of heavy drinking was immense in eighteenth and early nineteenth-century America. Early U.S. census reports estimate that in 1792 the per capita consumption of spirits was 2.5 gallons a year; by 1823, the figure had risen to 7.5 gallons. Almost every grocery store sold beer or liquor, and the 1810 census revealed there were 14,000 distilleries in the country, producing some 25 million gallons of liquor every year, for which the public spent about $12 million—more than the total budget of the federal government.

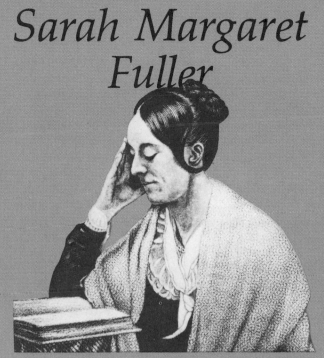

Sarah Margaret Fuller

(1810–1850)

Journalist, critic, social reformer, Margaret Fuller was a contradictory person whose forceful character had considerable impact upon her generation. She was born into a well-to-do Boston household with a strong Puritan heritage. Her father, a state politician and later a congressman, took full charge of her education, while her mother cared for the other children. When six-year-old Sarah (she later dropped that name) showed ability, she began to read Latin and by the age of eight was reading Shakespeare and Cervantes as well. Two years at boarding school turned out to be disastrous, and Margaret subsequently blamed the regimen forced upon her as a child for chronic ill health and fits of hysteria. Later, she observed that children should not read too early and thus through the printed word acquire knowledge predating actual experience.

By the time Fuller was twenty-five, she was associating with Channing, Emerson, Thoreau, and other Boston intellectuals and, like them, often was the butt of sly jokes concerning Transcendentalism and the experimental Brook Farm. Following several years as teacher and translator, from 1839 to 1844 she conducted her famous "conversation" classes for bright, rich young ladies characterized by one observer as "gorgeous pedants." Yet the "conversations" supplied material for Fuller's *Women in the Nineteenth Century* (1845), a work encompassing aspects of the women's movement but in phrases too philosophical for militants of that era. Nevertheless, through this publication she became known as one of the leading feminists of the period.

For a brief period Fuller helped edit the *Dial*, the mouthpiece of the Transcendentalists. George Ripley and Emerson were coeditors, but she seems to have done most of the work. She then moved on to New York City for two years as a literary critic on Horace Greeley's *Tribune*. In this role Fuller made foes but performed well, even brilliantly. She sailed for Europe in the summer of 1846 to meet and talk with leading literary figures and had some success in England and France. Letters describing visits with Carlyle, Wordsworth, George Sand, and others appeared in the *Tribune*.

In Italy, Fuller became deeply involved with both revolution and romance, a fateful combination. There she met Angelo Ossoli (an officer in the service of the republican insurgent Giuseppe Mazzini), who was handsome, penniless, and ten years younger than she. But they fell in love, had a son (born in September 1848), and at some undisclosed date were married, thus making her the Marquesa Ossoli. In mid-1849 the French army suppressed Mazzini's uprising, and the Marquesa—shocked by this turn of events—spent the next few months writing that revolution's history.

In May 1850 the Ossolis sailed for America on an ill-fated voyage that ended in tragedy. The captain died of smallpox and Margaret's child nearly succumbed to the dreaded disease. Then, on the eve of their arrival in New York, the ship was wrecked in a storm off Fire Island, and the entire family perished. The child's body was recovered, but those of his parents and the manuscript describing the revolution were never seen again.

Margaret Fuller was a puzzle to her contemporaries and remains something of an enigma. Virtually an invalid, nevertheless she did the editorial work of three people and in Rome left her son with a nurse to participate in a rebellion. Eccentric and outspoken, she easily made enemies. Yet she obviously was an accomplished intellectual who could hold her own with the best minds of her day. More clearly than many others agitating for women's rights, she saw the full scope of the movement they espoused.

Why Americans drank so much is a question that has elicited many theories. Liquor was, first of all, cheap and plentiful; in the early days of the West, for instance, whiskey was used as currency and even taxes and the salaries of ministers were paid in liquor. In rural areas many farmers ran stills, which helped to fend off boredom, fatigue, and loneliness. In the cities the poverty and confusion of people newly arrived from American farms or from Europe could be forgotten, at least for a moment, in drink. Also, drinking was often a cultural tradition, one means of keeping alive "old ways." The problem was that imbibing was done on a massive scale, and each group—the Irish, Germans, and so on—had their favorite drinks and ingrained social habits that rivals often found offensive and crude.

To reformers, this cause-and-effect pattern seemed strange; in their eyes liquor was not a symptom of poverty but rather the disease that created it. During the antebellum period, Americans were not equipped conceptually to see poverty as anything but the result of vice or laziness on the part of the underprivileged; to be poor was, in some sense, to be immoral. For the temperance worker liquor—rather than low wages, unemployment, or lack of opportunity—was the cause of urban poverty.

Temperance societies sprang up across the country, all of them working hard to convince Americans to sign the pledge against drinking. As early as 1826 a broader society, known as the American Society for the Promotion of Temperance, was formed in Boston. It was a dynamic group that sent lecturers throughout the country, published numerous pamphlets, placed stories in newspapers, and awarded prizes for the best temperance essays. By 1835, 3,000 ministers had signed a pledge promising to abstain altogether from liquor; with the aid of a large number of women supporters, schoolteachers, and hundreds of doctors, these ministers, in turn, campaigned for the cause.

In 1836 the first national convention of the American Temperance Union, a federation of temperance societies, met, and it was during this convocation that the movement split into two factions. The controversy was over how to define temperance. The majority of the delegates opposed only the consumption of hard liquor or "ardent spirits"; but they stopped short of demanding total abstinence. A radical minority (the "ultras") wished to broaden the abstinence pledge to include malt and

The *Drunkard's Progress,* a lithograph published in 1846, when Neal Dow was crusading for prohibition.

fermented liquors, even wine taken during communion. This group supported legislative action to ban the production and retailing of all alcoholic beverages and introduced a resolution that "the traffic in ardent spirits, as a drink, is *morally wrong;* and that the inhabitants of cities, towns, and other local communities, should be permitted by law to prohibit the said traffic within their respective jurisdictions."

Several states experimented with regulating intoxicants. Enthusiasm for Prohibition ran especially high in Maine; under the leadership of Neal Dow (see the accompanying biographical sketch), that state passed the first comprehensive statewide prohibition act in 1846. A year earlier, New York had approved a bill giving local communities the option to forbid the sale of alcohol. Soon five-sixths of the state voted against licensing liquor stores, although the communities rescinded their hasty action in 1847. In 1852 the legislatures of Vermont and Rhode Island enacted statewide prohibition. Michigan became dry in 1853; Connecticut and New York in 1854; and New Hampshire, Tennessee, Delaware, Illinois, Indiana, Iowa, and Wisconsin by 1855. By the end of the 1850s, thirteen states had approved prohibition legislation. The statutes on the books were flagrantly ignored, however, and the sale of hard liquor continued in scores of communities. Also, as numerous states learned, one group of legislators could quickly undo the work of their predecessors. By 1868, only Maine still retained its law establishing statewide Prohibition.

Wards of the State

One of the most significant areas of reform in the antebellum period was the movement to ameliorate the conditions of social offenders, paupers, deaf-mutes, the blind, the insane, and the retarded. The fervent belief of the humanitarian reformers that human beings were basically good and rational except when corrupted by evil institutions and a bad environment produced dramatic innovations in the treatment of prisoners, delinquents, dependent children, and other wards of the state.

Penal reform was influenced by the idea that human beings were made antisocial by the society about them. Rather than being born criminal, offenders learned to be that way by imitating bad

Neal Dow

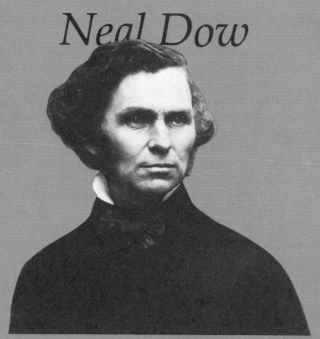

1804–1897

The "Napoleon of Temperance," father of the Maine Law, and a leading citizen of his native Portland for several decades, Neal Dow was a well-to-do businessman and landowner. Dow believed that the world was on the verge of anarchy and that it was necessary to check individual license for the sake of social order. To stem this tide of evil, he waged an unending campaign against liquor and spirits in all forms, tobacco, slavery, and failure to observe the Sabbath in proper fashion. Temperance, however, was his special crusade, and it was an ongoing battle because no legislation, no matter how contrived, could be properly enforced if local authorities winked at bootleggers and "blind tigers" (illicit saloons). During Dow's long life, most Maine residents undoubtedly endorsed his views, but lumberjacks piling into brawling cities such as Bangor after a season in the woods and sailors ashore for a few hours of fun made a mockery of most efforts to regulate the sale of whiskey, rum, and beer.

Dow, born into a family of English-Quaker descent, wanted to be a lawyer, but after basic academic schooling he entered his father's tanning business. A short, alert man (5 ft. 6 in.), Dow soon was married, raising a family, and in the thick of civic affairs; and, as his real estate investments grew, he devoted more and more time to thwarting Demon Rum. Soon at the center of controversy, Dow took boxing lessons to protect himself.

In 1846 Maine passed an antiliquor law that authorities were unable or unwilling to enforce. Five years later, as mayor of Portland, Dow engineered more stringent measures at both local and state levels. These moves won him national, even international attention as the prime spokesman for temperance.

During the Civil War, Dow became a colonel in the Maine Volunteers, was twice wounded, and was captured while recuperating behind Union lines. Eventually he was exchanged for Robert E. Lee's nephew, Fitzhugh Lee, later governor of Virginia. With peace, Dow resumed the liquor fight, running for President on the Prohibition party ticket in 1880.

A spirited campaigner almost until his death, Neal Dow wrote extensively and accumulated a fine library. His battles against evil were waged on many fronts; even celebrities who were guests in his home had to conform to his views. In 1885, for example, neighbors watched with amusement as the Reverend Phillips Brooks leaned far out of a bedroom window to puff contentedly, if precariously, on a huge cigar.

examples. In the eighteenth century (and well into the nineteenth) prisoners were confined in large groups, men and women together, young and old, debtors with hardened criminals. This mixture allowed confirmed wrongdoers to corrupt first offenders. The theory of solitary confinement (considered humane in the nineteenth century, though today most people regard it as cruel) attempted to correct this.

In New York state the prison that opened at Auburn in 1816 confined prisoners in tiny cells at night but gathered them by day in general workshops—or hired them out as contract labor. This contract labor arrangement turned the prison into a paying concern; in 1829 its operating expenses were about $34,000, but its receipts were nearly $40,000. Profits were given to prisoners when their sentences were up in order to encourage them to enter an honest occupation. Life at Auburn was harsh indeed. Convicts had to remain silent at all times, shuffle to and from work with one hand on the shoulder of the person in front of them, and risk flogging for even the most minor violation. Isolated cells were introduced in 1829 in the construction of Pennsylvania's Eastern State Penitentiary just outside Philadelphia. These two systems—inmate silence and separate confinement—were widely imitated in other states, but by midcentury the Auburn method of silence had triumphed over that of Pennsylvania.

Prison reform naturally led to the notion that juvenile offenders might be better treated in correctional institutions. Reform schools were started in which an equal emphasis was placed on education and moral rehabilitation. New York took the lead and built the New York House of Refuge in 1825. In the next few years, other areas of the Northeast established institutions for juvenile delinquents (in 1847 Massachusetts started the first home for girls). By 1850 Americans generally accepted the principle that a youthful offender should be a ward of the state.

Imprisonment for debt also came under attack, especially after the depression in 1819 sent many new debtors to jail. In 1816, even before the panic, there were almost two thousand imprisoned debtors in New York alone, half of them confined for debts of less than $50. Imprisoning debtors was not only cruel but also futile and self-defeating, since in jail the debtor could not earn the money necessary for paying his creditors. In effect, debtors' prisons held people for ransom: some relative usu-

ally came forward and paid the debt so an individual could be released.

In 1817 New York passed a law making $25 the lowest amount for which a debtor could be sentenced. Other states imitated New York, some of them adding clauses stipulating that women could not be imprisoned for any amount of indebtedness. In 1821 Kentucky became the first state to abolish imprisonment for debt altogether. And within two decades it was eliminated from the statute books of almost all of the states.

The mentally ill also received the attention of reformers. In fact, interest in the treatment of the insane grew out of prison reform, since the mentally ill were often incarcerated with prisoners. Quakers opened the first asylum to experiment with more humane forms of treatment in Philadelphia in 1817. In 1836 New York built a state lunatic asylum at Utica to house insane patients formerly lodged in almshouses and jails.

But as late as 1841, most of the insane in America still were brutally neglected and mistreated. Large numbers were housed in cages, jail cells, poorhouses, and even in outhouses. After a chance visit to the women's division of the House of Correction in East Cambridge, Massachusetts, Dorothea Dix (1802–1887), a schoolteacher, was so moved by the spectacle of suffering she observed that she resolved to conduct an investigation of the plight of the insane. In 1843 she presented a report of conditions endured by the indigent insane in almshouses and local jails throughout Massachusetts. She declared in blunt tones, "I tell what I have seen," and called attention "to the *present* state of insane persons confined within the Commonwealth, in *cages, closets, cellars, stalls, pens! Chained, naked, beaten with rods, and lashed into obedience!*"

Dix's exposé prompted the Massachusetts legislature to appropriate funds to build a large addition to a hospital for the insane. Her success in that state was followed by similar triumphs in other parts of the country. She was aided in her campaign by Samuel Gridley Howe (1801–1876), one of the great humanitarians of the day. He not only aided Dix but also pioneered in the education of the blind, the deaf-mutes, and the mentally retarded. He instructed blind children in reading with the aid of raised letters—the Braille system of raised dots representing characters, which was invented in France, was not introduced until later in the century—and he taught deaf-mutes to speak rather than to rely exclusively on sign language.

Dorothea Dix, a pioneer in the movement to provide specialized treatment for the insane.

In the 1850s Dix vainly attempted to obtain land from Congress for institutions for the care of the insane. Since land had been given for educational purposes and some citizens thought it should be granted to railroads to promote construction, she believed the federal government might provide for national hospitals as well. The bill passed after a hard fight but was vetoed by President Franklin Pierce, who thought it unwise for the federal government to support the nation's poor and unconstitutional to grant land for such purposes. Only long after the Civil War was her ambition to build such institutions realized.

Prison reform and improvement in the treatment of the afflicted and handicapped reflected the antebellum conviction that every aspect of human existence—from the soul of the sinner to the ravings of the lunatic—could be cured. Christian charity, a belief in perfectibility, and scientific euphoria had come together to usher in an age of unbounded confidence—what has been dubbed "the cult of curability."

Despite this "cult of curability," the general health of the public at large was almost too vast a subject for reformers to tackle. One could perhaps ameliorate specific social wrongs, but most Americans viewed epidemics and disease as facts of daily life which each person had to deal with as best he or she could. Yet by mid-century European research had begun to stir interest in a new science called "sanitation," and hard lessons learned during the Civil War made more and more Americans aware of possible connections between unsanitary living conditions and certain illnesses. (The essay at the end of this chapter, "To The Health of The American People," traces the development of concern for public health in America and growing efforts by local, state, and national agencies in behalf of the well-being of all citizens.)

The Peace Movement

Confidence in the perfectibility of human nature understandably led American reformers to condemn warfare and espouse pacifism. The War of 1812 spawned new pacifists, but a truly organized peace movement emerged only in 1828 when William Ladd (1778–1841), a retired merchant living in Maine, founded the American Peace Society. Although Ladd's enthusiasm was inexhaustible, the peace movement was torn by internal strife after 1837. Two factions arose: one, a forceful minority that condemned all war, recommended nonresistance to violence, and recognized no government as legitimate; and another that simply condemned "offensive" wars. This second faction, for instance, maintained that the uprisings of Indians against white encroachments such as the Seminole War in Florida were justified—in fact, were "defensive" wars that should be applauded.

Although sympathetic to the conditions of American Indians and black slaves in revolt, William Lloyd Garrison (1805–1879) believed in moral suasion rather than force. Garrison, a young man from a broken, poverty-stricken home, served a seven-year apprenticeship on the Newburyport (Mass.) *Herald,* and then moved on to Boston, where he dabbled not only in peace reform, but temperance and abolition as well. The latter eventually became his road to national recognition. By the late 1830s, Garrison advocated absolute nonresistance and total nonparticipation in government. With other radical pacifists, Garrison withdrew from the American Peace Society in 1838 and founded the New England Non-Resistance Society.

Most pacifists, however, remained within the American Peace Society. The entire peace movement, whether preaching nonresistance or simply an end to wars of aggression, was thrown into confusion by the Mexican War, which broke out in 1846. One strong opponent of the war was Charles Sumner (1811–1874) of Massachusetts; he feared the annexation of potential slave territory in the Southwest. In Boston on the Fourth of July, 1845, Sumner had given a rousing oration in which he concluded that "War is utterly and irreconcilably inconsistent with true grandeur."

Shortly thereafter, Elihu Burritt (1810–1879), a blacksmith, who had taught himself Latin, Greek, Hebrew, French, German, Spanish, and Italian, founded the League of Universal Brotherhood in 1846. This man, called "the Learned Blacksmith,"

Chicago Historical Society.
William Lloyd Garrison, pacifist and abolitionist.

became an advocate of international peace after a study of languages and science convinced him that all people are interdependent. He attempted to secure pledges from the members of his League that they would not serve in the military and would not support war in any way. Although Burritt enlisted some 30,000 converts in England, his campaign was a failure in America. By 1850, the peace movement was dying out in the United States. For scores of pacifists the cause of abolition was far more important than the cause of peace, and eventually many reformers (including Garrison) discarded their pacifist sentiments.

Abolitionism

Of all the reform movements of the antebellum period, abolitionism was the most explosive since it threatened the economic basis of the South. Given the widespread belief that progress was unlimited and perfection inevitable, the antislavery movement was only natural. One obstacle, however, always stymied even those most troubled by slavery—what was to be done with the slaves once they were freed? For no matter how sympathetic some whites were to the plight of the slaves, many feared that a large, free black population could not be integrated into American society.

The first Southerners to work actively for emancipation were the Quakers of the Upper South. In 1819 Tennessee Quaker Elihu Embree (1782–1820) began publishing the *Manumission Intelligencer* (later the *Emancipator*), the first periodical in America dedicated exclusively to abolitionism. Other Quakers distributed antislavery literature and organized societies that called for gradual abolition of slavery and an immediate improvement of the lives and fortunes of slaves by repealing laws that forbade whites to educate them. The number of abolition societies grew rapidly in the South. By 1827 three southern states—North Carolina, Tennessee, and Virginia—had more abolition societies than existed in the North. In addition to participating in such societies, Quakers in the South protested slavery by boycotting products made with slave labor and by helping runaway slaves.

Emancipation and abolition sentiment stirred interest in assisting free blacks to return to Africa and resulted, in 1817, in the founding of the American Colonization Society. This organization had its headquarters in Washington and was supported by conservative northern reformers and leading clergy and statesmen from the Upper South. The large, rural free black population of the Upper South posed problems of social control, and the leaders of that region were especially interested in getting rid of free blacks. The organization purchased land in Africa and created the Republic of Liberia ("Land of Freedom") with its capital at Monrovia (named after President Monroe, who supported this colonization plan).

The effort was a failure, however, because transportation to Africa was too costly and significant federal support was not forthcoming. In addition, farmers and fishermen in the Upper South depended on free blacks for labor; plantation owners in the Lower South equated colonization with abolitionism; and, most importantly, free blacks generally opposed the undertaking. Free blacks did more than protest colonization; they organized opposition so tightly that few emigrants could be found. Only a small percentage of free blacks ever supported the plan, most of them recently emancipated slaves who gladly agreed to colonization in return for freedom. Those emigrating to Africa were viewed as "traitors to their race" by opponents of colonization who argued that if these colonists were sincerely concerned with the welfare of blacks, they would work to improve their condition *in* America. As a result, by 1860 only about 15,000 blacks had moved to Liberia under the auspices of the American Colonization Society.

The rise of evangelical religion and the spirit of reform caused abolitionists in the North to abandon a gradual approach and demand an *immediate* end to slavery. This doctrine, called "immediatism," was championed by the most famous abolitionist of all, William Lloyd Garrison. About 1828 Garrison met Benjamin Lundy and the next year began to work with this Quaker on his *Genius for Universal Emancipation*. In 1831 Garrison founded his own paper, the militant *Liberator*, published in Boston.

Garrison told his readers that moderation in the face of such a great sin as slavery was unthinkable. As he put it, "Tell the mother to gradually extricate her babe from the fire into which it has fallen, but urge me not to use moderation in a cause like the present." Garrison's approach, as embodied in the American Anti-Slavery Society, which he helped found in 1833, demanded immediate abolition without compensation on the grounds that, since slavery is immoral, slaveholders should not be rewarded for their sinful behavior. Garrison and his followers opposed colonization in Africa and fought to achieve full equality for blacks within the American social system. And, the Garrisonians pursued these goals with militant determination; Garrison himself announced, "I am earnest—I will not equivocate—I will not excuse—I will not retreat a single inch—AND I WILL BE HEARD."

Garrison's assault, coupled with the shock waves from the Nat Turner rebellion in Virginia in 1831, marks a turning point in this crusade; and,

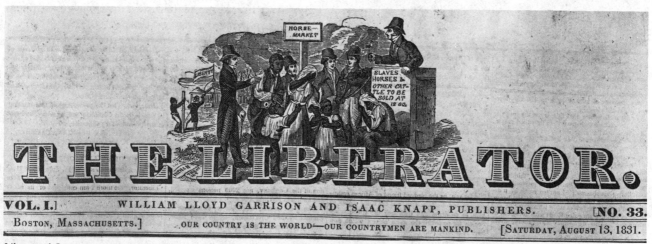

The masthead from *The Liberator*, published in Boston by William Lloyd Garrison. Most of the subscribers to this abolitionist paper were free blacks in the North.

as a result, the 1830s became a watershed in the saga of American reform. Within a decade or so, backed by experienced workers and some 1,350 societies with a quarter of a million members, abolition was a force to be reckoned with; and, as antislavery agitation moved from the local to national level and grew more and more political, it also emerged as *the* reform. Nearly all other movements had to mark time until this great question was resolved. Three main centers of abolitionist strength emerged: New England dominated by Garrison, New York state where wealthy Manhattan philanthropists such as Lewis and Arthur Tappan provided considerable assistance, and Ohio with Lane Seminary and Oberlin College as training grounds for both leaders and workers. Since the movement grew so fast, great diversity as well as conflicts and contradictions were evident. Some societies were segregated and others barred blacks from membership. By no means did all abolitionists subscribe to Garrison's "immediatism," and many were unsure how to play their cards in the political arena.

Thousands of northern whites, who were alarmed by the turmoil of this antislavery protest, detested Garrison and frequently mobbed him when he gave public speeches. His chief supporters were free blacks. Unlike many reformers, Garrison felt at home among blacks and they with him; his demand for black equality was repugnant to the vast majority of northern whites. Even many of his fellow abolitionists were dismayed by Garrison's support of other controversial causes such as women's rights.

The abolitionists used various means, not unlike the tactics of civil rights workers in the 1960s, to fight prejudice. In 1841 and 1842, fifty abolitionists, both white and black, protested segregated trains in Massachusetts by sitting indiscriminately in cars reserved for each race. A boycott of the trains, coupled with a threat of coercive legislation against segregation, led the railroads in that state to desegregate by 1843. Some abolitionists also attempted to integrate churches (most blacks were forced to occupy the "Negro pews" in the rear of churches or in balconies). They believed that the various Christian sects were responsible in large measure for the perpetuation of slavery; if the churches would band together and condemn slavery, they argued, blacks would soon be set free. By the end of the 1840s, abolitionists had integrated hundreds of churches in the North, though many blacks, frustrated by the ill will they continued to

meet, began to organize their own sects and independent houses of worship. Segregation in northern schools also was very widespread, and invariably the blacks had inferior primary schools, if any at all. By the 1840s, however, most of the secondary schools and half of the institutions of higher learning in New England were accepting black students.

Garrison was the most outspoken abolitionist, but not always the most effective, since his techniques often alarmed white Northerners, even those sympathetic to his general views. Charles G. Finney, the well-known evangelist, won many supporters to the cause of antislavery through his religious approach. And Theodore Dwight Weld (1803–1895) may have secured more converts to abolitionism than any other figure of his day. He was a Presbyterian evangelist who first preached with Finney; in 1830 Weld declared war on slavery. After that, not only did he preach abolitionism throughout the West but he also organized a band of seventy agents of the American Anti-Slavery Society who saturated towns with lecturers until a sufficient number of converts were found to form local abolition societies.

Abolitionist propaganda struck Southerners, especially after Nat Turner's revolt in 1831, as a dangerous and inflammatory encouragement of slave uprisings. In the summer of 1835 a mob of whites in Charleston, South Carolina, destroyed sacks of U.S. mail containing abolitionist literature. In response to pressure from southern whites, President Andrew Jackson recommended to Congress in December 1835 that it prohibit circulation through the mail in the South of all "incendiary publications" designed to promote slave insurrections. The measure was not adopted, but from 1836 until the eve of the Civil War, the U.S. Post Office permitted the extralegal censorship of the mails. Local postmasters in the South reviewed and destroyed publications they thought offensive.

In an effort to silence the abolitionists, southern influence in the House of Representatives produced a gag rule, which was in force between 1836 and 1844. Under this rule, petitions against slavery were automatically tabled without debate so that the subject of abolition could not be discussed in Congress. The fight against tabling was led by former President John Quincy Adams, who was now a congressman from his native state of Massachusetts. Converted to the antislavery cause by Theodore Dwight Weld, Adams never was an abolitionist stalwart, but he was greatly concerned over the

Library of Congress.
On November 7, 1837, an antiabolitionist mob in Alton, Illinois, stormed and set fire to the warehouse where Elijah P. Lovejoy stored his newspaper press. Lovejoy was killed as he left the building.

rights of citizens to petition Congress on any subject. And, during those eight years when the gag rule was in force, he presented hundreds of petitions against slavery, many of them from women in various states.

Even in the North, abolitionists found considerable opposition. In 1835, when an English abolitionist canceled a speech in Boston, Garrison spoke in his place. An angry mob of several thousand people, who had come to tar-and-feather the Englishman, vented their anger on Garrison, dragging him through the streets with a rope around his neck. In Alton, Illinois, the abolitionist newspaper editor Elijah P. Lovejoy (1802–1837) defied the townspeople and published fiery articles calling for an immediate end to slavery. When he announced in 1837 the organization of a state branch of the American Anti-Slavery Society, some Alton citizens destroyed his press. Each time he received a new press, mobs wrecked it until on November 7 Lovejoy recruited sixty young abolitionists to protect a newly arrived press. That night an armed mob stormed the warehouse where the press was stored. When the citizens attempted to set the warehouse on fire, Lovejoy rushed out to drive them away and was shot dead.

Although public opinion in both the North and the South pictured abolitionists as advocates of black equality and miscegenation, in fact many abolitionists were not free of a condescending paternalism toward blacks, whom they could describe as a race that was "genial . . . docile . . . in whom the affections rule . . . and who overflow with the exuberance of childhood." Indeed, few white aboli-

tionists treated their black counterparts as equals, and even Garrison once suggested to a former slave, Frederick Douglass, that he talk more like a slave and less like an educated man when addressing white audiences. (Douglass, who probably was the most prominent black in America during the nineteenth century, is the subject of a biographical sketch later in this chapter.)

The North was no utopia for either free blacks or abolitionists, but during the antebellum period, public sympathy for their cause grew, especially after irate Southerners began to suppress freedom of speech and use extralegal efforts to insulate themselves from antislavery sentiments. Many Northerners who were unsympathetic to abolition came to support the movement once the South violated constitutional rights.

Education and Reform

In the early decades of the nineteenth century, American primary and secondary schools generally were expensive, private, and affiliated with particular religious groups. Although New England had a tradition of public education, the reality had declined sadly from the ideal. Schoolhouses were dilapidated, teachers incompetent, textbooks inadequate and scarce, and school terms extremely short (often no more than two months long). Elementary schoolteachers were very poorly paid. The emphasis was on religion, with the Bible central to the curriculum of elementary schools. No state had a public education system that was truly free in 1830, but in the decade that followed, considerable innovation occurred. These changes were engineered by reformers who feared what might happen if voters remained ignorant and illiterate and by factory workers and immigrants who were increasingly eager to have their children learn at least the "three Rs." There also was a general desire on the part of many citizens to have nationalism (as they understood it) taught in order to strengthen the republic.

A turning point in the fight for free, public education was the decision by Massachusetts in 1827 to make tax support of common schools compulsory; seven years later a permanent school fund was established. By 1850, every state in the Union had a similar fund, and all except Arkansas had experimented with permissive tax legislation in one form or another. Instruction and enrollment in public educational facilities differed greatly from state to state and between urban and rural areas within states. In the state of New York, 675,221 students were attending public classrooms, while in Virginia, which had a white population about half as large as that of the Empire State, only a tenth as many students were in public classrooms.

However, at least in theory, the concept of the common school free to all children, one that was supported and controlled by the community where they lived, had won widespread acceptance. All states had made some progress toward this goal, although New England, New York, Pennsylvania, Ohio, and Michigan led the way. Of 3,644,928 individuals enrolled in all of the nation's educational institutions at mid-century, 90 percent were in a public facility of some sort. Nevertheless, only about one school-aged white child out of seven actually was in a classroom.

Educational reform extended not only to children but also to adults throughout the entire community because of the growth of a system of lyceums, which sponsored lectures, debates, scientific demonstrations, and other educational activities. The American Lyceum, founded in 1826 by Josiah Holbrook (1788–1854), was the name of this system, which had branches in every state in the Union within two years after it was established. The lyceum also served as a platform for proponents of the various reform programs.

The leading educational reformer of the day was Horace Mann (1796–1859). A frail youth who grew up in poverty, Mann had a dismal educational background and did not begin to prepare for college until he was twenty. Nevertheless, he posted a brilliant record at Brown University. He became a lawyer and then enjoyed a successful career in the Mas-

Frederick Douglass

ca. 1818–1895

Born into slavery, Douglass was the son of an unknown white man and a slave mother. He grew up on Maryland's Eastern Shore and in Baltimore under the name of Frederick Bailey, which he later changed to Douglass when he managed to escape to the North. At an early age he learned to read, which was forbidden by slave codes, and throughout his life he remained an avid scholar. As an adolescent, he showed his fighting spirit by being so rebellious that one of his masters sent him to a professional slavebreaker; however, six months of continual punishment only strengthened his will to be free.

The first two decades of his life were a frustrating mixture of good and bad treatment at the hands of varous masters. An initial attempt to escape to the North landed Douglass behind bars in the Easton County jail for a short time. However, in 1838 he borrowed the identification papers of a free black sailor whom he met on the docks in Baltimore where he worked as a ship calker and took public transportation to freedom. It was at this point that he changed his name to Douglass to avoid recapture. After settling in Massachusetts and marrying Anna Murray, a free black woman he had met in Baltimore and persuaded to finance his escape, Douglass became active in the abolition movement. Within a short time he became so eloquent a spokesman for the cause of emancipation that the Anti-Slavery Society hired him as a lecturer. Frequently when denouncing slavery before a large group, he would whip off his shirt and turn his back to show the shocked audience that he knew what he was talking about from firsthand experience.

Over six feet tall, endowed with a fine voice and a commanding presence, this ex-slave attracted so much attention that some who heard him began to question his credentials. In 1845, to prove to skeptics that despite his learning and polish he was a fugitive slave, he published his *Narrative*, an autobiographical account of his slave days. The book, however, revealed his true identity. In order to avoid being returned to bondage, Douglass fled to England where he enjoyed great success as an anti-slavery speaker. While abroad, treated as an equal for the first time, he began to think of emancipation as social equality and economic opportunity, not mere physical freedom.

When he returned to the United States, he edited a newspaper, *The North Star*, later called *Frederick Douglass' Newspaper*, published from 1847 to 1863. It was the leading black newspaper of the antebellum period. In its pages Douglass not only espoused abolition but also numerous other causes including women's rights. In fact, Douglass perceived the connection between the plight of women and that of slaves at an early date, and he was among those who encouraged feminists to fight for the vote.

In 1859 Douglass met with John Brown, an association that prompted Virginia authorities to seek his arrest as a co-conspirator in Brown's raid against the Federal arsenal at Harper's Ferry. Although Douglass had refused to join Brown's forces, he fled the country for several months, living first in Canada and then in England, until news of his daughter's death brought him back to the United States.

The outbreak of the Civil War gave him his great opportunity. Slavery, he told all who would listen, was the real cause of the conflict, and soon President Abraham Lincoln was among those listening to his closely reasoned arguments. In their meetings, Douglass urged the President to turn the war into a battle to end slavery. He also encouraged blacks to enlist and helped obtain black recruits, among them his own sons, to fill the ranks of two Massachusetts regiments.

After the war Douglass became a prominent voice in Republican circles and worked hard to obtain voting rights for newly freed blacks. He was rewarded with a variety of federal appointments. He was the first black man to hold the positions of a U.S. marshal (appointed 1877) and Recorder of Deeds (appointed 1881) in the District of Columbia, but the most important office he held was U.S. Minister and Consul General to Haiti (1889–1891). After his first wife died, Douglass married in 1884 his former secretary, who was white. This caused some outcry, but Douglass replied that he was only being impartial: his first wife was the color of his mother; his second, the color of his father. In 1894 Douglass prepared his last great address, "The Lesson of the Hour," an attack on "lynch law" in the South. Less than a month before his death in 1895, a young man asked Douglass what he would advise for a young, black man starting out in life. Douglass' response reflected his life's work: "Agitate! Agitate! Agitate!"

The Museum of the City of New York.

A lyceum lecturer, a meteorologist, and his audience about 1838, in New York City.

Library of Congress.

Horace Mann, nineteenth-century educational reformer.

sachusetts legislature from 1827 to 1837. To everyone's surprise, he suddenly abandoned politics to accept a position as secretary of the state's new board of education. In this capacity, he worked hard to win public support for improvements in the quality of instruction, teachers' salaries, school buildings, and educational materials. As secretary of the Massachusetts state board until 1848, Mann set the minimum school year at six months, persuaded the legislature to put up $2 million for better schoolhouses and equipment, doubled appropriations for public education, and increased the salaries of public school masters by sixty-two percent. During his administration some fifty new high schools were built in Massachusetts.

With the help of Henry Barnard (1811–1900), who later became the first U.S. Commissioner of Education in 1867, Mann successfully campaigned for free public education throughout the North. Teacher training institutes were opened, textbooks were improved, and bills were passed providing for public tax support of the schools. Although Mann envisioned schools as agents promoting social control, he was not willing to see them become sectarian. As a Unitarian, Mann agreed that the Bible could be read in classrooms, but he insisted that it be read without comment. One church after another attacked him for raising a generation of godless children. Mann, however, courageously defended his ideals and triumphed. All the same, the schools of his day were far more moralistic in their instruction than are schools of today. Even ordinary textbooks such as the *McGuffey Reader* carried a message of moral uplift. A typical McGuffey lesson, "The Creator," included several paragraphs concerning the glory and perfection of God and four verses by the English clergyman John Keble, one of which reads as follows:

The glorious sky, embracing all,
Is like the Father's love;
Wherewith encompassed, great and small
In peace and order move.

At the same time that public primary and secondary education was gaining ground, America's colleges and universities began to take the business of learning more seriously as better prepared students applied to enter their classrooms. They raised their standards and, for the first time, became much more than glorified preparatory schools. However, change and expansion in higher education depended directly upon the success of Mann, Barnard, and their associates. The true revolution at that level did not occur until after the Civil War.

A handful of colleges, in keeping with the spirit of the times, opened their doors to women as well as men—or devoted their efforts exclusively to the education of the "fair" sex. Yet, for the most part, neither coeducation nor women's higher education made much headway until after the Civil War. Seminaries founded by Emma Willard at Troy, New York (1821), by Catherine Beecher at Hartford, Connecticut (1823), and by Mary Lyon at South Hadley, Massachusetts (1836) were noteworthy, but Georgia Female College at Macon, which opened in 1836, was the first woman's college in America. One year later in 1837, Oberlin College in Ohio enrolled four females in its freshman class, but fewer than a half dozen other institutions of higher learning became coed before 1860, one of these being the University of Iowa (1855).

Utopianism

Paradoxically, although the spirit of the antebellum reform movement was highly individualistic, it found its purest expression in idealistic schemes for communal living. One obvious way to create the perfect world, at least in miniature or experimental

form, was to live apart from the imperfect world with other fellow believers. If the new version proved superior, and no dedicated reformer ever had any doubts concerning the outcome, then the "old" imperfect world would soon emulate the perfect.

The Mormons
One such effort was the Mormon Church. This faith, also called the Church of Jesus Christ of Latter-day Saints, was founded in 1830 by Joseph Smith (1805–1844), a young man of Vermont stock who was cast into the turmoil of religious controversies swirling around him. Smith claimed visions and personal meetings with two persons of the Trinity—the Father and the Son. These and other revelations allegedly led Smith to the discovery of buried gold plates on which were inscribed the scriptures of the new sect, *The Book of Mormon*. (Mormon was an angel who had originally created the plates.) This work, which resembles the King James translation of the Bible is believed by Mormons to be the record of ancient Hebrew settlers who came to America and also the record of the coming of Christ to the New World after the Resurrection. The central message of *The Book of Mormon* is the need for repentance. Rejecting Calvinist determinism altogether, the Mormon text states that all people are free to choose and attain salvation if they give up their life of sin and seek Christ.

Smith attracted large numbers of followers who believed his claim that he was a prophet chosen by God to receive direct and continuing heavenly revelations. The sect was attractive to some Protestant Americans, in part because of its strong emphasis on equality, its endorsement of democracy, and its assertion that America is the Promised Land. The Mormons formed a closely organized communal group; Joseph Smith expected all laymen to serve as priests in the church and advocated the communal sharing of goods.

Other Americans were much less receptive to Smith's ideas, and for a decade and a half (1831–1846) the sect faced violent opposition as the members tried to build their new Zion in various parts of Ohio, Illinois, and Missouri. Critics were incensed by their success, their missionary work with Indians, and their religious innovations, such as plural marriage, which were, in the eyes of some, heretical. When in 1844, a mob killed Joseph Smith and his brother in their fourth settlement at Nauvoo, Illinois, 148 of the faithful set out for the Far

West, although a large number dissented and refused to go. A six months' trek, begun in the dead of winter of 1846–1847 and marked by considerable hardship, was led by Brigham Young (1801–1877), who emerged as a very able organizer, a shrewd leader, and a man of great determination. At Salt Lake in Utah, where Young and his band finally settled, the religion flourished and became a worldwide movement. Young and his followers set up an elaborate irrigation system that turned the valley of the Great Salt Lake into an agricultural paradise. At the time of his death, the Mormon community consisted of 357 towns and villages with some 140,000 residents, many of them lured by promises of free land and a new life. This strongly communal religion is one of the most lasting legacies of antebellum revivalism.

The Shakers

In the second quarter of the nineteenth century, another religious sect attracted a substantial number of followers—the Shakers, or more properly, the United Society of Believers in Christ's Second Appearing. Called the "Shakers" because of the bodily movements some members evinced during religious ecstasies, the group was founded in the late eighteenth century by Ann Lee (1736–1784), an uneducated Englishwoman. After her four children died in childbirth, Ann Lee had a revelation in which she learned that the source of all sin and evil

was sex. Soon "Mother Ann," as she was addressed, had a number of adherents, all of whom joined her in practicing celibacy.

An additional revelation instructed the Shakers to move to America in 1774. By 1787, Mother Ann and her followers had established a successful community at New Lebanon, New York. By the Civil War era, there were some 6,000 believers living in nineteen different communities in the United States.

The Shakers suffered from public scorn and ridicule in antebellum America because of their celibacy and what opponents considered peculiar religious practices. Nevertheless, the Shakers slowly won grudging respect because of their organized and benevolent way of life. Members were strictly segregated according to sex in church, in dormitories, at meals, and on the job. Shaker farms were well run and prosperous; diversified agriculture was the rule, and members processed and sold dairy products and herbs. They were responsible for numerous practical inventions, including the buzz saw (invented by a woman), the apple parer, metal pen point, and flat broom. All work was shared, and all profits distributed equally among members.

Because the Shakers believed that the sexes were totally equal, male and female elders ruled the communities. These authorities had absolute power, and the Shaker world was not in any sense democratic. Childless, the Shakers had only two ways of

National Archives.
The exodus of the persecuted Mormons from Nauvoo, Illinois.

recruiting new members—through making converts and through adopting orphans. The Shakers, however, were not interested in forcing people to join their faith. Even the orphans they raised were free to leave the sect upon reaching twenty-one. Although scattered Shaker outposts appeared in various states east of the Mississippi River, the center of strength at their peak (perhaps 6,000 members in 1850) was in New England. Today only a handful of Shakers remain, yet the industrious, practical nature of their nineteenth-century counterparts, and especially the handsome, simple furniture and other artifacts they created, are now universally admired.

The Oneida Community

John Humphrey Noyes (1811–1886) carried the idea of Christian perfection farther than any other American of the antebellum period. He believed that true Christians could live without sin altogether and organized a community at Putney, Vermont, in 1836, where this ideal might be attained, but horrified neighbors soon forced the group to move elsewhere.

In Oneida, New York, their new home, the Perfectionists, as they were called, became extremely prosperous from farming and manufacturing various items including silverware. All property was held communally, the sexes were regarded as equal, and women adopted the Bloomer costume of short skirts worn over pantalettes. Children remained with their mothers until they could walk and then entered nurseries, freeing most of the women to pursue trades and occupations. The community was regularly entertained by plays, concerts, and lectures.

The most controversial aspect of the Oneida Community was the form of sex relationship practiced there. The conventional family system of parents and children remained, but Noyes felt a deep hostility towards the institution of marriage. In its place he introduced the practice of "complex marriage." Every woman was considered the wife of every man, and every man the husband of every woman. Sexual intercourse was permitted, but the act could only be performed with the agreement of both partners and community approval, and only certain members were supposed to produce offspring. The exclusive love of one person for another (called "special love") was frowned on and forbidden. Another unique feature of life at Oneida was a session or "cure" devoted to criticism of a member. The entire community participated in this ordeal, but such measures helped to maintain social control and provided an opportunity for the release of aggression and guilt feelings. Although this was a successful experiment, mounting hostility from nearby towns and villages led the Oneida group to abandon complex marriage in 1879 and in the following year to incorporate as a joint-stock company that carried on various manufactures such as silverplate. Noyes and a few followers then migrated to Canada.

Robert Owen and New Harmony

Robert Owen, who was born in North Wales in 1771, grew up in a poor, religious family. Before he was fourteen he lost his faith, but retained a commitment to universal charity. Owen rose to be one of the major industrialists of Great Britain, and, in 1825, he decided to put his ideas into practice in New Harmony, Indiana, where he, his sons, and about a thousand settlers from Europe and the northeastern part of the United States established a utopian community. Owen sought to free people from the dogma of religion by attacking institutionalized churches. (On Sunday mornings lectures were delivered at New Harmony.) To combat the alleged destructive influences of capitalism, he socialized the means of production and declared that after the first nine months, complete communism would be in effect. And Owen attacked sexism by making women full partners in this enterprise. Legislative power was delegated to an assembly made up of all adult residents, both male and female. Indeed, in his Declaration of Mental Independence, issued on the Fourth of July, 1826, Owen condemned private property, organized religion, and the institution of marriage—thereby alienating most Americans outside of his little community.

Internal dissension over ideological questions—combined with a liberal admissions policy—quickly ended this dream. By 1827 Owen, having lost four-fifths of his fortune, began to dissolve New Harmony. Critics attributed the failure to many causes. Some pointed to Owen's ambitious program to reform every aspect of ordinary life all at once. Others asserted that the community devoted too much time to music and dancing and too little to meeting the practical problems of survival. Still others observed that true democracy had been missing at New Harmony, since members from the upper classes refused to mix with those from the lower ranks of society.

Religion, Reform, and Utopianism

Fourierist Phalanxes

Like some abolitionists, the Fourierists were utopian thinkers who rejected gradualism in favor of immediatism. Charles Fourier (1772–1837), a French philosopher and socialist who left a great impact on American social experimentation, believed that the passions of people could attain harmony only in a simple society close to nature. He rejected a society based on the machine, and proposed in its place a reorganization of society into so-called "phalanxes" or associations large enough for all social industrial requirements and arranged in groups according to occupations, capabilities, attractions, and so on. According to Fourier, the phalanxes would guarantee every participant the means of self-support and the opportunity to develop personal interests. Each phalanx was to have 1,620 people cultivating 5,000 acres of land and working on handicrafts. Unlike Owen's effort in New Harmony, which attempted to change human nature from competitiveness to cooperation by altering the social environment, Fourier's phalanxes took into account individual differences.

Many phalanxes were formed—almost fifty in all, including six in New York, six in Pennsylvania, eight in Ohio, and three in Massachusetts. The longest-lived was the North American Phalanx, established in 1843 and situated near Red Bank, New Jersey. The colony lasted until 1854, when the members voted to disband it. Almost a hundred people worked the farmlands and operated a few small industries in a congenial atmosphere. The phalanx did not fail because of economic difficulties, since the value of the property alone was increased 1,000 percent during the years of its existence. Surplus vegetables were shipped to Manhattan, only fifty miles away, and everyone—male and female—received wages. Members worked only as much as they chose to and were paid accordingly; higher wages were given to those who performed "necessary but repulsive" jobs. Although the system functioned smoothly, the quality of life at Red Bank was extremely severe.

Brook Farm

The most famous experiment in utopian socialism was Brook Farm in West Roxbury, Massachusetts. Organized in 1841 by a group of New England intellectuals headed by a Unitarian minister and Transcendentalist, George Ripley (1802–1880), it grew dramatically in size after it became a Fourierist phalanx in 1845.

Life at Brook Farm was highly stimulating, since some of the best minds in the country were members or frequent visitors. Margaret Fuller, Ralph Waldo Emerson, Bronson Alcott, Nathaniel Hawthorne, Robert Owen, and many others took a strong interest in the community. The educational system was outstanding and for the first time in American history students were instructed in the subtleties of the music of Mozart, Haydn, and Beethoven and became familiar with the literary works of the present as well as of the past. Classes in agriculture also were part of the curriculum, and students did many chores about the farm, since the objectives of the community, according to Ripley, were "to insure a more natural union between intellectual and manual labor than now exists; to combine the thinker and the worker, as far as possible in the same individual."

Yet the experiment was not an economic success, and it dissolved in 1846 after a major fire destroyed the largest building. Bankruptcy seemed inevitable, and a few cases of smallpox frightened off those who remained. Nevertheless, Brook Farm was a utopian community that came close to realizing the dream of a peaceful, fraternal organization in which the life of the mind and the life of labor were fused.

Étienne Cabet and Ícaria

Utopianism was as much a European as an American phenomenon, and one of the longest-lived experiments in communal living was founded and peopled almost entirely by French radicals. Étienne Cabet (1788–1856) was exiled from France for five years as a punishment for his political beliefs. While living in England, he became friendly with Robert Owen. Under Owen's influence, Cabet wrote an enormously popular novel titled *Voyage en Icarie*, published in 1840. By 1847 there were, according to one estimate, some four million European adherents to Cabet's utopian ideas. The following year some 300 people set out for the American state of Texas to found a community of their own. There the French and German Icarians hoped to live in a society in which elected officials would control all economic activity and supervise social affairs in an environment free of the constraints of organized religion.

The original settlement proved to be a disaster. The million acres Cabet bought in Texas were arid and scattered in many small plots, far from all forms of transportation. Early in February 1849, Cabet himself arrived in New Orleans with fresh manpower. This group, hearing that the Mormons had abandoned Nauvoo, Illinois, for Utah, purchased the community. All went well in Nauvoo for five years, and the Icarians prospered from the profits of their sawmill, flour mill, and distillery. But soon an anti-Cabet faction developed, and Cabet withdrew with 180 faithful followers and moved to St. Louis. A week after the migration Cabet died of apoplexy. The Panic of 1857 impoverished the two communities, although a group in Iowa survived until 1895 before disbanding and distributing the property to the individual members.

Contributions to American Life

These various utopian societies, whether religious or secular, sometimes have been dismissed as naive experiments in folly. Nevertheless, although almost all of the communities were short-lived and many were poorly planned, some made important contributions to American life. They served as a testing ground for ideas about equality of the sexes, the integration of physical and intellectual labor, and the viability of socialist ideas. Utopian leaders seriously challenged such hallowed institutions as private property, the family, and marriage. In the second half of the twentieth century, these questions again have been raised as Americans reevaluate industrialization, racial and sexual equality, and the prevailing forms of social organization.

During the decades just before the Civil War, these would-be reformers of American life faced tremendous, seemingly impossible, obstacles. Their experiments, in the eyes of their critics, were often much too radical and failed to come to grips with what many Americans viewed as the most serious defect in the "Grand Experiment," which was, of course, slavery. Until something was done about the black man's place in the emerging democracy, little could be gained by discussing secondary issues. In fact, if the slave-free controversy was not resolved, then the "Grand Experiment" itself was in jeopardy.

To the Health of the American People

Library of Congress.
Vaccinating the baby, from *Harper's Weekly*, 1870.

Today the World Health Organization (WHO) defines public health as "the science and art of preventing disease, prolonging life, and promoting health and efficiency through organized community efforts." But, during a rather fumbling and often uncertain career, public health in America has masqueraded under a variety of names such as public hygiene, preventive medicine, community sanitation, and even social welfare. To a great extent, modern medical knowledge was the work of the Old World, not the New, and at least until 1850 Americans who resided some distance from "doctors" may have been better off and may even have lived longer than those who had them as neighbors. Yet during the preceding century two vital innovations were evident in Europe. First, leading researchers in England, France, and Germany abandoned the age-old, often fruitless hunt for miraculous "quickie" cures and began to study the nature of various diseases. The second step was careful examination by microscope, stethoscope, clinical statistics, experimentation, and autopsies to learn still more about the nature of human illnesses.

Colonial Americans certainly passed health ordinances; tried, at times, to isolate those thought ill with contagious diseases in pesthouses; drained marshes; sought out adequate supplies of fresh water; and endeavored to keep streets free of garbage, refuse, and sewage. But as cities grew and industrialization increased, these efforts were not enough. The life expectancy of school-aged children actually declined somewhat between 1789 and 1850.

One basic problem was a series of great epidemics that swept through the nation from time to time. The worst offenders—yellow fever, cholera, smallpox, and malaria—ravaged not only cities and towns but the countryside as well. To complicate matters, most doctors blamed uncontrollable natural phenomena or cosmic conditions and failed to realize how diseases were transmitted from one individual to another. Even if they suspected this possibility, they rarely understood the incubation period of germs and similar factors basic to disease control. Of course, vaccination for smallpox was known, but it was done from arm to arm until 1870 (not with calf lymph), and this method sometimes spread erysipelas, syphilis, and other dreaded maladies. Many consequently shunned vaccination and with good reason.

For the most part, these epidemics were caused by environmental factors such as polluted water, poor housing conditions, bad milk, decayed food, great swarms of flies, poor nutrition, overwork, ignorance, and carelessness. In their eagerness to stem these disasters our forefathers cleaned up their cities substantially (especially the more affluent neighborhoods), which was a step in the right di-

Courtesy of the New-York Historical Society, New York City.

The statistics for one day during a cholera epidemic, in the *New York City Health Reporter* for July 29, 1832.

315
To the Health of the American People

rection. But, since they did not comprehend how epidemics spread, these onslaughts continued. Researchers of today can pinpoint the ship that brought cholera, for example, to New Orleans, list its first victims, and trace its progress into the countryside and upriver to St. Louis and beyond. Asiatic cholera is a devastating, swift killer. A healthy young man who feels dizzy in the morning, by noon becomes ill with vomiting and dies, not in a few days, but in hours. An estimated 50,000 Americans succumbed to cholera in 1866 alone, but the last great epidemic five years later had one solid dividend: it gave birth to a nationwide program of ship quarantines. This quarantine program was an outgrowth of a congressional act of 1798—the first move by the federal government in behalf of public health—that sought to provide medical care for merchant seamen. In time, this quarantine program of 1871 grew into the United States Public Health Service. The Constitution, by the way, is silent on the subject of health, so most measures designed to promote community or public health in the nine-teenth century originated in cities and state capitals, not in Washington.

Although cholera, yellow fever, smallpox, and malaria were dramatic, the real enemies of much of nineteenth century America were familiar illnesses that aroused little interest. These killers invaded every household and claimed their victims in a slow, occasionally casual manner. They were tuberculosis, infant diarrhea, dysentery, typhoid fever, pneumonia, and childhood diseases such as scarlet fever and diphtheria. Tuberculosis, a disease closely associated with industrialization and poor living conditions, evidently reached its peak at mid-century; after that date, a slow decline in the death rate is apparent. Just why is not entirely clear, since the true nature of the disease was not yet understood. Some historians believe more intelligent citizens began to appreciate the value of fresh air, good food and water, and the dangers of indiscriminate coughing and spitting; thus a sanitary awakening turned the tide against "TB." Others point to better nutrition as a key factor, and still

The United States Sanitary Commission at work as portrayed in an engraving by Thomas Nast.

Religion, Reform, and Utopianism

others maintain that those most susceptible died off, producing a naturally immune populace.

A Massachusetts native, Lemuel Shattuck (1793–1859), laid the foundations for modern public health in America with his *Report of the Sanitary Commission of Massachusetts* (1850). Shattuck, an amateur genealogist, became interested in vital statistics while writing histories of his own family and of the town of Concord. In 1847, as a member of the Boston City Council and the state legislature, he engineered creation of a "Sanitary Commission" empowered to prepare a statewide survey. This undertaking clearly was Shattuck's own idea. He became commission chairman and, not surprisingly, also prepared the now famous report. At every step Shattuck faced stern opposition from medical men because he seemed to be invading their territory.

In his four-part study, Shattuck paid special attention to diseases caused by industrial-urban growth, demonstrating that the average age of all those who died in Boston between 1810 and 1820 was 27.85 years, but in the 1840s it was only 21.43 years, a decline in life expectancy of 6.42 years. Data collected for New York and Philadelphia revealed similar disturbing trends. Shattuck presented fifty recommendations aimed at creating local and state health programs, thirty-six of which now are accepted throughout America. These included state boards of health, local boards, careful compilation of vital statistics, special emphasis upon environmental factors such as smoke abatement; supervised construction of buildings; control of the sale and manufacture of food, drink, and medicine; compulsory vaccination against smallpox; schools for nurses; and institutions to train sanitary workers. Most important of all, Shattuck stressed the prevention of disease, not its cure.

Despite an appeal to practical New England common sense, a bill incorporating Shattuck's far-reaching proposals got nowhere in the Massachusetts legislature. He and his ideas were much too radical and far ahead of the times. Nevertheless, recurring epidemics and conditions created by the Civil War pushed sanitation to the forefront of the public mind and slowly some of his concepts began to be accepted. Because of yellow fever, Louisiana in 1855 set up a quarantine to be administered by a state board of health, the first in the nation. Massachusetts established a similar body in 1869, and during the early 1870s, six other states followed these examples: California, Minnesota, Virginia, Michigan, Maryland, and Alabama.

Emergence of the United States Sanitary Commission in June 1861, a voluntary group designed to promote the health and welfare of northern volunteers, was not viewed with much enthusiasm by Abraham Lincoln. Like Franklin Pierce who crushed Dorothea Dix's hopes for federally supported mental institutions with his veto in 1854, at first Lincoln was not impressed with the aims of a group composed of clergymen, do-gooder women, and a few doctors who, in his opinion, might become "a fifth wheel to the coach." Nevertheless, he gave reluctant approval, and a few weeks later the first battle of Bull Run demonstrated that the army's medical service alone could not possibly cope with thousands of sick and wounded.

The primary work of the commission was to inspect camps (this made workers very unpopular with military officers); to supply furniture, blankets, clothing, and some food to hospitals; and to provide nurses. Dorothea Dix headed up the corps of nurses. Out of these wartime experiences, considerable information was gained concerning malaria and "crowd" diseases, the proper disposal of human waste, the value of fresh vegetables, the use of ether and chloroform during surgery, and the need for nursing training.

During the next century, the pace of public health awareness quickened considerably throughout America, but progress often has been uneven as four sectors struggled to stake out their jurisdictions and protect their special interests. These were local health departments in cities, counties, and towns; state services under the control of state boards; federal departments and agencies; and voluntary groups and associations. Cooperation and competition were clearly possible and, predictably, both have occurred.

Like the Civil War, the crisis of the Great Depression of the 1930s stimulated considerable interest in public health, especially when local and state coffers were empty. Franklin D. Roosevelt's Social Security Act of 1935 contained sweeping provisions authorizing annual grants to states for health purposes and greatly increased federal-state cooperation in this realm. However, not until 1953 did public health win cabinet status with creation of the Department of Health, Education, and Welfare (HEW). At last, the nation had a national health organization, but whether it has a national health program is another matter. Despite this reorganization, public health work continues to be carried on by a variety of agencies and boards in the federal government, and efforts to pass national health care legislation have met stiff opposition from doctors and physicians who belong to the American Medical Association.

What has been accomplished in America during this century is indeed impressive. In 1900 the death rate from all causes was 17.2 per 1,000 population; in 1970 it was 9.4. Since the turn of the century, the life expectancy of Americans has increased by more than two decades, from forty-seven to seventy years. Epidemics have been eliminated, and tuberculosis—once the silent killer—has been virtually wiped out. Chronic diseases such as cancer, cardiovascular disorders, arthritis, neurological defects, and mental illness—often problems associated with aging—now are the special concern of public health research.

Treatment for any sickness, even basic hospital care, has become so expensive that a substantial number of Americans cannot bear the costs involved. A prolonged illness may mean heavy debt and mental anguish perhaps fully as disruptive as the illness itself. A cure that cripples cannot be viewed as a true corrective.

To assist the elderly, those hit hardest by expensive bouts with sickness, the Congress in 1965 created Medicare, two insurance programs administered by the Social Security Administration, now part of the Department of Health and Human Services, the successor to HEW, and financed by funds working Americans pay to that agency. Medicare provides hospital benefits and voluntary medical insurance to everyone over sixty-five years of age. Since 1973, Medicare also has provided help for some disabled individuals who are less than sixty-five. Closely related to Medicare is Medicaid, a state-administered program to give medical assistance to persons with low incomes. Supported by local, state, and federal funds, both eligibility and benefits vary somewhat from state to state.

For the past four decades, legislation designed to provide similar health care for all Americans, regardless of age, has failed to win congressional approval, and the merits of such proposals are hotly debated. Epidemics, wars, and economic disasters seem to have been the phenomena that nudged public health along the path of its hit-and-miss development and growth. And, as medical bills and hospital costs continue to soar, too many Americans can only pay lip service to Lemuel Shattuck's plea to seek the advice of a physician "while in health." Yet, although public health activity in America is a hodgepodge of boards and agencies, public and private, at various levels of society, the system works reasonably well; it certainly has come a long way since the days when a President dared to veto a bill designed to provide hospitals for the mentally ill and when another chief executive, a man known for his charity and wisdom, could approve, only with reluctance, voluntary efforts to ease the pain and suffering of wounded soldiers.

SELECTED
READINGS

General Accounts

E. Douglas Branch, *The Sentimental Years 1836–1860* (1934)

Russell B. Nye, *Society and Culture in America, 1830–1860* (1974)

Alice Felt Tyler, *Freedom's Ferment: Phases of American Social History from the Colonial Period to the Outbreak of the Civil War* (1944)

Harvey Wish, *Society and Thought in Early America* (1950)

Religion and Religious Benevolence

John R. Bodo, *The Protestant Clergy and Public Issues, 1812–1848* (1954)

Whitney R. Cross, *The Burned-Over District: The Social and Intellectual History of Enthusiastic Religion in Western New York, 1800–1850* (1950)

Clifford S. Griffin, *Their Brothers' Keepers: Moral Stewardship in the United States, 1800–1865* (1960)

Donald G. Mathews, *Religion in the Old South* (1977)

Timothy L. Smith, *Revivalism and Social Reform in Mid-Nineteenth Century America* (1957)

William W. Sweet, *Religion in the Development of American Culture, 1765–1840* (1963)

Bernard A. Weisberger, *They Gathered at the River: The Story of the Great Revivals and Their Impact upon Religion in America* (1958)

Some Varieties of Reform

Frederick M. Binder, *The Age of the Common School, 1830–1865* (1974)

Peter Brock, *Pacifism in the United States: From the Colonial Era to the First World War* (1968)

Frank L. Byrne, *Prophet of Prohibition: Neal Dow and his Crusade* (1961)

Merton L. Dillon, *The Abolitionists: The Growth of a Dissenting Minority* (1974)

Helen E. Marshall, *Dorothea Dix: Forgotten Samaritan* (1937)

David J. Rothman, *The Discovery of the Asylum: Social Order and Disorder in the New Republic* (1971)

Ronald G. Walters, *American Reformers, 1815–1860* (1978)

Utopianism

Edward D. Andrews, *The People Called Shakers: A Search for the Perfect Society* (1953)

Leonard J. Arrington and Davis Britton, *The Mormon Experience: A History of the Latter-Day Saints* (1979)

Arthur E. Bestor, Jr. *Backwoods Utopias: The Sectarian Origins and the Owenite Phase of Communitarian Socialism in America, 1663–1829* (2nd ed., 1971)

Mark Holloway, *Heavens on Earth: Utopian Communities in America, 1680–1880* (rev. ed., 1966)

Gairdner B. Moment and Otto F. Kraushaar, eds., *Utopias: The American Experience* (1980)

Thomas F. O'Dea, *The Mormons* (1964)

Robert D. Thomas, *The Man Who Would be Perfect: John Humphrey Noyes and the Utopian Impulse* (1977)

Carol Weisbrod, *The Boundaries of Utopia* (1980)

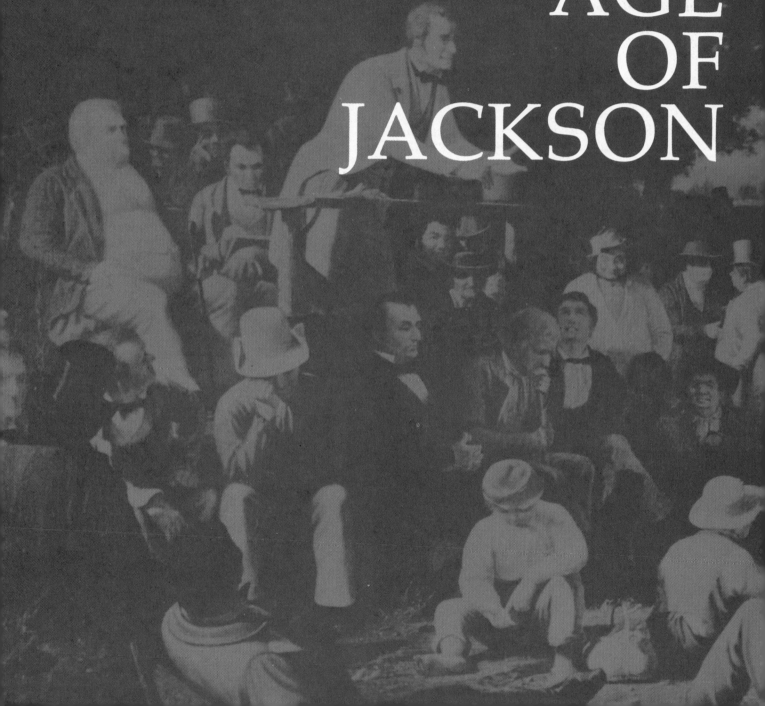

CHAPTER 11

THE AGE OF JACKSON

TIMELINE

1825
House of Representatives elects John Quincy Adams President

1828
John C. Calhoun writes *South Carolina Exposition and Protest*

1828
Democrat Andrew Jackson elected President

1830
Webster-Hayne Debate

1830
Land law permits purchase of up to 160 acres for $1.25 per acre

1831
Nat Turner slave revolt

1832
Jackson vetoes renewal of BUS charter

1832
South Carolina declares "Tariff of Abominations" null and void in *Ordinance of Nullification*

1832
Jackson reelected President

1833
Jackson issues *Nullification Proclamation*

1836
Democrat Martin Van Buren elected President

1837
United States recognizes Republic of Texas

1837
Onset of severe depression

1840
Congress approves Independent Treasury Plan

1840
Whig William Henry Harrison elected President

1841
John Tyler assumes presidency after Harrison's death

1841
Pre-Emption Act encourages frontier land settlement

1842
Webster-Ashburton Treaty

1844
Democrat James K. Polk elected President

1845
Texas annexed to the United States

1846
Clash between Mexican and American troops leads to war

1848
Treaty of Guadalupe Hildago ends war with Mexico

CHAPTER OUTLINE

The ballyhoo that surrounds presidential elections today began with Andrew Jackson's campaign in 1828 as shrewd politicians realized that the public would respond more fully to slogans, rallies, cartoons, and other forms of propaganda than to sober discussions of the issues. Jackson's campaign not only marked the introduction of new tactics but also the "rise of the common man"—if not in fact, at least in political rhetoric. Once in office, Jackson strengthened the presidency and wrestled for a position of dominance over Congress. A two-party system of sorts developed around Jackson as opposition to his policies and programs increased. Territorial expansion was tied increasingly to the question of slavery in the new territories. The split between the North and South over this expansion widened after the Mexican War in the late 1840s and the acquisition of vast new lands.

New Political Competition

After the War of 1812, the Federalist party, which had long been ailing, finally died as a national organization. During James Monroe's terms as President, from 1816 to 1824, Republicans became more national in outlook and actively modified their party so it might accommodate the view of ex-Federalists who wanted national government to do more than play a small, strictly custodial role.

Although the election of 1824 revolved to some extent around national questions such as internal improvements, the fate of slavery, the direction of banking policy, and the disposition of public lands, to a greater degree the competition was regional. Of the five candidates, Henry Clay was from Kentucky, Andrew Jackson from Tennessee, John C. Calhoun from South Carolina, William Harris Crawford from Georgia, and John Quincy Adams from Massachusetts.

Competition for votes caused the aspirants to search for issues with broad, national appeal. These issues, however, were often vague, and the candidates descended to attacking each other on the basis of personal characteristics: Adams was ridiculed for the way he dressed; Calhoun for his overzealous ambition; Clay for his drinking and gambling;

This painting of "Old Hickory" by Thomas Sully, a student of Gilbert Stuart and Benjamin West, depicts Andrew Jackson as the hero of New Orleans.

Crawford for once having advocated intermarriage of whites and Indians as an alternative to the latter's removal from Georgia; and Jackson for his alleged lack of experience in politics.

The electoral vote in 1824 was split among the four candidates, no one of whom received a majority. In accordance with the Twelfth Amendment, the election went to the House of Representatives, where the top three candidates—Jackson with 99 electoral votes, Adams with 84, and Crawford with 41—were under consideration. Clay, who won only 37 electoral votes, had dropped out of the race, but as Speaker of the House he was in a position of influence and threw his support to Adams, who was elected. Because Jackson won more popular votes than Adams and because the newly elected President appointed Clay as his Secretary of State, Jacksonians charged that a "corrupt bargain" had cheated "the people." Calhoun, meanwhile, became Vice President.

Further complicating matters for Adams, a highly intellectual man, were his own shortcomings as a political leader. Adams was no newcomer to

public life; he had held several important diplomatic posts abroad, including that of minister plenipotentiary to Russia and minister to England and had served in the U.S. Senate before becoming Secretary of State under President James Monroe in 1817. Yet like his father, former President John Adams, he lacked the common touch and seemed disagreeably patrician and puritanical to many Americans. He greatly distressed his fellow Republicans because he opposed partisan politics and refused to use his power of patronage for political advantage. Indeed, his lack of political sagacity prevented him from harnassing the surging political democracy of the 1820s, which made Andrew Jackson its beneficiary in the election of 1828.

The Adams Presidency

In his first annual message to Congress in December 1825, Adams proposed a reasonable protective

John Quincy Adams, scholar, diplomat, and President. This daguerreotype portrait was taken in 1843 when Adams was serving in the U.S. House of Representatives.

tariff that would aid native industry, provide domestic markets for farmers, and enrich the federal government. He asked for the creation of a department of the interior that would sell lands at low rates but discourage wildcat speculation and an overly rapid settlement of the West. Such a government agency would facilitate a rational allocation of lands and provide for the conservation of natural resources. The sale of public lands would provide money to be used in removing Indians on a voluntary basis to areas west of the Mississippi River. Indian removal, Adams urged, should not violate treaty rights.

Finally, Adams called for reforms that would benefit the nation intellectually. He asked for funds to support scientific research (especially explorations), to build a national observatory, and to pay for public lectures on scientific subjects. Reviving an old idea of George Washington, Adams suggested Congress build a national university in Washington, D.C. He recommended a more effective patent law and a uniform standard of weights and measures based upon the metric system. Adams's proposed reforms extended even to the Navy; he pointed out to Congress the "want of a naval school of instruction," corresponding with the Military Academy at West Point, for the training of scientific and accomplished officers.

The nationalistic plan that Adams outlined won little support since it required extensive central planning and control. In general, Adams failed to understand the changing nature of American politics. He did not recognize that the ordinary voter had become more influential. Rather than taking his controversial proposals to the people, Adams addressed himself to Congress alone. He held fast to the eighteenth-century idea that the voters elected the best and wisest men who, in turn, were free to make policies and laws without referring back to their constituents. This concept of government was fast being replaced by one more responsive to public opinion. Characteristically, Adams instructed Congress to adopt his program and not be "palsied by the will of our constituents"—an unfortunate phrase that his opponents later used to convince the voters that the President was an enemy of the people.

Even in the area of foreign affairs, in which Adams was an expert, he had little success. His efforts to increase trade with the British West Indies were rebuffed, and an attempt at hemispheric cooperation ended in confusion. The Adams administration received secret information that Spain was intent upon recovering its lost colonies in South America. Wanting to block Spain's ambitions, Adams proposed in December 1825 that the United States send a diplomatic mission to a congress of newly independent Latin American states. The meeting was to be held in Panama, and attendance by the United States would signal hemispheric solidarity. In March 1826, after many delays, Congress complied with the President's request—but so late that the diplomatic effort had been wrecked. One of the American delegates to Panama died en route, and the other arrived after the conference was over.

One of the deep differences between Adams and his enemies was over states' rights. In 1802 Georgia ceded its western land claims to the United States and assumed its present boundaries in return for the promise that the federal government would extinguish Indian title to lands within the state as soon as possible. Georgia was to be given full jurisdiction over those lands. Although the federal government had pledged to dissolve Creek and Cherokee land holdings in Georgia, this process was very slow. Finally, in 1825, the Treaty of Indian Springs was signed in which the "Creek Nation" agreed to surrender its lands in Georgia and a portion in Alabama in exchange for a tract in present-day Oklahoma.

Adams discovered that the chiefs who signed the treaty represented only eight of the forty-six Creek towns and that federal officers backing the treaty had acted more as Georgians than as representatives of Washington. Accordingly, Adams ordered Georgia to halt the surveying and sale of Creek lands to white settlers until a new, fairer treaty could be drawn up. The governor of Georgia threatened civil war if Adams attempted to stop the proceedings.

Some Southerners warned that if the federal government could defend the existence of Indian "nations" within states it could also interfere in the internal affairs of the slave states and emancipate bondsmen. Like the tariff issue, the Indian question caused Southerners to suspect the intentions of the federal government even though before leaving office Adams recommended removal of the Indians on a voluntary basis to territory west of the Mississippi.

The Tariff of Abominations

Another problem confronting Adams's administration was the tariff. The rise of American industry during the antebellum period made it an important political issue. New England manufacturers and sheep raisers, hurt by the Panic of 1819, sought protective tariffs. Congress responded by enacting the mild Tariff of 1824. It failed to satisfy the protectionists, who pressed for higher duties. When the tariff question came up again at the end of Adams's term, some of Jackson's supporters backed a bill designed to appeal to the Middle Atlantic states of New York and Pennsylvania and the western states. If Jackson could win the large bloc of electoral votes of these regions, he would enhance his chances of winning the upcoming election.

The Tariff of 1828 was a hodgepodge, poorly thought out and unfair, nothing more than a naked bid for votes. Oddly enough, the very Jacksonians who framed the bill never thought it would be passed. They had reasoned that the South, opposed to tariffs of any sort, would vote it down, and that the North, irritated by the high rates on raw materials, would also reject it. Defeat of the bill would win affection for Jackson from the antiprotectionist South. At the same time, Jackson would presumably secure the devotion of farmers in the West and manufacturing interests in the Middle Atlantic states for supporting the bill in the first place. Thus Jackson would be considered a friend of the western farmer, a protectionist in the North, and a free-trader in the South.

When the bill unexpectedly passed in mid-1828, it was immediately labeled "the tariff of abominations" by the South. John Calhoun, the Vice President, wrote the *South Carolina Exposition and Protest* (though he did not sign the essay) in which he called the tariff unconstitutional and recommended state nullification. Calhoun, once an ardent nationalist, was now a strong sectionalist. This switch reflected an economic trend. The average price for cotton had been dropping steadily for several years, bringing hardship to South Carolina (in 1816 cotton sold at 27 cents a pound, in 1820 at 17 cents, in 1824 at 13 cents, and in 1827 at 9 cents). The Tariff of 1828, by imposing high duties (and thus reaffirming the principle of protection), aroused great resentment in South Carolina. Calhoun's views on nullification of federal law did not, however, prevent him from running for reelection as Vice President on the Jackson ticket in 1828.

The Election of 1828

Between Jackson's defeat in 1825 and his triumph in 1828, his supporters in and out of Congress

Chicago Historical Society.

Martin Van Buren was a brilliant political manipulator. This daguerreotype portrait of the "Little Magician" is from the late 1840s.

forged a new political entity, the Democratic party, with the sole purpose of putting "Old Hickory" (a nickname given to Jackson by his men in the War of 1812) into office.

A key figure in this campaign was Martin Van Buren (1782-1862), a politician possessed of considerable shrewdness, wit, charm, and a keen sense of public relations. Van Buren became a U.S. Senator in 1821, yet kept his hand in New York state politics with the aid of a small band of associates. In 1824 he supported Crawford, but three years later was in Jackson's camp; and, in 1828, Van Buren became one of "Old Hickory's" closest advisers.

Historians have written of the "Revolution of 1828" and the sudden "rise of the common man." Actually ordinary citizens gained new prominence before Jackson's victory. In the election of 1824, the voters in all but six states chose presidential electors, and by that time universal white male suffrage was common in many areas. The great change that took place in 1828 had more to do with the creation of elaborate political machinery through which the ordinary citizen could make his influence felt, and men like Martin Van Buren played important roles in manipulating that machinery.

The political race of 1828 also signaled renewed emphasis upon smear tactics. The Jacksonians spent about a million dollars to elect their man. No lie, insult, or calumny was excluded from their attacks on President Adams. They accused the puritanical man from Massachusetts of having procured an American girl for the sexual pleasure of the Czar of Russia; this favor was alleged to be the basis of Adams's success as a diplomat. Other charges held that Adams nursed dreams of becoming a king, a fantasy that the Jacksonians attempted to substantiate by listing White House expenditures (later proved false) with public funds for ivory chessmen, a billiard table, and other "royal extravagances." Jacksonians told recent immigrants the President's father was the author of the Alien and Sedition Acts and that the son was equally prejudiced against foreigners, whom he reputedly insulted daily. The most publicized accusation was that Adams struck a corrupt bargain with Clay to win the election of 1824.

Supporters of the President were equally active in vilifying Jackson. Even Jackson's mother was smeared as being a "common prostitute." More damaging was the story that Jackson was an adulterer. His wife, Rachel, previously was married to Lewis Robards. Unbeknownst to her, she married Jackson before the divorce being sought by Robards actually was granted; as a consequence, Jackson and Rachel were forced to marry a second time. All of this was ancient history in 1828, since the second marriage took place in 1794, but the slurs continued and contributed to Rachel's death after the election. The General's personality was not exempt from criticism. Enemies portrayed him as a drunken bully, a rowdy, a duelist, and a gunfighter, as well as a villain who indulged in cock-fighting, horse-racing, and sabbath breaking, to say nothing of fornication, murder, and treason.

The election campaign of 1828 was among the dirtiest in American history. Much of the mud-slinging was done in the columns of the nations's newspapers. The Jacksonians were particularly effective in organizing a partisan press. Interestingly enough, much of the cost of reaching the public was ultimately borne by the American taxpayer since partisan congressmen used their franking privilege to distribute campaign literature. In the opinion of many observers, it was not spontaneous anti-Adams sentiment among the populace that drove the President from the White House but rather it was a well-coordinated campaign against him.

Jacksonians used stump speeches, parades, public rallies, barbecues, dinners, cartoons, and jokes. At the same time, they aroused the fears of minorities, implying, for example, that Adams was anti-Catholic and had made vague promises to special interest groups. The Jacksonian Democrats, anticipating modern tactics, even published results of public opinion polls favoring their candidate—in the hope of convincing fence sitters that Jackson was the inevitable choice, the winner whom they must support. In addition, they built up local political organizations in various states.

The Adams campaign never matched this effort, despite the efforts of Clay, members of the cabinet, and other supporters. Adams himself was hard to sell. As he once said of himself with deadly accuracy, "I am a man of reserved, cold, austere, and forbidding manners."

Jackson won a sweeping electoral victory, taking 178 votes in the Electoral College compared to 83 for Adams, though in the popular election he secured only 56 percent of the vote. Despite scattered opposition, John C. Calhoun easily won the vice presidency. The election demonstrated that reduced suffrage requirements had given the vote to a greater populace, and more than a million of these new voters had been lured to the polls by a vigorous campaign. (The turnout, however, did not exceed the previous highs in most recent state elections.) Once again, the nation seemed to have a two-party system, and this rebirth of competition meant that from now on candidates would have to fight for mass support. Though the situation encouraged demagoguery, it also had the merit of drawing huge numbers of Americans into the democratic process.

Establishing Jacksonian Democracy

Soon after Jackson was in office it was clear that he intended to reward his supporters with political appointments. His cabinet selections paid off political debts. Martin Van Buren of New York became Secretary of State. Although Van Buren became an important adviser, Jackson generally relied less on his official cabinet for guidance than on a small group of political friends who came to be known as his "Kitchen Cabinet." Amos Kendall and Isaac Hill, both Treasury officials for a time, and Francis P. Blair, on his way to becoming editor of the Washington *Globe*, were prominent members of this inner circle.

Unlike John Quincy Adams, whose refusal to dismiss anyone on the basis of political affiliation kept his enemies in office, Jackson and his followers were eager to place loyal men in control of the national patronage. Jackson even defended "rotation in office" as a democratic process. Yet he did not initiate a clean sweep in 1829. Indeed, in 1830, after 18 months in office, only 919 of 10,093 officeholders had been replaced. Unfortunately, not all of the former employees were removed for good cause. Jackson and his followers sanctioned replacement of subordinate officers for personal or purely partisan reasons; all other Presidents (with the exception of Jefferson who was bent in 1801–1802 on ridding the government of Federalists) had replaced most officeholders on well-justified grounds. Although Jackson's dismissals were not extensive (he probably divested himself of no more than 20 percent of all officeholders during his tenure), the spoils system was much more apparent on the state level, especially in New Hampshire and New York. Indeed, it was New York Senator William Learned Marcy, a Jacksonite, who had coined the phrase "to the victor belongs the spoils."

Nor did Jackson's appointments coincide with his stated concern for "the common man." Most of his choices for the higher public offices were rich, educated men from the same ethnic groups that Adams and his other predecessors had favored. Unfortunately, the spoils system led to a decline in the efficiency of public service, since incompetent men sometimes used their new offices to fill their pockets through graft and corruption. Yet not all of

Museum of the City of New York.
This lithograph portrays Jackson as a devil dangling the spoils of office above the heads of political supporters.

the new appointees were unqualified. Some were capable men with a broad experience in public life who had a strong desire to compile a record of constructive achievement.

The Jackson-Calhoun Split

Jackson's victory in 1828 was, in part, the result of support in the North by Martin Van Buren and in the South by Vice President John C. Calhoun. Both men wanted to be President, and each hoped to succeed Old Hickory, who had intimated he would serve only one term (he was sixty-one in 1828). Soon after Jackson came into the White House, it became clear that his sympathies lay with Van Buren.

One cause of the break with Calhoun was the Peggy Eaton affair. On January 1, 1829, Jackson's Secretary of War and fellow Tennessean, John Eaton, married Margaret ("Peggy") O'Neale Timberlake. A vivacious, beautiful widow, daughter of a Washington tavernkeeper, it was rumored that she "kept company" with Eaton, who frequently stayed at her father's establishment, while married to another man. Jackson refused to admit that Peggy Eaton might be a loose woman. His own wife, Rachel, died shortly before Jackson became President, and he was certain that the slanderous accusations of adultery against her had hastened her death. Jackson drew a parallel between the persecution his wife suffered and the coldness that official Washington was showing Mrs. Eaton.

Although at first Calhoun was not involved in the Eaton controversy, his wife, Floride, refused to acknowledge the woman's existence and other cabinet wives followed her example. Soon the President became convinced that Calhoun himself was leading the conspiracy against Mrs. Eaton. Van Buren—a widower without daughters and thus having no women in his family who might be "stained" through contact with Mrs. Eaton—ardently defended the lady's virtue. In doing so, Van Buren gained the President's confidence at the same time that Calhoun lost it, although the New Yorker's very obvious political skills had won his approbation long before Floride Calhoun refused to receive Peggy Eaton.

Other factors of much greater importance than any social fracas underlay the break between Jackson and Calhoun. Calhoun opposed most of Jackson's cabinet appointees and attempted to fill some vacant government offices with his own allies. To add to the tension, Jackson learned that Calhoun, as Secretary of War, had wanted to punish him back in 1818 for his invasion of Florida, then Spanish territory. But the most substantial issue that divided the President and the Vice President was the nullification controversy.

States' Rights and Nullification

Jackson's view of states' rights versus federalism is subtle and difficult to pinpoint, though it can be argued that he acted in accord with his attitude, elusive as it might seem to be. At times he was an old Jeffersonian Republican upholding the doctrine of state sovereignty, but not all of his actions in defense of states' rights were based simply on a philosophical adherence to that doctrine. In 1830, for example, Jackson vetoed the Maysville Road Bill, which called for a highway between Maysville and Lexington in Kentucky, on the grounds that federal aid to intrastate projects was unconstitutional. Yet the evidence indicates that the President's motive was purely political, for he signed other internal improvement bills equally as local. His veto was really a slap at Kentuckian Henry Clay, who, according to Jackson, was trying to compel him to publicly accept his views on internal improvements. Yet there can be no doubt that Jackson did have a far different conception of the role of the federal government than Clay. The President's states' rights leaning, however, did not prevent him from being a fervent nationalist, a role that especially suited the occupant of the White House. He entertained a vision of Americans from every state and territory indissolubly bound together in a common destiny unfolding as their nation expanded across the continent—though without direction from the federal government.

The President's nationalism gave him ample room to make use of federal authority to set aside any impediments to the fulfillment of the great destiny he felt certain was awaiting America. The Indian removal policy, for instance, was a natural corollary to his views about the American Union and its glorious future. Regretable as the harm done to the Indians might be, they could not be allowed to stand in the way of the white man's westward expansion, Jackson thought. Although Jackson's Indian policy led Southerners and other contemporaries to view him as a states' rights supporter, it soon became apparent that the President and Vice President Calhoun had different views about the proper balance between states' rights and federalism.

Daniel Webster replies to Robert Y. Hayne, who is sitting in the front center with his hands together. Vice President John C. Calhoun, at the extreme left, is listening intently and leaning on his desk.

In 1830 a debate arose in the Senate between Daniel Webster of Massachusetts (a biographical sketch in this chapter discusses his career) and South Carolinian Robert Y. Hayne (1791–1839) concerning sectionalism. This issue developed when senators from Connecticut and Missouri became embroiled over a proposal to limit land sales in the West. New Englanders clearly hoped to curb the emigration of settlers from their region—a population drain that diminished their wealth, manpower, and political influence. Southern senators came to the aid of Westerners in opposing this scheme. What seemed to be in the offing was a strong coalition of the South and the West against the Northeast, which favored high tariffs and high land prices. Hayne attempted to bolster this coalition by introducing the subject of states' rights.

He warned against the dangers of a strong central government and, basing his arguments on Calhoun's *South Carolina Exposition*, declared that each state possessed the ultimate authority to determine whether or not acts of Congress were constitutional.

Webster dropped in on the middle of Hayne's speech and decided that a reply to it would provide him with an excellent opportunity for speaking out against the dangerous doctrine of states' rights. The federal government and not the states, he reasoned, is sovereign over the people. Acts of Congress passed in accordance with the Constitution are the supreme law of the land. At the end of his second reply to Hayne, Webster concluded, "Liberty *and* Union, now and forever, one and inseparable!"

Webster's reply to Hayne is the most famous

congressional oration in American history. Its glowing patriotism and its forceful assertion that the authority of the federal government rests with the people, not with states, has resounded down through the years from the throats of both orators and schoolchildren. Americans everywhere responded to it enthusiastically, not only in New England but also in the South and West. A Virginian, former president James Madison, wrote, "It crushes 'nullification' and must hasten an abandonment of secession."

The nullification crisis completed the break between Jackson and Calhoun. At the annual Jefferson Day Dinner, held on April 13, 1830, Jackson pointedly made the following toast while looking at Vice President Calhoun: "Our *Federal* Union—It *must* be *preserved*." Van Buren, perhaps not the most impartial reporter, later asserted that the Vice President shook under Jackson's harsh gaze. In any event, Calhoun was ready with his reply: "The Union—Next to our liberty most dear."

Meanwhile the decline in the price of cotton led some South Carolinians to speak of nullifying the "Tariff of Abominations." Calhoun counseled delay, hoping that the new Congress scheduled to assemble in December 1831 would adopt a more moderate tariff, but former President John Quincy Adams, now a congressman from Massachusetts,

secured a victory for protection in the Tariff of 1832, a bill that removed most of the aspects of the 1828 measure objectionable to manufacturers.

South Carolina, one of two states (the other was Virginia) whose senators solidly opposed the new tariff, responded by calling a state convention that on November 24, 1832, declared the tariffs of 1828 and 1832 "null, void, and no law, nor binding upon this State, its officers or citizens." Furthermore, South Carolina's Ordinance of Nullification threatened secession from the Union if the federal government used force in implementing the tariff. Calhoun, who resigned the vice presidency late in 1832, was elected to the U.S. Senate, where he proceeded to defend energetically his state's actions.

The virtual hysteria with which South Carolina responded to the Tariff of 1832 concealed another fear that was plaguing the rich Low Country plantation owners—the abolition of slavery. Although the abolition movement was only in its infancy in 1832, many white Southerners feared that the federal government might someday ban the further expansion of slavery, or even intrude on the legality of slavery where it already existed. Worse, South Carolina had witnessed a bloody slave uprising, led by Denmark Vesey in 1822, and many whites lived in terror of a general insurrection among blacks. This fear was only heightened when Nat Turner led

This contemporary comment on the nullification crisis depicts John C. Calhoun reaching for a crown while his victims, the Constitution and the Union, lie dead at the bottom of the steps leading to despotism. President Andrew Jackson at the far right restrains a nullifier and threatens to hang all disunionists.

his unsuccessful revolt in Virginia in 1831. White Southerners began to blame abolitionists for these outbreaks of violence. The fear of slave uprisings fostered "a garrison mentality," especially in Low Country counties where blacks greatly outnumbered whites or where blacks had access to ports that sailors who were "infected" with the abolitionist virus might visit.

President Jackson responded to the nullification crisis with a determination to enforce federal law and to preserve the Union. He transported troops to the forts in Charleston harbor, sent arms and ammunition to nearby areas in North Carolina, named General Winfield Scott (1786–1866) as his special emissary to South Carolina, and encouraged Unionists within the rebellious state to temper the situation and oppose nullification and secession.

On December 10, 1832, after being reelected by an overwhelming majority with Van Buren as his running mate, Jackson was in an excellent position to issue his *Nullification Proclamation*, in which he declared that the federal government was supreme, nullification absurd, and "disunion by armed forces" treasonous.

Jackson was prepared, if necessary, to use federal troops to enforce the tariff. While Congress was at work drafting legislation that would give him the power to do so, Henry Clay introduced a compromise tariff. On the same day, March 1, 1833, that Congress gave Jackson power to enforce his *Proclamation*, it also passed Clay's tariff. This measure called for a gradual reduction of duties over a ten-year period; it was championed by Calhoun, still ambitious for the presidency and eager to head off an open war between his state and the Union. The new tariff and Jackson's Indian removal policy appeased all of the southern states except South Carolina, which had no option now but to rescind its *Ordinance of Nullification*.

The Bank War

If Jackson is remembered today as the friend of the "common man" and the defender of democracy, to a large degree it is because of his actions in the Bank War, and even more so to the rhetoric generated by his supporters in that conflict.

The Second Bank of the United States (called BUS) was incorporated in 1816 under a twenty-year charter. Its constitutionality was upheld in *McCulloch* v. *Maryland* (1819) by Chief Justice John Marshall. Although the BUS was mismanaged and suffered during the Panic of 1819, it subsequently

Daniel Webster

1782–1852

Son of a New Hampshire farmer who served in the state militia and was a judge in the county court, Daniel Webster graduated from Dartmouth College in 1801 and then studied law and taught school until he was admitted to the Boston bar in 1805.

There Webster became associated with the conservative mercantile interests of the population and soon became their champion. At the outbreak of the War of 1812, Webster opposed the federal government so vigorously and espoused the cause of peace so eloquently that the Federalists sent him to Congress. Though he never suggested that New England secede from the Union, he did recommend nullification of the conscription bill that would have drafted soldiers into the federal army. (The bill failed, so his suggestion was not put to the test.)

In Congress, Webster originally opposed high protective tariffs (duties designed to protect manufacturers and industries), for at this point he was the friend of merchants and shippers whose interests would be hurt by protection. After the war, Webster withdrew from Congress and became famous as a lawyer representing clients before the Supreme Court. His brilliant performance in court earned him the reputation of being the best legal mind in the country.

By the time Webster became a senator in 1827, his loyalties had shifted from the mercantile to the industrial sector of New England, reflecting a basic metamorphosis of the regional economy and a shift in Webster's own interests, as he now owned cotton mill stock. In Washington, he became an aggressive defender of the protective tariff and of the central government. Webster's movement from states' rights to nationalism reflected the concerns of his part of the country, just as Calhoun's shift in the opposite direction revealed South Carolina's economic interests. During the nullification crisis, Webster championed nationalism in his most famous oration, his second reply to Hayne in January 1830. In that speech he argued that the Constitution set up a government that was sovereign over its own domain and was not a compact that could be dissolved; the only body that could judge constitutionality was the Supreme Court, not the states. For this position Webster came to be known as the "Defender of the Constitution."

At this time Webster also championed the Bank of the United States against Andrew Jackson and the Democrats. Once again, principle and personal interest came together, for Webster was deeply in debt to the Bank. His defense of the Bank brought him one of the regional Whig nominations for the presidency in 1836, but in the election he received only the electoral vote of Massachusetts.

When Harrison became President in 1841, he appointed Webster Secretary of State, a position he retained after Tyler succeeded to the presidency. As Secretary of State, he brought a peaceful and successful conclusion to the border dispute between Canada and the United States in the Webster-Ashburton Treaty of 1842.

Throughout his life, marked by several changes of attitude, Webster was always consistent in his opposition to slavery; and toward the end of his life, he fought against the acquisition of Texas, which he felt certain would trigger new North-South friction. Although he believed that the question of continuing slavery within the southern states was a matter "within the exclusive control of the States themselves," Webster consistently supported the Wilmot Proviso, which would exclude slavery from territories acquired as a result of the Mexican War. In 1852, when he died of cirrhosis of the liver exacerbated by excessive drinking, Webster was worried about the fate of the Union he had done so much to preserve.

recovered under the capable management of the Philadelphian Nicholas Biddle (1785–1844), who assumed control in 1823. Biddle led the bank to great prosperity, and during his rule it did a business of $70 million a year and had branches in twenty-nine cities. The bank provided sound currency and inexpensive commercial credit. Among the advantages it offered the country were a source of money for industrial expansion, a clearinghouse for the nation's finances, and a deterrent to poorly capitalized, wildcat banks that, if left unchecked, overheated the economy by making easy loans and encouraging speculation in western land.

But not everyone appreciated these advantages. Many Westerners, including Andrew Jackson, saw the institution as a vast, powerful monopoly with all the influence of a branch of the government but not subject to federal supervision. More importantly, Jackson regarded the BUS as a dangerous foe to American liberties. He was convinced that the Bank, responsible only to its American and foreign stockholders and possessing almost limitless funds, could buy off congressmen, rig elections, and shape public opinion through newspapers owned by or indebted to it. This conviction was only strengthened in 1829 when several of his advisers assured him that Bank officials had campaigned against him in the recent election.

In 1832 Henry Clay, who had just received the National Republican presidential nomination, urged Nicholas Biddle to submit the Bank's charter to Congress for renewal. Although the charter would not expire for four years, Clay hoped to gain a major campaign issue if Jackson vetoed the new charter. Biddle thought that Jackson would never make the Bank a political issue, so he decided to follow Clay's suggestion.

This proposal enraged the President. As he told Van Buren, "The bank is trying to kill me, but I will kill it!" And, indeed, he did when Congress failed to override his veto of the recharter bill. More importantly, it became a factor in the 1832 election since the veto message was political propaganda designed to arouse the public to vote for Old Hickory in his struggle against "privilege and aristocracy."

In the 1832 presidential campaign, Henry Clay, nominee of the National Republicans, seized upon the Bank issue. National Republican politicians and their newspapers frequently linked Jackson's veto with his alleged "nullification" of the Supreme Court mandate in *Worchester* v. *State of Georgia*.

Courtesy of the New-York Historical Society, New York City.

"Doctor" Jackson's prescription for "Mother U.S. Bank." At the far left,
Jackson insists that his medicine will "clean out" the bank's "foul stomach."
In the center, leading anti-Jacksonites—Clay, Webster, and Calhoun—dis-
cuss remedies for the bank's predicament, while, at the far right, Nicholas
Biddle tries to stop the removal of the bank's deposits.

However, Jackson's war against the Bank rallied the
support of a majority of the electorate, and the
Democrats won a sweeping victory; they received
over fifty-four percent of the votes cast. Clay did
not carry a single state of the Lower South or the
New West where the BUS was held in such disre-
pute. In the Electoral College, Jackson had 219 votes
to Clay's 49 votes. There was a third candidate in
the race; William Wirt, a former Attorney General,
led the Anti-Masonic Party, a short-lived reaction
against the secrecy of the Masonic Order fueled by
the alleged murder of a member who supposedly
divulged its secrets. Wirt drew less than eight percent of the popular vote and only seven electoral
votes. Even if all of Wirt's votes had gone to Clay,

Jackson's victory would still have been impressive.
The President clearly sensed and reflected public
opinion far better than his opponents.

Jackson now decided to remove federal deposits from the BUS. When his Secretary of the Treasury, Louis McLane, opposed this move, Jackson replaced him with William J. Duane, who also spoke
out against the policy. A few months later, Jackson
nominated yet another man, Roger B. Taney (1777–
1864), to head the Treasury. Clay's supporters delighted in calling Jackson a tyrant because of this
constant reshuffling of the cabinet.

The President took the funds withdrawn from
the BUS and deposited them in "pet banks" controlled by his allies. Before the end of 1833, Clay

333

Establishing Jacksonian Democracy

introduced Senate resolutions censuring Jackson for his actions; these resolutions were aimed primarily against his war on the BUS but also against his repeated vetoes of congressional bills (Jackson used the veto more often than any previous chief executive), and his constant tampering with the cabinet. When Jackson's opponents gained a temporary majority in the Senate in 1834, they passed a formal act of censure against the President for his "executive tyranny." Jackson vigorously protested the move, but only after a three-year battle was he able to succeed in having it expunged from the Senate record. However, by the time these resolutions were being discussed, the Bank issue was no longer a sectional matter; instead it was a political question being hotly debated by Henry Clay's new Whig party and the Jacksonian Democrats.

Jackson's war against the Bank of the United States contributed to a series of severe economic reverses, including a nationwide financial crisis in 1833–1834. Biddle only hastened this disaster when he called in outstanding loans and contracted credit, partly to protect the Bank's investors but mainly to force congressional reconsideration of the BUS charter.

The "Biddle panic" lasted only a short time, and the country soon returned to what seemed like prosperity. But actually the economy had entered a dangerous inflationary spiral brought on, at least in part, by the tendency of state banks to lend newly acquired federal funds for the purpose of speculating in public lands and internal improvements. A land law of 1830 allowing settlers to purchase up to 160 acres at the new low price of $1.25 an acre greatly increased public land sales and encouraged reckless speculation. Between 1831 and 1836 federal land sales totalled 46 million acres as opposed to only 10 million for the years 1821 to 1830. To finance the construction of roads, canals, and railroads, states piled up enormous debts and local banks extended extensive credit. Between 1830 and 1838, states went into debt to the amount of $150 million, and two-thirds of the money was spent for internal improvements.

Those state banks that fueled this speculative mania were generally short of specie—gold and silver. They issued paper money without sufficient specie to back it up. Jackson himself finally noticed this dangerous trend and attempted to curtail it on July 11, 1836, when he published his Specie Circular ordering the U.S. Treasury to stop accepting paper money for the sale of public lands; only gold and silver could be received in the future. This policy not only curtailed land sales but contributed to a loss of public confidence in state banks. Distrustful of paper money, people began to hoard gold and silver—and this damming of the flow of specie helped to bring on a severe depression shortly after Jackson left office. Although Jackson justified his war on the Bank of the United States in the name of the common people, it was ultimately the average small investor who suffered the most in the depression that followed.

Jackson and Foreign Policy

Jackson had far more success in foreign affairs than his predecessor. Great Britain long had restricted U.S. trade with the West Indies, and the United States, in turn, had forbidden American goods to be carried in British ships to the islands. Jackson, an admitted and confirmed Anglophobe, issued a proclamation on October 5, 1830, announcing that West Indian and American ports would be free and open to ships from either nation. The trade, so beneficial to southern planters and northern merchants, reopened two months later.

Jacksonian diplomacy opened other parts of the world to American trade. In 1831, for example, the first treaty between the United States and Turkey was obtained. This agreement not only opened Turkey to American trade on a "most-favored-nation" basis but also provided a special legal status for Americans residing there. Then in 1833, Edmund Roberts (1784–1836), a New England merchant who had been commissioned by President Jackson as a special secret agent to negotiate treaties in the Far East, signed most-favored-nation treaties with Siam (present-day Thailand) and Muscat (capital and leading port of today's Oman on the southeastern Arabian Peninsula).

Another diplomatic success for President Jackson involved the French Spoilation Claims. France had never compensated Americans for ships and goods seized during the Napoleonic wars. At the end of 1834, Jackson recommended that French property in the United States should be seized if American claims were not promptly settled. Talk of war rumbled on both sides of the ocean, but finally in April 1835 the French Chamber of Deputies voted the necessary funds—but the American debt was to be paid only after Jackson had offered an explanation and an apology for his threats. "*From me, she will get neither,*" Jackson exclaimed, damning France. Despite these brave words, Jackson was careful to tell Congress that he had no intention "to menace or insult" the French government, and those words sufficed to appease the French. By the spring of 1836, Jackson was able to announce that four of the six installments on the debt had been paid.

While Americans were welcoming Jackson's triumph over France with keen approval, the President's attention was concentrated upon events in Texas, a loosely administered part of the young Republic of Mexico where thousands of Americans had settled in recent years. Alarmed by these trends, in 1830 Mexico adopted stringent laws which prohibited additional American emigration, enforced that nation's ban on slavery, reimposed customs duties that curtailed direct trade between Texas and United States ports such as New Orleans, and provided for garrisons of Mexican troops in Texas to see that these regulations were obeyed.

It should be emphasized that Mexico had every right to act as it did. Texas was Mexican soil and so recognized by the United States government, and Americans who lived there, many of whom had become Mexican citizens, were subject to Mexican law. But the result was a two-pronged campaign by Texas to revive the Constitution of 1824 (which emphasized federalism) and thus make Texas a separate state within the Republic of Mexico or to become free from Mexican rule. Older settlers, men who had received land for 6 cents an acre (or even less) at a time when an acre cost $1.25 in United States territories, at first tended to favor statehood; newcomers, less tolerant of Mexican customs and legal practices, especially the absence of trial by jury, opted for independence. The crux of the matter was, those who got there first rarely paid taxes on their huge ranches, had learned how to deal with local officialdom, and—if the easy relationship of the 1820s could be revived—were willing to remain under Mexican rule.

In 1833, Stephen F. Austin (1793–1836), a large landowner who had developed settlement schemes initiated by his Connecticut-born father, went to Mexico City with petitions for statehood. A representative in a provincial legislature and a man with considerable experience in Mexican politics, Austin also contrived while there to have the decrees of 1830 repealed. However, en route home he was thrown into jail and remained there for eighteen months without formal charges or a trial. Suddenly set free when a new government granted a general amnesty, Austin returned to Texas broken in health and his loyalty as a Mexican citizen much impaired. Once home, he quickly discovered that the new regime in Mexico City, led by Dictator Antonio López de Santa Anna (ca. 1795–1876), had launched a bitter campaign to snuff out all opposition and abolish federalism, which, of course, fanned the fires of the Texas independence movement.

Early in 1836, Santa Anna, having subdued other trouble spots within the republic, brought his main force of several brigades to Texas. In February, his men laid seige to a small rebel garrison lodged in an old mission complex near San Antonio known as the Alamo. After thirteen days the walls were scaled and some 150 to 200 Texans slaugh-

Siege of the Alamo on March 6, 1836. News of the siege, and the subsequent massacre of it's defenders, stiffened Texan resistance. Two months later, under the rallying cry "Remember the Alamo!" Texans defeated the Mexican army and captured General Santa Anna at San Jacinto.

tered. Strangely, those who died there were fighting not under an independent banner but under the red, white, and green flag of Mexico with "1824" (representing the liberal constitution of that year) superimposed upon it. However, four days before the Alamo fell, a formal Declaration of Independence was proclaimed by other Texans some hundred miles to the east, and this action, coupled with the useless bloodshed at the Alamo, sparked a true revolution.

Two months later, with the cry "Remember the Alamo!" ringing across the plains, the Texas army, led by Sam Houston (1793–1863), who was a former congressman, an ex-governor of Tennessee, and perhaps a secret agent in the pay of Andrew Jackson, defeated Santa Anna at San Jacinto and Texas achieved its independence. Yet this was not exactly what many citizens of the new nation really wanted; instead, they were eager to become part of the United States.

Jackson, who had long wanted to buy Texas and had permitted American diplomats to use bribery, blackmail, and even loan-shark tactics to obtain it, now hesitated before taking any precipitous action, for he feared war with Mexico. More importantly, if Texas was admitted as a state, the annexation could engender a new dispute between Northerners and Southerners over whether the region would be slave or free, and that dispute might jeopardize the chances of Jackson's party in the 1836 election. As a result, the President did not recognize the republic until the day before he left the White House in 1837.

The Jacksonian Heritage

Jackson's most significant accomplishment was his redefinition of the presidency. Forceful in manner and confident of his popularity, Jackson reshaped the office into a position of enormous power and influence by using his veto power, by removing government workers from office and naming their replacements, and by heading up a political party based on mass participation and organized for national action. Jackson became a symbol of the people's aspirations for democracy and participation in government. Yet the expanded presidency was a mixed blessing. The positive aspects of a strong chief executive are quick, well-directed responses to domestic needs and international crises. The negative aspects are the distortion of the traditional constitutional balance among the three branches of government and the possibility that the executive branch could mislead the people or limit their options through biased propaganda and management of the news.

A New Party System: Whigs and Democrats

His conduct as President won Jackson both friends and enemies. Members of the coalition opposed to him formed a new political party—the Whigs, named after the party that fought royal supremacy in England and sought to restore a "proper" constitutional balance by giving more weight to Parliament. In American terms, "King Andrew" was the monarch and foe and Congress the friend of liberty. The Whigs brought together disparate elements: the National Republicans such as John Quincy Adams and Henry Clay, the states' rights Democrats led by John C. Calhoun and John Tyler, of Virginia, and the Anti-Masons led by William Wirt. This last group, the first "third party" in U.S. political history, was especially strong in Vermont, New York, and Pennsylvania during the 1830s. In 1832 it drew support from Clay and helped reelect Jackson, but by 1838 the party merged with the Whigs. More important interest groups that came together in the Whig party included industrialists and merchants from the Northeast, led by Daniel Webster; champions of internal improvements from the West, led by Clay; and states' righters and wealthy planters from the South, led by John Tyler.

Although opposition to Jackson was the immediate goal of the Whigs, they offered voters an optimistic picture of the nation's future and, in contrast to Jacksonian laissez-faire, recommended a vigorous role for the federal government as a promoter of a healthy economy. Clay's American System lay at the heart of the Whig economic program; the Whigs called for a protective tariff that would promote American economic independence and lessen the country's reliance on foreign products and backed internal improvements that would bind together the industrial Northeast, the agricultural West, and the cotton South.

The Whigs, staunchly Protestant, tended to be

Andrew Jackson portrayed as "King Andrew," using his veto power to place his will above that of the Constitution, the federal courts, and the needs of the people.

churchgoing men who admired respectability and feared the alarming influx of foreigners, especially Irish Catholics. In spite of the elitist temper of the party, it included workers (especially those who resented immigrant competition for jobs). The Whigs also won support from free blacks in the North, since Jackson and most Democrats opposed equal suffrage rights for blacks and the Whigs, despite some doubletalk, seemed more sympathetic to black political aspirations.

A major factor that forged these disparate elements into a new political party was support for the Bank of the United States. Unity on the issue of the Bank and a general dislike for Jackson joined those Southerners, who abhorred the idea of a protective tariff and had threatened secession, with New Englanders who favored the tariff and abhorred states' rights. The Bank was very useful to southern planters, to northern manufacturers and merchants, and to western entrepreneurs. The battle over rechartering the BUS had very significant results in the political realm since it helped to create the Whig party and establish rigid alignments that lasted for nearly a quarter of a century.

The Election of 1836

The election of 1836 pitted the Whigs against Van Buren, Jackson's Vice President. Whig leaders knew that their party was not yet well organized, that it was full of conflicting views. In choosing a candidate, the party bypassed Clay, who had not done well in the 1832 election, and put up strong sectional candidates in various states. Webster was the candidate in New England. In Tennessee, Hugh L. White ran with Whig support after he broke with Jackson when it became clear that Van Buren, never popular in Tennessee, had received the Democratic nomination. William Henry Harrison of Ohio campaigned under the Whig banner in the West and the Middle Atlantic states.

The Democrats were riddled with factionalism. Many Southerners refused to support New Yorker Van Buren, and others were still seething with discontent over Jackson's handling of the South Carolina nullifiers. The party attempted to stress its record, accusing the Whigs of favoring that bastion of privilege, the BUS, a "wasteful" system of internal improvements, nullification, and high tariffs.

Jackson's own personality, however, was the chief issue, and the election returns were not much comfort to him. Van Buren received only fifty-one percent of the popular vote. No vice presidential candidate received a majority of the electoral votes, so the Senate eventually chose Richard M. Johnson, the Democratic contender for that office. The two parties, with almost an equal number of supporters, appeared to dominate no particular region and a truly national two-party system seemed to be emerging.

Van Buren and Economic Problems

In his inaugural address, Van Buren stressed the need for national unity—an emphasis that reflected the factionalism he knew existed within his own party. To still the fears of southern whites, Van Buren promised that his administration would not interfere with the institution of slavery—a promise

THE TIMES.

The Clarence Davies Collection, Museum of the City of New York.

A Whig cartoonist's view of the Panic of 1837. A caricature of President Andrew Jackson watches over idle ships and workers while bank depositors clamor for their money, a mother and child beg, a husband drinks his troubles away, and a pawnbroker's shop prospers.

that infuriated abolitionists. But also he intimated that he would not push for annexation of Texas, which Southerners wanted to become a slave state.

Slavery, however, was not the first problem Van Buren had to tackle. Rather, it quickly became apparent that he had inherited a major depression. The Panic of 1837 was brought about by Jackson's destruction of BUS, which had restricted the issuance of paper money by state banks. The Specie Circular of 1836 sharply decreased the demand for public land but at the same time it fed inflation by freeing money for other uses. Simultaneously, a depression in England lowered the price of south-

ern cotton. By mid-1837 banks all over the nation were in deep trouble, plantations were selling at low prices, food prices were soaring, and factories were shutting down.

Although many people, including loyal Democrats, clamored for the President to revoke Jackson's Specie Circular, Van Buren refused. A complete break between the government and all banks was what Van Buren wanted, and in 1840 Congress finally passed his Independent Treasury Act, which required the deposit of all federal funds in government-owned vaults in various parts of the country. In the process, Van Buren lost the support of those

The Age of Jackson

Democrats who had a personal interest in keeping federal funds in state banks. The only political gain of Van Buren's move was the return of Calhoun to the Democratic party. Calhoun never had been at ease with such Whig policies as the advocacy of a strong central government in charge of high tariffs and extensive internal improvements. He had long been in favor of an independent Treasury, and he welcomed Van Buren's bill as an opportunity for returning to the Democratic fold.

Although northern and southern Whigs disagreed about the efficacy of a Bank of the United States, a protective tariff, and internal improvements, nevertheless they closed ranks in blaming the depression on Democratic policies. Other issues also hurt Van Buren's chances for re-election. Some Southerners held that the President's failure to arrange for the annexation of Texas meant that he was secretly sympathetic to abolition. Conversely, abolitionists (such as Congressman Joshua Reed Giddings, whose leadership and contributions are described in an accompanying biographical sketch) maintained that Van Buren was proslavery because he endorsed the bloody Seminole War, which they viewed as a federally financed effort to return fugitive slaves living among the Indians to their white masters. Van Buren therefore had the disadvantage of seeming antislavery in the South and proslavery in the North. Moreover, abolitionists were especially incensed by the refusal of both houses of Congress to discuss petitions relating to slavery. After 1836, by tacit agreement, the Senate received antislavery petitions but rejected them. At the beginning of each session from 1836 to 1844 the House adopted a gag rule that automatically tabled any petition relating to slavery.

Whig Triumph of 1840

As the election of 1840 approached, the Whigs sensed victory. Remembering that William Henry Harrison had made the best showing among Whigs in the previous election, they offered him the nomination. An attractive candidate, Harrison had defeated Tecumseh's forces at the Battle of Tippecanoe in 1811. Harrison, who was of southern ancestry (born in Virginia), had a popular following in the Old Northwest. Best of all, his political sentiments were vague.

Harrison was the choice of the New York Whig boss, Thurlow Weed, a man who did for the Whigs in 1840 what Van Buren had done for the Democrats in 1828. Weed, grasping the nature of modern pol-

Joshua Reed Giddings

1795–1864

A strident voice against slavery during the middle decades of the nineteenth century, Joshua Giddings represents a maverick point of view that maintained that the federal government should do nothing that supported the institution of slavery.

Born in Pennsylvania to a restless frontier family of New England stock, Giddings grew up in Ohio. After rudimentary schooling and a brief career as an Indian fighter during the War of 1812, he taught school, farmed, married a girl from Connecticut, and began to study law in the town of Canton. Admitted to the bar in 1821, he set up a general practice in nearby Jefferson and, except for a term in the state legislature (1826), showed little interest in politics.

It was the financial crisis of 1837 and association with Abolitionist Theodore D. Weld that altered Giddings' life. The money panic ruined his dreams of a real estate fortune, and new antislavery zeal inspired him to seek a seat in Congress when the local incumbent decided to retire. During the next two decades Giddings moved from Whig to Free

Soiler to Republican, always on the attack against slavery. The illicit slave trade, Texas, the Mexican War, the Wilmot Proviso—all felt his scorn. In 1842 the House of Representatives censured him because of his relentless and bitter opposition to the U.S. coastal slave trade. Giddings immediately resigned but obtained the overwhelming endorsement of his district when he ran for reelection, winning by a vote of 7469 to 393.

During the 1847–1848 session, Giddings and young Abraham Lincoln shared the same lodgings, but not the same opinions. Giddings found the tall man from Illinois too timid on slavery and several of their table discussions led to heated words. Nevertheless a relationship emerged that lasted for many years. Because of ill health, Giddings quit Congress in 1858 and in that same year published *The Exiles of Florida: or, The Crimes Committed by our Government Against the Maroons, Who Fled from South Carolina and Other Slave States, Seeking Protection Under Spanish Laws.* This attack upon the machinations of southern Presidents (Madison, Monroe, and Jackson) brought to light the cruelty experienced by both runaway slaves and Indians of the Southeast.

Despite misgivings, Giddings backed Lincoln in 1860 and also worked hard (and successfully) to get cabinet posts for Ohio politicians. In 1861 Lincoln named Giddings consul general for Canada where he died suddenly three years later at the home of a Montreal friend while analyzing a difficult, three-cushion billiard shot.

A parade assembling at Whig Headquarters in Philadelphia in 1840. Whig politicians, following the Democratic strategy of 1828 and even appropriating the Democratic label, presented candidate William Henry Harrison as a homespun, log-cabin hero.

itics, argued that tactics not principles win campaigns. To assure Harrison's election, Weed secured the vice presidential nomination for Virginian John Tyler, a states' rights Democrat alienated from his party by Jackson's war on the Bank and his handling of the South Carolina nullifiers. Weed hoped that Tyler would attract southern votes.

The Whigs followed the Democratic precedent of 1828 by using parades, rallies, songs, and slogans in order to paint Van Buren as an aristocrat and Harrison as a frontiersman and military hero. They decided not to have a platform at all, since their fragmented party might fall apart over stated principles. Instead the party relied exclusively on ballyhoo.

Harrison garnered fifty-three percent of the popular vote and won 234 electoral votes compared to 60 votes for Van Buren. The popular margin was about 146,500 votes. Now politicians were certain that ballyhoo techniques could capture the White House.

Politics, Expansion, And Slavery

Victory in 1840 did not bring the factions in the Whig party together. Harrison never really commanded much respect among his fellow Whigs, and one month after he assumed office he died of pneumonia. Differences within the Whig Party quickly came out into the open.

John Tyler, the first Vice President to inherit through death the position of chief executive, shared very few of the ideas of Whig leaders, and Henry Clay had no intention of letting him head the party. Tyler used the presidential veto to stop Whig efforts to revive the Bank of the United States, to pass internal improvement bills, to institute higher tariffs, and to distribute proceeds of public land sales to the states. All of the original members of Harrison's cabinet except Secretary of State Daniel Webster resigned in disgust after six months.

Webster remained in the cabinet because he was entering upon delicate negotiations with Great Britain. American feelings toward England, never too cordial, became still more hostile in the late 1830s and early 1840s. At least five areas of disagreement existed between the two nations during these years. They included two Canadian border disputes, the Oregon question, the African slave trade, and the British intrigue in Texas.

In 1837 Canadian insurgents, dissatisfied with London's rule, fled to an island in the Niagara River, where Americans supplied them with recruits and arms. One American steamer, the *Caroline*, aided the rebellious Canadians. The British sent a small force to seize the vessel; when they discovered that the *Caroline* had moved to the American side of the Niagara River, the British force continued its mission and burned and sank the ship. One American was killed and others wounded. Americans were incensed when the British government refused to apologize to the United States.

A second border incident erupted in February 1839 as Canadian and American lumberjacks tried to oust each other from the Aroostook Valley, an area claimed by both Maine and New Brunswick. In March President Van Buren sent General Winfield Scott to Maine to negotiate an end to the undeclared and, fortunately, bloodless war. A truce was arranged by May, but the border continued to be vaguely defined.

Many Americans in the late 1830s and early 1840s were also troubled by British claims in the Oregon country. American interest in Oregon can be traced back at least to the Louisiana Purchase and the Lewis and Clark expedition. During the 1830s, thousands of Americans traveled the tortuous 2,000 mile-long Oregon Trail from Independence, Missouri, to settle in Oregon's Willamette Valley, and they were anxious to obtain formal recognition of the region as a part of the United States.

Another source of difficulty between the two nations was the African slave trade. Both governments had outlawed this traffic in humans; but, unlike the United States, the British vigorously enforced their prohibition. Americans resented British searches of suspected slave ships; indeed, they had gone to war in 1812 to protest similar actions. This ill feeling intensified in November 1841 when the blacks aboard the American brig *Creole* en route to New Orleans from Virginia mutineed, killed a passenger, and sailed the ship to the British Bahamas. There the authorities charged the ringleaders with mutiny and murder but freed the rest of the blacks, despite protests by the United States. Southerners may have been the most vocal group denouncing the British actions, but Americans in all parts of the nation were angered by these events.

British intrigues in Texas also stirred Americans. Britain favored an independent Texas, for it hoped that the new republic would provide both an alternative supply of cotton and a market for British goods outside of the American tariff system. Southerners especially feared that British influence in Texas might eventually lead to the abolition of slavery there.

In order to settle some of the major Anglo-American disputes and to prevent a third war between the two nations, Secretary of State Daniel Webster met with England's envoy, Lord Ashburton, in a series of conferences in 1842. Webster and Ashburton got along remarkably well; Ashburton was sympathetic to Webster's arguments since he was a businessman married to an American heiress and had large investments in the United States. Both men recognized that Britain's colonial holdings were less important to its economy than continued trade with America. Ashburton expressed regret that "some explanation and apology" had not been made for the sinking of the *Caroline* and Webster also accepted the vague promise that "officious interference" by British authorities with American vessels like the *Creole* would not reoccur. On the larger question of the African slave trade, both nations agreed to suppress the traffic by stationing separate but cooperating fleets in African waters. The Maine boundary dispute was settled by a compromise line, the present boundary, which gave the United States some 7,000 of the 12,000 square miles of wilderness under dispute. Without any reciprocal concession, Ashburton agreed to a Canadian-U.S. boundary between Lake Superior and the Lake of the Woods. Left unsettled was the question of Oregon and British intrigue in Texas.

Though Webster conducted an extensive propaganda campaign to sell the Webster-Ashburton Treaty of 1842, the citizens of Maine resented the treaty and felt shortchanged. And nearly a century later it turned out they were right. The famous "red line" map found in Madrid in 1933, a copy of the map used during the peace negotiations of 1783, validated American claims in that region. Nevertheless, the treaty preserved peace between England and the United States, firmed up the border with Canada and awarded the United States 6,500 square miles in Minnesota that contained the priceless Mesabi iron deposits. Webster resigned from the cabinet in 1843 at the completion of the negotiations.

His Accidency and Whig Troubles

Despite the fact that he was a chief executive almost without a party, Tyler's administration produced other solid results such as reorganization of the Navy, establishment of facilities that developed into the National Observatory, promotion of the use of the telegraph, and negotiation of a treaty opening up trade with China. Early in 1841 Tyler supported the successful effort by Whigs in Congress to repeal Van Buren's Independent Treasury law; for the next five years the federal government deposited its money in state banks.

Jacksonian Democrats long had wanted a land policy that would benefit the poor settler, and in 1841 the Preemption Act finally realized this goal. It allowed settlers to squat on land—up to 160 acres. When the land was put up for sale by the govern-

ment, the squatter had the right to buy it without fear of competitive bids and at the lowest government price. Preemption was a major triumph for the West. Called the "Log Cabin Act," it was linked to a proposal made by Henry Clay to distribute some of the proceeds of public land sales to the debt-burdened states, but this distribution bill was further connected with a provision for low tariff rates (distribution would be stopped if tariffs exceeded 20 percent). Since the tariff rate soon moved upward, distribution never went into effect.

In fact, in order to pay the growing national debt, Tyler was forced in 1842 to sign a high tariff bill, which restored duties back to the 1832 level. Statesmen of that period had a horror of federal debt; although the country had been quite free of debt in 1836, the government debt rose to $13,500,000 by 1842. The new tariff had to be revised three times before it could get past Tyler without a veto; many congressmen, including John Quincy Adams, were so angry at "His Accidency," as they called the President, that they unsuccessfully attempted to pass a constitutional amendment that would allow Congress to override a veto by a simple rather than a two-thirds majority.

The day after Tyler signed the Tariff of 1842 into law, Clay resigned from the Senate to prepare for the 1844 election. Tyler, anxious to win the presidency in his own right, now looked for new sources of support. To create a power base of his own, Tyler appointed a fellow Southerner, Calhoun, as Secretary of State in 1844. He also worked to add Texas, an area that would be likely to vote for him and would be a new slavery stronghold, to the Union. Even after he failed to win the party's nomination and while serving as a lame duck President, he sent American forces to the Gulf of Mexico and along the southwestern frontier of Texas without telling Congress or receiving the necessary authorization. Later, when Tyler submitted a treaty of annexation to the Senate, antislavery senators blocked its ratification, and Whig newspapers began to call for the President's impeachment. Tyler then proposed annexation by a joint resolution of Congress, one that would require only a simple rather than the usual two-thirds majority. Although some old Jeffersonian Republicans denounced this step as a violation of the Constitution, Texas finally was annexed by a joint resolution as Tyler was preparing to leave the White House in March 1845.

The Election of 1844

By 1844 a two-party system was fully reestablished and party loyalty had begun to outweigh the merits of the individual candidates. Ignoring Tyler, the Whigs nominated Clay as their candidate; Clay then received a visit from Van Buren, who seemed the obvious Democratic candidate, and the two men probably agreed not to bring up the issue of Texas, which could plunge the country into sectionally divisive debates over the explosive issue of slavery. Shortly before the Democrats met in Baltimore, both Clay and Van Buren published letters against the annexation of Texas on the grounds that it would lead to war with Mexico, since that country did not recognize the independence of Texas. The Whigs indeed remained silent on the subject of slavery, wary of alienating voters in both the North and South.

But the Democrats undermined this strategy by passing over Van Buren and nominating a dark horse, James K. Polk (1795–1849), Speaker of the House of Representatives and a former governor of Tennessee. Polk was a hard-money, Independent-Treasury Jacksonian, an expansionist, and a Democratic stalwart who enjoyed the confidence of Andrew Jackson. Whigs laughed at Polk's qualifications and asked, "Who is James K. Polk?", but they faced a tough electoral campaign in which Polk tried to remove the proslavery stigma of annexation of Texas by linking Texas with the "reoccupation" of Oregon.

The contest between Polk and Clay was complicated by the entrance of a third party, an antislavery faction active on the national scene since 1840, which was known as the Liberty party. In 1840 its candidate, James G. Birney, a moderate abolitionist (who is the subject of an accompanying biographical sketch), polled only 7,000 votes, despite the fact that there were some 1,500 antislavery societies in the country. At that point most abolitionists rejected a political solution to the slave issue and relied on moral suasion. By 1844, however, the party was gaining ground and won nearly 16,000 votes in New York alone—votes that otherwise might have gone to the Whig candidate Clay. Indeed, the Liberty party votes in New York allowed Polk to take that state—and thereby win the election, despite the fact that his views on slavery were even less acceptable to abolitionists than Clay's.

The Liberty party may have inadvertently given the election to Polk, but it received only 2.3 percent of the popular vote. Polk won with 49.6 percent compared to Clay's 48.1 percent; in the Electoral College Polk took 170 votes, Clay 105. Despite the Liberty party's poor showing, it soon won more converts as the events of the Polk administration convinced many Northerners that southern slaveholders were conspiring to control the federal government and promote their own interests over those of the rest of the country. As the debate over slavery heated up, the old coalitions of Northerners and Southerners began to break down in both of the major parties.

Young Hickory in Office

As his nickname indicates, Polk was a convinced Jacksonian and, like his mentor, an enemy to the Bank of the United States, a foe of federally financed internal improvements, and a champion of cheap land. As he said in his first message to Congress, the duty of government is to help citizens "become the owners of small portions of our vast public domain at low and moderate prices." Polk pledged to work for a lower tariff, a policy that made him attractive to Calhoun and many Southerners. After his election but before his inauguration, Polk, the youngest man (49 years old) to be elevated to the presidency up to that time, worked hard to promote the annexation of Texas, which Congress approved by joint resolution in February 1845.

With the Texas issue settled, Polk announced four objectives in his inaugural address on March 4, 1845. These were: (1) reduction of the tariff; (2) reestablishment of the Independent Treasury; (3) settlement of the Oregon boundary; and (4) acquisition of California. Polk accomplished the first three goals with the cooperation of Congress before the end of the first session of the Twenty-Ninth Congress. The acquisition of California was achieved by the end of his term.

Polk's administration, in many ways the culmination of the Jacksonian philosophy, was an outstanding success—if one accepts these goals as criteria. He revived the Monroe Doctrine (in fact, he was the first to use that term) to prevent European colonization in Yucatan, even though residents there were eager to accept rule by either Spain or Great Britain. He struggled mightily with the spoils

James Gillespie Birney

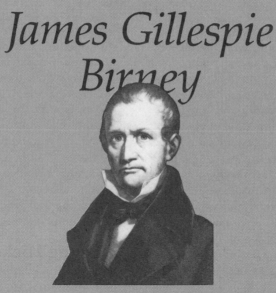

1792–1857

Born in Danville, Kentucky, and the only son of an Irish immigrant who became one of the state's wealthiest men, Birney was educated at Transylvania University in Kentucky and at the College of New Jersey (now Princeton). The elder Birney, though a slaveholder, favored emancipation and obviously imparted some of his ideas to his son, who returned to Kentucky to practice law and became, by marriage, master of several slaves.

In 1818, Birney moved to Alabama where, although not a member of a state constitutional convention, he seems to have influenced certain provisions designed to encourage emancipation and prohibit the introduction of slaves into the state for sale. As a result of gambling and neglect of his lands, he plunged into debt; early in 1823 he sold his plantation with its slaves and moved to Huntsville where he developed a successful law practice.

The decade from 1825 to 1835 marked Birney's transition from emancipationist to active abolitionist. Brought up an Episcopalian, at the urging of his wife in 1826 he became a Presbyterian, a move that coincided with his interest in African colonization for freed slaves and in the general restriction of slavery. A visit to New England three years later convinced him of the superiority of free institutions, and in 1832 he began touring the South as an agent of the American Colonization Society.

In 1834 he freed six of his own slaves and soon after quit the colonization movement. No longer able to reconcile colonization and gradual emancipation with his religious and social ideals, he took up the cause of immediate emancipation. As his campaign against slavery intensified, Birney had to leave the Lower South, living briefly in Kentucky and Ohio before moving to New York in 1837. While living in Ohio he aided the "Underground Railroad." By 1837, Birney's standing as an abolitionist was sufficient for him to be elected executive secretary of the American Anti-Slavery Society, yet he was not in total accord with the more radical abolitionists headed by Garrison. They were opposed to the Constitution (since it endorsed slavery) and felt that moral suasion, not political power, should bring about emancipation. Birney, by contrast, supported the Constitution and argued for political action. Accordingly, Birney was nominated in 1840 as the first presidential candidate of the new antislavery organization, the Liberty party. He was the presidential candidate of the Liberty party again in 1844 and received 62,000 votes. A fall from a horse in the summer of 1845 partially paralyzed him and led to his retirement from public life.

Birney, a prize catch for northern abolitionists, nevertheless was a strange figure in their midst. He never supported slavery yet owned slaves, accepting the institution as he found it and seeking gradually to change it. He was a reasonable man who understood the law and thus incurred the wrath of radicals such as Garrison.

system and was an unusually conscientious administrator; yet, the intraparty feuds within the Democratic party led him to pledge that he would only serve one term.

Continental Expansion and Manifest Destiny

In the early 1840s many Americans believed God had decreed that Texas, Oregon, and much of the rest of North America should be part of the United States. Evidence of this strong faith in America's "Manifest Destiny" could be found in the press, in the halls of Congress, and on the political hustings. One of the most influential voices was that of John L. O'Sullivan (1813–18??), ?? the *United States Magazine and* ?? a journal that was Democratic in comp?? ardently expansionist. By 1845, according?? O'Sullivan, it had become America's "manifest destiny to overspread the continent alloted by Providence for the free development of our yearly multiplying millions."

During the previous decade Jacksonian democracy had transformed confident nationalism and the idea of progress into a natural law of territorial expansion, expansion seen not only as inevitable but also as carrying out the will of God. Viewed in this light, the "reoccupation" of Oregon was ordained by both natural and divine forces.

Collection of Harry T. Peters, Jr.

This John Gast painting entitled *Manifest Destiny* **shows Indians and wild animals fleeing in terror before the Spirit of Progress, who wears the star of empire on her forehead, carries a book representing common-school education, and strings telegraph wire as she skims the ground. Joining the Spirit of Progress on her westward trek are the various forms of transportation and people representing the different occupations that characterized the years leading to the fulfillment of America's destiny.**

Interest in the Oregon country was stirred by missionaries who agitated for American control of the region. By 1842 the Oregon Trail, roughly traced in the 1830s by explorers and fur traders, was beaten into rutted roadways by wagon trains. In the so-called "great migration" of 1843 about a thousand people and twice as many animals followed the trail west. Additional wagon trains traveled the now famous route in 1844 and 1845 as "Oregon fever" spread.

Although the Democratic platform and Polk himself had asserted that the United States had "clear and unquestionable" title to the "whole" of Oregon—that is, north to the southern boundary of Russian Alaska at 54°40'—Polk was not eager to go to war with Britain. Under the Treaty of Joint Occupation of 1818, the Oregon country, stretching northward from the forty-second parallel to the line of 54°40', was open to settlement by both the United States and England. After his inaugural, Polk *publicly* called for recognition of American title as far north at 54°40', but *privately* he was willing to settle for the forty-ninth parallel. This duplicity misled many Westerners, and the cry of "Fifty-four forty or fight!" soon echoed across the land.

When the English offered in 1846 to set the boundary line at the forty-ninth parallel, Secretary of War John C. Calhoun used his influence to promote acceptance of the plan. Calhoun especially warned southern expansionists that British markets for southern cotton might be endangered if they insisted on 54°40'. Polk and the Senate accepted the English offer, but many Americans on the West coast objected. Antislavery forces grumbled, since they felt that Polk, suspected of southern sympathies, had fought hard to annex all of Texas, where slavery was already established, but had not held out for all of the Oregon country, where slavery would not be introduced. If many senators readily accepted England's offer of the forty-ninth parallel, they did so primarily because the United States already was involved in a war with Mexico and could not risk another international conflict.

The Mexican War

While staving off war with mighty England, Polk provoked weak Mexico into open hostility. In determining the southern border of Texas, Polk was in no mood for compromise; he demanded the Rio Grande. To secure that border (and to acquire California in the process), Polk was willing to shed American blood. He sent General Zachary Taylor to occupy the disputed territory between the Rio Grande and the Nueces River. In April 1846, American and Mexican troops skirmished. Polk, disregarding the constitutional stipulation that Congress alone had the power to declare war and aware that many Northerners were opposed to war, simply announced the opening of hostilities. He then shrewdly attached the declaration of war to an appropriations bill designed to pay for fighting already in progress. If congressmen now failed to endorse the war, they would be accused of refusing to fund loyal American troops already in the field—a stand that would appear unpatriotic, even traitorous. This ploy was a striking demonstration of Polk's determination to compel a reluctant Congress to support his aggressive foreign policy in the Southwest. In reality, Polk was interested in much more than Texas; he hoped to seize the northern provinces of Mexico and all of California. That Polk met most of his territorial objectives testifies to his success in using the power of the presidency to get what he wanted, a technique sometimes emulated by his successors. (The essay at the end of this chapter, "Polk and the Problems of a Powerful Presidency," explores this issue in greater detail.)

Many political leaders opposed the war, calling it unnecessary and unconstitutional. Abraham Lincoln, a first-term Whig congressman from Illinois in 1847–1848, was among those who denounced Polk. For the most part, this opposition was both sectional and partisan, that is, it came largely from northern Whigs. The President had defended his actions by saying that the war was not aggressive but defensive. Lincoln aroused intense controversy when he introduced his "Spot Resolutions" calling upon Polk to name the very "spot" where American blood had been spilled on American soil. According to Lincoln, the land where the first skirmish took place was not legitimately part of the United States but rather Mexican (and certainly the boundary was unclear).

Antislavery Whigs and abolitionists called the conflict "Mr. Polk's War." Early in 1846, Pennsylvania Congressman David Wilmot, a Democrat, introduced a proviso to an appropriations bill stipulating that none of the territory won from Mexico should be open to slavery. Although the Wilmot Proviso passed the House twice, it met defeat in the Senate. Nevertheless, the proviso became a rallying point for free soil Northerners and helped to dramatize the split between the North and the South.

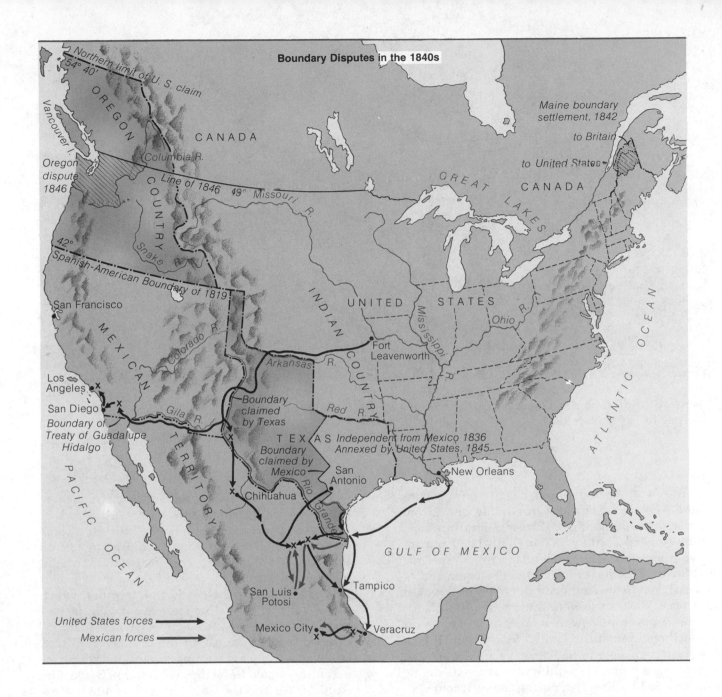

Boundary Disputes in the 1840s

Northern limit of U.S. claim
54° 40'

OREGON

CANADA

Vancouver I.

Columbia R.

Oregon dispute 1846

Line of 1846   49°   Missouri R.

GREAT LAKES

CANADA

Maine boundary settlement, 1842

to Britain

to United States

42°

Snake R.

OREGON COUNTRY

Spanish-American Boundary of 1819

San Francisco

UNITED   STATES

Mississippi R.

Ohio R.

INDIAN   COUNTRY

MEXICAN

Colorado R.

Fort Leavenworth

Arkansas   R.

Los Angeles   X

San Diego

Boundary of Treaty of Guadalupe Hidalgo

Gila R.

TERRITORY

X

X

Boundary claimed by Texas

Red   R.

T E X A S   Independent from Mexico 1836
Annexed by United States, 1845

Boundary claimed by Mexico

San Antonio

New Orleans

X

Chihuahua

Rio Grande

GULF OF MEXICO

ATLANTIC OCEAN

PACIFIC   OCEAN

San Luis Potosi

Tampico

United States forces ➝

Mexican forces ➝

Mexico City   X   X   Veracruz

American soldiers under General Winfield Scott storm the Castle of Chapultepec in September 1847.

The war, lasting about twenty-one months (1846–1848), consisted of a frustrating and inconclusive invasion southward from Texas by forces led by General Zachary Taylor (1784–1850) and another more successful march inland from Vera Cruz to Mexico City by units under the command of General Winfield Scott. Although Polk provoked this war, Mexican leaders must share the blame. Political opportunists were more than willing to stir up feelings against the United States; but, if Polk had not been determined to have California, the other issues probably could have been settled. The war cost $73 million and during the next four decades $64 million in pensions. Some 120,000 Americans were in uniform; of these, 1.5 percent died in battle, over 10 percent of disease, and 9,207 deserted.

The war ended with the Treaty of Guadalupe Hidalgo in 1848, which gave the United States its present southwestern boundaries, save for a small area along the Mexican border acquired in 1853 in the Gadsden Purchase. The treaty also brought many problems in its wake—a fight over the extension of slavery into the newly won territory, which intensified sectional strife and encouraged the disruption of political parties—circumstances that contributed to the outbreak of the Civil War. In fact, this war served as a training ground for young officers who would be facing each other in battle after April 1861. "The United States will conquer Mexico," Ralph Waldo Emerson had prophesied, "but it will be as the man who swallows the arsenic which brings him down in turn. Mexico will poison us."

Essay

Polk
and the Problems of a
Powerful Presidency

James Knox Polk, a rather frail man of iron will, is unique among the small band of men who have lived at 1600 Pennsylvania Avenue. He conceived and accomplished a very ambitious program in one term; he apparently never intended to seek another term; he kept an extensive diary; and he literally worked himself to death as chief executive. Every Tuesday and Saturday he held cabinet meetings at which he demanded reports, and he sometimes visited departments to see how his orders were being carried out. Polk's only diversion was daily walks, one just before sunrise and another after sunset. After more than a year in office, he noted with pride that he had dined out on one occasion and made only four social visits; only once had he been outside of the District of Columbia, a brief excursion to Mount Vernon.

A humorless, serious-minded individual who thought pleasure wasteful, Polk aged more dramatically during his White House tenure than most presidents have. Portraits of him at age forty-nine, the youngest man up to that time to win the presidency, and at fifty-four look almost like those of son and father. Within three months of his successor's inaugural, Polk was buried in the garden of his new home in Nashville, Tennessee, although his remains and those of his wife later were removed to the state capitol.

Polk Home, Columbia, Tennessee.
James K. Polk, the People's Choice in 1844.

Polk was inaugurated in the rain, amid what John Quincy Adams called "a large assemblage of umbrellas," and his address left little doubt that he planned to assert American claims to Oregon, reduce the tariff, and set up an independent treasury system. Privately Polk told friends that he also hoped to acquire California, and he might have added that he planned to annex Texas, since, though such a step was approved by Congress several days before he took office, the final negotiations with that young republic were still going on.

James Knox Polk, protégé of Andrew Jackson, did all of these things but is best remembered today as a strong chief executive who had his way and rounded out the western half of the nation from Texas to Puget Sound. Polk hoped to use money, bluff, and diplomatic bargaining to get what he wanted. But the Mexicans refused to sell and Polk soon found himself involved in a bitter confrontation between the White House and Capitol Hill.

Before this skirmishing ended, Polk greatly enlarged presidential power and the right of a President to withhold information from Congress. Polk's predecessor, Tyler, had given Webster $5,460 to defray his expenses while negotiating the border dispute between the United States and England. Later, when the House wanted to investigate how

This 1845 cartoon illustrates that the Texas and Oregon questions aroused strong feelings among Americans.

the money was spent, Polk refused to surrender the necessary documents. "The experience of every nation on earth," he told the House, "has demonstrated that emergencies may arise in which it becomes absolutely necessary for the public safety or the public good to make expenditures the very object of which would be defeated by publicity." If the President yielded to the House's request, then "he must answer similar calls for every expenditure of a confidential character, made under every Administration, in war and in peace, from the organization of the Government to the present period." The only time the House could *force* a President to hand over such documents was when it was conducting an investigation leading to possible impeachment. In an impeachment proceeding, Polk said, "the power of the House in pursuit of this object would penetrate into the most secret recesses of the Executive Departments."

The greatest outcry to that time against executive secrecy had concerned relations with Texas and Mexico. Without consulting Congress, Tyler had sent American forces to protect Texans against a possible Mexican invasion—before Texas had become part of the United States. When these secret arrangements and his treaty engineering the annexation of Texas were revealed, many Whig newspapers began to call for Tyler's impeachment. Once the annexation of Texas seemed assured, these objections died out, however.

When the Mexican government refused to receive Polk's envoy offering money for its lands between Texas and the Pacific, Polk concluded war was inevitable. Since many northern Congressmen opposed hostilities that they thought were designed solely to increase "The Slave Power," he looked for a way around this impediment. Mexico long had owed American citizens money for damage claims; the country was too poor, however, to honor these claims, and Polk considered declaring war on Mexico, using the unpaid debts as his pretext. He was on the verge of asking Congress to authorize war when he received information that gave him a better excuse.

Polk had sent General Zachary Taylor and a large force into the area between the Rio Grande and the Nueces River. Texas, partly at Polk's insistence, claimed the Rio Grande as its southern border; the Mexicans had a good case for designating the Nueces as the border; for, when Texas was a department of Mexico, that river had been its boundary. When Taylor moved into the disputed territory, Mexico regarded the action as a provocation. Polk instructed Taylor to consider any Mexican crossing of the Rio Grande as an act of war. Late in April a force of 1,600 Mexicans did just that and killed a small deputation of American soldiers. When this news reached Washington on May 9, Polk had his excuse for action.

In his war message to Congress, Polk announced that a state of war already existed since Mexico "has passed the boundary of the United States, has invaded our territory, and shed American blood upon the American soil." Polk declared war against Mexico without waiting for a congressional declaration as specified in the Constitution. He then stuck the declaration in the preamble to an appropriations bill for the prosecution of a war already in progress.

John Quincy Adams, formerly President and now a Congressman, denounced Polk in 1847. He said the war "has never to this day been declared by the Congress of the United States. It has [only] been recognized as existing by the Act of Mexico, in direct and notorious violation of the truth. . . . The most important conclusion from all this, in my mind, is the failure of that provision in the Constitution of the United States, that the power of declaring War is given exclusively to Congress." Adams dreaded the consequences of Polk's act.

Abraham Lincoln, a first-term member of the House of Representatives, also understood the dangerous implications of Polk's act. He felt that if the President was allowed to determine on his own when a foreign country was threatening invasion and must be repelled by a "defensive" war, then the chief executive had taken warmaking powers away from Congress. Warmaking had been the prerogative of kings, and the Constitution, Lincoln said, specifically denied this royal privilege to the President. The Founding Fathers, Lincoln wrote, "resolved to so frame the Constitution that *no one man* should hold the power of bringing the oppression upon us."

Polk clearly got what he wanted, claiming as he pursued his goals that he represented the will of the American people and that Congress could speak only for various districts and states. This stance was rather dangerous since reading the minds of millions of Americans was and always will be an obscure, uncertain art; in addition, his narrow victory at the polls in 1844 certainly was no mandate to do much of anything. To get his way, he withheld patronage, twisted arms, and evoked patriotism.

Yet, although Polk enhanced the power of the office he held and remained steadfast in the "continental vision" that greatly enlarged the territory of the United States of America, he was, in a sense, a failure. It is the duty of every President, as leader of his party, to keep his party unified so as to win reelection or to be sure his successor will continue the policies of his administration. This Polk did not do. Also, while he may have been blessed with "continental vision," this man comprehended neither the changing nature of the slavery debate nor the awesome effect the acquisition of new territory would have upon that controversy.

Just as other chief executives striving to be known as "strong" Presidents would learn, an aggressive foreign policy may turn sour; what the electorate seems to want at the outset—an overseas empire or complete victory in Korea or Vietnam, for example—can become so elusive and so costly that the voters change their minds. Polk was luckier than some of those who followed in his wake. The Mexican War was soon over, successfully and relatively cheaply; the Civil War, which followed, was a quite different conflict. But, by the time the true cost of Polk's adventure in nation building became apparent in the heightened rhetoric over slave and free territory, he was dead. Polk evidently thought that whatever domestic ruckus he stirred up by seizing some 5,000 square miles of territory could be solved by compromise, but by the early 1860s effective compromise on this smoldering issue was no longer possible.

SELECTED
READINGS

General Accounts

John R. Howe, *From the Revolution Through the Age of Jackson: Innocence and Empire in the Young Republic* (1973)

Edward Pessen, *Jacksonian America: Society, Personality, and Politics* (rev. ed., 1978)

Leonard L. Richards, *The Advent of American Democracy: 1815–1848* (1977)

Arthur M. Schlesinger, Jr., *The Age of Jackson* (1945)

Glyndon G. Van Deusen, *The Jacksonian Era: 1828–1848* (1959)

Politicians and Political Parties

Samuel Flagg Bemis, *John Quincy Adams and the Union* (1956)

Lee Benson, *The Concept of Jacksonian Democracy: New York as a Test Case* (1964)

Kinley J. Brauer, *Cotton Versus Conscience: Massachusetts Whig Politics and Southwestern Expansion, 1843–1848* (1967)

James C. Curtis, *The Fox at Bay: Martin Van Buren and the Presidency, 1837–1841* (1970)

Ronald P. Formisano, *The Birth of Mass Political Parties: Michigan, 1827–1861* (1971)

Robert G. Gunderson, *The Log Cabin Campaign* (1957)

Daniel W. Howe, *The Political Culture of the American Whigs* (1980)

Richard B. Latner, *The Presidency of Andrew Jackson: White House Politics, 1829–1837* (1979)

Richard P. McCormick, *The Second American Party System: Party Formation in the Jacksonian Era* (1966)

Charles A. McCoy, *Polk and the Presidency* (1960)

Marvin Meyers, *The Jacksonian Persuasion: Politics & Belief* (1960)

Robert J. Morgan, *A Whig Embattled: The Presidency under John Tyler* (1954)

Lorman Ratner, *Anti-Masonry: The Crusade and the Party* (1969)

Robert V. Remini, *Andrew Jackson* (1966)

Expansion and Slavery

K. Jack Bauer, *The Mexican War, 1846–1848* (1974)

Ernest M. Lander, Jr., *Reluctant Imperialists: Calhoun, the South Carolinians, and the Mexican War* (1980)

Fredrick Merk, *Manifest Destiny and Mission in American History: A Reinterpretation* (1963)

Chaplain W. Morrison, *Democratic Politics and Sectionalism: The Wilmont Proviso Controversy* (1967)

David M. Pletcher, *The Diplomacy of Annexation: Texas, Oregon, and the Mexican War* (1973)

Charles G. Sellers, Jr., *James K. Polk: Continentalist, 1843–1846* (1966)

Special Studies

William H. Freehling, *Prelude to Civil War: The Nullification Controversy in South Carolina* (1966)

Robert V. Remini, *Andrew Jackson and the Bank War* (1967)

Ronald N. Satz, *American Indian Policy in the Jacksonian Era* (1975)

Peter Temin, *The Jacksonian Economy* (1969)

John William Ward, *Andrew Jackson: Symbol for an Age* (1955)

Leonard D. White, *The Jacksonians: A Study in Administrative History, 1829–1861* (1954)

Paul A. Varg, *United States Foreign Relations, 1820–1860* (1979)

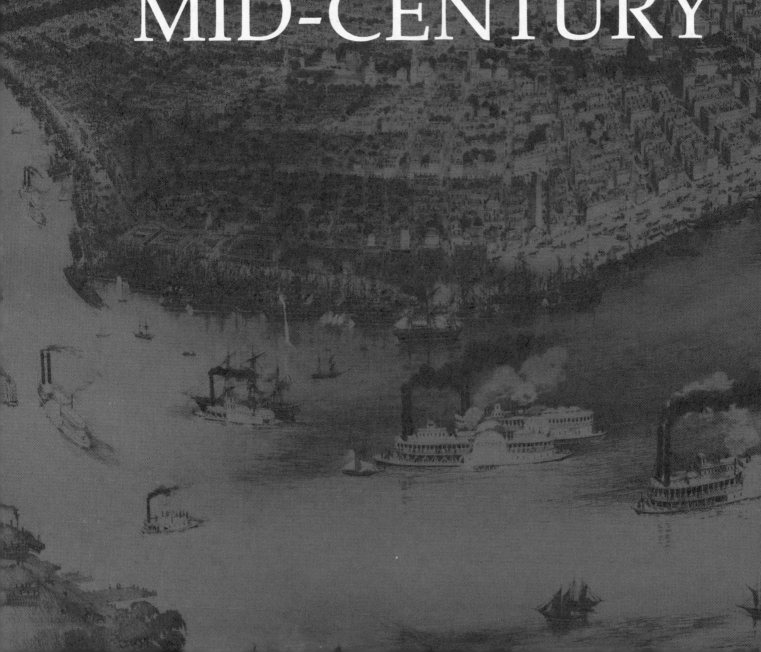

CHAPTER 12
AMERICA AT MID-CENTURY

TIMELINE

1841
Passage of Preemption Act

1842
William Gilmore Simms publishes *Beauchampe*

1844
Treaty of Wanghia opens Chinese ports to American trade

1846
Iowa becomes a state

1848
Discovery of gold in California

1849
Francis Parkman publishes *The California and Oregon Trail*

1850
The nation's population reaches 23,191,876

1850
California admitted to the Union

1851
Stephen Foster Publishes "The Old Folks at Home"

1853
Gadsden Purchase adds land south of the Gila River

1854
Know-Nothing party becomes a strong political force

1854
Graduation Act reduces price of unsold federal lands

1854
Commodore Perry secures treaty with Japan

1857
Panic of 1857 increases unemployment

1858
Minnesota becomes a state

1859
Oregon admitted to the Union

CHAPTER OUTLINE

By focusing upon the decade before 1860 as merely a prelude to the Civil War, some historians have obscured significant developments that were shaping the character of the United States in the first half of the nineteenth century. Now that the tragic division of North and South is finally being healed, historians are in a better position to analyze the decade before the Civil War. The focus is shifting to what previously were dismissed as secondary issues, such as the growth of industry and cities, the dramatic increase in immigration, social and cultural diversity and the territorial and economic expansion of the country. Of all these factors, only territorial expansion is of little concern today. The other matters now are more pressing than ever before as modern Americans wrestle with the problems of decaying cities, a troubling economy, and the inclusion of minority populations within the dominant society.

Expansion and Growth

In 1850, the nation had a population of 23,191,876 composed of 19,553,114 whites, 3,204,313 slaves, 434,449 free blacks, and, according to the compiler of the 1850 Census, there were 400,764 "unrepresented and untaxed Indians." There were 100 white males to 95 females (a ratio that had remained virtually unchanged since 1790). At mid-century the male-female slave population was about equal, although free female blacks outnumbered males by eight percent.

Virginia had the largest number of slaves (472,528), and five other states had a quarter of a million or more: North Carolina (288,548), South Carolina (384,984), Georgia (381,682), Mississippi (309,878), and Alabama (342,844). New Jersey (236), and the Utah Territory (26) were the only areas in the traditionally "free" sector which reported slaves within their borders that year. Maryland had the nation's largest free black population (74,723), followed closely by Virginia (54,333), Pennsylvania (53,626), and New York (49,069). About four-fifths of all free blacks lived in the state where they were born.

Only five states had more than a million inhabitants: New York (3,097,394), Pennsylvania (2,311,786), Ohio (1,980,329), Virginia (1,421,661), and Tennessee (1,002,717), although Massachusetts, Georgia, Kentucky, and Indiana each had almost that many residents. Massachusetts and Rhode Island were the only states with over 100 inhabitants per square mile. The national average was 7.90 persons, but ranged all the way from 861.45 in the District of Columbia to .04 in the Utah Territory.

New York, with slightly more than half a million people, was the nation's largest metropolis, followed by Philadelphia (340,045), Baltimore (169,054), Boston (136,881), New Orleans (116,375), and Cincinnati (115,435), with six percent of the total population living in these six cities. Some 2.2 million Americans were foreign born, Ireland (961,719), Germany (573,225), England (278,675), and "British America" or Canada (147,711) providing nearly all of this immigrant population. About two-thirds of these individuals lived in six states, each of which had over 100,000 foreigners within its borders: New York (651,801), Pennsylvania (294,871), Ohio (218,512), Massachusetts (160,909), Illinois (110,593), and Wisconsin (106,695).

The nation was, of course, overwhelmingly agricultural. About half of all free male workers over the age of fifteen worked on farms, and about a thirteenth of all land was improved and used for that purpose. Generally, by far the most important crop grown on America's farms was Indian corn, valued at nearly $300 million in 1850; three other crops each were worth about a third as much: wheat, hay, and cotton. Nevertheless, it was cotton that figured most prominently in overseas exports, seventy percent of the total production going to British factories. Butter valued at over $50 million was produced in 1850, slightly surpassing the oat harvest (nearly $44 million). Other crops of considerably less importance included Irish and sweet potatoes, tobacco, cane sugar, rye, orchard products, buckwheat, peas, beans, and market garden produce.

Wages varied greatly, so much so that no distinct pattern emerges. A laborer working without board could get as little as 54 cents a day in North Carolina, about twice as much in Florida, Louisiana, Maine, Massachusetts, Texas, and Wisconsin, and ten times as much on the Pacific coast.

Census takers of that year recognized over twenty major religious groupings from Baptist to Universalist with 38,183 churches and property valued at $87.4 million. The Methodists with 13,338 congregations and the Baptists with 9,360 clearly dominated the religious scene. In 1850, about four million young people were attending schools, colleges, and universities; only 26,461 of these students were black

Although manufacturing did not loom large, employing less than one-fifth of all free workers, factories of one sort or another could be found everywhere throughout the nation. New York, with 199,349 establishments having an annual output worth $500 or more, led the list, followed closely by Massachusetts (165,938) and Pennsylvania (146,766); the territories of Minnesota (63) and Utah (51) brought up the rear. Cotton and woolen mills and factories turning out pig iron and iron castings could be found in virtually every state, although, as one would expect, New England dominated textiles; Massachusetts, New York, Pennsylvania, Kentucky, and Ohio, the iron industry. Some 1,217 distilleries and breweries scattered throughout the nation (Pennsylvania had 371; Alabama, California, the District of Columbia, Vermont, and Utah Territory, one each) employed 6,140 individuals and in 1850 produced 1,179,495 barrels of ale, 6,500,500 gallons of rum, and 41,364,224 gallons of "whiskey and high wines."

Expansion into New Lands

The settlement of the Oregon question with England in 1846, the acquisition of land from Mexico in 1848, and the Gadsden Purchase in 1853 together gave the United States its present continental limits (except for Alaska). By 1853 the nation stretched from the Atlantic to the Pacific and embraced three million square miles. Of this land, three-quarters was in the public domain of the federal government, which could sell the lands as it saw fit. Despite the rapid settlement of the West, in 1860 two-thirds of the American territory was still in federal hands.

One result of the acquisition of new lands was a shift in the population. Only a quarter of the total population of 12,866,020 Americans lived west of the Appalachian Mountains in 1830, but by 1850, half of the total population of 23,191,876 had moved west. As a result of this pattern of settlement, by 1860 about one-fourth of all the 31,443,321 people in the United States were living in a state other than the one they had been born in.

Cheap land and opportunity (fact or fiction) lured Americans beyond the mountains. The Preemption Act of 1841 guaranteed squatters the

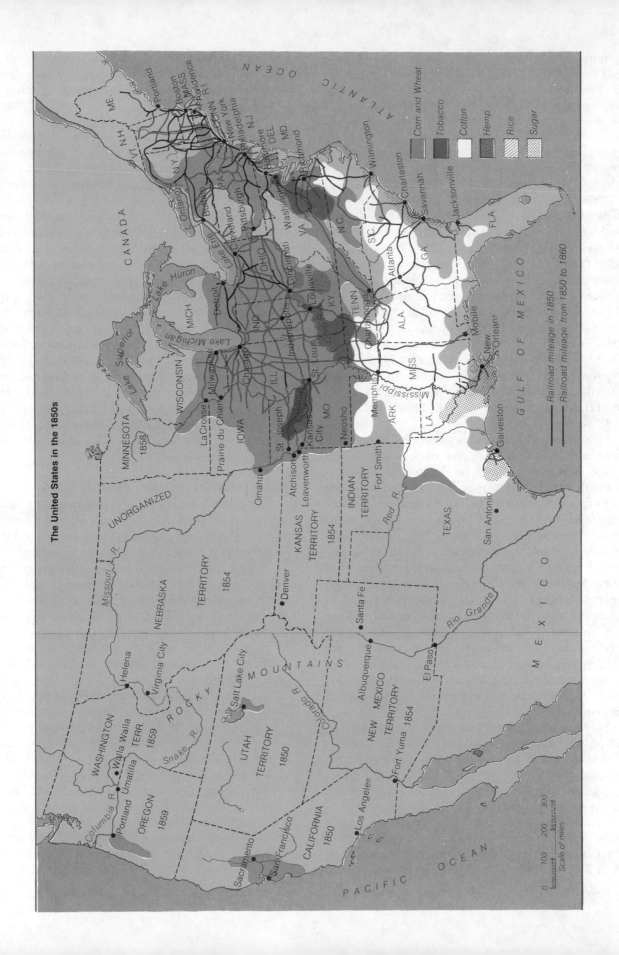

The United States in the 1850s

Corn and Wheat
Tobacco
Cotton
Hemp
Rice
Sugar

Railroad mileage in 1850
Railroad mileage from 1850 to 1860

0   100   200   300
Scale of miles

PACIFIC OCEAN

ATLANTIC OCEAN

GULF OF MEXICO

CANADA

MEXICO

WASHINGTON TERR. 1859
OREGON 1859
Portland
Walla Walla
Umatilla
Columbia R.
Snake R.
Helena
Virginia City
ROCKY MOUNTAINS
Salt Lake City
UTAH TERRITORY 1850
Colorado R.
Denver
NEBRASKA TERRITORY 1854
Missouri R.
Omaha
UNORGANIZED
MINNESOTA 1858
La Crosse
Prairie du Chien
WISCONSIN
Milwaukee
Lake Superior
Lake Michigan
Lake Huron
MICH
Detroit
Lake Erie
Lake Ontario
Buffalo
Cleveland
Pittsburgh
OHIO
Cincinnati
IND
Indianapolis
ILL
Chicago
IOWA
St. Joseph
Atchison
Leavenworth
Kansas City
KANSAS TERRITORY 1854
MO
St. Louis
Ohio R.
Louisville
KY
TENN
Memphis
Charleston
Chattanooga
Atlanta
GA
ALA
MISS
LA
New Orleans
Mobile
ARK
Fort Smith
Neosho
INDIAN TERRITORY 1854
Red R.
TEXAS
San Antonio
Galveston
Rio Grande
El Paso
Fort Yuma
NEW MEXICO TERRITORY 1854
Albuquerque
Santa Fe
CALIFORNIA 1850
Los Angeles
San Francisco
Sacramento
N.H.
VT.
ME.
Portland
Boston
MASS
Providence
R.I.
CONN
New York
N.J.
PA
Philadelphia
DEL
MD
Baltimore
Washington
VA
Richmond
N.C.
S.C.
Wilmington
Charleston
Savannah
Jacksonville
FLA

right to purchase up to 160 acres of land at the lowest government price; nor were squatters subjected to competitive bidding. Despite these generous concessions to venturesome, land-hungry settlers, Westerners pressed Congress for still more liberal terms. In 1854 the Graduation Act provided that all unsold public lands on the market for ten or more years were to be offered up at a price varying between 12.5 cents and $1 an acre, depending on how long the land had gone without a buyer. During the next eight years, nearly 40 million acres were settled under these provisions. Agitation for free land continued in the 1850s as Americans and recent immigrants sought homesteads and real estate for farming, herding, or speculation.

Southerners strongly opposed a free land policy for two reasons. First, they feared that such a policy would deprive the Treasury of necessary funds and the government would make up the difference by raising tariffs—which would hurt the South, dependent as it was on international trade. Second, free land in the West would attract antislavery settlers from the North, thereby making it likely that western territories would eventually enter the Union as free states. Southern opposition was so adamant that the nation did not embark on a free land policy until after the Civil War began. Nevertheless, the Preemption and Graduation Acts were sufficiently generous to promote rapid settlement. Iowa became a state in 1846, Wisconsin 1848, California in 1850, Minnesota in 1858, and Oregon in 1859; they were all free states.

The Transportation Revolution

In the late 1840s there were only 6,000 miles of railroad track in the United States, most of it along the East Coast. In 1860 there were 30,626 miles, and most of the increase was west of the Appalachians. Milwaukee, St. Louis, Memphis, and New Orleans all were served by railroads, and Chicago had become the very hub of transportation in the West, the terminus of fifteen separate lines. This explosion of railroad building not only increased traffic, it also moved it faster. For instance, the trip from New York to Chicago required three weeks in 1840 via water and land; in 1860 the same trip by train took only forty-eight hours.

Most cities of the Old Northwest were joined to the East Coast by lines emanating from Baltimore, New York, and Philadelphia. The economic interdependence of these two regions welded together a strong political unit, the North. This alliance dashed efforts of the South to form ties with the West. Western crops and other commodities that once went to southern markets (especially New Orleans) were now being diverted to the Northeast.

The emerging national system of transportation also stimulated regional specialization. Western farmers were producing foodstuffs that could be shipped to the industrial and financial centers of the Northeast, which in turn supplied the West with manufactured goods and capital. Southerners participated in this flow of goods and cash by sending cotton bales to the mills of the Northeast. All of these transactions were facilitated by trains,

Courtesy Clarke Historical Library, Central Michigan University.

A pioneer farm family in Michigan in the 1850s. The Graduation Act of 1854 did not end agitation for free land by Americans and recent immigrants.

The Illinois Central depot in Chicago. The main line of this railroad, the first great north-south railroad in America, was completed in 1854 and ran from Chicago to Cairo. The Illinois Central helped to open for development a wide expanse of fertile land. Southern Illinois, which otherwise might easily have gravitated into the orbit of St. Louis, was tied to Chicago.

though railroads affected the South much less markedly than the West and the Northeast. The South had far fewer tracks, and what it had often failed to form a continuous network. Southern railroads frequently did little more than carry goods from a plantation to a river or bay to be shipped to foreign or domestic ports.

The chart below shows the rapid increase in railroad mileage in the United States between 1830 and 1860.

Year	Miles of Track
1830	23
1835	1,098
1840	2,818
1845	4,633
1850	9,021
1855	18,374
1860	30,626

Industrial Expansion

In 1843 George Tucker, a professor at the University of Virginia, observed that industrial employment was increasing more rapidly than agricultural employment and that towns with a population of 10,000 or more were growing faster than the overall population. Industrialization and urbanization were indeed remarkable aspects of the United States in the 1840s and 1850s. In these two decades the number of agricultural workers increased from 3,570,000 to 5,880,000; but, as a percentage of the total work force, farm labor declined from 63.4 percent to 53.2 percent; in the same years, factory employees rose from 13.9 percent to 18.5 percent (in actual numbers, from 500,000 to 1,530,000).

By mid-century many of the conditions necessary for a true age of industrialization were emerging. Railroad track linked most urban centers to one another and permitted relatively easy exchange of goods, raw materials, and machine tools. Extensive coal mining allowed factories to be built anywhere, since they were no longer dependent on waterpower for fuel. Mechanized factory production benefited from the introduction of interchangeable and standardized parts, the rise of the machine tool industry, mass immigration from Europe (which provided a cheap source of labor), and new markets along the western frontier.

But industrialization requires capital, and a great deal of the capital that developed the United States came from overseas. One estimate holds that foreign capital in the United States rose from $222 million in 1853 to $400 million in 1860. Another source for industrial investment came from the gold mines of California. Between 1848 and 1853, more than half a billion dollars' worth of gold was extracted from California. Indeed, the nation's supply of hard money climbed from $90 million in 1843 to $283 million in 1862.

As industry grew, corporations developed to

control more and more of the new factories. New York passed a general corporation act in 1848 which permitted any group of investors to incorporate if they met certain standardized requirements (previously each group had to apply individually to the legislature). This new law and similar legislation elsewhere facilitated incorporation; nearly half of the business corporations established in America between 1800 and 1860 came into existence in the last decade before the Civil War. Traditionally businessmen took a concerned, paternalistic interest in the welfare of their employees, but as the real control of any corporation passed into the hands of management and the number of employees grew, even managers were separated from the rank and file by an intermediate hierarchy of foremen. The owners of a corporation, in short, were absent, and the managers were sequestered away in private offices.

Most Americans took no part in corporation life. The country's farmers, laborers, retail merchants, and professionals remained unorganized, while business was becoming organized on a grand scale. But it would be a mistake to see the early corporations simply as sinister cartels, that is, combinations within a single industry designed to restrict competition and maintain high profits. They were merely the first indications of the high degree of organization that would eventually characterize almost every aspect of American life.

"Yankee ingenuity" accounted to a large extent for both the increased efficiency of American industry and the appeal of its products. Separate industries had grown up by 1850 around such inventions as the sewing machine, telegraph, reaper, Colt revolver, vulcanized rubber, and circular saws. The most impressive American inventions were improvements of agricultural machinery, only natural in a county still primarily devoted to farming. American farmers were quite alert to every innovation; the farm press described inventions in detail and farmers examined them at county and state fairs. American plows, cornplanters, revolving rakes, and wheat drills surpassed those produced in other countries. Western farmers were especially attracted to these implements, which augmented production and reduced human toil and which often performed much better on the flat lands of the upper Mississippi Valley than in the hilly Northeast.

After agriculture, transportation was the next most important field to be improved by American ingenuity. American locomotives were roomier, more comfortable, and more durable than their European counterparts, and the American T-rail was designed so that it could be laid rapidly and easily, thereby saving money and effort. Yet another American enterprise that benefited from inventions was the textile industry. Inventions involving most other industries, however, lagged behind; English machines were simply too good and too cheap to invite American competition. Nevertheless, the United States was caught in an inventive fever in the decades before the Civil War; the U.S. Patent Office registered one-third more inventions in 1856 than it had in 1855, and every subsequent year saw increases.

In the 1850s manufacturers became more interested in foreign markets. Total exports were double what they had been in the 1840s, though the main commodities sold abroad were not factory goods but agricultural produce. Cotton, in fact, made up more than half of all exports, and other kinds of southern produce (tobacco, sugar, and rice, for instance) accounted for another quarter. Whereas Europe in general and England in particular bought the bulk of American cotton, manufactured goods made in the United States were sold primarily to Mexico, the West Indies, and China.

Farsighted American merchants considered the

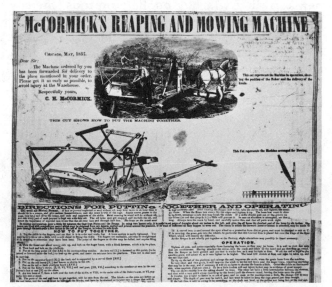

State Historical Society of Wisconsin.

Instructions for assembling a McCormick reaper-mower dated May 1857.

vast Chinese population a great potential market, and the treaties that America and other western powers forced a weak Chinese government to sign were all designed to enhance the profits of foreigners trading there. The Treaty of Wanghia, signed in 1844, for instance, opened five major Chinese ports to Americans and stipulated that very low tariffs would be imposed on American goods.

In 1853 and 1854, the show of naval force by Commodore Matthew C. Perry, (whose remarkable naval career is reviewed in an accompanying biographical sketch) led Japan in 1854 to conclude a treaty with the United States. The treaty permitted limited American trade on a most-favored-nation basis in two Japanese fishing villages. An abortive attempt to annex the Hawaiian Islands by the Pierce administration and a treaty with Siam (Thailand) in 1856 represent other attempts to extend American overseas trade.

Urban Expansion

By 1860 there were 6,216,518 Americans living in 101 urban centers with a population of 10,000 or more inhabitants. Port cities such as New York, Boston, and Philadelphia underwent tremendous growth between 1840 and 1860, and the inland cities on the Great Lakes experienced even more dramatic development. Chicago, a settlement of about fifty people in 1830, had 109,260 inhabitants in 1860.

At first Chicago had served as a place where new arrivals could buy public farmlands; the city was little more than a real estate office. After the Panic of 1837 slowed down speculation in land, it became a center for outfitting homesteaders with farm equipment. The railroad boom in the 1850s turned Chicago into a depot for farm produce streaming from the West to the East. Chicago's slaughterhouses and porkpacking plants enabled it to process the livestock of the region. By 1853 the city had seven daily newspapers, factories such as those of Cyrus McCormick, which manufactured reapers and other agricultural machines, as well as numerous iron mills and lumberyards. It owed its size and prosperity to its role as a center of industry, finance, and transportation.

Two other centers, older and somewhat larger, reflect similar trends, although both Cincinnati and St. Louis clung for too long to river commerce and saw Chicago and its railroads overtake them. Cincinnati grew rich supplying salt pork, flour, and foodstuffs to the one-crop cotton South. St. Louis,

its commerce much like that of Cincinnati—supplying the Lower South—had nineteen flour mills in 1850 and an assortment of foundries and food-processing plants. The two cities had other similarities: very large immigrant populations (more than 30,000 Germans settled in St. Louis before 1850) and close ties to the South. As a result, these commercial centers were torn apart by divided loyalties in 1861.

Cleveland and Buffalo, much more closely allied with the industrial Northeast and the burgeoning frontier states of Illinois, Michigan, and Wisconsin, present a somewhat different picture. In 1850, Cleveland was about one-tenth as large as Cincinnati but recently had "planked" its main streets and built a huge pier out into Lake Erie, the first of its kind. Like Buffalo, which was much larger, Cleveland was producing a variety of goods to be shipped westward to new settlements of the upper Midwest or to the East via the Erie Canal. By 1845, Buffalo was manufacturing tools, steam engines, stoves, nails, mirrors, picture frames, soap, candles, millstones, and porcelain bathtubs. Neither city had much difficulty deciding where its sympathies lay as the Civil War approached.

The South was much more agricultural than urban but nevertheless some major cities had risen by 1850. The census of 1860 numbered some thirty towns or cities in the South with a population of 8,000 or more. Most of these communities were state capitals or crossroads trading centers. Memphis, the largest city in antebellum Tennessee, was a typical southern boomtown. It was founded in 1819 and until the late 1840s, remained a sleepy Mississippi River town. But a good railroad connection with Charleston on the Atlantic coast (completed in 1857) and prosperous cotton production in the hinterland turned Memphis into a true metropolis. In 1850 factors, agents who bought and sold agricultural produce, were handling 150,000 bales of cotton valued at $7,520,000; by 1860 the figures had tripled. Accordingly, prosperity brought a leap in the city's population from 8,841 in 1850 to 22,623 in 1860.

New Orleans, by far the South's largest city in 1850 (116,375), was fed by the produce of the Mississippi Valley and the commerce created by bumper crops of corn, tobacco, and cotton. Exotic and somewhat atypical because of its rich French-Spanish heritage, this city battled fires, hurricanes, and yellow fever from 1812 to 1860 but continued to prosper despite the competition of railroads in the Old

Matthew Calbraith Perry

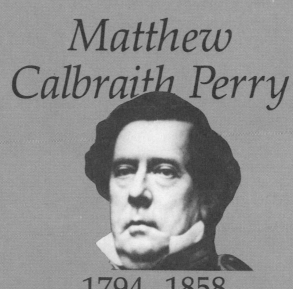

1794–1858

Son of a distinguished naval officer four times taken prisoner during the Revolutionary War, brother to four other U.S. Navy officers and brother-in-law to still two more, the sea and service to the nation clearly shaped the life of this Rhode Island-born youth and that of his family as well. At one time no fewer than 17 Perry cousins were enrolled at Annapolis.

After basic schooling in his native Newport, Perry became a midshipman in 1809 and during the hectic years leading up to the War of 1812 saw action on a vessel commanded by his brother, Oliver Hazard Perry (1785–1819); however, he spent most of that conflict aboard a ship bottled up in New London by the British. Late in 1814 he married Jane Slidell, sister of John Slidell of Civil War fame. They had ten children, one of their daughters marrying wealthy August Belmont.

During the next twenty years Perry traveled widely suppressing piracy, conducting diplomatic missions, and helping to establish the ex-slave nation of Liberia. In 1833 he began a decade of shore duty in Brooklyn and New York City where he developed an interest in steam transport, naval education, and nautical engineering. Elevated to captain in 1837, this brusk, irascible, and somewhat pompous man soon was in the forefront of a nautical revolution that culminated a few years later in establishment of the U.S. Naval Academy and adoption of radical changes in sea warfare.

In 1843 Perry commanded a squadron dispatched to Africa to suppress the slave trade, subsequently directed a large naval force sent to Vera Cruz during the Mexican War, and then was selected to lead a fleet to Japan when the United States decided to establish diplomatic ties with that mysterious realm. President Millard Fillmore's personal letter to the emperor stressed that America desired trading rights because of increasing commerce between California and China. Vessels wrecked near Japan and those requiring coal might need assistance, the President added. The objects of Perry's visit, he stressed, were "friendship, commerce, a supply of coal, and provisions and protection for our ship-wrecked people."

In November 1853 Perry set out from Norfolk with a fleet of ten vessels. Sailing by way of the south Atlantic, the Indian Ocean, and China, he reached Japanese waters six months later. After nine days marked by boldness, threats, and cajoling, Perry departed for China, promising to return the following year.

Alarmed by the sudden appearance of French and Russian warships and fearing their commanders might also be seeking special privileges in Japan then enjoyed only by Holland, Perry hurried back in February 1854 and within six weeks secured trading rights in two ports. This agreement, perhaps aided by the emergence of a new regime, was cemented by an exchange of gifts.

Perry's arrival back in New York was barely noted by the Pierce administration, but in 1856, assisted by Francis Lister Hawks, he published three remarkable volumes describing his exploits. Perry died suddenly two years later while about to assume command of a Mediterranean squadron.

Historic New Orleans Collection.

This illustration of urban life in the antebellum South shows a scene in Lafayette Square in New Orleans.

Northwest. It was a colorful, highliving mix of bars, gambling, red-light districts, immigrants, opera, and theater that set it apart from all other southern towns and cities and from most urban centers of the rest of the nation as well.

Compared with the thriving, thronged northern cities of New York, Philadelphia, and Boston, southern cities often appeared sleepy and a bit forlorn, especially since their well-being was tied to agricultural cycles and little influenced by immigration and industry. Except on Saturdays or during the busy fall harvest season, streets frequently were deserted. Many cities lacked adequate sidewalks, paved streets, sewers, or supplies of fresh water. Lurking just behind the imposing homes of white citizens were the miserable shanties of urban blacks, whether free or enslaved. Fear of a nocturnal black uprising haunted many southern cities; New Orleans employed more night watchmen than daytime police, and these nighttime officials patrolled the streets accompanied by trained dogs. Free blacks, moreover, were required by the city council to wear badges as well as to obey a strictly enforced curfew.

There were numerous attractions of urban life in the antebellum South. The public schools were better and more numerous than in the country. Towns and cities also offered other educational advantages, including lyceums, public libraries, theaters, circuses, concerts, and musical performances of many varieties. In the 1850s, athenaeums and mechanics' institutes sprang up in the larger southern cities; they sponsored lectures on useful subjects and provided both libraries and exhibits to the public. By 1860 nearly a thousand readers belonged to the Kentucky Mechanic's Institute in Louisville. In the last decade before the Civil War, libraries showed marked growth in the South, especially in South Carolina, which rivaled Massachusetts in its number of books per capita.

Social And Cultural Diversity

The sheer size of the United States and its division into distinctive regions often dominated by quite different groups of people—urban and rural; slave and free; New Englanders, New Yorkers, cotton-growing Southerners, and trans-Appalachian Westerners; residents of stable, settled areas and wild, untamed frontiersmen; natives and newcomers—created an unusual social and cultural diversity. Probably at no earlier time in American history could one have found such marked differences of outlook and of social habits as in the middle decades of the nineteenth century. The War of 1812 and the Mexican War had not woven these random viewpoints into distinctive themes, and changes wrought in communication, transportation, and industry, although certainly impressive when compared with earlier times, had not yet drastically altered American life.

Immigration and Nativism

By 1860, about one-eighth of the American population of some thirty-one million people were foreign born. Although many immigrants settled in the Old Northwest, an even larger number moved into enclaves already established in America's rapidly growing cities, especially in the Northeast. About 4.2 million foreigners arrived in the United States between 1840 and 1860 seeking new jobs and opportunities.

Most of the new immigrants came from Britain and Ireland or Germany; almost all the rest came from Scandinavia, Switzerland, and Holland. In fact, about ninety-five percent of the immigrants in the decades before the Civil War were from northern Europe. In general the immigrants were in the prime of life, able-bodied and productive workers; relatively few were under ten years old or over forty.

The largest group of immigrants were the Irish. Driven out of their own country by the potato crop failure and the famine that followed it in 1845 and 1846, more than 1.5 million of them had arrived in the United States by 1860, and they constituted about 40 percent of all foreign-born residents in America. Generally, the Irish were too poor to move inland from the coastal cities after they landed in the United States. They settled mainly in the port cities of the Northeast, though some traveled west and south seeking employment as day laborers building canals or railroads; only a very few ever turned to farming in America. The next numerous nationality were 1,301,136 Germans.

Foreigners were unevenly distributed in the 1850s with more than eighty-five percent of the new arrivals living in the North. Indeed, in such rapidly expanding cities as Chicago, Milwaukee, and St. Louis, over half of the population was foreign-born in 1860. The heaviest concentrations of immigrants were in eastern states such as Massachusetts, New York, and Pennsylvania and in such states in the Old Northwest as Illinois, Ohio, and Wisconsin. The Irish tended to concentrate in northeastern industrial cities, the Germans on farms or in the cities of the Ohio and Mississippi River valleys such as Cincinnati and St. Louis. The percentage of foreign-born citizens in various cities in 1860 is given in the table on the following page.

There was strong anti-Catholic sentiment in many parts of America and the presence of large numbers of Irish Catholics aroused deep suspicions

From the collections of the Michigan History Division.

"Come to America." This advertisement encouraged Germans to settle in Michigan. During the antebellum period, entire German villages left en masse for America, which was attractively pictured in numerous pamphlets and letters.

Over 50%	45% to 50%	35% to 45%	25% to 35%
Chicago	Buffalo	Boston	Baltimore
Milwaukee	Cincinnati	Brooklyn	Philadelphia
St. Louis	Detroit	Louisville	
	New York	Newark	
		New Orleans	
		Pittsburgh	

Based on Ira M. Leonard and Robert D. Parmet, *American Nativism, 1830–1860* (New York: Van Nostrand Reinhold, 1971), p. 33.

that had subtle, long-range effects. The political radicalism and antireligious convictions of some German refugees also frightened conservative Americans. A wave of unsuccessful liberal uprisings in Germany in 1848 sent many revolutionaries fleeing to the United States, bringing with them ideas that alarmed many Americans. Irish Catholicism on the one hand and German liberalism on the other were distressing and unsettling; when these ideological differences were coupled with the frustration and despair resulting from rapid social and economic change and severe competition for jobs, the result was the rise in the 1850s of a virulent nativism. The nativist or Know-Nothing party (so named because of the vow of secrecy members swore) emerged as a strong national force in 1854 and enlisted many adherents to its platform calling for restrictions against immigrants. Know-Nothings wanted to ban all foreign-born citizens from holding political office, deprive aliens of the vote, and delay naturalization of foreigners for at least twenty-one years after their arrival in this country.

Immigration to the South never matched the flood that inundated the North. The foreign-born were reluctant to settle in the South for a number of reasons. Southern cities were less industrialized than those in the North and consequently did not have as many factory jobs. The climate was unfamiliar, and growing conditions in the North more closely resembled those of northern Europe. Passage from Europe to southern ports was less frequent than to New York, Boston, or other northern cities. Finally, many immigrants had a strong aversion to slavery.

Among those foreigners who did go to the South were Germans, Irish Catholics, and Jews,

Library of Congress.

Title page of the "K N Quickstep" (1854), "dedicated to the Know Nothings"—a movement that attracted recruits from the middle class who were fascinated by secret handshakes, passwords, and distress signals, and who supported efforts at anti-immigrant legislation. Public opinion, however, was largely outraged by nativist mobbings and other excesses.

often lured below the Mason-Dixon line by relatives or neighborhoods in seaport communities long dominated by their fellow countrymen. Most immigrants settled in cities where they became merchants, peddlers, skilled craftsmen, or laborers. Relatively few became farmers. Although there were notable exceptions, most immigrants who settled in the South soon accepted the southern proslavery view.

Despite this assimilation of beliefs, immigrants often encountered a strong hatred of the foreign-born in the South. In the 1850s the Know-Nothings frequently dominated southern city elections. In an effort to find an issue that would distract attention from more dangerous sectional rivalries, the Know-Nothings fanned the sparks of xenophobia (hatred of foreigners) and mobs killed more than a score of foreigners in Louisville on election day in 1855 and led riots against immigrants in several other cities. Nativists won control of most of the large cities of the South by contending that immigrants were opposed to slavery. Southern nativism, unlike that in the North, was more antiforeign than anti-Catholic, partly because there were fewer Catholic immigrants in the South and partly because Catholics who settled in the South became defenders of slavery.

Cultural Diversity

The Northeast and its institutions by its sheer numbers and through its control of the leading printing presses, growth of metropolitan centers, and development of a convergent network of railroad tracks, tended to dominate the cultural life of mid-century America. New York, because of its size, wealth, and close ties to Europe, exerted influence throughout the entire nation and was, in a sense, its cultural capital, perhaps sharing the educational and literary realms with Boston to some degree. If nothing else, much that was done in Savannah, St. Louis, Buffalo, Baltimore, and even Boston or Philadelphia, was measured against standards set in Manhattan.

Immigration turned much of the North into a rich cultural mix. Scores of newspapers published in foreign languages gave enclaves of newcomers a sense of community and informed them of events back home. Each nationality, moreover, practiced in America the arts of its native land. The Germans of Cincinnati, for instance, were dedicated to music and the city had numerous choral societies and instrumental groups. Similarly, the Irish of Boston formed Catholic and fraternal organizations in which they preserved their own customs.

Most Americans were too busy and too unsophisticated to appreciate the fine arts, but they nonetheless had cultural activities, some of them unfamiliar to their twentieth-century descendants. For instance, oratory was highly admired during the antebellum period. Whether addressing a court room, a legislative body, or a church congregation, the orator won praise for a fine voice, effective gestures, perfect diction, and well-organized ideas. People would travel miles to hear an outstanding preacher or a stirring political speaker.

Theaters provided another form of popular entertainment. The characteristic fare presented good triumphing over evil. Actors recreated famous Rev-

Library of Congress.
The Irish Brigade of New York. Military companies like this Irish one were primarily social organizations. In addition to target practice and parades, the companies provided immigrants with such activities as balls, picnics, and lectures.

olutionary War battles and Indian raids for audiences who came early and nibbled on peanuts or hard-boiled eggs as they soaked up the patriotic melodrama. Minstrels were another popular form of entertainment with some of the best-known minstrel songs, many of them still popular today, being the work of Stephen Foster. (A biographical sketch in this chapter discusses in greater detail his career and minstrels.) At home, Americans played and sang minstrel songs as well as favorite hymns; they also entertained themselves with board games such as "The Reward of Virtue" and "The Mansion of Happiness."

Literature and History
The 1840s and 1850s marked the declaration of American independence from European literary traditions. American writers in the Northeast were no longer content to imitate the works of older cultures. The essays of Emerson and Thoreau, the novels of Nathaniel Hawthorne (1804–1864) and Herman Melville (1819–1891), and the poetry of Edgar Allan Poe (1809–1849) and Walt Whitman (1819–1892) are all examples of a new American voice. Hawthorne's *The Scarlet Letter* and *The House of Seven Gables* treated native themes—in both cases the Puritan heritage. The stern morality of New England, the religious, even mystical, approach to experience, and the pessimism about the sinfulness of humanity imbue these brilliantly written novels, much acclaimed on both sides of the Atlantic. Melville's *Moby Dick*, a far more original exploration of the nature of evil, dealt with a maritime way of life—whaling. Melville and Whitman both were virtually self-educated and thoroughly steeped, as were so many Americans, in the Bible.

Southern readers especially enjoyed the works of Sir Walter Scott (1771–1832), a Scotsman and author of *Ivanhoe*. It was he who pictured a medieval era of chivalry and courage, of deference to ladies and *noblesse oblige* towards servants—a view of society that Southerners were able to translate into the terms of their own world. The best-known American counterpart to Scott in the South was the South Carolinian novelist William Gilmore Simms (1806–1870). In 1842 he published his *Beauchampe*, the tale of an aristocratic Southerner who kills a Kentucky colonel in order to avenge the seduction of his wife. Simms wrote more than twenty novels and sixty stories and became well known in the North and in European literary circles.

The most popular writers of the day were

National Archives.
Nathaniel Hawthorne, of Salem, Massachusetts, wrote *The Scarlet Letter* in 1850 and *The House of the Seven Gables* in 1851. These novels established him in fiction as the classic interpreter of the Puritan mind.

poets; indeed poetry dominated American letters between 1830 and 1870. William Cullen Bryant (1794–1878) with his lyrical hymns to nature, and the American laureate, Henry Wadsworth Longfellow (1807–1882), with epics on native themes ("Evangeline" and "Hiawatha"), reached a vast public. Longfellow's poems were memorized by schoolchildren and his birthday was a national holiday for students. John Greenleaf Whittier (1807–1892) also won recognition for his fine regional poem about winter in New England, *Snowbound*. For all of these writers the one great subject was Nature (which they always capitalized); Romantics on both sides of the Atlantic believed that God's ways could be deduced by the painter and poet from a flower, a bird, or a landscape.

Some of the popular writers of this period were "scribbling women," female authors who supported

Stephen Foster

1826–1864

Born in Pittsburgh, Pennsylvania, Foster displayed at an early age a gift for music: however his parents opposed a musical career (a pursuit that scarcely existed as a full-time occupation in America at that time) and sent him to Jefferson College in July 1841 when he was barely fifteen years of age. Within a few weeks he quit, planning to continue his studies with tutors as home. Even at this tender age he had written several compositions, including "The Tioga Waltz," a melody for four flutes. Other songs followed, but five years later his parents sent young Foster to Cincinnati to keep books for his brother. There his ballads about black Americans became so popular that in 1848 he published a collection, *Songs of the Sable Harmonists*, that proved music could be profitable. With this success behind him, Foster left Cincinnati and returned to his family's home in Allegheny City to pursue his chosen career in earnest.

His early songs were written for minstrels—that is, white singers wearing blackface—and his ballads were performed by such groups as the famous Christy's Minstrels and the New Orleans Serenaders. His connection with E. P. Christy proved to be a very profitable arrangement for both men, each contributing greatly to the popularity of the other. "The Old Folks at Home" and "Massa's in the Cold Ground," two of Foster's best-loved songs, appeared in 1851 and 1852, respectively. The following year he deserted black dialect for a time and produced "My Old Kentucky Home" and "Old Dog Tray," the latter selling 125,000 copies in only eighteen months. For the next few years, Foster remained in Pittsburgh where he wrote little of any consequence; then in 1860 he reasserted his former power with "Old Black Joe," one of his most enduring ballads. Despite the fact that most of these lyrics celebrated the South, Foster only visited New Orleans briefly in 1852.

In that same year he moved to New York, having separated from Jane Denny McDowell whom he married in Pittsburgh in 1850. Poverty and obscurity marked Foster's final years as he drank heavily and wrote constantly (forty-eight songs in one twelve-month period), but his output was repetitive and uninspired. Frequently he sold these songs to music stores, not publishers, for only a few dollars. He died in 1864 in a charity ward at Bellevue Hospital after a brief illness. Foster's work was somewhat limited and obviously uneven, but his most enduring songs evoking a nostalgia for the security of bygone times and faraway places clearly express a unique, even exotic phase of American life and development.

themselves and their families by writing and were famous during their lifetime. Among them was Lydia Howard Huntley Sigourney (1791–1865), a New Englander who at first sold poems and other literary works so she could contribute to charitable causes. Later, when her husband's business fell upon hard times, she sold poems and sketches to magazines and published books in order to help support her family. Her literary reputation reached a high point in 1849 with the publication of *Illustrated Poems,* a sumptuously bound book comparable to similar publications of Bryant and Longfellow. One indication of her appeal is that publisher Louis Godey paid her $500 a year between 1840 and 1842 merely for the use of her name on the title page of *Godey's Lady's Book.* Also Edgar Allan Poe begged her to write for his publication. Although Sigourney had outlived her fame when she died in 1865, she is remembered as one of the first American women to have a successful career as a writer.

One of the South's greatest poets, Edgar Allan Poe (1809–1849), was actually born in Boston but moved to Virginia as a child. Like many other Southerners, he was lost in fantasies about an earlier, chivalrous, semimythical era, although for Poe this dream world was not ordered and calm but streaked through with doom and despair. Though he edited the *Southern Literary Messenger* for a brief period, he lived much of his adult life in the North, primarily in New York. Creator of the first detective stories, he was a master of psychological thrillers, an astute critic at a time when virtually no other American could express any opinion about literature beyond simple approval or disapproval, and the inventor of a kind of poetry so melodious and so original that it inspired generations of writers, not only in the United States but also in Europe.

With the exception of Poe, the South produced no major literary figures before the Civil War, and this paucity of talent can be attributed in part to slavery. Slavery was an institution so under attack from northern abolitionists that southern white intellectuals devoted much of their energy to defending it. Another penalty slavery imposed on southern culture was repression. As the slaveowning society became more and more embattled, the local post offices refused to distribute inflammatory publications from the North, professors in southern universities were dismissed or harassed for their criticism of the system, preachers who condemned

Fashions from *Godey's Lady's Book* (1857) showing a bridal gown, a young lady's outdoor costume, and a girl's dress. *Godey's* stressed the role of the family in society and women's work in the home. During Sarah J. Hale's career as editor, the magazine gained a then impressive circulation of 150,000 subscribers.

slavery were replaced, and the free play of ideas and inquiry was generally stifled.

Then as now Americans were addicted to a nonartistic form of literature—self-improvement and how-to-do-it books. As *The Farmer's Companion* optimistically observed, the "agriculturalist . . . may devote his earnings, or most of them, to study." He could learn ways to rebuild his house from an issue of a popular magazine, *The Horticul-*

turist. Or he could study one of the many technical treatises, such as *The Useful Arts Considered in Connexion with the Applications of Science*. If he had a taste for more abstract subjects, he could read Professor Denison Olmsted's *Letters on Astronomy* or a book written by three New England scholars, *Essays on Ancient Literature and Art*. His religious appetite was fed by millions of religious tracts.

The sacredness of the family was an entrenched aspect of the American ethic. Indicative of this attitude was the popularity of *Godey's Lady's Book* in which the editor, Sarah J. Hale, reputedly the author of "Mary Had a Little Lamb," dictated manners, dress, and taste to millions of women in all parts of the nation. (Hale's distinguished career as an arbiter of manners, dress, and taste for American women and as a crusader for female education and teaching careers for women is highlighted in an accompanying biographical sketch.)

The most famous American historian of the antebellum period (and for many years after the Civil War) was George Bancroft (1800–1891). In 1834 he published the first book of his ten-volume *History of the United States*, a gigantic effort that came to a conclusion only in 1876. In the intervening years Bancroft, a staunch Democrat and one-time political boss of Massachusetts, served as Secretary of the Navy under Polk and then as minister to Great Britain and later to Berlin. His *History*, which covered only the colonial and Revolutionary periods, was strongly patriotic and as such enjoyed wide popularity. As a defender of Jacksonian democracy, Bancroft read the early events of American history as sure signs of the rise of the common man.

The other major historian of the period was Francis Parkman (1823–1893), less grandiloquent but more scholarly. Throughout his life Parkman was tortured by a mysterious nervous ailment that kept him in a nearly constant state of exhaustion and confusion, sometimes allowing him to write only six lines a day. Despite this terrible disorder, he was able to write *The California and Oregon Trail* in 1849 and the two-volume *History of the Conspiracy of Pontiac*, published in 1851. In subsequent years he published several impressive histories of the struggle between the British and French for the domination of North America, a theme developed with genuine literary distinction in his monumental series, *France and England in North America* (published between 1865 and 1892).

Sarah Josepha Buell Hale

1788–1879

Born on a farm in New Hampshire, Sarah Buell had an appetite for, but few opportunities to acquire a formal education, though her mother taught her to read and an older brother instructed her in Latin and philosophy. When, at the age of twenty-five she married David Hale, a lawyer in Newport, she found in him a new teacher. Her husband also encouraged her to submit occasional articles to local newspapers.

The death of her husband in 1822 left her with the responsibility of providing for five children. She then entered upon a serious career as an author and began to publish poems and fiction. In 1828 she was named the editor of a Boston magazine for women, the *Ladies' Magazine*. In 1837 Louis A. Godey bought out the magazine and established his highly successful *Godey's Lady's Book*, with Sarah Hale as the literary editor. It became the most famous and widely read American periodical for women. In its pages she argued for sensible dress, better homes, scientific housekeeping, and women doctors.

Although Hale never endorsed feminism and even opposed feminists of her day, she was a champion of education for women, and her articles on this subject profoundly influenced Matthew Vassar, the founder of Vassar College for women. Sarah Hale also made the public aware of the accomplishments of women through the 2,500 biographical sketches she wrote and collected under the title *Woman's Record, or Sketches of Distinguished Women,* first published in 1853. (She omitted Lucy Stone, Elizabeth Stanton, and Susan Anthony. Her mention of Lucretia Mott, another feminist, was acidic.) She herself was one of the most distinguished women of her era. In 1877 she retired after half a century of editing the *Lady's Book,* a publication she considered to be "a beacon-light of refined taste, pure morals, and refined wisdom." Though she always believed that women were best suited to act as moral guides to men, her role in promoting higher education for women left an enduring mark on America.

Painting and Artists

Painting was not a pursuit that commanded much respect in the American public during the colonial period and the early years of the Republic. Americans frowned on painting for two major reasons—it was thought worldly and sinful and not a useful occupation. In the Jacksonian era, however, this point of view went through a transformation, attributable primarily to the Romantic cult of nature. In the thinking of European and English Romantic artists and writers, which was echoed by Americans, nature was God's handiwork. The artist was peculiarly gifted to see and capture the spiritual qualitites of nature in landscape painting. Thus, for an ordinary man or woman to contemplate a landscape painting was much the same as attending a sermon—it was a religious act. Armed with this reasoning, Americans suddenly felt justified in patronizing an art form that had previously struck them as frivolous and trivial.

An impressive new development in American art, called the Hudson River School, came into being about 1825 under the leadership of an English immigrant, Thomas Cole (1801–1848). An entirely self-taught painter, he began to do portraits, wandering from house to house and eking out a living from tiny commissions. In his travels, however, he saw the moody landscapes of Thomas Doughty, an older American artist. Despite the fact that young Cole never had seen a first-rate landscape painting by a major artist, he nevertheless fused this brief glimpse of Doughty's work with his own stored-up impressions of the American wilderness to produce canvases of an astonishing originality and power. When he took a walking tour through the Catskills along the Hudson River valley, Cole sketched directly from nature. Later, after meditating on these subjects, he executed his vast canvases. Even his earliest works speak of the grandeur of the American scene and reveal in startling clarity every detail of the vast panoramas he executed. After he converted to the Anglican Church in 1842, his works were infused with a more religious tone.

Soon a whole school of painters had formed around Cole's concept of nature. Among the most outstanding was Asher B. Durand (1796–1886), a man who worked as an engraver until he was forty years old and only then turned full-time to painting. Like Cole, Durand painted the Catskills, the White Mountains, the Adirondacks, and the Berkshires. Ironically, at the very moment when the countryside in the Northeast was becoming almost daily more and more built up and industrialized, American artists decided to create their immense, empty wilderness scenes. One of Durand's most famous canvases is *Kindred Spirits,* which shows William Cullen Bryant and Thomas Cole communing with nature, a fitting tribute to two of the American architects of the cult of nature.

The last of the great artists of the Hudson River School was Frederic Edwin Church (1826–1900). Church was Cole's only student and under his influence painted the ambitious, allegorical landscape, *Moses Viewing the Promised Land.* After Cole's death, Church took on a mighty subject that his teacher considered but rejected as too demanding—Niagara Falls. When Church exhibited his *Niagara* in New York and London in 1857, it drew hordes of excited spectators, and the dean of English art critics, John Ruskin, finally had to admit that perhaps there was such a thing as American landscape. Breathtaking vistas, scrupulously observed details, and religious symbolism imbued most of Church's landscapes; typically, in 1862 he pictured the reflection of the sun in a lake as the sign of the Cross.

American painters of the antebellum period achieved recognition not only for their landscapes and awesome technique. John James Audubon (1785–1851) and George Catlin (1796–1872) both left imaginative records of the wonders of a new land.

Audubon was born in Haiti in 1785 and raised in France but immigrated to the United States when he was eighteen. There he married and settled in Kentucky, earning his living as a merchant and land speculator. When he was thirty-five, in 1820, he exhibited his first bird drawings in Cincinnati, Ohio. They were greeted with such acclaim that Audubon, who was barely scratching out a living, decided to turn his attention to paintings of the birds of America. This new occupation soon became an obsession, and Audubon often worked seventeen hours a day. He collected specimens of birds from everywhere in the United States and, after many years of hard work, completed more than 1,000 paintings and 435 engravings. This monumental effort was unappreciated in America; consequently, in 1826, Audubon sailed to England. There he arranged for some of his plates to be published, but it was not until 1838 that Audubon was able to issue in England his four-volume *The Birds of America from Original Drawings, with 435 Plates Showing 1,065 Figures.*

Audubon's zealous study of birds was matched

The New York Public Library, Astor, Lenox & Tilden Foundations.
"Kindred Spirits" by Asher B. Durand (1849).

by the vivid and fascinating pictures of American Indians by George Catlin. Like Cole and so many other American artists of this period, the Pennsylvania-born Catlin was entirely self-taught. To please his father he practiced law for a few years, but when he was twenty-seven, in 1823, he became a full-time artist. He did many unimportant portraits until one day, in the late 1820s, he saw a delegation of splendidly dressed Indians in Philadelphia. Catlin then and there resolved to devote all his talents to portraying Indians. In 1830 he went to St. Louis, where he remained for the next two years, painting the Indian chiefs who came to that city, which was then a territorial capital. He subsequently made a trip up the Missouri River as far as South Dakota, sketching members of various tribes he encountered.

A year later Catlin, after refining his paintings, showed them to enormous crowds in Pittsburgh, Cincinnati, and Louisville. The exhibitions were so successful that he next journeyed through the Southwest, visited the Rockies, and then sailed up the Mississippi to its headwaters, all the while

"Carolina Paroquet" by John James Audubon (ca. 1825).

"Four Bears, Chief of the Missouri River Mandans" by George Catlin (1832).

painting the Indians, their regalia, their dwellings, and their weapons and tools. Aside from its considerable charm and vivacity, his work remains a valuable anthropological record of Indian ways of life. In 1837 Catlin opened an exhibition of 600 pictures in New York City, charging each visitor 50 cents. With the profits he sailed for Europe, taking along with him "Catlin's Indian Gallery." In London, Paris, and in Holland immense crowds flocked to the exhibitions, all eager to see the various colorful guises of the fabled Red Man.

By 1851, unfortunately, the public, both in Europe and in America, was losing interest in traveling exhibits of this sort, perhaps because of the increasing vogue of photography. Catlin attempted to sell his paintings to the United States government. As the modern art critic John Canaday has written, "Daniel Webster and the northern senators sponsored the acquisition, but the southern block

fought it. They saw the West as an area for the expansion of slavery at the expense of Indian rights and feared that Catlin's paintings would stir up sympathy for the tribes—as well they might have." As a result of southern opposition, the paintings were not bought by the government but rather by a rich American manufacturer.

At a time when Romantic artists in Europe were picturing medieval knights and ladies or conjuring up fantasies of devils and fair maidens or studying the exotic faces of Morocco, American painters were expertly capturing in paint the vast, haunting depths of the American landscape, the imposing splendors of the country's wildlife, and the haunting faces of its Indian population. The antebellum period saw the emergence not only of the first internationally important American writers (Hawthorne, Emerson, Poe, Melville, Thoreau, and Whitman) but also of its first major painters.

Contrasts and Contradictions

The very nature of the federal system of government, complicated by the addition of vast new lands, millions of immigrants, and industrial growth in what still was an agricultural economy, not only created cultural diversity within the United States but numerous contradictions as well. The greatest of these was, of course, slavery in an emerging democracy.

Because of these regional contrasts, any attempt to measure the achievements of a reform movement or even compare conditions in various regions ends up in a sea of qualifying statements. Different states reported statistics in different ways. Perhaps this was inevitable in an age not yet accustomed to standardization even within a single state. A simple matter such as basic, primary education can become hopelessly confused. Many states by 1850 did not have free common schools and the length of terms varied greatly (as did instruction).

The 1850 census indicates that the illiteracy rate among native-born whites in the South over the age of twenty was 20.3 percent, compared with 3.0 percent in the Middle Atlantic states, and .42 percent in New England. These statistics do not include the immigrant population of the North and disguise the fact that southern cities such as Charleston, New Orleans, Memphis, and Louisville were developing creditable school systems, certainly better than those found in smaller communities in many other states. And, in the 1850s, while the common school flourished in the North and languished in the South, private academies abounded below the Mason-Dixon line. Virginia, for example, had more colleges and more college graduates and was expending more money on higher education than Massachusetts.

Yet much more than differing educational standards set one region—the Lower South—apart from all others. There slavery had few critics, industry and immigrants were sparse, and economic well-being rested, in the final analysis, on one crop. As the antislavery fury mounted, this arc of states from South Carolina to Texas became more and more unified in opposition to abolition (and everything else northern as well) and came to see itself and, in turn, be seen as a distinct section somewhat apart from the main pulse of national life.

Cotton and Slavery

In 1850, U.S. exports were valued at $135 million and cotton bales produced by slave labor constituted over fifty percent of that total, or $72 million. Ten years later exports had increased to $316 million, and cotton's share was even greater, $192 million, or about sixty-one percent. About two-thirds of all cotton and tobacco grown in America was shipped overseas, virtually all other agricultural produce being consumed within the nation, although corn exports were mounting rapidly.

One of the unexpected results of the cotton economy was the way it tied the South to the North economically; in fact, the South was almost a northern "colony." Northern men, and particularly New Yorkers, were the middlemen, shippers, bankers, and insurers who took a large share of the South's agricultural profits.

The end of the War of 1812 marked an important shift of cotton production to the West as settlers moved into the fertile soils of Georgia, Alabama, and Mississippi. The rich bottom land of the lower Mississippi River and its tributaries provided an excellent environment for growing cotton. Western Tennessee, eastern Arkansas, and western Texas also became centers of cotton production. The Indian removal policy made possible white expansion into most of these areas. By 1860 these cotton-producing states outstripped the older states of Georgia and the Carolinas.

There were fifteen slave states in the Union in 1850. The dramatic rise in cotton production—which was generating more national income, for instance, than the entire northern iron industry—was based on slave labor. As slavery became more and more central to the southern economy, prospects of gradual and peaceful abolition became dimmer.

Yet it would be a mistake to think of the typical Southerner as the owner of a large plantation staffed with hundreds of slaves. In 1860 there were 1,516,000 white families in the South, but only 385,000 owned slaves—that is, almost seventy-five percent of the white southern families owned no slaves at all. Of those families that did own slaves, in 1850 almost fifty percent owned fewer than five. The planter aristocracy (that is, the group that owned more than fifty slaves) numbered only 10,000 families.

The well-to-do farmer who held ten to thirty slaves typically lived on his own land and personally supervised the management of his estate. He usually did not hire an overseer. Among the slaves there was some specialization of labor; a few of the slaves worked part-time as carpenters or cooks, but they generally had to do field work as well. Only on farms with more than thirty slaves was there much specialization. For instance, one wealthy Virginia planter in 1854 had eight plowmen, ten hoe hands, two wagoners, four oxcart drivers, a carriage driver, a hostler, a stableboy, a shepherd, a cowherd, a swineherd, two carpenters, five masons, two smiths, a miller, two shoemakers, five spinners, a weaver, a butler, two waitresses, four maids, a nurse, a laundress, a seamstress, a dairymaid, a gardener, and two cooks.

During these antebellum decades, because of an abundance of cheap land, an expanding economy, and a rapidly developing democracy, the plain people of the South, the less-affluent whites, did not think of themselves as a distinct class. In fact, the Northeast with its native-foreign, urban-rural, industrial-agricultural divisions perhaps had more easily defined class groupings. In the South, as elsewhere, it was not impossible for a poor lad to become a lawyer, editor, doctor, or politician, and perhaps, at the same time, a slaveowning planter. Most importantly, whites, regardless of wealth or education, considered themselves superior to blacks and maintained a high degree of solidarity to ensure white supremacy. And the general association of rich and poor at church and at various social functions created a sense of unity between the plain folk and the cotton aristocracy, a unity sometimes supplemented by kinship and a bond that would speak louder than politics in 1861.

The concentration of blacks in the South varied. In the cotton lands of the Deep South, the concentration was particularly dense, as it was in the bottom lands of the Mississippi River and in the parts of southern Texas that drained into the Gulf of Mexico. By 1850 the Gulf area was the largest cotton-growing region in the world, far surpassing Egypt and the East Indies, the closest rivals. Of the 2.8 million black slaves engaged in agriculture in the United States in 1850, at least 1,815,000 were employed in the cotton fields.

Heavy reliance on agriculture entailed constant financial problems for the South. Planters used factors (commission merchants) to sell their crops for them, as they had in colonial days. The factors, usually residing in a port city such as New Orleans, shipped crops, provided planters with credit, and sent supplies for their plantations in return for a commission. Between six and nine percent of the sale price of cotton went to the factor in return for providing services, such as insurance, storing the cotton, handling it at the wharf, and so on. The planters borrowed money from the factors, usually at the going rate of eight percent. In return, a planter promised most or all of a crop to his factor. This crop lien system, which became the principal means of borrowing money in the South, reinforced reliance on cotton as the mainstay of the economy, since factors regarded it as the safest crop and generally required planters to grow it in return for loans and advances.

While industrialization and urbanization were transforming the North, the South in many ways remained much as it had been in the eighteenth century—rural and agricultural. Immigrants brought to the North new ideas, customs, and trades, and in the big northern cities these cultural innovations passed quickly from one individual to another.

Slavery and Southern Society

The presence of slaves created special pressures in southern life. A slave could not be educated, even taught to read or write; to do so was against the law. Nevertheless, on some occasions the laws were broken. The Grimké sisters, the daughters of a liberal South Carolina judge, recalled the excitement of teaching blacks in an atmosphere of secrecy: "The lights were put out, the keyhole secured, and flat on our stomachs before the fire, with spelling books in our hands, we defied the laws of South Carolina." White supremacists were convinced that education would arouse a spirit of rebellion in blacks. Thus schools for free blacks were closed and masters were forbidden to teach their slaves. Georgia prohibited blacks from holding jobs requiring education (such as typesetting); and Virginia refused to let its free blacks educated in the North return to their homes. Nevertheless, in the face of an almost total banning of black education, some slaves did manage to learn—in secret schools run in the city, from the white children on plantations, and through self-instruction.

Southern Protestantism in the decades before the war was characterized by anti-intellectualism. Specifically, the fundamentalism of southern Christianity, linked with a Romantic adherence to intuition, led many Southerners in the 1850s to take up arms against the dangerous ideas of modern science. The new study of geology, of the cosmic system, of fossils and the remains of ancient civilization—all of these scientific pursuits brought into doubt many of the literal statements in the Bible concerning the age of the world, human origins, and the creation and development of the earth. As a result, by 1860 a Protestant dogma emphasizing the infallibility of the Scriptures and the vital need for conversion, along with a belief in the inherent good of slavery, had become firmly rooted in the southern way of life.

The rise of abolitionism in the North after the 1830s and the growing fear of slave rebellions caused Southerners to seek new ways of justifying slavery. The Baptist, Methodist, and Presbyterian churches, which had earlier condemned slavery, now defended the institution. By the mid-1840s, southern churches separated from their counterparts in the North as a result of the split over slavery. Leading southern ministers wrote books and delivered sermons demonstrating that slavery was upheld in the Old Testament and that, according to the New Testament, the Apostle Paul urged fugitive slaves to return to their masters.

A Clash of Cultures

Although it is incorrect to think of the United States as divided into two distinct regions, North and South, by mid-century the Northeast and sections of the satellite regions tied to it by railroad tracks (such as the Old Northwest) were becoming more urban and more industrial, less agricultural, and increasingly unwilling to tolerate much longer the institution of slavery. A fringe of states stretching from Maryland and Virginia westward through Kentucky and Missouri exhibited some aspects of this emerging urban-industrial life, yet by sentiment and blood tended to be deeply rooted in an agricultural past. To the South, except for a handful of river towns and seaports, agriculture's sway was unchallenged and so was the belief in a slave society. In some regions such as North Carolina, east Tennessee, and upland areas of several states, there was diversified, general farming, but cotton and those who grew it represented the real power throughout much of the Lower South.

While the North felt it was surging forward into a new era of greater prosperity for greater numbers of its citizens, much of the South was clinging to a romantic image of its slave society. Southerners often regarded Yankees as money-grubbing city slickers desperate for gain, indifferent to the suffering of their employees, and devoid of all personal charm; at the same time, they liked to see themselves as refined gentlefolk, more interested in a life of stately, cultivated ease than in making money, as kindly masters to their slaves, and as excellent hosts and fluent conversationalists. The North, however, saw the South as a land of moral and educational backwardness, perversely indifferent to progress, unjustifiably snobbish, more emotional than intellectual, and, above all else, as a land of slavery.

The North was a region marked by considerable cultural, linguistic, and religious diversity, the result of mass immigration; the South remained overwhelmingly Protestant and Anglo-Saxon, except, of course, for several million blacks who had a subtle but passive influence upon southern folkways. The mobility of people in the North (from farm to city, from city to frontier) was loosening the ties of family solidarity; in the South individuals grew up amongst relatives and maintained lasting loyalties even to distant cousins. The North was the scene of widespread and effective reform movements; the South was more content with traditional social arrangements. Education in the North was more and more directed towards practical benefit; in the South it continued to be oriented towards classical learning and the other ornaments of "civilized" life.

But the growing conflict over protective tariffs and slavery were the great divisive issues, and different styles of life, of thought, and of temperament merely exacerbated sectional hostilities. To the Southerner, the Northerner was an unfeeling machine; to a Northerner such as Henry Adams, historian and grandson of John Quincy Adams, the Southerner was a mindless creature of impulse. As Adams put it, "Strictly, the southerner had no mind; he had temperament. He was not a scholar, he had no intellectual training; he could not analyze an idea and he could not conceive of admitting two; but in life one could get along very well without ideas if one had only the social instinct." No matter how great the differences between Northerners and Southerners might have been, they were only exaggerated by ignorance. "We are, I fear," wrote one astute Southerner in 1857, "within a few years of disunion & perhaps of civil war; and all because neither side knows the other."

Essay

The Face
of
America at Mid-Century

Engine Company Casco No. 1 responding to a fire in Middle Street in Portland, Maine. Daguerreotype, 1848.

In its variant forms, photography—no less than television a century later—had a profound impact on American life and society. Whereas television reflects in image, sound, and motion what is going on, early daguerreotypes, tintypes, and glass-plate negatives caught instantaneous glimpses of the nation for all to see. (For more information on the development of photography in subsequent decades, see Chapter 17 and the essay on George Eastman and Kodak.)

This handful of views—figures and landscapes frozen in time—shows us precisely how America's towns, cities, and countryside appeared in the eyes of the people of the 1850s and 1860s. It is apparent that one dressed up and posed for a photographer much as one had done for a portrait painter, that Niagara Falls was already attracting tourists (and in top hats, no less), and that the bustle of Manhattan had already begun. (Insofar as they are known, the dates and photographic processes are cited in the accompanying captions.)

New York's Broadway with hacks and crowds, looking south from Duane Street to Chambers Street.

Niagara Falls. Ambrotype or glass negative, ca. 1854.

Looking down Boston's Brattle Street. Daguerreotype, 1852.

Planting sweet potatoes on Edisto Island, South Carolina, in 1862.

A Minnesota youth dreams of trekking to California for gold.

Proud parents and their six children, an unidentified family group.

A young seamstress pauses in her work and looks at the camera.

A cooper's shop near Titusville, Pennsylvania, ca. 1865. These barrels probably were soon filled with oil.

SELECTED
READINGS

Many of the books listed in Chapers 8 through 11 are relevant to the topics covered in this chapter. In addition, see the following sources.

General Accounts

Allan Nevins, *Ordeal of the Union* (2 vols., 1947)

Rush Welter, *The Mind of America, 1820–1860* (1975)

Expansion and Growth

Wyatt W. Belcher, The Economic Rivalry Between Chicago and St. Louis, 1850–1880 (1947)

Ray Allen Billington, *Westward Expansion: A History of the American Frontier* (4th ed., 1974)

Everett Dick, *The Lure of the Land: A Social History of the Public Lands from the Articles of Confederation to the New Deal* (1970)

Albert Fishlow, *American Railroads and the Transformation of the Ante-Bellum Economy* (1965)

Robert W. Fogel, *Railroads and American Economic Growth* (1964)

Paul W. Gates and Robert W. Swenson, *History of the Public Land Law Development* (1968)

Peter R. Knight, *The Plain People of Boston, 1830–1860: A Study in City Growth* (1971)

Samuel Eliot Morison, *Old Bruin: Commodore Matthew Calbraith Perry* (1967)

Merl E. Reed, *New Orleans and the Railroads: The Struggle for Commercial Empire, 1830–1860* (1966)

John D. Unruh, Jr. *The Plains Across: The Overland Emigrants and the Trans-Mississippi West, 1840–1860* (1979)

Richard W. Van Alstyne, *The Rising American Empire* (1960)

Arthur Walworth, *Black Ships off Japan: The Story of Commodore Perry's Expedition* (1946)

Social and Cultural Diversity

Irving H. Bartlett, *The American Mind in the Mid-Nineteenth Century* (1967)

Donald B. Cole, *Immigrant City: Lawrence, Massachusetts, 1845–1921* (1963)

Susan P. Conrad, *Perish the Thought: Intellectual Women in Romantic America, 1830–1860* (1976)

David Grimsted, ed., *Notions of the Americans, 1820–1860* (1970)

Francis O. Matthiessen, *American Renaissance: Art and Expression in the Age of Emerson and Whitman* (1941)

Perry Miller, *The Life of the Mind: From the Revolution to the Civil War* (1965)

Earl F. Niehaus, *The Irish in New Orleans, 1800–1860* (1965)

William R. Taylor, *Cavalier and Yankee: The Old South and the American National Character* (1961)

Contrasts and Contraditions

Clement Eaton, *The Growth of Southern Civilization, 1790–1860* (1961)

Clement Eaton, *The Mind of the Old South* (1964)

Clement Eaton, *A History of the Old South* (3rd ed., 1975)

Howard R. Floan, *The South in Northern Eyes, 1831–1861* (1958)

Eugene Genovese, *The Political Economy of Slavery* (1965)

Eugene Genovese, *The World the Slaveholders Made* (1969)

Eugene Genovese, *Roll, Jordan, Roll: The World the Slaves Made* (1974)

CHAPTER 13

SECTIONALISM AND SECESSION

TIMELINE

1848
Whig Zachary Taylor defeats Democrat Lewis Cass in presidential election

1849
California ratifies antislavery state constitution

1850
Zachary Taylor dies and Millard Fillmore becomes President

1850
Congress approves Compromise of 1850

1852
Harriet Beecher Stowe publishes *Uncle Tom's Cabin*

1852
Democrat Franklin Pierce elected President

1854
George Fitzhugh publishes *Sociology for the South*, a defense of slavery

1854
Kansas-Nebraska Act repeals Missouri Compromise

1854
Ostend Manifesto urges annexation of Cuba

1855
Settlers in Kansas clash over slavery

1856
Senator Charles Sumner attacked on the Senate floor

1856
Democrat James Buchanan elected President

1857
Dred Scott decision declares blacks are not citizens and opens territories to slavery

1857
President Buchanan recommends admission of Kansas as a slave state

1858
Abraham Lincoln and Stephen Douglas debate extension of slavery into the territories

1859
Abolitionist John Brown attacks federal arsenal at Harper's Ferry

1860
Abraham Lincoln elected President

1861
In February seven southern states establish a provisional government of the Confederate States of America

CHAPTER OUTLINE

The sectional conflicts that dominated American life in the 1850s arose from issues not always sharply defined in the minds of most Americans of the time. In one sense this very obscurity was deliberately cultivated in the mid-nineteenth century by the nation's major political parties. Just as many elected officials today frequently back away from decisive statements on such controversial questions as welfare, busing, and economic planning by the central government, so the Whigs and Democrats in the decades before the Civil War attempted to retain their followings by straddling the great problems—abolition, the tariff, and the spread of slavery into new territories.

Territorial Expansion And Politics

By the end of Polk's administration (1845–1849), congressmen were heatedly disputing the status of slavery in the territories. Southerners claimed the right to bring their property, including slaves, into any new area. They denied the contention that Congress had the authority to prohibit the movement of slavery into the territories. Democrat Lewis Cass (1782–1866) of Michigan tried to reduce tensions by advocating the principle of "squatter sovereignty," whereby the people of each territory might decide for themselves whether or not to permit slavery within their borders. Although this position might seem, at first glance, to favor southern ambitions, in fact southern extremists rejected it. They argued that territorial legislatures possessed no autonomy and ruled only by permission of Congress; they could not ban or endorse slavery. Congress alone had authority over territories, and that body, the Southerners reasoned, was constrained by the Constitution to guarantee an individual the freedom to use property (slaves) as he or she saw fit.

The Election of 1848
In the election of 1848 the Democrats nominated Cass, thereby endorsing his principle of squatter sovereignty, but avoided any mention of the con-

tainment of slavery in their platform. The notion of squatter sovereignty was in any event a calculated appeal to moderates on either side of the Mason-Dixon line. The Whigs nominated Zachary Taylor (1784–1850) of Louisiana, a man who owned slaves and cotton fields but who stated that, if elected President, he would not abuse his veto power. With this statement Taylor implied that he would not fight decisions made by Congress concerning slavery in recently acquired lands. But his party refused to adopt a platform or even announce its principles.

The Whigs attempted to capitalize on the war record of Taylor, who had won distinction during the Mexican War by defeating a superior Mexican force under General Santa Anna at Buena Vista. But Taylor, dubbed "Old Rough and Ready," was one of the strangest choices for the presidency in American history, since he had no previous political experience, had never cast a vote, lacked formal education, and remarked when asked if he would accept the nomination, "I will not say I would not serve if the good people were imprudent enough to elect me." This was, of course, a repeat of the "Tippecanoe and Tyler, too" strategy of 1840; once more the Whigs hoped to ride the coat tails of a celebrated battlefield hero to victory. Taylor's running mate was Millard Fillmore (1800–1874), a dig-

nified, high-minded political leader from New York state.

Cass, the Democratic nominee, was a loyal party man with considerable ability and political experience. A confirmed expansionist in the 1840s, he was, above all else, a nationalist. Even slavery with all of its ramifications was, in his view, a subordinate issue. The selection of Cass was an effort to win the western vote and to promote sectional harmony.

Antislavery politicians in both parties found it difficult to accept either Taylor or Cass. In New York and New England, Democratic dissidents were called "barnburners" by their enemies. Because of their dislike for Cass, it was said these dissidents were treating their party as the exasperated farmer who would burn down his barn to kill the rats infesting it. Antislavery or "conscience" Whigs, who bolted from their party as a result of Taylor's nomination, joined the barnburners and members of Birney's Liberty party to create the new Free Soil party founded on the principles of "Free Soil, Free Speech, Free Labor, and Free Men." The Free Soilers nominated ex-President Martin Van Buren, who had openly opposed the annexation of Texas and forthrightly repudiated slavery. This new party took away enough Democratic votes in New York to give that state—and the election—to Taylor and the Whigs. Nationwide, Van Buren won 10.1 percent of the popular vote; Cass, 42.5 percent; and Taylor, 47.3 percent.

Although a slaveholder, Taylor's military experience had given him a national outlook. He recommended that California, along with the rest of the land ceded by Mexico, be allowed to bypass territorial status and apply for statehood as quickly as possible. Immediate statehood, he believed, would settle the issue of slavery in the West without subjecting the nation to bitter sectional debates in Congress.

The Compromise of 1850

Following the discovery of gold in California in 1848 and the rush of settlers to the region, many Americans were eager to bring California into the Union. By October 1849, Californians had drawn up a state constitution outlawing slavery, which was overwhelmingly ratified two months later. The prospect of California's entrance into the Union as a free state alarmed Southerners, since it would upset the existing balance of fifteen slave states and fifteen free states. Should any new territory (New

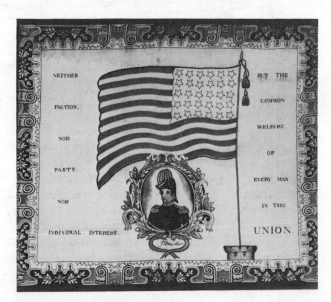

The Smithsonian Institution.

As this banner demonstrates, the Whigs attempted to capitalize on the war record of their candidate, Zachary Taylor, during the 1848 presidential campaign.

Mexico, Oregon, or Utah) also become a free state in the near future, the political power of the South in the Senate would be destroyed. Nevertheless, President Taylor, a Southerner, steadfastly urged the admission of California and warned that any attempt to block its entrance into the Union on purely sectional grounds would be unwise. In spite of Taylor's warning, southern extremists called for a convention to meet in Nashville, Tennessee, in the summer of 1850 to consider the possibility of secession.

Henry Clay, always a great nationalist, attempted to stage a reconciliation between the North and the South. Though he was seventy-one and in poor health, he recognized that sectional hostilities were explosive; a majority of Northerners in the House of Representatives were ready to pass the Wilmot Proviso, banning slavery from all territory acquired from Mexico, and southern congressmen under the leadership of Calhoun were openly threatening secession.

Beginning on January 29, 1850, Clay presented a number of compromise proposals to the Senate, which later were organized into an omnibus bill. He recommended that Congress admit California without any stipulation concerning slavery (he knew it would be free), and organize the Utah and New Mexico territories so that the people there could decide the slavery question for themselves when they applied for admission to the Union. (He assumed these areas would be free, too.) He suggested that the federal government pay part of the debt of the Republic of Texas, in return for which Texas would give up its claims to land that would become part of the New Mexico territory. He urged the prohibition of the slave trade in the District of Columbia in order to end the spectacle of manacled slaves being led through the streets of the nation's capital. To pacify the South in return for ending that trade, he urged enactment of a stronger fugitive slave law; Northerners, he said, must return runaway slaves to their owners. The last of Clay's eight resolutions stated that Congress "has no power to prohibit or obstruct the trade in slaves between the slaveholding states; but that the admission or exclusion of slaves brought from one into another of them, depends exclusively upon their own particular laws." These proposals were a strong bid for nationalism, and Clay closed with a fervent plea that everyone consider carefully before advocating secession or war.

Southerners were deeply unhappy with these suggestions, though they were offered in the spirit of compromise. Calhoun, too feeble to speak, had his objections voiced for him by Senator James M. Mason of Virginia. The South Carolinian threatened secession if the North took any action to thwart the spread of slavery or to curtail the domestic slave trade. What Calhoun did not anticipate was that his extreme remarks, by raising the distinct possibility of disunion and civil war, actually worked against his purposes and convinced moderate Southerners to cooperate with Clay.

But, strong opposition to Clay's proposals also came from the North. A leading opponent, Senator William H. Seward of New York (who is the subject of an accompanying biographical sketch), supported the Wilmot Proviso and denounced the Clay proposals as a failure of principle; even if the protection of slavery should be considered constitutional, Seward said, "there is a higher law than the Constitution"—an assertion that outraged conservatives, especially in the South. Jefferson Davis (1808–1889) of Mississippi upheld the right of the South to extend slavery to the territories. He argued that the proposals offered nothing of value to the South and insisted that the least the South would accept would be an extension of the Missouri Compromise line to the Pacific, permitting slavery to exist everywhere south of that line. Clay refused this counterproposal, pointing out that Mexican law had prohibited slavery and that it did not exist in new lands acquired from Mexico.

Daniel Webster made the most important speech on behalf of Clay's proposals. He assured his northern colleagues that agricultural, climactic, and geographic conditions made the new western territories acquired from Mexico unsuited for slavery. Thus it was not necessary to include the Wilmot Proviso or any similar prohibition against slavery.

Despite the efforts of Clay and Webster, dissension continued. But with the death of President Taylor in July 1850, Vice President Millard Fillmore, a strong advocate of Clay's compromise resolutions, moved into the White House and began to exert his influence. Even with the President's help, those favoring compromise faced serious opposition in the Senate until Democrat Stephen A. Douglas from Illinois (the man who framed the bills providing territorial governments for Utah and New Mexico) spoke eloquently in its behalf. Douglas decided to separate the various measures that were part of an omnibus bill and to push them through Con-

William Henry Seward

1801–1872

Born in Florida, New York, Seward graduated from Union College in 1820 and at the age of twenty-one settled in Auburn, New York, which he considered his home for the rest of his life. He was trained as a lawyer, but in his thirties became active in politics and joined the Whig party. Running as the Whig candidate, he was elected governor of New York in 1838, a position he held for four years. As governor, Seward was able to establish nonsectarian schools in New York City, despite the opposition of nativists.

Although at first rather lukewarm to the slavery issue, Seward soon moved squarely into the abolitionist camp before his second term as governor ended. Fearful he was too far in advance of public opinion and eager to replenish his financial resources, he chose not to seek another term and returned to his lucrative law practice. By 1848, however, antislavery sentiment was rising and Seward won a seat in the United States Senate. There he engaged actively in the debates concerning the Compromise of 1850. Seward was guided by a "higher law than the Constitution" and sought to abolish slavery and the slave trade in the District of Columbia and exclude slavery altogether from the western territories. He argued that "all legislative compromises [are] radically wrong and essentially vicious."

The early 1850s were difficult years for Seward. He had backed both Zachary Taylor and Winfield Scott wholeheartedly, but the declining power of the Whigs and the rise of the Know-Nothings in New York state called for fancy footwork. Nevertheless, Seward proved equal to the challenge, and in 1854, while seeking reelection, he took a strong, antislavery stand to please local Whigs and managed to secure Know-Nothing backing. A year later both the Know-Nothings and the Whigs were fast disappearing as the Republican party became a recognizable entity, and Seward now was in the forefront of the antislavery campaign.

From 1855 to 1860, Seward, now a Republican, served as one of the most vehement spokesmen of this growing movement. In 1858 he made a speech in which he characterized the North-South dispute over slavery as "an irrepressible conflict," a phrase that soon became famous. In 1860 Seward hoped to win the Republican presidential nomination, but he was judged too outspoken against slavery. After Lincoln won the election, however, he was quick to name Seward as his Secretary of State.

During the Civil War, Seward was in charge of the difficult task of keeping England and France from coming to the aid of the Confederacy. In this assignment he performed admirably, by appealing to the antislavery sentiment in Europe.

By temperament an expansionist, Seward negotiated the purchase of Alaska in 1867. During the Reconstruction period, he continued to act as Secretary of State under Andrew Johnson and was influential in convincing the President to take a conciliatory posture towards the defeated South. Although Seward often made reckless statements, sometimes showed poor judgment, and occasionally shifted opinions in order to appeal to voters, he was one of the earliest and staunchest antislavery leaders. As such, he earned the respect of many of his northern contemporaries.

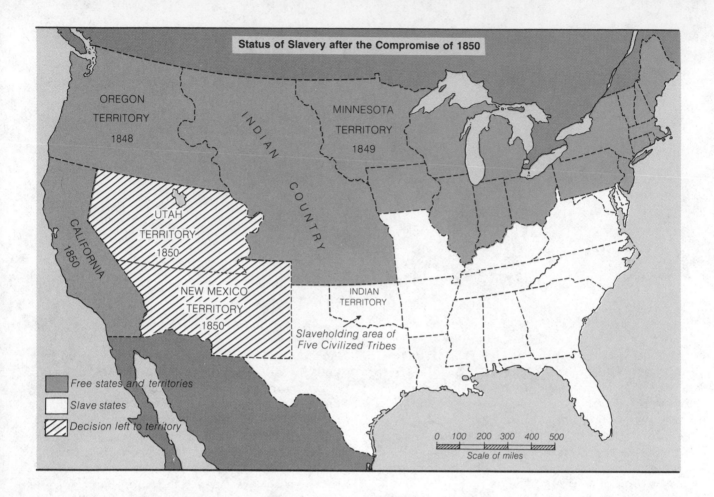

Status of Slavery after the Compromise of 1850

OREGON
TERRITORY
1848

MINNESOTA
TERRITORY
1849

INDIAN COUNTRY

CALIFORNIA
1850

UTAH
TERRITORY
1850

NEW MEXICO
TERRITORY
1850

INDIAN
TERRITORY

Slaveholding area of Five Civilized Tribes

Free states and territories

Slave states

Decision left to territory

0 100 200 300 400 500
Scale of miles

gress one by one. Soon, all but the District of Columbia bill, which banned the slave trade in Washington, passed, and on September 17 even that bill became law. Douglas's successful strategy involved finding different coalitions in Congress to support each measure. For instance, he secured the admission of California as a free state by putting together an alliance of Clay supporters and those antislavery men who, though they were against some of the other measures (such as the Fugitive Slave Law), were naturally in favor of gaining another state where slavery would be outlawed. The Fugitive Slave Law was in turn passed by a different coalition of proslavery Southerners and moderate Northerners.

The Fugitive Slave Law

The one provision of the compromise that everyone scrutinized carefully was the new, stricter Fugitive Slave Law. Southerners were waiting to see if it would be upheld in the North, and antislavery

Northerners recommended that it be ignored. As early as September 1850, one Ohio newspaper was predicting that the law "will be a dead letter upon the statute book," and an editorial in Maine recommended strenuous resistance. As one Florida editor complained, "No sooner has this Fugitive Slave Law gone into effect, [than] the cry of repeal . . . resounds from one end of the Northern States to the other."

Antislavery Northerners objected strenuously to several provisions of the Fugitive Slave Law in particular. Slave owners had only to submit an affidavit showing ownership to a special federal commission to recover a runaway slave and the alleged slave could not testify in his or her defense. Federal marshals were authorized to call on bystanders to help them enforce the law, and citizens preventing the arrest of a fugitive, or aiding in his or her concealment or rescue, were subject to a heavy fine, civil damages, and imprisonment for up to six months.

Fugitive slaves at a station on the "underground railroad."

Southerners viewed the election to the Senate in 1851 of Charles Sumner, an antislavery champion from Massachusetts, as a victory for northern opponents of the Fugitive Slave Law. Despite considerable evidence of northern opposition to the law, state election results indicate that a slight majority of southern voters looked upon the compromise with hope, or at least with a wait-and-see attitude. In Mississippi, South Carolina, and Alabama, moderates won narrow victories over secessionists. Nevertheless, some of these moderates warned that the success of the compromise depended largely on northern willingness to obey the Fugitive Slave Law.

The "underground railroad," a secret system for conveying escaped slaves on boats, wagons, and trains from one hiding place to another, brought a substantial number of fugitives to northern cities before 1850. Under the new law, those fugitives who settled in the North found their freedom once again threatened. Even free blacks who were not escaped slaves feared for their safety since they might be falsely charged with having escaped from their "owners" and "returned" to whites posing as former masters. One result of the passage of the law of 1850 was the movement of about 3,000 fugitive slaves to Canada within three months. Harriet Tubman (ca. 1821–1913), a slave who escaped from Maryland's Eastern Shore, was one of the most able conductors on the "underground railroad." Known by the slaves as "Moses," she made nineteen trips into slave territory to lead fellow blacks to freedom; and, after 1850, she guided runaways to Canada.

Although some 8,000 to 15,000 blacks fled from slavery in the period from 1850 to 1860, only 191 slaves were claimed in the courts under the provisions of the Fugitive Slave Law. Many Southerners sincerely believed by 1860 that hostile northern

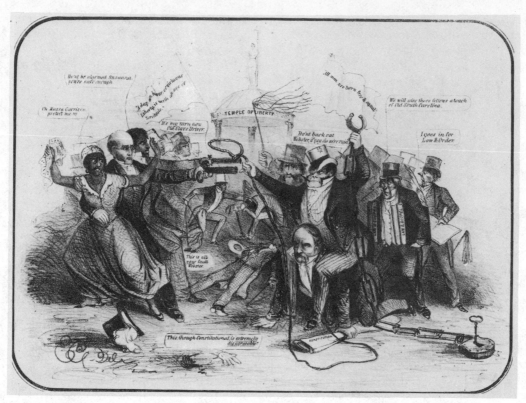

Courtesy of the New-York Historical Society, New York City.

This 1850 caricature entitled "Practical Illustration of the Fugitive Slave Law" depicts contemporary views of one of the most controversial congressional enactments in the 1850s. The leading figures include William Lloyd Garrison and Daniel Webster.

public opinion made this portion of the Compromise of 1850 unenforceable. Indeed many northern communities formed "vigilance committees" in the 1850s to protect fugitives. In Boston, for example, such a committee headed by Unitarian minister Theodore Parker (1810–1860) smuggled two slaves out of the country in 1850 to put them beyond the reach of slave catchers. Vermont passed a "Personal Liberty Law" in 1850 designed to impede enforcement of the Fugitive Slave Law, to discourage slave owners from pursuing their slaves, and to prevent kidnapping of free blacks. In New England, where hostility to the law ran highest, only three claims for the return of runaway slaves were made before 1854, and none after that year. Between 1855 and 1859 Connecticut, Rhode Island, Massachusetts, Michigan, Maine, Ohio, and Wisconsin also enacted personal liberty laws.

Despite the establishment of vigilance com-

mittees and the enactment of personal liberty laws, what Southerners thought was happening (wholesale disregard of the law) was not actually taking place. In the 191 cases calling for enforcement of the Fugitive Slave Law before 1860, 157 slaves, or over eighty-two percent, were returned to their masters by federal tribunals. Of the thirty-four fugitives who were not returned, twenty-two, or 11.5 percent of the total, were rescued from federal custody, one escaped, and 11, or less than six percent, were released. These statistics, however, hide the fact that many fugitive slaves were captured by their own masters, or other slave owners, and returned to slavery without recourse to the judicial machinery provided by law. U.S. Senator Stephen A. Douglas of Illinois, for example, claimed that:

"In nineteen cases out of twenty when a fugitive

slave enters Illinois, he is arrested and returned without any judicial process whatever. Those portions of the State which border on the Kentucky and Missouri lines are in harmony with their neighbors on the other side, and a fugitive slave is returned as regularly as a stolen horse."

———

Even among the majority of Northerners who opposed slavery, only a few citizens actually tried to thwart enforcement of the Fugitive Slave Law. In spite of much hostility and opposition to the law, federal court officials did their duty.

Though the Fugitive Slave Law may have been enforced in the North, nevertheless, it incurred considerable sectional animosity. Earlier the slavery question centered around whether slavery should be allowed to enter the western territories, but the 1850 Fugitive Slave Law raised a more sensitive question for some Northerners—the treatment and fate of individual blacks in their own hometowns.

Northern antislavery feeling was further aroused by the publication in 1852 of *Uncle Tom's Cabin*, written by Harriet Beecher Stowe (whose life and contributions to the antislavery movement are discussed in a biographical sketch in this chapter). The book itself was inspired by Stowe's revulsion against the Fugitive Slave Law, which she regarded as immoral and un-Christian. Many Northerners, never before sympathetic to abolitionist propaganda, agreed with her that the return of fugitive slaves was insupportable on humanitarian grounds. The Fugitive Slave Law unified the abolitionists since it was a common rallying point for all shades of opinion; those favoring pacifism, political action, and even disunion found it an issue upon which they could all agree.

In Defense of Slavery

As abolitionism and antislavery sentiment grew in the North, more and more Southerners came to the defense of their peculiar institution. South Carolina, with the largest proportion of slaves to whites in the South in 1850 (57.6 percent) and Virginia, with the greatest number of slaves (nearly half a million) led in forging the proslavery argument that became an ingenious defense of an institution condemned earlier by the South's finest minds.

Southerners cited the Scriptures, turned to the words and deeds of colonial statesmen, and drew upon the Roman and Greek classics—and they pointed to the prosperity of their region and to the living and working conditions of factory workers in the North—to prove the superiority of their slave society.

Two books by Virginian George Fitzhugh—*Sociology for the South; or, The Failure of Free Society* (1854) and *Cannibals All! or, Slaves Without Masters* (1857)—tried to forge this view into an aggressive, positive philosophy. The South must, he concluded, defend not merely black slavery, "but the principle of slavery as part of man's nature," a view that sent chills throughout much of the North, especially immigrant quarters peopled by those fresh from Europe. (A biographical sketch in this chapter discusses Fitzhugh's life and defense of slavery.

Another Virginian, Edmund Ruffin (1794–1865), was one of slavery's most ardent defenders. An agriculturalist and publisher who wrote scores of ar-

Courtesy of the New-York Historical Society, New York City.
"God wrote it," Harriet Beecher Stowe once said of her famous novel *Uncle Tom's Cabin* (1852).

Harriet Beecher Stowe

1811–1896

The woman destined to awaken a nation to the evils of slavery was born into a highly religious family. She was the seventh child of the famous Congregational minister and evangelist, Lyman Beecher. Although born in Litchfield, Connecticut, she moved with her family to Cincinnati, Ohio, in her early twenties when her father, eager to save the souls of Westerners, became the president of Lane Theological Seminary. In Cincinnati she met and married Calvin Ellis Stowe, a professor of Biblical Literature at Lane.

During the first seven years of marriage Mrs. Stowe bore five children, and for a time the cares of maternity kept her from pursuing a career as a writer. In 1843 a collection of her stories was published under the title *The Mayflower*.

In 1850 her husband received an appointment as a professor at Bowdoin College, and the family moved to Brunswick, Maine, where they existed in "genteel poverty." Mrs. Stowe began to immerse herself in published accounts of slavery, and contemplated writing a novel on that subject. While living in Cincinnati she had crossed the Ohio River into Kentucky on several occasions and even visited briefly a plantation; she and her husband had also helped one of their own black servants, who was claimed as a slave, to escape from federal officers. Aside from these incidents, Mrs. Stowe had few direct contacts with slavery, though she lived among fiery abolitionists, including two of her brothers, who were constantly denouncing slavery from their pulpits.

Mrs. Stowe's response to the Fugitive Slave Law of 1850 was to begin writing *Uncle Tom's Cabin; or, Life Among the Lowly*, which was published in weekly installments in the *National Era*, an abolitionist paper, beginning in 1851. Published in book form in 1852, it became one of the most widely read novels of the nineteenth century, not only in America but also in Europe. Within a year after its publication, *Uncle Tom's Cabin* had sold over 300,000 copies. The popularity of her antislavery novel had little to do with its literary merit, for Mrs. Stowe was clearly a second-rate writer. She adopted the idealized and sentimental style of the day and created sharply contrasted stereotypes such as the saintly slave, Uncle Tom, and the fiendish transplanted Yankee overseer, Simon Legree. Yet, because she avoided the vindictive and self-righteous tone that characterized abolitionist literature and because she attacked the institution of slavery by arousing sympathy for its individual victims, her novel was more persuasive and influential than contemporary abolitionist tracts, which condemned the South. *Uncle Tom's Cabin* proved especially effective on the stage, and northern impresarios were quick to stage dramatic readings and other performances based on the plot.

The book not only won Mrs. Stowe the vast admiration of Northerners but also the undying hatred of southern whites, although her "concluding remarks" pointed out that the North must share the blame and burden of slavery. Her book spawned some thirty anti-*Uncle Tom's Cabin* novels in the South within three years. To defend herself against accusations of inaccuracy and ignorance, Mrs. Stowe documented her case against slavery in *A Key to Uncle Tom's Cabin* (published in 1853). And in 1856, she published yet another antislavery novel, *Dred*.

The Stowe family was supported chiefly by earnings from her writings, and between 1862 and 1884 she turned out about a book a year. Her responsibilities were large, since she supported a number of poor relatives, but her skill in handling money was faulty. Nevertheless, she was able to build a modest house in Hartford, Connecticut, and buy a home in Florida with the profits of her pen. The best of her later novels (*The Pearl of Orr's Island* and *Oldtown Folks*, for instance) were based on recollections of her girlhood in New England.

ticles and pamphlets on a subject that became a personal obsession, his *Anticipations of the Future* (1860) went beyond the ideas of Fitzhugh, who always sought to convert the North to his point of view. Ruffin argued that secession was a necessity as he extolled the glories of an independent South. (Ruffin was permitted to fire the first shot against Fort Sumter in April 1861 and a few weeks later participated in the first Battle of Bull Run as a "temporary" private. When the Civil War ended four years later, he committed suicide.)

The Election of 1852

The results of the election of 1852 can be interpreted as a sign that most American voters favored the Compromise of 1850, or at least they were searching for a basis for national unity. Whig politicians bypassed the incumbent, Fillmore, while Southerners tended to favor him because he supported the compromise. However, many Northerners looked elsewhere for a candidate for a variety of reasons: some because he had southern support; others because they thought another military man like Harrison or Taylor could lead them to victory; and still others because they were already thinking of an antisouthern, abolitionist, and purely sectional movement. To replace Fillmore, the Whigs nominated vain, pompous General Winfield Scott (1786–1866), nicknamed by his enemies "Old Fuss and Feathers" because of his notorious punctiliousness, quarrelsome nature, and pompous bearing. Scott was chosen—though on the fifty-third ballot—because he was a hero of the Mexican War. Although Scott himself was a champion of the 1850 compromise, many Whigs, especially in the North, deplored that settlement; in fact the compromise badly divided the party.

By contrast, the Democrats endorsed the compromise, though they did not proclaim it to be a final settlement of the slavery problem. Their candidate was Franklin Pierce (1804–1869) of New Hampshire, who was selected as a compromise candidate on the forty-ninth ballot. Though only forty-eight at the time of the election, Pierce had served in the legislature of New Hampshire and in the United States Senate. A loyal Jacksonian Democrat, Pierce respected southern rights and harbored an antipathy for abolitionists, whom he considered dangerous activists bent upon destroying the Union. He was an ardent nationalist who hoped to promote the public well-being by harmonizing the conflicting aspirations of the various sections of the nation.

Pierce carried a majority of northern and southern states and received the largest plurality of votes ever recorded up to that time. He garnered 1,607,510 popular votes, or 50.8 percent; Scott won 1,386,942 or 43.9 percent of the popular vote. The Free Soil candidate, John P. Hale (1806–1873) of New Hampshire, polled only about five percent of the votes with a platform that condemned the Compromise of 1850 and the institution of slavery. Despite Pierce's large plurality, his majority was slender—just 51,896, or 1.6 percent of the votes. Although his victory may have been a sign that the public endorsed the compromise, some historians believe the voters saw little real choice between Scott and Pierce.

Nevertheless, the election of 1852 had an important impact on the political party system. Both major parties recognized that the Catholic vote was becoming important, and their candidates attempted to demonstrate they were not hostile to that religion or that their opponent was. In addition, defeat at the polls indicated the further disintegration of the Whigs into "cotton" (proslavery) and "conscience" (antislavery) factions. The Whigs were never again a national party after 1852. The Free Soil party also showed weakness. The Democrats appeared to be the only political organization in which both Northerners and Southerners still were trying to accommodate sectional differences.

The Kansas-Nebraska Controversy

Until 1854, only the territories of Utah and New Mexico were open to slavery on the basis of local self-determination. In that year, however, Senator Stephen A. Douglas of Illinois (called "The Little Giant") proposed the territorial organization of the land west of Missouri and Iowa.

Douglas, a firm advocate of continental expansionism, viewed slavery as a "curse beyond computation" but he refused to acknowledge that a moral issue was at stake. He seemed to see slavery as a local matter and tried to relegate the question to the sidelines as he dealt with territorial government and problems presented by national growth. Whatever his reasoning, Douglas did not want the ques-

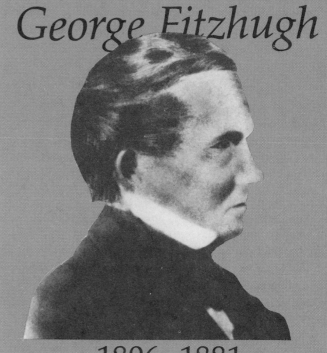

George Fitzhugh

1806–1881

A staunch defender of the institution of slavery, George Fitzhugh was born on November 4, 1806, in an isolated rural community along the Potomac River in Prince William County, Virginia. His father, an army surgeon and small planter, soon moved the family to a 500-acre plantation near Alexandria. Although the Fitzhughs undoubtedly used slave labor, they were not affluent, and when the elder Fitzhugh died about a dozen years later the land passed out of the family's hands. Nevertheless, young Fitzhugh remained wedded to the ideals of the planter class and concocted a genealogy (never verified) which connected him to an aristocratic Virginia dynasty.

Although George Fitzhugh's formal education was quite modest (he may have attended an academy), he was an avid reader and began to study law. In 1829 he married Mary Brockenbrough of Port Royal, Caroline County, and took up residence in that small Tidewater community.

For the most part, Fitzhugh found legal work boring and much of his time was devoted to his favorite topic—slavery and the race question. During early manhood he presumably shared the Jeffersonian belief that the extinction of slavery was imminent, but by the 1840s he became convinced that slavery was a force for good in society, not evil, and was indeed a constructive form of labor. Unlike many other reactionaries who came to the defense of slavery as the abolition fury mounted, this man took great pains to read antislavery literature. In 1849 he began writing for a Virginia newspaper and soon was a leading proslavery voice.

Fitzhugh, greatly distressed by the poverty and misery of the industrial poor in the North, concluded that the socialists were right in believing that capitalism led to the exploitation of workers. But he did not think that a socialist revolution was the solution to America's problem. Rather, he proposed that the entire country should embrace the paternalistic relationship between master and slave that supposedly existed on southern plantations. This idea Fitzhugh expressed in his two best-known works, *Sociology for the South; or, the Failure of Free Society* (1854) and *Cannibals All! or, Slaves without Masters* (1857). Only if a person actually *owned* workers, Fitzhugh argued, would their health and morale be guarded. Until the eve of the Civil War, Fitzhugh still hoped to introduce slavery into the North as a more beneficient system than free labor. Somewhat more realistically, Fitzhugh was also an early advocate of the industrialization of the South, though he hoped it would be accomplished, of course, with slave labor which could be made readily available by reopening the African slave trade.

Despite his proslavery views, George Fitzhugh was a late convert to secession, opposing it until the last moment. He worked for the Confederate Treasury in Richmond during the war, served as a Freedmen's Bureau agent in Reconstruction, and following his wife's death in 1877 moved west to live with his children, first in Kentucky and then Texas. Strangely, in the wake of a war that ended an institution he revered, Fitzhugh busied himself arranging labor contracts between ex-slaves and plantation owners and also was an associate judge, along with several blacks, on a freedmen's court.

tion of slavery to interfere with the rapid settlement and exploitation of the continent. He focused on two specific goals: first, removal of the Indian barrier to expansion and settlement west of Missouri and Iowa, that is, in Kansas and Nebraska; second, the building of a railroad to the Pacific, which would weld the East and West into a single nation.

In order to accomplish these goals, Douglas proposed that the people of the Kansas and Nebraska territories be allowed to determine the slavery question for themselves according to the principle of "popular sovereignty," which already had been instituted in New Mexico and Utah by the Compromise of 1850. Unfortunately, Douglas's Kansas-Nebraska Bill only further endangered the already uneasy truce achieved by the Compromise of 1850.

From many northern members of Congress, Douglas faced very strong opposition to his proposals. Senator Charles Sumner of Massachusetts denounced the Kansas-Nebraska Bill and warned his constituents that "the Nebraska bill opens anew the whole slavery question." Sumner joined other antislavery Democrats in publishing "An Appeal" against Douglas's bill. This document declared that the new bill was "a gross violation of a sacred pledge" made in 1820. That pledge was the Missouri Compromise. The "Appeal" charged that Douglas had joined hands with southern slaveholders to violate the Compromise of 1820. Douglas himself, Sumner claimed, was "that human anomaly—a Northern man with Southern principles."

Despite such opposition, Douglas fought very hard for the passage of the bill. Popular sovereignty, he believed, was necessary to break up the Indian barrier in the West and provide a pathway to the Pacific coast for white settlers. If the bill were enacted, it would win Douglas southern votes should he run in the 1856 presidential election. Finally, he had another personal motive: he was associated with real estate and railroad interests and had speculated in land along the projected central and northern routes to the West. If Kansas and Nebraska were not immediately open to settlers upon the principle of "popular sovereignty," Douglas feared that Secretary of War Jefferson Davis (an apologist for slavery) might decide to run the transcontinental railway line through Texas and New Mexico. Although the debates over the Kansas-Nebraska Bill were heated in both houses of Congress, it was approved and became law in 1854.

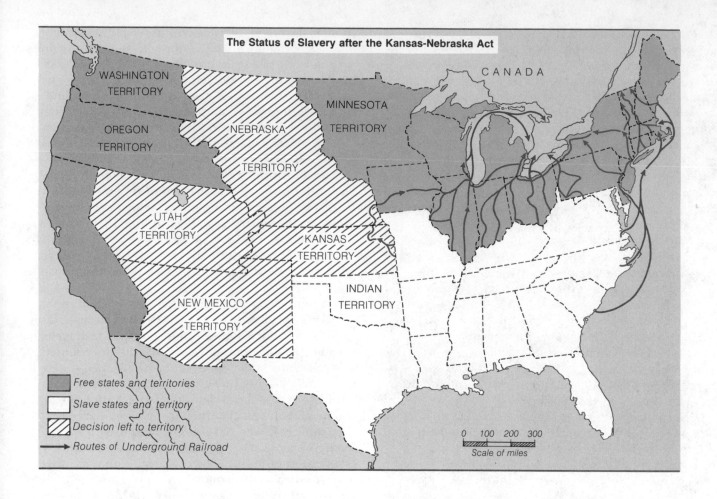

The Status of Slavery after the Kansas-Nebraska Act

WASHINGTON TERRITORY

OREGON TERRITORY

NEBRASKA TERRITORY

MINNESOTA TERRITORY

CANADA

UTAH TERRITORY

KANSAS TERRITORY

NEW MEXICO TERRITORY

INDIAN TERRITORY

Free states and territories

Slave states and territory

Decision left to territory

Routes of Underground Railroad

0   100   200   300
Scale of miles

The immediate result of the passage of the bill was the fragmentation of both political parties. Northern Democrats in the House had split over the issue, 44 in favor and 42 opposed to it. Opponents of the new law burned Douglas in effigy in every free state. The Whigs also were divided by the measure. Northern "conscience" Whigs fought the bill as had some southern Whigs. Most southern "cotton" Whigs joined the overwhelming majority of southern Democrats who supported it—a step that led to the absorption of most southern Whigs into the Democratic party. In short, the Whigs had split irrevocably over the bill and the Democratic party was badly divided as well; the Kansas-Nebraska Bill had clearly weakened both national parties.

Northern "conscience" Whigs drifted into other parties such as the short-lived Know-Nothings and the young Republican party. The latter included many diverse elements—abolitionists and other moral reformers, antislavery proponents, Negrophobes who disliked blacks as well as slavery, and zealous Protestant evangelicals, among others. All of these groups shared a common antipathy to the spread of slavery in the western territories. The Republican party grew with startling speed because millions of Americans in the North regarded the Kansas-Nebraska Act as the opening battle in a last-ditch struggle between the southern and northern ways of life. Some citizens viewed slavery as an immoral institution while others only concerned themselves with the prospect that it might become a national institution and force white workers to compete with slaves for jobs. Regardless of their particular orientation, the diverse elements comprising the new Republican party all agreed that slavery was a menace that had to be contained.

The Ostend Manifesto

While this new political realignment was forming,

sectional suspicions were growing as a result of the efforts of proslavery American ministers in Britain, France, and Spain to annex Cuba. Southerners were worried that Spain, which owned Cuba, was planning to free the slaves there and turn it into a black republic much like Haiti. The Ostend Manifesto—actually a secret dispatch issued by James Buchanan, American minister to Britain, John Mason, minister to France, and Pierre Soulé, minister to Spain, and sent to Secretary of State William Marcy in October 1854—offered two recommendations. The United States should make an earnest attempt to buy Cuba from Spain, but, if unsuccessful, the American government should seize the island by force. When news of this leaked to the press, northern politicians found additional grounds for denouncing southern schemes. And the new Republican party found its membership growing.

Bleeding Kansas

In Kansas, a race was on between free soilers and proslavery Southerners to determine whether the territory would enter the Union as a free or slave state. Nebraska faced no such problem. It lay west of a free state and would be settled by an antislavery population, but proslavery Missourians saw Kansas as a natural area for slave expansion (some Missourians even insisting that the security of their state depended upon a proslavery government in Kansas). While the New England Emigrant Aid Society and other organizations financed free soil settlers to the region, Missourians poured into Kansas

and packed the Kansas territorial legislature with seeking to turn Kansas into a slave state. During the course of his loftily worded speech (which included quotations from Cicero, Livy, Vergil, Dante, and Milton), Sumner lowered his tone to aim some choice insults at Senator Andrew P. Butler of South Carolina, whom he called the "Don Quixote of Slavery," a man who had "chosen a mistress to whom he has made his vows and who, though ugly to others, is always lovely to him; though polluted in the sight of the world, is chaste in his sight . . . the harlot, Slavery." Several days later in retaliation for this affront to the absent Butler, South Carolina Congressman Preston Brooks, Butler's nephew, at-proslavery representatives. The free soil voters, however, refused to recognize the proslavery government. They drew up their own constitution that prohibited slavery as well as the entrance of blacks into Kansas, and in January 1856 elected a governor and a legislature. Virtual civil war erupted between supporters of the two rival governments as troublemakers on both sides staged frequent raids against each other. Brooklyn clergyman Henry Ward Beecher (1813–1887) gave his blessings to shipments of rifles to free soilers in Kansas; the weapons came to be known as "Beecher's Bibles." Missourians and free soilers came to the aid of their beleaguered brethren, and both sides added fuel to the guerrilla war that was ravaging Kansas.

On May 19, 1856, Charles Sumner rose in the Senate to speak about what he called "The Crime Against Kansas." In a three-hour diatribe he denounced the "murderous robbers" of Missouri

SOUTHERN CHIVALRY — ARGUMENT versus CLUB'S.

This 1856 lithograph portrays the attack on Charles Sumner by Preston Brooks and ridicules "Southern Chivalry."

seeking to turn Kansas into a slave state. During the course of his loftily worded speech (which included quotations from Cicero, Livy, Vergil, Dante, and Milton), Sumner lowered his tone to aim some choice insults at Senator Andrew P. Butler of South Carolina, whom he called the "Don Quixote of Slavery," a man who had "chosen a mistress to whom he has made his vows and who, though ugly to others, is always lovely to him; though polluted in the sight of the world, is chaste in his sight . . . the harlot, Slavery." Several days later in retaliation for this affront to the absent Butler, South Carolina Congressman Preston Brooks, Butler's nephew, attacked Sumner at his desk and struck him repeatedly over the head with a cane. The assault on Sumner by "Bully Brooks" greatly increased sectional tension.

Meanwhile in Kansas, a transplanted Northerner named John Brown (1800–1859), who had settled with his four sons at Osawatomie and joined the free-state partisans in their struggle against the proslavery forces, was preparing to strike a blow for the antislavery cause. Several days after the attack on Senator Sumner, Brown and a small band of his followers descended upon the cabins of proslavery families on Pottawatomie Creek, brutally murdered five of the unsuspecting settlers, and mutilated their bodies. Several hundred proslavery partisans retaliated for the murders by attacking and burning Osawatomie. One of Brown's sons was killed, and Brown soon fled to the East. News of bloody raids and skirmishes in Kansas influenced the 1856 presidential campaign.

The Election of 1856

Democrats passed over Douglas since his Kansas-Nebraska Act was so unpopular in the North. Instead they chose the shrewd and conservative Pennsylvanian James Buchanan, a sixty-five-year-old bachelor who had served as U.S. minister to Britain during the controversy over the Kansas-Nebraska Act and thus escaped association with that issue. Despite his coolness and impartiality, gained during some forty years in public life, Buchanan was known as a "Doughface"—a Northerner with southern sympathies. His advocacy of the southern side during the recent Ostend Manifesto affair seemed to support this claim. In fact, Buchanan was a strict constructionist of the Constitution who believed that the slavery question could best be solved by the judiciary.

The Nativist American or Know-Nothing party chose ex-President Millard Fillmore who, like Buchanan, saw compromise as the only way the nation could survive sectional tensions. Republicans, reflecting the Whig inclination for military heroes, selected the glamorous soldier-explorer, John C. Frémont (1813-1890), as their standardbearer. In 1846 and 1847 Frémont fought the Mexican army in California and served briefly as civil governor of the region. He knew little about politics, having spent only a year as a United States Senator, but came out vigorously in favor of a free-soil Kansas and against the enforcement of the Fugitive Slave Law.

Although Buchanan won the election, Frémont and the Republican party showed extraordinary strength in many former Democratic strongholds in the North. Buchanan, with 45.3 percent of the ballots and 174 electoral votes, swept the South but carried only five of the free states. Frémont, with 33.1 percent and 114 electoral votes, took the rest of the free states. Ominous for the future of the Democratic party was the fact that the Republican vote in the free states exceeded that of the Democrats by well over 100,000. Millard Fillmore and the Know-Nothings ran a poor third.

The Dred Scott Decision and Its Effects

Two days after Buchanan's inauguration on March 4, 1857, the Supreme Court rendered a decision in the case of *Dred Scott* v. *Sanford*. Dred Scott, once a slave, had belonged to Dr. John Emerson of Missouri. In 1834 Emerson took Scott with him to the free state of Illinois and in 1836 to the upper Louisiana Purchase Territory, which, under the Missouri Compromise of 1820, was also free. Two years later, in 1838, Emerson returned Scott to Missouri. After Emerson died, Scott and his family were inherited by Emerson's widow. Asserting that his earlier residence in a free state and a free territory made him free, Scott then sued in the courts of Missouri. The lower court decided in his favor, the Missouri Supreme Court decided against him—and after several years the case finally reached the Supreme Court.

After the Supreme Court heard arguments on the case in February 1856, seven of the justices concluded that the Court had no jurisdiction, a ruling that would have sustained the Missouri Supreme Court. However, two antislavery justices, John McLean and Benjamin Curtis, declared that they intended to dissent and defend Dred Scott's free-

This cartoon presents Republican John C. Frémont as the candidate of "Popery, Fourierism, Free Love, Woman's rights, the Maine Law, & . . . the Equality of our Colored brethren (sic)." The "Maine Law" (1851) was the nation's first experiment in statewide Prohibition.

dom. Because the dissenting opinions would discuss the status of slavery in the territories, each of the judges in the majority decided to write an opinion. Therefore, when the ruling against Dred Scott was issued on March 6, 1857, there were seven different majority opinions, no two of them stressing the same arguments or citing the same statutes to support the views expressed.

Since the majority opinion was so divided, Chief Justice Roger B. Taney's opinion received the greatest attention. According to Taney, Dred Scott was not an American citizen since the Constitution recognized a "perpetual and impassible barrier" between blacks and whites and denied citizenship to blacks. Dred Scott was a black and also possibly still a slave; he had no right, on either score, to sue

in the courts of the nation. But Taney did not stop with the fate of Dred Scott. He proceeded to deliver an opinion concerning the whole gnarled question of slavery in the territories. Citing the Fifth Amendment, which prohibits the government from depriving persons of life, liberty, or property without due process of law, Taney condemned the Missouri Compromise of 1820 as unconstitutional. The Compromise, he said, had attempted to deprive Southerners in the Louisiana Purchase Territory north of 36°30' of their slaves—that is, their property—and it therefore was invalid.

The Court's ruling wrecked the machinery of political compromise. Opposition by the Republican party to slavery in the territories suffered a serious blow. The fate of the Democrats, the only re-

STEPHEN FINDING "HIS MOTHER."

Library of Congress

Using a whip to represent the Maine Law, Miss Columbia punishes Senator Stephen Douglas of Illinois for his anti-Lecompton position while Uncle Sam (who bears a striking resemblence to President James Buchanan) watches approvingly.

maining national party, depended on its various factions accepting popular sovereignty and compromise. Yet, if the Constitution and the Supreme Court prohibited Congress and territorial legislatures from excluding slavery, how could the settlers themselves ever do so?

The Dred Scott decision was only one of many far-reaching decisions handed down by the Supreme Court during these years. (For an in-depth description of how the Court works and settles landmark cases, see the essay on "The Supreme Court and Its Work" at the end of this chapter.)

Showdown in Kansas

The question of the status of slavery in the territories came to a showdown in Kansas where there were two territorial governments, each vying for authority. One, located in Lecompton, was proslavery and the other legislature, in Lawrence, was just as vigorously free soil. President Buchanan officially recognized the Lecompton legislature, but the Lawrence government maintained its own militia—and eventually commanded the allegiance of the majority of settlers.

In March 1857 the new territorial governor of Kansas, Robert Walker, called for the election of delegates to a new constitutional convention. But the free soilers, who deliberately abstained from voting, claimed with considerable accuracy that the election was rigged. Although the constitution drafted by the proslavery delegates contained a clause that protected slavery, Kansas voters were only given the option of ruling on the future introduction of slaves to Kansas. In an election marked by fraud and the abstention of free soilers, the proslavery forces easily triumphed.

Under pressure from southern leaders, President Buchanan recommended that Congress accept Kansas as a slave state governed by the Lecompton Constitution. As a result of Buchanan's actions, the Democratic party split sharply into northern and southern factions, and Kansas was not admitted until 1861. By that time, Buchanan was preparing to leave office and a number of southern states had seceded. Kansas entered the Union as a free state in 1861, following the admission of Minnesota in 1857 and Oregon in 1859, both also free states.

The Dred Scott decision and Buchanan's recommendation of the Lecompton Constitution destroyed the principle of "popular sovereignty." Consequently, more and more Northerners, disillusioned with the President, the Supreme Court, and the Democratic party, turned to the Republican party.

Growth of the Republican Party

The Compromise of 1850, the Kansas-Nebraska Act, and the Dred Scott decision, as well as numerous other political facts of life—the demise of the Whigs, the failure of the Know-Nothings, the conflict in Kansas, and the apparent impossibility of compromise on the expansion of slavery—aided greatly the youngest of political parties, the Republicans. Their ideology, very appealing to an emerging middle class and those who were or sought to become part of it, was centered on the concept of free as opposed to slave labor. They came to believe that the expanding, competitive society was nothing less than the direct result of free labor, and social, upward mobility was an integral part of that society.

Economic Issues

The Panic of 1857, a depression which lasted until 1859, exacerbated the nation's problems and had important political consequences. The industrial areas of the Northeast and the agricultural Midwest were hardest hit. Unemployment was greater than at any previous time in American history. Only in the South were the effects of the depression negligible. Southerners saw their own continued prosperity, which was based on the steady and lucrative cotton export trade, as confirmation the cotton and slave economy was preferable to the free northern industrial and agricultural economy.

Meanwhile, the Republicans took up the cry of impoverished Northerners for free homesteads of 160 acres in the West. To court the votes of eastern business interests, the Republicans called for a higher protective tariff, thus appealing to businessmen who were convinced that the low tariff had brought on the depression. By taking up these two causes, the Republicans hoped to attract farmers, industrial workers, and businessmen in the North who might be indifferent to the whole question of slavery.

The Lincoln-Douglas Debates

In the midst of the terrible depression that had begun in 1857, the Republicans in Illinois convened in Springfield in June 1858 to nominate Abraham Lincoln (1809–1865) as their candidate for the seat in the United States Senate held by Stephen A. Douglas. Lincoln, an admirer of Henry Clay and a former Whig who had served in the Illinois legislature (1834–1842) and the United States House of Representatives (1847–1849), was an outstanding lawyer and an energetic campaigner. Though not an abolitionist, he regarded slavery as an evil that should not spread. He joined the Republicans only after it became clear that their party was not merely a collection of abolitionists. Although he was an ambitious man, membership in the Republican party was not a cynical move. Lincoln considered the containment of slavery a paramount issue and the Republican party as the proper vehicle for addressing the problem.

Between August 21 and October 15, 1858, Lincoln and Senator Douglas met in various locations in Illinois for seven joint debates. The major topic at issue was the status of slavery in the territories.

Douglas still defended the principle of popular sovereignty, but the Dred Scott decision and Buchanan's acceptance of the Lecompton Constitution seriously undermined that approach to the slavery problem. Lincoln, by contrast, was determined to contain slavery, although he pledged to support the Fugitive Slave Law and to oppose northern interference with slavery where it already existed in the South. He favored gradual, compensated emancipation as the best way to end slavery.

Eager to denigrate his rival, Douglas accused Lincoln of thinking "that the negro was made his equal, and hence is his brother, but for my own part, I do not regard the negro as my equal, and positively deny that he is my brother or any kin to me whatever." Lincoln hastened to contradict this assertion. He announced that he was opposed to citizenship and suffrage for blacks and did not approve of racial intermingling. As he put it, "I have no purpose to introduce political and social equality between the white and black races. There is a physical difference between the two, which . . . will probably forever forbid their living together on the footing of perfect equality." Lincoln shared and accepted prevailing northern racist attitudes. He desired freedom for blacks but not social and political equality. Nevertheless, Lincoln believed that blacks were entitled to "all the rights enumerated in the Declaration of Independence," and that position was in itself remarkably progressive in his time.

Before Lincoln encountered Douglas in the debates, he had made a speech accepting the Republican nomination that inflamed Southerners. Lincoln argued:

"A house divided against itself cannot stand. I believe this government cannot endure, permanently half *slave* and half *free*.

I do not expect the Union to be *dissolved*—I do not expect the house to *fall*—but I *do* expect it will cease to be divided.

It will become *all* one thing, or *all* the other.

Either the *opponents* of slavery will arrest the further spread of it, and place it where the public mind shall rest in the belief that it is in course of ultimate extinction; or its *advocates* will push it forward, till it shall become alike lawful in *all* states, *old* as well as *new*—North as well as South.

Have we no *tendency* to the latter condition?"

In this last ominous-sounding question, Lincoln was pointing out that the Kansas-Nebraska Act and the Dred Scott decision indicated a tendency toward the expansion of slavery. Popular sovereignty, Lincoln reasoned, was a step towards the "Africanization" of the United States—that is, Douglas's popular sovereignty was really a proslavery doctrine.

In the seven debates with Douglas, Lincoln maintained that slavery was the principal threat to the Union and that the Kansas-Nebraska Act had only intensified sectional conflict. He urged the exclusion of slavery from all territories despite the Dred Scott decision and warned that popular sovereignty, if allowed to go unchecked, would eventually lead to the reopening of the African slave trade. Although Douglas had specifically condemned the clamor of southern extremists for a renewed African slave trade, Lincoln argued that, given the senator's popular sovereignty position, such a condemnation was logically inconsistent.

Douglas not only denied his alleged approval of the African slave trade, he also reaffirmed his belief that popular sovereignty was the only democratic means for putting the slavery question to rest.

At Freeport, in northern Illinois, Lincoln forced Douglas to admit that the Dred Scott decision had badly eroded the popular sovereignty argument. If a territory could exclude slavery only when it voted to become a state, might that not be too late to take effective action against the institution? Was there any lawful way for residents to exclude slavery from a territory *before* it became a state? Douglas responded with what has come to be known as his "Freeport Doctrine." He argued that regardless of how the Supreme Court ruled concerning the exclusion of slavery from a territory, it still could be excluded since:

"slavery cannot exist a day or an hour anywhere unless it is supported by local police regulations. These police regulations can only be established by the local legislature, and if the people are opposed to slavery they will elect representatives to that body who will by unfriendly legislation effectually prevent the introduction of it into their midst."

Lincoln challenged the Freeport Doctrine as a "bare absurdity" that maintained "a thing may be

lawfully driven from a place where it has a lawful right to stay," but in 1858 it served to win Douglas reelection in Illinois. Yet Douglas's Freeport Doctrine angered southern voters who already were disturbed by his stand against the admission of Kansas into the Union under the proslavery Lecompton Constitution. (Douglas took the view that the constitution had to be submitted to the voters to become legal.) Traditionally, historians have asserted that although the Freeport Doctrine won Douglas reelection to the Senate in 1858, it lost him the presidency in 1860. But the treatment accorded Douglas in the southern press during the early months of 1858 provides adequate proof that Douglas had already sacrificed much of his southern support long before he began to debate with Lincoln. Many Southerners simply could not forget Douglas's opposition to the Lecompton Constitution in Kansas.

In the debates Lincoln held his own against Douglas, one of the most formidable figures in American politics. And he received remarkable publicity. The Chicago *Times* and the Chicago *Press and Tribune* printed all seven debates—an innovation in American political coverage. The campaign of 1858 was Douglas's last triumph and marked Lincoln's emergence as a national figure in the Republican party.

Emotionalism at High Tide

Republican gains in the 1858 elections alarmed even moderate Southerners, and their uneasiness was only intensified when Republican Senator William H. Seward predicted that the nation was headed toward an "irrepressible conflict" between freedom and slavery. Although Lincoln was careful to urge the containment—not the abolition—of slavery, some Southerners quoted his "House-Divided" speech out of context to imply that he actually was an abolitionist.

Southerners became still more apprehensive when they learned that on July 5, 1859, the Kansas constitutional convention had replaced the proslav-

This etching depicts John Brown kissing a black baby on his way to the gallows. Brown's execution created a martyr for northern abolitionists.

ery Lecompton Constitution with a new document that prohibited slavery; this free-soil constitution was ratified by the people of Kansas on October 4. Thoroughly alarmed by the drift of events, some extremists urged reopening the African slave trade. In May 1859 delegates at the Southern Commercial Convention in Richmond adopted resolutions in favor of reopening the African slave trade.

Harper's Ferry, Virginia

On October 16, 1859, abolitionist John Brown and a group of eighteen devoted followers, both white and black, attacked the federal arsenal at Harper's Ferry with the hope of instigating a slave revolt. The entire nation was electrified by the news. President Buchanan immediately instructed Colonel Robert E. Lee (1807–1870) to lead a group of marines and defeat the insurgents. The battle lasted two days and no slaves came to Brown's aid. Two of Brown's sons died during the night, eight other members of his band were either killed or mortally wounded, and eight, including Brown, taken prisoner.

Brown was a poor farmer who settled in Kansas and was convinced that he had been appointed by Providence to set up a stronghold somewhere in the mountains from which fugitive slaves and their white friends could incite a general rebellion among the blacks in the South. On a visit to New England, Brown got money, supplies, and arms from various abolitionists.

The attack on a federal arsenal and the attempt to incite a slave insurrection played into the hands of southern disunionists who charged that the "Black Republicans" had supported the raid. Brown's actions, they warned, were only a logical step in the developing program of Republicans. To some Northerners, the raid seemed an unnecessary and misguided act of violence, but to others Brown was a martyr. Within a week after the raid, the Circuit Court of Virginia convicted Brown of treason against the state and of conspiracy to incite a slave rebellion. Throughout the proceedings Brown behaved with dignity and even cheerfulness. On the day he was hanged, he said that "the crimes of this guilty land will never be purged *away:* but with Blood." In the North, Emerson stated that Brown had made the "gallows glorious like the cross."

The Election of 1860

When Congress convened on December 5, 1859, three days after John Brown was hanged, many members attended sessions fully armed, so heated had the political climate become. Secession, a concept bandied about in some circles since the nullification fight of the early 1830s, gradually became more attractive to many Southerners. Whether it was a practical solution or not, talk about secession provided southern whites with an emotional release—a means of getting rid of tension aroused by outside criticisms of southern institutions. At the same time, the South was limiting freedom of expression; it became extremely dangerous for an editor to print criticism of southern policies. Free blacks were banished from many areas, manumission was forbidden, and apologists for the South were promulgating the theory that slavery, far from being a necessary evil, was a positive good.

Many Americans in the North and the South believed that Stephen A. Douglas was the only person who, if elected President, could prevent a fatal rupture between the North and the South. But the struggle between Douglas and Buchanan over the admission of Kansas into the Union had badly disrupted the Democratic party. When the Democrats

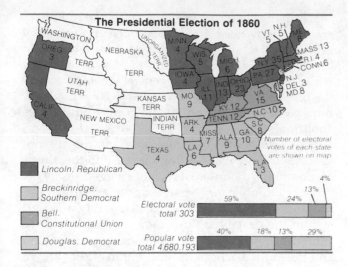

The Presidential Election of 1860

Number of electoral votes of each state are shown on map

Lincoln. Republican

Breckinridge. Southern Democrat

Bell. Constitutional Union

Douglas. Democrat

Electoral vote total 303 — 59% 24% 13% 4%

Popular vote total 4,680,193 — 40% 18% 13% 29%

met in Charleston on April 23, 1860, to nominate a candidate for President (Buchanan refused to serve more than one term), Southerners proposed that the party endorse a statement stipulating that no territory could abolish or prohibit the introduction of slavery and that it was the obligation of Congress to protect slavery in the territories. When this proposal was defeated, the convention voted to leave the question of the power of territories over slaves to the Supreme Court, and the delegates from most of the southern states withdrew. These southern Democrats held their own meeting at Richmond, Virginia, and nominated Vice President John C. Breckinridge of Kentucky; the northern faction of the party, reconvening in Baltimore, nominated Douglas.

The Republicans, bypassing such leading candidates as William H. Seward, who seemed too radical, and a contender from Missouri, Edward Bates (1793–1869), who offended immigrant voters because of his flirtation with nativism, picked a moderate, Abraham Lincoln. As a candidate, Lincoln had much to offer. He had taken a strong moral stand against slavery over a number of years and had quietly but firmly built an historical and ethical case against the institution. Now that the country was polarized and the Republican party could hope to appeal only to the northern antislavery and free-soil vote, Lincoln's reputation as a foe of slavery seemed an advantage. Since 1856 Lincoln had been building his own power base in the North, and he had the advice and aid of a shrewd political manager, David Davis (1815–1886), a wealthy and flamboyant 300-pound circuit court judge from central

Illinois who made a series of deals to ensure his nomination.

In the months following his nomination, Lincoln did little campaigning beyond growing a beard because a young girl informed him that "all the ladies like whiskers." But if the candidate was dignified and inactive, his party was energetically soliciting votes. The Republicans appealed to many different groups by standing for a higher tariff, free homesteads, a transcontinental railroad, and the rights of immigrants. The strongest and most solid arguments, however, were those against the extension of slavery and proposals to revive the African slave trade.

The campaign of 1860 was complicated even further by the presence of a fourth presidential candidate. The Constitutional Union party, composed of conservative remnants of several defunct parties, especially nativist Americans or Know-Nothings and old-line Whigs in the border states, chose John Bell of Tennessee as their candidate. Though Bell was a slave owner, he was one of only two southern Whigs who voted in 1858 against admitting Kansas into the Union as a slave state. The Constitutional Union party condemned sectionalism and stood for the preservation of the Union.

In the presidential race, Douglas stood for local self-determination or "popular sovereignty," Breckinridge upheld slavery and its extension into the territories, Lincoln preached containment of slavery, and Bell stood for "no political principle other than the *Constitution of the Country, the Union of the States, and the Enforcement of the Laws.*"

The question of the status of slavery in the territories was the crucial issue of the campaign, for by 1860 Southerners had come to recognize that the power to decide the status of slavery in the territories was the power to determine the future of slavery itself. Of the four nominees, Douglas was the only one to campaign actively, a practice considered unseemly in those days. Perhaps the best known politician in the country, Douglas understood that the Union was imperiled. He traveled widely reaffirming the principle of popular sovereignty and pleading with voters to stand by the Union, even if Lincoln were elected.

When the votes were counted, the worst fears of the South were realized. Despite the fact that Lincoln's three opponents piled up a plurality that surpassed his count by nearly a million votes, he had a clear majority in the electoral college. Lincoln's support, however, was the most sectional of all of the candidates. He won the electoral votes of every free state except three of New Jersey's seven electors, received virtually no votes in the southern states, and won only fourth place in the border states. Breckinridge received more popular votes in the North than Lincoln in the South. His strength, however, was in the Lower South; in the border states, he carried only Delaware and Maryland. Bell received the electoral votes of Tennessee, Kentucky, and Virginia. Douglas, whose popular vote fell short of Lincoln's by 485,706 ballots, won only Missouri's nine electoral votes and three of New Jersey's seven. Douglas obviously enjoyed widespread support, and only the four-man race denied him more votes. Indicative of the fact that a majority of voters were moderates, Douglas and Bell between them received 100,000 more votes than Lincoln, and their votes were more evenly distributed around the country than those received by Lincoln or Breckinridge.

Candidate	Electoral	Popular	Percentage of Popular Vote
Lincoln	180	1,865,908	39.8
Douglas	12	1,380,202	29.5
Breckinridge	72	848,019	18.1
Bell	39	590,901	12.6

The New York Public Library.
Political Cartoon of 1860 shows Lincoln easily outsprinting opponents (from left to right) Bell, Breckinridge, and Douglas.

Southerners were irate because a Republican would be inaugurated as a "minority president" in March 1861. Had they paid closer attention to the election results, however, they might have found some solace. The Republicans would be the minority party in Congress. But the prospect of a "Black Republican" in the White House enraged Southerners, and many subsequently focused attention on their state capitals rather than the national capital for political action.

Secession

A South Carolina woman traveling in Florida recorded in her diary for November 8, 1860:

_____

"Yesterday on the train . . . before we reached Fernandina a woman cried out—

'That settles the hash.'

Tanny touched me on the shoulder.

—'Look out!—Lincoln's elected.'

'How do you know?'—

'The man over there has a telegram. . . .'

'Now did you ever!' was the prevailing exclamation, and some one cried out: 'Now that the black radical Republicans have the power I suppose they will Brown us all. No doubt of it.'"

_____

Lincoln's election was seen as the beginning of more assaults like John Brown's. On December 20, 1860, a South Carolina convention announced the state's secession from the Union, saying that "a sectional party" had engineered the "election of a man to the high office of President of the United States whose opinions and purposes are hostile to slavery." For these reasons the "People of South Carolina" announced that their union with "the other states of North America" was "dissolved."

By February 1, 1861, all of the other states of the Lower South had followed suit. A week later, at Montgomery, Alabama, a provisional government of the Confederate States of America was established composed of South Carolina, Georgia, Florida, Alabama, Mississippi, and Louisiana. Soon, Texas joined the Confederacy. Meanwhile, Delaware, North Carolina, Maryland, Virginia, Kentucky, Tennessee, Arkansas, and Missouri were still clinging to the Union, but strong secession groups in most of these states were campaigning for withdrawal from the Union.

Southern moderates had kept Breckinridge from sweeping their region in the election, but a few months later Southerners had established their own confederacy. The secession movement was achieved through representatives sent by the electorate to state conventions; among Lower South states, only in Texas was the decision to secede submitted directly to the voters. Often, as in Virginia, a public referendum meant little since fighting had already begun. In each convention, except that held in South Carolina, members voiced both objections

Courtesy of the New-York Historical Society, New York City.
A cartoon showing the American eagle as it appeared when James Buchanan became President in 1857 and when he left office in 1861.

to and serious reservations about the momentous course upon which they were embarking.

Although there was still strong support for the Union in the South, especially in areas where there were few slaves, numerous influential Southerners were eventually emboldened to secede because they became convinced that the North would not fight. These leaders believed that northern merchants were too interested in making profits through trade to wage war against both their best market and their prime source of cotton—customer-suppliers who owed them $200 million. Nor could the North fight, some Southerners reasoned, since factory workers were "wage slaves" who were obviously too weak and spiritless to enter combat; in addition, the North lacked tested military leaders whom the South had in abundance. Should war break out, secessionists emphasized, the South would win. In Britain and France, the South had powerful allies who were dependent on southern cotton. And if the South did not act now, some extremists argued, soon it would be too late, for every year the North was becoming stronger, richer, and more populous.

The events in the wake of Lincoln's election would have taxed any lame-duck administration, but for a chief executive as weak as James Buchanan, they were overwhelming. To make matters worse, Lincoln, who promised not to interfere with slavery where it already existed, nevertheless was regarded in the South as a symbol of abolitionism.

What Caused the Civil War?

As the major internal disruption in American history, the Civil War has invited many different interpretations that often reflect as much about the period in which they were written as about the Civil War. During and immediately after the conflict, some historians explained it as a struggle between the principles of freedom (the North) and of bondage (the South) and others as a struggle between the principles of "localism" (the South) and of uniformity (the North). When the United States was emerging as a world power in the 1890s, historians wrote accounts of the war which stressed the deep-seated, irreconcilable differences such as slavery between sections of the nation. The war, according to their interpretation, made possible America's rise to greatness because it preserved the Union.

In the 1920s economic and class determinism began to color historical thinking, and Charles and Mary Beard in their *Rise of American Civilization* (1927) construed the war as a struggle for power between two economic sections of the country; in this context "the institution of slavery as a question of ethics was not the fundamental issue." Since the 1920s other interpretations have flourished. Some scholars have argued that the conflict was "irrepressible," while others have doubted that the war was inevitable and point to the "fanatical" abolitionists and the southern "extremists" as major contributing factors to the outbreak of hostilities. In recent years, the whole question of the causation of the Civil War has been lost in general discussions of racism and the subordination of blacks, not only during the Civil War but throughout American history.

These theories on the causes of the war can be reduced to four basic interpretations. Especially fashionable among antislavery writers during and after the war was the *slavery interpretation*. According to this view, the war was a crusade against the South's evil and "peculiar" institution. The South was blind and irrational. The various compromises worked out in 1820, 1850, and 1854 had failed to stop the growth of "The Slave Power." The war was the result of the ideological differences between a free and a slave society. Those who adhere to this interpretation today frequently argue that moral judgments are necessary in an evaluation of the past and that slavery clearly was an abominable institution that had to be destroyed.

Critics of the *slavery interpretation* hold that good and evil are never so neatly divided that one side can be considered to be composed of "the good guys" and the other of "the bad guys." And they point out that while many Northerners opposed the extension of slavery, only a very few were actually abolitionists or even sympathetic to abolitionism. Lincoln, for example, was not an abolitionist. Moreover, there was little concern for the welfare of blacks among segments of northern society. Nor can the slavery argument explain why a Southerner such as Robert E. Lee went to war; his loyalty to the South was not based on devotion to the institution of slavery.

Secondly, there is the *states' rights interpretation*, which holds that the oldest debate in America was between champions of states' rights and nationalists. According to southern apologists, the North was threatening the South, and states' rights and secession were legitimate means of self-defense. This position was expressed by the President of the Confederacy, Jefferson Davis, whose two-volume *Rise and Fall of the Confederate Government*, published in 1881, summarized the major arguments. Davis claimed that secession was a conservative and legal action to preserve the Constitution and laws of the "Old Union" against northern assaults.

Opponents of this view maintain, however, that states' rights was only a derivative issue worked up by Southerners who were really concerned about more pressing matters. States' rights had not led to civil war in 1798, 1814, 1828, or 1850. Why should 1861 be any different? States' rights was not a conservative action to preserve the "Old Union" but a radical action to destroy it.

The third main point of view can be called the *economic interpretation*. This was especially popular in the late 1920s and 1930s. According to this position, the war was a "Second American Revolution" or a struggle of self-conscious economic groups for control of the government resulting in the triumph of capitalists, laborers, and farmers of the North and West over the southern plantation aristocracy. What the North wanted and achieved as a result of the war was a protective tariff, land grants, cheap southern raw materials, southern markets, internal improvements at federal expense, and national banks. The South fought the North to protect its property and its profits, both embodied in slavery. This point of view echoes that expressed in Charles and Mary Beard's previously mentioned *Rise of American Civilization*. This work traced the evils associated with the rise of big business to the triumph of northern capitalists in the Civil War.

Critics of the *economic interpretation* note that northern crops and manufactures sold in southern markets just as southern crops sold in northern markets. Indeed, big business in the North, far from promoting the conflict, actually worked for compromise in 1860. Nor was the South truly threatened by the North. Lincoln was not an abo-litionist, and the Congress would not have been in Republican control if the southern states had stayed in the Union. The Supreme Court led by Chief Justice Taney had, moreover, acted to protect the property interests of southern planters.

Finally, there is the interpretation that highlights the importance of *emotions*. This approach flourished markedly during the 1930s as the threat of war grew. According to this interpretation, southern nationalism may have been growing before the Civil War, but the war itself was brought on by extremists in both the South and the North who inflamed sectional prejudices. Abolitionists began to malign the South itself rather than just the institution of slavery. Southern fanatics demanded the reopening of the nefarious African slave trade. All the pride, fear, frustration, and hatred to be found in each section became focused on the North-South division, which led to a breakdown in democratic processes and a release of the same powerful passions that were earlier vented in waves of religious revivalism and in the hysteria of various nativist groups. This *emotional interpretation* was voiced by Avery O. Craven in *The Repressible Conflict, 1820–1861* (1939) and by James G. Randall in an article, "The Blundering Generation" (1940).

Some of those dissenting from this *emotional interpretation* hold that moral judgment in politics is necessary. According to them, the problem of slavery in a free society had to be solved and the abolitionists were right in calling slavery an evil that had to be eradicated.

If the question "What caused the Civil War?" is so difficult to answer, the difficulty may in part lie with the question. A direct answer assumes that the causes were equal to the events leading to secession. But this is not necessarily the case. Few people, in either the North or the South, expected war; it came about through a series of incidents and miscalculations. A more fruitful question might be, "Why did the southern states secede from the Union?"

Secession was a deliberate decision prompted by specific causes and motives. Some of these causes can be quickly summarized. Southern nationalism had matured by 1861. The states' rights arguments similarly had been worked out by 1860 and many Southerners believed that their rights were being abused. Northern abolitionists were aiding slaves to flee the South and preventing their return under the Fugitive Slave Law. In Congress Northerners were denouncing Southerners as agents of Satan or as proud, unrepentant sinners. Southerners were being denied the right to take slaves into western territories. John Brown's raid only strengthened the southern belief that their property was being jeopardized. For these reasons, champions of states' rights were willing to join with southern nationalists to plot secession.

Yet another cause of secession was the personal interests of southern leaders. Some owed considerable sums of money to northern creditors; secession might cancel these debts. A southern republic also would provide new opportunities for ambitious politicians. And once the excitement of the moment swept aside all caution and deliberation, many Southerners—those trained in the ideals of valor and martial glory and gallantry—could not turn back. Instead, they looked forward to the prospect of chivalrous exploits in battle.

Essay

The Supreme Court and Its Work

Alexis de Tocqueville (1805–1859), that often-quoted nineteenth century observer of American life, customs, and mores, noted that "scarcely any political question arises in the United States that is not resolved, sooner or later, into a judicial question." And, he might have added, if that question becomes important enough it ends up before the United States Supreme Court. For the most part, the Court is an appellate court, that is, it listens to appeals regarding decisions rendered by lower courts. According to Article III of the Constitution, it also has original jurisdiction "in all Cases affecting Ambassadors, other public Ministers and Consuls, and those in which a State shall be a Party."

The regular term of the Supreme Court opens on the first Monday of October and usually lasts about nine months. During the first six months or so, the justices hear arguments for perhaps three days of each week, spending the remainder of their time in conferences concerning matters before them. Once an appeal by someone dissatisfied with a lower-court ruling reaches the Supreme Court, the justices can deal with it in several ways. They may decide rather quickly that the case is not worth hearing and merely reaffirm the lower court's action, in effect letting that decision stand. Sometimes they proceed a bit further and, without hearing arguments, issue short, unsigned opinions on an issue they believe needs clarification. If an appeal involves a question that deserves consideration—perhaps circuit justices are ruling differently on an important matter—then lawyers representing those involved in a case will be invited to present oral arguments lasting thirty minutes to an hour. Even at this point the justices may conclude a case contains nothing of much relevance and decline to proceed further. However; if arguments are completed, then the justices weigh the issue involved.

Some weeks or months later, but within the same term, an opinion is announced, usually on a

Culver Pictures.

A nineteenth-century view of the chamber of the Supreme Court in the Capitol.

Monday. One of the justices customarily delivers a brief summation for the majority of the Court; and, if a dissenting member feels strongly about the matter, he may speak for the minority. At the same time, rough copies of these opinions, later polished and published, are distributed to some thirty or thirty-five reporters, and the basic elements of the decision are soon communicated through the nation's newspapers and its television and radio networks. Some cases elicit little attention; others deserve and get bold headlines. The *Dred Scott* decision of 1857, delivered two days after President Buchanan took office, was clearly a landmark case which fueled passions that led to war.

There have been many more cases, less emotionally charged, which have influenced profoundly national growth and development. In *Marbury* v. *Madison* (1803), Chief Justice John Marshall used the appeal of a would-be justice of the peace for his commission as an instrument to affirm that the Supreme Court alone had the power to interpret the Constitution and to decide if laws conflicted with that document. In 1824, the Court faced a very different matter in *Gibbons* v. *Ogden*, a case originating from a state-granted monopoly to a steamboat company owned by Colonel Aaron Ogden that served New York harbor and nearby areas. Thomas Gibbons had a small coastal boat in New Jersey that supplied customers to Ogden's line, which in turn took them on to New York, Gibbons decided to challenge the New York monopoly, claiming that he was involved in coastal trade that was actually interstate commerce; hence, the federal government had authority in this realm, not an individual state. A key question was, of course, whether navigation was commerce. The Marshall Court agreed it was, emphasizing that the federal government was already regulating interstate commerce. Within months, fares dropped drastically on steamboat lines along the East Coast as service increased. This decision meant that the federal government would have considerable influence on the development and growth of railroads and other modes of transportation that followed in the wake of the steamboat.

The Dred Scott case, mentioned earlier, involved a slave who sought his freedom through court actions as a result of residence in a free state and a free territory controlled by the U.S. Congress. The case raised a perilous issue in troubled times, and Chief Justice Taney's opinion, one of seven majority opinions issued, was much more than a simple ruling.

Taney first examined the Constitution in an attempt to demonstrate that *people* of the United States meant those citizens "who were members of the different political communities in the several states" and that the sacred document recognized "the Negro race as a separate class of persons" apart from the *people* or citizens then forming a government. Nowhere does the Constitution specifically mention blacks, instead referring to them in a vague fashion as "other Persons" and "such Persons." Nevertheless, Taney interpreted Article I, Section 9, which prohibits any ban on the migration or importation of "such Persons" prior to 1808 to his own ends. Also, in a deft turn of phrase, to buttress his opinion he cited the words of the Fugitive Slave Law of 1850 as if it were part of the Constitution and had been written in 1787.

Not surprisingly, with the aid of such judicial gymnastics, the Chief Justice concluded that Scott, a slave, could not sue in the courts; and, in addition, since he was property, the Constitution could not deny his master the right to transport him to territorial land. And, even if Scott had become free while living in Illinois or the Upper Louisiana Purchase Territory, upon his return to a slave state (Missouri), state law, not national, established his status. Ironically, a few months after Dred Scott's name became known throughout the nation, his new owner granted him his freedom. So Scott got what he wanted despite Taney's provocative ruling.

Missouri Historical Society.
Dred Scott, the slave who looked in vain to the Supreme Court for his freedom.

Nearly forty years later, in 1896, another case involving the matter of race came before the Supreme Court; it, too, had profound social implications. The question was whether an act passed by Louisiana in 1890 providing separate railway carriages for whites and blacks violated the Thirteenth and Fourteenth Amendments to the Constitution. A majority of Supreme Court justices ruled that it did not. The plaintiff's underlying fallacy, they said, was an assumption that "enforced separation of the two races stamps the colored race with a badge of inferiority." If blacks became the domi-

Chief Justice Roger B. Taney ruled that blacks were not included under the word "citizen" in the Constitution and were, therefore, ineligible to claim the rights and privileges guaranteed to American citizens.

nant power in Louisiana, the justices noted, then they probably would pass similar laws favoring their race. They also refused to accept arguments that social prejudice could be overcome by legislation or that only by enforced commingling of the races could blacks secure equal rights. One justice, John M. Harlan (an appointee of President Hayes), vigorously dissented. Citing many of the same sections of the Constitution used by Taney in the 1850s, he concluded that the Louisiana statute was inconsistent with the personal liberty of *all* citizens in that state, white and black, and "hostile to both the spirit and letter of the Constitution of the United States of America." Despite this plea, *Plessy* v. *Ferguson* bestowed legality upon a Jim Crow rule that reigned largely unchallenged in many parts of America until after 1950.

Eight years after *Plessy* v. *Ferguson,* a decision with implications similar to those flowing from *Gibbons* v. *Ogden* changed the nature of American capitalism. A group of railroad potentates, J. P. Morgan, James J. Hill, and Edward H. Harriman, decided to organize a supermonopoly to control transportation in the northwestern United States. The Northern Securities Company, organized by Morgan, was supposed to end competition among his Northern Pacific, Hill's Great Northern, and Harriman's Burlington. In February 1902, President Theodore Roosevelt let the press know that he and his Attorney General planned to enforce the Sherman Antitrust Act of 1890 and break up the Northern Securities Company.

Since the Sherman Act was previously ignored, Morgan was dazed by this revelation and hurried to the White House where he reportedly told the President: "If we have done anything wrong, send your man to my man and they can fix it up." As Morgan viewed matters, one corporation (his) was dealing with another of equal status (The United States of America). Roosevelt did not agree. The administration first sought relief in the federal courts of Minnesota, which had state legislation forbidding a railroad to buy control of parallel or competing lines; however, the railroads won, the courts concluding that a stockholding company such as Northern Securities was a legal venture.

But a short time later, Morgan, filled with self-confidence, told a group of New York reporters that his Northern Securities actually was "a community of interests," an admission that it was not merely a stockholding company as claimed. During the ensuing months Roosevelt went on the offensive, charging that a too powerful monopoly such as Northern Securities actually destroyed the rights of others, and in 1904 the Supreme Court agreed with him. This decision by no means ended efforts by American businessmen to create monopolies, cartels, and similar groupings designed to restrict competition and to increase profits, but Roosevelt's aggressive policy put new teeth into antitrust legislation by serving notice that the U.S. government would not tolerate blatant restraints of trade that threatened the public interest.

Important decisions have often involved un-

Culver Pictures.

President Theodore Roosevelt's offensive against monopoly and illegitimate practices in railroad transportation was supported by the Supreme Court in 1904.

"GET RID OF YOUR FRIENDS"

likely protagonists. Elsie Parrish, like Dred Scott, was one of the last people one would expect to become the principal in a Supreme Court case. In 1935 Parrish, a chambermaid in a Washington state hotel, received notice that she was being discharged. She had been getting 25 cents an hour when, by state law, her hourly income should have been 35 cents. When management refused to pay her $216.92 in back salary, she and her husband went to an attorney. A local court said the state minimum wage law was unconstitutional, but a state court reversed that ruling.

Unhappy with the latter decision, Mrs. Parrish's former employers appealed to the Supreme Court. Unfortunately for the justices, *West Coast*

Hotel Co. v. *Parrish* arrived before them in 1937 at a most inopportune time since they were involved in a bitter confrontation with President Franklin D. Roosevelt. They were striking down much of his hastily contrived New Deal legislation, and the President, in turn, fresh from a sweeping reelection victory, was threatening to enlarge the Court's membership so as to get his own way. This case created a special dilemma for the entire Court: should they uphold the state minimum wage law (similar to much of FDR's social legislation); or should they rule against it and thus take an indirect slap at their adversary's overall program? Elsie Parrish won, and with this decision and others in the same vein, much of the rancor embittering the relations between the White House and the Supreme Court was dissipated.

Undoubtedly the most celebrated decision of recent years was *Brown* v. *Board of Education of Topeka* (1954), overturning the previous racial segregation rulings such as *Plessy* v. *Ferguson* (1896), which had sanctioned a dual, segregated society throughout much of the United States. The *Brown* case, really an amalgam of several similar cases, climaxed at least three decades of change as separation on the basis of race alone in schools, transportation, and housing came under fire. It proved very graphically that the court *can* change its mind, a fact that distressed thousands of segregationists as integration in nearly all aspects of everyday life became increasingly common. It also vindicated Justice John Harlan's dissenting opinion in *Plessy* v. *Ferguson*.

In July 1974, the Supreme Court, headed by Chief Justice Warren Burger, heard and quickly disposed of one of the most sensational cases of recent decades: *United States* v. *Nixon, President of the United States*. Leon Jaworski, special prosecutor appointed by Nixon to probe the Watergate affair, was seeking White House tapes and documents he thought vital to his investigation. Nixon, claiming "executive privilege," refused to turn over those materials to Jaworski. By executive privilege, Nixon meant the acknowledged need to protect communications between high government officials and those who advise them, also asserting that this dispute was within the executive department and that to accede to Jaworski's request would violate the doctrine of separation of powers.

Ruling against Nixon, the Court observed that nowhere in the Constitution was there "any explicit reference to a privilege of confidentiality," yet the justices agreed that to exercise his office the President must be able to speak in confidence with his associates. But, since the materials that were sought related to criminal proceedings, to withhold such evidence "would cut deeply into the guarantee of due process of law and gravely impair the basic function of the courts." In short, no President is above the law.

This case, like *Marbury* v. *Madison*, which was quoted several times in the Supreme Court opinion, did not involve great numbers of people, but like the earlier case, and others mentioned in this essay, was of great significance to the nation. It reaffirmed the widely held belief that all citizens are equal before the law and, interestingly, substantiated Tocqueville's observation made nearly 150 years ago that almost any American political question is resolved "sooner or later" into a judicial matter.

SELECTED
READINGS

General Accounts

Michael F. Holt, *The Political Crisis of the 1850's* (1978)

Allan Nevins, *The Ordeal of the Union* (2 vols., 1947)

David M. Potter and Don E. Fehrenbacher, *The Impending Crisis, 1848–1861* (1976)

Territorial Expansion and Politics

Fredrick J. Blue, *The Free Soilers: Third Party Politics, 1848–1854* (1973)

Stanley W. Campbell, *The Slave Catchers: Enforcement of the Fugitive Slave Law, 1850–1860* (1972)

William J. Cooper, Jr., *The South and the Politics of Slavery, 1828–1856* (1978)

Larry Gara, *The Liberty Line: The Legend of the Underground Railroad* (1961)

Holman Hamilton, *Zachary Taylor: Soldier in the White House* (1951)

Holman Hamilton, *Prologue to Conflict: The Crisis and Compromise of 1850* (1964)

William S. Jenkins, *Pro-Slavery Thought in the Old South* (1935)

E. Bruce Kirkham, *The Building of Uncle Tom's Cabin* (1977)

Roy F. Nichols, *Franklin Pierce: Young Hickory of the Granite Hills* (2nd ed., 1958)

Robert J. Rayback, *Millard Fillmore: Biography of a President* (1959)

Harvey Wish, *George Fitzhugh: Propagandist of the Old South* (1944)

The Kansas-Nebraska Controversy

David Donald, *Charles Sumner and the Coming of the Civil War* (1960)

Don Fehrenbacher, *The Dred Scott Case: Its Significance in American Law and Politics* (1978)

Robert W. Johannsen, *Stephen A. Douglas* (1973)

Phillip S. Klein, *President James Buchanan* (1962)

James C. Malin, *The Nebraska Question, 1852–1854* (1953)

Roy F. Nichols, *The Disruption of American Democracy* (1948)

Basil Rauch, *American Interest in Cuba, 1848–1855* (1948)

James A. Rawley, *Race and Politics: "Bleeding Kansas" and the Coming of the Civil War* (1969)

Growth of the Republican Party

Don E. Fehrenbacher, *Prelude to Greatness: Lincoln in the 1850's* (1962)

Eric Foner, *Free Soil, Free Labor, Free Men: The Ideology of the Republican Party before the Civil War* (1970)

Ronald P. Formisano, *The Birth of Mass Political Parties in Michigan, 1827–1861* (1971)

Michael F. Holt, *Forging a Majority: The Formation of the Republican Party in Pittsburgh, 1848–1860* (1969)

Harry V. Jaffa, *Crisis of the House Divided: The Lincoln-Douglas Debates* (1959)

Allan Nevins, *The Emergence of Lincoln* (2 vols., 1950)

Emotionalism at High Tide

William L. Barney, *The Road to Secession* (1972)

Don E. Fehrenbacher, *The South and Three Sectional Crises* (1980)

John McCardell, *The Idea of a Southern Nation: Southern Nationalists and Southern Nationalism, 1830–1860* (1979)

Stephen B. Oates, *To Purge this Land with Blood: John Brown* (1970)

David M. Potter, *The South and the Sectional Conflict* (1968)

Kenneth M. Stampp, *And the War Came: The North and the Secession Crisis, 1860–1861* (1950)

Ronald T. Takaki, *Pro-Slavery Crusade: The Agitation to Reopen the African Slave Trade* (1971)

Ralph A. Wooster, *The Secession Conventions of the South* (1962)

What Caused the Civil War?

Thomas J. Pressly, *Americans Interpret Their Civil War* (1965)

Edwin C. Rozwenc, ed., *The Causes of the American Civil War* (2nd. ed., 1972)

Kenneth M. Stampp, ed., *The Causes of the Civil War* (rev. ed., 1974)

CHAPTER 14

THE WAR TO SAVE THE UNION

TIMELINE

February 1861
Seven seceding southern states meet to form the government of The Confederate States of America

March 1861
Lincoln inaugurated President
Congress passes Morrill Tariff

April 1861
Fort Sumter surrenders

April-May 1861
Virginia, Arkansas, Tennessee, and North Carolina join the Confederacy

July 1861
Confederates win the first Battle of Bull Run

November 1861
The *Trent* Affair

February 1862
Grant gains control of Tennessee and Cumberland rivers

March 1862
Congress passes Homestead Act

April 1862
Battle of Shiloh

April 1862
New Orleans falls to David G. Farragut

September 1862
Battle of Antietam

September 1862
Lincoln issues Preliminary Emancipation Proclamation

March 1863
Congress passes Conscription Law

July 1863
Battle of Gettysburg

July 1863
Vicksburg surrenders to Grant

May 1864
Sherman begins campaign into Georgia

November 1864
Lincoln reelected

April 1865
Lee surrenders to Grant at Appomattox

April 1865
Lincoln assassinated

CHAPTER OUTLINE

The Civil War marked the beginning of the modern American nation, a major economic power governed by a strong chief executive. This dramatic turning point in American history established the supremacy of the Union over the individual states and brought a dramatic shift in the country's political life. In a sense, the original republic of 1789 collapsed in 1860, and a four-year struggle brought an effective end to the dual sovereignty of a federal-state system.

After the Civil War, the Union no longer seemed to be a federation of quasi-independent states but rather a solid political body in its own right. Similarly, the role of the President was transformed from that of a caretaker to a potent leader. Equally important, the victory of the North represented the triumph of one economy and way of life over another. The impersonal, urban, industrial Northeast, which was dependent on free labor (much of it supplied by immigration), had conquered the paternalistic, rural, agricultural South, based on slave labor and a static caste system.

Few people on either side foresaw how long and bloody a struggle lay ahead of them when war broke out in April 1861—or realized how profoundly their world would change before the fighting ceased. Few understood that the outcome of the war would be the transformation of the United States into a centralized, modern nation. Northerners imagined that the Confederacy would be quickly defeated and just as swiftly restored to the Union. Confederates believed that the North would have to accept the independence of the Confederacy once it secured the diplomatic recognition of European powers and proved that its armies were formidable on the battlefield.

The Path to War

When the first southern states seceded following Lincoln's election, James Buchanan was still President. Although eager to preserve the Union, he was hamstrung by his interpretation of his own powers as stated in the Constitution. He believed that secession was unconstitutional, but at the same time was convinced he had no right to make aggressive war upon any state, though he was empowered to use military force defensively to overcome resistance to federal officers and to protect federal property. Moreover, Buchanan sympathized with advocates of southern rights. Many of his advisers, including several members of his cabinet, were from the South. The President, nearly seventy, feared that some act by the North would provoke the South into war. Consequently, he and his colleagues worked for a reconciliation through compromise.

But these efforts got nowhere. Kentucky Senator John J. Crittenden proposed a plan embracing popular sovereignty, enforcement of the Fugitive Slave Law, and bans on both abolition and revival of the African slave trade. Two days after Crittenden unveiled his scheme, South Carolina seceded.

On February 4, 1861, a Peace Convention, called by the state of Virginia, assembled in Washington, led largely by old men whose views on the question of the hour were well-known. Representatives from twenty-one states eventually recommended to Congress seven amendments to the Constitution which reflected Crittenden's ideas. Congress, the Lower South, and much of the North generally ignored both the proceedings of this convention and its proposals.

Throughout this interregnum, President-elect Lincoln refused to make any concessions to the South regarding the question of the extension of slavery. He instructed a congressman from Illinois, for example, to "entertain no proposition for a compromise in regard to the *extension* of slavery. The instant you do, they have us under again; all our labor is lost, and sooner or later must be done over. . . . Have none of it. The tug has to come, &

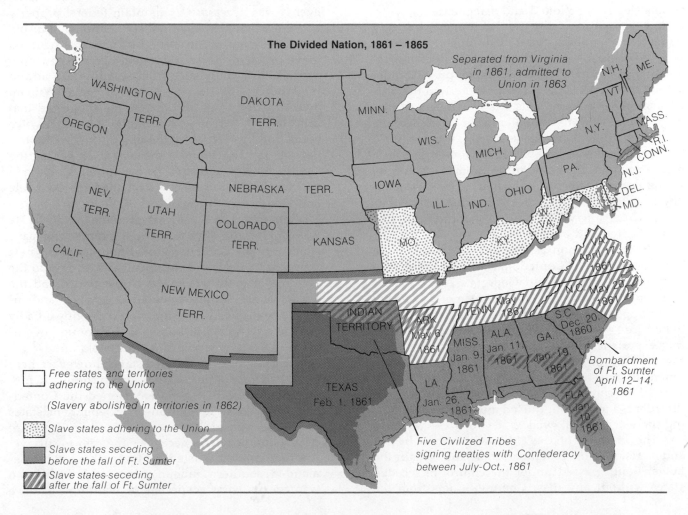

The Divided Nation, 1861 – 1865

Separated from Virginia in 1861, admitted to Union in 1863

Bombardment of Ft. Sumter April 12–14, 1861

Five Civilized Tribes signing treaties with Confederacy between July-Oct., 1861

Free states and territories adhering to the Union

(Slavery abolished in territories in 1862)

Slave states adhering to the Union

Slave states seceding before the fall of Ft. Sumter

Slave states seceding after the fall of Ft. Sumter

TEXAS Feb. 1, 1861
LA. Jan. 26, 1861
MISS. Jan. 9, 1861
ALA. Jan. 11, 1861
GA. Jan. 19, 1861
FLA. Jan. 10, 1861
S.C. Dec. 20, 1860
ARK. May 6, 1861
TENN. May, 1861
N.C. May 20, 1861
VA. April 17, 1861

better now than later." Though Lincoln was willing to say that he would not interfere with slavery where it already existed and would back a rigorous enforcement of the Fugitive Slave Law, his conciliatory attitudes on these points either were not known or not believed in the South. Instead, Southerners quoted his "House-Divided" speech and invariably pictured him as an implacable foe to their way of life.

Rival Governments

Delegates from the seceding southern states meeting in Montgomery, Alabama, on February 4, 1861, adopted a constitution and established a provisional government. The Confederate Constitution largely copied the federal Constitution, lifting wholesale much of its language, but there were some significant changes. First, the "sovereign and independent character" of the individual states in the Confederacy was recognized and states' rights specifically guaranteed. Second, the southern politicians clearly sanctioned and safeguarded slavery; no law "denying . . . the right of property in negro slaves" was to be passed. Extremists, however, were disappointed by the prohibition of the reopening of the African slave trade, a provision designed to win diplomatic recognition from the British and French governments. Many of the mechanics of government were also altered. For instance, the President, elected for a six-year term, was ineligible for reelection. Presumably this would give him more freedom in formulating policies since he would not be compelled to maneuver for reelection. There were to be no protective tariffs; this stipulation dispensing with a practice that the South had long resented and opposed.

Though Jefferson Davis (1808–1889) was not a rabid secessionist, Confederate leaders chose him to be their President and Georgia's Alexander H. Stephens (1812–1883), a Douglas Democrat who actively opposed secession in his state's convention, to be Vice President. Davis clearly was an outstanding, experienced statesman, but his course during the ensuing months caused some diehard Southerners to question his credentials. Moreover, he wanted to command the South's armies, not be President, a factor that caused much confusion during the war that followed.

The breakup of the Union proceeded by fits and starts, as most federal arsenals and forts in the Lower South passed under the control of seceded states without any fuss. Commissioners from the

Confederacy, like traveling salesmen peddling their wares, scurried and lobbied throughout the rest of the slave states in an effort to increase the size of their nation. In general, their travels were unproductive; politicians in the Upper South (Virginia, North Carolina, Tennessee, and Arkansas) and in the Border states (Delaware, Maryland, Kentucky, and Missouri) were adopting a "wait-and-see" attitude. Yet the anxiety created by delay aided the secessionist cause. Congressmen from states that might secede hurried home to keep an eye on conventions debating the issue, to mend political fences, and to seek, perhaps, positions with the government of a new nation. This vacuum at the national level decreased the last hope of compromise and, because most of those who left Washington were Democrats of one sort or another, enhanced the power of the Republicans in Congress.

Meanwhile, on March 4, 1861, in his inaugural speech, Lincoln urged a reconciliation, but he promised to use the full powers of his office wherever it was necessary to maintain federal property and collect duties and imposts. Although Lincoln closed with a plea for unity, he knew that he faced grave problems as he attempted to keep the Upper South and Border states from seceding. To add to his trouble, his own Secretary of State, William Seward, tried to dictate policy. He suggested that Lincoln pick a fight with a foreign power, involve the nation in a war—and thereby unify the country. Seward fancied himself the actual leader of the United States, Lincoln's prime minister. Quietly and firmly the President established his own rule and won Seward's respect.

Jefferson Davis had his problems as well. He was looking for ways to bring the remaining slave states into the Confederacy; without them the new "country" would find it difficult to stand up to the Union. Not only would the Upper South and the Border states supply valuable manpower and industry, but their admission would provide a badly needed psychological boost for the young government and deal a severe blow to the old one.

Even among the seceded states, however, there were warring political factions and a conflict in ideology between those who envisioned the Confederacy as a loose federation of independent states and those who recognized that a certain degree of central authority was necessary in order to survive. Another conflict existed between those who demanded southern independence and those who wanted—or were suspected of wanting—to have

National Archives.
President Abraham Lincoln.

Chicago Historical Society.
President Jefferson Davis.

the South rejoin the United States under more favorable terms. Jefferson Davis often was accused of belonging to this second group, dubbed the "reconstructionist" faction. Numerous other tensions also existed. Old Whigs disliked old Democrats; early advocates of secession were suspicious of recent converts; those eager to reopen the African slave trade vilified their opponents; and those content with a slave-based Confederacy condemned anyone who advocated the admission of free states.

The First Shot

Efforts of the Buchanan administration to resupply Fort Sumter in Charleston Harbor had failed, and Lincoln inherited this unresolved problem. Any action that provoked the Confederacy might lead to the secession of the Border states, but any indecisiveness on Lincoln's part might be disastrous to the Union. Lincoln decided to provision the fort and notified South Carolina in early April that an

expedition was on its way; the expedition would be peaceful if possible but would use force if necessary. Now the South decided to act. When Major Robert Anderson refused to surrender the fort to Confederate General Pierre G. T. Beauregard (1818–1893), the southern forces opened fire at 4:30 A.M. on April 12, 1861. The next day Anderson surrendered.

There are conflicting opinions among historians concerning Lincoln's role in the Sumter affair and also about which side began the war. Some argue that Lincoln deliberately maneuvered the Confederacy into firing the first shot, while others place the blame on Davis and the Confederates, who, they believe, were spoiling for a fight and were in an increasingly desperate position. The Confederacy needed Border state help to survive, and its leaders were confident that after the first shot rang out, Virginia and Maryland, even Delaware, would join the Confederates. One Alabaman, fearful of Unionists in the Confederacy, wrote, "There is another way of avoiding the calamity of reconstruction and that is war. Now pardon me for suggesting that South Carolina has the power of putting us beyond the reach of reconstruction by taking Fort Sumter at any cost." In any event, the war had begun; the attack on Fort Sumter instantly won public opinion in the North to the defense of the Union.

The Upper South and the Border States

On April 15, 1861, following the Confederate attack on Fort Sumter, President Lincoln called upon the states to provide him with militia to resist the "insurrection," to enforce the federal law, and to preserve the Union. But the great question, for both Lincoln and Davis, was what would the Upper South and the Border states do?

Although seven states in the Lower South seceded from the Union before the attack on Fort Sumter, not a single state of the Upper South had joined the Confederacy. Their reluctance to pull out of the Union derived from several sources. If they joined the Confederacy, they would be cut off from their markets and sources of credit and manufactured goods in the North. But if they remained in the Union, they would lose their sources of some agricultural staples and would forfeit the money lent individuals in the Confederacy. Furthermore, the cultural affinity between the Upper South and the Lower South was not absolute. Although the states of the Upper South had slaves, most of them had far fewer than states in the Deep South, and these slaves were generally treated far more mildly.

In effect, the firing on Fort Sumter, forced the states of the Upper South to take sides. Virginia (April 17), Arkansas (May 6), Tennessee (May 7), and North Carolina (May 20) went over to the Confederacy. Now that Virginia was part of the Confederacy, Richmond became the southern capital, despite the veto of President Jefferson Davis. The move to within 100 miles of Washington was one of defiance because the new capital was vulnerable indeed, but it also rewarded Virginians for casting their lot with the Confederacy and provided lawmakers with a more congenial urban setting of 40,000 in which to deliberate. With the addition of Virginia, the Confederacy also gained a great military leader—Robert E. Lee. When his native state withdrew from the Union, Lee resigned from the U.S. Army, despite the fact that Lincoln offered him

Following the Confederate attack on Fort Sumter, President Lincoln called upon the states to provide him with troops to preserve the Union. This recruitment poster urges all patriots to resist the treason.

command of it. (A biographical sketch in this chapter highlights Lee's impressive career.)

Yet none of these events led to the secession of the Border states. Delaware, Maryland, Kentucky, and Missouri remained loyal to the Union. This decision, however, was preceded and followed by fierce debates in each of the states except Delaware, and only military coercion kept Missouri in the Union.

In addition to these four Border states, the mountainous western section of Virginia refused to secede. The western counties, physically isolated from slavery and long resentful of the economic and political dominance exerted by slaveholders along the coast, entered the Union as the new state of

Robert E. Lee

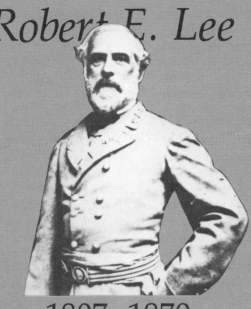

1807–1870

This peerless Confederate leader was the son of a famous cavalry officer of the Revolution and governor of Virginia, Henry ("Light-Horse Harry") Lee, who was ill-fitted for civilian life and, overwhelmed by a sea of debt, died when Robert was eleven. The youth grew up in Alexandria where his widowed mother was supported by her father's estate. In 1825 he entered West Point and distinguished himself as a student and as a military man, graduating second in his class in 1829.

After winning a name for himself in the Mexican War, Lee served as superintendent of West Point. In 1859 he led the troops sent to quell the rebellion at Harper's Ferry. At the outbreak of the Civil War, he commanded the Department of Texas. Lee had mixed feelings about secession. He did not approve of the Confederacy, but he was torn between allegiance to his native state of Virginia and fidelity to the United States. On April 18, 1861, Lincoln offered him the command of the United States Army, but Lee declined the offer and cast his lot with Virginia and the Confederacy.

After Confederate General Joseph E. Johnston was wounded in May 1862, Lee took command of the "Army of Northern Virginia" (as Lee himself dubbed his troops). It was not until February 1865 that Lee became General-in-Chief of all Confederate armies. Nevertheless, in the intervening years Lee was certainly the ablest southern general and the author of most of the Confederate strategy. His military successes were brilliant. Aided by the daring and intelligent "Stonewall" Jackson, Lee won virtually every encounter in the early years of the war. He was turned back and defeated only in July 1863 at the Battle of Gettysburg. After that defeat Lee was on the defensive—from the Battle of the Wilderness in early May 1864 until the final surrender at Appomattox Courthouse on April 9, 1865. Gifted with a great acumen for strategy and rare courage, Lee lacked only one quality, the ability to force his subordinates to conform to his own plans. Too courteous to browbeat his officers, Lee sometimes went along with the ideas of lesser men. Occasionally, for example, Lee yielded to General James Longstreet's obstinancy and adopted what proved to be inferior battle plans. Lee was a great strategist, but at times he gave excessive consideration to the feelings of subordinates like Longstreet.

After the war Lee applied for a pardon. Though indicted for treason, he was never brought to trial. He became president of Washington College in Lexington, Virginia (later renamed Washington and Lee). Avoiding all discussion of politics, until his death in 1870 he urged fellow Southerners to work hard, keep the peace, and accept the decision reached at Appomattox. No other Confederate leader was so revered; he was a man in whom the South saw the embodiment of its best ideals and a man who, in time, became a national hero as well. In 1976 the United States Congress, in a final act of forgiveness and reconciliation, belatedly restored Lee's citizenship.

West Virginia on June 20, 1863. Lincoln, although he disapproved of splitting Virginia in this fashion, accepted the admission of West Virginia on the basis of expediency. There was practically, if not constitutionally, in his opinion, a difference between secession in favor of the Union and secession in favor of the Confederacy.

The Opposing Forces

The North's strength was strikingly superior to that of the South, though Confederates usually refused to admit their handicaps. There were approximately twenty-two million people living in the twenty-three states remaining in the Union. Continued high immigration increased this numerical superiority; immigrants were encouraged to settle in the North in order to free factory workers to fight on the battlefield. In 1861, 91,918 immigrants came to America and settled mostly in the North; in 1862, 91,985; in 1863, 176,282; in 1864, 193,418; and in 1865, 248,120. The foreign-born not only worked for the Union in factories, nearly 400,000 also served in the Union army.

In 1860 the North enjoyed a highly diversified economy that included 110,000 manufacturing establishments employing 1,300,000 industrial workers. Numerous farms produced an ample supply of food for its citizens. Northern cities had sound banks and other financial institutions. The wealth of the North can be gauged by the value of its manufactured products ($1,700 million) and its iron production (480,000 tons). A railroad system, 22,000 miles long, bound the Northeast to the Mississippi and Ohio River valleys. Moreover, the North could boast of naval supremacy.

The Confederacy, by contrast, had 9.1 million people living in eleven states. Of this population, over 3.6 million were blacks (3.5 million slaves and the rest free blacks). Though these blacks contributed to the southern economy, they were not used as soldiers. The agricultural South had little banking capital and few industrial resources. Manufactured products were valued at $156 million and annual iron production was only 31,000 tons. The region had only 9,283 miles of track, much of it in scattered sections not joined together. The South had only a few good ports, and these could be blockaded easily. An even greater disadvantage to military security were the Mississippi and Tennessee rivers and the Great Valley of Virginia, which offered tempting routes for invasion. Despite these disadvantages, the Confederacy did possess excellent military leaders.

Confederate Strategy

The Confederates thought that the North would not wage war; since Northerners were primarily interested in profits, why would they bother fighting good customers and suppliers? Moreover, the South was confident that Great Britain and France, both dependent on southern crops, especially cotton, would grant diplomatic recognition and aid; backed up by these European powers, surely the South would be invincible.

The chief strategy of the Confederacy, once the war broke out, was defensive. Southerners in the seceded states reasoned that if the Confederacy still remained in existence after the fighting ceased, then it would be the victor, regardless of who won on the battlefield. But this strategy had the disadvantage of forcing the Confederacy to spread its armies over the full length of its northern borders as well as along the Atlantic coast. This dilution of manpower made the Confederacy vulnerable to heavy concentrations of Union soldiers attacking at a particular point. The South's "perimeter defense" meant that Union forces generally had the initiative in battle.

Union Strategy

The problem of reuniting the nation quickly led Lincoln and his Cabinet to reject most of the strategy of the elderly General Winfield Scott (1786–1866). Scott's plan, referred to as the "Anaconda" by impatient Northerners, seemed to require too much waiting and too much time. It called for a policy of tightening the grip of the North around the body of the South by blockading Confederate ports until a Union invasion could be organized. Scott recommended that some Union forces protect the nation's capital while others be sent down the Mississippi River to fragment the Confederacy and thereby force it into submission.

The blockade proposal was immediately adopted, but because Northerners were looking for a speedy conquest of the South and a swift reunification of the country, they decided to go on the offensive. Only after numerous failures and defeats did the Union finally revert to Scott's plan—the Anaconda pattern that eventually brought success. Northern hopes for a short war received a dramatic setback when Union troops under Brigadier Gen-

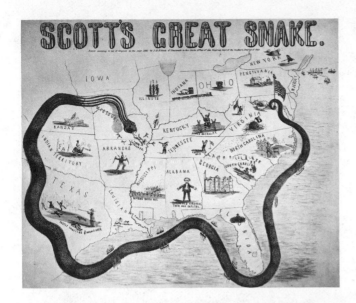

A contemporary depiction of General Winfield Scott's "Anaconda" strategy that eventually brought success to the Union.

eral Irvin McDowell (1818–1885) came rushing back to Washington in July 1861 after a brief encounter with a force of Confederate troops under Generals Joseph E. Johnston and P. G. T. Beauregard. This was the first Battle of Bull Run (also called Manassas); during this conflict, the gallant Thomas J. Jackson (1824–1863), a Confederate officer, won his nickname of "Stonewall" by repulsing a Union charge. The ill-prepared Union troops at first left the field in an orderly fashion, but the retreat soon deteriorated into a rout.

This defeat led the North to a sobering reappraisal of the military situation. President Lincoln replaced the defeated McDowell with General George B. McClellan (1826–1885) and, in November 1861, upon Scott's retirement named McClellan general-in-chief. There was an effort to raise not just short-term militia units but a real army in which soldiers would serve for longer periods. The army in the West was regrouped, placed under the command of General Henry W. Halleck (1815–1872) and based at St. Louis. In Congress a group of Republicans pressured Lincoln to bring the war to a speedy and triumphant conclusion. This faction was led by Senators Benjamin F. Wade (1800–1878) of Ohio and Zachariah Chandler (1813–1879) of

Michigan and Representative Thaddeus Stevens (1792–1868) of Pennsylvania. Known by 1862 as the Radical Republicans, this group established a congressional Joint Committee on the Conduct of the War that called for immediate military success and the emancipation of the slaves.

A Contest of Arms And Ideas

From July 1861 to March 1862, McClellan methodically trained and drilled his troops, believing that if he could put together a well-organized force of a quarter of a million soldiers he could simply march on Richmond and end the war quickly. Lincoln, impatient with continuing delay, ordered McClellan to take Richmond immediately. McClellan, however, preferred to advance on the city by way of the peninsula between the York and James rivers. By the first of May 1862, McClellan was leading an army of 112,000 men up the peninsula and demanding still more soldiers, but Lincoln denied the request, retaining 40,000 men to protect the national capital.

While McClellan moved cautiously up the peninsula, a Confederate force of 85,000 men was preparing for battle. In the early stages of the peninsular campaign, Robert E. Lee, commander of the Army of Northern Virginia, replaced Confederate General Joseph E. Johnston, who was wounded. Together with "Stonewall" Jackson, Lee forced McClellan to retreat after the so-called Seven Days' Battle, fought between June 26 and July 2, 1862, near Richmond. The last battle of this engagement, fought at Malvern Hill, was one of the bloodiest encounters of the war. McClellan failed to capture Richmond and was driven back. Some 36,000 men were killed, wounded, or missing in action—over twenty thousand of them Confederate and nearly

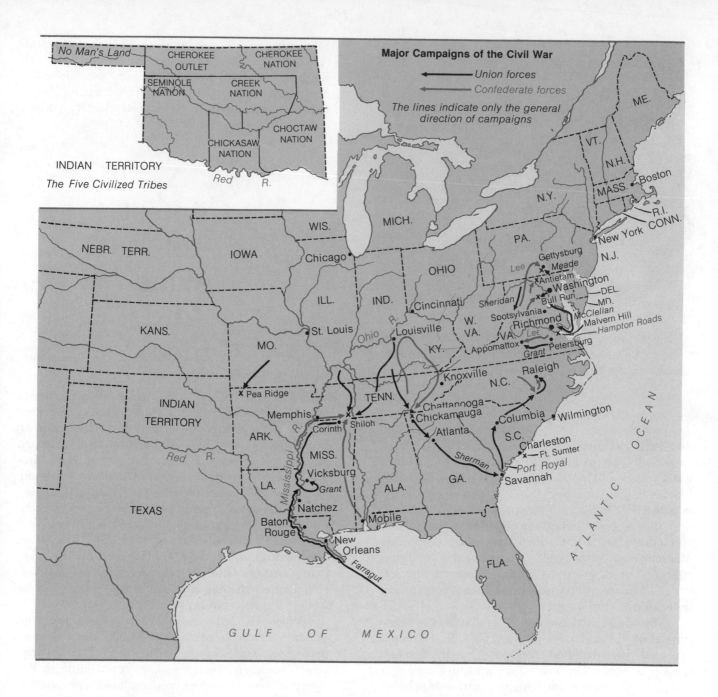

The Five Civilized Tribes

Major Campaigns of the Civil War

⟵ *Union forces*
⟵ *Confederate forces*

The lines indicate only the general direction of campaigns

sixteen thousand of them Union men. Despite such heavy losses, Lee's defense of Richmond encouraged the Confederacy.

Second Bull Run and Antietam

Lincoln was so dissatisfied with McClellan's failure to capture Richmond that he named Halleck general-in-chief of the Army and Halleck then brought John Pope (1822–1892) from the West to lead the forces in Virginia. Pope, a handsome, dashing, Kentucky-born West Point graduate, had scored some easy victories in the West, but actually he was a weak leader given to incessant storytelling and vanity. Jackson and Lee easily outmaneuvered him in August 1862, and his effort to seize Richmond also failed. Jackson led his force to the rear of the Union Army and broke its communications; then, before Pope could isolate Jackson, the Confederate detachment had rejoined Lee. United, Lee and Jackson defeated Pope on August 29–30 at the second Battle of Bull Run and forced him to retreat.

Lincoln replaced Pope with McClellan, whose name now had been vindicated. McClellan's task was to stop Lee, who decided to press his advantage by seeking a decisive victory on northern soil and perhaps isolating the city of Washington. In early September Lee crossed the Potomac into Maryland and on September 15 some of his troops under "Stonewall" Jackson seized the federal garrison at Harper's Ferry, capturing 11,000 men and 13,000 small arms. But Lee soon walked into a trap. His orders giving the disposition of troops fell into McClellan's hands. A Union private found the orders wrapped around three cigars that a Confederate officer had accidentally dropped. Lee quickly recognized the hazards of his smaller army facing McClellan's forces with the Potomac River at his rear and made plans to withdraw back across the river into Virginia.

On September 17, McClellan attacked Lee at Sharpsburg on Antietam Creek, the goriest battle in American history up to that point. Lee had 40,000 men with him and all were actively engaged; McClellan, 70,000, but only about 46,000 took part in the battle. Lee lost one-fourth of his army—killed, wounded, captured, or missing, McClellan, about 12,000. McClellan failed to follow up his advantage, and Lee slipped out of his hands and back to Virginia. The South's most ambitious attempt so far to threaten Washington by cutting the rail lines to the city had ended in defeat.

The Abolition of Slavery

At the outset of the war, Lincoln had stated that his goal was to restore the Union, not to free the slaves. Indeed, to retain the loyalty of the Border states he resisted the growing demands of Radical Republicans for abolition. Lincoln questioned the legality of his right to free the slaves and worried about the effect of liberation on the country. Yet on the field of battle, northern military officers were taking the matter into their own hands. In May 1861 at Fortress Monroe in Virginia, General Benjamin F. Butler (1818–1893) refused to return to their masters slaves who escaped to his lines. Simon Cameron (1799–1889), Lincoln's first Secretary of War, recommended to the President as early as the end of 1861 that slaves be emancipated and armed. In the West, Major General John C. Frémont proclaimed a state of martial law in Missouri in August 1861 and freed all slaves belonging to Confederates. Lincoln was embarrassed by this order and made Frémont retract it, though at the very same time Congress was passing the first Confiscation Act, which provided that any slaves used for "insurrectionary purposes" in war against the United States would be freed.

Not only were there good military reasons to free the slaves, there were also humanitarian reasons; and to these arguments Lincoln was always responsive. Week after week he received petitions and delegations from religious and reform groups demanding emancipation. One of the most outspoken proponents for immediate abolition was Frederick Douglass, the former slave, who urged the President to enlist northern free blacks into the Union Army. Douglass's suggestion was seconded by military men for practical reasons. When McClellan's peninsular campaign faltered, some Northerners suggested the Union Army recruit blacks to increase its strength. This proposal was closely tied to the question of abolition since slaves were flocking to Union lines and eager to fight for the Union cause, which they perceived as a war to end slavery. Meanwhile, Congress was taking steps towards general emancipation. In April 1862 Congress abolished slavery in the District of Columbia; in June, Congress abolished slavery in all U.S. territories. And in July, the second Confiscation Act declared "forever free" all escaped or captured slaves in Union hands who belonged to any master in rebellion against the federal government.

Lincoln himself favored abolition by state law (not federal decree) with compensation for masters and eventual colonization of the blacks. Indeed, the April 1862 act abolishing slavery in the capital provided $1 million for compensation to masters (not to exceed $300 for any one slave) and $100,000 for the voluntary emigration of freed men to Haiti and Liberia. The colonization plan, however, did not succeed. Lincoln addressed a deputation of free blacks from the District of Columbia on August 14, 1862, and outlined the advantages of settling in Central America. The blacks, however, did not respond favorably to the idea of colonization.

By the middle of 1862, Lincoln concluded that a presidential proclamation freeing the slaves in Confederate-held territory was becoming a military necessity. On July 22 the President told his Cabinet of his intention to issue a proclamation of emancipation but hesitated until the right moment. The

Harper's Weekly.

Thousands of slaves fled from their masters after news of Lincoln's Emancipation Proclamation reached them.

proclamation was to be issued in the interests of the Union, not that of the slaves. Lincoln wrote New York editor Horace Greeley on August 22, 1862, before the proclamation had been made public: "My paramount object in this struggle *is* to save the Union, and is *not* either to save or to destroy slavery. If I could save the Union without freeing *any* slave I would do it, and if I could save it by freeing *all* the slaves I would do it; and if I could save it by freeing some and leaving others alone I would also do that. What I do about slavery, and the colored race, I do because I believe it helps to save the Union; and what I forebear, I forebear because I do *not* believe it would help to save the Union." He concluded his remarks by noting, "I have here stated my purpose according to my view of *official* duty; and I intend no modification of my oft-expressed *personal* wish that all men everywhere could be free."

McClellan's success in turning back Lee's invasion of Maryland in the middle of September provided Lincoln with a suitable opportunity to act. The abolition of slavery, he now believed, was necessary for winning the war. The freed slaves would swell the ranks of the Union Army, and the act of freeing them would win the sympathy of European powers and persuade them not to recognize the Confederacy. Nearly a generation earlier, during the Mexican War, Lincoln had expressed fears about President Polk's unprecedented wartime powers, and even now he worried that freeing the slaves went beyond a President's constitutional authority. Lincoln issued his proclamation, therefore,

"as a fit and necessary measure" supposedly "warranted by the Constitution upon military necessity."

The Preliminary Emancipation Proclamation of September 22, 1862, warned the Confederacy that after January 1, 1863, all slaves in areas still in rebellion against the United States would be "thenceforward, and forever free." Lincoln's Proclamation was designed to entice the slave states back into the Union; if they returned to the fold, he was saying, they could keep their slaves. Should a majority of qualified voters in any southern state elect representatives to Congress before January 1, 1863, that state would escape enforced emancipation. At the same time, Lincoln was willing to seek federal aid for any state that voluntarily put into effect a program of compensated emancipation.

In spite of the limited nature of Lincoln's Proclamation, it was the turning point of the Civil War. It shattered the Confederacy's hopes for foreign recognition, gave Union commanders presidential authority to recruit ex-slaves, and turned the war into the crusade that blacks and abolitionists had hoped for—a war to end slavery. Not until the Thirteenth Amendment was ratified in 1865, however, was slavery abolished *everywhere*, rather than only in areas in rebellion.

Wartime Diplomacy

Although the South's campaign to win recognition as an independent nation had the overwhelming approval of European aristocracy, slavery was a heavy burden, and Confederate diplomats never seemed to appreciate the depth of antislavery feeling throughout the Continent. And, while many aristocrats in England and France (the major continental nations) disliked the liberal, emerging democracy of the Union, once Lincoln transformed the Civil War into a struggle to end slavery, any possibility of European intervention vanished.

Several factors played into northern hands and frustrated southern schemes. England began the war years with a huge surplus of American cotton and, despite later shortages, was soon importing bales from Egypt and India. Also, England was becoming increasingly dependent upon northern wheat, and the British faced a naval dilemma as well. As the world's leading sea power, Great Britain had long insisted upon the blockade as a recognized weapon of war. Breaking the northern blockade to aid the Confederacy could establish a dangerous precedent. In addition, England was booming as a result of the Civil War; she was selling supplies to both sides, and Confederate raiders were sweeping rival Yankee merchantmen from the seas, diverting more and more trade to British bottoms. Yet the key issue was the failure of the South to mount a sustained drive that promised ultimate victory. As a result, no European nation granted official recognition of the Confederate States of America, although several southern statesmen lobbied hard throughout various capitals.

Despite Union objections, the European powers proclaimed their official neutrality soon after war erupted. This diplomatic maneuver granted the Confederacy belligerent status. In the years that followed, there were transatlantic crises from time to time, but Charles Francis Adams (1807–1886), the son of one President and the grandson of another, was Lincoln's minister in London. He performed brilliantly and no break in diplomatic relations with Great Britain ever occurred. The most provocative episode, the *Trent* affair, took place in November 1861 when an impetuous Yankee captain, Charles Wilkes, stopped a British steamer, the *Trent,* and seized two southern diplomats, James M. Mason and John Slidell, who respectively were heading for London and Paris, and took them in triumph to Boston. The British were furious; the populace of the North elated. But cooler heads won out, and eventually the two men were permitted to proceed to Europe where they accomplished little.

Confederate purchase of sea raiders and ironclad warships from English shipyards precipitated more angry words, but nothing as volatile as the *Trent* affair. (After the war ended, the United States presented Britain with a huge bill for damages done by these raiders and, in time, collected.) Following McClellan's limited victory at Antietam and issuance of Lincoln's Emanciption Proclamation, the North was in a position to speak more forcefully, and the British government belatedly decided to terminate Confederate contracts with English shipbuilders. Displeased at the failure of cotton diplomacy, Southerners became increasingly critical of the British and late in 1863 gave up any hope of diplomatic recognition and expelled all British consuls from the Confederate states.

Napoleon III of France, eager to meddle in America to promote his colonial dreams, also helped the Confederacy outfit raiders and used a Mexican debt to French, English, and Spanish creditors as an excuse to occupy Mexico City in June 1863 and to set up a puppet empire in that country. This was, of course, a flagrant affront to the Monroe Doctrine, but the United States could do nothing about it until the war ended.

From Antietam to Appomattox

Lee was turned back at the Battle of Antietam and the engagement afforded Lincoln an opportunity to issue the Emancipation Proclamation, but Lee and the Confederate armies still were a force to be reckoned with. In October 1862 a gallant southern officer, James E. B. "Jeb" Stuart (1833–1864), led a cavalry raid behind McClellan's army, rushed up into Pennsylvania, and then returned to Lee's side, virtually unharmed. This daring feat made the cautious McClellan look ridiculous. When he told Lincoln that his horses were too tired to move, Lincoln caustically asked "what [have] the horses of your army done since the battle of Antietam that fatigues anything?" In early November Lincoln replaced McClellan with General Ambrose E. Burnside (1824–1881). Although the army nearly mutinied upon hearing of McClellan's removal, Lincoln expected great things of his new commander.

A month later at Fredericksburg, Burnside

committed one of the worst blunders of the war. After neglecting to move against smaller Confederate forces that were exposed to attack, Burnside then foolishly struck, charging the musketry and artillery fire of well-entrenched Confederates. When the smoke cleared, Burnside's losses totalled 12,600 men killed or wounded as compared with Lee's 5,300 casualties. In January 1863, a few weeks after Fredericksburg, Lincoln replaced Burnside with Major General Joseph Hooker (1814–1879).

The year 1863 was filled with dramatic events. It opened with Lincoln's proclamation that slaves in areas still in rebellion were henceforth free. In the spring, Hooker led an army twice as large as Lee's, and crossing the Rappahannock River above Fredericksburg, he attempted to cut southern supply lines in Virginia and force the Confederates to retreat. But "Fighting Joe" Hooker failed to take the initiative, and Lee, with the aid of "Stonewall" Jackson, defeated the Union Army on May 3 near Chancellorsville. The Confederate victory at Chancellorsville, however, was marred by heavy casualties, including the death of Jackson, who was accidentally shot by his own troops—thereby robbing the Army of Northern Virginia of one of its great commanders. Nevertheless, Lincoln still had not found a general who could outmaneuver Lee.

The War in the West

Union armies were having greater successes in the West. In February 1862, General Ulysses S. Grant struck hard at several Confederate positions and quickly gained control of the Tennessee and Cumberland rivers. This gave him easy access to the heart of the South, and Nashville soon fell to Union forces. These victories marked the beginning of Grant's rise to prominence and eventually led to his appointment as general-in-chief of the Union armies. (A biographical sketch in this chapter reviews Grant's military career and the two terms he served as President.)

Several weeks later as Grant's army of 33,000 advanced into the South, the Confederates attacked at Shiloh Church near the Tennessee-Mississippi border. The two-day Battle of Shiloh (April 6 and 7, 1862) was one of the bloodiest battles of the war, with both sides suffering heavy casualties. The death of General Albert S. Johnston (1803–1862) and the loss of about 11,000 Confederate troops so weakened southern forces that they were unable to push Grant out of western Tennessee.

Further south, naval Commander David G.

Ulysses S. Grant

1822–1885

This Civil War hero was born in humble circumstances and grew up in Georgetown, Ohio, the son of a poor tanner. In his late teens he attended the United States Military Academy at West Point but was graduated without distinction in the middle of his class. After graduation in 1843, he served in the army in Missouri and Louisiana. He first saw action a few years later during the Mexican War.

In the early 1850s, Grant was transferred to the Pacific coast where, lonely for his wife and young son, he became so bored and despondent that he drank too much and was urged to tender his resignation to the Secretary of War, Jefferson Davis. After eleven years of service, Grant was without money or employment and had the responsibility of supporting a family. He tried farming, selling real estate, and clerking in a customs house, but he was unsuccessful in all these enterprises.

His prospects improved considerably with the outbreak of the Civil War. He received an appointment as colonel of the Twenty-first Illinois Volunteers and, soon after, as a brigadier general. He served for two years in the West where he scored some stunning successes, especially at the Battle of Vicksburg, which he captured on July 4, 1863. This victory cut the Confederacy in half and gave the Union control of the Mississippi River.

After another victory that fall near Chattanooga, Grant was appointed general-in-chief of the Union armies and subsequently devised the strategy that helped to win the war. He recognized that the North had to destroy southern armies, not merely capture southern cities. In addition, the Union had to engage all the Confederate armies at once, so that the various enemy forces could not come to each other's aid. Finally, he sought to cut the Confederacy into fragments. In all these goals, Grant was successful.

After the war Grant was acclaimed everywhere as a great hero and, in time, became a contender for the presidency. In 1868 he ran as the Republican candidate and won. Unfortunately, he made many inept decisions during his two terms and surrounded himself with advisors who were both corrupt and involved in major scandals. An unsuccessful candidate for the Republican nomination in 1880, Grant entered the world of business and again encountered failure. In the last year of his life, as he was dying of cancer, Grant recouped his fortunes, repaired his reputation, and bequeathed his family a fortune by writing his memoirs, two volumes that had an emormous sale and earned his survivors almost half a million dollars.

Farragut (1801–1870) of the West Gulf Blockading Squadron launched the Battle of New Orleans on April 18, 1862, and went on to destroy most of the Confederate fleet, which hastened the fall, ten days later, of the city. During the summer of 1862 federal gunboats defeated the remnants of the Confederate fleet at Memphis and opened up most of the Mississippi River to Union forces, but the Confederacy still controlled some 200 miles of the river between Port Hudson, Louisiana, and Vicksburg, Mississippi. All previous attempts to take Vicksburg by either naval assault or by land had failed. The river city, held by General John C. Pemberton (1814–1881) and 30,000 Confederates, was strongly fortified and protected by natural defenses. General Grant, taking a calculated risk of great magnitude, left his base at Memphis in late March of 1863 with 20,000 troops and moved down the Mississippi to a point below Vicksburg. On May 22, aided by reinforcements, he laid seige to the city. During the next seven weeks each side suffered about 10,000 casualties. Finally, on July 4, Pemberton accepted Grant's demand for an unconditional surrender.

Although public attention was focused on the almost simultaneous Confederate defeat at Gettysburg, many military experts believe Grant's victory at Vicksburg was one of the decisive battles of the Civil War. Five days after the fall of Vicksburg, Port Hudson was in Union hands and the Mississippi River flowed "unvexed to the sea." Grant's triumph, perhaps his greatest achievement of the war, gave heart to the North, impressed European nations with the strength of the United States, and split the Confederacy by separating the states of the South from the Southwest.

From Gettysburg to the Wilderness

The fall of Vicksburg in the summer of 1863 coincided with Lee's second unsuccessful invasion of the Union in the East. In early June, hoping to force the North to sue for peace, Davis and Lee decided to risk everything on an assault into Pennsylvania.

Lee led his army up the Shenandoah Valley toward Pennsylvania, which he entered on June 28. At the same time Major General George G. Meade (1815–1872) replaced Hooker as the Commander of the Union Army of the Potomac. Lee and Meade locked horns at Gettysburg in July in the greatest battle of the war after the two armies chanced upon one another on June 30. In the opening maneuvers on July 1, Lee was clearly victorious. But during the next two days, July 2 and 3, the tide turned.

General Grant's siege of Vicksburg as depicted by an unknown artist. Grant's triumph, one of the decisive battles of the Civil War, raised northern spirits.

On the afternoon of July 2, Lee's men battered mercilessly at Union positions, but Meade held on—though at a terrible cost, since he lost 20,000 men. At noon on July 3 the Confederate forces fired 140 cannons at the Union lines on Cemetery Ridge. The whole valley, two miles long and half a mile wide, was filled with thick black smoke. But when the smoke cleared, Lee could see that his gunners had failed to knock out the Union artillery. Grimly, Lee ordered 15,000 of his infantry to charge the Ridge. Union muskets and artillery mowed down the brave Confederate soldiers but on they came. When they reached the top of Cemetery Ridge, the mass of Union and Confederate soldiers was so thick that some men were firing accidentally at their own comrades.

Lee's army eventually was driven back and he retreated into Virginia once more. Each side had casualties numbering about 25,000 men, but the North could far better afford such losses than the already weakened South. This invasion of the North took so terrible a toll of lives that Lee never again was able to mount an attack north of the Potomac. On November 19, 1863, several months after the battle, a cemetery at Gettysburg was dedicated. The principal oration was delivered by a famous public speaker, Edward Everett (1795–1865), but President Lincoln made a few remarks that have resounded over the decades—the Gettysburg Address.

"Four score and seven years ago our fathers brought forth on this continent, a new nation, conceived in Liberty, and dedicated to the proposition that all men are created equal.

Now we are engaged in a great civil war, testing whether that nation, or any nation so conceived and so dedicated, can long endure. We are met on a great battle-field of that war. We have come to dedicate a portion of that field, as a final resting place for those who here gave their lives that that nation might live. It is altogether fitting and proper that we should do this.

But, in a larger sense, we can not dedicate—we can not consecrate—we can not hallow—this ground. The brave men, living and dead, who struggled here, have consecrated it, far above our poor power to add or detract. The world will little note, nor long remember what we say here, but it can never forget what they did here. It is for us the living, rather, to be dedicated here to the unfinished work which they who fought here have thus far so nobly advanced. It is rather for us to be here dedicated to the great task remaining before us—that from these honored dead we take increased devotion to that cause for which they gave the last full measure of devotion—that we here highly resolve that these dead shall not have died in vain—that this nation, under God, shall have a new birth of freedom—and that government of the people, by the people, for the people, shall not perish from the earth."

———

Following the Battle of Gettysburg, there was a period of relative calm on the eastern front. In the West, General Grant cleared Tennessee of Confederate troops in November 1863 and opened the way for a Union drive eastward through the mountain barrier into Georgia and South Carolina. President Lincoln rewarded Grant for his successes by summoning him to Washington and naming him general-in-chief of the Union forces in March 1864.

Three major campaigns eventually resulted in the Union's victory in the war. Grant led one of these campaigns toward the Confederate capital of Richmond. On May 5 and 6 Grant and Meade, leading 100,000 men, met Lee in the Wilderness region of Virginia; the engagement was inconclusive. From May 8 to May 12, Grant suffered heavy losses at Spotsylvania Court House, but continued to march toward Richmond. On June 1 Lee rebuffed Grant at Cold Harbor. Though Lee lost only 30,000 men in these engagements, compared with Grant's loss of 60,000, Lee could ill afford any losses, however small. In June Grant settled down to a pro-longed siege of Petersburg, just twenty miles below Richmond.

In August 1864 Grant sent his ablest cavalry commander, Philip Sheridan (1831–1888), to push the enemy south and destroy all supplies in the Shenandoah Valley. Sheridan defeated Confederate General Jubal A. Early (1816–1894) in several engagements in the fall and proceeded to devastate the valley in order to deny its crops to the Confederate Army. As Sheridan himself put it, "A crow would have to carry its rations if it had flown across the valley." Later Sheridan turned the flank of the Confederate Army on April 1, 1865, thus forcing it to evacuate Petersburg and retreat to Appomattox Courthouse.

While Grant and Sheridan were hammering away at Confederate forces in the East, General William Tecumseh Sherman (1820–1891) was completing his campaign against Atlanta in the fall of 1864. Sherman had left Chattanooga in May with about 100,000 men. Early in September, his "march through Georgia" led to the capture of Atlanta. Sherman, an early practitioner of total war, then led 60,000 men from Atlanta to Savannah, destroying everything in their path—war supplies, public and private buildings, railroads, homes, and household goods. Sherman believed that only such extreme measures would convince southern civilians that their cause was hopeless. The pillaging of Georgia, moreover, devastated a vital source of food and

General Sherman ordered his troops to destroy everything in their path on their "march through Georgia".

supplies for the Confederate armies. The city of Savannah was occupied on December 21 and presented to Lincoln as a Christmas present. Then Sherman began a march northward through the Carolinas. In mid-February 1865 the Union Army reached Columbia, South Carolina's capital city, much of which it burned to the ground.

Wartime Politics in the North

In Grant, Lincoln finally found a general who could fight, but this discovery did not instantly win Lincoln much support from weary, restless Union voters. Grant's heavy losses in his drive toward Richmond did not inspire Northerners with much enthusiasm. As a result, the Democrats gained supporters from a growing peace movement that undoubtedly harbored southern sympathizers eager for a negotiated settlement of some sort. Republicans accused the members of various organizations in Illinois, Indiana, and Ohio of plotting to aid the South with arms or attempting to establish a separate Confederacy in the North that would side with the South.

The Republicans did have cause for alarm. In fact, some members of these secret organizations promoted resistance to the draft, encouraged and protected deserters, and engaged in outright acts of espionage and sabotage. As a result of such activities, loyal Unionists came to view all Peace Democrats as "Copperheads"—poisonous snakes that strike without warning. Most Peace Democrats, however, did not deserve the label. The groups comprising the ranks of the Peace Democrats, excluding southern sympathizers, included eastern merchants eager for the restoration of profitable southern markets, workers and poor farmers suffering from inflation and fearful of the draft, and numerous citizens who were weary of a seemingly endless bloody war. Although most were loyal Unionists, they became stigmatized as "Copperheads."

From the beginning of the war, Lincoln was dissatisfied with the failure of the courts and government prosecutors to convict and punish people guilty of conspiracy and treason. Accordingly, he suspended the habeas corpus privilege, designed to protect citizens from arbitrary arrest, and imprisoned thousands of people without benefit of trial. And in 1862 he issued a general proclamation providing that all persons who discouraged enlistment, resisted the draft, or were disloyal in any way were subject to trial by courts-martial or military commissions. Over 13,000 individuals eventually were arrested and confined in federal penitentiaries or state prisons.

Lincoln's best-known northern opponent was Clement L. Vallandigham (1820–1871). A lawyer, editor, and Democratic politician, Vallandigham lived most of his life in Ohio, but his father's family was from Virginia and he idealized the southern way of life. Vallandigham led the Peace Democrats in the Old Northwest with such vigor that he was arrested. Then Lincoln shrewdly arranged his release and banished him to the South under threat of imprisonment should he return north.

Courtesy of the New-York Historical Society, New York City.
The Conscription Act of 1863 triggered an antidraft riot in New York City that cost hundreds of lives and $1.5 million in property damage. The troops used to quell the riot came from the army of General George G. Meade. The lack of these soldiers contributed to Meade's failure to stage an offensive against Lee after the Battle of Gettysburg.

Republican defeats in the 1862 congressional elections cut the Republican majority to a margin of just eighteen votes in the House of Representatives. Even this slim majority was achieved only through intervention by the Lincoln Administration in the Border states. Furthermore, the Union Army's failure to force Lee's surrender led many Northerners to question Lincoln's wartime leadership and his choice of generals.

In March 1863 Lincoln's popularity suffered another blow when he signed a conscription law. Before the law was passed, most of the soldiers were volunteers, moved by patriotism or enticed by bounties paid by federal, local, or state governments. (These bounties also caused problems, since many men would desert as soon as they had collected the money and then reenlist in order to receive more money.) The 1863 Conscription Law made men between twenty and forty-five subject to the draft and made them liable, if drafted, for three years' service. But prosperous men could hire substitutes or pay the federal government $300 in order to get out of fighting. When authorities published the draft calls, the names of the poor and foreign-born dominated the list. Enraged workers in many communities protested against the distinction between "rich men's money and poor men's blood." The outburst in New York in mid-July 1863 was an especially ugly affair as gangs, often led by Irish-Americans, turned their wrath against blacks, killing, pillaging, and looting. Several hundred people were killed and the Colored Orphan Asylum was burned to the ground before troops could restore order.

In spite of strong dissatisfaction among Republicans, Lincoln received the nomination of his party in June 1864. To improve his chances of winning the election, he selected Andrew Johnson (1808–1875), a Tennessee "War Democrat," as his running mate and the two men campaigned under the banner of the National Union party.

War Democrats chose General McClellan as the candidate of the Democratic party and permitted Peace Democrats to draft a platform calling for the immediate cessation of hostilities and the restoration of the "Federal Union of the States." After serious soul-searching, McClellan repudiated this peace plank—though he was not above playing on the widespread feeling of frustration with both Lincoln and the war which permeated the North.

By midsummer the strength of pacifism and defeatism made Lincoln's reelection seem doubtful.

Even within Republican ranks there was much dissension. Although the party agreed on three aims—victory in the war, reunion of the North and South, and emancipation of slaves everywhere in the country—it was split over the crucial question of reconstruction.

Lincoln hoped that when the war was over, the southern states would swiftly reenter the Union with a minimum of rancor. Accordingly, he proposed that when ten percent of the voters of 1860 in each rebel state had pledged allegiance to the United States, they could form a new state government and rejoin the Union. But two Republicans, Senator Benjamin Wade and Representative Henry Winter Davis, pushed a bill through Congress that required a majority of voters of 1860 in each southern state to pledge allegiance to the United States and to declare that they had never held office or voluntarily fought for the Confederacy before civil government could be restored. Lincoln was already setting up reconstruction governments in Louisiana and Arkansas and feared the Wade-Davis Bill might jeopardize their foundation. He found its terms so unacceptable that he pocket-vetoed it, sparking a short-lived movement to nominate another Republican candidate for President. Lincoln himself conceded that he probably would not be reelected.

Sheridan's scorching of the Shenandoah Valley and Sherman's entry into Atlanta greatly aided Lincoln's search for votes and finally won Radical Republicans to his side. Indeed, it was probably the votes of Union soldiers that put New York, Connecticut, Pennsylvania, Maryland, Indiana, and Illinois (a total of 101 electoral votes) in his column. McClellan carried only one state, Kentucky, decisively and won less handily in New Jersey and Delaware. Overall, Lincoln amassed 2,218,388 ballots, fifty-five percent of the popular vote, to 1,812,807 for McClellan. He had an electoral majority of 212 to 21.

Although patriotism and battlefield victories contributed to Lincoln's reelection, a booming wartime economy and enactment of the economic planks of the Republican platform of 1860 aided him considerably. The departure of southern leaders from Congress following secession gave the Republicans a unique opportunity. The Morrill Tariff Act of 1861 and its subsequent revisions designed to foster native industry pleased manufacturing interests. In 1862 the long-awaited Homestead Act gave 160 acres of surveyed public domain for a nominal fee to any settler who would farm the land for five years. Nearly 20,000 homesteads came into existence during the remaining war years. The Morrill Land Grant Act of 1862 provided states with public land earmarked to assist colleges and universities. During that same year, the Pacific Railway Act authorized subsidies for the construction of a transcontinental railway from Omaha to San Francisco. The national banking system established in 1863 and 1864, despite major defects, gave the country a uniform currency, served the needs of dominant groups in banking and business, and, in general, benefited the whole economy. After 1861, government purchases of goods and related services for the war effort stimulated the economy. At the same time, a series of bad harvests in western Europe boosted the prices of agricultural commodities. Thus, by the time many Americans went to the polls in the fall of 1864, they had numerous reasons to support Lincoln's bid for reelection.

The Collapse of the Confederacy

By the beginning of 1865 the South was collapsing. The federal blockade cut off badly needed imported supplies. Union occupation and destruction of production centers and the breakdown of transportation created chaos throughout large areas. Four years of conflict took a huge toll, reducing agricultural production, depreciating land values, stifling industry, demoralizing commerce, and disrupting whatever banking facilities existed. Omitting slave property, southern wealth shrank in value by some forty-three percent.

Morale in the Confederate Army was shattered; desertions were high. Jefferson Davis even contemplated arming the slaves, but the Confederate Congress acted too late for this measure to take effect before the conflict ended. Davis also had trouble commandeering goods and services from some states, especially from South Carolina, which jealously guarded its rights as a sovereign state. The southern plight became so desperate that Davis permitted Vice President Stephens and two other Confederate officials to meet with Lincoln and Secretary of State Seward aboard the Union vessel *River Queen* at Hampton Roads on February 3, 1865, to discuss peace proposals. But the Confederate commissioners stubbornly insisted that a prerequisite for peace was Union recognition of southern independence. Lincoln found this stipulation unacceptable, and this last ditch effort at peacemaking failed.

The end came in the spring of 1865. By continually bludgeoning Confederate forces and cutting Lee's supply lines, Grant and Sheridan forced the Confederate military leader to abandon both Petersburg and Richmond early in April. Fearing that Lee might escape into central North Carolina and join up with another large Confederate force, Grant and Sheridan rushed after Lee and trapped him in south central Virginia. On the 9th of April Grant and Lee met in the village of Appomattox Courthouse southwest of Richmond. In accordance with President Lincoln's desire to treat the South with generosity, Grant seized all weapons but gave the soldiers their freedom after they had pledged not to take up arms against the United States again. Grant also permitted the men to retain their horses, which they needed for spring ploughing. The once magnificent Army of Northern Virginia disbanded, and the last major Confederate forces surrendered on May 26. Although the Civil War was over, it would have a profound impact on Americans for generations to come. (For an analysis of this impact, see the essay at the end of this chapter: "War: Its Effects and Costs.")

The People Who Fought the War

In both the North and the South the actual waging of the war involved hundreds of thousands of people. Estimates of the sizes of the two armies are only approximate, but one expert calculated that during the war 1,556,678 men (eventually outfitted in dark blue uniforms) served the Union and 1,082,119 (many of whom wore a light gray uniforms) fought on behalf of the Confederacy. The war cost about a million casualties, including 360,222 deaths on the Union side and 258,000 on the Confederate side.

The Blue and the Gray
The northern Army faced many problems. In the

Harper's Weekly.

An improvised hospital, flanked on the right by reserves waiting to be called into action. On the outdoor operating table, in front of the house, is a bottle of whiskey—the only anesthetic available; about the table, scattered on the ground, lie amputated limbs.

first years of the war uniforms differed from regiment to regiment, which led to terrible confusion on the battlefield. Greedy and unscrupulous private contractors supplied soldiers with expensive but inadequate food. At the beginning of the war, each soldier cooked his own food; only much later were cooks detailed to prepare food for large numbers.

Weapons also were inadequate. Only after Edwin Stanton (1814–1869) took over the War Department in January 1862 did the supplies of weapons begin to improve; by 1864 most northern troops were outfitted with the Spencer breech-loading, single shot rifle, which allowed a soldier to fire several rounds a minute. This efficient weapon raised Union morale considerably.

Food, clothing, and campsites were so dirty that the army was plagued by bouts of diarrhea, dysentery, and typhoid, which killed thousands of soldiers. Only toward the end of the war did the Union have more stringent rules of hygiene, a larger medical corps, and an increased number of hospital beds. The United States Sanitary Commission, a quasi-volunteer women's auxiliary to the Army Medical Corps, coordinated care of Union soldiers. It provided nurses, supplied and staffed hospitals, and did whatever it could to aid the sick and wounded. The Commission spent $50 million, most of it raised at local sanitary fairs.

The democratic quality of American life made it difficult for officers to maintain discipline. Soldiers ignored orders with which they disagreed. After repeated defeats on the battlefield, the morale of the northern troops deteriorated steadily. Only toward the end of 1863 did army discipline improve, though desertions remained frequent. There were about 200,000 men who permanently deserted their outfits, many of them in order to return to support their impoverished families; the federal government did nothing to compensate the wives and children of soldiers, and army wages were low—eleven dollars a month at the beginning of the war, though by 1864 this amount had risen to sixteen dollars. However, because of inflation a soldier's pay in 1864 purchased less than in 1861.

Reports filtering back about southern camps for prisoners of war did not help Union morale. Until 1862, captured Union soldiers were released or exchanged, but after that they were interned in prisons such as Andersonville, where some 13,000 prisoners died. Of the nearly 200,000 Union prisoners captured during the war, about 30,000 died in various prisons.

Confederate soldiers also faced numerous problems. Pay was low, inflation high, soldiers suffered from a poor diet, and medical care was inadequate. The Confederacy found it difficult to maintain discipline, a problem aggravated by the 1862 Conscription Act, passed a year earlier than in the North. This law also discriminated against the poor. Men who owned more than twenty slaves were exempt from the draft, which led angry soldiers to call the conflict "a rich man's war and a poor man's fight." The morale of southern troops in the closing years of the war was far lower than that of the northern troops, since the Confederates were conscious of their dwindling fortunes.

Blacks

The war was a mixed experience for blacks both in the South and in the North. Northern blacks argued that the war could not be won nor the Union restored without ending slavery. Their expectations were buoyed up especially by the Emancipation Proclamation of 1863, which sanctioned the enlistment of black soldiers, and by the Thirteenth Amendment (ratified in 1865), which ended slavery.

In the early years of the war, Union armies did not allow blacks to enlist; northern generals sometimes returned escaped southern slaves to their masters; and Lincoln announced that the purpose of the war was not to end slavery but to preserve the Union. After the Emancipation Proclamation, however, blacks were allowed to serve in the army. In Massachusetts blacks formed the famous Fifty-fourth Regiment, and soon filled another, the Fifty-fifth. In the Mississippi Valley some 76,000 blacks formed twenty black regiments. Northern officers recruited nearly 100,000 black volunteers in the South.

Equal service in the army did not lead to equal benefits. Black soldiers were paid lower wages, received fewer and shoddier supplies, and suffered from very inadequate medical care, which accounted for the astonishingly high death toll among black soldiers—some thirty-seven percent of their number. Nor did emancipation and military service ensure northern blacks the vote. Only the New England states (with the exception of Connecticut) allowed blacks to vote on the same terms as whites; elsewhere, they generally were denied the ballot. Only the ratification of the Fifteenth Amendment in 1870 opened the polls to all northern blacks.

In the South conditions for blacks were still worse. Black slaves were forced to serve in the armies, not as soldiers but in noncombat positions as cooks, teamsters, and laborers. Some free blacks volunteered to serve in the Confederate Army, but they were never used in combat; and others, like their slave brothers, were compelled to aid the Confederate cause in numerous ways. Many more blacks deserted their masters and formed armed bands that lived off the land or joined the Union Army.

The Five Civilized Tribes

Though Southerners had been extremely reluctant to recruit blacks for battle, they eagerly sought military alliances with the Indians living west of the Arkansas-Missouri line. In particular, Confederate supply officers hoped to secure beef, hides, horses, grain, salt, and lead from the "Five Civilized Tribes"—the Cherokees, Chickasaws, Choctaws, Creeks, and Seminoles. The Confederacy was also eager to recruit Indian warriors to guard its western border from Union troops. The territory inhabited by the Five Civilized Tribes was located between Kansas and Texas. If the Confederates controlled this area, they would be able to defend the western approaches to Arkansas, Texas, and Louisiana against a Union invasion from Kansas. In order to accomplish this end, the Confederacy sent Albert Pike (1809–1891) of Arkansas to negotiate treaties of alliance with the Five Civilized Tribes.

The Confederacy found numerous allies among the Five Civilized Tribes. Many Indian leaders were mixed-blood slaveowners who identified with the South. Furthermore, as Union forces withdrew eastward from the vicinity of the Indian Territory, Indians found themselves surrounded by the Confederacy on three sides. Between May and October 1861, while public attention in the North focused

Stand Watie, a Cherokee who was a Confederate general and also Chief of the pro-southern wing of his tribe.

on battlefields in Virginia, Confederate Commissioner Pike negotiated treaties with tribal leaders. In return for their pledges of military support, the Indians received several concessions including the right to control white traders, the exclusive right to exercise police power in their domain, and a guarantee that the Confederacy would be financially liable for the actions of any intruders on Indian lands. Although Pike's efforts to secure treaties were successful, not all the members of the tribes supported the Confederacy.

Indians fought on both sides during the Civil War. Factionalism within each of the tribes led to the creation of rival governments, each claiming to speak for the tribe. Outstanding leaders among the Indians included Opothleyahola (1790–1862), a Creek who headed the Union faction, and Stand Watie (1806–1871), a Cherokee who accepted a commission in the Confederate Army.

In early March 1862, Stand Watie commanded a regiment of Cherokee Indians at the Battle of Pea Ridge in Arkansas. The Union forces were victo-

rious, but his warriers continued to harass and raid Union settlements on the western border until the end of the war. Indeed, Watie, who surrendered over two months after Lee's surrender at Appomattox, was the last Confederate general to lay down his arms.

The Civil War wreaked havoc in the Indian Territory inhabited by the Five Civilized Tribes. Union Indians fought their Confederate tribesmen, and Union volunteers from Kansas participated in numerous operations in the area. Guerrilla bands from Arkansas and Missouri such as the one led by the infamous William C. Quantrill (1837–1865) roamed through Indian communities stealing livestock and spreading destruction and slaughter. These bushwackers, though proslavery in sympathy, were indiscriminate in their raiding and attacked both Union and Confederate Indian settlements.

War also had a significant impact on other Indians in the trans-Mississippi West. As Union military forces withdrew eastward, some Indians seized the opportunity to avenge previous wrongs and went on the warpath. Others were harassed by local Indian-haters or by other whites who coveted their lands. These events provide the background to the earliest of the Indians wars on the plains, which increased in numbers and intensity after the Civil War.

Women

Except for the blacks in the South, no group in American society was more deeply affected by the Civil War than were the women of this nation. Union women and Confederate women supported the war effort by encouraging enlistment, aiding in the provisioning of the soldiers, caring for the wounded, raising funds, serving as spies, and assuming the tasks of their husbands or brothers back home. Yet male chauvinism did not die easily.

Male doctors, especially in the North, were hostile to the idea of using women nurses, who never constituted more than twenty percent of the Union nursing staff. Although this hostility was veiled as concern for the welfare of the "weaker sex," it was in fact more often an antifemale attitude. Yet one female doctor, Mary Walker (1832–1919) won the coveted Medal of Honor, the only member of her sex ever to do so, for her work on behalf of Union troops. Women nurses tended the wounded and dying on the battlefield, some 3,200 of them on both sides during the Civil War.

Dr. Mary Walker won the Medal of Honor for her work on her behalf of the Union soldiers.

In the North, female nurses were under the direction of Dorothea Dix, who stipulated that only women over thirty who were "plain in appearance" could serve. Clara Barton (1821–1912), who helped organize the International and American Red Cross in the 1880s, was one of the best-known nurses of the war. Born in Massachusetts, she gave up a teaching career because of a throat ailment and moved to Washington in 1854 to work in the Patent Office. Distressed by the treatment given Union soldiers, she went out to the Virginia battlefields without any official affiliation to care for the wounded and sick and to cook nourishing food for them. In time, she became superintendent of nurses with the Army of the James.

In the South, only the tremendous need for medical aid tempered male chauvinism and resulted in some women nurses gaining official status. The Confederacy on occasion even used slaves and free black women as nurses. One white woman, Sally Tompkins (1833–1916), organized a hospital in Richmond, and Jefferson Davis commissioned her a captain in order to keep "Sally's hospital" open. Another woman, Ella Newsom (1828–1919), dedicated herself and her deceased husband's substantial fortune to establish military hospitals in the South. Her efforts won her the title "Florence Nightingale of the South."

Women aided the war effort in many other ways. One of their chief activities was forming clubs and societies that raised money to finance the commissioning of troops or to provide care for the wounded. The United States Sanitary Commission, an enterprise largely organized, supported, and staffed by northern women, performed noble service.

Some women participated in the war more directly; about 400 of them presumably posed as male soldiers and actually saw combat. Other women, working either for the Confederacy or the Union, functioned as spies; Rose O'Neal Greenhow (1815–1864), a society hostess in the District of Columbia, for instance, fed valuable information to Confederate officers that helped them win the first Battle of Bull Run. Still other women became camp followers, some of them traveling with their husbands, others working the camps as prostitutes.

On the home front, women stepped into the jobs abandoned by soldiers. For the first time they became "government girls," clerks in federal offices. In the retail trades, women found jobs as salesladies. Northern women such as Lucy and Sarah Chase (whose activities are described in an accompanying biographical sketch) followed Union troops into the South and established schools to educate newly liberated slaves; eventually southern women took their places teaching school. (By the turn of the century, most of the nation's teachers were women.) In the South, women turned their houses and farms into supply centers and improvised factories, manufacturing clothes, shoes, and medicines needed by troops. In many ways, the Civil War was a watershed in the struggle of women for new roles outside their homes.

Harper's Weekly.

This sketch by Winslow Homer depicts the federal arsenal at Watertown, Massachusetts, where women participated in munitions making.

Aftermath

The Civil War resolved several issues that had long divided the nation. Slavery, the South's "peculiar institution," was finally abolished by the Thirteenth Amendment. The federal government under President Lincoln had forcefully asserted its dominant role in the nation's political structure. Manufacturing also flourished as the Congress, dominated by the Northeast after the exodus of Southerners, pushed through legislation long sought by industrialists. By the end of the war, business values had clearly emerged as the national ethic. Other issues, however, were still left pending. The nation would now have to grapple with the vexing problems of reconstruction and race relations in the defeated southern states.

After Lee's surrender at Appomattox, Lincoln's major concern was to bring the South back into the Union quickly and without malice. In his Second Inaugural Address on March 4, 1865, about a month before Lee's capitulation, Lincoln made his intentions explicit: "With malice toward none; with charity for all; with firmness in the right, as God gives us to see the right, let us strive on to finish the work we are in; to bind up the nation's wounds; to care for him who shall have borne the battle, and for his widow, and his orphan—to do all which may achieve and cherish a just and a lasting peace, among ourselves, and with all nations."

On April 14, five days after Lee's surrender, Lincoln attended a play at Ford's Theater in Washington. The President's party arrived after the curtain went up, and an ovation from the audience interrupted the actors. Less than a block from the theater, four men were conspiring to kill Lincoln. The ringleader was John Wilkes Booth (1838–1865), a handsome, twenty-six-year-old actor from a Maryland family. Booth, who was subject to fits of temper, had a sentimental attachment to the South but had ignored its plight throughout the war and continued to act on northern stages. Now that the Confederacy was collapsing, Booth saw an opportunity to avenge the South's defeat.

At a little after 10:00 P.M. Booth gained access to the presidential box, coolly shot the President through the head, leapt to the stage, and shouted *"Sic semper tyrannis!* The South is avenged!" The Latin words, the motto of the state of Virginia, meant loosely that a tyrant will always be destroyed. In jumping from the box, Booth broke a leg; with great pain he limped to the stage door and rode away into the night. A few days later, federal troops tracked him down in a barn near Bowling Green, Virginia. One of his accomplices surrendered, but Booth refused to do so and federal authorities set the structure on fire. In the uproar Booth either committed suicide or was shot by his pursuers. Although rumors of his escape persisted for many years, little doubt exists that Lincoln's assassin met his death in the Virginia tobacco barn.

The wounded President breathed his last at 7:22 in the morning of April 15, 1865. His death was a national calamity. Even some Southerners openly wept at the news. With Lincoln's death, it seemed to many people, the chances of a moderate reconstruction of the South had vanished.

Sarah Chase   Lucy Chase

Sarah Chase (bottom left) and Lucy Chase (bottom center) with a group of normal schoolteachers in Norfolk, Virginia in 1865.

1836–1913   1822–1909

Lucy Chase and her sister Sarah grew up in a large, intellectually stimulating, and prosperous Quaker household in Worchester, Massachusetts. They both shared the reforming fervor of the pre-Civil War decades, and when war erupted, proposed to become army nurses. However, perhaps because of protests from their brothers and father, they decided to work instead among freedmen now under the control of the U.S. Army. In December 1862 they received appointments as teachers and orders to report to Craney Island near Norfolk, Virginia. Each received $20 with which to purchase "an outfit;" their salary was to be $25 per month.

A few weeks later they were in the midst of 2,000 homeless, hungry, destitute ex-slaves. They worked from dawn to dusk handing out clothing, patching and sewing, and visiting the aged and ill. They encouraged the industrious, scolded those who were lazy, listened to complaints, wrote letters for their charges, and, incidentally, taught the three Rs to all eager to learn. Although under nominal military discipline, these sisters operated with considerable independence, striving to prepare blacks to take their place in a postwar South.

For all their zeal, the Chase sisters also looked out for their own well-being much of the time. They spent each summer back in Worcester far from the heat of Virginia, managed to attend inaugural balls in Washington in March 1865, and a month later joined a party touring Richmond, capital of the defeated Confederacy. On April 18, 1865, Lucy wrote from Richmond to friends in Boston:

"The colored people will need little help except in helping themselves. We are not going to make beggars of them. Will you please consult your Society in regard to getting a box of straw & materials for braiding—and yarn & needles & other materials for manufacture. . . . I will be most grateful if you can give a contract for work of any kind or send any plans for materials. You will forgive the writing in consideration of my tired, *shaken* hand, and also inasmuch as I am using the pen and holder that Grant used just before he left his headquarters at City Point for Richmond. One Monday I was in our Capital, the next Monday in Jeff Davis's . . . the slave pens and Libby. I have thanked God for this day."

During the winter of 1865–1866, the two sisters visited Georgia with an eye to teaching there but decided not to do so. Lucy, the stronger of the two and fourteen years older than Sarah, taught in Richmond and Florida until 1869, but Sarah retired to the serenity of Worcester.

The Chase sisters spent the rest of their lives in genteel repose. Lucy died in 1909, Sarah a few years later. Their work of the 1860s is chronicled in penetrating detailed letters, some of them surprisingly modern in outlook, edited for publication by Henry L. Swint in 1966: *Dear Ones At Home*. Their words provide a dramatic portrait of an aspect of life in the Civil War period—contraband camps for ex-slaves—about which we know little.

Essay

War: Its Effects and Costs

The costs of waging war, both apparent and hidden, are enormous. Almost any historian or statistician can dredge up eye-boggling figures detailing how many millions or billions a modern conflict cost in money for bombs, materiel, manpower, and aircraft . . . how many buildings were destroyed in air raids . . . how many people were killed or maimed . . . how many thousands of dollars were spent on veterans' pensions after the fighting ceased . . . how many dams, schools, and hospitals could have been built with the funds expended in battle. The 600,000 men lost in the Civil War or the 291,000 Americans who died in World War II and the destruction accompanying their deaths obviously are only a small part of the total picture. But war has its positive side, too. Under pressure of war, nations often undertake research in medicine, technology, and industry that, because of great cost, might be unthinkable in peacetime. The growth of the American automobile industry in 1917–1918 and of atomic research during World War II are examples of this phenomenon.

Yet, in the final analysis, the true costs of war have little to do with dollar signs, daring projects rushed to completion in hush-hush secrecy, cities destroyed or cities not built. The real costs are to be found in the impact of a war experience upon those who survive and upon their way of life. Interestingly, however, books on why or how a war was fought probably outnumber by a hundred to one those dealing with its effects.

The Civil War is, admittedly, the great traumatic experience in our national life. It somehow touched practically every household of the 1860s and for a half-century or more had considerable impact on how many Americans thought, voted, and viewed the world about them. It greatly increased presidential power, made an industrial giant out of the northeastern quarter of the United States, and paralyzed the South for several decades. The South had to deal almost singlehandedly with the physical, moral, and social problems spawned by defeat.

These problems included recurring racial turmoil and widespread misunderstanding that still bear bitter fruit.

In addition, the confrontation of the 1860s released pentup forces favoring nation building such as transcontinental railroads, land-grant education, and a more centralized federal banking structure—measures long frustrated by southern voices in Congress until April 1861.

During the war, an acute manpower shortage on northern farms produced a dramatic shift from handheld to horsedrawn machinery. Observers remarked upon this unexpected development. An official of the Ohio State Board of Agriculture wrote that "machinery and improved implements have been employed to a much greater extent during the years of the rebellion than ever before. . . . Without drills, cornplanters, reapers and mowers, horserakes, hay elevators, and threshing machines, it would have been impossible to have seeded and gathered the crops of 1863 with the implements in use forty or fifty years ago. . . ." World War II produced a similar shift on the nation's farms from horses to tractor-drawn or gas-propelled machinery. Before 1940 many farmers tilled their fields with a combination of animal- and gas-powered implements, but by 1945 the sturdy horse and mule had all but disappeared.

Many of these wartime results were by no means anticipated. In fact, Americans usually have fought wars for what seem to be very specific goals such as independence, preservation of the Union, making the world safe for democracy, or the containment of Communism. At the outset, they were secure in the belief that victory would guarantee an automatic return to things as they were before the current trouble erupted. But peace very often has arrived hand-in-hand with unforeseen dilemmas and numerous byproducts, some bad, some good. The Peace of Paris (1783) brought an independence of sorts and a chaotic five- or six-year interim that gave birth to a stronger, more workable federal structure. The War of 1812 perhaps nailed down the fact of independence and certainly stirred a flurry of national spirit; more importantly, as European imports declined, that brief encounter and the acrimony surrounding it generated an economic boom that gave birth to scores of mills and factories and set in motion forces that would come into conflict at Fort Sumter a half-century later. And, of course, the Mexican War hastened the showdown on slavery.

The major conflicts of this century—two world wars and the so-called Cold War with its warmer moments in Korea and Vietnam—also have had profound economic impact. World War I fed a boom that ended in a depression which, in turn, had much to do with the onset of World War II. The latter conflict certainly provided jobs and ended unemployment, ushering in a generation of prosperity; but, by the 1970s, many Americans were beginning to question seriously the merits of unrestricted growth and development.

Among the specific effects of World War I were a quickening of black migration from the South to the North with vast social and political implications, a disillusionment with the great crusade to make the world safe for democracy, and a lowering or a shift in social mores that produced flappers, bathtub gin, and the Roaring Twenties. World War II greatly accelerated the black demand for full equality, increased the flow of women into the work force where many remained, and initiated a baby boom with an untold effect in ensuing decades for realms such as education, housing, department-store sales, and even for the protest marches of the 1960s. Korea produced the conservative backlash of McCarthyism and a silent generation of young people fearful to speak out, eager to hide within a safe corporate structure by day and in surburbia at night. The slow involvement in Vietnam, apparently engineered or at least condoned by forces Americans had been taught to revere—officials at the highest level of the federal government, corporate executives, and military experts—eventually led to anything but silence. In fact, the ongoing ripples from faraway Vietnam are still felt today in recurring waves of inflation and heated debate over national goals.

Over a quarter-century of "nonpeace" has bestowed upon America something it never had before: a gigantic peacetime military force centered in the Pentagon, which seems to wield more and more power in many realms of American life. No less a

The War to Save the Union

Cornell Capa/Magnum.

Inger Elliott/Rapho-Photo Researchers.

These scenes of business activity on the floor on the New York Stock Exchange and the rows of graves in Arlington National Cemetery provide two different perspectives on the impact of war on American society.

The great migration of blacks from the South to northern cities that began during World War I was a major watershed in the history of American blacks. Today, blacks live mainly in urban areas.

military man than Dwight D. Eisenhower (West Point graduate, career man, five-star general) in his Farewell Address (1961) as President leveled a warning finger at America's military-industrial complex:

"Now this conjunction of an immense military establishment and a large arms industry is new to the American experience. The total influence— economic, political, even spiritual—is felt in every city, every state house, every office of the Federal Government. We recognize the imperative need for this development. Yet we must not fail to comprehend its grave implications. Our toil, resources and livelihood are all involved; so is the very structure of our society."

The answer, according to the retiring President, was to guard against the unwarranted influence of the military-industrial complex. It was the duty of the nation's leaders, he concluded, to mold, balance, and integrate such forces so as to be certain that a free, democratic society would survive.

Just as the Civil War elevated industrialists to

a position from which they ruled America for over half a century, World War II and its aftermath did much of the same for the Pentagon generals and their think-tank, computerized satellites. Only the future can tell whether their reign also will go unchallenged, but chinks in the armor are evident, Vietnam being the most obvious. Nevertheless, the military-industrial complex, a necessary fact of life in present-day America, is the most obvious byproduct of World War II. This combination of military and industrial self-interest influences all of our lives and pocketbooks directly and if reckoned as a "cost of war" becomes too staggering to contemplate.

In essence, war is an unpredictable force in the life of any nation. In fact, sometimes it is those who win who must face the greatest dilemmas. The vanquished wipe the slate clean and begin anew; their adversaries are encumbered by the spoils of war and the responsibility for reestablishing peacetime modes of life, if that is truly possible. Clearly the costs and the effects of war extend far beyond the months or years between the first and last salvo; they are intricately woven into the fabric of every nation, sadly even into that of those who choose to remain aloof and neutral.

SELECTED
READINGS

General Accounts

Robert Cruden, *The War that Never Ended: The American Civil War* (1973)

David Donald, *Liberty and Union* (1978)

David Donald, ed., *Why the North Won the Civil War* (1960)

Allan Nevins, *The War for the Union* (4 vols., 1959–1971)

Peter J. Parish, *The American Civil War* (1975)

James G. Randall and David Donald, *The Civil War and Reconstruction* (rev., 2nd ed., 1973)

The Road to War

William B. Catton and Bruce Catton, *Two Roads to Sumter* (1963)

Richard N. Current, *Lincoln and the First Shot* (1963)

Robert G. Gunderson, *Old Gentlemen's Convention: The Washington Peace Conference of 1861* (1961)

Kenneth M. Stampp, *And the War Came: The North and the Secession Crisis, 1860–1861* (1950)

Military History

Bruce Catton, *The Centennial History of the Civil War* (3 vols., 1961–1965)

Marcus Cunliffe, *Soldiers and Civilians: The Martial Spirit in America, 1775–1865* (1968)

Burke Davis, *Sherman's March* (1980)

Shelby Foote, *The Civil War: A Narrative* (3 vols., 1958–1974)

John F. C. Fuller, *Grant and Lee* (1957)

William B. Hesseltine, *Civil War Prisons: A Study in War Psychology* (1930)

James A. Rawley, *Turning Points of the Civil War* (1966)

The Union

William L. Barney, *Flawed Victory: A New Perspective on the Civil War* (1975)

Leonard P. Curry, *Blueprint for Modern America: Nonmilitary Legislation of the First Civil War Congress* (1968)

Norman B. Ferris, *The Trent Affair: A Diplomatic Crisis* (1977)

George M. Frederickson, *The Inner Civil War: Northern Intellectuals and the Crisis of the Union* (1965)

Louis S. Gerteis, *From Contraband to Freedom: Federal Policy Toward Southern Blacks, 1861–1865* (1973)

Frank L. Klement, *The Limits of Dissent: Clement L. Vallandigham and the Civil War* (1970)

James McCague, *Second Rebellion: The Story of the New York City Draft Riots of 1863* (1968)

James A. Rawley, *The Politics of Union: Northern Politics During the Civil War* (1974)

Joel H. Silbey, *A Respectable Minority: The Democratic Party in the Civil War Era, 1860–1868* (1977)

The Confederacy

Thomas L. Connelly and Archer Jones, *The Politics of Command: Factions and Ideas in Confederate Strategy* (1973)

Robert F. Durden, *The Gray and the Black: The Confederate Debate on Emancipation* (1972)

Clement Eaton, *A History of the Southern Confederacy* (1954)

Paul D. Escott, *After Secession: Jefferson Davis and the Failure of Confederate Nationalism* (1978)

Frank L. Owsley and H. C. Owsley, *King Cotton Diplomacy: Foreign Relations of the Confederate States of America* (rev. 2nd ed., 1959)

Charles W. Ramsdell, *Behind the Lines in the Southern Confederacy* (1944)

Emory M. Thomas, *The Confederacy as a Revolutionary Experience* (1971)

W. Buck Yearns, *The Confederate Congress* (1960)

The People Who Fought the War

Annie H. Abel, *The American Indian as Participant in the Civil War* (1919)

John R. Brumgardt, ed., *Civil War Nurse: The Diary and Letters of Hannah Ropes* (1980)

Kenny A. Franks, *Stand Watie and the Agony of the Cherokee Nation* (1979)

Majorie B. Greenbie, *Lincoln's Daughters of Mercy* (1944)

Mary E. Massey, *Bonnet Brigades: American Women and the Civil War* (1966)

James McPherson, *The Negro's Civil War: How American Negroes Felt and Acted During the War for the Union* (1965)

David A. Nichols, *Lincoln and the Indians: Civil War Policy and Politics* (1978)

Ben I. Wiley, *The Common Soldier of the Civil War* (1975)

Bell I. Wiley, *Confederate Women* (1975)

CHAPTER 15
RESTORING THE UNION

TIMELINE

December 1863
Lincoln announces "Ten Percent Plan"

May 1865
Johnson offers presidential pardon to Confederates

December 1865
Ratification of the Thirteenth Amendment

February 1866
Freedmen's Bureau expands to counteract "black codes"

July–October 1866
Reconstruction treaties between federal government and the Five Civilized Tribes

November 1866
Republican party sweeps congressional elections

March 1867
Congress places southern states under military rule

March 1867
Passage of Tenure of Office Act

February 1868
House of Representatives votes to impeach Johnson

May 1868
Senate acquits Johnson of impeachment charges

July 1868
Ratification of Fourteenth Amendment

November 1868
Ulysses S. Grant wins presidential election

May and November 1869
National Woman Suffrage Association and American Woman Suffrage Association formed

March 1870
Ratification of Fifteenth Amendment

November 1872
Grant reelected President

November 1876
Hayes versus Tilden in disputed election

March 1877
Compromise of 1877 makes Hayes President and ends Reconstruction

CHAPTER OUTLINE

The end of the Civil War on the battlefield ushered in many problems relating to the restoration of the Union. The South, stunned by defeat, lay prostrate and bloody. Four years of war had disrupted business and agriculture, labor was in chaos, and many institutions of normal daily life—especially in Virginia, the Carolinas, and Georgia where fighting only recently ceased—were virtually nonexistent.

An immediate question for the North was the readmission of the seceded states: when, how, and under what terms were they to rejoin the Union? Though the North was solidly committed to the ideal of unification, no such solidarity was evident in proposals concerning readmission, treatment of the defeated South, enfranchisement of blacks, and reestablishment of state governments.

Lincoln and Preparations for Reconstruction

The question of Reconstruction arose as early as 1861, when Lincoln raised the subject in his address to a special session of Congress on July 4th. Although Lincoln assured Congress that he would be guided by the Constitution in his policy toward the rebellious states after their insurrection was suppressed, the Constitution provided no guidelines for Reconstruction, since nowhere in it was the issue of secession raised. (This, in fact, was the great argument of the southern states: they had not violated the Constitution, since it had not explicitly forbidden secession.) Lincoln argued that the perpetuity of the Union was implied if not expressed in the Constitution. He insisted that, since the Union was older than the states, no state could reserve for itself the power to secede, nor could an individual state have entered the Union in the first place without having tacitly surrendered some of its sovereignty.

Attitude of Conciliation

In December 1863, Lincoln informed the nation of his intention to provide for the full restoration of the southern states to the Union. Such restoration could occur after one-tenth of the citizens in each state who voted in the presidential election of 1860 swore allegiance to the Constitution and formed a new state government that abolished slavery and repudiated secession. Lincoln's Ten Percent Plan, as it came to be called, provided a system whereby the states could reestablish their former relationships with the federal government.

Lincoln's plan aimed at a speedy restoration with a minimum of federal intervention in internal state affairs. He intended to give the majority of Southerners amnesty and full powers to restore loyal state governments. Even Confederate leaders might be pardoned, though the primary architects of rebellion, Lincoln hoped, would go into exile. Southern Whigs, who had been at the forefront of opponents to secession, would be established in powerful positions in state governments and urged to affiliate themselves with the Republican party.

As early as 1862, Lincoln appointed military governors in Tennessee, Louisiana, Arkansas, and the sea islands off South Carolina and encouraged loyal citizens to establish pro-Union governments. Indeed, he was willing to pardon Confederate soldiers who would take oaths of loyalty to the Constitution and to exonerate all citizens who had not borne arms.

Though Lincoln's benevolence influenced his policy toward the South, he was nevertheless a shrewd politician. He adhered to the conservative principles of the Whig party which had given him his start. Throughout his difficulties with Congress, particularly with Radical Republicans, his political acumen alone kept the administration functioning with reasonable harmony and efficiency.

Despite opposition from Radical Republicans, Lincoln adhered to his Ten Percent Plan. By January of 1865, Tennessee followed Louisiana and Arkansas in offering Washington a loyal state government. Technically, these states were ready to be restored to their full privileges within the Union under Lincoln's plan, but Congress remained adamant in its refusal to seat senators and representatives from these states.

The Thirteenth Amendment

In February 1865 Congress proposed the Thirteenth Amendment, which would abolish slavery throughout the nation. Since acceptance of the amendment would void the three-fifths clause of the Constitution, the southern states might return to the Union with larger congressional delegations than they had in 1861. Southern whites might even be able to coerce the freedmen into supporting conservative Democrats rather than Republican candidates. Also, black suffrage in the South might bring increased black suffrage in the North—but would northern whites accept black voters? Such matters perplexed congressional Republicans, and the stalemate between them and the President continued until Lincoln's death.

The question of dealing with active Confederate supporters was also thorny. Both Lincoln and Congress agreed as early as 1862 that no mass executions for treason would take place. But in the summer of that same year, Congress passed a sweeping measure based on the idea of treason, the so-called Second Confiscation Act. The first act (August 6, 1861) had ordered the seizure of all property used for insurrectionary purposes. The second (July 17, 1862) provided for the punishment of treason by fines and imprisonment as well as by death and the punishment of actions of "rebellion or insurrection" by fine, imprisonment, and confiscation of property, including slaves. Although the Act of 1862 confirmed the government's position against wholesale executions, enforcement would have redistributed the huge landed estates and destroyed the planter aristocracy. Lincoln, however, doubted the constitutionality of this measure and his attorney-general made no serious effort to enforce it.

Shortly after Lincoln's death, Senator Benjamin F. Wade of Ohio (who is the subject of a biographical sketch in this chapter) and a small group of Radical Republican members of the Congressional Committee on the Conduct of the War met in Washington to plan their reconstruction strategy. Some of them believed that the President's death was "a godsend to the country." They sincerely felt that a "soft" peace, which enabled Confederate leaders to regain political and economic power, would make a mockery of much of the hardship the Union had endured.

Benjamin Franklin Wade

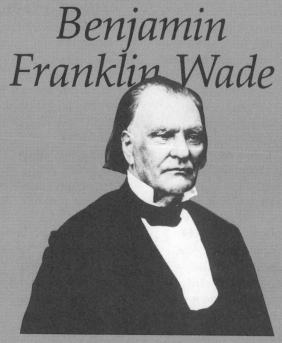

1800–1878

One of Lincoln's severest critics during the Civil War, Wade was a Republican Senator from Ohio. He was reared in New England but moved to Andover, Ohio when he was a young man. There he tried a number of professions, working as a farmer, drover, laborer, medical student, and teacher before he finally decided to study law. As a lawyer he had one of the most successful practices in northeastern Ohio, but quickly turned to politics. From the very beginning, he allied himself with the antislavery forces.

After serving as a state senator and as a judge, in 1851 he was elected by the Ohio legislature to the United States Senate, where he served continuously until 1869. Wade attempted in 1852 to repeal the Fugitive Slave Law and later denounced the Kansas-Nebraska Bill. During the secession crises of 1860 and 1861, he took a militant stand against all compromise plans including the Crittenden proposals.

Once war broke out, Wade was a passionate advocate of a stern, relentless offensive. When McClellan stalled after the first Battle of Bull Run, Wade tongue-lashed him repeatedly. As chairman of the Committee on the Conduct of the War, a congressional group that heaped criticism on the administration, he personally attacked the President and his generals. He disliked Lincoln intensely, especially after the President suggested a moderate Reconstruction policy in 1863. In reponse to that proposal, Wade and Henry Winter Davis drew up a punitive congressional plan, dubbed the Wade-Davis Bill.

Lincoln pocket vetoed this measure, prompting its authors to issue the Wade-Davis Manifesto, condemning Lincoln's action as a "studied outrage on the legislative authority" of Congress; according to Wade, Congress alone should establish a policy for the Reconstruction of the South. The President's plan, Wade announced, was "absurd, monarchical and anti-American."

After Lincoln's assassination, Wade clearly expected President Johnson to cooperate more fully with the Radical Republicans. When Johnson surprised the Radicals by endorsing Lincoln's plan, Wade joined forces with his fellow Radicals Charles Sumner and Thaddeus Stevens in attacking the new President. In 1867 Wade became president pro tempore of the Senate, a position that in those days made him next in line for the presidency. Wade fully expected that the impeachment proceedings against Johnson would lead to the President's re-

Johnson and Reconstruction

Tennessean Andrew Johnson (1808–1875), the new Vice President, was a dedicated Unionist. Johnson, a Democrat, had repudiated secession and refused to abandon his seat in the Senate when Tennessee seceded. In addition, he served at Lincoln's request on the Committee on the Conduct of the War and worked without rancor with such Radicals as Wade and Chandler. In 1862, after Union troops occupied much of Tennessee, Lincoln appointed him military governor, and in 1864 the President made him his vice presidential running mate.

Johnson was a self-educated man who had risen from poverty in North Carolina and Tennessee and who hated the aristocrats of the South. The Radicals hoped that he shared their views on Reconstruction, and they had good reasons to believe he did. He had fought hard to preserve the integrity of the Union. Like them, he had supported ratification of the Thirteenth Amendment. Moreover, his vitriolic remarks about the southern aristocrats who had "dragooned" the ordinary Southerners, the humble men, into the war warmed their hearts, as did his contention that the aristocratic class had to be destroyed. Johnson's efforts to undermine the southern planters helps to explain his reconstruction program, which barred those with sizable property from taking the oath of allegiance. This prohibition, Johnson hoped, would transfer political power and economic benefits from large property holders to the yeomanry.

The Radicals soon discovered, however, that Johnson was not *their* man. Congress was in recess when Lincoln was assassinated, and Johnson was President from April to December 1865 before it reconvened. His actions during this period dismayed the Radicals. He recognized the new loyal governments of Arkansas, Louisiana, Tennessee, and Virginia established under Lincoln's Ten Percent Plan. On May 29, 1865 Johnson offered presidential amnesty to Confederates taking the oath of allegiance, although he excluded several classes (holders of taxable property worth $20,000 or more, for example). But even the wealthy under this plan could petition the President for special pardons.

moval from office; accordingly, the Ohioan began to choose his own Cabinet members. When Johnson was acquitted, Wade had to abandon his dreams of power.

Meanwhile, Democrats had gained control of the Ohio legislature. Knowing he could not win reelection, Wade made an unsuccessful bid to become Grant's running mate. At the end of his Senate term in 1869, he returned to his Ohio law practice.

Wade was a fervent (if sometimes tactless) advocate of black suffrage, better wages for labor, and equal rights for women, including suffrage. In 1866 he joined seven other senators in supporting legislation designed to enfranchise both blacks and women in the District of Columbia. Controversial stands such as this caused some senators to hesitate as they pondered the fate of Andrew Johnson. Putting Wade in the White House, they concluded, was no solution to problems facing the nation.

Wade's last official role in government service was as a member of the Commission of Investigation that visited Santa Domingo in 1871 and recommended its annexation. Seven years later, in 1878, he died in Ohio.

Andrew Johnson in a photograph taken in 1865.

Indeed, to the surprise of Confederates and Unionists alike, Johnson granted these pardons rather liberally. Moreover, he began organizing provisional governments for the remaining ex-Confederate states and empowered provisional governors to assemble conventions composed of "loyal" citizens to amend state constitutions, ratify the Thirteenth Amendment, and repudiate the Confederate war debt. By December 1865 when Congress reconvened, every Confederate state except Texas had fulfilled his requirements (Texas did so by April 1866). Johnson then informed Congress that these states were ready to seat their senators and representatives in Congress.

Johnson's Motives

Why did Johnson take a new approach to Reconstruction after he had convinced the Radicals that he and they had so much in common? There is a distinct possibility that Johnson was influenced by his adroit Secretary of State, William H. Seward, who had been urging the establishment of a new national conservative political party that would attract Southerners. Perhaps Johnson wanted the presidential nomination in 1868 in his own right

and realized he needed a firm political base in order to achieve that goal. Some historians have maintained that, sobered by the responsibility of power, Johnson began to see no alternative to leniency once he recognized duly elected southern officials. Others suggest that his change of policy resulted from weakness or fear; either he lacked the ruthlessness necessary to implement a harsh reconstruction plan or his growing fear of northern capitalists made him see the political value of retaining the planter class as a balancing force.

Part of the reason for Johnson's failure to implement either Lincoln's plan or the policy of the Radical Republicans lies in the fact that the planter aristocrats proved to be far more astute politicians than he. Johnson's vanity was fed when members of the planter aristocracy came to him seeking special pardons. Had Johnson not been a vain man, they would have found nothing to exploit. But once they discovered his weakness, they easily led him to compromise his positions to such an extent that finally he had to side with them against the Radicals or to admit he had failed—and thus invite Congress to take over the responsibility of Reconstruction.

Johnson's reputation has undergone a number of historical reevaluations. For much of the twentieth century, he usually was portrayed as courageous, a man who defended constitutional rights and popular democracy in a spirit of reconciliation against vengeful Radicals and rapacious northern capitalists. The pro-Johnson literature led to a 1942 Hollywood film, *Tennessee Johnson*, in which Johnson was portrayed as a heroic fighter for democracy and justice. In 1960, Eric L. McKitrick challenged this view, portraying Johnson as stubborn, provincial, and inept, a President who misunderstood public sentiment, particularly in the North, and who misled the South about northern intentions. Johnson alienated moderates in Congress, thus losing whatever bargaining power he may have had there. In McKitrick's view Johnson's failure can be attributed to his being an "outsider." Though he had undeniable abilities, he was a maverick. The same plebeian origins that made him independent, also made him vulnerable.

Criticism of the President similar to that expressed by the Radical Republicans themselves has emerged in recent years. Hans L. Trefousse and Michael Les Benedict argued in the 1970s, for example, that Johnson was a cunning politician who misused and abused the powers of his office and whose obstructionism prevented a true reconstruction of the South. Writing in 1979, historian Albert Castel offered a middle ground between the neo-Radical interpretation and the pro-Johnson approach. According to Castel, Johnson was inept in using the power he had so suddenly and unexpectedly inherited. Nevertheless, he must be viewed as a "strong" President for his courage and for upholding the integrity, if not always the dignity, of the presidency. Historians have disagreed, and un doubtedly will continue to do so, about this controversial President who was buried in 1875 with an American flag wrapped around his body and with his well-thumbed copy of the U.S. Constitution beneath his head.

The Black Codes

Perhaps Johnson's greatest failure was his decision to abandon the southern freedmen to the mercy of their former masters. Johnson demanded that the southern states accept the Thirteenth Amendment, but he did not require Southerners to deal fairly with the freedmen. The new governments in the South barred freedmen from voting, failed to make any provision for educating them, and took other steps to keep them illiterate, unskilled, and without property. These governments enacted "black codes" between 1865 and 1866 as a system of social control.

The codes condemned blacks to a subordinate and carefully regulated position in the social order in the hope of providing a manageable and inexpensive labor force for southern planters. They declared that blacks who were unemployed or without permanent residence should be treated as vagrants subject to fine, arrest, imprisonment, or forced labor. The words "master" and "slave" actually appeared in the labor contracts utilized in some of the southern states. Laws were passed that legalized marriages between blacks but banned interracial marriages. Blacks in South Carolina were required to obtain special licenses before they could enter any occupation other than agriculture. In Mississippi, blacks could not rent or lease land. Throughout the South, the codes led to racial segregation in public facilities and subjected blacks to discrimination in court procedures and in making contracts.

Within a few years sharecropping emerged as the replacement for the former slave-labor system in the South. As the freedmen were forced to buy their goods at plantation stores, a system of taking liens on their crops emerged, which led to debt peonage. Thus, the new postwar governments in the South promoted disenfranchisement, discrimination, segregation, sharecropping, and debt peonage.

The black codes replaced slavery in the South and virtually established a system of peonage for blacks. Here, a freedman's services are being sold to pay his fine.

Congressional Reconstruction

When the first session of the Thirty-ninth Congress assembled in December 1865, Radical Republicans Thaddeus Stevens, Charles Sumner, and Benjamin Wade sought to have Congress take control of the course of Reconstruction. At that time, there were four caucuses in Congress: The Radical Republicans, a demoralized Democratic minority, a small band of Republican conservatives, and a potentially powerful body of Republican moderates. The latter, who wavered between supporting the President and siding with the Radicals, seemed inclined to go along with the administration when Congress convened. Johnson had nearly completed his reconstruction program and it apparently enjoyed general approval throughout the North.

Soon, however, the Radicals began to exert new strength as President Johnson became increasingly inflexible and tactless in dealing with Congress. In addition, politicians in control of governments he had helped establish in the southern states took actions that angered northern public opinion. Not only had they passed the black codes, they were also completely indifferent to the reactions of many Northerners. Finally, the Radicals knew what they wanted in terms of Reconstruction in contrast to Johnson's seemingly inconsistent policies, and they worked strenuously to achieve their ends. As a result, some moderate Republicans were drawn into their camp. By the summer of 1866, the Radicals were able to control Congress and to take over the direction of Reconstruction.

The Motivation of the Radicals

What motivated the Radicals in their policies toward the South? Long historical debate has not yet settled this controversy. Some men like Thaddeus Stevens of Pennsylvania apparently were motivated by a combination of factors: vindictiveness toward the South, idealism, and an equally powerful desire to maintain the ascendancy of the Republican party in the South. A commitment to the interests of northern capitalism was a fourth and perhaps even the principal motive, according to some historians.

Almost from the beginning of the historical examination of Reconstruction, American writers condemned it as "tragic," a national disgrace, and "an age of hate." Early in the twentieth century a talented professor of history, William A. Dunning (1857–1922) of Columbia University, defined the attitude toward Radical Reconstruction that was to dominate American thought for the next fifty years. This interpretation held that the Radicals were motivated by vindictiveness. Driven by hatred of the South and selfish economic and political interests, only Lincoln's compassion for human suffering held them in check. Once Lincoln died, they used that tragedy to push through Congress their program for southern humiliation. In this view, Johnson is seen as sincerely trying to foster Lincoln's original plans, for which the Radicals viciously attempted to impeach him. Failing this, they elected Ulysses S. Grant President and engineered a corruption of government hitherto unprecedented. Finally, the triumph of states' rights in the South with the removal of federal troops signaled the redemption of decency in politics.

More recently, scholars such as Kenneth M. Stampp have noted that the program of the Radicals had its roots in the antislavery crusade. Like the abolitionists, the Radicals spoke of regenerating the South and talked much of their sacred duties, of the will of God, and the evils of compromise.

Black suffrage was politically advantageous for the Republican party. Thaddeus Stevens himself frankly admitted that he favored black suffrage in the South because "it would insure the ascendancy" of the party. Before he became an advocate of black suffrage, however, Stevens had hoped to provide the freedmen with an economic base of confiscated land to protect them from the exploitation of southern planters. He had argued that forty acres, a mule, and a hut would be more valuable to each freed black than suffrage.

Other Northerners had always pinned their hopes for the freedmen on their obtaining the right to vote. Radicals like Charles Sumner and Benjamin Wade warned that the franchise was needed to protect freed blacks. Moderate Republicans, however, hoped to find some alternative between the black codes of the southern states and the position of these Radicals. Eventually, Sumner and Wade won other Radicals and the moderates over to their suffrage ideas. They were unwilling to reward the South by allowing the seceded states to return to Congress with more representatives as a result of the abolition of Slavery and of the three-fifths clause than when they had left the Union. Many Republi-

AWKWARD COLLISION ON THE GRAND TRUNK COLUMBIA R. R.

A. J. (Driver of Engine "President")—"LOOK HERE! ONE OF US HAS GOT TO BACK."
Thaddeus (Driver of Engine "Congress")—"WELL, IT AIN'T ME THAT'S GOING TO DO IT.—YOU BET!"

Library of Congress.

This cartoon shows President Andrew Johnson and Radical Republican leader Thaddeus Stevens on a collision course concerning Reconstruction.

cans thus saw the enfranchisement of blacks and their alignment with Republicanism as the only solution to this perplexing problem.

Even moderate Republicans feared the prospect of a southern-western agrarian alliance in the Democratic party dominating national politics. In addition, the adoption of the black codes convinced many congressmen that a plot existed to maintain slavery in disguise. Thus they decided to carry out a more vigorous Reconstruction program than that proposed by President Johnson.

The Radicals, like the early nineteenth century reformers, viewed their work as a great crusade. Many had come from the ranks of the abolitionists or at least shared their moral idealism. Their pleas for justice to blacks and their warnings that the black codes were restoring a form of slavery reflect this idealism.

The Freedmen's Bureau
Congress sought to counteract the black codes by

an act of February 19, 1866, that enlarged the Freedmen's Bureau. First established in March 1865 as a temporary bureau to care for the freedmen and the abandoned lands of the South, this paternalistic agency headed by General Oliver O. Howard (1830–1909) provided assistence to thousands of refugees, white Unionists, and freed blacks.

Within four years the Bureau, which worked closely with the U.S. Army, issued twenty-one million rations, established forty hospitals, and spent more than $2 million in treating 450,000 sick people of both races. Harassed Bureau agents were especially active in the fields of labor relations and education. They fought hard to make certain that ex-slaves were treated fairly and that, in turn, ex-masters received a reasonable amount of work for wages paid.

The Bureau's greatest success was in education. Its agents established a variety of schools that included day schools, Sunday schools, industrial schools, and even colleges and universities. By 1870, more than 250,000 blacks were in 4,300 schools aided by the Bureau and various philanthropic and religious groups. Howard University (named for the Bureau's director), Hampton Institute, and Atlanta and Fisk universities are among the best known of the institutions that flourished with Bureau help.

Nevertheless, the Bureau had its troubles. Though Howard, known as "the Christian General," viewed the problems of the ex-slaves as an opportunity for evangelical and charitable service, some bureau agents were incompetent, some corrupt, and others were converted to the argument that white Southerners "knew their people best." Also, the Bureau always faced open scorn from conservative white Southerners and, in time, incurred the enmity of President Johnson as well. Despite these handicaps, the Bureau accomplished a great deal, and the Radicals still hoped to make the agency even more effective by extending its life and by empowering its agents to protect the civil rights of the freed blacks.

Johnson's Responses
Early in 1866, President Johnson vetoed the bill seeking to extend the life of the Freedmen's Bureau. The President also vetoed a civil rights bill that guaranteed blacks the same rights and protection as whites, regardless of local laws; this bill authorized the use of federal troops to enforce the rights of

**The greatest success of the Freedmen's Bureau was in education. In 1869
more than 9,000 teachers worked in about 4,000 schools. A majority of the
white teachers came from the North.**

black citizens. These vetoes alienated even the
moderates and precipitated open warfare between
Johnson and Congress. The President's suggestion,
after his vetoes, that the Radical Republican
"traitors" were trying to seize control of the government united moderate and Radical Republicans
as never before, and together on April 9, 1866, they
overrode his veto of the Civil Rights Act. Then Congress passed a new Freedmen's Bureau Bill, and
again the President vetoed it. Finally, on July 16,
1866, despite Johnson's obstinate insistence that
the legislation encroached on states' rights, moderate and Radical Republicans worked together to
override that veto as well.

The open political conflict between the majority of Congress and the President set the stage for
the congressional elections of 1866. Many Northerners condemned President Johnson's abortive attempt to forge a new national political party composed of moderates and conservatives of both major
parties. Johnson's "swing around the circle"—a
speaking tour between late August and mid-Sep-
tember that took him as far west as St. Louis—was
a disaster. His speeches were vindictive, and they
met with jeers from crowds in the Midwest.

Johnson's continued opposition to the Fourteenth Amendment (passed by Congress in mid-
June and submitted to the states for ratification)

also provided the Radicals with ammunition against him. This Amendment, the most detailed of the three so-called Civil War Amendments to the Constitution, had four principal provisions: (1) all persons, born or naturalized in the United States and subject to its jurisdiction, are entitled to all the privileges of citizenship and no state can deprive anyone of life, liberty, or property without "due process of law"; (2) if any state seeks to deprive any *male* citizen of the suffrage, then its representation in the Congress will be reduced proportionally; (3) anyone who had renounced his oath to uphold the federal government and engaged in rebellion could not hold state or federal office (however, by a two-thirds vote in each house Congress could remove this disability); and (4) the public debt incurred by the federal government during the Civil War "shall not be questioned," but all debts and obligations of the Confederacy and its states, including "any claim for the loss or emancipation of any slave" are "illegal and void."

Radicals, eager to form a firm alliance with the moderates in the struggle against Johnson, supported the measure even though they preferred a less ambiguous definition of black rights. President Johnson opposed the Fourteenth Amendment and encouraged Southerners to reject the measure. Ironically, Johnson's home state (Tennessee) spurned his advice, adopted the measure, returned to the Union in July 1866, and thus escaped the military rule that Congress soon imposed on the rest of the South. However, in ensuing months, ten other ex-Confederate states followed Johnson's lead and rejected the Amendment. Meanwhile Johnson emerged from the 1866 congressional elections discredited. The Republicans, led by the Radicals, waved "the bloody shirt of the rebellion" (a tactic by which they portrayed the Democratic party as the standardbearer of rebellion) and obtained more than two-thirds of the seats in both houses of Congress, won every gubernatorial contest, and captured control of every northern state legislature.

There are many explanations for this sweeping victory—Johnson's political mistakes as well as northern opposition to the black codes, a bloody race riot in Memphis, and the support of both businessmen and Union Army veterans. The Republican victory, however, was based primarily on the fear among Northerners that Johnson was encouraging unreconstructed southern whites to ignore their defeat in war and to reestablish their old privileges—and even to reintroduce slavery.

Radical Reconstruction

Two years after Civil War ended, the Republicans, firmly in control of Congress, voted to return the defeated states of the South to military rule, thus beginning the process of Reconstruction anew. Congress deemed its actions necessary for a number of reasons: the President, who remained hostile and uncoopertive, had to be chastened; ten of the former states of the Confederacy refused to adopt the Fourteenth Amendment; and the freedmen in the South were still subject to continual abuse. On March 2, 1867, Congress passed its First Reconstruction Act over Johnson's veto. This measure divided the South into five military districts subject to martial law. In order to return to their original status within the Union, the southern states were required to call new constitutional conventions elected by all adult males, black and white, except ex-Confederates. These conventions had to establish state governments guaranteeing black suffrage and had to ratify the Fourteenth Amendment.

Military authorities were required to register voters and to supervise the election of delegates to the constitutional conventions. Yet Southerners defeated ratification of the proposed constitutions by staying away from the polls. The laws clearly had provided that the new documents were to be ratified by a majority of registered voters. In March 1868, Congress ruled that the new constitutions could be ratified by merely a majority of voters, no matter how small the turnout.

State conventions dominated by Radical Republicans met in ten southern states in 1868. Blacks participated in every state convention, though they formed a majority only in South Carolina (See chart on next page.).

The new constitutions, the most progressive the South had ever known, were similar to those in effect in the rest of the nation except for the articles guaranteeing civil rights for blacks, establishing universal manhood suffrage, and disqualifying ex-Confederates from voting or holding public office. Some documents introduced more equitable systems of legislative apportionment and made appointive offices elective. Most of these constitutions encouraged state support of education, the poor, and the physically and mentally handicapped. Other

An interracial jury in the South during Reconstruction.

State Convention	Delegates			
	Black	White	Total	% Black
Alabama	18	90	108	17
Arkansas	8	58	66	12
Florida	18	27	45	40
Georgia	33	137	170	19
Louisiana	49	49	98	50
Mississippi	17	83	100	17
North Carolina	15	118	133	11
South Carolina	76	48	124	61
Virginia	25	80	105	24
Texas	9	81	90	10

Based on W. E. B. DuBois, *Black Reconstruction in America* (New York: Atheneum, 1969 reprint), p. 372.

subjects addressed by the various constitutional conventions included the rights of women, reform of penal codes, and establishment of a more equitable tax structure. Indeed, the new constitution adopted in South Carolina was that state's first truly democratic frame of government.

By June 1868, seven states satisfied the requirements and their representatives were readmitted to Congress: Arkansas, Alabama, Florida, Georgia, Louisiana, North Carolina, and South Carolina. Early in 1869, Congress proposed the Fifteenth Amendment to the Constitution, which barred any state from depriving a citizen of his right to vote because of race, color, or previous condition of servitude. By 1870, Mississippi, Texas, and Virginia were restored to the Union. Admission of these states was delayed because of their refusal to approve constitutional clauses disenfranchising ex-Confederates, but these states were finally readmitted following their ratification of the Fifteenth Amendment. Georgia, first admitted in 1868, was returned to military rule by Congress after whites there expelled duly elected blacks from the state legislature. The state was readmitted in 1870 only after the Reconstruction Acts and the Fourteenth Amendment were fully enforced there; Georgia also had to ratify the Fifteenth Amendment and to seat expelled black legislators.

In essence, the era of congressional Reconstruction was relatively brief. Within a short time, the former Confederate states were back in the Union and their governments once more were being directed by old-line conservatives. There were, however, several exceptions to this general picture: Tennessee was restored to the Union in July 1866 before congressional Reconstruction began; conservatives were in power in Virginia before its readmission; and three states (Florida, Louisiana, and South Carolina) experienced a measure of military rule until after the disputed election of 1876.

Congress versus President Johnson

The anti-Johnson Republican victories in the 1866 congressional elections enabled the Radicals to

Between 1869 and 1901, two blacks served in the U.S. Senate and twenty in the House of Representatives. This illustration shows those serving in the Forty-first and Forty-second Congress, 1869–1873.

State	Readmitted to Union	Conservatives Win Control
Alabama	June 25, 1868	November 14, 1874
Arkansas	June 22, 1868	November 10, 1874
Florida	June 25, 1868	January 2, 1877
Georgia	July 15, 1870	November 1, 1871
Louisiana	June 25, 1868	January 2, 1877
Mississippi	February 23, 1870	November 3, 1875
North Carolina	June 25, 1868	November 3, 1870
South Carolina	June 25, 1868	November 12, 1876
Tennessee	July 24, 1866	October 4, 1869
Texas	March 30, 1870	January 14, 1873
Virginia	January 26, 1870	October 5, 1869

Based on John Hope Franklin, *Reconstruction: After the Civil War* (Chicago: University of Chicago Press, 1961), p. 231.

override President Johnson's vetos of their Reconstruction Acts. Radical Republican leaders next sought to take advantage of their increased strength to weaken Johnson's ability to thwart their measures. Between 1866 and 1868, the Radicals passed several acts that increased congressional control over the military, over the process of amending the Constitution, and over presidential appointments. Congress even sought to prevent the Supreme Court from declaring its Reconstruction Acts unconstitutional by limiting the Court's jurisdiction over civil rights cases.

Passage of the Tenure of Office Act in March 1867 precipitated a final confrontation between Congress and the President. This law prohibited Johnson from removing officials appointed by and with the advice and consent of the Senate without that body's approval. Designed to prevent Johnson from undermining the Radicals by using his patronage power against them, it also was an attempt to keep him from removing Secretary of War Stanton, the only member of the Cabinet still in sympathy with the Radicals. Johnson decided to test the constitutionality of these inroads into executive authority. While Congress was in recess in the summer of 1867, he dismissed Stanton. In close communication with the Radicals, Stanton barricaded himself in his office and refused to leave.

Johnson's attempt to oust Stanton outraged Congress. On February 24, 1868, the House of Representatives voted to impeach the President for "high crimes and misdeameanors." Strictly speaking, Johnson had done nothing to justify such a drastic procedure, but the Radicals were convinced that he meant to sabotage their programs, and some felt that he actually was planning to return ex-Confederates and Copperheads to power. In addition to his alleged violation of the Tenure of Office Act, the Radicals charged Johnson with attempting to bring disgrace and ridicule upon Congress. Yet only after Congress had decided to impeach Johnson did it actually appoint a committee to prepare the articles of impeachment. In the eyes of many congressmen, Johnson unquestionably was unsuited for office and assembling a list of his misdemeanors constituted, as it were, only an afterthought.

President Johnson's trial lasted from late March to mid-May, 1868. According to constitutional provisions, Chief Justice Salmon P. Chase (1808–1873) presided over the Senate proceedings. Chase was a strong advocate of black suffrage. Despite his

A ticket of admission to the impeachment trial of President Andrew Johnson.

sympathies for the Radicals, he soon was accused by members of Congress of being in Johnson's party. In fact, Chase questioned the constitutionality of the Tenure of Office Act and the procedures of the Senate; his avowed purpose was to sustain the integrity of the Supreme Court and prevent Congress from reducing the Chief Justice to a mere figurehead in the proceedings.

On May 16, 1868, the Senate voted on whether or not Johnson had committed high misdemeanors as charged. The vote was 35 for conviction and 19 for acquittal, *one* vote short of the two-thirds necessary for conviction. Voting for acquittal were seven Republicans and twelve Democrats, who did not wish to convict Johnson for dismissing a cabinet member whom he had not even appointed. Following the impeachment trial, Stanton resigned his office, and Congress adjourned.

The Election of 1868

A few days after Johnson's acquittal, the Republican national convention met in Chicago to prepare for the 1868 presidential campaign. On the first ballot the Republicans nominated General Ulysses S. Grant, the Union war hero. Indiana Radical Schuyler Colfax (1823–1885), former Speaker of the House, was selected as Grant's running mate. The Republican platform condemned Johnson and the Democratic party, and praised the Reconstruction Acts of Congress. It equivocated, however, on the question of black suffrage by calling for it in the South but stating that the "question of suffrage in all of the loyal states properly belongs to the people of those states."

The Radicals attracted a number of formidable enemies by insisting on black suffrage. This issue not only divided Republicans but became the rallying point for unity among Democrats who attacked the incumbents for advocating the "Africanization" of the South and black equality for the rest of the nation. In fact, Grant himself had little sympathy with the Radical view of racial relations. He lived much of his life in border states and was married to a Missouri lady whose father, an unreconstructed rebel, declared that the President really was "a good Democrat but did not know it."

The Democrats convened in New York on July 4. After considerable political maneuvering, the delegates nominated Horatio Seymour (1810–1886), a former governor of New York, as their candidate and Francis P. Blair, Jr. (1821–1875), a Unionist from Kentucky, as his running mate.

Throughout the campaign, the Republicans again made "the bloody shirt of the rebellion" their primary campaign issue. (Invoking the Democrats' role in the Civil War remained a standard Republican tactic for many years to come.) The result in 1868 was an easy electoral victory for Grant, 214 to 80, though the popular vote was much closer: 3,013,360 to 2,708,744 (52.7 percent to 47.3 percent). Interestingly, Grant's popular margin of slightly over 300,000 votes was provided by more than 500,000 black voters who were mostly southern blacks enfranchised by the Reconstruction Acts. Viewed in this light, it can be argued that Seymour was the choice of a majority of white voters both North and South. Indeed, the closeness of the vote in such states as Indiana (where Grant won by only about 10,000 votes) and New York (where he lost by a similar number) convinced many Republicans that their continued political hegemony necessitated enfranchising blacks in the North as well as in the South.

The Fifteenth Amendment

Ratification of the Fourteenth Amendment in July 1868 should have given black males throughout the nation the right to vote, but this extension of suffrage met considerable opposition in the North. Nevertheless, on February 27, 1869, Congress passed the Fifteenth Amendment to the Constitution, which forbade *any* state to deprive any citizen of his vote because of race, color, or previous condition of servitude (no mention was made of sex). The result was a vigorous fight, since voters in Connecticut, Ohio, Michigan, Minnesota, and Kansas had rejected proposals for black suffrage after the Civil War. Indeed, ratification of the Amendment in March 1870 was assured only by the support of southern states. Ironically, four of the southern states listed as ratifying the Amendment (Texas, Mississippi, Virginia, and Georgia) had not yet been fully restored to the Union by Congress when they participated in the task of amending the Constitution.

Blacks and former abolitionists praised the passage of the Fifteenth Amendment, yet failure to put the supervision of elections under federal control eventually allowed Southerners to subvert the law. Blacks in the South found they were denied the vote on technicalities; thus there was no effective way of securing true national suffrage. Only in the twentieth century was the Amendment invoked by the Supreme Court to strike down discriminatory practices.

The South under Radical Rule

The eleven states of the former Confederacy were under the control of the Radical Republicans during all or part of the decade between 1867 and 1877. The legend of "Black Reconstruction" enunciated by conservative Southerners and propagated by prosouthern historians claims that a Radical coalition of carpetbaggers, scalawags, and blacks ruined the South. Members of this coalition, according to this interpretation, increased state and local taxes until they nearly ruined the white property holding class. The governments controlled by the coalition were corrupt and wasteful. Indeed, they incurred shocking increases in state debts and brought some states to the edge of bankruptcy. Finally, according to the proponents of this view, the governments run by this coalition were destroying southern civilization by Africanizing it.

In the last twenty years historians have done much to correct this distorted picture of Reconstruction. Admittedly, the carpetbaggers were recent northern settlers who actively supported the Radicals. But many were simply experienced frontier promoters and developers who moved South rather than West. Reconstruction, in other words entailed a diversion of the frontier movement into the relatively undeveloped South. A large number of so-called "carpetbaggers" (so named because they could supposedly carry all their assets in a satchel made of carpeting) were Union Army veterans who believed the South was a land of opportunity. Hostile southern whites included among the carpetbaggers all the teachers, clergymen, and officers of the Freedmen's Bureau as well as many other agents of charitable organizations sent to relieve and give aid to the blacks. Some of these men and women were motivated by personal gain, some by humanitarianism, and some by a combination of both. There were, undeniably, some plunderers and parasites who fitted the stereotype invented by Southerners, but no matter how carpetbaggers behaved, southern whites denounced them as corrupt. The real complaint, however, was that these Northerners were organizing blacks for political action.

Most white Southerners were especially contemptuous of groups such as the Union League. Organized in the North in 1862 to bolster sagging wartime morale, the League demanded unconditional loyalty to the Union. Although some groups remained largely social, others became blatantly political and, with peace, embraced the Radical cause. Agents who went south at first were welcomed by upland Unionists who wanted to use the League to wrest power from lowland aristocrats; however, admission of blacks to membership provoked controversy and by 1870 the Union League (also called the Loyal League) ceased to exert influence in the South.

According to the southern version of Radical Reconstruction, degraded poor whites and other opportunists betrayed the South and aided the Radical Republicans. These so-called scalawags actually consisted of four distinct groups. First, there were the southern Unionists, who had suffered severe persecution from their Confederate neighbors during the war and who now wanted retaliation for their grievances; this group usually scorned equal rights for blacks. Second, there was a group of poor white yeoman farmers who hoped for the confiscation of the rich planters' lands. Third, were those southern entrepreneurs who favored Republican economic policies and hoped to bring industry to the South. Fourth, there was a group of upperclass Southerners previously affiliated with the Whigs; they believed they could control the black voters and thus gain power at the expense of their old political foes, the Democrats, whom they especially distrusted.

Southern blacks constituted the third element in the Radical coalition. Blacks had some influence in all the southern Radical governments but controlled none of them. Contrary to the charges advanced by southern conservatives, at *no* time were blacks in control of any southern state during Radical Reconstruction. Moreover, blacks developed their own leadership and seldom were vindictive in their use of political power or in their treatment of southern whites. Their goal was equal political rights, not subjugation or vengeance. Among prominent black leaders was Robert Smalls of Beaufort, South Carolina. (For an account of his interesting life as a slave, naval hero, legislator, and spokesman for his race see the biographical sketch later in this chapter.

The Radical coalitions in the South brought about more equitable tax systems, the promotion of physical reconstruction, the expansion of state railroad systems, the increase of public services, and the creation or expansion of public school systems.

Southern conservatives and their later apologists contended that the carpetbaggers, scalawags, and blacks brought economic chaos to the South. Corruption did flourish in some of the new governments. Legislators awarded themselves high salaries and padded their expense accounts. The high cost of state government admittedly arose from corruption. Yet blame for such activities must be carefully assessed. The highest cost of state government arose, for example, from corruption connected with railroad construction and railroad subsidies, and in these ventures Democrats participated fully as much as Republicans. And corruption was evident in the post-Reconstruction governments as much or more than those of the Radical Republicans. Radical rule may have had its shortcomings, but it was not synonymous with incompetence and wrongdoing. On the contrary, the Radical governments were the most democratic the South had ever known. The basic grievance of white conservatives who attacked the Radical governments was not really against corruption, but against a tolerant race policy. The conservatives who "redeemed" the South viewed themselves as the saviors of southern democracy, but they were willing to relegate poor whites and blacks to political obscurity.

Moreover, contrary to the charges of contemporary southern conservatives, the presence of blacks, scalawags, and carpetbaggers in government was not in itself the source of corruption. The South was being affected by the same forces disturbing the rest of the country. The social disorganization that accompanied the war hit the de-

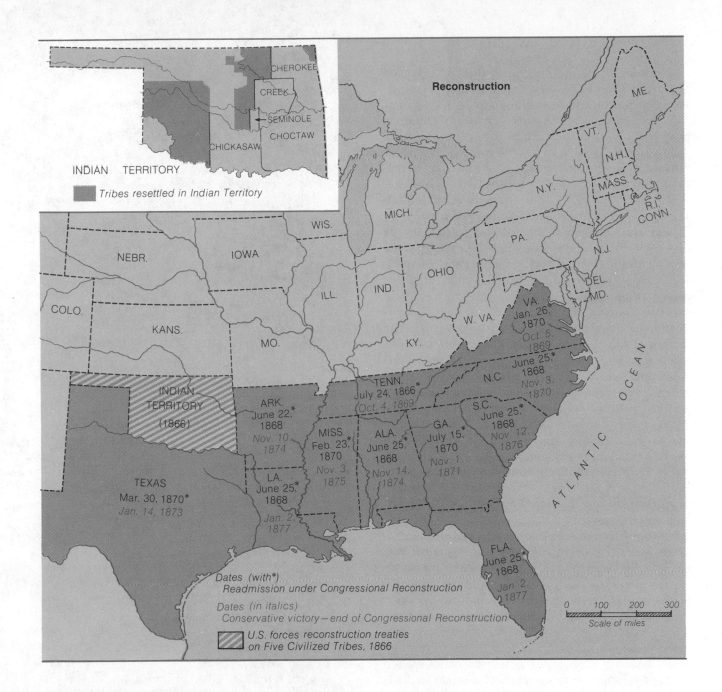

INDIAN TERRITORY

Tribes resettled in Indian Territory

CHEROKEE

CREEK

SEMINOLE

CHICKASAW CHOCTAW

ME.

VT.

N.H.

N.Y. MASS.

R.I. CONN.

MICH.

WIS.

PA.

N.J.

NEBR. IOWA

DEL.
MD.

OHIO

COLO. ILL. IND.

KANS. MO. KY. W. VA.

VA.
Jan. 26,
1870
Oct. 5,
1869

INDIAN TERRITORY (1866)

ARK.
June 22,*
1868
Nov. 10,
1874

TENN.
July 24, 1866*
Oct. 4, 1869

N.C.
June 25,*
1868
Nov. 3,
1870

MISS.
Feb. 23,*
1870
Nov. 3,
1875

ALA.
June 25,*
1868
Nov. 14,
1874

GA.
July 15,*
1870
Nov. 1,
1871

S.C.
June 25,*
1868
Nov. 12,
1876

TEXAS
Mar. 30, 1870*
Jan. 14, 1873

LA.
June 25,*
1868
Jan. 2,
1877

FLA.
June 25*
1868
Jan. 2,
1877

ATLANTIC OCEAN

Dates (with *)
Readmission under Congressional Reconstruction

Dates (in italics)
Conservative victory—end of Congressional Reconstruction

U.S. forces reconstruction treaties
on Five Civilized Tribes, 1866

0   100   200   300
Scale of miles

feated South with particular severity, but postwar economic expansion was dominated by entrepreneurs whose loose standards of public morality infected contemporary politicians above the Mason-Dixon line as well.

Grantism and National Disgrace

Ulysses S. Grant came to the White House in March 1869 with little prior political experience and few direct ties to any faction. It was only when he broke with President Johnson in 1867 during the controversy over the dismissal of Secretary of War Stanton that the Radicals began to view Grant with favor. Lacking administrative experience outside of the military, Grant ran his office with the aid of a military staff. He failed to consult with party leaders in Congress and ended up, through inept appointments to important offices and poor decisions, alienating some Republicans and naming several scoundrels to high positions.

Perhaps the most notorious scandal involved the Crédit Mobilier, a construction company that helped build the Union Pacific Railroad. That company, owned by a few Union Pacific stockholders, received fraudulent contracts from the railroad, enabling it to pocket huge sums, some of which came from federal subsidies. To thwart a government inquiry, the company gave Crédit Mobilier stock to key politicians, among them, Schuyler Colfax, who later became Grant's Vice President.

Exposure of the Crédit Mobilier scandal by the *New York Sun* in September 1872 cast an ugly shadow upon Grant's bid for reelection in 1872. Joining the Democrats in their distrust of Grant were a number of Liberal Republicans (as those who favored civil service reform and opposed corruption in government came to be known). The election of 1872 saw an attempt at coalition between Democrats and Liberal Republicans. The Liberal movement, which was a conservative movement by modern definitions of the word, was composed of political neophytes. The nomination of Horace Greeley, well-known editor of the *New York Tribune,* as the Liberal party's candidate for President not only shocked the Democrats, but stunned many within Liberal Republican ranks as well. Yet, Democratic leaders, anxious to overtake the Republicans, gambled and endorsed the impulsive and unpredictable Greeley.

The result of the election was a second term for Grant, which proved even more reprehensible than the first. On March 3, 1873, just one day before his second inauguration, Congress approved a bill that doubled the President's salary and raised other government salaries, including their own. Grant signed the bill. Public indignation against the so-called "Salary Grab Act" led to a repeal of portions of the law less than a year later. To make matters worse, Grant's private secretary, General Orville E. Babcock, was indicted in 1875 for involvement in a whiskey ring that defrauded the government of the tax on whiskey. Then Secretary of War William Belknap (1829–1890) resigned from office in 1876 under threat of impeachment because of charges that he had accepted bribes from an Indian trader. Corruption in office appeared to be rampant.

Similar conditions were evident at the state and municipal levels. New York's William Marcy Tweed (1823–1878) was an infamous example of

Robert Smalls

1839–1916

Born a slave in Beaufort, South Carolina, Smalls obtained some basic education with his master's help and in 1851 moved with that family to Charleston. There he worked as a hotel waiter, hack driver, and ship rigger; at the age of seventeen he was permitted to marry the woman of his own choice, Hannah, who died in 1883.

In 1861 Confederate authorities pressed Smalls into service on the *Planter*, a large steam vessel used to supply ordnance and other materials to forts in Charleston harbor. Laying his plans carefully, at about 3:00 A.M. on May 13, 1862, he assumed command of the ship (despite orders to the contrary, all of the white officers were ashore). Together with his wife, his two small children, and a dozen black crewmen, Smalls sailed unmolested past the guns of Fort Sumter and out to the open sea. There he received a hero's welcome as he joined up with the federal blockade. As a reward he was given part of the prize money granted for the *Planter* and a job as a pilot in the U.S. Navy. His knowledge of Charleston Harbor and its fortifications was of great service to the Union Navy.

On December 1, 1863, Smalls added to his laurels when the captain of the *Planter* panicked in the face of heavy enemy fire. The youthful pilot promptly took over the vessel and guided it to safety, an exploit that won him permanent command of the *Planter* and the rank of captain, a position he held until the ship was decommissioned in 1866. Smalls was the only black man who served at that rank during the Civil War.

Meanwhile, in 1864 he represented the Port Royal, South Carolina, area at the Republican-National-Union Convention in Baltimore, Maryland. He was one of three blacks and thirteen whites in the South Carolina delegation that was seated but never officially recognized by the convention. Four years later in 1868 he helped draw up a new state constitution for South Carolina.

A moderate in racial matters, affable, poised, and good-humored, Smalls won the begrudging respect of the Reconstruction whites who found him less objectionable than some of his black associates. Following six years in the South Carolina legislature, he won in 1874 a seat in the U.S. House of Representatives where he served for nearly a dozen years—elected four times, defeated three times. Despite a bribery conviction in 1877 (for which he was pardoned a year or so later) and a bitterly contested election in 1880 (in which he finally was declared the winner in July 1882), Robert Smalls proved to be one of the most resilient of Reconstruction black politicos. A thoroughly partisan Republican, he opposed civil service reform, favored pension bills, and worked for equal accommodation for blacks on interstate conveyances.

In 1890 Smalls was one of six black delegates to another state constitutional convention, this one called to legalize Jim Crow and ballot box discrimination. Because whites planned to codify a ban on racial intermarriage in effect since 1879, Smalls proposed an amendment denying public office to whites who were found guilty of cohabiting with blacks and decreeing that the children of such unions receive the same paternal recognition—name and inheritance—as accorded legitimate children. This caused much consternation and was voted down.

From 1899 to 1913 Smalls served under three Republican presidents as duty collector of the port of Beaufort. An able, brave individual, somewhat hampered by his lack of formal training, he was an exceptional black man, one who led a full and varied life as a slave, naval hero, legislator, and spokesman for his race.

political corruption. His organization, Tammany Hall, dominated Manhattan politics from the late 1850s until 1871. It is estimated that he and his ring filched between $30 million and $200 million during their regime.

The public reaction to Grantism greatly aided Democrats. In the 1874 congressional elections, they regained control of the House of Representatives for the first time since before the Civil War, improved their standing in the Senate, and won control in many states. These accomplishments were clear signals that Radical Reconstruction was coming to an end.

The End of Reconstruction Politics

In the 1860s and the 1870s, many southern whites perceived blacks as a threat to their economic security and dominant status. White Southerners used a variety of methods to "redeem" the South from Republicanism and black rule. They joined a number of secret terrorist societies such as the Ku Klux Klan (the KKK), the Knights of the White Camelia, the Pale Faces, and the Shotgun Club. The Klan, founded in Pulaski, Tennessee, in the winter of 1865–1866, was the most notorious of these organizations.

Redeeming the South—The KKK
Originally organized as a social club, the KKK was soon transformed into a powerful political organization. Ex-Confederate General Nathan Bedford Forrest (1821–1877) became "Grand Wizard of the Empire" in 1867. "Realms," or state organizations headed by "Grand Dragons," began to appear throughout the South in the late 1860s. By such tactics as night rides of white-robed and hooded men to frighten the allegedly superstitious blacks, by physical violence and by keeping blacks from the polls, the KKK sought to overthrow Radical rule. In

K.K.Klan Ala 1868

Rutherford B. Hayes Library.

The Ku Klux Klan used physical violence to keep blacks from voting and to overthrow Radical Republican rule.

Born of the night, and vanish by day;
Leaguers and niggers, get out of the way!

Quoted in E. Merton Coulter, *The South During Reconstruction 1865–1877* (Baton Rouge: Louisiana State University Press, 1947), pp. 167–168.

The violence that ensued not only offended northern public opinion, but also led to the withdrawal of the more respectable members of the KKK. In 1869 Imperial Wizard Forrest ordered the dissolution of the organization. One problem the Klan faced from the outset was lawlessness and crime committed in its name by those who took advantage of their anonymity to pillage and steal. Shortly after Forrest told members to disband, Congress passed the first of several Enforcement Acts designed to protect blacks. These measures provided for federal supervision of elections and, in time, specifically declared the KKK an illegal organization. They also gave the President power to suspend the writ of habeas corpus and to proclaim martial law in areas where unlawful combinations were inciting "rebellion." In 1871 Grant used this authority to quell unrest, notably in North and South Carolina. Meanwhile, Congress held hearings in Washington and sent committees scurrying about the South to investigate the Klan. Despite passage of the Enforcement Acts, the congressional probes of the KKK, and indictment of several thousand suspected Klan members, few convictions were obtained. In 1894 Congress repealed many of the Enforcement Acts.

addition to blacks, the chief targets of the KKK also included the carpetbaggers, scalawags, and the Union Leaguers. The *Southern Enterprise* of Greenville, South Carolina, published the following warning to these groups in April 1868:

Niggers and leaguers, get out of the way,
We're born of the night and we vanish by day.
No rations have we, but the flesh of man—
And love niggers best—the Ku Klux Klan;
We catch 'em alive and roast 'em whole,
Then hand 'em around with a sharpened pole.
Whole Leagues have been eaten, not leaving a man,
And went away hungry—the Ku Klux Klan;

Alabama Department of Archives and History.
A Ku Klux Klan warning to carpetbaggers.

In retrospect, the rise of the Ku Klux Klan had both immediate and long-range effects. Federal investigations into its activities brought to light often chaotic conditions in the South, paving the way for changes (largely on southern terms), and the work of the Klan left a legacy of violence directed at keeping blacks and "outsiders" in subservient roles. Klan terrorism (or the threat of it) weakened the will of those white Republicans who had little sympathy for racial equality. The net result was that conservatives regained control of the state political machinery in Tennessee (1869), Virginia (1870), North Carolina (1870), and Georgia (1871). By 1874 Southerners elsewhere were openly using economic pressure and physical violence to keep blacks from exercising their right to vote. By the autumn of 1876, only Florida, South Carolina, and Louisiana were still under Republican rule.

The Contested Election of 1876

Looking for a reform candidate to help overcome the criticism that they were the party of "Grantism," Republicans nominated Governor Rutherford B. Hayes (1822–1893) of Ohio as their presidential candidate. Hayes was a former Union Army general whose military service was varied and capable but not very distinguished. In addition, he had served a brief term in Congress (1864–1867) before his election to the governorship of Ohio. In that office he proved to be an astute politician and acquired a reputation as an honest and courageous administrator.

The Democrats nominated Governor Samuel J. Tilden (1814–1886) of New York as their candidate. Tilden, who was a corporation lawyer, had opposed the election of Lincoln and disapproved of the war from the beginning. In 1866 he became chairman of the Democratic state committee and gained a reputation as a reform politician. He played a prominent role in bringing about the fall of Boss Tweed's corrupt machine in New York City and, as governor after 1874, made a good reform candidate.

Democrat Tilden received a popular margin in the presidential election of over 250,000 votes. The Republicans, however, refused to concede Tilden's election and claimed that the returns in Florida, Louisiana, and South Carolina were in dispute. Both the Democrats and Republicans sent representatives to watch the official election count in these critical states. The situation in all three states was similar. Republicans, in control of the state governments and the election machinery, relied upon the black masses for votes and practiced widespread frauds. By threats, intimidation, and even violence, Democrats kept blacks from the polls and, where possible, also resorted to fraud. Although the efforts of white conservatives made a full and fair *vote* impossible, Republican control of the states made a fair vote *count* impossible.

On January 29, 1877, with Inauguration Day in early March quickly approaching, Congress created an Electoral Commission to settle the disputed election. The original plan called for the selection of seven Republicans and seven Democrats, while the fifteenth member was to be Supreme Court Justice David Davis, an independent. Davis became ineligible, however, when he resigned from the Court to become a senator from Illinois. A Republican justice was then appointed to fill his place on the commission which, by a vote of 8 to 7, proceeded to support the Republicans in each disputed state election. On March 2, 1877, a final count gave Hayes the victory by one electoral vote, a decision that was approved by the Senate, and Hayes, after one of the most disputed and uncertain elections in the nation's history, was inaugurated three days later.

The Compromise of 1877

In order to secure southern support for the decisions of the Electoral Commission, the Republicans made three basic pledges: (1) they would withdraw federal troops from the South; (2) they would be fair to Southerners when it came time to distribute federal patronage and make sure a Southerner would be appointed to Hayes's Cabinet; and (3) they would provide federal funds for internal improvements in the South. In return, southern Democrats acquiesced in the election of Hayes and promised to deal fairly with blacks.

Both the South and the North were in a severe depression in the winter of 1876–1877. Unemployment provoked radical labor groups into a violent mood portending insurrectionary rioting. Among the Republicans, deep concern for the privileges promised by various new statutes regarding money, banks, tariffs, land, and railroads overshadowed whatever civil libertarian sentiments still remained among them. In addition, both parties feared that the election crisis would result in violence reminiscent of the crisis of 1860–1861.

The South's extreme poverty and desperate need for capital, coupled with its longstanding hatred for the remaining carpetbaggers, were primary causes for the cooperation between southern

Democrats and Republicans. In return for the promise of state autonomy over civil rights, for a share of the federal patronage, and for access to federal funds, Southerners agreed to the election of Hayes. Upon entering office, Hayes appointed David M. Key of Tennessee, who had served in the Confederate Army, as Postmaster General and ordered the withdrawal of federal troops from all former Confederate states. The Compromise of 1877 signaled the end of Radical Reconstruction and the "redemption" of the South.

Reconstruction in Retrospect

Although Republicans retained the White House in 1877 and a basis for sectional reconciliation was laid, both achievements were accomplished at the expense of the black people of the South. In the rural South, sharecropping and debt peonage replaced slavery. Despite the Fourteenth and Fifteenth Amendments, whites in the "redeemed" South denied blacks civil and political rights.

Several factors help to explain why the North abandoned southern blacks. Many Radicals had died or retired. Others showed little concern or understanding of the problems of the ex-slaves. Indeed, as immigrants from southern and eastern Europe poured into America in the 1870s, many old middle class families—with whom most Radicals identified—came to view the problems of southern whites in a new light. Although some Republican congressmen continued to push for civil rights laws, the Congress, the Supreme Court, and the executive branch increasingly turned their attention to other issues. A new group of Republican leaders with ties to industrialists was emerging. Consequently, economic development in the South rather than the promotion of black suffrage there increasingly received greater attention.

By the 1870s, the Republicans no longer needed southern black votes to win elections. The states of the Old Northwest, which had consistently voted Democratic before 1860, were now Republican strongholds. The growth of urban industrial centers in this region had helped to align it with the industrial Northeast and the Republican party. In the

eleven presidential elections between 1868 and 1908, the states of the Old Northwest went Republican eight times. All of these factors contributed to the demise of idealism and zeal for social reform engendered by the antislavery crusade. The Republican party was becoming a party of the status quo.

Ironically, neither the Republican party's abandonment of southern blacks to local white rule by the Compromise of 1877 nor congressional repeal of the Force Acts in 1894 necessarily alienated northern blacks from the party. Frederick Douglass, for example, continued to assure blacks that the Republican party was their party.

Southern Segregation

Historians still disagree about the origins and development of widespread segregation. Clearly, there was de facto segregation in parts of the South soon after emancipation, but it is disputed whether this pattern prevailed throughout the South. Jim Crow laws (the term is derived from white minstrel songs stereotyping blacks), which made segregation a rigid institution everywhere in the South, emerged only in the 1890s.

Segregation had appeared in southern cities before the Civil War as a mosaic of customs, ordinances, state laws, public pressures, and convenience intended to serve as a means of social control over slaves who often performed various services without close supervision. The avowed goal of antebellum segregation was to prevent fraternization between whites and blacks, and between slaves and free blacks. During the period of congressional Reconstruction, some Radicals such as Charles Sumner hoped that the due process and equal protection clauses of the Fourteenth Amendment would protect the civil and personal rights of the former slaves. In order to guarantee blacks "the full and equal enjoyment of the accommodations . . . of inns, public conveyances on land or water, theatres, and other places of public amusement" and to "mete out equal and exact justice to all," Congress passed the Civil Rights Act of 1875.

Southerners denied that Congress had the right to interfere with matters that were supposedly purely social, and the Supreme Court supported this contention. The Court held in *Hall* v. *De Cuir* (1878) that a state law forbidding discrimination on public carriers was an undue burden on interstate commerce. In the *Civil Rights Cases* of 1883, the Supreme Court declared the Civil Rights Act of 1875 unconstitutional and ruled that the federal government had no legal jurisdiction over discrimination practiced by individuals or private organizations. The federal government had jurisdiction only over the invasion of civil rights by states.

The Thirteenth, Fourteenth, and Fifteenth Amendments had ended slavery, pledged equal protection of the laws and due process, and guaranteed black *males* their voting rights. Yet blacks were denied these rights by spurious arguments, devious subterfuge, and extralegal coercion. They were, in truth, only half-emancipated.

Indian Territory

After the Civil War, not only the eleven former states of the Confederacy but the Five Civilized Tribes also underwent a reconstruction process.

Following the collapse of the Confederacy, the tribes living in Indian Territory (present-day Oklahoma) were subjected to new federal policies. Although large segments of the Creeks, Seminoles, and Cherokees had remained steadfastly loyal to the Union, other members of these tribes as well as the Chickasaws and the Choctaws ultimately joined the Confederacy.

The Five Civilized Tribes signed Reconstruction treaties with the federal government in 1866. All five tribes soon recovered from the hard times that "the white man's war" brought to Indian Territory. The mixed bloods, with the aid of hired laborers who replaced their slaves, rebuilt their homes, and raised livestock and were soon relatively prosperous once more. The full bloods also

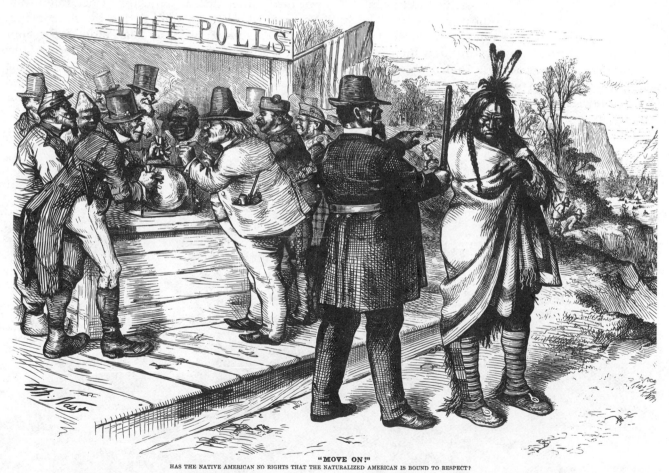

"MOVE ON!"
HAS THE NATIVE AMERICAN NO RIGHTS THAT THE NATURALIZED AMERICAN IS BOUND TO RESPECT?

The New York Public Library, Picture Collection.
This Reconstruction cartoon depicts blacks and immigrants at the ballot box, while an Indian is being rudely pushed away.

returned to their homes and resumed a subsistence agriculture. With the signing of the treaties in 1866 and the subsequent restoration of their annuities, the tribes reopened their schools for the first time in five years.

But the Reconstruction treaties provided a convenient opportunity for the federal government to attempt to achieve two long sought goals: (1) the reduction of tribal land holdings; and (2) the establishment of a territorial government over the Indians in order to regulate their activities. The latter effort failed, but the first goal was accomplished. The Reconstruction treaties of 1866 took away nearly one-half of the domain previously granted the Five Civilized Tribes "in perpetuity" under the removal policy of the Jacksonian era. In essence, the Reconstruction treaties were used as a means to circumvent the old removal treaties and concentrate other tribes in the territory guaranteed to the Five Civilized Tribes, thus releasing additional land for white settlement in other states as well as in Indian Territory. The treaties also forced the tribes to allow railroads to pass through their territory with tragic consequences. Their land lost its alleged protection from white society as railroad promoters, lawless and disorderly railroad crews, and many unscrupulous whites preyed on them.

Reconstruction was both a unique and tragic experience for the Five Civilized Tribes, and the treaties of 1866 served as a convenient means of reasserting social control over the Indians, regardless of whether they had been "loyal" or "disloyal" to the Union.

Women's Rights

During the Civil War, American feminists generally subordinated their own programs to an all-out effort to abolish slavery. In return, they expected the support of the abolitionists in the campaign to enfranchise women. But that did not happen. Some abolitionist leaders, like Wendell Phillips, believed that merging women's rights and the rights of blacks would only confuse both issues in the public mind. Other politicians, eager to acquire at least two million potential Republican *male* black voters in the South, were reluctant to endanger ratification of the Fourteenth and Fifteenth Amendments and passage of civil rights legislation by incorporating women's suffrage in their bills. Indeed, the Fourteenth and Fifteenth Amendments not only failed to prohibit discrimination by sex, but the former actually highlighted sexual discrimination in federal law by reducing representation only for denial of suffrage to a man.

To some women like Susan B. Anthony

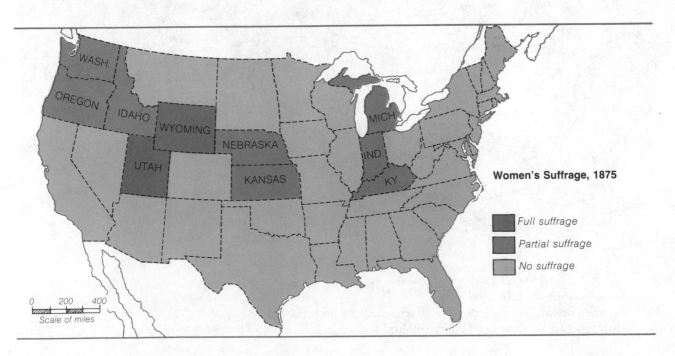

Women's Suffrage, 1875

Full suffrage
Partial suffrage
No suffrage

Victoria Claflin Woodhull

1838–1927

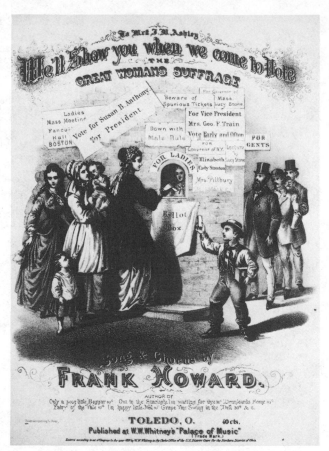

Courtesy of the American Antiquarian Society.

American feminists who subordinated their own program to an all-out effort to abolish slavery during the Civil War felt that they, as well as the freedmen, should have been enfranchised by the constitutional amendment passed during Reconstruction.

(1820–1906) and Elizabeth Cady Stanton (1815–1902) the reiteration of the word "male" three times in the Fourteenth Amendment, always in connection with the term "citizen," opened the question of whether or not women were really citizens of the United States. Nevertheless, some women did try to vote during the Reconstruction years. Virginia Louisa Minor (1824–1894) filed suit in 1872 against an election official who refused to let her vote. The Supreme Court told her that the Fourteenth Amendment did not apply to women.

In May 1869, some feminists set up the National Woman Suffrage Association to push for a

During the decade after the Civil War, the first woman to campaign for the presidency, Victoria Claflin Woodhull, flashed across the American scene like a meteor. A woman of great charm and considerable beauty, she scorned the moral code of her day, acted as if the fight for women's rights had already been won, and ended up dying at 89 much revered and very rich.

One of ten children, Victoria was born in near poverty in the country village of Homer, Ohio, not far from Columbus. Three of the children—Victoria, Tennessee Celeste, and Hebron—possessed a mix of remarkable guile, ambition, and showmanship. Along with their father, they put together a troupe that bottled and sold a variety of nostrums, including an "Elixir of Life" with Tennessee's lovely features on the label and a cancer cure concocted by brother Hebron. By the time Victoria was sixteen, she had married a young doctor named Woodhull. They had two children, one of whom, Zula Maud, was associated with some of her later enterprises in England.

In the late 1860s, Victoria and Tennessee moved to New York City. Within a short time, they captured the attention (if not the heart) of Commodore Cornelius Vanderbilt, age 74, who for a brief moment apparently considered marrying Tennessee; nevertheless, the trio remained good friends. He enjoyed their company, their dabbling in mesmerism and the occult; they, in turn, enjoyed his favors, his tips on the stock market, and above all else, his willingness to set them up as a full-fledged brokerage house: Woodhull and Claflin.

The personal relationships of the two sisters defy easy classification, but it would appear that both embraced a "free love" philosophy, while Victoria became involved with numerous reforms, including women's suffrage.

In April 1870, Victoria announced she wanted to be President, and six weeks later with the assistance of Stephen P. Andrews, a radical reformer, the first issue of *Woodhull & Claflin's Weekly* appeared. It was a "strident, eccentric, vulgar" sheet designed to propel her toward the White House, to promote feminism, a single standard of morality, and free love, and to attack injustice in all forms.

Woodhull's announcement attracted the attention of suffrage leaders, especially Elizabeth Cady Stanton and Susan B. Anthony, who were even more impressed when she wangled an invitation to address a congressional committee on the subject of women's suffrage. During 1871 she used her connection with Stanton and Anthony to pursue her candidacy for President, coming close to taking over the National Woman Suffrage Association (NWSA). Early in 1872, after Anthony forced her out of the NWSA, Woodhull formed the Equal Rights party, which nominated her for the presidency with ex-slave Frederick Douglass as her running mate. Douglass, who supported Grant, ignored the nomination, and the Equal Rights party received virtually no votes.

While Victoria was trying to unseat Ulysses S. Grant, Tennessee was using the *Weekly* to blackmail some of her boyfriends. She let it be known that the records of a famous Manhattan brothel would soon be published in its columns—names, addresses, everything. Apparently, a lot of money appeared since the brothel records were never published.

In November 1872, the *Weekly* broke the story of Preacher Henry Ward Beecher's presumed intimacies with Mrs. Theodore Tilton, a parishioner.

Tilton, who eventually sued Beecher, was a close friend of Victoria, and the trial, which ended in a hung jury, was one of the most sensational of the century. To get even, the Beechers and their friends drove the two sisters to the brink of financial ruin. Then, in 1877, two years after the trial was over, Commodore Vanderbilt died, leaving the bulk of his estate to his son William. The rest of the family contested the will, claiming that Vanderbilt was incompetent because of his involvement with the Claflin sisters. Fearful of what Tennessee and Victoria might reveal if called as witnesses, William hustled them off to England to live, presumably with a large sum of spending money. Victoria married a very rich banker; Tennessee, a prominent businessman who subsequently became a baronet.

During the next half century Victoria made some efforts to conceal her past, but nevertheless remained a vibrant, alert person. A donor of Washington's ancestral home, Sulgrave Manor, and an avid promoter of Anglo-American relations, at the age 76 she formed the Women's Aerial League of England to promote transatlantic flight and offered $5,000 to the first person to fly between America and the British Isles. Inconoclastic, dynamic, and interesting, Victoria Woodhull's life reflected much of the flamboyance of the late nineteenth and early twentieth centuries.

constitutional amendment enfranchising women, but insisted upon excluding men from its membership because the founders believed that male abolitionists had betrayed women's interests. In the same year, Susan B. Anthony and Elizabeth Cady Stanton, with the aid of an eccentric financier and Democrat, George Francis Train (1829–1904), founded a weekly newspaper, *The Revolution*, whose motto was: "Men, their rights and nothing more; women, their rights and nothing less!"

A division in the ranks of the women's movement occurred when Henry Blackwell and his wife Lucy Stone joined with others in November 1869 to establish the American Woman Suffrage Association, which worked to enfranchise women through state organization and through the efforts of women and men. In early 1870, on the anniversary of the founding of *The Revolution*, Lucy Stone began a rival publication, *Woman's Journal*. The field was too small for more than one feminist paper, and *The Revolution* failed several months later. The explanation for this schism was more economic and political than ideological. The American Woman Suffrage Association and *Woman's Journal* represented the interests of clubwomen, writers, and women in professions—in short, middle class women who were more or less conservative by feminist standards. The National Woman Suffrage Association and *The Revolution* were concerned with exploited workingwomen, social outcasts, and women who were far more radical in their political orientation.

The split between "respectability" (The American Woman Suffrage Association) and "radicalism" (The National Woman Suffrage Association) greatly weakened the women's rights movement for more than a generation. The divided groups, however, complemented each other in quietly adding new converts to the cause and in lobbying for women's suffrage at local and national levels. These accomplishments went nearly unnoticed by Americans absorbed by the economic development and social change of the 1870s and 1880s. Nevertheless, women leaders continued to press their cause, sometimes with the aid of colorful figures such as Victoria Claflin Woodhull. (A biographical sketch in this chapter highlights her very unusual and interesting life.)

Reconstruction, a decade of tension, high drama, some successes and many disappointments, left the nation a bit tired in body and spirit. As Americans celebrated the end of their first hundred

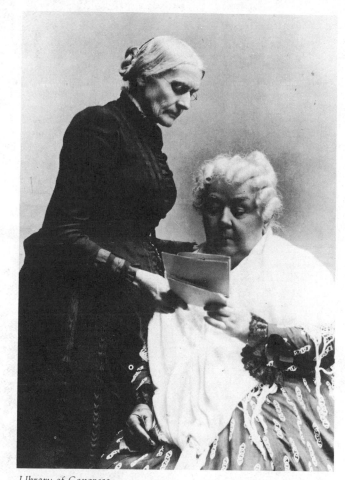

LIbrary of Congress.

In 1869 Elizabeth Cady Stanton (seated) and Susan B. Anthony organized the National Woman Suffrage Association.

years, most citizens were quite eager to put behind them the war, the turmoil in its wake, the fate of the free blacks, and, in great measure, social reform as well. Instead, they turned their energies inward to develop the West and the South, to build new industries and new factories, and to make one unified nation out of what almost had become two.

Essay

Turning Points: America Comes of Age

The five decades from 1830 to 1880 represent an era of tremendous growth and expansion in American life. The population rose from 12.8 to 50.1 million people and fourteen new states, representing a vast expanse of plains, mountains, and rich farmlands, were admitted to the Union. Politically it was a time of considerable turmoil. Parties tended to splinter and disappear to be replaced by those with new slogans and new leaders. Only three Presidents won reelection (two of them generals), and fragile compromises and hesitant accommodations at length gave way to bloodshed and confusion.

In view of these rather erratic trends, which

W. H. S.—"*Look, Uncle—there's a bully pear! let me pluck it for you.*"
Uncle Sam—"*Wait a bit, Willy—when it's ripe t'will fall into our grounds.*"

Secretary of State William H. Seward was among those Americans who cast covetous eyes on Cuba during the 1860s, as this cartoon in the October 24, 1863, issue of *Harper's Weekly* demonstrates.

were accompanied by unprecedented industrial development and substantial social change, it is somewhat difficult to see these fifty years as a unified whole. Yet even in the midst of great diversity, certain underlying themes are evident.

First and foremost, these years were dominated by internal concerns that usually related foreign affairs directly to strivings for national growth. The Oregon controversy and the Mexican War can be seen in this light, since by the time Americans of that era got down to the business of talking or shooting, they had already convinced themselves that United States soil was involved. The same can be said concerning Maine's contested Aroostook Valley, and some Southerners undoubtedly saw Cuba as a natural outlet for internal growth. After

all, if Texas and California could become states—both essentially Spanish and one of them cut off from the rest of the nation by many miles of desert and high mountains—why not Cuba? It was much closer to eastern population centers and had a long history of commercial ties to New Orleans, Charleston, and other ports of the United States.

A second major theme was the spirit of reform, so evident in virtually all realms of American life during the middle years of the nineteenth century and eventually focused in one great reform: emancipation. Inherent in any such movement seeking change are conflicting moods of doubt, misgiving, and confidence. That change was thought necessary indicates many Americans believed their forefathers had made incorrect decisions, which were now taking them down the wrong road. At the same time, in an expanding age rich with new inventions, new thought, new immigrants, these reformers were possessed with an air of confident self-assurance that they had the power, the God-given right, and the innate good sense to put things back on a proper course. Not everyone agreed, however, that they had such powers and abilities, let alone any mandate from above, or that the changes they envisioned were either necessary or beneficial. Hence, these years were marked by conflict, most notably in the Civil War.

As secessionists, the states of the Confederacy were cast in a reform mold. That armies and cannon were involved (and not solely words and proclamations)—that emancipation eventually succeeded and secession failed—should not obscure the true nature of what was happening in the 1860s. The Confederate government was a massive effort by one section of the American nation to go its own way, to alter the course of internal development according to its own viewpoint, to restore a balance which over the years the federal-state system of 1787 presumably had lost. Seen in this context, the Confederate experiment was a reform movement concerned with internal matters of vital importance to Southerners.

And there can be little doubt that both Johnny Reb and Billy Yank emerged from that four-year conflict with confidence in their abilities seriously impaired. One went down to defeat, an experience

Carl Schurz, a German-born statesman and political reformer, took up the cause of abolitionism when he emigrated to the United States in 1852. Following his service in the Union Army during the Civil War, he was active in the movement to bring new standards of honesty to the government. Here he is depicted addressing a reform conference in New York.

always damaging to individual self-esteem; the other prevailed, but only after a struggle that proved to be embarrassingly long and extremely costly. The turmoil and confusion of the Reconstruction decade that followed did little to relieve the somber mood prevalent on both sides of the Mason-Dixon line.

On the eve of the Centennial, the editor of *Scribner's Monthly* surveyed the troubled scene and suggested in very strong terms that this was an ideal moment for the United States to take stock of itself. The outcome of the Civil War indicated this was to be one nation "integral, indissoluble, indestructable." All states, he added, should defend their legitimate rights but not to a degree that makes the Union "a rope of sand" or a mere assortment of "petty nationalities." The point to remember, he continued, is that "for richer for poorer, in sickness and health, until death do us part, these United States constitute a nation; that

we are to live, grow, prosper, and suffer together, united by bands that cannot be sundered . . . and if we are to celebrate anything worth celebrating, it is the birth of a nation."

These words are indeed sober in tone, what one might call plain, straight-from-the-shoulder talk. The abrasive assertiveness of the reformers of the 1840s and 1850s is gone, and so are the exultant claims of many Americans, both North and South, who said far too much in the 1860s. In their place is a solid assessment of things as they were in 1876—not the way some Americans might have wanted them to be. After one hundred years a note of realism, instead of conflicting moods of nagging doubt and exuberant self-confidence, seemed to be creeping into the American character. That this was realism born of frustration, bloodshed, and disappointment, no one would deny, but it could be a most useful trait to develop more fully in the years ahead.

SELECTED
READINGS

General Accounts

David Donald, *Liberty and Union* (1978)

W. E. B. DuBois, *Black Reconstruction, 1860–1880* (1935)

John Hope Franklin, *Reconstruction after the Civil War* (1961)

James G. Randall and David Donald, *The Civil War and Reconstruction* (rev., 2nd ed., 1973)

Kenneth M. Stampp, *The Era of Reconstruction, 1865–1877* (1965)

Reconstruction during the Civil War

Herman Belz, *Reconstructing the Union: Theory and Policy during the Civil War* (1969)

Herman Belz, *A New Birth of Freedom: The Republican Party and Freedmen's Rights, 1861 to 1866* (1977)

William B. Hesseltine, *Lincoln's Plan of Reconstruction* (1960)

Willie L. Rose, *Rehearsal for Reconstruction: The Port Royal Experiment* (1964)

T. Harry Williams, *Lincoln and the Radicals* (1965)

Reconstruction after Appomattox

Michael Les Benedict, *A Compromise of Principle: Congressional Republicans and Reconstruction, 1863–1869* (1974)

Albert Castel, *The Presidency of Andrew Johnson* (1979)

David Donald, *Charles Sumner and the Rights of Man* (1970)

William S. McFeely, *Yankee Stepfather: General O. O. Howard and the Freedmen* (1968)

Eric L. McKitrick, *Andrew Johnson and Reconstruction* (1960)

Martin E. Mantell, *Johnson, Grant and the Politics of Reconstruction* (1973)

Donald G. Nieman, *To Set the Law in Motion: The Freedmen's Bureau and the Legal Rights of Blacks, 1865–1868* (1979)

James E. Setton, *Andrew Johnson and the Uses of Constitutional Power* (1980)

Hans L. Trefousse, *Impeachment of a President: Andrew Johnson, the Blacks, and Reconstruction* (1975)

Blacks, Indians, and Women

M. Thomas Bailey, *Reconstruction in Indian Territory: A Story of Avarice, Discrimination, and Opportunism* (1972)

Lois W. Banner, *Elizabeth Cady Stanton: A Radical for Women's Rights* (1980)

Robert Cruden, *The Negro in Reconstruction* (1969)

Elinor R. Hays, *Lucy Stone: One of America's First and Greatest Feminists* (1961)

Leon F. Litwack, *Been in the Storm So Long: The Aftermath of Slavery* (1980)

Alma Lutz, *Susan B. Anthony: Rebel, Crusader, Humanitarian* (1959)

Theda Perdue, *Nations Remembered: An Oral History of the Five Civilized Tribes, 1865–1907* (1980)

Roger L. Ramsom and Richard Sutch, *One Kind of Freedom: The Economic Consequences of Emancipation* (1977)

The End of Reconstruction

William Gillette, *Retreat from Reconstruction: A Political History 1869–1879* (1980)

Samuel P. Hirshson, *Farewell to the Bloody Shirt: Northern Republicans and the Southern Negro, 1877–1893* (1962)

Keith I. Polakoff, *The Politics of Inertia: The Election of 1876 and the End of Reconstruction* (1973)

Allen W. Trelease, *White Terror: The Ku Klux Klan Conspiracy and Southern Reconstruction* (1971)

C. Vann Woodward, *Reunion and Reaction: The Compromise of 1877 and the End of Reconstruction* (rev. ed., 1966)

C. Vann Woodward, *The Strange Career of Jim Crow* (3rd rev. ed., 1974)

Appendixes

The
Declaration
of
Independence

When in the Course of human events, it becomes necessary for one people to dissolve the political bands which have connected them with another, and to assume among the Powers of the earth, the separate and equal station to which the Laws of Nature and of Nature's God entitle them, a decent respect to the opinions of mankind requires that they should declare the causes which impel them to the separation.

We hold these truths to be self-evident, that all men are created equal, that they are endowed by their Creator with certain unalienable Rights, that among these are Life, Liberty and the pursuit of Happiness. That to secure these rights, Governments are instituted among Men, deriving their just powers from the consent of the governed, That whenever any Form of Government becomes destructive of these ends, it is the Right of the People to alter or to abolish it, and to institute new Government, laying its foundation on such principles and organizing its powers in such form, as to them shall seem most likely to effect their Safety and Happiness. Prudence, indeed, will dictate that Governments long established should not be changed for light and transient causes; and accordingly all experience hath shown, that mankind are more disposed to suffer, while evils are sufferable, than to right themselves by abolishing the forms to which they are accustomed. But when a long train of abuses and usurpations, pursuing invariably the same Object evinces a design to reduce them under absolute Despotism, it is their right, it is their duty, to throw off such Government, and to provide new Guards for their future security.—Such has been the patient sufferance of these Colonies; and such is now the necessity which constrains them to alter their former Systems of Government. The history of the present Great Britain is a history of repeated injuries and usurpations, all having in direct object the establishment of an absolute Tyranny over these States. To prove this, let Facts be submitted to a candid world.

He has refused his Assent to Laws, the most wholesome and necessary for the public good.

He has forbidden his Governors to pass Laws of immediate and pressing importance, unless suspended in their operation till his Assent should be obtained; and when so suspended, he has utterly neglected to attend to them.

He has refused to pass other Laws for the accomodation of large districts of people, unless those people would relinquish the right of Representation in the Legislature, a right inestimable to them and formidable to tyrants only.

He has called together legislative bodies at places unusual, uncomfortable, and distant from the depository of their Public Records, for the sole purpose of fatiguing them into compliance with his measures.

He has dissolved Representative Houses repeatedly, for opposing with manly firmness his invasions on the rights of the people.

He has refused for a long time, after such dissolutions, to cause others to be elected; whereby the Legislative Powers, incapable of Annihilation, have returned to the People at large for their exercise; the State remaining in the mean time exposed to all the dangers of invasion from without, and convulsions within.

He has endeavoured to prevent the population of these States; for that purpose obstructing the Laws of Naturalization of Foreigners; refusing to pass others to encourage their migration hither, and raising the conditions of new Appropriations of Lands.

He has obstructed the Administration of Justice, by refusing his Assent to Laws for establishing Judiciary Powers.

He has made Judges dependent on his Will alone, for the tenure of their offices, and the amount and payment of their salaries.

He has erected a multitude of New Offices, and sent hither swarms of Officers to harass our People, and to eat out their substance.

He has kept among us, in times of peace, Standing Armies without the Consent of our legislature.

He has affected to render the Military independent of and superior to the Civil Power.

He has combined with others to subject us to a jurisdiction foreign to our constitution, and unacknowledged by our laws; giving his Assent to their acts of pretended legislation:

For quartering large bodies of armed troops among us:

For protecting them, by a mock Trial, from Punishment for any Murders which they should commit on the Inhabitants of these States:

For cutting off our Trade with all parts of the world:

For imposing taxes on us without our Consent:

For depriving us in many cases, of the benefits of Trial by Jury:

For transporting us beyond Seas to be tried for pretended offences:

For abolishing the free System of English Laws in a neighbouring Province, establishing therein an Arbitrary government, and enlarging its Boundaries so as to render it at once an example and fit instrument for introducing the same absolute rule into these Colonies:

For taking away our Charters, abolishing our most valuable Laws, and altering fundamentally the Forms of our Governments:

For suspending our own Legislature, and declaring themselves invested with Power to legislate for us in all cases whatsoever.

He has abdicated Government here, by declaring us out of his Protection and waging War against us.

He has plundered our seas, ravaged our Coasts, burnt our towns, and destroyed the lives of our people.

He is at this time transporting large armies of foreign mercenaries to compleat the works of death, desolation and tyranny, already begun with circumstances of Cruelty & perfidy scarcely paralleled in the most barbarous ages, and totally unworthy the Head of a civilized nation.

He has constrained our fellow Citizens taken Captive on the high Seas to bear Arms against their Country, to become the executioners of their friends and Brethren, or to fall themselves by their Hands.

He has excited domestic insurrections amongst us, and has endeavoured to bring on the inhabitants of our frontiers, the merciless Indian Savages, whose known rule of warfare, is an undistinguished destruction of all ages, sexes and conditions.

In every stage of these Oppressions We have Petitioned for Redress in the most humble terms: Our repeated Petitions have been answered only by repeated injury. A Prince, whose character is thus marked by every act which may define a Tyrant, is unfit to be the ruler of a free People.

Nor have We been wanting in attention to our British brethren. We have warned them from time to time of attempts by their legislature to extend an unwarrantable jurisdiction over us. We have reminded them of the circumstances of our emigration and settlement here. We have appealed to their native justice and magnanimity, and we have conjured them by the ties of our common kindred to disavow these usurpations, which, would inevitably interrupt our connections and correspondence. They too have been deaf to the voice of justice and of consanguinity. We must, therefore, acquiesce in the necessity, which denounces our Separation, and hold them, as we hold the rest of mankind, Enemies in War, in Peace Friends.

We, therefore, the Representatives of the United States of America, in General Congress, Assembled, appealing to the Supreme Judge of the world for the rectitude of our intentions, do, in the Name, and by the Authority of the good People of these Colonies, solemnly publish and declare, That these United Colonies are, and of Right ought to be Free and Independent States; that they are Absolved from all Allegiance to the British Crown, and that all political connection between them and the State of Great Britain, is and ought to be totally dissolved; and that as Free and Independent States, they have full Power to levy War, conclude Peace, contract Alliances, establish Commerce, and to do all other Acts and Things which Independent States may of right do. And for the support of this Declaration, with a firm reliance on the Protection of Divine Providence, we mutually pledge to each other our Lives, our Fortunes and our sacred Honor.

The Constitution of the United States

We the people of the United States, in Order to form a more perfect Union, establish Justice, insure domestic Tranquility, provide for the common defense, promote the general Welfare, and secure the Blessings of Liberty to ourselves and our Posterity, do ordain and establish this CONSTITUTION for the United States of America.

ARTICLE I

Section 1. All legislative Powers herein granted shall be vested in a Congress of the United States which shall consist of a Senate and House of Representatives.

Section 2. The House of Representatives shall be composed of Members chosen every second Year by the People of the several States, and the Electors in each State shall have the Qualifications requisite for Electors of the most numerous Branch of the State Legislature.

No Person shall be a Representative who shall not have attained to the Age of twenty-five Years, and been seven Years a Citizen of the United States, and who shall not, when elected, be an inhabitant of that State in which he shall be chosen.

Representatives and direct Taxes shall be apportioned among the several States which may be included within this Union, according to their respective Numbers, which shall be determined by adding to the whole Number of free Persons, including those bound to Service for a Term of Years and excluding Indians not taxed, three fifths of all other Persons. The actual Enumeration shall be made within three Years after the first Meeting of the Congress of the United States, and within every subsequent Term of ten Years, in such Manner as they shall by Law direct. The Number of Representatives shall not exceed one for every thirty Thousand, but each State shall have at Least one Representative; and until such enumeration shall be made, the State of New Hampshire shall be entitled to chuse three, Massachusetts eight, Rhode-Island and Providence Plantations one, Connecticut five, New-York six, New Jersey four, Pennsylvania eight, Delaware one, Maryland six, Virginia ten, North Carolina five, South Carolina five, and Georgia three.

When vacancies happen in the Representation from any State, the Executive Authority thereof shall issue Writs of Election to fill such Vacancies.

The House of Representatives shall chuse their Speaker and other Officers; and shall have the sole Power of Impeachment.

Section 3. The Senate of the United States shall be composed of two Senators from each State, chosen by the Legislature thereof, for six Years; and each Senator shall have one Vote.

Immediately after they shall be assembled in Consequence of the first Election, they shall be divided as equally as may be into three Classes. The Seats of the Senators of the first Class shall be vacated at the Expiration of the second Year, of the second Class at the Expiration of the fourth Year, and of the third Class at the Expiration of the sixth Year, so that one-third may be chosen every second

Year; and if Vacancies happen by Resignation, or otherwise, during the Recess of the Legislature of any State, the Executive thereof may make temporary Appointments until the next Meeting of the Legislature, which shall then fill such Vacancies.

No Person shall be a Senator who shall not have attained to the Age of thirty Years, and been nine Years a Citizen of the United States, and who shall not, when elected, be an Inhabitant of that State in which he shall be chosen.

The Vice President of the United States shall be President of the Senate, but shall have no vote, unless they be equally divided.

The Senate shall chuse their other Officers, and also a President pro tempore, in the absence of the Vice President, or when he shall exercise the Office of the President of the United States.

The Senate shall have the sole Power to try all Impeachments. When sitting for that purpose, they shall be on Oath or Affirmation. When the President of the United States is tried, the Chief Justice shall preside; And no person shall be convicted without the Concurrence of two thirds of the Members present.

Judgment in Cases of Impeachment shall not extend further than to removal from Office, and disqualification to hold and enjoy any Office of honor, Trust, or Profit under the United States: but the Party convicted shall nevertheless be liable and subject to Indictment, Trial, Judgment, and Punishment, according to Law.

Section 4. The Times, Places and Manner of holding Elections for Senators and Representatives, shall be prescribed in each state by the Legislature thereof; but the Congress may at any time by Law make or alter such Regulations, except as to the Places of Chusing Senators.

The Congress shall assemble at least once in every Year, and such Meeting shall be on the first Monday in December, unless they shall by Law appoint a different Day.

Section 5. Each House shall be the Judge of the Elections, Returns and Qualifications of its own Members, and a Majority of each shall constitute a Quorum to do Business; but a smaller number may adjourn from day to day, and may be authorized to compel the Attendance of absent Members, in such Manner, and under such Penalties, as each House may provide.

Each House may determine the Rule of its Proceedings, punish its Members for disorderly Behavior, and with the Concurrence of two thirds, expel a Member.

Each House shall keep a Journal of its Proceedings, and from time to time publish the same, excepting such Parts as may in their Judgment require Secrecy; and the Yeas and Nays of the Members of either House on any question shall, at the Desire of one fifth of those Present, be entered on the Journal.

Neither House, during the Session of Congress, shall, without the Consent of the other, adjourn for more than three days, nor to any other Place than that in which the two Houses shall be sitting.

Section 6. The Senators and Representatives shall receive a Compensation for their Services, to be ascertained by Law, and paid out of the Treasury of the United States. They shall in all Cases, except Treason, Felony, and Breach of the Peace, be privileged from Arrest during their Attendance at the Session of their respective Houses, and in going to and returning from the same; and for any Speech or Debate in either House, they shall not be questioned in any other Place.

No Senator or Representative shall, during the Time for which he was elected, be appointed to any civil Office under the Authority of the United States, which shall been created, or the Emoluments whereof shall have been increased, during such time; and no Person holding any Office under the United States shall be a Member of either House during his continuance in Office.

Section 7. All Bills for raising Revenue shall orginate in the House of Representatives; but the Senate may propose or concur with Amendments as on other bills.

Every Bill which shall have passed the House of Representatives and the Senate, shall, before it become a Law, be presented to the President of the United States; if he approve he shall sign it, but if not he shall return it, with his Objections, to that House in which it shall have originated, who shall enter the Objections at large on their Journal, and proceed to reconsider it. If after such Reconsideration two thirds of that House shall agree to pass the bill, it shall be sent, together with the objections, to the other House, by which it shall likewise be reconsidered, and if approved by two thirds of that House, it shall become a Law. But in all such Cases the Votes of both Houses shall be determined by Yeas and Nays, and the Names of the Persons voting for and against the Bill shall be entered on the Journal of each House respectively. If any Bill shall not be returned by the President within ten Days (Sunday excepted) after it shall have been presented to him, the Same shall be a Law, in like Manner as if he had signed it, unless the Congress by their Adjournment prevent its Return, in which Case it shall not be a Law.

Every Order, Resolution, or Vote to which the Concurrence of the Senate and House of Representatives may be necessary (except on a question of Adjournment) shall be presented to the President of the United States; and before the Same shall take Effect, shall be approved by him, or being disapproved by him, shall be repassed by two thirds of the Senate and House of Representatives, according to the Rules and Limitations prescribed in the Case of a Bill.

Section 8. The Congress shall have Power To lay and collect Taxes, Duties, Imposts and Excises, to pay the Debts and provide for the common Defence and general Welfare of the United States; but all Duties, Imposts and Excises shall be uniform throughout the United States;

To borrow money on the credit of the United States;

To regulate Commerce with foreign Nations, and among the several States, and with the Indian Tribes;

To establish an uniform Rule of Naturalization, and uniform Laws on the subject of Bankruptcies throughout the United States;

To coin Money, regulate the Value thereof, and of foreign Coin, and fix the Standard of Weights and Measures;

To provide for the Punishment of counterfeiting the Securities and current Coin of the United States;

To establish Post Offices and post Roads;

To promote the Progress of Science and useful Arts, by securing for limited Times to Authors and Inventors the exclusive Right to their respective Writings and Discoveries;

To constitute Tribunals inferior to the Supreme Court;

To define and punish Piracies and Felonies committed on the high Seas, and Offences against the Law of Nations;

To declare War, grant Letters of Marque and Reprisal, and make Rules concerning Captures on Land and Water;

To raise and support Armies, but no Appropriation of Money to that Use shall be for a longer Term than two Years;

To provide and maintain a Navy;

To make Rules for the Government and Regulation of the land and naval forces;

To provide for calling forth the Militia to execute the Laws of the Union, suppress Insurrections and repel Invasions;

To provide for organizing, arming, and disciplining the Militia, and for governing such Part of them as may be employed in the Service of the United States, reserving to the States respectively, the Appointment of the Officers, and the Authority of training the Militia according to the discipline prescribed by Congress;

To exercise exclusive Legislation in all Cases whatsoever, over such District (not exceeding ten Miles square) as may, be Cession of particular States, and the acceptance of Congress, become the Seat of Government of the United States, and to exercise like Authority over all Places purchased by the Consent of the Legislature of the States in which the Same shall be, for the Erection of Forts, Magazines, Arsenals, dock-Yards, and other needful Buildings;—And

To make all Laws which shall be necessary and proper for carrying into Execution the foregoing Powers, and all other Powers vested by this Constitution in the Government of the United States, or in any Department or Officer thereof.

Section 9. The Migration or Importation of such Persons as any of the States now existing shall think proper to admit, shall not be prohibited by the Congress prior to the Year one thousand eight hundred and eight, but a tax or duty may be imposed on such Importation, not exceeding ten dollars for each Person.

The privilege of the Writ of Habeas Corpus shall not be suspended, unless when in Cases of Rebellion or Invasion the public Safety may require it.

No Bill of Attainder or ex post facto Law shall be passed.

No capitation, or other direct, Tax shall be laid unless in Proportion to the Census or Enumeration herein before directed to be taken.

No Tax or Duty shall be laid on Articles exported from any State.

No Preference shall be given by any Regulation or Revenue to the Ports of one State over those of another: nor shall Vessels bound to, or from, one State, be obliged to enter, clear, or pay Duties in another.

No Money shall be drawn from the Treasury, but in Consequence of Appropriations made by Law; and a regular Statement and Account of the Receipts and Expenditures of all public Money shall be published from time to time.

No Title of Nobility shall be granted by the United States: And no Person holding any Office of Profit or Trust under them, shall, without the Consent of the Congress, accept of any present, Emolument, Office, or Title, of any kind whatever, from any King, Prince, or foreign State.

Section 10. No State shall enter any Treaty, Alliance, or Confederation; grant Letters of Marque and Reprisal; coin Money; emit Bills of Credit; make any Thing but gold and silver Coin a Tender in Payment of Debts; pass any Bill of Attainder, ex post facto Law, or Law impairing the Obligation of Contracts, or grant any Title of Nobility.

No State shall, without the Consent of the Congress, lay any Imposts or Duties on Imports or Exports, except what may be absolutely necessary for executing its inspection Laws: and the net Produce of all Duties and Imposts, laid by any State on Imports or Exports, shall be for the Use of the Treasury of the United States; and all such Laws shall be subject to the Revision and Control of the Congress.

No State shall, without the Consent of Congress, lay any duty of Tonnage, keep Troops, or Ships of War in time of Peace, enter into any Agreement or Compact with another State, or with a foreign Power, or engage in War, unless actually invaded, or in such imminent Danger as will not admit of delay.

ARTICLE II

Section 1. The executive Power shall be vested in a President of the United States of America. He shall hold his Office during the Term of four years, and, together with the Vice-President, chosen for the same Term, be elected, as follows:

Each State shall appoint, in such Manner as the Legislature thereof may direct, a Number of Electors, equal to the whole Number of Senators and Representatives to which the State may be entitled in the Congress; but no Senator or Representative, or Person holding an Office of Trust or Profit under the United States, shall be appointed an Elector.

The Electors shall meet in their respective States, and vote by Ballot for two persons, of whom one at least shall not be an Inhabitant of the same State with themselves. And they shall make a List of all the Persons voted for, and of the Number of Votes for each; which List they shall sign and certify, and transmit sealed to the Seat of the Government of the United States, directed to the President of the Senate. The President of the Senate shall, in the Presence of the Senate and House of Representatives, open all the Certificates, and the Votes shall then be counted. The Person having the greatest Number of Votes shall be the President, if such Number be a Majority of the whole Number of Electors appointed; and if there be more than one who have such Majority, and have an equal Number of Votes, then the House of Representatives shall immediately chuse by Ballot one of them for President; and if no Person have a Majority, then from the five highest on the List the said House shall in like Manner chuse the President. But in chusing the President, the Votes shall be taken by States, the Representation from each State having one Vote; a quorum for this Purpose shall consist of a Member or Members from two-thirds of the States, and a Majority of all the States shall be necessary to a Choice. In every Case, after the Choice of the President, the Person having the greatest Number of Votes of the Electors shall be the Vice President. But if there should remain two or more who have equal votes, the Senate shall chuse from them by Ballot the Vice-President.

The Congress may determine the Time of chusing the Electors, and the Day on which they shall give their Votes; which Day shall be the same throughout the United States.

No person except a natural-born Citizen, or a Citizen of the United States, at the time of the Adoption of this Constitution, shall be eligible to the Office of President; neither shall any Person be eligible to that Office who shall not have attained to the Age of thirty-five years, and been fourteen Years a Resident within the United States.

In Case of the Removal of the President from Office, or of his Death, Resignation, or Inability to discharge the Powers and Duties of the said Office, the same shall devolve on the Vice President, and the Congress may by Law provide for the Case of Removal, Death, Resignation, or Inability, both of the President and Vice President, declaring what

Officer shall then act as President, and such Officer shall act accordingly, until the disability be removed, or a President shall be elected.

The President shall, at stated Times, receive for his Services a Compensation, which shall neither be increased nor diminished during the Period for which he shall have been elected, and he shall not receive within that Period any other Emolument from the United States, or any of them.

Before he enter on the execution of his Office, he shall take the following Oath or Affirmation:—"I do solemnly swear (or affirm) that I will faithfully execute the Office of President of the United States, and will, to the best of my Ability, preserve, protect, and defend the Constitution of the United States."

Section 2. The President shall be Commander in Chief of the Army and Navy of the United States, and of the Militia of the several States, when called into the actual Service of the United States; he may require the Opinion, in writing, of the principal Officer in each of the executive Departments, upon any subject relating to the Duties of their respective Offices, and he shall have Power to Grant Reprieves and Pardons for Offences against the United States, except in Cases of Impeachment.

He shall have Power, by and with the Advice and Consent of the Senate, to make Treaties, provided two thirds of the Senators present concur; and he shall nominate, and by and with the Advice and Consent of the Senate, shall appoint Ambassadors, other public Ministers and Consuls, Judges of the supreme Court, and all other Offices of the United States, whose Appointments are not herein otherwise provided for, and which shall be established by Law: but the Congress may by Law vest the Appointments of such inferior Officers, as they think proper, in the President alone, in the Courts of Law, or in the Heads of Departments.

The President shall have Power to fill up all Vacancies that may happen during the Recess of the Senate, by granting Commissions which shall expire at the End of their next Session.

Section 3. He shall from time to time give to the Congress Information of the State of the Union, and recommend to their Consideration such Measures as he shall judge necessary and expedient; he may, on extraordinary occasions, convene both Houses, or either of them, and in Case of Disagreement between them, with respect to the Time of Adjourn-

ment, he may adjourn them to such Time as he shall think proper; he shall receive Ambassadors and other public Ministers; he shall take Care that the Laws be faithfully executed, and shall Commission all the Officers of the United States.

Section 4. The President, Vice President and all civil Officers of the United States, shall be removed from Office on Impeachment for, and Conviction of, Treason, Bribery, or other high Crimes and Misdemeanors.

ARTICLE III

Section 1. The judicial Power of the United States, shall be vested in one supreme Court, and in such inferior Courts as the Congress may from time to time ordain and establish. The Judges, both of the supreme and inferior Courts, shall hold their Offices during good Behaviour, and shall, at stated Times, receive for their Services, a Compensation, which shall not be diminished during their Continuance in Office.

Section 2. The judicial Power shall extend to all Cases, in Law and Equity, arising under this Constitution, the Laws of the United States, and treaties made, or which shall be made, under their Authority;—to all Cases affecting ambassadors, other public ministers and consuls;—to all cases of admiralty and maritime Jurisdiction;—to Controversies to which the United States shall be a Party;—to Controversies between two or more States;—between a State and Citizens of another State;—between Citizens of different States,—between Citizens of the same State claiming Lands under Grants of different States, and between a State, or the Citizens thereof, and foreign States, Citizens or Subjects.

In all Cases affecting Ambassadors, other public Ministers and Consuls, and those in which a State shall be Party, the supreme Court shall have original Jurisdiction. In all the other Cases before mentioned, the supreme Court shall have appellate Jurisdiction, both as to Law and Fact, with such Exceptions, and under such Regulations as the Congress shall make.

The trial of all Crimes, except in Cases of Impeachment, shall be by Jury; and such Trial shall be held in the State where the said Crimes shall have been committed; but when not committed within any State, the Trial shall be at such Place or Places as the Congress may by Law have directed.

Section 3. Treason against the United States, shall consist only in levying War against them, or in adhering to their Enemies, giving them Aid and Comfort. No Person shall be convicted of Treason unless on the Testimony of two Witnesses to the same overt Act, or on Confession in open Court.

The Congress shall have power to declare the Punishment of Treason, but no Attainder of Treason shall work Corruption of Blood, or Forfeiture except during the Life of the Person attainted.

ARTICLE IV

Section 1. Full Faith and Credit shall be given in each State to the public Acts, Records, and judicial Proceedings of every other State. And the Congress may by general Laws prescribe the Manner in which such Acts, Records and Proceedings shall be proved, and the Effect thereof.

Section 2. The Citizens of each State shall be entitled to all Privileges and Immunities of Citizens in the several States.

A Person charged in any State with Treason, Felony, or other Crime, who shall flee from Justice, and be found in another State, shall on demand of the executive Authority of the State from which he fled, be delivered up, to be removed to the State having Jurisdiction of the crime.

No Person held to Service or Labour in one State, under the Laws thereof, escaping into another, shall, in Consequence of any Law or Regulation therein, be discharged from such Service or Labour, but shall be delivered up on Claim of the Party to whom such Service or Labour may be due.

Section 3. New States may be admitted by the Congress into this Union; but no new State shall be formed or erected within the Jurisdiction of any other State; nor and State be formed by the Junction of two or more States, or parts of States, without the Consent of the Legislatures of the States concerned as well as of the Congress.

The Congress shall have Power to dispose of and make all needful Rules and Regulations respecting the Territory or other Property belonging to the United States; and nothing in this Constitution shall be so construed as to Prejudice any Claims of the United States, or of any particular State.

Section 4. The United States shall guarantee to every State in this Union a Republican Form of Government, and shall protect each of them against Invasion; and on Application of the Legislature, or the Executive (when the Legislature cannot be convened) against domestic Violence.

ARTICLE V

The Congress, whenever two-thirds of both Houses shall deem it necessary, shall propose Amendments to this Constitution, or, on the Application of the Legislatures of two-thirds of the several States, shall call a Convention for proposing Amendments, which, in either Case, shall be valid to all Intents and Purposes, as part of this Constitution, when ratified by the Legislatures of three-fourths of the several States, or by Conventions in three-fourths thereof, as the one or the other Mode of Ratification may be proposed by the Congress; Provided that no Amendment which may be made prior to the Year One thousand eight hundred and eight shall in any Manner affect the first and fourth Clauses in the Ninth Section of the first Article; and that no State, without its Consent, shall be deprived of its equal Suffrage in the Senate.

ARTICLE VI

All Debts contracted and Engagements entered into, before the Adoption of this Constitution, shall be as valid against the United States under this Constitution, as under the Confederation.

This Constitution, and the Laws of the United States which shall be made in Pursuance thereof; and all Treaties made, or which shall be made, under the Authority of the United States, shall be the supreme Law of the Land; and the Judges in every State shall be bound thereby, any Thing in the Constitution or Laws of any State to the Contrary notwithstanding.

The Senators and Representatives before mentioned, and the Members of the several State Legislatures, and all executive and judicial Officers, both of the United States and of the several States, shall be bound by Oath or Affirmation to support this Constitution; but no religious Test shall ever be required as a qualification to any Office or public Trust under the United States.

ARTICLE VII

The Ratification of the Conventions of nine States shall be sufficient for the Establishment of this Constitution between the States so ratifying the same.

Done in Convention by the Unanimous Consent of the States present the Seventeenth Day of September in the Year of our Lord one Thousand seven hundred and Eighty seven, and of the Independence of the United States of America the Twelfth. In Witness whereof We have hereunto subscribed our names.

Articles in Addition to, and Amendment of, the Constitution of the United States of America. Proposed by Congress, and Ratified by the Legislatures of the Several States, Pursuant to the Fifth Article of the Original Constitution.

AMENDMENT I [1791]

Congress shall make no law respecting an establishment of religion, or prohibiting the free exercise thereof; or abridging the freedom of speech, or of the press; or the right of the people peacably to assemble, and to petition the Government for a redress of grievances.

AMENDMENT II [1791]

A well regulated Militia, being necessary to the security of a free State, the right of the people to keep and bear Arms shall not be infringed.

AMENDMENT III [1791]

No Soldier shall, in time of peace, be quartered in any house, without the consent of the Owner, nor in time of war, but in a manner to be prescribed by law.

AMENDMENT IV [1791]

The right of the people to secure in their persons, houses, papers, and effects, against unreasonable searches and seizures, shall not be violated, and no Warrant shall issue, but upon probable cause, supported by Oath or affirmation, and particularly describing the place to be searched, and the persons or things to be seized.

AMENDMENT V [1791]

No person shall be held to answer for a capital or otherwise infamous crime, unless on a presentment or indictment of a Grand Jury, except in cases arising in the land or naval forces, or in the Militia, when in actual service in time of War or public danger; nor shall any person be subject for the same offence to be twice put in jeopardy of life or limb; nor shall be compelled in any criminal case to be a witness against himself, nor be deprived of life, liberty, or property, without due process of law; nor shall private property be taken for public use, without just compensation.

AMENDMENT VI [1791]

In all criminal prosecutions, the accused shall enjoy the right to a speedy and public trial, by an impartial jury of the State and district wherein the crime shall have been committed, which district shall have been previously ascertained by law, and to be informed of the nature and cause of the accusation; to be confronted with the witnesses against him; to have compulsory process for obtaining witnesses in his favor, and to have the Assistance of Counsel for his defence.

AMENDMENT VII [1791]

In suits at common law, where the value in controversy shall exceed twenty dollars, the right of trial by jury shall be preserved, and no fact tried by a jury, shall be otherwise reexamined in any Court of the United States, than according to the rules of the common law.

AMENDMENT VIII [1791]

Excessive bail shall not be required, nor excessive fines imposed, nor cruel and unusual punishments inflicted.

AMENDMENT IX [1791]

The enumeration in the Constitution, of certain rights, shall not be construed to deny or disparage others retained by the people.

AMENDMENT X [1791]

The powers not delegated to the United States by the Constitution, nor prohibited by it to the States, are reserved to the States respectively, or to the people.

AMENDMENT XI [1798]

The Judicial power of the United States shall not be construed to extend to any suit in law or equity, commenced or prosecuted against one of the United States by Citizens of another State, or by Citizens or Subjects of any Foreign State.

AMENDMENT XII [1804]

The Electors shall meet in their respective States and vote by ballot for President and Vice-President, one of whom, at least, shall not be an inhabitant of the same State with themselves; they shall name in their ballots the person voted for as President, and in distinct ballots the person voted for as Vice-President, and they shall make distinct lists of all persons voted for as President, and of all persons voted for as Vice-President, and of the number of votes for each, which lists they shall sign and certify, and transmit sealed to the seat of the government of the United States, directed to the President of the Senate;—The President of the Senate shall, in the presence of the Senate and House of Representatives, open all the certificates and the votes shall then be counted;—The person having the greatest number of votes for President, shall be the President, if such number be a majority of the whole number of Electors appointed; and if no person have such majority, then from the persons having the highest numbers not exceeding three on the list of those voted for as President, the House of Representatives shall choose immediately, by ballot, the President. But in choosing the President, the votes shall be taken by states, the representation from each state having one vote; a quorum for this purpose shall consist of a member or members from two-thirds of the states, and a majority of all the states shall be necessary to a choice. And if the House of Representatives shall not choose a President whenever the right of choice shall devolve upon them, before the fourth day of March next following, then the Vice-President shall act as President, as in the case of the death or other constitutional disability of the President.—The person having the greatest number of votes as Vice-President, shall be the Vice President, if such number be a majority of the whole number of Electors appointed, and if no person have a majority, then from the two highest numbers on the list, the Senate shall choose the Vice-President; a quorum for the purpose shall consist of two-thirds of the whole number of Senators, and a majority of the whole number shall be necessary to a choice. But no person constitutionally ineligible to the office of President shall be eligible to that of Vice-President of the United States.

AMENDMENT XIII [1865]

Section 1. Neither slavery nor involuntary servitude, except as a punishment for crime whereof the party shall have been duly convicted, shall exist within the United States, or any place subject to their jurisdiction.

Section 2. Congress shall have power to enforce this article by appropriate legislation.

AMENDMENT XIV [1868]

Section 1. All persons born or naturalized in the United States, and subject to the jurisdiction thereof, are citizens of the United States and of the State wherein they reside. No State shall make or enforce any law which shall abridge the privileges or immunities of citizens of the United States; nor shall any State deprive any person of life, liberty, or property, without due process of law; nor deny to any person within its jurisdiction the equal protection of the laws.

Section 2. Representatives shall be apportioned among the several States according to their respective numbers, counting the whole number of persons in each State, excluding Indians not taxed. But when the right to vote at any election for the choice of electors for President and Vice-President of the United States, Representatives in Congress, the Executive and Judicial officers of a State, or the members of the Legislature thereof, is denied to any of the male inhabitants of such State, being twenty-one years of age, and citizens of the United States, or in any way abridged, except for participation in rebellion, or other crime, the basis of representation therein shall be reduced in the proportion which the number of such male citizens shall bear to the whole number of male citizens twenty-one years of age in such State.

Section 3. No person shall be a Senator or Representative in Congress, or elector of President and Vice-President, or hold any office, civil or military, under the United States, or under any State, who, having previously taken an oath, as a member of Congress, or as an officer of the United States, or as a member of any State legislature, or as an executive or judicial officer of any State, to support the Constitution of the United States, shall have engaged in insurrection or rebellion against the same, or given aid or comfort to the enemies thereof. But Congress may by a vote of two-thirds of each House, remove such disability.

Section 4. The validity of the public debt of the United States, authorized by law, including debts incurred for payment of pensions and bounties for services in suppressing insurrection or rebellion, shall not be questioned. But neither the United States nor any State shall assume or pay any debt or obligation incurred in aid of insurrection or rebellion against the United States or any claim for the loss or emancipation of any slave; but all such debts, obligations, and claims shall be held illegal and void.

Section 5. The Congress shall have the power to enforce, by appropriate legislation, the provisions of this article.

AMENDMENT XV [1870]

Section 2. The right of citizens of the United States to vote shall not be denied or abridged by the United States or by any State on account of race, color, or previous condition of servitude—

Section 2. The Congress shall have power to enforce this article by appropriate legislation.

AMENDMENT XVI [1913]

The Congress shall have power to lay and collect taxes on incomes, from whatever source derived, without apportionment among the several States, and without regard to any census or enumeration.

AMENDMENT XVII [1913]

The Senate of the United States shall be composed of two Senators from each State, elected by the people thereof, for six years; and each Senator shall have one vote. The electors in each State shall have the qualifications requisite for electors of the most numerous branch of the State legislatures.

When vacancies happen in the representation of any State in the Senate, the executive authority of such State shall issue writs of election to fill such vacancies: *Provided,* That the legislature of any State may empower the executive thereof to make temporary appointments until the people fill the vacancies by election as the legislature may direct.

This amendment shall not be so construed as to affect the election or term of any Senator chosen before it becomes valid as part of the Constitution.

AMENDMENT XVIII [1919]

Section 1. After one year from the ratification of this article the manufacture, sale, or transportation of intoxicating liquors within, the importation thereof into, or the exportation thereof from the United States and all territory subject to the jurisdiction thereof for beverage purposes is hereby prohibited.

Section 2. The Congress and the several States shall have concurrent power to enforce this article by appropriate legislation.

Section 3. This article shall be inoperative unless it shall have been ratified as an amendment to the Constitution by the legislatures of the several States, as provided in the Constitution, within seven years from the date of the submission hereof to the States by the Congress.

AMENDMENT XIX [1920]

The right of citizens of the United States to vote shall not be denied or abridged by the United States or by any State on account of sex.

Congress shall have power to enforce this article by appropriate legislation.

AMENDMENT XX [1933]

Section 1. The terms of the President and Vice-Preisdent shall end at noon on the 20th day of January, and the terms of Senators and Representatives at noon on the 3d day of January, of the years in which such terms would have ended if this article had not been ratified; and the terms of their successors shall then begin.

Section 2. The Congress shall assemble at least once in every year, and such meeting shall begin at noon on the 3d day of January, unless they shall by law appoint a different day.

Section 3. If, at the time fixed for the beginning of the term of the President, the President elect shall have died, the Vice-President elect shall become

President. If a President shall not have been chosen before the time fixed for the beginning of his term, or if the President elect shall have failed to qualify, then the Vice-President elect shall act as President until a President shall have qualified; and the Congress may by law provide for the case wherein neither a President elect nor a Vice-President elect shall have qualified, declaring who shall then act as President, or the manner in which one who is to act shall be selected, and such person shall act accordingly until a President or Vice-President shall have qualified.

Section 4. The Congress may by law provide for the case of the death of any of the persons from whom the House of Representatives may choose a President whenever the right of choice shall have devolved upon them, and for the case of the death of any of the persons from whom the Senate may choose a Vice-President whenever the right of choice shall have devolved upon them.

Section 5. Sections 1 and 2 shall take effect on the 15th day of October following the ratification of this article.

Section 6. This article shall be inoperative unless it shall have been ratified as an amendment to the Constitution by the legislatures of three-fourths of the several States within seven years from the date of its submission.

AMENDMENT XXI [1933]

Section 1. The eighteenth article of amendment to the Constitution of the United States is hereby repealed.

Section 2. The transportation or importation into any State, Territory, or possession of the United States for delivery or use therein of intoxicating liquors, in violation of the laws thereof, is hereby prohibited.

Section 3. This article shall be inoperative unless it shall have been ratified as an amendment to the Constitution by conventions in the several States, as provided in the Constitution, within seven years from the date of the Submission hereof to the States by the Congress.

AMENDMENT XXII [1951]

No person shall be elected to the office the President more than twice, and no person who has held the office of President, or acted as President, for more than two years of a term to which some other person was elected President shall be elected to the office of the President more than once.

But this Article shall not apply to any person holding the office of President when this Article was proposed by the Congress, and shall not prevent any person who may be holding the office of President, or acting as President, during the term within which this Article becomes operative from holding the office of President or acting as President during the remainder of such term.

AMENDMENT XXIII [1961]

Section 1. The District constituting the seat of Government of the United States shall appoint in such manner as the Congress may direct:

A number of electors of President and Vice President equal to the whole number of Senators and Representatives in Congress to which the District would be entitled if it were a State, but in no event more than the least populous State; they shall be in addition to those appointed by the States, but they shall be considered, for the purposes of the election of President and Vice President, to be electors appointed by a State; and they shall meet in the District and perform such duties as provided by the twelfth article of amendment.

Section 2. The Congress shall have power to enforce this article by appropriate legislation.

AMENDMENT XXIV [1964]

Section 1. The right of citizens of the United States to vote in any primary or other election for President or Vice President, for electors for President or Vice President, or for Senator or Representative in Congress, shall not be denied or abridged by the United States or any State by reason of failure to pay any poll tax or other tax.

Section 2. The Congress shall have the power to enforce this article by appropriate legislation.

AMENDMENT XXV [1967]

Section 1. In case of the removal of the President from office or his death or resignation, the Vice President shall become President.

Section 2. Whenever there is a vacancy in the office of the Vice President, the President shall nominate a Vice President who shall take the office upon confirmation by a majority vote of both houses of Congress.

Section 3. Whenever the President transmits to the President pro tempore of the Senate and the Speaker of the House of Representatives his written declaration that he is unable to discharge the powers and duties of his office, and until he transmits to them a written declaration to the contrary, such powers and duties shall be discharged by the Vice President as Acting President.

Section 4. Whenever the Vice President and a majority of either the principal officers of the executive departments, or of such other body as Congress may by law provide, transmit to the President pro tempore of the Senate and the Speaker of the House of Representatives their written declaration that the President is unable to discharge the powers and duties of his office, the Vice President shall immediately assume the powers and duties of the office as Acting President.

Thereafter, when the President transmits to the President pro tempore of the Senate and the Speaker of the House of Representatives his written declaration that no inability exists, he shall resume the powers and duties of his office unless the Vice President and a majority of either the principal officers of the executive departments, or of such other body as Congress may by law provide, transmit within four days to the President pro tempore of the Senate and the Speaker of the House of Representatives their written declaration that the President is unable to discharge the powers and duties of his office. Thereupon Congress shall decide the issue, assembling within 48 hours for that purpose if not in session. If the Congress, within 21 days after receipt of the latter written declaration, or, if Congress is not in session, within 21 days after Congress is required to assemble, determines by two-thirds vote of both houses that the President is unable to discharge the powers and duties of his office, the Vice President shall continue to dicharge the same as Acting President; otherwise, the President shall resume the powers and duties of his office.

AMENDMENT XXVI [1971]

Section 1. The right of citizens of the United States who are eighteen years of age or older, to vote shall not be denied or abridged by the United States or by any State on account of age.

Section 2. The Congress shall have power to enforce this article by appropriate legislation.

Admission of States to the Union

1 Delaware	Dec. 7, 1787	26 Michigan	Jan. 26, 1837
2 Pennsylvania	Dec. 12, 1787	27 Florida	Mar. 3, 1845
3 New Jersey	Dec. 18, 1787	28 Texas	Dec. 29, 1845
4 Georgia	Jan. 2, 1788	29 Iowa	Dec. 28, 1846
5 Connecticut	Jan. 9, 1788	30 Wisconsin	May 29, 1848
6 Massachusetts	Feb. 6, 1788	31 California	Sept. 9, 1850
7 Maryland	Apr. 28, 1788	32 Minnesota	May 11, 1858
8 South Carolina	May 23, 1788	33 Oregon	Feb. 14, 1859
9 New Hampshire	June 21, 1788	34 Kansas	Jan. 29, 1861
10 Virginia	June 25, 1788	35 West Virginia	June 20, 1863
11 New York	July 26, 1788	36 Nevada	Oct. 31, 1864
12 North Carolina	Nov. 21, 1789	37 Nebraska	Mar. 1, 1867
13 Rhode Island	May 29, 1790	38 Colorado	Aug. 1, 1876
14 Vermont	Mar. 4, 1791	39 North Dakota	Nov. 2, 1889
15 Kentucky	June 1, 1792	40 South Dakota	Nov. 2, 1889
16 Tennessee	June 1, 1796	41 Montana	Nov. 8, 1889
17 Ohio	Mar. 1, 1803	42 Washington	Nov. 11, 1889
18 Louisiana	Apr. 30, 1812	43 Idaho	July 3, 1890
19 Indiana	Dec. 11, 1816	44 Wyoming	July 10, 1890
20 Mississippi	Dec. 10, 1817	45 Utah	Jan. 4, 1896
21 Illinois	Dec. 3, 1818	46 Oklahoma	Nov. 16, 1907
22 Alabama	Dec. 14, 1819	47 New Mexico	Jan. 6, 1912
23 Maine	Mar. 15, 1820	48 Arizona	Feb. 14, 1912
24 Missouri	Aug. 10, 1821	49 Alaska	Jan. 3, 1959
25 Arkansas	June 15, 1836	50 Hawaii	Aug. 21, 1959

Population of the United States, 1790–1980

Year	Total population (in thousands)	Number per square mile of land area (continental United States)	Year	Total population (in thousands)	Number per square mile of land area (continental United States)
1790	3,929	4.5	1837	15,843	
1791	4,056		1838	16,264	
1792	4,194		1839	16,684	
1793	4,332		1840	17,120	9.8
1794	4,469		1841	17,733	
1795	4,607		1842	18,345	
1796	4,745		1843	18,957	
1797	4,883		1844	19,569	
1798	5,021		1845	20,182	
1799	5,159		1846	20,794	
1800	5,297	6.1	1847	21,405	
1801	5,486		1848	22,018	
1802	5,679		1849	22,631	
1803	5,872		1850	23,261	7.9
1804	5,065		1851	24,086	
1805	6,258		1852	24,911	
1806	6,451		1853	25,736	
1807	6,644		1854	26,561	
1808	6,838		1855	27,386	
1809	7,031		1856	28,212	
1810	7,224	4.3	1857	29,037	
1811	7,460		1858	29,862	
1812	7,700		1859	30,687	
1813	7,939		1860	31,513	10.6
1814	8,179		1861	32,351	
1815	8,419		1862	33,188	
1816	8,659		1863	34,026	
1817	8,899		1864	34,863	

Figures are from pp. 7, 8; *Statistical Abstract of the United States: 1974*, p. 5; Census Bureau for 1974 through 1980.

Year	Total population (in thousands)	Number per square mile of land area (continental United States)	Year	Total population (in thousands)	Number per square mile of land area (continental United States)
1818	9,139		1865	35,701	
1819	9,379		1866	36,538	
1820	9,618	5.6	1867	37,376	
1821	9,939		1868	38,213	
1822	10,268		1869	39,051	
1823	10,596		1870	39,905	13.4
1824	10,924		1871	40,938	
1825	11,252		1872	41,972	
1826	11,580		1873	43,006	
1827	11,909		1874	44,040	
1828	12,237		1875	45,073	
1829	12,565		1876	46,107	
1830	12,901	7.4	1877	47,141	
1831	13,321		1878	48,174	
1832	13,742		1879	49,208	
1833	14,162		1880	50,262	16.9
1834	14,582		1881	51,542	
1835	15,003		1882	52,821	
1836	15,423		1883	54,100	
1884	55,379		1932	124,840	
1885	56,658		1933	125,579	
1886	57,938		1934	126,374	
1887	59,217		1935	127,250	
1888	60,496		1936	128,053	
1889	61,775		1937	128,825	
1890	63,056	21.2	1938	129,825	
1891	64,361		1939	130,880	
1892	65,666		1940	131,669	44.2
1893	66,970		1941	133,894	
1894	68,275		1942	135,361	
1895	69,580		1943	137,250	
1896	70,885		1944	138,916	
1897	72,189		1945	140,468	
1898	73,494		1946	141,936	
1899	74,799		1947	144,698	
1900	76,094	25.6	1948	147,208	
1901	77,585		1949	149,767	
1902	79,160		1950	150,697	50.7
1903	80,632		1951	154,878	
1904	82,165		1952	157,553	
1905	83,820		1953	160,184	
1906	85,437		1954	163,026	
1907	87,000		1955	165,931	
1908	88,709		1956	168,903	

Year	Total population (in thousands)	Number per square mile of land area (continental United States)	Year	Total population (in thousands)*	Number per square mile of land area (continental United States)
1909	90,492		1957	171,984	
1910	92,407	31.0	1958	174,882	
1911	93,868		1959	177,830	
1912	95,331		1960	178,464	60.1
1913	97,227		1961	183,672	
1914	99,118		1962	186,504	
1915	100,549		1963	189,197	
1916	101,966		1964	191,833	
1917	103,414		1965	194,237	
1918	104,550		1966	196,485	
1919	105,063		1967	198,629	
1920	106,466	35.6	1968	200,619	
1921	108,541		1969	202,599	
1922	110,055		1970	203,875	57.5†
1923	111,950		1971	207,045	
1924	114,113		1972	208,842	
1925	115,832		1973	210,396	
1926	117,399		1974	211,894	
1927	119,038		1975	213,631	
1928	120,501		1976	215,142	
1929	121,770		1977	216,817	
1930	122,775	41.2	1978	218,931	
1931	124,040		1979	220,584	
			1980	222.807	62.9†

* Figures after 1940 represent total population including Armed Forces abroad, except in official census years.
† Figure includes Alaska and Hawaii.

Presidential Elections, 1789–1980

Year	Candidates	Party	Popular Vote	Electoral Vote
1789	**George Washington**			69
	John Adams			34
	Others			35
1792	**George Washington**			132
	John Adams			77
	George Clinton			50
	Others			5
1796	**John Adams**	Federalist		71
	Thomas Jefferson	Democratic-Republican		68
	Thomas Pinckney	Federalist		59
	Aaron Burr	Democratic-Republican		30
	Others			48
1800	**Thomas Jefferson**	Democratic-Republican		73
	Aaron Burr	Democratic-Republican		73
	John Adams	Federalist		65
	Charles C. Pinckney	Federalist		64
1804	**Thomas Jefferson**	Democratic-Republican		162
	Charles C. Pinckney	Federalist		14
1808	**James Madison**	Democratic-Republican		122
	Charles C. Pinckney	Federalist		47
	George Clinton	Independent-Republican		6
1812	**James Madison**	Democratic-Republican		128
	Dewitt Clinton	Federalist		89
1816	**James Monroe**	Democratic-Republican		183
	Rufus King	Federalist		34
1820	**James Monroe**	Democratic-Republican		231
	John Quincy Adams	Independent-Republican		1
1824	**John Quincy Adams**	Democratic-Republican	113,122 (30.9%)	84
	Andrew Jackson	Democratic-Republican	151,271 (41.3%)	99
	Henry Clay	Democratic-Republican	47,531 (12.9%)	37
	William H. Crawford	Democratic-Republican	40,856 (11.1%)	41
1828	**Andrew Jackson**	Democratic	642,553 (55.9%)	178
	John Quincy Adams	National Republican	500,897 (43.6%)	83

Year	Candidates	Party	Popular Vote	Electoral Vote
1832	**Andrew Jackson**	Democratic	701,780 (54.2%)	219
	Henry Clay	National Republican	484,205 (37.4%)	49
	William Wirt	Anti-Masonic	100,715 (7.7%)	7
1836	**Martin Van Buren**	Democratic	764,176 (50.8%)	170
	William H. Harrison	Whig	550,816 (36.6%)	73
	Hugh L. White	Whig	146,107 (9.7%)	26
	Daniel Webster	Whig	41,201 (2.7%)	14
1840	**William H. Harrison** (**John Tyler,** 1841)	Whig	1,275,390 (52.8%)	234
	Martin Van Buren	Democratic	1,128,854 (46.8%)	60
1844	**James K. Polk**	Democratic	1,339,494 (49.5%)	170
	Henry Clay	Whig	1,300,004 (48.0%)	105
	James G. Birney	Liberty	62,103 (2.3%)	
1848	**Zachary Taylor** (**Millard Fillmore,** 1850)	Whig	1,361,393 (47.2%)	163
	Lewis Cass	Democratic	1,223,460 (42.4%)	127
	Martin Van Buren	Free Soil	291,501 (10.1%)	
1852	**Franklin Pierce**	Democratic	1,607,510 (50.8%)	254
	Winfield Scott	Whig	1,386,942 (43.8%)	42
1856	**James Buchanan**	Democratic	1,836,072 (45.2%)	174
	John C. Frémont	Republican	1,342,345 (33.1%)	114
	Millard Fillmore	American	873,053 (21.5%)	8
1860	**Abraham Lincoln**	Republican	1,865,908 (39.8%)	180
	Stephen A. Douglas	Democratic	1,382,202 (29.4%)	12
	John C. Breckinridge	Democratic	848,019 (18.0%)	72
	John Bell	Constitutional Union	591,901 (12.6%)	39
1864	**Abraham Lincoln** (**Andrew Johnson,** 1865)	Republican	2,218,388 (55.0%)	212
	George B. McClellan	Democratic	1,812,807 (44.9%)	21
1868	**Ulysses S. Grant**	Republican	3,013,650 (52.6%)	214
	Horatio Seymour	Democratic	2,708,744 (47.3%)	80
1872	**Ulysses S. Grant**	Republican	3,598,235 (55.6%)	286
	Horace Greeley	Democratic	2,834,761 (43.8%)	66
1876	**Rutherford B. Hayes**	Republican	4,034,311 (47.9%)	185
	Samuel J. Tilden	Democratic	4,288,546 (50.9%)	184
1880	**James A. Garfield** (**Chester A. Arthur,** 1881)	Republican	4,446,158 (48.2%)	214
	Winfield S. Hancock	Democratic	4,444,260 (48.2%)	155
	James B. Weaver	Greenback-Labor	305,997 (3.3%)	155

Year	Candidates	Party	Popular Vote	Electoral Vote
1884	**Grover Cleveland**	Democratic	4,874,621 (48.5%)	219
	James G. Blaine	Republican	4,848,936 (48.2%)	182
	Benjamin F. Butler	Greenback-Labor	175,096 (1.7%)	
1888	**Benjamin Harrison**	Republican	5,44,892 (47.8%)	233
	Grover Cleveland	Democratic	5,534,488 (48.6%)	168
1892	**Grover Cleveland**	Democratic	5,551,883 (46.0%)	277
	Benjamin Harrison	Republican	5,179,244 (42.9%)	145
	James B. Weaver	People's	1,024,280 (8.5%)	22
1896	**William McKinley**	Republican	7,108,480 (51.9%)	271
	William J. Bryan	Democratic; Populist	6,511,495 (46.7%)	176
1900	**William McKinley** **(Theodore Roosevelt,** 1901)	Republican	7,218,039 (51.6%)	292
	William J. Bryan	Democratic; Populist	6,358,345 (45.5%)	155
1904	**Theodore Roosevelt**	Republican	7,626,593 (56.4%)	336
	Alton B. Parker	Democratic	5,082,898 (37.6%)	140
	Eugene V. Debs	Socialist	402,489 (2.9%)	
1908	**William H. Taft**	Republican	7,676,258 (51.5%)	321
	William J. Bryan	Democratic	6,406,801 (43.0%)	162
	Eugene V. Debs	Socialist	420,380 (2.8%)	
1912	**Woodrow Wilson**	Democratic	6,293,152 (41.8%)	435
	Theodore Roosevelt	Progressive	4,119,207 (27.3%)	88
	William H. Taft	Republican	3,486,383 (23.1%)	8
	Eugene V. Debs	Socialist	900,369 (5.9%)	8
1916	**Woodrow Wilson**	Democratic	9,126,300 (49.2%)	277
	Charles E. Hughes	Republican	8,546,789 (46.1%)	254
1920	**Warren G. Harding** **(Calvin Coolidge,** 1923)	Republican	16,133,314 (60.3%)	404
	James M. Cox	Democratic	9,140,884 (34.1%)	127
	Eugene V. Debs	Socialist	913,664 (3.4%)	
1924	**Calvin Coolidge**	Republican	15,717,553 (54.0%)	382
	John W. Davis	Democratic	8,386,169 (28.8%)	136
	Robert M. La Follette	Progressive	4,814,050 (16.5%)	13
1928	**Herbert C. Hoover**	Republican	21,411,991 (58.2%)	444
	Alfred C. Smith	Democratic	15,000,185 (40.7%)	87
1932	**Franklin D. Roosevelt**	Democratic	22,825,016 (57.4%)	472
	Herbert C. Hoover	Republican	15,758,397 (39.6%)	59
	Norman Thomas	Socialist	883,990 (2.2%)	

Year	Candidates	Party	Popular Vote	Electoral Vote
1936	**Franklin D. Roosevelt**	Democratic	27,747,636 (60.7%)	523
	Alfred M. Landon	Republican	16,679,543 (36.5%)	8
	William Lemke	Union	892,492 (1.9%)	
1940	**Franklin D. Roosevelt**	Democratic	27,263,448 (54.7%)	449
	Wendell L. Wilkie	Republican	22,336,260 (44.8%)	82
1944	**Franklin D. Roosevelt**	Democratic	25,611,936 (53.3%)	432
	(Harry S Truman, 1945)			
	Thomas E. Dewey	Republican	22,013,372 (45.8%)	99
1948	**Harry S Truman**	Democratic	24,105,587 (49.8%)	303
	Thomas E. Dewey	Republican	21,970,017 (45.1%)	189
	J. Strom Thurmond	States' Rights	1,169,134 (2.4%)	39
	Henry A. Wallace	Progressive	1,157,057 (2.3%)	
1952	**Dwight D. Eisenhower**	Republican	33,936,137 (55.1%)	442
	Adlai E. Stevenson	Democratic	27,314,649 (44.3%)	89
1956	**Dwight D. Eisenhower**	Republican	35,585,245 (57.3%)	457
	Adlai E. Stevenson	Democratic	26,030,172 (41.9%)	73
1960	**John F. Kennedy**	Democratic	34,221,344 (49.7%)	303
	(Lyndon B. Johnson, 1963)			
	Richard M. Nixon	Republican	34,106,671 (49.5%)	219
1964	**Lyndon B. Johnson**	Democratic	43,126,584 (61.0%)	486
	Barry M. Goldwater	Republican	27,177,838 (38.4%)	52
1968	**Richard M. Nixon**	Republican	31,783,148 (43.4%)	301
	Hubert H. Humphrey	Democratic	31,274,503 (42.7%)	191
	George C. Wallace	Amer. Independent	9,901,151 (13.5%)	46
1972	**Richard M. Nixon**	Repubican	47,170,179 (60.6%)	520
	George S. McGovern	Democratic	29,171,791 (37.5%)	17
1974	**Gerald R. Ford**	Republican	Appointed on August 9, 1974 as President after the resignation of Richard M. Nixon. No election was held.	
1976	**Jimmy Carter**	Democrat	40,828,587 (50.1%)	297
	Gerald R. Ford	Republican	39,147,613 (48.0%)	240
1980	**Ronald Reagan**	Republican	43,899,248 (50.9%)	489
	Jimmy Carter	Democrat	35,481,435 (41.1%)	49
	John Anderson	Independent	5,719,437 (6.6%)	0

Because only the leading candidates are listed, popular vote percentages do not always total 100. The elections of 1800 and 1924, in which no candidate received an electoral-vote majority, were decided in the House of Representatives.

Election Returns are from *Congressional Quarterly, Presidential Elections, Since 1789* (1975), *Congressional Quarterly Weekly Reports* (March 19, 1977), and *Facts on File* (January 9, 1981).

Presidents, Vice Presidents, and Cabinet Members (1789–1980)

President	Vice President	Secretary of State	Secretary of Treasury	Secretary of War
George Washington 1789–97	John Adams 1789–97	Thomas Jefferson 1789–94 Edmund Randolph 1794–95 Timothy Pickering 1795–97	Alexander Hamilton 1789–95 Oliver Wolcott 1795–97	Henry Knox 1789–95 Timothy Pickering 1795–96 James McHenry 1796–97
John Adams 1797–1801	Thomas Jefferson 1797–1801	Timothy Pickering 1797–1800 John Marshall 1800–01	Oliver Wolcott 1797–1801 Samuel Dexter 1801	James McHenry 1797–1800 Samuel Dexter 1800–01
Thomas Jefferson 1801–09	Aaron Burr 1801–05 George Clinton 1805–09	James Madison 1801–09	Samuel Dexter 1801 Albert Gallatin 1801–09	Henry Dearborn 1801–09
James Madison 1809–17	George Clinton 1809–13 Elbridge Gerry 1813–17	Robert Smith 1809–11 James Monroe 1811–17	Albert Gallatin 1809–14 George Campbell 1814 Alexander Dallas 1814–16 William Crawford 1816–17	William Eustis 1809–13 John Armstrong 1813–14 James Monroe 1814–15 William Crawford 1815–17
James Monroe 1817–25	Daniel D. Tompkins 1817–25	John Quincy Adams 1817–25	William Crawford 1817–25	George Graham 1817 John C. Calhoun 1817–25
John Quincy Adams 1825–29	John C. Calhoun 1825–29	Henry Clay 1825–29	Richard Rush 1825–29	James Barbour 1825–28 Peter B. Porter 1828–29
Andrew Jackson 1829–37	John C. Calhoun 1829–33 Martin Van Buren 1833–37	Martin Van Buren 1829–31 Edward Livingston 1831–33 Louis McLane 1833–34 John Forsyth 1834–37	Samuel Ingham 1829–31 Louis McLane 1831–33 William Duane 1833 Roger B. Taney 1833–34 Levi Woodbury 1834–37	John H. Eaton 1829–31 Lewis Cass 1831–37 Benjamin Butler 1837
Martin Van Buren 1837–41	Richard M. Johnson 1837–41	John Forsyth 1837–41	Levi Woodbury 1837–41	Joel R. Poinsett 1837–41

Secretary of Navy	Postmaster General	Attorney General	Secretary of Interior
	Samuel Osgood 1789–91 Timothy Pickering 1791–95 Joseph Habersham 1795–97	Edmund Randolph 1789–94 William Bradford 1794–95 Charles Lee 1795–97	
Benjamin Stoddert 1798–1801	Joseph Habersham 1797–1801	Charles Lee 1797–1801	
Benjamin Stoddert 1801 Robert Smith 1801–09	Joseph Habersham 1801 Gideon Granger 1801–09	Levi Lincoln 1801–05 John Breckinridge 1805–07 Caesar Rodney 1807–09	
Paul Hamilton 1809–13 William Jones 1813–14 Benjamin Crowninshield 1814–17	Gideon Granger 1809–14 Return Meigs 1814–17	Caesar Rodney 1809–11 William Pinkney 1811–14 Richard Rush 1814–17	
Benjamin Crowninshield 1817–18 Smith Thompson 1818–23 Samuel Southard 1823–25	Return Meigs 1817–23 John McLean 1823–25	Richard Rush 1817 William Wirt 1817–25	
Samuel Southard 1825–29	John McLean 1825–29	William Wirt 1825–29	
John Branch 1829–31 Levi Woodbury 1831–34 Mahlon Dickerson 1834–37	William Barry 1829–35 Amos Kendall 1835–37	John M. Berrien 1829–31 Roger B. Taney 1831–33 Benjamin Butler 1833–37	
Mahlon Dickerson 1837–38 James K. Paulding 1838–41	Amos Kendall 1837–41 John M. Niles 1840–41	Benjamin Butler 1837–38 Felix Grundy 1838–40 Henry D. Gilpin 1840–41	

President	Vice President	Secretary of State	Secretary of Treasury	Secretary of War
William H. Harrison 1841	John Tyler 1841	Daniel Webster 1841	Thomas Ewing 1841	John Bell 1841
John Tyler 1841–45		Daniel Webster 1841–43 Hugh S. Legaré 1843 Abel P. Upshur 1843–44 John C. Calhoun 1844–45	Thomas Ewing 1841 Walter Forward 1841–43 John C. Spencer 1843–44 George M. Bibb 1844–45	John Bell 1841 John C. Spencer 1841–43 James M. Porter 1843–44 William Wilkins 1844–45
James K. Polk 1845–49	George M. Dallas 1845–49	James Buchanan 1845–49	Robert J. Walker 1845–49	William L. Marcy 1845–49
Zachary Taylor 1849–50	Millard Fillmore 1849–50	John M. Clayton 1849–50	William M. Meredith 1849–50	George W. Crawford 1849–50
Millard Fillmore 1850–53		Daniel Webster 1850–52 Edward Everett 1852–53	Thomas Corwin 1850–53	Charles M. Conrad 1850–53
Franklin Pierce 1853–57	William R. King 1853–57	William L. Marcy 1853–57	James Guthrie 1853–57	Jefferson Davis 1853–57
James Buchanan 1857–61	John C. Breckinridge 1857–61	Lewis Cass 1857–60 Jeremiah S. Black 1860–61	Howell Cobb 1857–60 Philip F. Thomas 1860–61 John A. Dix 1861	John B. Floyd 1857–61 Joseph Holt 1861
Abraham Lincoln 1861–65	Hannibal Hamlin 1861–65 Andrew Johnson 1865	William H. Seward 1861–65	Salmon P. Chase 1861–64 William P. Fessenden 1864–65 Hugh McCulloch 1865	Simon Cameron 1861–62 Edwin M. Stanton 1862–65
Andrew Johnson 1865–69		William H. Seward 1865–69	Hugh McCulloch 1865–69	Edwin M. Stanton 1865–67 Ulysses S. Grant 1867–68 John M. Schofield 1868–69
Ulysses S. Grant 1869–77	Schuyler Colfax 1869–73 Henry Wilson 1873–77	Elihu B. Washburne 1869 Hamilton Fish 1869–77	George S. Boutwell 1869–73 William A. Richardson 1873–74 Benjamin H. Bristow 1874–76 Lot M. Morrill 1876–77	John A. Rawlins 1869 William T. Sherman 1869 William W. Belknap 1869–76 Alphonso Taft 1876 James D. Cameron 1876–77

Secretary of Navy	Postmaster General	Attorney General	Secretary of Interior
George E. Badger 1841	Francis Granger 1841	John J. Crittenden 1841	
George E. Badger 1841 Abel P. Upshur 1841–43 David Henshaw 1843–44 Thomas Gilmer 1844 John Y. Mason 1844–45	Francis Granger 1841 Charles A. Wickliffe 1841–45	John J. Crittenden 1841 Hugh S. Legaré 1841–43 John Nelson 1843–45	
George Bancroft 1845–46 John Y. Mason 1846–49	Cave Johnson 1845–49	John Y. Mason 1845–46 Nathan Clifford 1846–48 Isaac Toucey 1848–49	
William B. Preston 1849–50	Jacob Collamer 1849–50	Reverdy Johnson 1849–50	Thomas Ewing 1849–50
William A. Graham 1850–52 John P. Kennedy 1852–53	Nathan K. Hall 1850–52 Sam D. Hubbard 1852–53	John J. Crittenden 1850–53	Thomas McKennan 1850 A. H. H. Stuart 1850–53
James C. Dobbin 1853–57	James Campbell 1853–57	Caleb Cushing 1853–57	Robert McClelland 1853–57
Isaac Toucey 1857–61	Aaron V. Brown 1857–59 Joseph Holt 1859–61 Horatio King 1861	Jeremiah S. Black 1857–60 Edwin M. Stanton 1860–61	Jacob Thompson 1857–61
Gideon Welles 1861–65	Horatio King 1861 Montgomery Blair 1861–64 William Dennison 1864–65	Edward Bates 1861–64 James Speed 1864–65	Caleb B. Smith 1861–63 John P. Usher 1863–65
Gideon Welles 1865–69	William Dennison 1865–66 Alexander Randall 1866–69	James Speed 1865–66 Henry Stanbery 1866–68 William M. Evarts 1868–69	John P. Usher 1865 James Harlan 1865–66 O. H. Browning 1866–69
Adolph E. Borie 1869 George M. Robeson 1869–77	John A. J. Creswell 1869–74 James W. Marshall 1874 Marshall Jewell 1874–76 James N. Tyner 1876–77	Ebenezer R. Hoar 1869–70 Amos T. Akerman 1870–71 G. H. Williams 1871–75 Edwards Pierrepont 1875–76 Alphonso Taft 1876–77	Jacob D. Cox 1869–70 Columbus Delano 1870–75 Zachariah Chandler 1875–77

President	Vice President	Secretary of State	Secretary of Treasury	Secretary of War	Secretary of Navy
Rutherford B. Hayes 1877–81	William A. Wheeler 1877–81	William M. Evarts 1877–81	John Sherman 1877–81	George W. McCrary 1877–79 Alexander Ramsey 1879–81	R. W. Thompson 1877–81 Nathan Goff, Jr. 1881
James A. Garfield 1881	Chester A. Arthur 1881	James G. Blaine 1881	William Windom 1881	Robert T. Lincoln 1881	William H. Hunt 1881
Chester A. Arthur 1881–85		F. T. Frelinghuysen 1881–85	Charles J. Folger 1881–84 Walter Q. Gresham 1884 Hugh McCulloch 1884–85	Robert T. Lincoln 1881–85	William E. Chandler 1881–85
Grover Cleveland 1885–89	T. A. Hendricks 1885	Thomas F. Bayard 1885–89	Daniel Manning 1885–87 Charles S. Fairchild 1887–89	William C. Endicott 1885–89	William C. Whitney 1885–89
Benjamin Harrison 1889–93	Levi P. Morton 1889–93	James G. Blaine 1889–92 John W. Foster 1892–93	William Windom 1889–91 Charles Foster 1891–93	Redfield Procter 1889–91 Stephen B. Elkins 1891–93	Benjamin F. Tracy 1889–93
Grover Cleveland 1893–97	Adlai E. Stevenson 1893–97	Walter Q. Gresham 1893–95 Richard Olney 1895–97	John G. Carlisle 1893–97	Daniel S. Lamont 1893–97	Hilary A. Herbert 1893–97
William McKinley 1897–1901	Garret A. Hobart 1897–1901 Theodore Roosevelt 1901	John Sherman 1897–98 William R. Day 1898 John Hay 1898–1901	Lyman J. Gage 1897–1901	Russell A. Alger 1897–99 Elihu Root 1899–1901	John D. Long 1897–1901
Theodore Roosevelt 1901–09	Charles Fairbanks 1905–09	John Hay 1901–05 Elihu Root 1905–09 Robert Bacon 1909	Lyman J. Gage 1901–02 Leslie M. Shaw 1902–07 George B. Cortelyou 1907–09	Elihu Root 1901–04 William H. Taft 1904–08 Luke E. Wright 1908–09	John D. Long 1901–02 William H. Moody 1902–04 Paul Morton 1904–05 Charles J. Bonaparte 1905–06 Victor H. Metcalf 1906–08 T. H. Newberry 1908–09
William H. Taft 1909–13	James S. Sherman 1909–13	Philander C. Knox 1909–13	Franklin MacVeagh 1909–13	Jacob M. Dickinson 1909–11 Henry L. Stimson 1911–13	George von L. Meyer 1909–13
Woodrow Wilson 1913–21	Thomas R. Marshall 1913–21	William J. Bryan 1913–15 Robert Lansing 1915–20 Bainbridge Colby 1920–21	William G. McAdoo 1913–18 Carter Glass 1918–20 David F. Houston 1920–21	Lindley M. Garrison 1913–16 Newton D. Baker 1916–21	Josephus Daniels 1913–21

Postmaster General	Attorney General	Secretary of Interior	Secretary of Agriculture	Secretary of Commerce and Labor	
David M. Key 1877–80 Horace Maynard 1880–81	Charles Devens 1877–81	Carl Schurz 1877–81			
Thomas L. James 1881	Wayne MacVeagh 1881	S. J. Kirkwood 1881			
Thomas L. James 1881 Timothy O. Howe 1881–83 Walter Q. Gresham 1883–84 Frank Hatton 1884–85	B. H. Brewster 1881–85	Henry M. Teller 1881–85			
William F. Vilas 1885–88 Don M. Dickinson 1888–89	A. H. Garland 1885–89	L. Q. C. Lamar 1885–88 William F. Villas 1888–89	Norman J. Colman 1889		
John Wanamaker 1889–93	W. H. H. Miller 1889–93	John W. Noble 1889–93	Jeremiah M. Rusk 1889–93		
Wilson S. Bissel 1893–95 William L. Wilson 1895–97	Richard Olney 1893–95 Judson Harmon 1895–97	Hoke Smith 1893–96 David R. Francis 1896–97	J. Sterling Morton 1893–97		
James A. Gary 1897–98 Charles E. Smith 1898–1901	Joseph McKenna 1897–98 John W. Griggs 1898–1901 Philander C. Knox 1901	Cornelius N. Bliss 1897–98 E. A. Hitchcock 1898–1901	James Wilson 1897–1901		
Charles E. Smith 1901–02 Henry C. Payne 1902–04 Robert J. Wynne 1904–05 George B. Cortelyou 1905–07 George von L. Meyer 1907–09	Philander C. Knox 1901–04 William H. Moody 1904–06 Charles J. Bonaparte 1906–09	E. A. Hitchcock 1901–07 James R. Garfield 1907–09	James Wilson 1901–09	George B. Cortelyou 1903–04 Victor H. Metcalf 1904–06 Oscar S. Straus 1906–09	

Postmaster General	Attorney General	Secretary of Interior	Secretary of Agriculture	Secretary of Commerce	Secretary of Labor
Frank H. Hitchcock 1909–13	G. W. Wickersham 1909–13	R. A. Ballinger 1909–11 Walter L. Fisher 1911–13	James Wilson 1909–13	Charles Nagel 1909–13	
Albert S. Burleson 1913–21	J. C. McReynolds 1913–14 T. W. Gregory 1914–19 A. Mitchell Palmer 1919–21	Franklin K. Lane 1913–20 John B. Payne 1920–21	David F. Houston 1913–20 E. T. Meredith 1920–21	W. C. Redfield 1913–19 J. W. Alexander 1919–21	William B. Wilson 1913–21

President	Vice President	Secretary of State	Secretary of Treasury	Secretary of War	Secretary of Navy
Warren G. Harding 1921–23	Calvin Coolidge 1921–23	Charles E. Hughes 1921–23	Andrew W. Mellon 1921–23	John W. Weeks 1921–23	Edwin Denby 1921–23
Calvin Coolidge 1923–29	Charles G. Dawes 1925–29	Charles E. Hughes 1923–25 Frank B. Kellogg 1925–29	Andrew W. Mellon 1923–29	John W. Weeks 1923–25 Dwight F. Davis 1925–29	Edwin Denby 1923–24 Curtis D. Wilbur 1924–29
Herbert C. Hoover 1929–33	Charles Curtis 1929–33	Henry L. Stimson 1929–33	Andrew W. Mellon 1929–32 Ogden L. Mills 1932–33	James W. Good 1929 Patrick J. Hurley 1929–33	Charles F. Adams 1929–33
Franklin Delano Roosevelt 1933–45	John Nance Garner 1933–41 Henry A. Wallace 1941–45 Harry S. Truman 1945	Cordell Hull 1933–44 E. R. Stettinius, Jr. 1944–45	William H. Woodin 1933–34 Henry Morgenthau, Jr. 1934–45	George H. Dern 1933–36 Harry H. Woodring 1936–40 Henry L. Stimson 1940–45	Claude A. Swanson 1933–40 Charles Edison 1940 Frank Knox 1940–44 James V. Forrestal 1944–45
Harry S Truman 1945–53	Alben W. Barkley 1949–53	James F. Byrnes 1945–47 George C. Marshall 1947–49 Dean G. Acheson 1949–53	Fred M. Vinson 1945–46 John W. Snyder 1946–53	Robert P. Patterson 1945–47 Kenneth C. Royall 1947	James V. Forrestal 1945–47

				Secretary of Defense	
				James V. Forrestal (1947–49) Louis A. Johnson (1949–50) George C. Marshall (1950–51) Robert A. Lovett (1951–53)	
Dwight D. Eisenhower 1953–61	Richard M. Nixon 1953–61	John Foster Dulles 1953–59 Christian A. Herter 1959–61	George M. Humphrey 1953–57 Robert B. Anderson 1957–61	Charles E. Wilson 1953–57 Neil H. McElroy 1957–61 Thomas S. Gates 1959–61	
John F. Kennedy 1961–63	Lyndon B. Johnson 1961–63	Dean Rusk 1961–63	C. Douglas Dillon 1961–63	Robert S. McNamara 1961–63	

Postmaster General	Attorney General	Secretary of Interior	Secretary of Agriculture	Secretary of Commerce and Labor	
Will H. Hayes 1921–22 Hubert Work 1922–23 Harry S. New 1923	H. M. Daugherty 1921–23	Albert B. Fall 1921–23 Hubert Work 1923	Henry C. Wallace 1921–23	Herbert C. Hoover 1921–23	James J. Davis 1921–23

Postmaster General	Attorney General	Secretary of Interior	Secretary of Agriculture	Secretary of Commerce	Secretary of Labor	Secretary of Health, Education and Welfare
Harry S. New 1923–29	H. M. Daugherty 1923–24 Harlan F. Stone 1924–25 John G. Sargent 1925–29	Hubert Work 1923–28 Roy O. West 1928–29	Henry C. Wallace 1923–24 Howard M. Gore 1924–25 W. M. Jardine 1925–29	Herbert C. Hoover 1923–28 William F. Whiting 1928–29	James J. Davis 1923–29	
Walter F. Brown 1929–33	J. D. Mitchell 1929–33	Ray L. Wilbur 1929–33	Arthur M. Hyde 1929–33	Robert P. Lamont 1929–32 Roy D. Chapin 1932–33	James J. Davis 1929–30 William N. Doak 1930–33	
James A. Farley 1933–40 Frank C. Walker 1940–45	H. S. Cummings 1933–39 Frank Murphy 1939–40 Robert Jackson 1940–41 Francis Biddle 1941–45	Harold L. Ickes 1933–45	Henry A. Wallace 1933–40 Claude R. Wickard 1940–45	Daniel D. Roper 1933–39 Harry L. Hopkins 1939–40 Jesse Jones 1940–45 Henry A. Wallace 1945	Frances Perkins 1933–45	
R. E. Hannegan 1945–47 Jesse M. Donaldson 1947–53	Tom C. Clark 1945–49 J. H. McGrath 1949–52 James P. McGranery 1952–53	Harold L. Ickes 1945–46 Julius A. Krug 1946–49 Oscar L. Chapman 1949–53	C. P. Anderson 1945–48 C. F. Brannan 1948–53	W. A. Harriman 1946–48 Charles Sawyer 1948–53	L. B. Schwellenbach 1945–48 Maurice J. Tobin 1948–53	
A. E. Summerfield 1953–61	H. Brownell, Jr. 1953–57 William P. Rogers 1957–61	Douglas McKay 1953–56 Fred Seaton 1956–61	Ezra T. Benson 1953–61	Sinclair Weeks 1953–58 Lewis L. Strauss 1958–61	Martin P. Durkin 1953 James P. Mitchell 1953–61	Oveta Culp Hobby 1953–55 Marion B. Folsom 1955–58 Arthur S. Flemming 1958–61
J. Edward Day 1961–63 John A. Gronouski 1963	Robert F. Kennedy 1961–63	Stewart L. Udall 1961–63	Orville L. Freeman 1961–63	Luther H. Hodges 1961–63	Arthur J. Goldberg 1961–62 W. Willard Wirtz 1962–63	A. H. Ribicoff 1961–62 Anthony J. Celebrezze 1962–63

President	Vice President	Secretary of State	Secretary of Treasury	Secretary of Defense	Postmaster General*	Attorney General
Lyndon B. Johnson 1963–69	Hubert H. Humphrey 1965–69	Dean Rusk 1963–69	C. Douglas Dillon 1963–65 Henry H. Fowler 1965–68 Joseph W. Barr 1968–69	Robert S. McNamara 1963–68 Clark M. Clifford 1968–69	John A. Gronouski 1963–65 Lawrence F. O'Brien 1965–68 W. Marvin Watson 1968–69	Robert F. Kennedy 1963–65 N. deB. Katzenbach 1965–67 Ramsey Clark 1967–69
Richard M. Nixon 1969–74	Spiro T. Agnew 1969–73 Gerald R. Ford 1973–74	William P. Rogers 1969–73 Henry A. Kissinger 1973–74	David M. Kennedy 1969–70 John B. Connally 1970–72 George P. Shultz 1972–74 William E. Simon 1974	Melvin R. Laird 1969–73 Elliot L. Richardson 1973 James R. Schlesinger 1973–74	Winston M. Blount 1969–71	John M. Mitchell 1969–72 Richard G. Kleindienst 1972–73 Elliot L. Richardson 1973 William B. Saxbe 1974
Gerald R. Ford 1974–77	Nelson A. Rockefeller 1974–77	Henry A. Kissinger 1974–77	William E. Simon 1974–77	James R. Schlesinger 1974–75 Donald H. Rumsfeld 1975–77		William B. Saxbe 1974–75 Edward H. Levi 1975–77

President	Vice President	Secretary of State	Secretary of Treasury	Secretary of Defense	Attorney General	Secretary of Interior
Jimmy Carter 1977–81	Walter F. Mondale 1977–81	Cyrus R. Vance 1977–80 Edmund S. Muskie 1980–81	W. Michael Blumenthal 1977–79 G. William Miller 1979–81	Harold Brown 1977–81	Griffin Bell 1977–79 Benjamin R. Civiletti 1979–81	Cecil D. Andrus 1977–81
Ronald Reagan 1981	George Bush 1981	Alexander M. Haig, Jr. 1981	Donald T. Regan 1981	Caspar W. Weinberger 1981	William French Smith 1981	James G. Watt 1981

Secretary of Interior	Secretary of Agriculture	Secretary of Commerce	Secretary of Labor	Secretary of Health, Education and Welfare	Secretary of Housing and Urban Development	Secretary of Transportation
Stewart L. Udall 1963–69	Orville L. Freeman 1963–69	Luther H. Hodges 1963–65 John T. Connor 1965–67 Alexander B. Trowbridge 1967–68 C. R. Smith 1968–69	W. Willard Wirtz 1963–69	Anthony J. Celebrezze 1963–65 John W. Gardner 1965–68 Wilbur J. Cohen 1968–69	Robert C. Weaver 1966–68 Robert C. Wood 1968–69	Alan S. Boyd 1966–69
Walter J. Hickel 1969–71 Rogers C. B. Morton 1971–74	Clifford M. Hardin 1969–71 Earl L. Butz 1971–74	Maurice H. Stans 1969–72 Peter G. Peterson 1972 Frederick B. Dent 1972–74	George P. Shultz 1969–70 James D. Hodgson 1970–73 Peter J. Brennan 1973–74	Robert H. Finch 1969–70 Elliot L. Richardson 1970–73 Caspar W. Weinberger 1973–74	George W. Romney 1969–73 James T. Lynn 1973–74	John A. Volpe 1969–73 Claude S. Brinegar 1973–74
Rogers C. B. Morton 1974–75 Stanley K. Hathaway 1975 Thomas D. Kleppe 1975–77	Earl L. Butz 1974–76	Frederick B. Dent 1974–75 Rogers C. B. Morton 1975 Elliot L. Richardson 1975–77	Peter J. Brennan 1974–75 John T. Dunlop 1975–76 W. J. Usery 1976–77	Caspar W. Weinberger 1974–75 Forrest D. Mathews 1975–77	James T. Lynn 1974–75 Carla A. Hills 1975–77	Claude S. Brinegar 1974–75 William T. Coleman 1975–77

Secretary of Agriculture	Secretary of Commerce	Secretary of Labor	Secretary of Health, Education and Welfare	Secretary of Housing and Urban Development	Secretary of Transportation	Secretary of Energy
Robert Bergland 1977–81	Juanita Kreps 1977–1979 Philip M. Klutznick 1979–81	F. Ray Marshall 1977–81	Joseph Califano 1977–79 Patricia Roberts Harris 1979–80	Patricia Roberts Harris 1977–79 Moon Landrieu 1979–	Brock Adams 1977–79 Neil E. Goldschmidt 1979–81	James R. Schlesinger 1977–79 Charles W. Duncan, Jr. 1979–81

Secretary of Health and Human Services	Secretary of Education
Patricia Roberts Harris 1980–81	Shirley M. Hufstedler 1980–81

Secretary of Agriculture	Secretary of Commerce	Secretary of Labor	Secretary of Health and Human Services	Secretary of Education	Secretary of Housing and Urban Development	Secretary of Transportation	Secretary of Energy
John R. Block 1981	Malcom Baldrige 1981	Raymond J. Donovan 1981	Richard S. Schweiker 1981	Terrel H. Bell 1981	Samuel R. Pierce, Jr. 1981	Andrew Lindsay Lewis, Jr. 1981	James B. Edwards 1981

PHOTO CREDITS/BIOGRAPHIES

Chapter 1 Pages 13 and 16: Library of Congress. Page 20: Rare Book Division, The New York Public Library, Astor, Lenox and Tilden Foundation. Page 21: National Portrait Gallery, Smithsonian Institute, Washington, D.C.

Chapter 2 Page 42: Culver Pictures. Page 46: Brown Brothers. Pages 53 and 57: Library of Congress.

Chapter 3 Page 84: Massachusetts Historical Society. Page 85: The Rhode Island Historical Society. Page 90: Massachusetts Historical Society.

Chapter 4 Page 114: Courtesy Museum of Fine Arts, Boston. Page 116: Library of Congress. Page 118: Courtesy Museum of Fine Arts, Boston, fund bequest of Winslow Warren. Page 120: Courtesy of The New-York Historical Society, New York City.

Chapter 5 Page 138: The New York Public Library, Picture Collection. Page 153: Historical Society of Pennsylvania. Page 157: The Library Company of Philadelphia.

Chapter 6 Page 169: Maryland Historical Society. Page 171: Library of Congress. Page 176: State Historical Society of North Dakota.

Chapter 7 Pages 197 and 204: Courtesy of The New-York Historical Society, New York City. Page 215: Chicago Historical Society.

Chapter 8 Page 238: The Metropolitan Museum of Art, Gift of I. N. Phelps Stokes, Edward S. Hawes, Alice Mary Hawes, Marion Augusta Hawes, 1937. Page 244: Library of Congress.

Chapter 9 Page 262: Culver Pictures. Page 268: Library of Congress. Page 277: (right) Sophia Smith Collection, Smith College.

Chapter 10 Pages 297, 300, and 307: Library of Congress.

Chapter 11 Page 331: Chicago Historical Society. Page 339: Library of Congress. Page 344: Sophia Smith Collection, Smith College.

Chapter 12 Page 363: Library of Congress. Page 369: Foster Hall Collection, University of Pittsburgh. Page 371: Library of Congress.

Chapter 13 Page 387: National Archives. Page 392: The Metropolitan Museum of Art, Gift of I. N. Phelps

Stokes, Edward S. Hawes, Alice Mary Hawes, Marion Augusta Hawes, 1937. Page 394: Courtesy of The New-York Historical Society, New York City.

Chapter 14 Page 423: Cook Collection, Valentine Museum, Richmond, Virginia. Page 430: National Archives. Page 442: Massachusetts Commandery, Military Order of the Loyal Legion and the U.S. Army Military History Institute.

Chapter 15 Page 452: Library of Congress. Page 466: The New York Public Library, Schromburg Collection. Page 473: (right) Courtesy of The New-York Historical Society, New York City.

PHOTO CREDITS/CHAPTER OPENINGS

Chapter 1 Library of Congress

Chapter 2 The Clarence J. Davies Collection, Museum of the City of New York.

Chapter 3 The New York Public Library Prints Division, Astor, Lenox and Tilden Foundations.

Chapter 4 The New York Public Library Prints Division.

Chapter 5 Abby Aldrich Rockefeller Folk Art Center, Williamsburg, Virginia.

Chapter 6 Library of Congress.

Chapter 7 Worcester Art Museum, Worcester Massachusettes.

Chapter 8 Yale University Art Gallery, Mabel Brady Garvan Collection.

Chapter 9 Philbrook Art Center, Tulsa, Oklahoma.

Chapter 10 Library of Congress.

Chapter 11 Collection of the Boatmen's National Bank of St. Louis.

Chapter 12 The New York Public Library Prints Division, The I. N. Phelps Stokes Collection of American Historical Prints.

Chapter 13 Courtesy New-York Historical Society.

Chapter 14 Library of Congress.

Chapter 15 Library of Congress.

desertions, 437
discipline, 437
dissent, 129
interpretations, 407–408
effects, 443–444
and European neutrality, 429
events leading to, 418–425
Fort Sumter, 421
in Georgia, 433
Harper's Ferry, 402–403, 427
hygiene, 437
and Indians, 438–439
Joint Committee on the Conduct of the War, 425
major campaigns (map), 426
Malvern Hill, 425
march on Richmond, 425–426
and Mexican War, 348
North:
  politics of: 434–436
  problems in, 436–438
  strategy of, 424–425
  superiority of, 424
  see also North
and nursing, 439–440
peace convention, 1861, 419
and Peace Democrats, 434
peace proposals, 436
peace societies, 129
and secession, 420–421
Shenandoah Valley, 433
Siege of Petersburg, 433
South:
  problems and disadvantages, 424, 438
  strategy of, 424
  see also South
Spotsylvania Courthouse, 433
in Tennessee, 433
Trent affair, 429
and U.S. Sanitary Commission, 317
in Virginia, 433
wartime diplomacy, 428–429
in West, 430
women and, 439–443
Clark, George Rogers, 122, 125
Clark, William, 176–177
Clatsop Indians, 190
Clay, Henry, 199, 208, 211, 341, 342
  "American System," 216, 234, 336
  and Bank War, 332–334
  censures Jackson, 333–334
  and Compromise of 1850, 386
  and compromise tariff, 331
  and election of 1824, 322–323
  and election of 1836, 337
  and Indian policy, 272
  "Log Cabin Act," 342
  and Missouri Compromise, 214
  presidential campaign of, 332, 343
  as Secretary of State, 217
  and states' rights, 328
  and Whigs, 336
Cleveland, Ohio:
  nineteenth century urban growth, 362
  see also Ohio
Clinton, DeWitt, 201, 231
Clinton, George, 179, 183
Coal mining, nineteenth century, 360

Coercive Acts, 111
Coffee, 149
Cohen, Daniel, 94
Coke, Edward, 85
Cold War, 444
Cole, Thomas, 372
Coleridge, Samuel Taylor, 296
Coles, Edward, 215–216
Colfax, Schuyler, 462, 466
College of William and Mary, 89
Colleges, see Education; specific institutions
Collier, John, 286
Collinson, Peter, 89
Colonies, see British colonies; French colonies
Colored Orphan Asylum, 435
Colt, Samuel, 236, 237
Colt revolver, 361
Columbia College (King's College), 89
Columbian Artillery, 367
Columbus, Christopher, 2, 6, 12–14, 26–30
Comanche Indians, 6
Commerce:
  in colonial era, 74
  John Marshall and, 213
  and slavery, 262
  see also Economy; Trade
Committee of Detail, 141
Committees of safety, 114, 138
Commonlaw courts, 106
Common Sense, 115, 116
Communism, Robert Owen and, 312
Complex marriage, 312
Compromise of 1820, see Missouri Compromise
Compromise of 1850, 385–387
Compromise of 1877, 469–470
Confederacy, 406, 408, 420–421
  amnesty to, 451, 453
  Civil War strategy, 424
  collapse of, 436
  conflict in ideology, 420–421
  and foreign aid, 429
  Indian alliance, 438–439
  See also Civil War
Confederate constitution, 420
Confiscation Acts, 427, 451
Congregationalism, 83–85, 88, 293
Congress, 126, 136–137, 139
  and abolition, 339
  and Adams, John Quincy, 324
  Civilization Fund, 268
  Constitutional Convention, 141
  and Freedmen's Bureau, 457
  Independent Treasury Act, 338
  and Johnson, Andrew, 454, 456, 458–459, 460, 462
  and Kansas-Nebraska Act, 395–396
  location of, 147
  and national land policy, 135–136
  and Northwest Ordinance (1787), 136
  and Polk, James K., 346
  and Reconstruction, 456–459
  during Revolution, 118, 119, 123, 126, 137
  and slavery, 214–215, 339
  see also House of Representatives; Senate
Congress of Vienna, 210
Connecticut:
  as British colony, 43, 45
  and corporate regulation, nineteenth

century, 241
  Indian war in, 52
  and ratification of Constitution, 142
  and slavery, 158
  temperance movement in, 299
Conquistadores, 14, 16–17
Conscription Act of 1863, 434, 435
Constitution, U.S., 137–139
  amendments to:
    First, 126
    Tenth, 145
    Twelfth, 323
    Thirteenth, 451, 455
    Fourteenth, 285–286, 458–459, 472
    Fifteenth, 286, 460–461, 463, 472
    Nineteenth, 286
  Bill of Rights, 144–145
  conflicts in drafting, 141
  and dissent, 131
  and Marshall, John, 212
  and Presidency, 145–146
  ratification of, 142
  and secession, 450
Constitutional Convention, 139–142
  during Reconstruction, 459–460
Constitutional Union Party, 404
Continental Army, 122, 123
  blacks in, 120–121
  competition with militia, 120
Continental Congress, first, 112–113, 114, 137
  blacks and, 121
  and dissent, 129
Continental Congress, second, recommendations of, 118
Continental dollars, 119
"Continentals," see Continental Army
"Continental Sunday," 281
Convention of 1801, 156
Cooper, James Fennimore, 163
Cooper, Peter, 232–233
Cooper Union, 232
Copley, John Singleton, 117
"Copperheads," 129, 434
Corn, 357
Cornwallis, Lord, 125
Corporation charters, 235
Corporations:
  development of, 241, 361
  regulations established, 241
  see also Business; Economy
Cortez, Hernando, 4
Cotton, 149, 249, 361
  boom, nineteenth century, 239
  and Indians, 268–269
  and depression in England, 338
  economy and, nineteenth century, 375
  factory system and, 251
  and Gulf of Mexico, 376
  and Panic of 1819, 212
  role in Civil War, 429
  and slavery, 185, 259, 375–376
  in South Carolina, 325
  and tariffs, 233, 330
  and trade:
    with Britain, 211–212
    nineteenth century, 357
Cotton gin, 185, 237
"Cotton Kingdom," 158, 239, 249

Edwards, Jonathan, 88, 92
Eisenhower, Dwight D., farewell address, 446
Elections, Presidential, *see* Presidential elections
Electoral College, 141, 167, 333
Electricity, 91
Elizabeth I, 18, 39, 83
Elkins, Stanley, 263
Ellsworth, Oliver, 177
Emancipation Proclamation, 428
Embargo of 1807, 182–183
Embree, Elihu, 303
Emerson, Ralph Waldo, 296, 368
  and abolitionist movement, 296
  at Brook Farm, 313
  and Indian removal policy, 274
Encomienda system, 16
Endymion, 172
Engerman, Stanley L., 264
England, *see* Britain; British Colonies; English immigrants; English settlements
England Emigrant Aid Society, 397
English colonial wars, 55–56
English-French war, 181–184
English immigrants, 34–36
English settlements, 18–19
  competition with France, 24
  early nonexpansion of, 25
  and farming, 25
  Parliament and, 25
  see also British colonies; *specific settlements*
Enlightenment philosophy, 293
Epidemics, 162, 315–316
Episcopalians, 293
"Era of Good Feelings," 209
Ericson, Leif, 9–10
Erie Canal, 230–231
Escott, Paul D., 265
Eskimos, 4, 8
"Essex Junta," 179
Everett, Edward, 274, 432
Executive privilege, and Washington, George, 149
Executive secrecy, and Polk, James K., 351
"Executive tyranny," 334
Expansionists of 1812, 199
Exports, nineteenth century, 241
  see also Trade

Factors, 376
Factory system, 235, 236, 241, 244, 247
  American *vs.* English, 240
  Boston Associates, 243, 251
  Boston Manufacturing Company, 250–252
  and Irish immigrants, 280
  Lowell, Massachusetts, 243, 245
Fallen Timbers, 147
Family:
  in colonial era, 77
  eighteenth century, 157
    decline in size, 220
  nineteenth century:
    and literature, 371
    North *vs.* South, 377
  and slavery, 259
Farmers:
  as anti-Federalists, 143
  in colonial era, 79

Farmer's Companion, The, 370
Farming:
  Brook Farm, 313
  in colonial era, 25, 70–74
  vs. factory system, 236
  Fourierist Phalanxes and, 313
  nineteenth century:
    early growth, 185
    and German immigrants, 281
    improvements, 361
    inventions, 236–237
    tenant, 36, 70
  see also Agriculture
Farragut, David C., 430–431
Federal government, *see* Government, federal
Federalist, The, 142
Federalists, 142, 151–152, 154
  and anti-Federalists, 142–143
  and Convention of 1801, 156
  and Embargo of 1807, 182–183
  and homesteading, 172
  influence on Democratic-Republicans, 200
  invasion of, 156
  lose power, 200
  and Madison, James, 183–184
  and Supreme Court, 177–179
  and War of 1812, 199, 200–201, 209
Federal Street Congregation, 295
Female Moral Reform Society, 275
Female Reform League, 245
Feminist movement:
  beginnings, 274
  and Fuller, Margaret, 297–298
  and Grimké sisters, 276
  and Industrial Revolution, 275
  New York Female Moral Reform Society, 275
  and Protestant ministry, 276–277
  Seneca Falls meeting, 278–279
  see also Women; Women's rights
Fenno, John, 152
Ferdinand VII, 210
Ferdinand and Isabella, 30
Field, Cyrus, 233
Fifteenth Amendment, 286, 460–461, 463, 472
Fillmore, Millard, 363, 385, 386, 393, 398
Finney, Charles Grandison, 94, 294, 295, 305
Firearms, assembly line and, 240
First Amendment, 126
First Americans, 2
Fiske, John, 137
Fitzhugh, George, 280, 391, 394–395
Fitzhugh, William, 72, 73
Five Civilized Tribes:
  in Civil War, 438–439
  and Reconstruction, 471–472
Florida:
  acquisition of, 209–210
  annexation by Madison, 187
  and Civil War, 406, 460–461
  Seminole removal, 273
  Spain and, 126, 175
  and War of 1812, 205
Fogel, Robert W., 264
Foreign capital, and nineteenth century industry, 360

Foreign policy:
  and Adams, John Quincy, 324
  and Hamilton, 148
  and Jackson, 334–336
  and Jefferson, 148
  and Polk, 346
  and Washington, George, 148, 152
  see also Diplomacy
Forrest, Nathan Bedford, 467
Fortas, Abe, 131
Fort Duquesne, 102
Fort Laramie, Treaty of, 274
Fort McHenry, 205, 206
Fort Mims, 205
Fort Necessity, 102
Fort Saint Marks, 209
Fort Sumter, 421
Fort Ticonderoga, 122, 124
Forty-Eighters, 280
Foster, Stephen, 368–369
Founding Fathers, 14, 157, 283
Fourier, Charles, 313
Fourierist Phalanxes, 313
Fourteenth Amendment, 285–286, 458–459, 472
France:
  and American Revolution, 125–126
  and Convention of 1801, 156
  and Jay's Treaty, 152, 154
  war with Britain, (1793), 148
Franklin, Benjamin, 64, 87, 91, 101, 108, 115
  and Constitutional Convention, 139, 140
  and Declaration of Independence, 119
  and Revolution, 126
Fredericksburg, Battle of, 429–430
Free African Society, 158
Free blacks, 261, 266–267, 356
  abolition and, 304–305
  and black codes, 455
  in Boston, 279
  education for, 376
  vs. Irish immigrants, 279
  North *vs.* South, 266–267
  taxation and, 266
  and urban expansion, 364
  Whigs and, 337
  see also Blacks
Freedmen's Bureau, 457–458, 464
  and Congress, 457
  and Johnson, Andrew, 457–458
"Freedom dues," 35, 81
Free land policy, 359
"Freeport Doctrine," 402
Free Soil Party, 385, 397, 400
Frelinghuysen, Theorodus, 92, 295
Frémont, John C., 398, 399, 427
French and Indian War (Seven Year's War), 56
  and Albany Congress, 100–101
  British victory, 101–103
French colonies, 23–25
French-English war, 181–184
French Revolution, 148–149
Freneau, Philip, 152, 153
Friends, *see* Quakers
Frontier, 135, 173
  and early labor movement, 247
  Jefferson and, 171–172
  see also Western expansion

Frontier Thesis, 247
Fugitive Slave Law, 257, 408, 419, 420, 452
  and abolitionists, 393
  and Compromise of 1850, 387, 389–391
Fuller, Margaret, 278, 286, 296–298, 313
Fuller, Thomas, 256
Fulton, Robert, 185, 229
Fur trade, French colonies and, 23, 25

Gadsden Purchase, 348
Gage, Thomas, 112, 113
Gallatin, Albert, 168, 200, 207, 226
Galloway, Joseph, 112
Galveston, Texas, slave markets in, 263
Garden, Alexander, 89
Garrett, Henry Highland, 267
Garrison, William Lloyd, 302, 303, 304, 344
Gaspee, 110
Gass, Patrick, 190
Gates, Horatio, 124, 125
Gates, Sir Thomas, 22
Gazette of the United States, 152, 153
General Land Office, 272
Genét, Edmond, 148
Genovese, Eugene, 265
Geography, eighteenth century, 162
Geology, nineteenth century, 377
George II, 105
George III, 106, 108, 283
Georgia:
  as British colony, 44, 45, 55, 58, 80
  in Civil War, 406, 433–434, 460–461
  cotton in, 375
  and Indians, 147, 272, 324
  population, nineteenth century, 357
  and ratification of Constitution, 142
  during Reconstruction, 460–461
  and slavery, 158, 356
Georgia, University of (Franklin College),
  160
German immigrants, 280–281
  in British colonies, 40
  supplant slaves in South, 259, 263
German mercenaries, American Revolution,
  123
Gerry, Elbridge, 154
Gettysburg, Battle of, 423, 431–432
Gettysburg Address, 432–433
Ghent, Treaty of, 127
Biggons v. *Ogden*, 213, 234, 410
Giddings, Joshua Reed, 339–340
Gilbert, Sir Humphrey, 18
Glebe House, 71
"Glorious Revolution" of 1688, 40–41
Godey's *Lady's Book*, 370, 371
Gold, in California, 360
Goodyear, Charles, 237
Goulding condenser, 237
Government:
  central:
    Articles of Confederation, 137
    assumption of state debt, 146–147
    created, 136–143
    "critical period," 137
    Federalists *vs.* anti-Federalists,
      142–143
    and Revolutionary debt, 146–147
  federal:
    Indian policy, 268–274, 328

nineteenth century:
  land policy, 234, 357–359
  and public health, 315–318
state, nineteenth century, 234–235
Graduation Act, 359
Graham, William Franklin, 94, 95
Granger, Gideon, 170
Grant, Ulysses, S., 430–431, 433, 462
  in Civil War, 433, 436
  elected President, 456, 463
  and Ku Klux Klan, 468–469
  and Liberal Republicans, 466
  Presidency, 466–467
Gray, Simon, 261, 262
Great Awakening, 88–89, 92, 95
  Second, 293
Great Depression, 317–318
Great Divide, 190
Great Lakes:
  Erie Canal and, 231
  and Treaty of Ghent, 209
  and urban expansion, 362
  and War of 1812, 208
"Great Migration" of 1843, 346
Great Northern Railroad, 412
Great Salt Lake, 311
Greeley, Horace, 249, 298, 428, 466
Greenback Party, 233
Greene, Nathaniel, 120, 125
Greenhow, Rose O'Neal, 440
Greenville, Treaty of, 147
Grenville, George, 108
Grimké sisters, 274, 276, 376
Grundy, Felix, 199
Guadalupe Hidalgo, Treaty of, 348
Guanahani (Watlings Island), 2
Guerriére, 203

Habeas corpus, Lincoln and, 434
Haiti:
  Columbus in, 12
  slave rebellion in, 257
Hale, Sarah Josepha, 371–372
Halfway covenant, 85
Halleck, Henry W., 425
Hall, Prince, 256
Hampden-Sydney (school), 160
Hamilton, Alexander, 152
  and Constitutional Convention, 139, 141
  duel with Burr, 179–180
  and Jefferson, 151, 167
  as Federalist, 142, 151
  and foreign policy, 148
  and national bank, 146–147
  and Revolutionary debt, 146–147
  as Secretary of Treasury, 145–146
  view of Supreme Court, 177
Hampton Institute, 457
Hancock, John, 117, 139
Hand-in-Hand Fire Company, 76
Harding, Warren G., 128
Harlan, John M., 412
Harman, Josiah, 147
Harper's Ferry, 402–403, 427
Harrison, William Henry, 185–187, 201, 270,
  341
  elected President, 339
  and election of 1836, 337
  Tippecanoe, 187

Hartford Convention, 127, 128, 200
Harvard University, 53, 88–89, 91, 160
  Indian college at, 50
Hassey, Obed, 237
Hat Act of 1732, 69
Hawaiian Islands, 362
Hawks, Francis Lister, 363
Hawthorne, Nathaniel, 296, 368, 313
Hayes, Rutherford B:
  and Compromise of 1877, 469–470
  contested election of, 469
Hayne, Robert Y., 329
"Headright system," 35
Health and Human Services, Department of,
  318
Health, Education and Welfare, Department
  of (HEW), 318
Hearst, William Randolph, 96
Hemp, 239
Henry, Patrick, 129, 139, 142
Henry VII, 18
Henry VIII, 18
Henry of Navarre, 39
Hicks, Elias, 278
Hill, James J., 412
Historians, nineteenth century, 371
Holbrook, Josiah, 307
Homestead Act of 1862, 435–436
Homesteading, 172
Honokam, 7
Hooker, Joseph, 430
Hopi Indians, 7
Horseshoe Bend, Battle of, 205, 209
Horticulturalist, The, 370
House of Burgesses, 25
House of Commons, 103, 104
  see also British Parliament
House of Lords, 104
  see also British Parliament
House of Representatives, 141
  and abolition, 305
  and election of 1800, 167
  and election of 1824, 323
  see also Congress; Senate
House of Seven Gables, The, 368
Houston, Sam, 268, 336
Howard, Oliver O., 457
Howard University, 457
Howe, Elias, 237, 238, 241–242
Howe, Richard, 123
Howe, William, 123–125
Howe, Samuel Gridley, 301
Hudson Bay, colonial wars and, 55
Hudson River School, 372–373
Hughes, John, 282
Huguenots, 39–40
Hull, John, 64
Hull, William, 201
Humanitarian reform, nineteenth century,
  296–310
Humbard, Rex, 95
Hutchinson, Anne, 46, 85
Hutchinson, Thomas, 111, 118

Ícaria, 313–314
Illinois:
  and immigrants, nineteenth century, 281,
    365, 366
  and temperance movement, 299

factory system in, 235, 243–244, 252
  and public health, 317
  and War of 1812, 199, 200
  and Western expansion, 329
  wool industry in, 185
  see also Northeast, nineteenth century
New England Confederation, 52–54
New England Non-Resistance Society, 302
Newfoundland:
  colonial wars and, 55
  Viking dwellings in, 9–10
New France, 102
New Hampshire:
  as British colony, 45, 58
  and Constitutional Convention, 139, 142
  and temperance movement, 299
New Harmony, 312
New Haven, Connecticut, colonial, 75
New Jersey:
  as British colony, 43, 58
  and ratification of Constitution, 142
  and slavery, 356
New Light Presbyterians, 89
New Netherlands, 52
New Orleans, Battle of, 431
New Orleans, Louisiana:
  and Pinckney's Treaty, 172
  nineteenth century:
    population growth, 219, 357
    urban expansion, 362
  slave markets in, 263
  and steamboats, 230
  and trade, 149
  see also Louisiana
New Orleans Serenaders, 369
Newsom, Ella, 440
Newspaper, first, 91
New York:
  and abolitionist movement, 305
  as British colony, 43, 45, 58, 75
  as capital, 147
  and Constitutional Convention, 139, 142, 143
  debt reform in, 301
  and Erie Canal, 230–231
  and Fourierist Phalanxes, 313
  free black population, 356
  immigrants in, nineteenth century, 281, 365, 366
  and General Corporation Act of 1848, 361
  and Lee Resolution, 119
  and penal reform, 301
  and revivalism, 294
  and Revolution, 123
  and Shakers, 311
  and temperance movement, 299
  tenant farmers in, 70
  wool industry in, 185
New York City, nineteenth century:
  as cultural center, 367
  industry in, 357
  population, 357
  prostitution in, 275
  urban expansion, 362
New York Female Moral Reform Society, 276
New York House of Refuge, 301
Nex Percé Indians, 190
Niagara, 373
Niagara Falls, War of 1812, 201

Nicot, Jean, 59
Niña, 12, 27
Nineteenth Amendment, 286
Nixon, Richard, and Supreme Court, 414
Nonimportation Act (1806), 182
Nonimportation Agreement, 113
Nonintercourse Act (1809), 183, 197
North:
  abandonment of southern blacks, 470
  and abolitionist movement, 303–306
  in Civil War, 420–413
  free blacks in, 266–267
  see also Civil War
North, Lord, 111
North, Simeon, 240
North American Phalanx, 313
North American Telegraph Company, 233
North Carolina:
  abolition societies in, 303
  becomes state, 145
  as British colony, 45, 47, 48, 75
    tobacco in, 66–67
  and Civil War, 406, 420, 422, 434
  and ratification of Constitution, 142
  and Revolution, 135
  and slavery, 356
  see also Carolinas
North Carolina, University of, 160
Northeast, nineteenth century:
  cultural development, 367
  and factory system, 236
  industrialization and, 235, 240
  see also New England
Northern Pacific Railroad, 412
Northern Securities Company, 412
North/South cultural differences, 377
North Star, The, 308
Northwest, statehood and, 136
Northwest Ordinance, 136, 147
Northwest Passage, 23, 189
Nova Scotia, colonial wars and, 55
Noyes, John Humphrey, 312
Nullification crisis, 330–332
Nullification Proclamation, 331
Nursing, 317
  and Civil War, 439–440

Oberlin College, 95, 294, 310
Ogden, William, 249
Oglethorpe, James, 45
Ohio:
  and abolitionist movement, 305
  becomes state, 172
  and Democratic-Republicans, 179
  free blacks in, 266
  immigrants in, nineteenth century, 281, 365, 366
  see also Cincinnati, Ohio; Cleveland, Ohio
Ohio Canal, 231
Ohio Company, 102
Ojeda, Alonso de, 14
Oklahoma, and Cherokee Indians, 273
"Old Hickory," see Jackson, Andrew
Old Northwest, immigrants and, 365, 366
Olmsted, Denison, 371
Oneida Community, 312
Onodaga Indians, 4
Opechancanough, 51
Opotheyahola, 439

Oratory, nineteenth century, 367
Ordinance of Nullification, 331
Ordinance of 1784, 135
Ordinance of 1785, 135
Oregon:
  becomes state, 359
  Spain and, 210
Oregon Trail, 346
Oregon question, 341, 345–346
Osawatomie, 397
Ossoli, Angelo, 298
Ostend Manifesto, 396–397
O'Sullivan, John L., 345
Otis, James, 105, 108, 110, 116
Owen, Robert, 312, 313
Owen, Ruth Bryan, 286.

Pacific Railway Act, 436
Paine, Thomas, 115, 116
Painting, nineteenth century, 372–375
Pakenham, Sir Edward, 206
Pamphleteering, Revolutionary, 114–116
Pamunkey Indians, 52
Panic of 1819, 211–212, 239, 325, 331–332
Panic of 1837, 338, 362
  and unionism, 247
Panic of 1857, 314, 400–401
Paper money, see Currency, paper money
Parker, Theodore, 390
Parkman, Francis, 371
Parrish, Elsie, 413
Pasha of Tripoli, 171
Patent law, John Quincy Adams and, 324
Patent Office, U.S., 234, 239, 361
Paternalism:
  industrial, nineteenth century, 243
  and slavery, 265
Patterson, William, 140
Peace Democrats, 434
  see also Democratic Party; Democrats; Jacksonian Democrats
Peace movement, nineteenth century, 302–303
Peace of Paris, 126, 444
Peace societies, Civil War, 129
Pea Ridge, Battle of, 439
Peggy Eaton Affair, 328
Pemberton, John C., 431
Penal reform, nineteenth century, 299–301
Penn, William, 43, 47, 86
Pennsylvania:
  as British colony, 43, 47, 58, 83
  free black population, 356
  nineteenth century:
    factory system, 236
    immigrants in, 365, 366
    industry, 357
    and Panic of 1819, 212
    population, 357
    and railroads, 235
    and slavery, 157–158
    wool industry in, 185
  see also Philadelphia, Pennsylvania
Pennsylvania, University of, 89
Penobscot Indians, 6, 245
Pepperell, William, 76
Pequot Indians, 52
Perfectionism, 296, 312
Perry, Matthew C., 362, 363

under colonial law, 81
in colonial Virginia, 37–38
and commerce, 262
and Compromise of 1850 (map), 387
and confiscation acts, 427
and Constitutional Convention, 141
cotton and, 185, 375–376
and cultural repression, 370
economics of, 38, 265
emancipation problems, 256–257
and Fitzhugh, George, 394–395
and Fugitive Slave Law, 387, 389–391
historians view, 263–265
and Kansas-Nebraska Act (map), 396
laws concerning, 257–259
and Lecompton Constitution, 402
Lincoln on, 401–402
maps of, 258
and Mexican War, 348
and Personal Liberty Law, 390
and Portuguese, 38
and religion, 37–38, 261
Southern defense of, 391, 393
and taxation, 141
in territories, 384–387
    and Dred Scott decision, 398–399
    and election of 1860, 404
    and Kansas-Nebraska Act, 394–397, 400
    and Northwest Territory, 136
    and Thirteenth Amendment, 451, 455
and tobacco, 38, 60
and "underground railroad," 389–390
urban, 261, 263
Van Buren and, 339
Slave trade, 68–69, 239, 263, 341–342, 363
Slidell, John, 429
Smallpox, 77, 89–91, 315
Smalls, Robert, 464, 466–467
Smear tactics, and election of 1828, 326
Smith, John, 20, 21, 49
Smith, Jonathan, 138
Smith, Joseph, 310
Smith, Robert, 170, 200
Social and cultural diversity, nineteenth
    century, 365–371
Social Security Act of 1935, 317–318
Social Security Administration, 318
Solitary confinement, 301
Sons of Liberty, 108
Soulé, Pierre, 397
South:
    and abolitionist movement, 303–306
    and agriculture, nineteenth century, 376
    antebellum 375–377
    in Civil War, 420–443
    and Compromise of 1850, 385–387
    cotton and, 149, 185, 239, 249, 259, 361,
        375–376, 429
    and Embargo of 1807, 183
    and Fifteenth Amendment, 463
    free blacks in, 266–267
    and immigrants, nineteenth century,
        366–367
    and Indians, 268–269, 271–274, 324
    and literature, nineteenth century, 368, 370
    Lower, see Lower South
    and nationalism, 408
    and nativism, 367
    planter aristocracy, 454

and public lands, 359
and Radical Republicans, 463–465
and railroads, 360
Reconstruction, 450–475
    during Revolution, 122, 125
    secession of, 403, 406–407
    and slavery, see Slavery
    and Tariff of Abominations, 325
    textile industry in, 240
    and unionization, 246
    urban expansion, nineteenth century, 249,
        362, 364
    and War of 1812, 199
    see also Lower South; Upper South
South America, Britain and, 210
South Carolina:
    and abolition, 330–331
    and Civil War, 406, 419, 421, 434, 436, 451
    and cotton, 325
    Huguenots in, 40
    and Ordinance of Nullification, 331
    and ratification of Constitution, 142
    during Revolution, 122
    and slavery, 158, 185, 356
    and states' rights, 330
    see also Carolinas
South Carolina Exposition, 325, 329
Southern colonies, 47–48
Southern planter, 72
South/North cultural differences, 377
Spain, 181, 324
    and Florida, 175, 209–210
    and Latin American colonies, dissolve of,
        210
    and Oregon, 210
    and Pinckney's Treaty, 149
Spanish-American War, 127–128
Spanish Empire, 3, 14, 16–17, 24
    map, 15
Spanish voyages, 12–17
Speaker of the House, first, 143
Speech, freedom of, 145
Spencer, Archibald, 91
Spinning jenny, 201
Spinning wheel, 237
"Spot Resolutions," 346
Spotsylvania Court House, 433
Squatter sovereignty, 384, 395
Stamp Act, 106–109
Stamp Act Congress, 108
Stampp, Kenneth, 263, 456
Stanton, Edwin, 437, 562
Stanton, Elizabeth Cady, 277–278, 472, 473,
    474, 475
Statehood, 135–136
States' rights, 135
    and Adams, John Quincy, 324
    as cause of Civil War, 408
    and Jackson, 328–332
    and Marshall, John, 212–213
    and Missouri Compromise, 214–215
    and Webster, Daniel, 329
Steamboat, invention of, 185, 229–231
Steam engines, 201
Steam locomotive, first, 232
Stephens, Alexander H., 420
Stevens, Thaddeus, 425, 452, 456
Stoddard, Solomon, 85
Stone, Barton W., 94

Stone, Lucy, 475
Stow, Harriett Beecher, 391–393
Stuart, James E.B. ("Jeb), 429
Suffolk County Convention, 113
Suffolk Resolves, 113
Suffrage, see Voting rights
Sugar, 149, 239
Sugar Act, 106
Sullivan, John, 122
Sumner, Charles, 303, 389, 452, 456, 470
    and Kansas-Nebraska Act, 395, 397
Sunday, William Ashley, 94, 95
Supreme Court, 178–179, 234, 409–410
    and blacks, 411–412
    Brown v. Board of Education of Topeka, 414
    Charles River Bridge case, 234
    Cherokee Nation v. State of Georgia, 272
    and citizenship, 285, 288
    and civil rights, 470–471
    Dartmouth v. Woodward, 212
    and Dred Scott decision, 410, 411
    under Federalists, 177–179
    Hamilton's view of, 177
    impeachment of justices, 179
    McCulloch v. Maryland, 212, 331
    Marbury v. Madison, 178–179, 410
    and Marshall, John, 177–179, 212–213
    and Missouri Compromise, 215
    and Nixon, Richard, 414
    Plessy v. Ferguson, 411–412
    and railroads, 410–412
    and treason, 181
    and Watergate affair, 414
    United States v. Nixon, President of the United
        States, 414
    West Coast Hotel Co. v. Parrish, 413
    and women's rights, 286
    Worcester v. State of Georgia, 272, 332
Susquehanna Indians, 52
Syphilis, 315

Tallapoosa River, 270
Talleyrand (Charles Maurice de
    Talleyrand-Périgord), 154
Tallmadge, James, 214
Tammany Hall, 467
Taney, Roger B., 234, 398–399, 411, 412
Tariff Bill of 1824, 209
Tariff of Abominations, 233, 324–325, 330
Tariff of 1824, 325
Tariff of 1828, 233, 325
Tariff of 1832, 330
Tariff of 1842, 342
Tariffs:
    and Adams, John Quincy, 324–324
    on cotton, 233
    protective, 209, 324
    on tobacco, 233
    and Tyler, John, 342
    and Whigs, 336
    see also Trade
Taxation:
    in colonial era, 105–111
    and Congress, 137
    and education, nineteenth century, 307
    and free blacks, 266
    during Revolution, 119
    and slavery, 141
    and Whiskey Rebellion, 147–148

World War II, 444
Wright, Frances, 277, 278
Writs of Assistance, 105

X,Y,Z affair, 154

Yahgan Indians, 4
Yale University, 89, 160, 242
"Yankee brag," 162
Yellow fever, 315, 317
York, Duke of (James II), 43

Yorktown, Battle of, 126
Young, Brigham, 311
Young Hickory, *see* Polk, James K.
Yucatan Peninsula, 4, 343

Color Plates

Plates 2 & 3:

John Morris

Plate 4:

The New-York Historical Society

Plate 5:

(top) The New-York Historical Society (bottom) Larry Chambers/Black Star

Plate 6:

(top, left) *The Cornell Farm* by Edward Hicks. National Gallery of Art, Washington. Gift of Edgar William and Berenice Chrysler Garbisch. (all others) The Bettmann Archive

Plate 7:

(top) The Bettman Archive (bottom) © 1979 Earl Roberge/Photo Researchers

Plate 8:

(bottom, right) The New York Public Library, Prints Division, Astor Lenox and Tilden Foundations (all others) The Bettmann Archive

Plate 9:

(top) Erich Lessing/Magnum (bottom) Jim Tute/Black Star

Plate 10:

(top) H. Jensen-Scala/Editorial Photocolor Archives (center, right) The New-York Historical Society (center, left) The New York Public Library, Prints Division, Eno Collection (bottom) The Bettmann Archive

Plate 11:

(top) © George E. Jones III 1975/Photo Researchers (bottom) © 1980 Herman J. Kokojan/Black Star

Plate 12:

(top, left) The Bettmann Archive (top, right) Abby Aldrich Rockefeller Folk Art Center, Williamsburg, Virginia (center, right) Museum of the City of New York (bottom, left) The Bettmann Archive (bottom, right) The Bettmann Archive

Plate 13:

(top) Robin Forbes/The Image Bank (bottom) Ellis Herwig/Stock, Boston

Plate 14:

(bottom) The Bettmann Archive (all others) The New-York Historical Society

Plate 15:

(top) George Hall ©/Woodfin Camp (center) Lester Sloan © 1978/Woodfin Camp (bottom) Charles M. Dollar

Plate 16:

© Wally McNamee 1980/Woodfin Camp

Notes

Notes

Notes

Notes

Notes

Notes

Notes